W9-AFV-874

Allen and Greenough's

NEW LATIN GRAMMAR

Allen and Greenough's

NEW LATIN GRAMMAR

J. H. ALLEN AND J. B. GREENOUGH

EDITED BY

J. B. GREENOUGH, G. L. KITTREDGE, A. A. HOWARD,
AND BENJ. L. D'OOGE

DOVER PUBLICATIONS, INC.
MINEOLA, NEW YORK

Bibliographical Note

This Dover edition, first published in 2006, is an unabridged republication of *Allen and Greenough's New Latin Grammar for Schools and Colleges,* originally published by Ginn and Company, Boston, in 1903.

International Standard Book Number: 0-486-44806-1

Manufactured in the United States of America
Dover Publications, Inc., 31 East 2nd Street, Mineola, N.Y. 11501

PUBLISHER'S NOTE

THIS Dover edition is an unaltered reprint of the famed 1903 edition of the *New Latin Grammar* created by Joseph Henry Allen (1820–1898) and James Bradstreet Greenough (1833–1901) and ably edited by Greenough himself along with George Lyman Kittredge, Albert Andrew Howard, and Benjamin Leonard D'Ooge. After all these years, the *New Latin Grammar* remains popular and invaluable for Latin study. It is seriously out of date, however, in one area: the sections (§§607–629, on pages 405–427) on rhythm and versification. Therefore, though we have left those sections untouched, we can not vouch for their accuracy. We would recommend that the student interested in Latin poetry turn to one of these sources as a supplement to this volume:

The Meters of Greek and Latin Poetry, by James W. Halporn, Martin Ostwald, and Thomas G. Rosenmeyer (Indianapolis: Hackett Publishing, 1994; ISBN: 0-872-20243-7)

A Guide to Latin Meter and Verse Composition, by David J. Califf (London: The Anthem Press, 2002; ISBN 1-898-85572-2)

PREFACE

THE present book is a careful revision of the edition of 1888. This revision was planned and actually begun in the lifetime of Professor Greenough and has been carried out in accordance with principles that met with his full approval. The renumbering of the sections has made it possible to improve the arrangement of material in many particulars and to avoid a certain amount of repetition which was inevitable in the former edition. Thus, without increasing the size of the volume, the editors have been able to include such new matter as the advance in grammatical science has afforded. The study of historical and comparative syntax has been pursued with considerable vigor during the past fifteen years, and the well-established results of this study have been inserted in their appropriate places. In general, however, the principles and facts of Latin syntax, as set forth by Professor Greenough, have stood the test both of scientific criticism and of practical use in the class-room, and accordingly the many friends of Allen and Greenough's Grammar will not find the new edition strange or unfamiliar in its method or its contents. The editors have seen no occasion to change long-settled nomenclature or to adopt novel classifications when the usual terms and categories have proved satisfactory. On the other hand, they have not hesitated to modify either doctrines or forms of statement whenever improvement seemed possible.

In the matter of "hidden quantity" the editors have been even more conservative than in the former revision. This subject is one of great difficulty, and the results of the most recent investigations are far from harmonious. In many instances the facts are quite undiscoverable, and, in general, the phenomena are of comparatively slight interest except to special students of the arcana of philology. No vowel has been marked long unless the evidence seemed practically decisive.

The editors have been fortunate in securing the advice and assistance of Professor E. S. Sheldon, of Harvard University, for the first ten pages, dealing with phonetics and phonology. They are equally indebted to Professor E. P. Morris, of Yale University, who has had the kindness to revise the notes on historical and comparative syntax. Particular acknowledgment is also due to Mr. M. Grant Daniell, who has coöperated in the revision throughout, and whose accurate scholarship and long experience as a teacher have been of the greatest service at every point.

SEPTEMBER 1, 1903.

CONTENTS

PART I — WORDS AND FORMS

PART II — SYNTAX

PROSODY

Allen and Greenough's

NEW LATIN GRAMMAR

LATIN GRAMMAR

Latin Grammar is usually treated under three heads: 1. Words and Forms; 2. Syntax; 3. Prosody. Syntax treats of the function of words when joined together as parts of the sentence; Prosody of their arrangement in metrical composition.

PART FIRST—WORDS AND FORMS

THE ALPHABET

1. The Latin Alphabet is the same as the English (which is in fact borrowed from it) except that it does not contain **J**, **U**, and **W**.

NOTE 1.—The Latin alphabet was borrowed in very early times from a Greek alphabet (though not from that most familiar to us) and did not at first contain the letters **G** and **Y**. It consisted of capital letters only, and the small letters with which we are familiar did not come into general use until the close of the eighth century of our era.

NOTE 2.—The Latin names of the consonants were as follows:—**B**, *be* (pronounced *bay*); **C**, *ce* (pronounced *kay*); **D**, *de* (*day*); **F**, *ef*; **G**, *ge* (*gay*); **H**, *ha*; **K**, *ka*; **L**, *el*; **M**, *em*; **N**, *en*; **P**, *pe* (*pay*); **Q**, *qu* (*koo*); **R**, *er*; **S**, *es*; **T**, *te* (*tay*); **X**, *ix*; **Z**, *zeta* (the Greek name, pronounced *dzayta*). The sound of each vowel was used as its name.

a. The character **C** originally meant **G**, a value always retained in the abbreviations **C.** (for **Gāius**) and **Cn.** (for **Gnaeus**).

NOTE.—In early Latin **C** came also to be used for **K**, and **K** disappeared except before **a** in a few words, as **Kal.** (**Kalendae**), **Karthāgō**. Thus there was no distinction *in writing* between the sounds of **g** and **k**. Later this defect was remedied by forming (from **C**) the new character **G**. This took the alphabetic place formerly occupied by **Z**, which had gone out of use. In Cicero's time (see N. D. ii. 93), **Y** (originally a form of **V**) and **Z** were introduced from the ordinary Greek alphabet to represent sounds in words derived from the Greek, and they were put at the end of the Latin alphabet.

b. **I** and **V** were used both as vowels and as consonants (see § 5).

NOTE.—**V** originally denoted the vowel sound **u** (*oo*), and **F** stood for the sound of our consonant **w**. When **F** acquired the value of our **f**, **V** came to be used for the sound of **w** as well as for the vowel **u**.

In this book **i** is used for both vowel and consonant **i**, **u** for vowel **u**, and **v** for consonant **u**:—**iūs**, **vir**, **iuvenis**.

Classification of Sounds

2. The simple Vowels are **a, e, i, o, u, y.**

The Diphthongs are **ae, au, ei, eu, oe, ui,** and, in early Latin, **ai, oi, ou.** In the diphthongs both vowel sounds are heard, one following the other in the same syllable.

3. Consonants are either voiced (*sonant*) or voiceless (*surd*). Voiced consonants are pronounced with the same vocal murmur that is heard in vowels; voiceless consonants lack this murmur.

1. The voiced consonants are **b, d, g, l, r, m, n, z,** consonant **i, v.**
2. The voiceless consonants are **p, t, c (k, q), f, h, s, x.**

4. Consonants are further classified as in the following table:

		Labials	Dentals	Palatals
Mutes	Voiced (*mediae*)	**b**	**d**	**g**
	Voiceless (*tenuēs*)	**p**	**t**	**c (k, q)**
	Aspirates	**ph**	**th**	**ch**
Nasals		**m**	**n**	**n** (before **c, g, q**)
Liquids			**l, r**	
Fricatives (Spirants)		**f**[1]	**s, z**	
Sibilants			**s, z**	
Semivowels		**v**		consonant **i**

Double consonants are **x** (= cs) and **z** (= dz); **h** is merely a breathing.

1. Mutes are pronounced by blocking entirely, for an instant, the passage of the breath through the mouth, and then allowing it to escape with an explosion (distinctly heard before a following vowel). Between the explosion and the vowel there may be a slight puff of breath (h), as in the Aspirates (**ph, th, ch**).[2]
2. Labials are pronounced with the lips, or lips and teeth.
3. Dentals (sometimes called Linguals) are pronounced with the tip of the tongue touching or approaching the upper front teeth.
4. Palatals are pronounced with a part of the upper surface of the tongue touching or approaching the palate.[3]
5. Fricatives (or Spirants) are consonants in which the breath passes continuously through the mouth with audible friction.
6. Nasals are like voiced mutes, except that the mouth remains closed and the breath passes through the nose.

[1] Strictly a *labio-dental*, pronounced with the under lip touching the upper teeth.

[2] The aspirates are almost wholly confined to words borrowed from the Greek. In early Latin such borrowed sounds lost their aspiration and became simply **p, t, c.**

[3] Palatals are often classed as (1) *velars*, pronounced with the tongue touching or rising toward the soft palate (in the back part of the mouth), and (2) *palatals*, in which the tongue touches or rises toward the hard palate (farther forward in the mouth). Compare the initial consonants in *key* and *cool*, whispering the two words, and it will be observed that before **e** and **i** the **k** is sounded farther forward in the mouth than before **a, o,** or **u.**

5. The vowels **i** and **u** serve as consonants when pronounced rapidly before a vowel so as to stand in the same syllable.[1] Consonant **i** has the sound of English consonant **y**; consonant **u** (**v**) that of English consonant **w**.

Consonant **i** and **u** (**v**) are sometimes called Semivowels.

NOTE 1.—The Latin alphabet did not distinguish between the vowel and consonant sounds of **i** and **u**, but used each letter (I and V) with a double value. In modern books **i** and **u** are often used for the vowel sounds, **j** and **v** for the consonant sounds; but in printing in capitals J and U are avoided:—IVLIVS (**Iūlius**). The characters J and U are only slight modifications of the characters I and V. The ordinary English sounds of **j** and **v** did not exist in classical Latin, but consonant **u** perhaps approached English **v** in the pronunciation of some persons.

NOTE 2.—In the combinations **qu**, **gu**, and sometimes **su**, **u** seems to be the consonant (**w**). Thus, **aqua**, **anguis**, **cōnsuētus** (compare English *quart*, *anguish*, *suave*). In these combinations, however, **u** is reckoned neither as a vowel nor as a consonant.[2]

ORTHOGRAPHY

6. Latin spelling varied somewhat with the changes in the language and was never absolutely settled in all details.

Thus, we find **lubet**, **vortō**, as earlier, and **libet**, **vertō**, as later forms. Other variations are **optumus** and **optimus**, **gerundus** and **gerendus**.

The spelling of the first century of our era, known chiefly from inscriptions, is tolerably uniform, and is commonly used in modern editions of the classics.

a. After **v** (consonant **u**), **o** was anciently used instead of **u** (**voltus**, **servos**), and this spelling was not entirely given up until the middle of the first century of our era.

b. The older **quo** became **cu** in the Augustan period; in the second century of our era the spelling **quu** established itself in some words:—

> **cum**, older **quom**;[3] **equos**, **ecus**, later **equus**; **sequontur**, **secuntur**, later **sequuntur**; similarly **exstinguont**, **exstingunt**, later **exstinguunt**.

NOTE.—In most modern editions the spelling **quu** is adopted, except in **cum**.

c. Between consonant **i** and a preceding **a**, **e**, **o**, or **u**, an **i** was developed as a transient sound, thus producing a diphthong **ai**, **ei**, etc., before the consonant **i**. In such cases but one **i** was written: as, **âiō** (for †**ai-iō**), **mâius** (for †**mai-ius**), **pêius** (for †**pei-ius**).

[1] Compare the English word *Indian* as pronounced in two syllables or in three.

[2] In such words it is possible that the preceding consonant was labialized and that no distinct and separate consonant **u** was heard.

[3] The spelling **quum** is very late and without authority.

d. Similarly in compounds of **iaciō** but one **i** was written (as, **con-iciō**, not **con-iiciō**); but the usual pronunciation probably showed consonant **i** followed by vowel **i** (see § 11. *e*).

NOTE. — Some variations are due to later changes in Latin itself, and these are not now recognized in classical texts.

1. Unaccented **ti** and **ci**, when followed by a vowel, came to be pronounced alike; hence **nūntiō** was later spelled with a **c** and **diciō** with a **t**.

2. The sound of **h** was after a time lost and hence this letter was often omitted (as, **arēna** for **harēna**) or mistakenly written (as, **hūmor** for **ūmor**).

3. The diphthong **ae** early in the time of the Empire acquired the value of long open **e** (about like English *e* in *there*), and similarly **oe** after a time became a long close **e** (about like the English *ey* in *they*); and so both were often confused in spelling with **e**: as, **coena** or **caena** for the correct form **cēna**.

Syllables

7. Every Latin word has as many syllables as it has vowels or diphthongs: —

a-ci-ē, mo-nē, fī-li-us, fe-rō-ci-tā-te.

a. In the division of words into syllables a single consonant (including consonant **i** and **v**) between two vowels is written and pronounced with the following vowel. Doubled consonants are separated: —

pa-ter, mī-li-tēs, in-iū-ri-a, dī-vi-dō; mit-tō, tol-lō.

NOTE 1. — Some extend the rule for single consonants to any consonant group (as **sp**, **st**, **gn**) that can begin a word. In this book, **dīx-it, sax-um**, etc. are preferred to **dī-xit, sa-xum**; the pronunciation was probably **dīc-sit, sac-sum**.

NOTE 2. — A syllable ending with a vowel or diphthong is called *open*: all others are called *close*. Thus in **pa-ter** the first syllable is open, the second close.

b. In compounds the parts are separated: —

ab-est, ob-lātus, dis-cernō, du-plex, dī-stō.

Pronunciation

8. The so-called Roman Pronunciation of Latin aims to represent approximately the pronunciation of classical times.

VOWELS:	**ā** as in *father*;	**ă** as in *idea*.
	ē as *eh?* (prolonged), or *a* in *date*;	**ĕ** as *eh?* (clipped) or *e* in *net*.
	ī as in *machine*;	**ĭ** as in *holiest* or *sit*.
	ō as in *holy*;	**ŏ** as in *obey*.
	ū as *oo* in *boot*;	**ŭ** as *oo* in *foot*.
	y between **u** and **i** (French **u** or German **ü**).	

DIPHTHONGS: **ae** like *ay*;	**ei** as in *eight*;	**oe** like *oy* in *boy*;
eu as *eh'oo*;	**au** like *ow* in *now*;	**ui** as *oo'ee*.

Consonants are the same as in English, except that —

c and g are as in *come*, *get*, never as in *city*, *gem*.

s as in *sea*, *lips*, never as in *ease*.

Consonant i is like *y* in *young;* v (consonant u) like *w* in *wing*.

n in the combinations ns and nf probably indicates nasalization of the preceding vowel, which was also lengthened; and final m in an unaccented syllable probably had a similar nasalizing effect on the preceding vowel.

ph, th, ch, are properly like p, t, k, followed by h (which may, for convenience, be neglected); but ph probably became like (or nearly like) f soon after the classical period, and may be so pronounced to distinguish it from p.

z is as *dz* in *adze*.

bs is like ps; bt is like pt.

Note. — Latin is sometimes pronounced with the ordinary English sounds of the letters. The English pronunciation should be used in Roman names occurring in English (as, *Julius Cæsar*); and in familiar quotations, as, *e pluribus unum; viva voce; vice versa; a fortiori; veni, vidi, vici*, etc.

Quantity

9. The Quantity of a Vowel or a Syllable is the time occupied in pronouncing it. Two degrees of Quantity are recognized, — *long* and *short*.

a. In syllables, quantity is measured from the beginning of the vowel or diphthong to the end of the syllable.

10. Vowels are either long or short *by nature*, and are pronounced accordingly (§ 8).

a. A vowel before another vowel or h is short: as in **vĭa**, **nĭhil**.

b. A diphthong is long: as in **aedēs**, **foedus**. So, also, a vowel derived from a diphthong: as in **exclūdō** (from †**ex-claudō**).

c. A vowel formed by contraction is long: as in **nīl** (from **nihil**).

d. A vowel before ns, nf, gn, is long: as in **cōnstāns**, **īnferō**, **māgnus**.

Note. — But the quantity of the vowel before gn is not certain in all cases.

e. A vowel before nd, nt, is regularly short: as in **amandus**, **amant**.

In this book all vowels known to be long are marked (ā, ē, etc.), and short vowels are left unmarked (a, e, etc.). Vowels marked with both signs at once (ă̄, ĕ̄, etc.) occur sometimes as long and sometimes as short.

Note. — The Romans sometimes marked vowel length by a stroke above the letter (called an apex), as, Á; and sometimes the vowel was doubled to indicate length. An I made higher than the other letters was occasionally used for ī. But none of these devices came into general use.

11. The Quantity of the Syllable is important for the position of the accent and in versification.

a. A syllable containing a long vowel or a diphthong is said to be *long by nature:* as, **mā-ter, aes, au-la.**

b. A syllable containing a short vowel followed by two consonants (except a mute before **l** or **r**) or by a double consonant (**x, z**) is said to be *long by position*, but the vowel is pronounced *short:* as, **est, ter-ra, sax-um, Me-zen-tius.**

NOTE.—When a consonant is doubled the pronunciation should show this distinctly. Thus in **mit-tō** both **t**'s should be pronounced as in *out-talk* (not merely a single **t** as in *better*).

c. A syllable containing a short vowel followed by a mute before **l** or **r** is properly short, but may be used as long in verse. Such a syllable is said to be *common*.

NOTE 1.—In syllables long by position, but having a short vowel, the length is partly due to the first of the consonants, which stands in the same syllable with the vowel. In syllables of "common" quantity (as the first syllable of **patrem**) the ordinary pronunciation was **pa-trem**, but in verse **pat-rem** was allowed so that the syllable could become long.

NOTE 2.—In final syllables ending with a consonant, and containing a short vowel, the quantity in verse is determined by the following word: if this begins with a vowel the final consonant is joined to it in pronunciation; if it begins with a consonant the syllable is long by position.

NOTE 3.—In rules for quantity **h** is not counted as a consonant, nor is the apparently consonantal **u** in **qu, gu, su** (see § 5. N. 2).

d. A syllable whose vowel is **a, e, o,** or **u,** followed by consonant **i,** is long whether the vowel itself is long or short: as, **â-iō, mâ-ior, pê-ius.**

In such cases the length of the syllable is indicated in this book by a circumflex on the vowel.

NOTE.—The length of a syllable before consonant **i** is due to a transitional sound (vowel **i**) which forms a diphthong with the preceding vowel: as, **â-iō** (for †**ai-iō**), **mâ-ior** (for †**mai-ior**). See § 6. *c.*

e. In some compounds of **iaciō** (as, **in-iciō**) the consonant **i** of the simple verb was probably pronounced (though not written). Thus the first syllable was long by position: as, **in-iciō** (for **in-iiciō**). See § 6. *d.*

In such cases the length of the syllable is not indicated in this book by a circumflex on the vowel.

f. When a syllable is long by position the quantity of the vowel is not always determinable. The vowel should be pronounced short unless it is known to be long.

NOTE.—The quantity of a vowel under these circumstances is said to be *hidden*. It is often determined with a greater or less degree of certainty by inscriptional evidence (see § 10. N.) or by other means. In this book, the quantity of all such vowels known to be long is marked.

Accent

12. Words of two syllables are accented on the first syllable: as, **Rō′ma, fi′dēs, tan′gō.**

Words of more than two syllables are accented on the Penult[1] if that is long (as, **amī′cus, monē′tur, contin′git**); otherwise on the Antepenult (as, **do′mĭnus, a′lăcris, dissociā′bĭlis**).

a. When an enclitic is joined to a word, the accent falls on the syllable next before the enclitic, whether long or short: as, **dĕă′que, ămārĕ′ve, tĭbĭ′ne, ită′que** (*and . . . so*), as distinguished from **i′tăque** (*therefore*). So (according to some) **ex′inde, ec′quandō,** etc.

Exceptions: 1. Certain apparent compounds of **faciō** retain the accent of the simple verb: as, **benefă′cit, calefă′cit** (see § 266. *a*).

NOTE. — These were not true compounds, but phrases.

2. In the second declension the genitive and vocative of nouns in **-ius** and the genitive of those in **-ium** retain the accent of the nominative: as, **Cornē′lī, Vergi′lī, inge′nī** (see § 49. *c*).

3. Certain words which have lost a final vowel retain the accent of the complete words: as, **illī′c** for **illī′ce, prōdū′c** for **prōdūce, sati′n** for **sati′sne.**

Combinations

13. In some cases adjacent words, being pronounced together, are written as one: —

> **ūnusquisque (ūnus quisque), sīquis (sī quis), quārē (quā rē), quamobrem (quam ob rem; cf. quās ob rēs), rēspūblica (rēs pūblica), iūsiūrandum (iūs iūrandum), paterfamiliās (pater familiās).**

NOTE. — Sometimes a slight change in pronunciation resulted, as, especially in the old poets, before **est** in **homōst (homō est), perīculumst (perīculum est), ausust (ausus est), quālist (quālis est).** Similarly there occur **vīn', scīn'** for **vīsne, scīsne, sīs (sī vīs), sōdēs (sī audēs), sūltis (sī vultis).** Compare in English *somebody, to breakfast; he 's, I 've, thou 'rt.*

Phonetic Changes

14. Latin, the language of the ancient Romans, was properly, as its name implies, the language spoken in the plain of Latium, lying south of the Tiber, which was the first territory occupied and governed by the Romans. It is a descendant of an early form of speech commonly called *Indo-European* (by some *Indo-Germanic*), from which are also descended most of the important languages now in use in Europe, including among others English, German, the Slavic and the Celtic languages, and further some now or formerly spoken in Asia, as Sanskrit, Persian, Armenian. Greek likewise

[1] The Penult is the last syllable but one; the Antepenult, the last but two.

belongs to the same family. The Romance (or Romanic) languages, of which the most important are Italian, French, Provençal, Spanish, Portuguese, and Roumanian, are modern descendants of spoken Latin.

The earliest known forms of Latin are preserved in a few inscriptions. These increase in number as we approach the time when the language began to be used in literature; that is, about B.C. 250. It is the comparatively stable language of the classical period (B.C. 80–A.D. 14) that is ordinarily meant when we speak of Latin, and it is mainly this that is described in this book.

15. Among the main features in the changes of Latin from the earliest stages of the language as we know it up to the forms of classical Latin may be mentioned the following:—

Vowel Changes

1. The old diphthong **ai** became the classical **ae** (**aedīlis** for old **aidīlis**), old **oi** became **oe** or **ū** (**ūnus** for old **oinos**), and old **ou** became **ū** (**dūcō** for old **doucō**).

2. In compound verbs the vowel **a** of the simple verb often appears as **i** or **e**, and **ae** similarly appears as **ī**:—

> **faciō, factum**, but **cōnficiō, cōnfectum**; **caedō**, but **occīdō**, and similarly **cecīdī**, perfect of **caedō** (cf. **cadō, occidō**; **cecidī**, perfect of **cadō**).

NOTE.—This change is commonly ascribed to an accentuation on the first syllable, which seems to have been the rule in Latin before the rule given above (see § 12) became established. The original Indo-European accent, however, was not limited by either of these principles; it was probably a musical accent so-called, consisting in a change of pitch, and not merely in a more forcible utterance of the accented syllable.

3. Two vowels coming together are often contracted:—

> **cōgō** for †**co-agō**; **prōmō** for †**pro-emō**; **nīl** for **nihil**; **dēbeō** for †**dē-hibeō** (†**dē-habeō**).

Consonant Changes

4. An old **s** regularly became **r** between two vowels (*rhotacism*), passing first through the sound of (English) **z**:—

> **eram** (cf. **est**); **generis**, genitive of **genus**.[1]

NOTE.—Final **s** sometimes became **r** by analogy: as, **honor** (older **honōs**), from the analogy of **honōris**, etc.

5. A dental (**t, d**) often became **s**, especially when standing next to **t, d**, or **s**: as, **equestris** for †**equettris**, **cāsus** for †**cadtus** (cf. 6, below).

6. Many instances of assimilation, partial or complete, are found:—

> **cessī** for †**ced-sī**; **summus** for †**supmus**; **scrīptus** for **scrībtus** (**b** unvoicing to **p** before the voiceless **t**); and in compound verbs (see § 16).

[1] A similar change can be seen in English: as, *were* (cf. *was*), *lorn* (cf. *lose*).

Dissimilation, the opposite kind of change, prevented in some cases the repetition of the same sound in succcessive syllables: —

Thus, **parīlia** for **palīlia** (from **Palēs**); **merīdiēs** for †**medīdiēs**; **nātūrālis** with suffix **-ālis** (after **r**), but **populāris** with **-āris** (after **l**).

7. Final **s** was in early Latin not always pronounced: as, **plēnu(s) fidēī.**

Note.—Traces of this pronunciation existed in Cicero's time. He speaks of the omission of final **s** before a word beginning with a consonant as "countrified" (*subrūsticum*).

8. A final consonant often disappears: as, **virgō** for †**virgōn**; **lac** for †**lact**; **cor** for †**cord.**

9. **G**, **c**, and **h** unite with a following **s** to form **x**: as, **rēx** for †**rēgs**; **dux** for †**ducs**; **trāxī** for †**trahsī.**[1]

10. **G** and **h** before **t** become **c**: as, **rēctum** for †**regtum**; **āctum** for †**agtum**; **trāctum** for †**trahtum.**[2]

11. Between **m** and **s** or **m** and **t**, a **p** is often developed: as, **sūmpsī** for †**sūmsī**; **ēmptum** for †**ēmtum.**

16. In compounds with prepositions the final consonant in the preposition was often assimilated to the following consonant, but usage varied considerably.

There is good authority for many complete or partial assimilations; as, for **ad**, **acc-**, **agg-**, **app-**, **att-**, instead of **adc-**, **adg-**, etc. Before a labial consonant we find **com-** (**comb-**, **comp-**, **comm-**), but **con-** is the form before **c**, **d**, **f**, **g**, cons. **i**, **q**, **s**, **t**, cons. **v**; we find **conl-** or **coll-**, **conr-** or **corr-**; **cō-** in **cōnectō**, **cōnīveō**, **cōnītor**, **cōnūbium**. **In** usually changes to **im-** before **p**, **b**, **m**. **Ob** and **sub** may assimilate **b** to a following **c**, **f**, **g**, or **p**; before **s** and **t** the pronunciation of prepositions ending in **b** doubtless had **p**; **surr-**, **summ-**, occur for **subr-**, **subm-**. The inseparable **amb-** loses **b** before a consonant. **Circum** often loses its **m** before **i**. The **s** of **dis** becomes **r** before a vowel and is assimilated to a following **f**; sometimes this prefix appears as **dī-**. Instead of **ex** we find **ef-** before **f** (also **ecf-**). The **d** of **red** and **sēd** is generally lost before a consonant. The preposition is better left unchanged in most other cases.

Vowel Variations

17. The parent language showed great variation in the vowel sounds of kindred words.[3]

a. This variation is often called by the German name *Ablaut.* It has left considerable traces in the forms of Latin words, appearing sometimes as a difference of quantity in the same vowel (as, **u**, **ū**; **e**, **ē**), sometimes as a difference in the vowel itself (as, **e**, **o**; **i**, **ae**):[4]—

tegō, *I cover*, **toga**, *a robe*; **pendō**, *I weigh*, **pondus**, *weight*; **fidēs**, *faith*, **fīdus**, *faithful*, **foedus**, *a treaty*; **miser**, *wretched*, **maestus**, *sad*; **dare**, *to give*, **dōnum**, *a gift*; **regō**, *I rule*, **rēx**, *a king*; **dux**, *a leader*, **dūcō** (for older **doucō**), *I lead*. Compare English *drive*, *drove* (*drave*), *driven*; *bind*, *bound*, *band*; *sing*, *sang*, *sung*; etc.

[1] Really for †**traghsī.** The **h** of **trahō** represents an older palatal sound (see § 19).

[2] Really for †**traghtum.** These are cases of partial assimilation (cf. 6, above).

[3] This variation was not without regularity, but was confined within definite limits.

[4] In Greek, however, it is more extensively preserved.

Kindred Forms

18. Both Latin and English have gone through a series of phonetic changes, different in the two languages, but following definite laws in each. Hence both preserve traces of the older speech in some features of the vowel system, and both show certain correspondences in consonants in words which each language has inherited from the old common stock. Only a few of these correspondences can be mentioned here.

19. The most important correspondences in consonants between Latin and English, in cognate words, may be seen in the following table: —[1]

Latin	English
p: pater	f: *father*, earlier *fader*[2]
f from bh: ferō, frāter	b: *to bear*, *brother*
b " " lubet, libet	v, f: *love*, *lief*
t: tū, tenuis	th: *thou*, *thin*[3]
d: duo, dent-	t: *two*, *tooth*
f from dh: faciō	d: *do*
d " " medius	d: *mid*
b " " ruber	d: *red*
c: cord-, cornū	h: *heart*, *horn*
qu: quod	wh: *what*
g: genus, gustus	c, k, ch: *kin*, *choose*
h (from gh): hortus, haedus	y, g: *yard*, *goat*
cons. i: iugum	y: *yoke*
v: ventus, ovis	w: *wind*, *ewe*
v from gv: vīvus (for †gvīvos), veniō (for †gvemiō).	qu, c, k: *quick*, *come*

NOTE 1. — Sometimes a consonant lost in Latin is still represented in English: as, niv- (for †sniv-), Eng. *snow*; ānser (for †hānser), Eng. *goose*.

NOTE 2. — From these cases of kindred words in Latin and English must be carefully distinguished those cases in which the Latin word has been taken into English either directly or through some one of the modern descendants of Latin, especially French. Thus faciō is kindred with Eng. *do*, but from the Latin participle (factum) of this verb comes Eng. *fact*, and from the French descendant (*fait*) of factum comes Eng. *feat*.

[1] The Indo-European parent speech had among its consonants voiced aspirates (bh, dh, gh). All these suffered change in Latin, the most important results being, for bh, Latin f, b (English has b, v, or f); for dh, Latin f, b, d (English has d); for gh, Latin h, g (English has y, g). The other mutes suffered in Latin much less change, while in English, as in the other Germanic languages, they have all changed considerably in accordance with what has been called Grimm's Law for the shifting of mutes.

[2] The th in *father* is a late development. The older form *fader* seems to show an exception to the rule that English th corresponds to Latin t. The primitive Germanic form was doubtless in accordance with this rule, but, on account of the position of the accent, which in Germanic was not originally on the first syllable in this word, the consonant underwent a secondary change to d.

[3] But to the group st of Latin corresponds also English st; as in Latin stō, English *stand*.

THE PARTS OF SPEECH

20. Words are divided into eight Parts of Speech: Nouns, Adjectives (including Participles), Pronouns, Verbs, Adverbs, Prepositions, Conjunctions, and Interjections.

a. A Noun is the name of a person, place, thing, or idea: as, **Caesar**; **Rōma**, *Rome;* **domus**, *a house;* **virtūs**, *virtue.*

Names of particular persons and places are called Proper Nouns; other nouns are called Common.

NOTE.—An Abstract Noun is the name of a quality or idea: as, **audācia**, *boldness;* **senectūs**, *old age.* A Collective Noun is the name of a group, class, or the like: as, **turba**, *crowd;* **exercitus**, *army.*

b. An Adjective is a word that attributes a quality: as, **bonus**, *good;* **fortis**, *brave, strong.*

NOTE 1.—A Participle is a word that attributes quality like an adjective, but, being derived from a verb, retains in some degree the power of the verb to assert: as,—Caesar cōnsul **creātus**, *Cæsar having been elected consul.*

NOTE 2.—Etymologically there is no difference between a noun and an adjective, both being formed alike. So, too, all names originally attribute quality, and any common name can still be so used. Thus, *King William* distinguishes this William from other Williams, by the attribute of royalty expressed in the name *king.*

c. A Pronoun is a word used to distinguish a person, place, thing, or idea without either naming or describing it: as, **is**, *he;* **quī**, *who;* **nōs**, *we.*

Nouns and pronouns are often called Substantives.

d. A Verb is a word which is capable of asserting something: as, **sum**, *I am;* **amat**, *he loves.*

NOTE.—In all modern speech the verb is usually the only word that asserts anything, and a verb is therefore supposed to be necessary to complete an assertion. Strictly, however, any adjective or noun may, by attributing a quality or giving a name, make a complete assertion. In the infancy of language there could have been no other means of asserting, as the verb is of comparatively late development.

e. An Adverb is a word used to express the time, place, or manner of an assertion or attribute: as, **splendidē mendāx**, *gloriously false;* **hodiē nātus est**, *he was born to-day.*

NOTE.—These same functions are often performed by cases (see §§ 214–217) of nouns, pronouns, and adjectives, and by phrases or sentences. In fact, all adverbs were originally cases or phrases, but have become specialized by use.

f. A Preposition is a word which shows the relation between a noun or pronoun and some other word or words in the same sentence: as, **per agrōs it**, *he goes over the fields;* **ē plūribus ūnum**, *one out of many.*

NOTE.—Most prepositions are specialized adverbs (cf. § 219). The relations expressed by prepositions were earlier expressed by case-endings.

g. A Conjunction is a word which connects words, or groups of words, without affecting their grammatical relations: as, **et**, *and;* **sed**, *but.*

NOTE.—Some adverbs are also used as connectives. These are called Adverbial Conjunctions or Conjunctive (Relative) Adverbs: as, **ubi**, *where;* **dōnec**, *until.*

h. Interjections are mere exclamations and are not strictly to be classed as parts of speech. Thus,—**heus**, *halloo!* **ō**, *oh!*

NOTE.—Interjections sometimes express an emotion which affects a person or thing mentioned, and so have a grammatical connection like other words: as, **vae victīs**, *woe to the conquered* (alas for the conquered)!

INFLECTION

21. Latin is an *inflected language.*

Inflection is a change made in the form of a word to show its grammatical relations.

a. Inflectional changes sometimes take place in the body of a word, or at the beginning, but oftener in its termination:—

> **vōx**, *a voice;* **vōcis**, *of a voice;* **vocō**, *I call;* **vocat**, *he calls;* **vocet**, *let him call;* **vocāvit**, *he has called;* **tangit**, *he touches;* **tetigit**, *he touched.*

b. Terminations of inflection had originally independent meanings which are now obscured. They correspond nearly to the use of prepositions auxiliaries, and personal pronouns in English.

Thus, in **vocat**, the termination is equivalent to *he* or *she;* in **vōcis**, to the preposition *of;* and in **vocet** the change of vowel signifies a change of mood.

c. Inflectional changes in the body of a verb usually denote relations of tense or mood, and often correspond to the use of auxiliary verbs in English:—

> **frangit**, *he breaks* or *is breaking;* **frēgit**, *he broke* or *has broken;* **mordet**, *he bites;* **momordit**, *he bit.*[1]

22. The inflection of Nouns, Adjectives, Pronouns, and Participles to denote gender, number, and case is called Declension, and these parts of speech are said to be *declined.*

The inflection of Verbs to denote voice, mood, tense, number, and person is called Conjugation, and the verb is said to be *conjugated.*

NOTE.—Adjectives are often said to have inflections of *comparison.* These are, however, properly stem-formations made by derivation (p. 55, footnote).

[1] The only *proper* inflections of verbs are those of the personal endings; and the changes here referred to are strictly changes of *stem*, but have become a part of the system of inflections.

23. Adverbs, Prepositions, Conjunctions, and Interjections are not inflected and are called Particles.

NOTE.—The term Particle is sometimes limited to such words as **num**, **-ne**, **an** (*interrogative*), **nōn**, **nē** (*negative*), **sī** (*conditional*), etc., which are used simply to indicate the form or construction of a sentence.

Root, Stem, and Base

24. The body of a word, to which the terminations are attached, is called the Stem.

The Stem contains the *idea* of the word without relations; but, except in the first part of a compound (as, **arti-fex**, *artificer*), it cannot ordinarily be used without some termination to express them.[1]

Thus the stem **vōc-** denotes *voice;* with **-s** added it becomes **vōx**, *a voice* or *the voice*, as the subject or agent of an action; with **-is** it becomes **vōcis**, and signifies *of a voice.*

NOTE.—The stem is in many forms so united with the termination that a comparison with other forms is necessary to determine it.

25. A Root is the simplest form attainable by analysis of a word into its component parts.

Such a form contains the main idea of the word in a very general sense, and is common also to other words either in the same language or in kindred languages.[2]

Thus the root of the stem **vōc-** is voc, which does not mean *to call*, or *I call*, or *calling*, but merely expresses vaguely the idea of calling, and cannot be used as a part of speech without terminations. With **ā-** it becomes **vocā-**, the stem of **vocāre** (*to call*); with **āv-** it is the stem of **vocāvit** (*he called*); with **āto-** it becomes the stem of **vocātus** (*called*); with **ātiōn-** it becomes the stem of **vocātiōnis** (*of a calling*). With its vowel lengthened it becomes the stem of **vōx**, **vōc-is** (*a voice:* that by which we call). This stem **vōc-**, with **-ālis** added, means *belonging to a voice;* with **-ŭla**, *a little voice.*

NOTE.—In inflected languages, words are built up from Roots, which at a very early time were used alone to express ideas, as is now done in Chinese. Roots are modified into Stems, which, by inflection, become fully formed words. The process by which roots are modified, in the various forms of derivatives and compounds, is called *Stem-building*. The whole of this process is originally one of composition, by which significant endings are added one after another to forms capable of pronunciation and conveying a meaning.

Roots had long ceased to be recognized as such before the Latin existed as a separate language. Consequently the forms which we assume as Latin roots never really existed in Latin, but are the representatives of forms used earlier.

[1] Another exception is the imperative second person singular in **-e** (as, **rege**).

[2] For example, the root STA is found in the Sanskrit *tishṭhāmi*, Greek ἵστημι, Latin **sistere** and **stāre**, German stehen, and English *stand*.

26. The Stem may be the same as the root: as in **duc-is**, *of a leader*, **fer-t**, *he bears;* but it is more frequently formed from the root —

1. By changing or lengthening its vowel: as in **scob-s**, *sawdust* (SCAB, *shave*); **rēg-is**, *of a king* (REG, *direct*); **vōc-is**, *of a voice* (VOC, *call*).

2. By the addition of a simple suffix (originally another root): as in **fugā-**, stem of **fuga**, *flight* (FUG + ā-); **regi-s**, *you rule* (REG + stem-ending $^e/_o$-); **sini-t**, *he allows* (SI + n$^e/_o$-).[1]

3. By two or more of these methods: as in **dūci-t**, *he leads* (DUC + stem-ending $^e/_o$-).

4. By derivation and composition, following the laws of development peculiar to the language. (See §§ 227 ff.)

27. The Base is that part of a word which is unchanged in inflection: as, **serv-** in **servus**; **mēns-** in **mēnsa**; **īgn-** in **īgnis.**

a. The Base and the Stem are often identical, as in many consonant stems of nouns (as, **rēg-** in **rēg-is**). If, however, the stem ends in a vowel, the latter does not appear in the base, but is variously combined with the inflectional termination. Thus the stem of **servus** is **servo-**; that of **mēnsa**, **mēnsā-**; that of **īgnis**, **īgni-**.

28. Inflectional terminations are variously modified by combination with the final vowel or consonant of the Stem, and thus the various forms of Declension and Conjugation (see §§ 36, 164) developed.

GENDER

29. The Genders distinguished in Latin are three: Masculine, Feminine, and Neuter.

30. The gender of Latin nouns is either *natural* or *grammatical.*

a. Natural Gender is distinction as to the sex of the object denoted: as, **puer** (M.), *boy;* **puella** (F.), *girl;* **rēx** (M.), *king;* **rēgīna** (F.), *queen.*

NOTE 1.—Many nouns have both a masculine and a feminine form to distinguish sex: as, **cervus**, **cerva**, *stag, doe;* **cliēns**, **clienta**, *client;* **victor**, **victrīx**, *conqueror.*

Many designations of persons (as **nauta**, *sailor*) usually though not necessarily male are always treated as masculine. Similarly names of *tribes* and *peoples* are masculine: as, **Rōmānī**, *the Romans;* **Persae**, *the Persians.*

NOTE 2.—A few neuter nouns are used to designate persons as belonging to a class: as, **mancipium tuum**, *your slave* (your chattel).

Many pet names of girls and boys are neuter in form: as, **Paegnium**, **Glycerium**.

NOTE 3.—Names of *classes* or *collections* of persons may be of any gender: as, **exercitus** (M.), **aciēs** (F.), and **agmen** (N.), *army;* **operae** (F. plur.), *workmen;* **cōpiae** (F. plur.), *troops;* **senātus** (M.), *senate;* **cohors** (F.), *cohort;* **concilium** (N.), *council.*

[1] These suffixes are Indo-European stem-endings.

b. Grammatical Gender is a formal distinction as to sex where no actual sex exists in the object. It is shown by the form of the adjective joined with the noun: as, **lapis māgnus** (M.), *a great stone;* **manus mea** (F.), *my hand.*

General Rules of Gender

31. Names of Male beings, and of Rivers, Winds, Months, and Mountains, are *masculine:*—

> **pater**, *father;* **Iūlius**, *Julius;* **Tiberis**, *the Tiber;* **auster**, *south wind;* **Iānuārius**, *January;* **Apennīnus**, *the Apennines.*

NOTE.—Names of Months are properly adjectives, the masculine noun **mēnsis**, *month*, being understood: as, **Iānuārius**, *January.*

a. A few names of Rivers ending in **-a** (as, **Allia**), with the Greek names **Lēthē** and **Styx**, are feminine; others are variable or uncertain.

b. Some names of Mountains are feminine or neuter, taking the gender of their termination: as, **Alpēs** (F.), *the Alps;* **Sōracte** (N.).

32. Names of Female beings, of Cities, Countries, Plants, Trees, and Gems, of many Animals (especially Birds), and of most abstract Qualities, are *feminine:*—

> **māter**, *mother;* **Iūlia**, *Julia;* **Rōma**, *Rome;* **Ītalia**, *Italy;* **rosa**, *rose;* **pīnus**, *pine;* **sapphīrus**, *sapphire;* **anas**, *duck;* **vēritās**, *truth.*

a. Some names of Towns and Countries are masculine: as, **Sulmō**, **Gabiī** (plur.); or neuter, as, **Tarentum**, **Illyricum.**

b. A few names of Plants and Gems follow the gender of their termination: as, **centaurēum** (N.), *centaury;* **acanthus** (M.), *bearsfoot;* **opalus** (M.), *opal.*

NOTE.—The gender of most of the above may also be recognized by the terminations, according to the rules given under the several declensions. The names of Roman women were usually feminine adjectives denoting their *gēns* or house (see § 108. *b*).

33. Indeclinable nouns, infinitives, terms or phrases used as nouns, and words quoted merely for their form, are *neuter:*—

> **fās**, *right;* **nihil**, *nothing;* **gummī**, *gum;* **scīre tuum**, *your knowledge* (to know); **trīste valē**, *a sad farewell;* **hōc ipsum diū**, *this very "long."*

34. Many nouns may be either masculine or feminine, according to the sex of the object. These are said to be of Common Gender: as, **exsul**, *exile;* **bōs**, *ox* or *cow;* **parēns**, *parent.*

NOTE.—Several names of animals have a grammatical gender, independent of sex. These are called *epicene.* Thus **lepus**, *hare*, is always masculine, and **vulpēs**, *fox*, is always feminine.

NUMBER AND CASE

35. Nouns, Pronouns, Adjectives, and Participles are declined in two Numbers, *singular* and *plural;* and in six Cases, *nominative*, *genitive*, *dative*, *accusative*, *ablative*, *vocative.*

a. The Nominative is the case of the Subject of a sentence.

b. The Genitive may generally be translated by the English Possessive, or by the Objective with the preposition *of.*

c. The Dative is the case of the Indirect Object (§ 274). It may usually be translated by the Objective with the preposition *to* or *for.*

d. The Accusative is the case of the Direct Object of a verb (§ 274). It is used also with many of the prepositions.

e. The Ablative may usually be translated by the Objective with *from, by, with, in,* or *at.* It is often used with prepositions.

f. The Vocative is the case of Direct Address.

g. All the cases, except the nominative and vocative, are used as object-cases; and are sometimes called Oblique Cases (*cāsūs oblīquī*).

h. In names of towns and a few other words appear traces of another case (the Locative), denoting the *place where:* as, **Rōmae**, *at Rome;* **rūrī**, *in the country.*

NOTE.—Still another case, the Instrumental, appears in a few adverbs (§ 215. 4).

DECLENSION OF NOUNS

36. Declension is produced by adding terminations originally significant to different forms of stems, vowel or consonant. The various phonetic corruptions in the language have given rise to the several declensions. Most of the case-endings, as given in Latin, contain also the final letter of the stem.

Adjectives are, in general, declined like nouns, and are etymologically to be classed with them; but they have several peculiarities of inflection (see § 109 ff.).

37. Nouns are inflected in five Declensions, distinguished by the final letter (*characteristic*) of the Stem, and by the case-ending of the Genitive Singular.

DECL.	CHARACTERISTIC	GEN. SING.
1	**ā**	**ae**
2	**ŏ**	**ī**
3	**ĭ** or a Consonant	**ĭs**
4	**ŭ**	**ūs**
5	**ē**	**ēī**

a. The Stem of a noun may be found, if a consonant stem, by omitting the case-ending; if a vowel stem, by substituting for the case-ending the characteristic vowel.

38. The following are General Rules of Declension:—

a. The Vocative is always the same as the Nominative, except in the singular of nouns and adjectives in **-us** of the second declension, which have **-e** in the vocative. It is not included in the paradigms, unless it differs from the nominative.

b. In neuters the Nominative and Accusative are always alike, and in the plural end in **-ă**.

c. The Accusative singular of all masculines and feminines ends in **-m**; the Accusative plural in **-s**.

d. In the last three declensions (and in a few cases in the others) the Dative singular ends in **-ī**.

e. The Dative and Ablative plural are always alike.

f. The Genitive plural always ends in **-um**.

g. Final **-i**, **-o**, **-u** of inflection are always *long*; final **-a** is *short*, except in the Ablative singular of the first declension; final **-e** is *long* in the first and fifth declensions, *short* in the second and third. Final **-is** and **-us** are *long* in plural cases.

Case-endings of the Five Declensions

39. The regular Case-endings of the several declensions are the following:—[1]

	Decl. I	Decl. II		Decl. III		Decl. IV		Decl. V
				Singular				
	F.	M.	N.	M., F.	N.	M.	N.	F.
Nom.	-a	-us / ——	-um	-s	(modified stem)	-us	-ū	-ēs
Gen.	-ae	-ī		-is		-ūs		-ēī (-ē)
Dat.	-ae	-ō		-ī		-uī (-ū)	-ū	-ēī (-ē)
Acc.	-am	-um	-um	-em (-im)	(like nom.)	-um	-ū	-em
Abl.	-ā	-ō		-e (-ī)		-ū		-ē
Voc.	-a	-e	-um	(like nom.)		-us	-ū	-ēs
				Plural				
N.V.	-ae	-ī	-a	-ēs	-a, -ia	-ūs	-ua	-ēs
Gen.	-ārum	-ōrum		-um, -ium		-uum		-ērum
D.Ab.	-īs	-īs		-ibus		-ibus (-ubus)		-ēbus
Acc.	-ās	-ōs	-a	-ēs (-īs)	-a, -ia	-ūs	-ua	-ēs

[1] For ancient, rare, and Greek forms (which are here omitted), see under the several declensions.

FIRST DECLENSION (*ā*-STEMS)

40. The Stem of nouns of the First Declension ends in **ā-**. The Nominative ending is **-a** (the stem-vowel shortened), except in Greek nouns.

41. Latin nouns of the First Declension are thus declined: —

stella, F., *star*
STEM **stellā-**

		SINGULAR	CASE-ENDINGS
NOM.	**stella**	*a star*	**-a**
GEN.	**stellae**	*of a star*	**-ae**
DAT.	**stellae**	*to* or *for a star*	**-ae**
ACC.	**stellam**	*a star*	**-am**
ABL.	**stellā**	*with, from, by,* etc. *a star*	**-ā**
		PLURAL	
NOM.	**stellae**	*stars*	**-ae**
GEN.	**stellārum**	*of stars*	**-ārum**
DAT.	**stellīs**	*to* or *for stars*	**-īs**
ACC.	**stellās**	*stars*	**-ās**
ABL.	**stellīs**	*with, from, by,* etc. *stars*	**-īs**

a. The Latin has no article; hence **stella** may mean *a star*, *the star*, or simply *star*.

Gender in the First Declension

42. Nouns of the first declension are Feminine.

Exceptions: Nouns masculine from their signification: as, **nauta**, *sailor*. So a few family or personal names: as, **Mūrēna, Dolābella, Scaevola**[1]; also, **Hadria**, *the Adriatic*.

Case-Forms in the First Declension

43. *a.* The genitive singular anciently ended in **-āī** (dissyllabic), which is occasionally found: as, **aulāī**. The same ending sometimes occurs in the dative, but only as a diphthong.

[1] **Scaevola** is really a feminine adjective, used as a noun, meaning *little left hand;* but, being used as the name of a man (originally a *nickname*), it became masculine. Original genders are often thus changed by a change in the sense of a noun.

b. An old genitive in **-ās** is preserved in the word **familiās**, often used in the combinations **pater** (**māter, fīlius, fīlia**) **familiās**, *father*, etc., *of a family* (plur. **patrēs familiās** or **familiārum**).

c. The Locative form for the singular ends in **-ae**; for the plural in **-īs** (cf. p. 34, footnote): as, **Rōmae**, *at Rome;* **Athēnīs**, *at Athens.*

d. The genitive plural is sometimes found in **-um** instead of **-ārum**, especially in Greek patronymics, as, **Aeneadum**, *sons of Æneas*, and in compounds with **-cŏla** and **-gĕna**, signifying *dwelling* and *descent:* as, **caelicolum**, *celestials;* **Trōiugenum**, *sons of Troy;* so also in the Greek nouns **amphora** and **drachma**.

e. The dative and ablative plural of **dea**, *goddess*, **fīlia**, *daughter*, end in an older form **-ābus** (**deābus, fīliābus**) to distinguish them from the corresponding cases of **deus**, *god*, and **fīlius**, *son* (**deīs, fīliīs**). So rarely with other words, as, **līberta**, *freed-woman;* **mūla**, *she-mule;* **equa**, *mare.* But, except when the two sexes are mentioned together (as in formulas, documents, etc.), the form in **-īs** is preferred in all but **dea** and **fīlia**.

NOTE 1.—The old ending of the ablative singular (**-ād**) is sometimes retained in early Latin: as, **praidād**, *booty* (later, **praedā**).

NOTE 2.—In the dative and ablative plural **-eis** for **-īs** is sometimes found, and **-iīs** (as in **taeniīs**) is occasionally contracted to **-īs** (**taenīs**); so regularly in words in **-âia** (as, **Bâīs** from **Bâiae**).

Greek Nouns of the First Declension

44. Many nouns of the First Declension borrowed from the Greek are entirely Latinized (as, **aula**, *court*); but others retain traces of their Greek case-forms in the singular.

	Electra, F.	*synopsis*, F.	*art of music*, F.
NOM.	Ēlectra (-ā)	epitomē	mūsica (-ē)
GEN.	Ēlectrae	epitomēs	mūsicae (-ēs)
DAT.	Ēlectrae	epitomae	mūsicae
ACC.	Ēlectram (-ān)	epitomēn	mūsicam (-ēn)
ABL.	Ēlectrā	epitomē	mūsicā (-ē)

	Andromache, F.	*Æneas*, M.	*Persian*, M.
NOM.	Andromachē (-a)	Aenēās	Persēs (-a)
GEN.	Andromachēs (-ae)	Aenēae	Persae
DAT.	Andromachae	Aenēae	Persae
ACC.	Andromachēn (-am)	Aenēān (-am)	Persēn (-am)
ABL.	Andromachē (-ā)	Aenēā	Persē (-ā)
VOC.	Andromachē (-a)	Aenēā (-a)	Persa

	Anchises, M.	*son of Æneas*, M.	*comet*, M.
Nom.	Anchīsēs	Aeneadēs (-a)	comētēs (-a)
Gen.	Anchīsae	Aeneadae	comētae
Dat.	Anchīsae	Aeneadae	comētae
Acc.	Anchīsēn (-am)	Aeneadēn	comētēn (-am)
Abl.	Anchīsē (-ā)	Aeneadē (-ā)	comētā (-ē)
Voc.	Anchīsē (-ā, -a)	Aeneadē (-a)	comēta

There are (besides proper names) about thirty-five of these words, several being names of plants or arts: as, crambē, *cabbage;* mūsicē, *music.* Most have also regular Latin forms: as, comēta; but the nominative sometimes has the a long.

a. Greek forms are found only in the singular; the plural, when it occurs, is regular: as, **comētae, -ārum**, etc.

b. Many Greek nouns vary between the first, the second, and the third declensions: as, **Boōtae** (genitive of **Boōtēs, -is**), **Thūcydidās** (accusative plural of **Thūcydidēs, -is**). See § 52. *a* and § 81.

Note.—The Greek accusative Scīpiadam, from Scīpiadēs, *descendant of the Scipios,* is found in Horace.

SECOND DECLENSION (*o*-STEMS)

45. The Stem of nouns of the Second Declension ends in **ŏ-**: as, **viro-** (stem of **vir**, *man*), **servo-** (stem of **servus** or **servos**, *slave*), **bello-** (stem of **bellum**, *war*).

a. The Nominative is formed from the stem by adding **s** in masculines and feminines, and **m** in neuters, the vowel **ŏ** being weakened to **ŭ** (see §§ 6. *a*, 46. N.[1]).

b. In most nouns whose stem ends in **rŏ-** the **s** is not added in the Nominative, but **o** is lost, and **e** intrudes before **r**,[1] if not already present: as, **ager**, stem **agrŏ-**[2]; cf. **puer**, stem **puero-**.

Exceptions: erus, hesperus, iūniperus, mōrus, numerus, taurus, umerus, uterus, vīrus, and many Greek nouns.

c. The stem-vowel **ŏ** has a variant form **ĕ**,[3] which is preserved in the Latin vocative singular of nouns in **-us**: as, **servĕ**, vocative of **servus**, *slave.*

Note.—In composition this ĕ appears as ĭ. Thus,—belli-ger, *warlike* (from bello/e-, stem of bellum, *war*).

46. Nouns of the Second Declension in **-us** (**-os**) and **-um** (**-om**) are thus declined:—

1 Compare the English *chamber* from French *chambre.*

2 Compare Greek ἀγρός, which shows the original o of the stem.

3 By so-called *Ablaut* (see § 17. *a*).

	servus, M., *slave* STEM servo-		**bellum**, N., *war* STEM bello-		**Pompêius**, M., *Pompey* STEM Pompêio-
		SINGULAR			
		CASE-ENDINGS		CASE-ENDINGS	
NOM.	servus (-os)	-us (-os)	bellum	-um	Pompêius
GEN.	servī	-ī	bellī	-ī	Pompêī
DAT.	servō	-ō	bellō	-ō	Pompêiō
ACC.	servum (-om)	-um (-om)	bellum	-um	Pompêium
ABL.	servō	-ō	bellō	-ō	Pompêiō
VOC.	serve	-e	bellum	-um	Pompêī (-eī)
		PLURAL			
NOM.	servī	-ī	bella	-a	Pompêī
GEN.	servōrum	-ōrum	bellōrum	-ōrum	Pompêiōrum
DAT.	servīs	-īs	bellīs	-īs	Pompêīs
ACC.	servōs	-ōs	bella	-a	Pompêiōs
ABL.	servīs	-īs	bellīs	-īs	Pompêīs

NOTE 1.—The earlier forms for nominative and accusative were -os, -om, and these were always retained after u and v up to the end of the Republic. The terminations s and m are sometimes omitted in inscriptions: as, Cornēlio for Cornēlios, Cornēliom.

NOTE 2.—Stems in quo-, like equo-, change qu to c before u. Thus,—ecus (earlier equos), equī, equō, ecum (earlier equom), eque. Modern editions disregard this principle.

47. Nouns of the Second Declension in -er and -ir are thus declined:—

	puer, M., *boy* STEM puero-	**ager**, M., *field* STEM agro-	**vir**, M., *man* STEM viro-	
		SINGULAR		CASE-ENDINGS
NOM.	puer	ager	vir	——
GEN.	puerī	agrī	virī	-ī
DAT.	puerō	agrō	virō	-ō
ACC.	puerum	agrum	virum	-um
ABL.	puerō	agrō	virō	-ō
		PLURAL		
NOM.	puerī	agrī	virī	-ī
GEN.	puerōrum	agrōrum	virōrum	-ōrum
DAT.	puerīs	agrīs	virīs	-īs
ACC.	puerōs	agrōs	virōs	-ōs
ABL.	puerīs	agrīs	virīs	-īs

NOTE.—When e belongs to the stem, as in puer, it is retained throughout; otherwise it appears only in the nominative and vocative singular, as in ager.

Gender in the Second Declension

48. Nouns ending in **-us** (**-os**), **-er**, **-ir**, are Masculine; those ending in **-um** (**-on**) are Neuter.

Exceptions: Names of countries and towns in **-us** (**-os**) are Feminine: as, **Aegyptus**, **Corinthus**. Also many names of plants and gems, with the following: **alvus**, *belly;* **carbasus**, *linen* (pl. **carbasa**, *sails*, N.); **colus**, *distaff;* **humus**, *ground;* **vannus**, *winnowing-shovel.*

Many Greek nouns retain their original gender: as, **arctus** (F.), *the Polar Bear;* **methodus** (F.), *method.*

a. The following in **-us** are Neuter; their accusative (as with all neuters) is the same as the nominative: **pelagus**, *sea;* **vīrus**, *poison;* **vulgus** (rarely M.), *the crowd.* They are not found in the plural, except **pelagus**, which has a rare nominative and accusative plural **pelagē**.

NOTE.—The nominative plural neuter **cētē**, *sea monsters*, occurs; the nominative singular **cētus** occurs in Vitruvius.

Case-Forms in the Second Declension

49. *a.* The Locative form of this declension ends for the singular in **-ī**: as, **humī**, *on the ground;* **Corinthī**, *at Corinth;* for the plural, in **-īs**: as, **Philippīs**, *at Philippi* (cf. p. 34, footnote).

b. The genitive of nouns in **-ius** or **-ium** ended, until the Augustan Age, in a single **-ī**: as, **fīlī**, *of a son;* **Pompêī**, *of Pompey* (**Pompêius**); but the accent of the nominative is retained: as, **ingĕ′nī**, *of genius.*[1]

c. Proper names in **-ius** have **-ī** in the vocative, retaining the accent of the nominative: as, **Vergĭ′lī**. So also, **fīlius**, *son;* **genius**, *divine guardian:* as, **audī, mī fīlī**, *hear, my son.*

Adjectives in **-ĭus** form the vocative in **-ie**, and some of these are occasionally used as nouns: as, **Lacedaemonie**, *O Spartan.*

NOTE.—Greek names in **-īus** have the vocative **-īe**: as, **Lyrcīus**, vocative **Lyrcīe**.

d. The genitive plural often has **-um** or (after **v**) **-om** (cf. § 6. *a*) instead of **-ōrum**, especially in the poets: as, **deum**, **superum**, **dīvom**, *of the gods;* **virum**, *of men.* Also in compounds of **vir**, and in many words of money, measure, and weight: as, **Sēvirum**, *of the Seviri;* **nummum**, *of coins;* **iūgerum**, *of acres.*

e. The original ending of the ablative singular (**-ōd**) is sometimes found in early Latin: as, **Gnaivōd** (later, **Gnaeō**), *Cneius.*

f. Proper names in **-âius**, **-êius**, **-ôius** (as, **Aurunculêius**, **Bôī**), are declined like **Pompêius**.

[1] The genitive in **-iī** occurs once in Virgil, and constantly in Ovid, but was probably unknown to Cicero.

g. **Deus** (M.), *god*, is thus declined: —

	SINGULAR	PLURAL
NOM.	deus	deī (diī), dī
GEN.	deī	deōrum, deum
DAT.	deō	deīs (diīs), dīs
ACC.	deum	deōs
ABL.	deō	deīs (diīs), dīs

NOTE. — The vocative singular of **deus** does not occur in classic Latin, but is said to have been **dee**; **deus** (like the nominative) occurs in the Vulgate. For the genitive plural, **dīvum** or **dīvom** (from **dīvus**, *divine*) is often used.

50. The following stems in **ero-**, in which **e** belongs to the stem, retain the **e** throughout and are declined like **puer** (§ 47): —

adulter, *adulterer*; **gener**, *son-in-law*; **puer**, *boy*;
socer, *father-in-law*; **vesper**, *evening*; **Līber**, *Bacchus*.

Also, the adjective **līber**, *free*, of which **līberī**, *children*, is the plural (§ 111. *a*), and compounds in **-fer** and **-ger** (stem **fero-**, **gero-**): as, **lūcifer**, *morning star*; **armiger**, *squire*.

a. An old nominative **socerus** occurs. So vocative **puere**, *boy*, as if from †**puerus** (regularly **puer**).

b. **Vir**, *man*, has genitive **virī**; the adjective **satur**, *sated*, has **saturī**; **vesper**, *evening*, has ablative **vespere** (locative **vesperī**, *in the evening*).

c. **Mulciber**, *Vulcan*, has **-berī** and **-brī** in the genitive. The barbaric names **Hibēr** and **Celtibēr** retain **ē** throughout.

51. The following, not having **e** in the stem, insert it in the nominative singular and are declined like **ager** (§ 47): —

ager, *field*, stem **agro-**; **coluber**, *snake*; **magister**, *master*;
aper, *boar*; **conger**, *sea eel*; **minister**, *servant*;
arbiter, *judge*; **culter**, *knife*; **oleaster**, *wild olive*;
auster, *south wind*; **faber**, *smith*; **onager** (**-grus**), *wild ass*;
cancer, *crab*; **fiber**, *beaver*; **scomber** (**-brus**), *mackerel*.
caper, *goat*; **liber**, *book*;

Greek Nouns of the Second Declension

52. Greek nouns of the Second Declension end in **-os**, **-ōs**, masculine or feminine, and in **-on** neuter.

They are mostly proper names and are declined as follows in the Singular, the Plural, when found, being regular: —

	mȳthos, M. *fable*	**Athōs**, M. *Athos*	**Dēlos**, F. *Delos*	**Īlion**, N. *Ilium*
		SINGULAR		
NOM.	mȳthos	Athōs (-ō)	Dēlos	Īlion
GEN.	mȳthī	Athō (-ī)	Dēlī	Īliī
DAT.	mȳthō	Athō	Dēlō	Īliō
ACC.	mȳthon	Athōn (-um)	Dēlon (-um)	Īlion
ABL.	mȳthō	Athō	Dēlō	Īliō
VOC.	mȳthe	Athōs	Dēle	Īlion

a. Many names in -ēs belonging to the third declension have also a genitive in -ī: as, **Thūcȳdidēs, Thūcȳdidī** (compare § 44. *b*).

b. Several names in -er have also a nominative in **-us**: as, **Teucer** or **Teucrus**. The name **Panthūs** has the vocative **Panthū** (§ 81. 3).

c. The genitive plural of certain titles of books takes the Greek termination **-ōn**: as, **Geōrgicōn**, *of the Georgics*.

d. The termination **-oe** (for Greek -οι) is sometimes found in the nominative plural: as, **Adelphoe**, *the Adelphi* (a play of Terence).

e. Greek names in **-eus** (like **Orpheus**) have forms of the second and third declensions (see § 82).

THIRD DECLENSION (CONSONANT AND *i*-STEMS)

53. Nouns of the Third Declension end in **a, e, ī, ō, y, c, l, n, r, s, t, x.**

54. Stems of the Third Declension are classed as follows:—

I. Consonant Stems
- *a.* Mute stems.
- *b.* Liquid and Nasal stems.

II. **I**-Stems
- *a.* Pure **i**-stems.
- *b.* Mixed **i**-stems.

55. The Nominative is always derived from the stem.

The variety in form in the Nominative is due to simple modifications of the stem, of which the most important are —

1. Combination of final consonants: as of **c** (or **g**) and **s** to form **x**; **dux, ducis**, stem **duc-**; **rēx, rēgis**, stem **rēg-**.

2. Omission of a final consonant: as of a final nasal; **leō, leōnis**, stem **leōn-**; **ōrātiō, ōrātiōnis**, stem **ōrātiōn-**.

3. Omission of a final vowel: as of final **i**; **calcar, calcāris**, stem **calcāri-**.

4. Change of vowel in the final syllable: as of **a** to **e**; **prīnceps** (for **-caps**), **prīncipis**, stem **prīncip-** (for **-cap-**).

Consonant Stems

Mute Stems

56. Masculine and Feminine Nouns with mute stems form the Nominative by adding **s** to the stem.

A labial (**p**) is retained before **s**: as, **prīncep-s.**

A lingual (**t, d**) is dropped before **s**: as, **mīles** (stem **mīlit-**), **cūstōs** (stem **cūstōd-**).

A palatal (**c, g**) unites with **s** to form **x**: as, **dux** (for †**duc-s**), **rēx** (for †**rēg-s**).

a. In dissyllabic stems the final syllable often shows **e** in the nominative and **i** in the stem: as, **prīnceps**, stem **prīncip-** (for **-cap-**).

57. Nouns of this class are declined as follows:

	prīnceps, C., *chief* STEM **prīncip-**	**rādīx**, F., *root* STEM **rādīc-**	**mīles**, M., *soldier* STEM **mīlit-**	
		SINGULAR		CASE-ENDINGS
NOM.	prīncep**s**	rādī**x**	mīle**s**	**-s**
GEN.	prīncip**is**	rādīc**is**	mīlit**is**	**-is**
DAT.	prīncip**ī**	rādīc**ī**	mīlit**ī**	**-ī**
ACC.	prīncip**em**	rādīc**em**	mīlit**em**	**-em**
ABL.	prīncip**e**	rādīc**e**	mīlit**e**	**-e**
		PLURAL		
NOM.	prīncip**ēs**	rādīc**ēs**	mīlit**ēs**	**-ēs**
GEN.	prīncip**um**	rādīc**um**	mīlit**um**	**-um**
DAT.	prīncip**ibus**	rādīc**ibus**	mīlit**ibus**	**-ibus**
ACC.	prīncip**ēs**	rādīc**ēs**	mīlit**ēs**	**-ēs**
ABL.	prīncip**ibus**	rādīc**ibus**	mīlit**ibus**	**-ibus**

	cūstōs, C., *guard* STEM **cūstōd-**	**dux**, C., *leader* STEM **duc-**	**rēx**, M., *king* STEM **rēg-**	
		SINGULAR		CASE-ENDINGS
NOM.	cūstō**s**	du**x**	rē**x**	**-s**
GEN.	cūstōd**is**	duc**is**	rēg**is**	**-is**
DAT.	cūstōd**ī**	duc**ī**	rēg**ī**	**-ī**
ACC.	cūstōd**em**	duc**em**	rēg**em**	**-em**
ABL.	cūstōd**e**	duc**e**	rēg**e**	**-e**

PLURAL

NOM.	cūstōd**ēs**	duc**ēs**	rēg**ēs**	**-ēs**
GEN.	cūstōd**um**	duc**um**	rēg**um**	**-um**
DAT.	cūstōd**ibus**	duc**ibus**	rēg**ibus**	**-ibus**
ACC.	cūstōd**ēs**	duc**ēs**	rēg**ēs**	**-ēs**
ABL.	cūstōd**ibus**	duc**ibus**	rēg**ibus**	**-ibus**

a. In like manner are declined —

ariēs, -etis (M.), *ram;* **comes, -itis** (C.), *companion;* **lapis, -idis** (M.), *stone;* **iūdex, -icis** (M.), *judge;* **cornīx, -īcis** (F.), *raven*, and many other nouns.

58. Most mute stems are Masculine or Feminine. Those that are neuter have for the Nominative the simple stem. But, —

a. Lingual Stems (**t, d**) ending in two consonants drop the final mute: as, **cor** (stem **cord-**), **lac** (stem **lact-**). So also stems in **ăt-** from the Greek: as, **poēma** (stem **poēmat-**).

b. The stem **capit-** shows **u** in the nominative (**caput** for †**capot**).

59. Nouns of this class are declined as follows: —

	cor, N., *heart* STEM **cord-**	**caput**, N., *head* STEM **capit-**	**poēma**, N., *poem* STEM **poēmat-**	CASE-ENDINGS
		SINGULAR		
NOM.	cor	caput	poēma	——
GEN.	cord**is**	capit**is**	poēmat**is**	**-is**
DAT.	cord**ī**	capit**ī**	poēmat**ī**	**-ī**
ACC.	cor	caput	poēma	——
ABL.	cord**e**	capit**e**	poēmat**e**	**-e**
		PLURAL		
NOM.	cord**a**	capit**a**	poēmat**a**	**-a**
GEN.	——	capit**um**	poēmat**um**	**-um**
DAT.	cord**ibus**	capit**ibus**	poēmat**ibus**	**-ibus**
ACC.	cord**a**	capit**a**	poēmat**a**	**-a**
ABL.	cord**ibus**	capit**ibus**	poēmat**ibus**	**-ibus**

60. The following irregularities require notice: —

a. Greek neuters with nominative singular in **-a** (as **poēma**) frequently end in **-īs** in the dative and ablative plural, and rarely in **-ōrum** in the genitive plural; as, **poēmatīs** (for **poēmatibus**), **poēmatōrum** (for **poēmatum**).

b. A number of monosyllabic nouns with mute stems want the genitive plural (like **cor**). See § 103. *g.* 2.

Liquid and Nasal Stems (*l, n, r*)

61. In Masculine and Feminine nouns with liquid and nasal stems the Nominative is the same as the stem.

Exceptions are the following: —

1. Stems in **ōn-** drop **n** in the nominative: as in **legiō**, stem **legiōn-**.
2. Stems in **din-** and **gin-** drop **n** and keep an original **ō** in the nominative: as in **virgō**, stem **virgin-**.[1]
3. Stems in **in-** (not **din-** or **gin-**) retain **n** and have **e** instead of **i** in the nominative: as in **cornicen**, stem **cornicin-**.[1]
4. Stems in **tr-** have **-ter** in the nominative: as, **pater**, stem **patr-**.[2]

62. Nouns of this class are declined as follows: —

	cōnsul, M., *consul* STEM **cōnsul-**	**leō**, M., *lion* STEM **leōn-**	**virgō**, F., *maiden* STEM **virgin-**	**pater**, M., *father* STEM **patr-**	
			SINGULAR		CASE-ENDINGS
NOM.	cōnsul	leō	virgō	pater	——
GEN.	cōnsul**is**	leōn**is**	virgin**is**	patr**is**	**-is**
DAT.	cōnsul**ī**	leōn**ī**	virgin**ī**	patr**ī**	**-ī**
ACC.	cōnsul**em**	leōn**em**	virgin**em**	patr**em**	**-em**
ABL.	cōnsul**e**	leōn**e**	virgin**e**	patr**e**	**-e**
			PLURAL		
NOM.	cōnsul**ēs**	leōn**ēs**	virgin**ēs**	patr**ēs**	**-ēs**
GEN.	cōnsul**um**	leōn**um**	virgin**um**	patr**um**	**-um**
DAT.	cōnsul**ibus**	leōn**ibus**	virgin**ibus**	patr**ibus**	**-ibus**
ACC.	cōnsul**ēs**	leōn**ēs**	virgin**ēs**	patr**ēs**	**-ēs**
ABL.	cōnsul**ibus**	leōn**ibus**	virgin**ibus**	patr**ibus**	**-ibus**

NOTE 1. — Stems in **ll-**, **rr-** (N.) lose one of their liquids in the nominative: as, **far, farris**; **mel, mellis**.

NOTE 2. — A few masculine and feminine stems have a nominative in **-s** as well as in **-r**: as, **honōs** or **honor**, **arbōs** or **arbor**.

NOTE 3. — **Canis**, *dog*, and **iuvenis**, *youth*, have **-is** in the nominative.

[1] These differences depend in part upon special phonetic laws, in accordance with which vowels in weakly accented or unaccented syllables are variously modified, and in part upon the influence of analogy.

[2] These, no doubt, had originally **ter-** in the stem, but this had become weakened to **tr-** in some of the cases even in the parent speech. In Latin only the nominative and vocative singular show the **e**. But cf. **Māspitris** and **Māspiteris** (**Mā[r]s-piter**), quoted by Priscian as old forms.

63. In Neuter nouns with liquid or nasal stems the Nominative is the same as the stem.

Exceptions: 1. Stems in **in-** have **e** instead of **i** in the nominative: as in **nōmen**, stem **nōmin-**.

2. Most stems in **er-** and **or-** have **-us** in the nominative: as, **genus**, stem **gener-**.[1]

64. Nouns of this class are declined as follows: —

	nomen, N., *name* STEM **nomin-**	**genus**, N., *race* STEM **gener-**	**corpus**, N., *body* STEM **corpor-**	**aequor**, N., *sea* STEM **aequor-**
	SINGULAR			
NOM.	nōmen	genus	corpus	aequor
GEN.	nōmin**is**	gener**is**	corpor**is**	aequor**is**
DAT.	nōmin**ī**	gener**ī**	corpor**ī**	aequor**ī**
ACC.	nōmen	genus	corpus	aequor
ABL.	nōmin**e**	gener**e**	corpor**e**	aequor**e**
	PLURAL			
NOM.	nōmin**a**	gener**a**	corpor**a**	aequor**a**
GEN.	nōmin**um**	gener**um**	corpor**um**	aequor**um**
DAT.	nōmin**ibus**	gener**ibus**	corpor**ibus**	aequor**ibus**
ACC.	nōmin**a**	gener**a**	corpor**a**	aequor**a**
ABL.	nōmin**ibus**	gener**ibus**	corpor**ibus**	aequor**ibus**

So also are declined **opus, -eris**, *work;* **pīgnus, -eris** or **-oris**, *pledge*, etc.

NOTE. — The following real or apparent liquid and nasal stems have the genitive plural in **-ium**, and are to be classed with the i-stems: **imber, linter, ūter, venter; glīs, mās, mūs, [†rēn]**; also **vīrēs** (plural of **vīs**: see § 79).

i-STEMS

65. Nouns of this class include —

1. Pure **i**-Stems:

a. Masculine and Feminine parisyllabic[2] nouns in **-is** and four in **-er**.
b. Neuters in **-e, -al**, and **-ar**.

2. Mixed **i**-Stems, declined in the singular like consonant stems, in the plural like **i**-stems.

[1] These were originally **s**-stems (cf. § 15. 4).
[2] I.e. having the same number of syllables in the nominative and genitive singular.

Pure *i*-Stems

66. Masculine and Feminine parisyllabic nouns in **-is** form the Nominative singular by adding **s** to the stem.

Four stems in **bri-** and **tri-** do not add **s** to form the nominative, but drop **i** and insert **e** before **r**. These are **imber, linter, ūter, venter.**

67. Nouns of this class are declined as follows: —

	sitis, F., *thirst*	**turris**, F., *tower*	**īgnis**, M., *fire*	**imber**, M., *rain*
	STEM **siti-**	STEM **turri-**	STEM **īgni-**	STEM **imbri-**
		SINGULAR		
NOM.	sit**is**	turr**is**	īgn**is**	imber
GEN.	sit**is**	turr**is**	īgn**is**	imbr**is**
DAT.	sit**ī**	turr**ī**	īgn**ī**	imbr**ī**
ACC.	sit**im**	turr**im** (**-em**)	īgn**em**	imbr**em**
ABL.	sit**ī**	turr**ī** (**-e**)	īgn**ī** (**-e**)	imbr**ī** (**-e**)
		PLURAL		
NOM.		turr**ēs**	īgn**ēs**	imbr**ēs**
GEN.		turr**ium**	īgn**ium**	imbr**ium**
DAT.		turr**ibus**	īgn**ibus**	imbr**ibus**
ACC.		turr**īs** (**-ēs**)	īgn**īs** (**-ēs**)	imbr**īs** (**-ēs**)
ABL.		turr**ibus**	īgn**ibus**	imbr**ibus**

68. In Neuters the Nominative is the same as the stem, with final **i** changed to **e**: as, **mare**, stem **mari-**. But most nouns[1] in which the **i** of the stem is preceded by **āl** or **ār** lose the final vowel and shorten the preceding **ā**: as, **animăl**, stem **animāli-**.[2]

a. Neuters in **-e**, **-al**, and **-ar** have **-ī** in the ablative singular, **-ium** in the genitive plural, and **-ia** in the nominative and accusative plural: as, **animal, animālī, -ia, -ium.**

1 Such are **animal, bacchānal, bidental, capital, cervīcal, cubital, lupercal, minūtal, puteal, quadrantal, toral, tribūnal, vectīgal; calcar, cochlear, exemplar, lacūnar, laquear, lūcar, lūminar, lupānar, palear, pulvīnar, torcular.** Cf. the plurals **dentālia, frontālia, genuālia, spōnsālia; altāria, plantāria, speculāria, tālāria**; also many names of festivals, as, **Sāturnālia.**

2 Exceptions are **augurāle, collāre, fōcāle, nāvāle, penetrāle, rāmāle, scūtāle, tībiāle; alveāre, capillāre, cochleāre.**

69. Nouns of this class are declined as follows: —

	sedīle, N., *seat* STEM **sedīli-**	**animal**, N., *animal* STEM **animāli-**	**calcar**, N., *spur* STEM **calcāri-**	
		SINGULAR		CASE-ENDINGS
NOM.	sedī**le**	animal	calcar	**-e** or —
GEN.	sedīl**is**	animāl**is**	calcār**is**	**-is**
DAT.	sedīl**ī**	animāl**ī**	calcār**ī**	**-ī**
ACC.	sedī**le**	animal	calcar	**-e** or —
ABL.	sedīl**ī**	animāl**ī**	calcār**ī**	**-ī**
		PLURAL		
NOM.	sedīl**ia**	animāl**ia**	calcār**ia**	**-ia**
GEN.	sedīl**ium**	animāl**ium**	calcār**ium**	**-ium**
DAT.	sedīl**ibus**	animāl**ibus**	calcār**ibus**	**-ibus**
ACC.	sedīl**ia**	animāl**ia**	calcār**ia**	**-ia**
ABL.	sedīl**ibus**	animāl**ibus**	calcār**ibus**	**-ibus**

Mixed *i*-Stems

70. Mixed **i**-stems are either original **i**-stems that have lost their **i**-forms in the singular, or consonant stems that have assumed **i**-forms in the plural.

NOTE. — It is sometimes impossible to distinguish between these two classes.

71. Mixed **i**-stems have **-em** in the accusative and **-e** in the ablative singular, **-ium** in the genitive[1] and **-īs** or **-ēs** in the accusative plural. They include the following: —

1. Nouns in **-ēs**, gen. **-is**.[2]
2. Monosyllables in **-s** or **-x** preceded by a consonant: as, **ars**, **pōns**, **arx**.
3. Polysyllables in **-ns** or **-rs**: as, **cliēns**, **cohors**.
4. Nouns in **-tās**, genitive **-tātis** (genitive plural usually **-um**)[1]: as, **cīvitās**.
5. **Penātēs**, **optimātēs**, and nouns denoting birth or abode (*patrials*) in **-ās**, **-īs**, plural **-ātēs**, **-ītēs**: as, **Arpīnās**, plural **Arpīnātēs**; **Quirīs**, plural **Quirītēs**.
6. The following monosyllables in **-s** or **-x** preceded by a vowel: **dōs**, **fraus**, **glīs**, **līs**, **mās**, **mūs**, **nix**, **nox**, **strix**, **vīs**.

[1] There is much variety in the practice of the ancients, some of these words having **-ium**, some **-um**, and some both.

[2] These are **acīnacēs**, **aedēs**, **alcēs**, **caedēs**, **cautēs**, **clādēs**, **compāgēs**, **contāgēs**, **famēs**, **fēlēs**, **fidēs** (plural), **indolēs**, **lābēs**, **luēs**, **mēlēs**, **mōlēs**, **nūbēs**, **palumbēs**, **prōlēs**, **prōpāgēs**, **pūbēs**, **sēdēs**, **saepēs**, **sordēs**, **strāgēs**, **struēs**, **subolēs**, **tābēs**, **torquēs**, **tudēs**, **vātēs**, **vehēs**, **veprēs**, **verrēs**, **vulpēs**; **aedēs** has also nominative **aedis**.

72. Nouns of this class are thus declined: —

	nūbēs, F., *cloud* STEM **nūb(i)-**	**urbs**, F., *city* STEM **urb(i)-**	**nox**, F., *night* STEM **noct(i)-**	**cliēns**, M., *client* STEM **client(i)-**	**aetās**, F., *age* STEM **aetāt(i)-**
			SINGULAR		
NOM.	nūbē**s**	urb**s**	no**x**	cliēn**s**	aetā**s**
GEN.	nūb**is**	urb**is**	noct**is**	client**is**	aetāt**is**
DAT.	nūb**ī**	urb**ī**	noct**ī**	client**ī**	aetāt**ī**
ACC.	nūb**em**	urb**em**	noct**em**	client**em**	aetāt**em**
ABL.	nūb**e**	urb**e**	noct**e**	client**e**	aetāt**e**
			PLURAL		
NOM.	nūb**ēs**	urb**ēs**	noct**ēs**	client**ēs**	aetāt**ēs**
GEN.	nūb**ium**	urb**ium**	noct**ium**	client**ium** [1]	aetāt**um** [2]
DAT.	nūb**ibus**	urb**ibus**	noct**ibus**	client**ibus**	aetāt**ibus**
ACC.	nūb**īs**(-**ēs**)	urb**īs**(-**ēs**)	noct**īs**(-**ēs**)	client**īs**(-**ēs**)	aetāt**īs**(-**ēs**)
ABL.	nūb**ibus**	urb**ibus**	noct**ibus**	client**ibus**	aetāt**ibus**

Summary of *i*-Stems

73. The i-declension was confused even to the Romans themselves, nor was it stable at all periods of the language, early Latin having i-forms which afterwards disappeared. There was a tendency in nouns to lose the i-forms, in adjectives to gain them. The nominative plural (-īs) [3] was most thoroughly lost, next the accusative singular (**-im**), next the ablative (-ī); while the genitive and accusative plural (**-ium**, **-īs**) were retained in almost all.

74. I-stems show the **i** of the stem in the following forms: —

a. They have the genitive plural in **-ium** (but some monosyllables lack it entirely). For a few exceptions, see § 78.

b. All neuters have the nominative and accusative plural in **-ia**.

c. The accusative plural (M. or F.) is regularly **-īs**.

d. The accusative singular (M. or F.) of a few ends in **-im** (§ 75).

e. The ablative singular of all neuters, and of many masculines and feminines, ends in **-ī** (see § 76).

75. The regular case-ending of the Accusative singular of **i**-stems (M. or F.) would be **-im**: as, **sitis, sitim** (cf. **stella, -am**; **servus, -um**); but in most nouns this is changed to **-em** (following the consonant declension).

[1] Rarely **clientum**. [2] Also **aetātium**. Cf. § 71. 4.
[3] An old, though not the original, ending (see p. 32, footnote 2).

a. The accusative in **-im** is found exclusively —

1. In Greek nouns and in names of rivers.
2. In **būris, cucumis, rāvis, sitis, tussis, vīs.**
3. In adverbs in **-tim** (being accusative of nouns in **-tis**), as, **partim**; and in **amussim.**

b. The accusative in **-im** is found sometimes in **febris, puppis, restis, turris, secūris, sēmentis,** and rarely in many other words.

76. The regular form of the Ablative singular of i-stems would be **-ī**: as, **sitis, sitī**; but in most nouns this is changed to **-e.**

a. The ablative in **-ī** is found exclusively —

1. In nouns having the accusative in **-im** (§ 75); also **secūris.**
2. In the following adjectives used as nouns: **aequālis, annālis, aquālis, cōnsulāris, gentīlis, molāris, prīmipīlāris, tribūlis.**
3. In neuters in **-e, -al, -ar**: except **baccar, iubar, rēte,** and sometimes **mare.**

b. The ablative in **-ī** is found sometimes —

1. In **avis, clāvis, febris, fīnis, īgnis,**[1] **imber, lūx, nāvis, ovis, pelvis, puppis, sēmentis, strigilis, turris,** and occasionally in other words.
2. In the following adjectives used as nouns: **affīnis, bipennis, canālis, familiāris, nātālis, rīvālis, sapiēns, tridēns, trirēmis, vōcālis.**

NOTE 1. — The ablative of **famēs** is always **famē** (§ 105. *e*). The defective **māne** has sometimes **mānī** (§ 103. *b*. N.) as ablative.

NOTE 2. — Most names of towns in **-e** (as, **Praeneste, Tergeste**) and **Sōracte**, a mountain, have the ablative in **-e. Caere** has **Caerēte.**

NOTE 3. — **Canis** and **iuvenis** have **cane, iuvene**

77. The regular Nominative plural of i-stems is **-ēs,**[2] but **-īs** is occasionally found. The regular Accusative plural **-īs** is common, but not exclusively used in any word. An old form for both cases is **-ēis** (diphthong).

78. The following have **-um** (not **-ium**) in the genitive plural:

1. Always, — **canis, iuvenis,**[3] **ambāgēs, mare** (once only, otherwise wanting), **volucris**; regularly, **sēdēs, vātēs.**
2. Sometimes, — **apis, caedēs, clādēs, mēnsis, struēs, subolēs.**
3. Very rarely, — patrials in **-ās, -ātis**; **-īs, -ītis**; as, **Arpīnās, Arpīnātum; Samnīs, Samnītum.**

[1] Always in the formula **aquā et īgnī interdīcī** (§ 401).

[2] The Indo-European ending of the nominative plural, **-ĕs** (preserved in Greek in consonant stems, as ὄρτυξ, ὄρτυγ-ες), contracts with a stem-vowel and gives **-ēs** in the Latin i-declension (cf. the Greek plural ὄεις). This **-ēs** was extended to consonant stems in Latin.

[3] **Canis** and **iuvenis** are really n-stems.

Irregular Nouns of the Third Declension

79. In many nouns the stem is irregularly modified in the nominative or other cases. Some peculiar forms are thus declined:—

	bōs, C. *ox, cow*	**senex**, M. *old man*	**carō**, F. *flesh*	**os**, N. *bone*	**vīs**, F. *force*
			SINGULAR		
NOM.	bōs	senex	carō	os	vīs
GEN.	bŏvis	senis	carnis	ossis	vīs (rare)
DAT.	bovī	senī	carnī	ossī	vī (rare)
ACC.	bovem	senem	carnem	os	vim
ABL.	bove	sene	carne	osse	vī
			PLURAL		
	cattle				*strength*
NOM.	bovēs	senēs	carnēs	ossa	vīrēs
GEN.	boum	senum	carnium	ossium	vīrium
DAT.	bōbus (būbus)	senibus	carnibus	ossibus	vīribus
ACC.	bovēs	senēs	carnēs	ossa	vīrīs (-ēs)
ABL.	bōbus (būbus)	senibus	carnibus	ossibus	vīribus

	sūs, C. *swine*	**Iuppiter**, M. *Jupiter*	**nix**, F. *snow*	**iter**, N. *march*
		SINGULAR		
NOM.	sūs	Iuppiter[1]	nix	iter
GEN.	suis	Iovis	nivis	itineris
DAT.	suī	Iovī	nivī	itinerī
ACC.	suem	Iovem	nivem	iter
ABL.	sue	Iove	nive	itinere
		PLURAL		
NOM.	suēs		nivēs	itinera
GEN.	suum		nivium	itinerum
DAT.	sŭbus (suibus)		nivibus	itineribus
ACC.	suēs		nivēs	itinera
ABL.	sŭbus (suibus)		nivibus	itineribus

[1] Also Iūpiter.

a. Two vowel-stems in ū-, **grū-** and **sū-**, which follow the third declension, add **s** in the nominative, and are inflected like mute stems: **grūs** has also a nominative **gruis**; **sūs** has both **suibus** and **sŭbus** in the dative and ablative plural, **grūs** has only **gruibus**.

b. In the stem **bov-** (**bou-**) the diphthong **ou** becomes **ō** in the nominative (**bōs, bŏvis**).

In **nāv-** (**nau-**) an **i** is added (**nāvis, -is**), and it is declined like **turris** (§ 67).

In **Iŏv-** (= Ζεύς) the diphthong (**ou**) becomes **ū** in **Iū-piter** (for **-păter**), genitive **Iŏvis**, etc.; but the form **Iuppiter** is preferred.

c. In **iter, itineris** (N.), **iecur, iecinoris** (**iecoris**) (N.), **supellēx, supellēctilis** (F.), the nominative has been formed from a shorter stem; in **senex, senis**, from a longer; so that these words show a combination of forms from two distinct stems.

d. In **nix, nivis** the nominative retains a **g** from the original stem, the **g** uniting with **s**, the nominative ending, to form **x**. In the other cases the stem assumes the form **niv-** and it adds **i** in the genitive plural.

e. **Vās** (N.), **vāsis**, keeps **s** throughout; plural **vāsa, vāsōrum**. A dative plural **vāsibus** also occurs. There is a rare singular **vāsum**.

The Locative Case

80. The Locative form for nouns of the third declension ends in the singular in **-ī** or **-e**, in the plural in **-ibus**: as, **rūrī**, *in the country;* **Carthāginī** or **Carthāgine**, *at Carthage;* **Trallibus**, *at Tralles.*[1]

Greek Nouns of the Third Declension

81. Many nouns originally Greek — mostly proper names — retain Greek forms of inflection. So especially —

1. Genitive singular in **-os**, as, **tigridos**.
2. Accusative singular in **-a**, as, **aethera**.
3. Vocative singular like the stem, as, **Periclē, Orpheu, Atlā**.
4. Nominative plural in **-ĕs**, as, **hērōĕs**.
5. Accusative plural in **-ăs**, as, **hērōăs**.

[1] The Indo-European locative singular ended in **-ĭ**, which became **-ĕ** in Latin. Thus the Latin ablative in **-e** is, historically considered, a locative. The Latin ablative in **-ī** (from **-īd**) was an analogical formation (cf. **-ā** from **-ād**, **-ō** from **-ōd**), properly belonging to **i**-stems. With names of towns and a few other words, a locative function was ascribed to forms in **-ī** (as, **Carthāginī**), partly on the analogy of the real locative of **o**-stems (as, **Corinthī**, § 49. *a*); but forms in **-ĕ** also survived in this use. The plural **-bus** is properly dative or ablative, but in forms like **Trallibus** it has a locative function. Cf. **Philippīs** (§ 49. *a*), in which the ending **-īs** is, historically considered, either locative, or instrumental, or both, and **Athēnīs** (§ 43. *c*), in which the ending is formed on the analogy of **o**-stems.

82. Some of these forms are seen in the following examples: —

	hērōs, M., *hero*	**lampas**, F., *torch*	**basis**, F., *base*	**tigris**, C., *tiger*	**nāis**, F., *naiad*
	STEM **hērō-**	STEM **lampad-**	STEM **basi-**	STEM { **tigrid-** / **tigri-** }	STEM **nāid-**
			SINGULAR		
NOM.	hērōs	lampas	basis	tigris	nāis
GEN.	hērōis	lampados	baseōs	tigris(-idos)	nāidos
DAT.	hērōī	lampadī	basī	tigrī	nāidī
ACC.	hērōa	lampada	basin	tigrin(-ida)	nāida
ABL.	hērōe	lampade	basī	tigrī(-ide)	nāide
			PLURAL		
NOM.	hērōĕs	lampadĕs	basēs	tigrēs	nāidĕs
GEN.	hērōum	lampadum	basium(-eōn)	tigrium	nāidum
D., A.[1]	hērōibus	lampadibus	basibus	tigribus	nāidibus
ACC.	hērōăs	lampadăs	basīs(-ēis)	tigrīs(-idăs)	nāidăs

	PROPER NAMES		
NOM.	Dīdō	Simoīs	Capys
GEN.	Dīdōnis(Dīdūs)	Simoentis	Capyos
DAT.	Dīdōnī(Dīdō)	Simoentī	Capyī
ACC.	Dīdōnem(-ō)	Simoenta	Capyn
ABL.	Dīdōne(-ō)	Simoente	Capyë
VOC.	Dīdō	Simoīs	Capy
NOM.	Orpheus	Periclēs	Paris
GEN.	Orpheī(-eōs)	Periclis(-ī)	Paridis
DAT.	Orpheī(-eō)	Periclī(-i)	Paridī
ACC.	Orphea(-um)	Periclem(-ea, -ēn)	{ Paridem, Parim(-in)
ABL.	Orpheō	Pericle	Paride, Parī
VOC.	Orpheu	Periclēs(-ē)	Pari

NOTE.—The regular Latin forms may be used for most of the above.

83. Other peculiarities are the following: —

a. **Delphīnus, -ī** (M.), has also the form **delphīn, -īnis**; **Salamīs, -is** (F.), has acc. **Salamīna**.

b. Most stems in **ĭd-** (nom. **-is**) often have also the forms of **i**-stems: as, **tigris**, gen. **-ĭdis** (**-ĭdos**) or **-is**; acc. **-ĭdem** (**-ĭda**) or **-im** (**-in**); abl. **-ĭde** or **-ī**. But many, including most feminine proper names, have acc. **-idem** (**-ida**), abl. **-ide**, — not **-im** or **-ī**. (These stems are irregular also in Greek.)

[1] Dative, **hērōisin** (once only).

c. Stems in **on-** sometimes retain **-n** in the nominative: as, **Agamemnōn** (or **Agamemnō**), genitive **-ŏnis**, accusative **-ŏna.**

d. Stems in **ont-** form the nominative in **-ōn**: as, **horizōn, Xenophōn**; but a few are occasionally Latinized into **ōn-** (nom. **-ō**): as, **Dracō, -ōnis**; **Antiphō, -ōnis.**

e. Like **Simoīs** are declined stems in **ant-, ent-,** and a few in **ūnt-** (nominative in **-ās, -īs, -ūs**): as, **Atlās, -antis**; **Trapezūs, -ūntis.**

f. Some words fluctuate between different declensions: as **Orpheus** between the second and the third.

g. **-ōn** is found in the genitive plural in a few Greek titles of books: as, **Metamorphōseōn,** *of the Metamorphoses* (Ovid's well-known poem); **Geōrgicōn,** *of the Georgics* (a poem of Virgil).

Gender in the Third Declension

84. The Gender of nouns of this declension must be learned by practice and from the Lexicon. Many are masculine or feminine by nature or in accordance with the general rules for gender (p. 15). The most important rules for the others, with their principal exceptions, are the following: —[1]

85. Masculine are nouns in **-or, -ōs, -er, -ĕs** (gen. **-itis**), **-ex** (gen. **-ĭcis**): as, **color, flōs, imber, gurges (gurgitis), vertex (verticis).**

Exceptions are the following: —

a. Feminine are **arbor**; **cōs, dōs**; **linter.**

b. Neuter are **ador, aequor, cor, marmor**; **ōs (ōris)**; also **os (ossis)**; **cadāver, iter, tūber, ūber, vēr**; and names of plants and trees in **-er**: as, **acer, papāver.**

86. Feminine are nouns in **-ō, -ās, -ēs, -is, -ūs, -x,** and in **-s** preceded by a consonant: as, **legiō, cīvitās, nūbēs, avis, virtūs, arx, urbs.** The nouns in **-ō** are mostly those in **-dō** and **-gō**, and abstract and collective nouns in **-iō.**

Exceptions are the following: —

a. Masculine are **leō, leōnis**; **ligō, -ōnis**; **sermō, -ōnis**; also **cardō, harpagō, margō, ōrdō, turbō**; and concrete nouns in **-iō**: as, **pugiō, ūniō, papiliō**;[2] **acīnacēs, ariēs, celēs, lebēs, pariēs, pēs**;

[1] Some nouns of doubtful or variable gender are omitted.

[2] Many nouns in **-ō** (gen. **-ōnis**) are masculine by signification: as, **gerō,** *carrier*; **restiō,** *ropemaker*; and family names (originally nicknames): as, **Cicerō, Nāsō.** See §§ 236. *c*, 255.

Nouns in **-nis** and **-guis** : as, **īgnis, sanguis**; also **axis, caulis, collis, cucumis, ēnsis, fascis, follis, fūstis, lapis, mēnsis, orbis, piscis, postis, pulvis, vōmis**;

mūs;

calix, fornix, grex, phoenīx, and nouns in **-ex** (gen. **-icis**) (§ 85);

dēns, fōns, mōns, pōns.

NOTE.—Some nouns in -is and -ns which are masculine were originally adjectives or participles agreeing with a masculine noun: as, Aprīlis (sc. mēnsis), M., *April;* oriēns (sc. sōl), M., *the east;* annālis (sc. liber), M., *the year-book.*

b. Neuter are **vās (vāsis)**; **crūs, iūs, pūs, rūs, tūs.**

87. Neuter are nouns in **-a, -e, -l, -n, -ar, -ur, -ŭs**: as, **poēma, mare, animal, nōmen, calcar, rōbur, corpus**; also **lac** and **caput.**

Exceptions are the following:—

a. Masculine are **sāl, sōl, pecten, vultur, lepus.**

b. Feminine is **pecus** (gen. **-udis**).

FOURTH DECLENSION

88. The Stem of nouns of the Fourth Declension ends in **u-**. This is usually weakened to **i** before **-bus**. Masculine and Feminine nouns form the nominative by adding **s**; Neuters have for nominative the simple stem, but with **ū** (long).

89. Nouns of the Fourth Declension are declined as follows:

	manus, F., *hand* STEM **manu-**	**lacus**, M., *lake* STEM **lacu-**		**genū**, N., *knee* STEM **genu-**	
		SINGULAR			
			CASE-ENDINGS		CASE-ENDINGS
NOM.	**manus**	**lacus**	**-us**	**genū**	**-ū**
GEN.	**manūs**	**lacūs**	**-ūs**	**genūs**	**-ūs**
DAT.	**manuī(-ū)**	**lacuī(-ū)**	**-uī(-ū)**	**genū**	**-ū**
ACC.	**manum**	**lacum**	**-um**	**genū**	**-ū**
ABL.	**manū**	**lacū**	**-ū**	**genū**	**-ū**
		PLURAL			
NOM.	**manūs**	**lacūs**	**-ūs**	**genua**	**-ua**
GEN.	**manuum**	**lacuum**	**-uum**	**genuum**	**-uum**
DAT.	**manibus**	**lacubus**	**-ibus(-ubus)**	**genibus**	**-ibus**
ACC.	**manūs**	**lacūs**	**-ūs**	**genua**	**-ua**
ABL.	**manibus**	**lacubus**	**-ibus(-ubus)**	**genibus**	**-ibus**

Gender in the Fourth Declension

90. Most nouns of the Fourth Declension in **-us** are Masculine.

Exceptions: The following are Feminine: **acus, anus, colus, domus, īdūs** (plural), **manus, nurus, porticus, quīnquātrūs** (plural), **socrus, tribus,** with a few names of plants and trees. Also, rarely, **penus, specus.**

91. The only Neuters of the Fourth Declension are **cornū, genū, pecū** (§ 105. *f*), **verū.**[1]

Case-Forms in the Fourth Declension

92. The following peculiarities in case-forms of the Fourth Declension require notice: —

a. A genitive singular in **-ī** (as of the second declension) sometimes occurs in nouns in **-tus**: as, **senātus,** genitive **senātī** (regularly **senātūs**).

b. In the genitive plural **-uum** is sometimes pronounced as one syllable, and may then be written **-um**: as, **currum** (Aen. vi. 653) for **curruum.**

c. The dative and ablative plural in **-ŭbus** are retained in **partus** and **tribus**; so regularly in **artus** and **lacus,** and occasionally in other words; **portus** and **specus** have both **-ubus** and **-ibus.**

d. Most names of plants and trees, and **colus,** *distaff*, have also forms of the second declension: as, **fīcus,** *fig*, genitive **fīcūs** or **fīcī.**

e. An old genitive singular in **-uis** or **-uos** and an old genitive plural in **-uom** occur rarely: as, **senātuis, senātuos; fluctuom.**

f. The ablative singular ended anciently in **-ūd** (cf. § 43. N. 1): as, **magistrātūd.**

93. **Domus** (F.), *house*, has two stems ending in **u-** and **o-**. Hence it shows forms of both the fourth and second declensions:

	SINGULAR	PLURAL
NOM.	dom**us**	dom**ūs**
GEN.	dom**ūs** (dom**ī**, loc.)	dom**uum** (dom**ōrum**)
DAT.	dom**uī** (dom**ō**)	dom**ibus**
ACC.	dom**um**	dom**ōs** (dom**ūs**)
ABL.	dom**ō** (dom**ū**)	dom**ibus**

NOTE 1. — The Locative is **domī** (rarely **domuī**), *at home.*

NOTE 2. — The Genitive **domī** occurs in Plautus; **domōrum** is late or poetic.

[1] A few other neuters of this declension are mentioned by the ancient grammarians as occurring in certain cases.

94. Most nouns of the Fourth Declension are formed from verb-stems, or roots, by means of the suffix **-tus** (**-sus**) (§ 238. *b*):

> **cantus**, *song*, CAN, **canō**, *sing;* **cāsus** (for †**cad-tus**), *chance*, CAD, **cadō**, *fall;* **exsulātus**, *exile*, from **exsulō**, *to be an exile* (**exsul**).

a. Many are formed either from verb-stems not in use, or by analogy:

> **cōnsulātus** (as if from †**cōnsulō, -āre**), **senātus, incestus.**

b. The accusative and the dative or ablative of nouns in **-tus** (**-sus**) form the Supines of verbs (§ 159. *b*): as, **spectātum, petītum**; **dictū, vīsū.**

c. Of many verbal derivatives only the ablative is used as a noun: as, **iussū** (**meō**), *by* (*my*) *command;* so **iniussū** (**populī**), *without* (*the people's*) *order.* Of some only the dative is used: as, **dīvīsuī.**

FIFTH DECLENSION (*ē*-STEMS)

95. The Stem of nouns of the Fifth Declension ends in **ē-**, which appears in all the cases. The Nominative is formed from the stem by adding **s.**

96. Nouns of the Fifth Declension are declined as follows: —

	rēs, F., *thing* STEM **rē-**	**diēs**, M., *day* STEM **diē-**	**fidēs**, F., *faith* STEM **fidē-**	CASE-ENDINGS
		SINGULAR		
NOM.	**rēs**	**diēs**	**fidēs**	**-ēs**
GEN.	**rĕī**	**diēī** (**diē**)	**fidĕī**	**-ēī** (**-ē**)
DAT.	**rĕī**	**diēī** (**diē**)	**fidĕī**	**-ēī** (**-ē**)
ACC.	**rem**	**diem**	**fidem**	**-em**
ABL.	**rē**	**diē**	**fidē**	**-ē**
		PLURAL		
NOM.	**rēs**	**diēs**		**-ēs**
GEN.	**rērum**	**diērum**		**-ērum**
DAT.	**rēbus**	**diēbus**		**-ēbus**
ACC.	**rēs**	**diēs**		**-ēs**
ABL.	**rēbus**	**diēbus**		**-ēbus**

NOTE. — The **ē** of the stem is shortened in the genitive and dative singular of **fidēs, spēs, rēs**, but in these it is found long in early Latin. In the accusative singular **e** is always short.

Gender in the Fifth Declension

97. All nouns of the Fifth Declension are Feminine, except **diēs** (usually M.), *day*, and **merīdiēs** (M.), *noon*.

a. **Diēs** is sometimes feminine in the singular, especially in phrases indicating a fixed time, and regularly feminine when used of time in general: as, **cōnstitūtā diē**, *on a set day;* **longa diēs**, *a long time.*

Case-Forms in the Fifth Declension

98. The following peculiarities require notice: —

a. Of nouns of the fifth declension, only **diēs** and **rēs** are declined throughout. Most want the plural, which is, however, found in the nominative or accusative in **aciēs**, **effigiēs**, **ēluviēs**, **faciēs**, **glaciēs**, **seriēs**, **speciēs**, **spēs**.[1]

b. The Locative form of this declension ends in **-ē**. It is found only in certain adverbs and expressions of time: —

hodiē, *to-day;*	**diē quārtō** (old, **quārtī**), *the fourth day;*
perendiē, *day after to-morrow;*	**prīdiē**, *the day before.*

c. The fifth declension is closely related to the first, and several nouns have forms of both: as, **māteria, -iēs**; **saevitia, -iēs**. The genitive and dative in **-ēī** are rarely found in these words.

d. Some nouns vary between the fifth and the third declension: as, **requiēs**, **satiēs** (also **satiās**, genitive **-ātis**), **plēbēs** (also **plēbs**, genitive **plēbis**), **famēs**, genitive **famis**, ablative **famē**.

NOTE. — In the genitive and dative **-ēī** (**-ĕī**) was sometimes contracted into **-ēî**: as, **tribūnus plēbêi**, *tribune of the people* (**plēbēs**). Genitives in **-ī** and **-ē** also occur: as, **diī** (Aen. i. 636), **plēbī-scītum**, **aciē** (B. G. ii. 23). A few examples of the old genitive in **-ēs** are found (cf. **-ās** in the first declension, § 43. *b*). The dative has rarely **-ē**, and a form in **-ī** is cited.

DEFECTIVE NOUNS

Nouns wanting in the Plural

99. Some nouns are ordinarily found in the Singular number only (*singulāria tantum*). These are —

1. Most proper names: as, **Caesar**, *Cæsar;* **Gallia**, *Gaul.*
2. Names of things not counted, but reckoned in mass: as, **aurum**, *gold;* **āēr**, *air;* **trīticum**, *wheat.*
3. Abstract nouns: as, **ambitiō**, *ambition;* **fortitūdō**, *courage;* **calor**, *heat.*

[1] The forms **faciērum**, **speciērum**, **speciēbus**, **spērum**, **spēbus**, are cited by grammarians, also **spērēs**, **spēribus**, and some of these occur in late authors.

100. Many of these nouns, however, are used in the plural in some other sense.

a. The plural of a proper name may be applied to two or more persons or places, or even things, and so become strictly common: —

> **duodecim Caesarēs**, *the twelve Cæsars.*
> **Galliae**, *the two Gauls* (Cis- and Transalpine).
> **Castores**, *Castor and Pollux;* **Iovēs**, *images of Jupiter.*

b. The plural of names of things reckoned in mass may denote *particular objects:* as, **aera**, *bronze utensils*, **nivēs**, *snowflakes;* or *different kinds* of a thing: as, **āerēs**, *airs* (good and bad).

c. The plural of abstract nouns denotes *occasions* or *instances* of the quality, or the like: —

> **quaedam excellentiae**, *some cases of superiority;* **ōtia**, *periods of rest;* **calōrēs, frīgora**, *times of heat* and *cold.*

Nouns wanting in the Singular

101. Some nouns are commonly or exclusively found in the Plural (*plūrālia tantum*). Such are —

1. Many names of towns: as, **Athēnae** (*Athens*), **Thūriī**, **Philippī**, **Vêiī**.

2. Names of festivals and games: as, **Olympia**, *the Olympic Games;* **Bacchānālia**, *feast of Bacchus;* **Quīnquātrūs**, *festival of Minerva;* **lūdī Rōmānī**, *the Roman Games.*

3. Names of classes: as, **optimātēs**, *the upper classes;* **mâiōrēs**, *ancestors;* **līberī**, *children;* **penātēs**, *household gods;* **Quirītēs**, *citizens* (of Rome).

4. Words plural by signification: as, **arma**, *weapons;* **artūs**, *joints;* **dīvitiae**, *riches;* **scālae**, *stairs;* **valvae**, *folding-doors;* **forēs**, *double-doors;* **angustiae**, *a narrow pass* (narrows); **moenia**, *city walls.*

NOTE 1. — Some words, plural by signification in Latin, are translated by English nouns in the singular number: as, **dēliciae**, *delight, darling;* **faucēs**, *throat;* **fidēs**, *lyre* (also singular in poetry); **īnsidiae**, *ambush;* **cervīcēs**, *neck;* **viscera**, *flesh.*

NOTE 2. — The poets often use the plural number for the singular, sometimes for metrical reasons, sometimes from a mere fashion: as, **ōra** (for **ōs**), *the face;* **scēptra** (for **scēptrum**), *sceptre;* **silentia** (for **silentium**), *silence.*

102. Some nouns of the above classes (§ 101. 1–4), have a corresponding singular, as noun or adjective, often in a special sense:

1. As noun, to denote a single object: as, **Bacchānal**, *a spot sacred to Bacchus;* **optimās**, *an aristocrat.*

2. As adjective: as, **Catō Mâior**, *Cato the Elder.*

3. In a sense rare, or found only in early Latin: as, **scāla**, *a ladder;* **valva**, *a door;* **artus**, *a joint.*

Nouns Defective in Certain Cases

103. Many nouns are defective in case-forms:[1] —

a. Indeclinable nouns, used only as nominative and accusative singular: **fās, nefās, īnstar, nihil, opus** (*need*), **secus.**

NOTE 1. — The indeclinable adjective **necesse** is used as a nominative or accusative.
NOTE 2. — The genitive **nihilī** and the ablative **nihilō** (from **nihilum**, *nothing*) occur.

b. Nouns found in *one case* only (monoptotes): —

1. In the nominative singular: **glōs** (F.).
2. In the genitive singular: **dicis, naucī** (N.).
3. In the dative singular: **dīvīsuī** (M.) (cf. § 94. *c*).
4. In the accusative singular: **amussim** (M.); **vēnum** (dative **vēnō** in Tacitus).
5. In the ablative singular: **pondō** (N.); **māne** (N.); **astū** (M.), *by craft;* **iussū, iniussū, nātū,** and many other verbal nouns in **-us** (M.) (§ 94. *c*).

NOTE. — **Māne** is also used as an indeclinable accusative, and an old form **mānī** is used as ablative. **Pondō** with a numeral is often apparently equivalent to *pounds.* A nominative singular **astus** and a plural **astūs** occur rarely in later writers.

6. In the accusative plural: **īnfitiās.**

c. Nouns found in *two cases* only (diptotes): —

1. In the nominative and ablative singular: **fors, forte** (F.).
2. In the genitive and ablative singular: **spontis** (rare), **sponte** (F.).
3. In the accusative singular and plural: **dicam, dicās** (F.).
4. In the accusative and ablative plural: **forās, forīs** (F.) (cf. **forēs**), used as adverbs.

d. Nouns found in *three cases* only (triptotes): —

1. In the nominative, accusative, and ablative singular: **impetus, -um, -ū** (M.)[2]; **luēs, -em, -ē** (F.).
2. In the nominative, accusative, and dative or ablative plural: **grātēs, -ibus** (F).
3. In the nominative, genitive, and dative or ablative plural: **iūgera, -um, -ibus** (N.); but **iūgerum,** etc., in the singular (cf. § 105. *b*).

e. Nouns found in *four cases* only (tetraptotes): —

In the genitive, dative, accusative, ablative singular: **diciōnis, -ī, -em, -e** (F.).

f. Nouns declined regularly in the *plural,* but defective in the *singular:* —

1. Nouns found in the singular, in genitive, dative, accusative, ablative: **frūgis, -ī, -em, -e** (F.); **opis, -ī** (once only), **-em, -e** (F.; nominative **Ops** as a divinity).
2. Nouns found in the dative, accusative, ablative: **precī, -em, -e** (F.).
3. Nouns found in the accusative and ablative: **cassem, -e** (F.); **sordem, -e** (F.).
4. Nouns found in the ablative only: **ambāge** (F.); **fauce** (F.); **obice** (C.).

g. Nouns regular in the *singular,* defective in the *plural:* —

[1] Some early or late forms and other rarities are omitted.
[2] The dative singular **impetuī** and the ablative plural **impetibus** occur once each.

1. The following neuters have in the plural the nominative and accusative only: **fel** (**fella**), **far** (**farra**), **hordeum** (**hordea**), **iūs**, *broth* (**iūra**), **mel** (**mella**), **murmur** (**murmura**), **pūs** (**pūra**), **rūs** (**rūra**), **tūs** or **thūs** (**tūra**).

NOTE.—The neuter **iūs**, *right*, has only **iūra** in classical writers, but a very rare genitive plural **iūrum** occurs in old Latin.

2. **calx**, **cor**, **cōs**, **crux**, **fax**, **faex**, **lanx**, **lūx**, **nex**, **ōs** (**ōris**),[1] **os** (**ossis**),[2] **pāx**, **pix**, **rōs**, **sāl**, **sōl**, **vas** (**vadis**), want the genitive plural.

3. Most nouns of the fifth declension want the whole or part of the plural (see § 98. *a*).

h. Nouns defective in both *singular* and *plural*:—

1. Noun found in the genitive, accusative, ablative singular; nominative, accusative, dative, ablative plural: **vicis**, **-em**, **-e**; **-ēs**, **-ibus**.

2. Noun found in the genitive, dative, accusative, and ablative singular; genitive plural wanting: **dapis**, **-ī**, **-em**, **-e**; **-ēs**, **-ibus**.[3]

VARIABLE NOUNS

104. Many nouns vary either in Declension or in Gender.

105. Nouns that vary in Declension are called *heteroclites*.[4]

a. **Colus** (F.), *distaff*; **domus** (F.), *house* (see § 93), and many names of plants in **-us**, vary between the Second and Fourth Declensions.

b. Some nouns vary between the Second and Third: as, **iūgerum**, **-ī**, **-ō**, ablative **-ō** or **-e**, plural **-a**, **-um**, **-ibus**; **Mulciber**, genitive **-berī** and **-beris**; **sequester**, genitive **-trī** and **-tris**; **vās**, **vāsis**, and (old) **vāsum**, **-ī** (§ 79. *e*).

c. Some vary between the Second, Third, and Fourth: as, **penus**, **penum**, genitive **penī** and **penoris**, ablative **penū**.

d. Many nouns vary between the First and Fifth (see § 98. *c*).

e. Some vary between the Third and Fifth. Thus,—**requiēs** has genitive **-ētis**, dative wanting, accusative **-ētem** or **-em**, ablative **-ē** (once **-ēte**); **famēs**, regularly of the third declension, has ablative **famē** (§ 76. N. 1), and **pūbēs** (M.) has once dative **pūbē** (in Plautus).

f. **Pecus** varies between the Third and Fourth, having **pecoris**, etc., but also nominative **pecū**, ablative **pecū**; plural **pecua**, genitive **pecuum**.

g. Many vary between different stems of the same declension: as, **femur** (N.), genitive **-oris**, also **-inis** (as from †**femen**); **iecur** (N.), genitive **iecinoris**, **iocinoris**, **iecoris**; **mūnus** (N.), plural **mūnera** and **mūnia**.

[1] The ablative plural **ōribus** is rare, the classical idiom being **in ōre omnium**, *in everybody's mouth*, etc., not **in ōribus omnium**.

[2] The genitive plural **ossium** is late; **ossuum** (from **ossua**, plural of a neuter u-stem) is early and late.

[3] An old nominative **daps** is cited.

[4] That is, "nouns of different inflections" (ἕτερος, *another*, and κλίνω, *to inflect*).

106. Nouns that vary in Gender are said to be *heterogeneous*.[1]

a. The following have a masculine form in **-us** and a neuter in **-um**: **balteus, cāseus, clipeus, collum, cingulum, pīleus, tergum, vāllum,** with many others of rare occurrence.

b. The following have in the Plural a different gender from that of the Singular: —

balneum (N.), *bath;*	**balneae** (F.), *baths* (an establishment).
caelum (N.), *heaven;*	**caelōs** (M. acc., Lucr.).
carbasus (F.), *a sail;*	**carbasa** (N.) (-ōrum), *sails.*
dēlicium (N.), *pleasure;*	**dēliciae** (F.), *pet.*
epulum (N.), *feast;*	**epulae** (F.), *feast.*
frēnum (N.), *a bit;*	**frēnī** (M.) or **frēna** (N.), *a bridle.*
iocus (M.), *a jest;*	**ioca** (N.), **iocī** (M.), *jests.*
locus (M.), *place;*	**loca** (N.), **locī** (M., usually *topics, passages* in books).
rāstrum (N.), *a rake;*	**rāstrī** (M.), **rāstra** (N.), *rakes.*

NOTE. — Some of these nouns are heteroclites as well as heterogeneous.

107. Many nouns are found in the Plural in a peculiar sense: —

aedēs, -is (F.), *temple;*	**aedēs, -ium,** *house.*
aqua (F.), *water;*	**aquae,** *mineral springs, a watering-place.*
auxilium (N.), *help;*	**auxilia,** *auxiliaries.*
bonum (N.), *a good;*	**bona,** *goods, property.*
carcer (M.), *dungeon;*	**carcerēs,** *barriers* (of race-course).
castrum (N.), *fort;*	**castra,** *camp.*
comitium (N.), *place of assembly;*	**comitia,** *an election* (*town-meeting*).
cōpia (F.), *plenty;*	**cōpiae,** *stores, troops.*
fidēs (F.), *harp-string;*	**fidēs,** *lyre.*
fīnis (M.), *end;*	**fīnēs,** *bounds, territories.*
fortūna (F.), *fortune;*	**fortūnae,** *possessions.*
grātia (F.), *favor* (rarely, *thanks*);	**grātiae,** *thanks* (also, *the Graces*).
hortus (M.), *a garden;*	**hortī,** *pleasure-grounds.*
impedīmentum (N.) *hindrance;*	**impedīmenta,** *baggage.*
littera (F.), *letter* (of alphabet);	**litterae,** *epistle, literature.*
locus (M.), *place* [plural **loca** (N.)];	**locī,**[2] *topics, places in books.*
lūdus (M.), *sport;*	**lūdī,** *public games.*
mōs (M.), *habit, custom;*	**mōrēs,** *character.*
nātālis (M.), *birthday;*	**nātālēs,** *descent, origin.*
opera (F.), *work;*	**operae,** *day-laborers* ("hands").
[**ops,**] **opis** (F.), *help* (§ 103. *f.* 1);	**opēs,** *resources, wealth.*
pars (F.), *part;*	**partēs,** *part* (on the stage), *party.*
rōstrum (N.), *beak of a ship;*	**rōstra,** *speaker's platform.*
sāl (M. or N.), *salt;*	**salēs,** *witticisms.*
tabella (F.), *tablet;*	**tabellae,** *documents, records.*

[1] That is, "of different genders" (ἕτερος, *another*, and γένος, *gender*).

[2] In early writers the regular plural.

NAMES OF PERSONS

108. A Roman had regularly three names:—(1) the **praenōmen**, or personal name; (2) the **nōmen**, or name of the *gēns* or house; (3) the **cōgnōmen**, or family name:—

Thus in **Mārcus Tullius Cicerō** we have—

Mārcus, the **praenōmen**, like our Christian or given name;

Tullius, the **nōmen**, properly an adjective denoting *of the Tullian gēns* (or *house*) whose original head was a real or supposed *Tullus*;

Cicerō, the **cōgnōmen**, or family name, often in origin a nickname,—in this case from **cicer**, *a vetch*, or small pea.

NOTE.—When two persons of the same family are mentioned together, the *cōgnōmen* is usually put in the plural: as, **Pūblius et Servius Sullae.**

a. A fourth or fifth name was sometimes given as a mark of honor or distinction, or to show adoption from another *gēns*.

Thus the complete name of Scipio the Younger was **Pūblius Cornēlius Scīpiō Āfricānus Aemiliānus: Āfricānus**, from his exploits in Africa; **Aemiliānus**, as adopted from the Æmilian *gēns*.[1]

NOTE.—The Romans of the classical period had no separate name for these additions, but later grammarians invented the word *āgnōmen* to express them.

b. Women had commonly in classical times no personal names, but were known only by the *nōmen* of their *gēns*.

Thus, the wife of Cicero was **Terentia**, and his daughter **Tullia**. A second daughter would have been called **Tullia secunda** or **minor**, a third daughter, **Tullia tertia**, and so on.

c. The commonest prænomens are thus abbreviated:—

A. Aulus.	L. Lūcius.	Q. Quīntus.
App. (Ap.) Appius.	M. Mārcus.	Ser. Servius.
C. (G.) Gāius (*Caius*) (cf. § 1. *a*).	M'. Mānius.	Sex. (S.) Sextus.
Cn. (Gn.) Gnaeus (*Cneius*).	Mām. Māmercus.	Sp. Spurius.
D. Decimus.	N. (Num.) Numerius	T. Titus.
K. Kaesō (*Caeso*).	P. Pūblius.	Ti. (Tib.) Tiberius.

NOTE 1.—In the abbreviations **C.** and **Cn.**, the initial character has the value of **G** (§ 1. *a*).

[1] In stating officially the full name of a Roman it was customary to include the *praenōmina* of the father, grandfather, and great-grandfather, together with the name of the tribe to which the individual belonged. Thus in an inscription we find M. TVLLIVS M. F. M. N. M. PR. COR. CICERO, i.e. **Mārcus Tullius Mārcī fīlius Mārcī nepōs Mārcī pronepōs Cornēliā tribū Cicerō.** The names of grandfather and great-grandfather as well as that of the tribe are usually omitted in literature. The name of a wife or daughter is usually accompanied by that of the husband or father in the genitive: as, **Postumia Servī Sulpiciī** (Suet. Iul. 50), *Postumia, wife of Servius Sulpicius;* **Caecilia Metellī** (Div. i. 104), *Caecilia, daughter of Metellus.*

ADJECTIVES

109. Adjectives and Participles are in general formed and declined like Nouns, differing from them only in their use.

1. In accordance with their use, they distinguish gender by different forms in the same word, and agree with their nouns in *gender*, *number*, and *case*. Thus,—

bonus puer, *the good boy.*
bona puella, *the good girl.*
bonum dōnum, *the good gift.*

2. In their inflection they are either (1) of the First and Second Declensions, or (2) of the Third Declension.

FIRST AND SECOND DECLENSIONS (*ā*- AND *o*-STEMS)

110. Adjectives of the First and Second Declensions (**ā**- and **o**-stems) are declined in the Masculine like **servus, puer,** or **ager**; in the Feminine like **stella**; and in the Neuter like **bellum.**

The regular type of an adjective of the First and Second Declensions is **bonus, -a, -um,** which is thus declined:—

bonus, bona, bonum, *good*

	MASCULINE STEM **bono-**	FEMININE STEM **bonā-**	NEUTER STEM **bono-**
		SINGULAR	
NOM.	bon**us**	bon**a**	bon**um**
GEN.	bon**ī**	bon**ae**	bon**ī**
DAT.	bon**ō**	bon**ae**	bon**ō**
ACC.	bon**um**	bon**am**	bon**um**
ABL.	bon**ō**	bon**ā**	bon**ō**
VOC.	bon**e**	bon**a**	bon**um**
		PLURAL	
NOM.	bon**ī**	bon**ae**	bon**a**
GEN.	bon**ōrum**	bon**ārum**	bon**ōrum**
DAT.	bon**īs**	bon**īs**	bon**īs**
ACC.	bon**ōs**	bon**ās**	bon**a**
ABL.	bon**īs**	bon**īs**	bon**īs**

NOTE. — Stems in **quo-** have nominative **-cus** (**-quos**), **-qua**, **-cum** (**-quom**), accusative **-cum** (**-quom**), **-quam**, **-cum** (**-quom**), to avoid **quu-** (see §§ 6. *b* and 46. N. 2). Thus, —

NOM.	**propincus** (**-quos**)	**propinqua**	**propincum** (**-quom**)
GEN.	**propinquī**	**propinquae**	**propinquī**, etc.

But most modern editions disregard this principle.

a. The Genitive Singular masculine of adjectives in **-ius** ends in **-iī**, and the Vocative in **-ie**; not in **-ī**, as in nouns (cf. § 49. *b*, *c*); as, **Lacedaemonius, -iī, -ie.**

NOTE. — The possessive **meus**, *my*, has the vocative masculine **mī** (cf. § 145).

111. Stems ending in **ro-** preceded by **e** form the Nominative Masculine like **puer** (§ 47) and are declined as follows: —

miser, misera, miserum, *wretched*

	MASCULINE STEM **misero-**	FEMININE STEM **miserā-**	NEUTER STEM **misero-**
		SINGULAR	
NOM.	**miser**	**misera**	**miserum**
GEN.	**miserī**	**miserae**	**miserī**
DAT.	**miserō**	**miserae**	**miserō**
ACC.	**miserum**	**miseram**	**miserum**
ABL.	**miserō**	**miserā**	**miserō**
		PLURAL	
NOM.	**miserī**	**miserae**	**misera**
GEN.	**miserōrum**	**miserārum**	**miserōrum**
DAT.	**miserīs**	**miserīs**	**miserīs**
ACC.	**miserōs**	**miserās**	**misera**
ABL.	**miserīs**	**miserīs**	**miserīs**

a. Like **miser** are declined **asper, gibber, lacer, līber, prosper** (also **prosperus**), **satur** (**-ura, -urum**), **tener**, with compounds of **-fer** and **-ger**: as, **saetiger, -era, -erum**, *bristle-bearing;* also, usually, **dexter**. In these the **e** belongs to the stem; but in **dextra** it is often omitted: as, **dextra manus**, *the right hand.*

NOTE. — Stems in **ēro-** (as **prōcērus**), with **mōrigĕrus, propĕrus**, have the regular nominative masculine in **-us**.

b. The following lack a nominative singular masculine in classic use: **cētera, īnfera, postera, supera.** They are rarely found in the singular except in certain phrases: as, **posterō diē**, *the next day.*

NOTE. — An ablative feminine in **-ō** is found in a few Greek adjectives: as, **lectīcā octōphorō** (Verr. v. 27).

112. Stems in **ro-** preceded by a consonant form the Nominative Masculine like **ager** (§ 47) and are declined as follows: —

niger, nigra, nigrum, *black*

	MASCULINE STEM **nigro-**	FEMININE STEM **nigrā-**	NEUTER STEM **nigro-**
		SINGULAR	
NOM.	niger	nigra	nigrum
GEN.	nigrī	nigrae	nigrī
DAT.	nigrō	nigrae	nigrō
ACC.	nigrum	nigram	nigrum
ABL.	nigrō	nigrā	nigrō
		PLURAL	
NOM.	nigrī	nigrae	nigra
GEN.	nigrōrum	nigrārum	nigrōrum
DAT.	nigrīs	nigrīs	nigrīs
ACC.	nigrōs	nigrās	nigra
ABL.	nigrīs	nigrīs	nigrīs

a. Like **niger** are declined **aeger, āter, crēber, faber, glaber, integer, lūdicer, macer, piger, pulcher, ruber, sacer, scaber, sinister, taeter, vafer**; also the possessives **noster, vester** (§ 145).

113. The following nine adjectives with their compounds have the Genitive Singular in **-īus** and the Dative in **-ī** in all genders:

alius (N. **aliud**), *other.* **tōtus**, *whole.* **alter, -terīus**, *the other.*
nūllus, *no, none.* **ūllus**, *any.* **neuter, -trīus**, *neither.*
sōlus, *alone.* **ūnus**, *one.* **uter, -trīus**, *which* (of two).

Of these the singular is thus declined: —

	M.	F.	N.	M.	F.	N.
NOM.	ūnus	ūna	ūnum	uter	utra	utrum
GEN.	ūnīus	ūnīus	ūnīus	utrīus	utrīus	utrīus
DAT.	ūnī	ūnī	ūnī	utrī	utrī	utrī
ACC.	ūnum	ūnam	ūnum	utrum	utram	utrum
ABL.	ūnō	ūnā	ūnō	utrō	utrā	utrō
NOM.	alius	alia	aliud	alter	altera	alterum
GEN.	alīus	alīus	alīus	alterīus	alterīus	alterīus
DAT.	aliī	aliī	aliī	alterī	alterī	alterī
ACC.	alium	aliam	aliud	alterum	alteram	alterum
ABL.	aliō	aliā	aliō	alterō	alterā	alterō

a. The plural of these words is regular, like that of **bonus** (§ 110).

b. The genitive in **-īus**, dative in **-ī**, and neuter in **-d** are pronominal in origin (cf. **illīus, illī, illud**, and § 146).

c. The i of the genitive ending **-īus**, though originally long, may be made short in verse; so often in **alterius** and regularly in **utriusque.**

d. Instead of **alīus, alterīus** is commonly used, or in the possessive sense the adjective **aliēnus,** *belonging to another, another's.*

e. In compounds — as **alteruter** — sometimes both parts are declined, sometimes only the latter. Thus, **alterī utrī** or **alterutrī,** *to one of the two.*

NOTE. — The regular genitive and dative forms (as in **bonus**) are sometimes found in some of these words: as, genitive and dative feminine, **aliae**; dative masculine, **aliō**. Rare forms are **alis** and **alid** (for **alius, aliud**).

THIRD DECLENSION (CONSONANT AND *i*-STEMS)

114. Adjectives of the Third Declension are thus classified: —

1. Adjectives of Three Terminations in the nominative singular, — one for each gender: as, **ācer, ācris, ācre.**

2. Adjectives of Two Terminations, — masculine and feminine the same: as, **levis** (M., F.), **leve** (N.).

3. Adjectives of One Termination, — the same for all three genders: as, **atrōx.**

a. Adjectives of two and three terminations are true i-stems and hence retain in the ablative singular **-ī**, in the neuter plural **-ia**, in the genitive plural **-ium**, and in the accusative plural regularly **-īs** (see §§ 73 and 74).[1]

Adjectives of Three and of Two Terminations

115. Adjectives of Three Terminations are thus declined: —

ācer, ācris, ācre, *keen,* STEM **ācri-**

	SINGULAR			PLURAL		
	M.	F.	N.	M.	F.	N.
NOM.	ācer	ācris	ācre	ācrēs	ācrēs	ācria
GEN.	ācris	ācris	ācris	ācrium	ācrium	ācrium
DAT.	ācrī	ācrī	ācrī	ācribus	ācribus	ācribus
ACC.	ācrem	ācrem	ācre	ācrīs (-ēs)	ācrīs (-ēs)	ācria
ABL.	ācrī	ācrī	ācrī	ācribus	ācribus	ācribus

[1] But the forms of some are doubtful.

a. Like **ācer** are declined the following stems in **ri-**: —

alacer, campester, celeber, equester, palūster, pedester, puter, salūber, silvester, terrester, volucer. So also names of months in **-ber**: as, **Octōber** (cf. § 66).

NOTE 1.—This formation is comparatively late, and hence, in the poets and in early Latin, either the masculine or the feminine form of these adjectives was sometimes used for both genders: as, **coetus alacris** (Enn.). In others, as **faenebris, fūnebris, illūstris, lūgubris, mediocris, muliebris**, there is no separate masculine form at all, and these are declined like **levis** (§ 116).

NOTE 2.—**Celer, celeris, celere**, *swift*, has the genitive plural **celerum**, used only as a noun, denoting a military rank. The proper name **Celer** has the ablative in **-e**.

116. Adjectives of Two Terminations are thus declined: —

levis, leve, *light*, STEM **levi-**

	SINGULAR		PLURAL	
	M., F.	N.	M., F.	N.
NOM.	lev**is**	lev**e**	lev**ēs**	lev**ia**
GEN.	lev**is**	lev**is**	lev**ium**	lev**ium**
DAT.	lev**ī**	lev**ī**	lev**ibus**	lev**ibus**
ACC.	lev**em**	lev**e**	lev**īs** (-**ēs**)	lev**ia**
ABL.	lev**ī**	lev**ī**	lev**ibus**	lev**ibus**

NOTE.—Adjectives of two and three terminations sometimes have an ablative in **-e** in poetry, rarely in prose.

Adjectives of One Termination

117. The remaining adjectives of the third declension are Consonant stems; but most of them, except Comparatives, have the following forms of **i**-stems: —[1]

-ī in the ablative singular (but often **-e**);
-ia in the nominative and accusative plural neuter;
-ium in the genitive plural;
-īs (as well as **-ēs**) in the accusative plural masculine and feminine.

In the other cases they follow the rule for Consonant stems.

a. These adjectives, except stems in **l-** or **r-**, form the nominative singular from the stem by adding **s**: as, **atrōx** (stem **atrōc-** + **s**), **egēns** (stem **egent-** + **s**).[2]

b. Here belong the present participles in **-ns** (stem **nt-**)[2]: as, **amāns, monēns.** They are declined like **egēns** (but cf. § 121).

[1] For details see § 121. [2] Stems in **nt-** omit **t** before the nominative **-s**.

118. Adjectives of one termination are declined as follows: —

	atrōx, *fierce*, STEM **atrōc-**		**egēns**, *needy*, STEM **egent-**	
		SINGULAR		
	M., F.	N.	M., F.	N.
NOM.	atrōx	atrōx	egēns	egēns
GEN.	atrōcis	atrōcis	egentis	egentis
DAT.	atrōcī	atrōcī	egentī	egentī
ACC.	atrōcem	atrōx	egentem	egēns
ABL.	atrōcī (-e)	atrōcī (-e)	egentī (-e)	egentī (-e)
		PLURAL		
NOM.	atrōcēs	atrōcia	egentēs	egentia
GEN.	atrōcium	atrōcium	egentium	egentium
DAT.	atrōcibus	atrōcibus	egentibus	egentibus
ACC.	atrōcīs (-ēs)	atrōcia	egentīs (-ēs)	egentia
ABL.	atrōcibus	atrōcibus	egentibus	egentibus

119. Other examples are the following: —

	concors, *harmonious* STEM **concord-**		**praeceps**, *headlong* STEM **praecipit-**	
		SINGULAR		
	M., F.	N.	M., F.	N.
NOM.	concors	concors	praeceps	praeceps
GEN.	concordis	concordis	praecipitis	praecipitis
DAT.	concordī	concordī	praecipitī	praecipitī
ACC.	concordem	concors	praecipitem	praeceps
ABL.	concordī	concordī	praecipitī	praecipitī
		PLURAL		
NOM.	concordēs	concordia	praecipitēs	praecipitia
GEN.	concordium	concordium	[praecipitium][1]	
DAT.	concordibus	concordibus	praecipitibus	praecipitibus
ACC.	concordīs (-ēs)	concordia	praecipitīs (-ēs)	praecipitia
ABL.	concordibus	concordibus	praecipitibus	praecipitibus

[1] Given by grammarians, but not found.

	iēns, *going* STEM **eunt-**		**pār**, *equal* STEM **par-**		**dīves**, *rich* STEM **dīvit-**	
	SINGULAR					
	M., F.	N.	M., F.	N.	M., F.	N.
NOM.	iēns	iēns	pār	pār	dīves	dīves
GEN.	euntis	euntis	paris	paris	dīvitis	dīvitis
DAT.	euntī	euntī	parī	parī	dīvitī	dīvitī
ACC.	euntem	iēns	parem	pār	dīvitem	dīves
ABL.	eunte (-ī)	eunte (-ī)	parī	parī	dīvite	dīvite
	PLURAL					
NOM.	euntēs	euntia	parēs	paria	dīvitēs	[dītia]
GEN.	euntium	euntium	parium	parium	dīvitum	dīvitum
DAT.	euntibus	euntibus	paribus	paribus	dīvitibus	dīvitibus
ACC.	euntīs (-ēs)	euntia	parīs (-ēs)	paria	dīvitīs (-ēs)	[dītia]
ABL.	euntibus	euntibus	paribus	paribus	dīvitibus	dīvitibus

	ūber, *fertile* STEM **ūber-**		**vetus**, *old* STEM **veter-**	
	SINGULAR			
	M., F.	N.	M., F.	N.
NOM.	ūber	ūber	vetus	vetus
GEN.	ūberis	ūberis	veteris	veteris
DAT.	ūberī	ūberī	veterī	veterī
ACC.	ūberem	ūber	veterem	vetus
ABL.	ūberī [1]	ūberī [1]	vetere (-ī)	vetere (-ī)
	PLURAL			
NOM.	ūberēs	ūbera	veterēs	vetera
GEN.	ūberum	ūberum	veterum	veterum
DAT.	ūberibus	ūberibus	veteribus	veteribus
ACC.	ūberēs	ūbera	veterēs	vetera
ABL.	ūberibus	ūberibus	veteribus	veteribus

NOTE. — Of these **vetus** is originally an s-stem. In most s-stems the **r** has intruded itself into the nominative also, as **bi-corpor** (for †**bi-corpos**), **dēgener** (for †**dē-genes**).

[1] An ablative in **-e** is very rare.

Declension of Comparatives

120. Comparatives are declined as follows: —

	melior, *better* STEM **meliōr-** for **meliōs-**		**plūs**, *more* STEM **plūr-** for **plūs-**	
		SINGULAR		
	M., F.	N.	M., F.	N.
NOM.	melior	melius	——	plūs
GEN.	meliōr**is**	meliōr**is**	——	plūr**is**
DAT.	meliōr**ī**	meliōr**ī**	——	——
ACC.	meliōr**em**	melius	——	plūs
ABL.	meliōr**e** (-**ī**)	meliōr**e** (-**ī**)	——	plūr**e**
		PLURAL		
NOM.	meliōr**ēs**	meliōr**a**	plūr**ēs**	plūr**a**
GEN.	meliōr**um**	meliōr**um**	plūr**ium**	plūr**ium**
DAT.	meliōr**ibus**	meliōr**ibus**	plūr**ibus**	plūr**ibus**
ACC.	meliōr**ēs** (-**īs**)	meliōr**a**	plūr**ēs** (-**īs**)	plūr**a**
ABL.	meliōr**ibus**	meliōr**ibus**	plūr**ibus**	plūr**ibus**

a. All comparatives except **plūs** are declined like **melior**.

b. The stem of comparatives properly ended in ŏ̄s-; but this became **or** in the nominative masculine and feminine, and ōr- in all other cases except the nominative and accusative singular neuter, where s is retained and ŏ is changed to ŭ (cf. **honŏr**, **-ōris**; **corpus**, **-ŏris**). Thus comparatives appear to have two terminations.

c. The neuter singular **plūs** is used only as a noun. The genitive (rarely the ablative) is used only as an expression of value (cf. § 417). The dative is not found in classic use. The compound **complūrēs**, *several*, has sometimes neuter plural **complūria**.

Case-Forms of Consonant Stems

121. In adjectives of Consonant stems —

a. The Ablative Singular commonly ends in -ī, but sometimes -e.

1. Adjectives used as nouns (as **superstes**, *survivor*) have **-e**.

2. Participles in **-ns** used *as such* (especially in the ablative absolute, § 419), or as nouns, regularly have **-e**; but participles used as adjectives have regularly **-ī**: —

> **dominō imperante**, *at the master's command;* **ab amante**, *by a lover;* **ab amantī muliere**, *by a loving woman.*

3. The following have regularly -ī: — **āmēns, anceps, concors** (and other compounds of **cor**), **cōnsors** (but as a substantive, -e), **dēgener, hebes, ingēns, inops, memor** (and compounds), **pār** (in prose), **perpes, praeceps, praepes, teres.**

4. The following have regularly -e: — **caeles, compos,** [†**dēses**], **dīves, hospes, particeps, pauper, prīnceps, sōspes, superstes.** So also patrials (see § 71. 5) and stems in **āt-, īt-, nt-, rt-,** when used as nouns, and sometimes when used as adjectives.

b. The Genitive Plural ends commonly in **-ium**, but has **-um** in the following:[1] —

1. Always in **compos, dīves, inops, particeps, praepes, prīnceps, supplex,** and compounds of nouns which have **-um**: as, **quadru-pēs, bi-color.**

2. Sometimes, in poetry, in participles in **-ns**: as, **silentum concilium,** *a council of the silent shades* (Aen. vi. 432).

c. The Accusative Plural regularly ends in **-īs**, but comparatives commonly have **-ēs.**

d. **Vetus** (gen. **-ĕris**) and **pūbes** (gen. **-ĕris**) regularly have **-e** in the ablative singular, **-a** in the nominative and accusative plural, and **-um** in the genitive plural. For **ūber**, see § 119.

e. A few adjectives of one termination, used as nouns, have a feminine form in **-a**: as, **clienta, hospita,** with the appellative **Iūnō Sōspita.**

Irregularities and Special Uses of Adjectives

122. The following special points require notice: —

a. Several adjectives vary in declension: as, **gracilis** (-us), **hilaris** (-us), **inermis** (-us), **bicolor** (-ōrus).

b. A few adjectives are indeclinable: as, **damnās, frūgī** (really a dative of service, see § 382. 1. N. [2]), **nēquam** (originally an adverb), **necesse,** and the pronominal forms **tot, quot, aliquot, totidem. Potis** is often used as an indeclinable adjective, but sometimes has **pote** in the neuter.

c. Several adjectives are defective: as, **exspēs** (only nom.), **exlēx** (**exlēgem**) (only nom. and acc. sing.), **pernox** (**pernocte**) (only nom. and abl. sing.); and **prīmōris, sēminecī,** etc., which lack the nominative singular.

d. Many adjectives, from their signification, can be used only in the masculine and feminine. These may be called *adjectives of common gender.*

Such are **adulēscēns,** *youthful;* [†**dēses**], **-idis,** *slothful;* **inops, -opis,** *poor;* **sōspes, -itis,** *safe.* Similarly, **senex,** *old man,* and **iuvenis,** *young man,* are sometimes called *masculine adjectives.*

For Adjectives used as Nouns, see §§ 288, 289; for Nouns used as Adjectives, see § 321. *c*; for Adjectives used as Adverbs, see § 214; for Adverbs used as Adjectives, see § 321. *d.*

[1] Forms in **-um** sometimes occur in a few others.

COMPARISON OF ADJECTIVES

123. In Latin, as in English, there are three degrees of comparison: the *Positive*, the *Comparative*, and the *Superlative*.

124. The Comparative is regularly formed by adding **-ior** (neuter **-ius**),[1] the Superlative by adding **-issimus** (**-a**, **-um**), to the stem of the Positive, which loses its final vowel: —

cārus, *dear* (stem **cāro-**);	cār**ior**, *dearer;*	cār**issimus**, *dearest.*
levis, *light* (stem **levi-**);	lev**ior**, *lighter;*	lev**issimus**, *lightest.*
fēlīx, *happy* (stem **fēlīc-**);	fēlīc**ior**, *happier;*	fēlīc**issimus**, *happiest.*
hebes, *dull* (stem **hebet-**);	hebet**ior**, *duller;*	hebet**issimus**, *dullest.*

NOTE. — A form of diminutive is made upon the stem of some comparatives: as, **grandius-culus**, *a little larger* (see § 243).

a. Participles when used as adjectives are regularly compared: —

patiēns, *patient;* patient**ior**, patient**issimus**.
apertus, *open;* apert**ior**, apert**issimus**.

125. Adjectives in **-er** form the Superlative by adding **-rimus** to the nominative. The comparative is regular: —

ācer, *keen;* āc**rior**, ācer**rimus**.
miser, *wretched;* miser**ior**, miser**rimus**.

a. So **vetus** (gen. **veteris**) has superlative **veterrimus**, from the old form **veter**; and **mātūrus**, besides its regular superlative (**mātūrissimus**), has a rare form **mātūrrimus**.

For the comparative of **vetus**, **vetustior** (from **vetustus**) is used.

126. Six adjectives in **-lis** form the Superlative by adding **-limus** to the stem clipped of its final **i-**. These are **facilis, difficilis, similis, dissimilis, gracilis, humilis.**

facilis (stem **facili-**), *easy;* facil**ior**, facil**limus**.

127. Compounds in **-dicus** (*saying*) and **-volus** (*willing*) take in their comparison the forms of the corresponding participles **dīcēns** and **volēns**, which were anciently used as adjectives: —

male**dicus**, *slanderous;* maledī**centior**, maledī**centissimus**.
male**volus**, *spiteful;* malevol**entior**, malevol**entissimus**.

[1] The comparative suffix (earlier **-iōs**) is akin to the Greek *-ιων*, or the Sanskrit *-iyans*. That of the superlative (**-issimus**) is a double form of uncertain origin. It appears to contain the **is-** of the old suffix **-is-to-s** (seen in ἥδ-ιστο-ς and English *sweetest*) and also the old **-mo-s** (seen in **prī-mus, mini-mus**, etc.). The endings **-limus** and **-rimus** are formed by assimilation (§ 15. 6) from **-simus**. The comparative and superlative are really new stems, and are not strictly to be regarded as forms of inflection.

a. So, by analogy, compounds in **-ficus**: —

māgni**ficus**, *grand;* māgnifi**centior**, māgnifi**centissimus**.

128. Some adjectives are compared by means of the adverbs **magis**, *more*, and **maximē**, *most.*

So especially adjectives in **-us** preceded by **e** or **i**: —

idōneus, *fit;* **magis** idōneus, **maximē** idōneus.

NOTE.—But pius has piissimus in the superlative,—a form condemned by Cicero, but common in inscriptions; equally common, however, is the irregular pientissimus.

Irregular Comparison

129. Several adjectives have in their comparison irregular forms: —

bonus, *good;*	mel**ior**, *better;*	opt**imus**, *best.*
malus, *bad;*	pê**ior**, *worse;*	pess**imus**, *worst.*
māgnus, *great;*	mâ**ior**, *greater;*	max**imus**, *greatest.*
parvus, *small;*	min**or**, *less;*	min**imus**, *least.*
multus, *much;*	plūs (N.) (§ 120), *more;*	plūr**imus**, *most.*
multī, *many;*	plūrēs, *more;*	plūr**imī**, *most.*
nēquam (indecl., § 122. *b*), *worthless;*	nēqu**ior**;	nēqu**issimus**.
frūgī (indecl., § 122. *b*), *useful, worthy;*	frūgāl**ior**;	frūgāl**issimus**.
dexter, *on the right, handy;*	dexter**ior**;	dext**imus**.

NOTE.—These irregularities arise from the use of different stems (cf. § 127). Thus frūgālior and frūgālissimus are formed from the stem frūgāli-, but are used as the comparative and superlative of the indeclinable frūgī.

Defective Comparison

130. Some Comparatives and Superlatives appear without a Positive: —

ōc**ior**, *swifter;*	ōc**issimus**, *swiftest.*
pot**ior**, *preferable;*[1]	pot**issimus**, *most important.*

a. The following are formed from stems not used as adjectives:[2] —

[1] The old positive potis occurs in the sense of *able, possible.*

[2] The forms in -trā and -terus were originally comparative (cf. alter), so that the comparatives in -terior are double comparatives. Īnferus and superus are comparatives of a still more primitive form (cf. the English comparative in *-er*).

The superlatives in -timus (-tumus) are relics of old forms of comparison; those in -mus like īmus, summus, prīmus, are still more primitive. Forms like extrēmus are superlatives of a comparative. In fact, comparison has always been treated with an accumulation of endings, as children say *furtherer* and *furtherest.*

cis, citrā (adv., *on this side*):	citer**ior**, *hither;*	cit**imus**, *hithermost.*
dē (prep., *down*):	dēter**ior**, *worse;*	dēter**rimus**, *worst.*
in, intrā (prep., *in, within*):	inter**ior**, *inner;*	int**imus**, *inmost.*
prae, prō (prep., *before*):	pr**ior**, *former;*	prī**mus**, *first.*
prope (adv., *near*):	prop**ior**, *nearer;*	pro**ximus**, *next.*
ultrā (adv., *beyond*):	ulter**ior**, *farther;*	ult**imus**, *farthest.*

b. Of the following the positive forms are rare, except when used as nouns (generally in the plural):—

exterus, *outward;*	exter**ior**, *outer;*	extr**ēmus** (ext**imus**), *outmost.*
īnferus, *below* (see § 111. *b*);	īnfer**ior**, *lower;*	īnf**imus** (**īmus**), *lowest.*
posterus, *following;*	poster**ior**, *latter;*	postr**ēmus** (post**umus**), *last.*
superus, *above;*	super**ior**, *higher;*	supr**ēmus** or sum**mus**, *highest.*

But the plurals, **exterī**, *foreigners;* **īnferī**, *the gods below;* **posterī**, *posterity;* **superī**, *the heavenly gods*, are common.

Note.—The superlative **postumus** has the special sense of *last-born*, and was a well-known surname.

131. Several adjectives lack the Comparative or the Superlative:—

a. The Comparative is rare or wanting in the following:—

bellus,	**inclutus** (or **inclitus**),	**novus,**
caesius,	**invictus,**	**pius,**
falsus,	**invītus,**	**sacer,**
fīdus (with its compounds),	**meritus,**	**vafer.**

b. The Superlative is wanting in many adjectives in **-ilis** or **-bilis** (as, **agilis, probābilis**), and in the following:—

āctuōsus	**exīlis**	**prōclīvis**	**surdus**
agrestis	**ingēns**	**propinquus**	**taciturnus**
alacer	**iēiūnus**	**satur**	**tempestīvus**
arcānus	**longinquus**	**sēgnis**	**teres**
caecus	**oblīquus**	**sērus**	**vīcīnus**
diūturnus	**opīmus**	**supīnus**	

c. From **iuvenis**, *youth*, **senex**, *old man* (cf. § 122. *d*), are formed the comparatives **iūnior**, *younger*, **senior**, *older*. For these, however, **minor nātū** and **mâior nātū** are sometimes used (**nātū** being often omitted).

The superlative is regularly expressed by **minimus** and **maximus**, with or without **nātū**.

Note.—In these phrases **nātū** is ablative of specification (see § 418).

d. Many adjectives (as **aureus**, *golden*) are from their meaning incapable of comparison.

Note.—But each language has its own usage in this respect. Thus, **niger**, *glossy black*, and **candidus**, *shining white*, are compared; but not **āter** or **albus**, meaning *absolute* dead black or white (except that Plautus once has **ātrior**).

NUMERALS

132. The Latin Numerals may be classified as follows: —

I. NUMERAL ADJECTIVES:

1. Cardinal Numbers, answering the question *how many?* as, **ūnus**, *one;* **duo**, *two*, etc.

2. Ordinal Numbers,[1] adjectives derived (in most cases) from the Cardinals, and answering the question *which in order?* as, **prīmus**, *first;* **secundus**, *second*, etc.

3. Distributive Numerals, answering the question *how many at a time?* as, **singulī**, *one at a time;* **bīnī**, *two by two*, etc.

II. NUMERAL ADVERBS, answering the question *how often?* as, **semel**, *once;* **bis**, *twice*, etc.

Cardinals and Ordinals

133. These two series are as follows: —

	CARDINAL	ORDINAL	ROMAN NUMERALS
1.	ūnus, ūna, ūnum, *one*	prīmus, -a, -um, *first*	I
2.	duo, duae, duo, *two*	secundus (alter), *second*	II
3.	trēs, tria, *three*	tertius, *third*	III
4.	quattuor	quārtus	IIII *or* IV
5.	quīnque	quīntus	V
6.	sex	sextus	VI
7.	septem	septimus	VII
8.	octō	octāvus	VIII
9.	novem	nōnus	VIIII *or* IX
10.	decem	decimus	X
11.	ūndecim	ūndecimus	XI
12.	duodecim	duodecimus	XII
13.	tredecim (decem (et) trēs)	tertius decimus (decimus (et) tertius)	XIII
14.	quattuordecim	quārtus decimus	XIIII *or* XIV
15.	quīndecim	quīntus decimus	XV
16.	sēdecim	sextus decimus	XVI
17.	septendecim	septimus decimus	XVII
18.	duodēvīgintī (octōdecim)	duodēvīcēnsimus (octāvus decimus)	XVIII

[1] The Ordinals (except **secundus, tertius, octāvus, nōnus**) are formed by means of suffixes related to those used in the superlative and in part identical with them. Thus, **decimus** (compare the form **īnfimus**) may be regarded as the last of a series of ten; **prīmus** is a superlative of a stem akin to **prō**; the forms in **-tus** (**quārtus, quīntus, sextus**) may be compared with the corresponding Greek forms in *-τος*, and with superlatives in *-ισ-το-ς*, while the others have the superlative ending **-timus** (changed to **-simus**). Of the exceptions, **secundus** is a participle of **sequor**; **alter** is a comparative form (compare *-τερος* in Greek), and **nōnus** is contracted from †**novenos**. The cardinal multiples of ten are compounds of **-gint-** 'ten' (a fragment of a derivative from **decem**).

	CARDINAL	ORDINAL	ROMAN NUMERALS
19.	ūndēvīgintī (novendecim)	ūndēvīcēnsimus (nōnus decimus)	XVIIII *or* XIX
20.	vīgintī	vīcēnsimus (vīgēnsimus)	XX
21.	vīgintī ūnus (*or* ūnus et vīgintī, *etc.*)	vīcēnsimus prīmus (ūnus et vīcēnsimus, *etc.*)	XXI
30.	trīgintā	trīcēnsimus	XXX
40.	quadrāgintā	quadrāgēnsimus	XXXX *or* XL
50.	quīnquāgintā	quīnquāgēnsimus	⊥ *or* L
60.	sexāgintā	sexāgēnsimus	LX
70.	septuāgintā	septuāgēnsimus	LXX
80.	octōgintā	octōgēnsimus	LXXX
90.	nōnāgintā	nōnāgēnsimus	LXXXX *or* XC
100.	centum	centēnsimus	C
101.	centum (et) ūnus, *etc.*	centēnsimus prīmus, *etc.*	CI
200.	ducentī, -ae, -a	ducentēnsimus	CC
300.	trecentī	trecentēnsimus	CCC
400.	quadringentī	quadringentēnsimus	CCCC
500.	quīngentī	quīngentēnsimus	D
600.	sescentī	sescentēnsimus	DC
700.	septingentī	septingentēnsimus	DCC
800.	octingentī	octingentēnsimus	DCCC
900.	nōngentī	nōngentēnsimus	DCCCC
1000.	mīlle	mīllēnsimus	∞ (CIↃ) *or* M
5000.	quīnque mīlia (mīllia)	quīnquiēns mīllēnsimus	IↃↃ
10,000.	decem mīlia (mīllia)	deciēns mīllēnsimus	CCIↃↃ
100,000.	centum mīlia (mīllia)	centiēns mīllēnsimus	CCCIↃↃↃ

NOTE 1.—The forms in **-ēnsimus** are often written without the **n**: as, **vīcēsimus**, etc.

NOTE 2.—The forms **octōdecim, novendecim** are rare, **duodēvīgintī** (*two from twenty*), **ūndēvīgintī** (*one from twenty*), being used instead. So 28, 29; 38, 39; etc. may be expressed either by the subtraction of *two* and *one* or by the addition of *eight* and *nine* respectively.

Declension of Cardinals and Ordinals

134. Of the Cardinals only **ūnus, duo, trēs,** the *hundreds* above one hundred, and **mīlle** when used as a noun, are declinable.

a. For the declension of **ūnus**, see § 113. It often has the meaning of *same* or *only*. The plural is used in this sense; but also, as a simple numeral, to agree with a plural noun of a singular meaning: as, **ūna castra**, *one camp* (cf. § 137. *b*). The plural occurs also in the phrase **ūnī et alterī**, *one party and the other* (the ones and the others).

b. **Duo**,[1] *two*, and **trēs**, *three*, are thus declined:—

[1] The form in **-o** is a remnant of the *dual number*, which was lost in Latin, but is found in cognate languages. So in **ambō**, *both*, which preserves **-ō** (cf. δύω and § 629. *b*).

	M.	F.	N.	M., F.	N.
Nom.	duo	duae	duo	trēs	tria
Gen.	duōrum	duārum	duōrum	trium	trium
Dat.	duōbus	duābus	duōbus	tribus	tribus
Acc.	duōs (duo)	duās	duo	trēs (trīs)	tria
Abl.	duōbus	duābus	duōbus	tribus	tribus

Note.—Ambō, *both*, is declined like duo.

c. The hundreds, up to 1000, are adjectives of the First and Second Declensions, and are regularly declined like the plural of **bonus**.

d. **Mīlle**, *a thousand*, is in the singular an indeclinable adjective:—

mīlle modīs, *in a thousand ways.*
cum **mīlle** hominibus, *with a thousand men.*
mīlle trahēns variōs colōrēs (Aen. iv. 701), *drawing out a thousand various colors.*

In the plural it is used as a neuter noun, and is declined like the plural of **sedīle** (§ 69): **mīlia**, **mīlium**, **mīlibus**, etc.

Note.—The singular mīlle is sometimes found as a noun in the nominative and accusative: as, mīlle hominum mīsit, *he sent a thousand* (of) *men;* in the other cases rarely, except in connection with the same case of mīlia: as, cum octō mīlibus peditum, mīlle equitum, *with eight thousand foot and a thousand horse.*

e. The ordinals are adjectives of the First and Second Declensions, and are regularly declined like **bonus**.

135. Cardinals and Ordinals have the following uses:—

a. In numbers below 100, if units precede tens, **et** is generally inserted: **duo et vīgintī**; otherwise **et** is omitted: **vīgintī duo.**

b. In numbers above 100 the highest denomination generally stands first, the next second, etc., as in English. **Et** is either omitted entirely, or stands between the two highest denominations:—**mīlle (et) septingentī sexāgintā quattuor**, 1764.

Note.—Observe the following combinations of numerals with substantives:—
ūnus et vīgintī mīlitēs, or vīgintī mīlitēs (et) ūnus, *21 soldiers.*
duo mīlia quīngentī mīlitēs, or duo mīlia mīlitum et quīngentī, *2500 soldiers.*
mīlitēs mīlle ducentī trīgintā ūnus, *1231 soldiers.*

c. After **mīlia** the name of the objects enumerated is in the genitive:

duo mīlia **hominum**, *two thousand men.*[1]
cum tribus mīlibus **mīlitum**, *with three thousand soldiers.*
mīlia **passuum** tria, *three thousand paces* (three miles).

d. For *million, billion, trillion*, etc., the Romans had no special words, but these numbers were expressed by multiplication (cf. § 138. *a*).

[1] Or, in poetry, bis mīlle hominēs, *twice a thousand men.*

e. Fractions are expressed, as in English, by cardinals in the numerator and ordinals in the denominator. The feminine gender is used to agree with **pars** expressed or understood:—*two-sevenths*, **duae septimae** (sc. **partēs**); *three-eighths*, **trēs octāvae** (sc. **partēs**).

One-half is **dīmidia pars** or **dīmidium**.

Note 1.—When the numerator is *one*, it is omitted and **pars** is expressed: *one-third*, **tertia pars**; *one-fourth*, **quārta pars**.

Note 2.—When the denominator is but one greater than the numerator, the numerator only is given: *two-thirds*, **duae partēs**; *three-fourths*, **trēs partēs**, etc.

Note 3.—Fractions are also expressed by special words derived from **as**, *a pound*: as, **triēns**, *a third*; **bēs**, *two-thirds*. See § 637.

Distributives

136. Distributive Numerals are declined like the plural of **bonus**.

Note.—These answer to the interrogative **quotēnī**, *how many of each?* or *how many at a time?*

1. singulī, *one by one*
2. bīnī, *two by two*
3. ternī, trīnī
4. quaternī
5. quīnī
6. sēnī
7. septēnī
8. octōnī
9. novēnī
10. dēnī
11. ūndēnī
12. duodēnī
13. ternī dēnī, *etc.*
18. octōnī dēnī *or* duodēvīcēnī
19. novēnī dēnī *or* ūndēvīcēnī
20. vīcēnī
21. vīcēnī singulī, *etc.*
30. trīcēnī
40. quadrāgēnī
50. quīnquāgēnī
60. sexāgēnī
70. septuāgēnī
80. octōgēnī
90. nōnāgēnī
100. centēnī
200. ducēnī
300. trecēnī
400. quadringēnī
500. quīngēnī
600. sescēnī
700. septingēnī
800. octingēnī
900. nōngēnī
1000. mīllēnī
2000. bīna mīlia
10,000. dēna mīlia
100,000. centēna mīlia

137. Distributives are used as follows:—

a. In the sense of *so many apiece* or *on each side*: as, **singula singulīs**, *one apiece* (one each to each one); **agrī septēna iūgera plēbī dīvīsa sunt**, i.e. *seven jugera to each citizen* (seven jugera each), etc.

b. Instead of cardinals, to express simple number, when a noun plural in form but usually singular in meaning is used in a plural sense: as, **bīna castra**, *two camps* (**duo castra** would mean *two forts*). With such nouns **trīnī**, not **ternī**, is used for *three*: as, **trīna** (not **terna**) **castra**, *three camps*; **terna castra** means *camps in threes*.

c. In multiplication: as, **bis bīna**, *twice two*; **ter septēnīs diēbus**, *in thrice seven days*.

d. By the poets instead of cardinal numbers, particularly where *pairs* or *sets* are spoken of: as, **bīna hastīlia**, *two shafts* (two in a set).

Numeral Adverbs

138. The Numeral Adverbs answer the question **quotiēns** (**quotiēs**), *how many times? how often?*

1. semel, *once*
2. bis, *twice*
3. ter, *thrice*
4. quater
5. quīnquiēns (-ēs)[1]
6. sexiēns
7. septiēns
8. octiēns
9. noviēns
10. deciēns
11. ūndeciēns
12. duodeciēns
13. terdeciēns
14. quaterdeciēns
15. quīndeciēns
16. sēdeciēns
17. septiēsdeciēns
18. duodēvīciēns
19. ūndēvīciēns
20. vīciēns
21. semel vīciēns,[2] *etc.*
30. trīciēns
40. quadrāgiēns
50. quīnquāgiēns
60. sexāgiēns
70. septuāgiēns
80. octōgiēns
90. nōnāgiēns
100. centiēns
200. ducentiēns
300. trecentiēns
1000. mīliēns
10,000. deciēns mīliēns

a. Numeral Adverbs are used with **mīlle** to express the higher numbers:

ter et trīciēns (centēna mīlia) sēstertium, *3,300,000 sesterces* (three and thirty times a hundred thousand sesterces).

vīciēs ac septiēs mīliēs (centēna mīlia) sēstertium, *2,700,000,000 sesterces* (twenty-seven thousand times a hundred thousand).

NOTE.—These large numbers are used almost exclusively in reckoning money, and **centēna mīlia** is regularly omitted (see § 634).

Other Numerals

139. The following adjectives are called Multiplicatives:—

simplex, *single;* **duplex**, *double, twofold;* **triplex**, *triple, threefold;* **quadruplex, quīnquiplex, septemplex, decemplex, centuplex, sēsquiplex** ($1\frac{1}{2}$), **multiplex** (*manifold*).

a. Proportionals are: **duplus, triplus, quadruplus, octuplus,** etc., *twice as great, thrice as great,* etc.

b. Temporals: **bīmus, trīmus,** *of two* or *three years' age;* **biennis, triennis,** *lasting two* or *three years;* **bimēstris, trimēstris,** *of two* or *three months;* **bīduum,** *a period of two days;* **biennium,** *a period of two years.*

c. Partitives: **bīnārius, ternārius,** *of two* or *three parts.*

d. Other derivatives are: **ūniō,** *unity;* **bīniō,** *the two* (of dice); **prīmānus,** *of the first legion;* **prīmārius,** *of the first rank;* **dēnārius,** a sum of *10 asses;* **bīnus** (distributive), *double,* etc.

[1] Forms in **-ns** are often written without the **n**.

[2] Also written **vīciēns et semel** or **vīciēns semel**, etc.

PRONOUNS

140. Pronouns are used as Nouns or as Adjectives. They are divided into the following seven classes: —

1. Personal Pronouns: as, **ego**, *I*.
2. Reflexive Pronouns: as, **sē**, *himself*.
3. Possessive Pronouns: as, **meus**, *my*.
4. Demonstrative Pronouns: as, **hīc**, *this;* **ille**, *that*.
5. Relative Pronouns: as, **quī**, *who*.
6. Interrogative Pronouns: as, **quis**, *who?*
7. Indefinite Pronouns: as, **aliquis**, *some one*.

141. Pronouns have special forms of declension.

NOTE.—These special forms are, in general, survivals of a very ancient form of declension differing from that of nouns.

Personal Pronouns

142. The Personal pronouns of the *first person* are **ego**, *I*, **nōs**, *we;* of the *second person*, **tū**, *thou* or *you*, **vōs**, *ye* or *you*. The personal pronouns of the *third person* — *he, she, it, they* — are wanting in Latin, a demonstrative being sometimes used instead.

143. Ego and **tū** are declined as follows: —

FIRST PERSON

	Singular	*Plural*
NOM.	**ego**, *I*	**nōs**, *we*
GEN.	**meī**, *of me*	**nostrum, nostrī**, *of us*
DAT.	**mihi (mī)**, *to me*	**nōbīs**, *to us*
ACC.	**mē**, *me*	**nōs**, *us*
ABL.	**mē**, *by me*	**nōbīs**, *by us*

SECOND PERSON

NOM	**tū**, *thou* or *you*	**vōs**, *ye* or *you*
GEN.	**tuī**, *of thee* or *you*	**vestrum, vestrī; vostrum (-trī)**
DAT.	**tibi**	**vōbīs**
ACC.	**tē**	**vōs**
ABL.	**tē**	**vōbīs**

a. The plural **nōs** is often used for the singular **ego**; the plural **vōs** is never so used for the singular **tū**.

Note.—Old forms are genitive **mīs**, **tīs**; accusative and ablative **mēd**, **tēd** (cf. § 43. N. 1).

b. The forms **nostrum**, **vestrum**, etc., are used *partitively*:—

ūnusquisque nostrum, *each one of us.*
vestrum omnium, *of all of you.*

Note.—The forms of the genitive of the personal pronouns are really the genitives of the possessives: **meī**, **tuī**, **suī**, **nostrī**, **vestrī**, genitive singular neuter: **nostrum**, **vestrum**, genitive plural masculine or neuter. So in early and later Latin we find **ūna vestrārum**, *one of you (women).*

c. The genitives **meī**, **tuī**, **suī**, **nostri**, **vestrī**, are chiefly used *objectively* (§ 347):—

memor sīs nostrī, *be mindful of us* (me).
mē tuī pudet, *I am ashamed of you.*

d. Emphatic forms of **tū** are **tūte** and **tūtemet** (**tūtimet**). The other cases of the personal pronouns, excepting the genitive plural, are made emphatic by adding **-met**: as, **egomet**, **vōsmet**.

Note.—Early emphatic forms are **mēpte** and **tēpte**.

e. Reduplicated forms are found in the accusative and ablative singular: as, **mēmē**, **tētē**.

f. The preposition **cum**, *with*, is joined enclitically with the ablative: as, **tēcum loquitur**, *he talks with you.*

Reflexive Pronouns

144. Reflexive Pronouns are used in the Oblique Cases to refer to the subject of the sentence or clause in which they stand (see § 299): as, **sē amat**, *he loves himself.*

a. In the *first* and *second* persons the oblique cases of the Personal pronouns are used as Reflexives: as, **mē videō**, *I see myself;* **tē laudās**, *you praise yourself;* **nōbīs persuādēmus**, *we persuade ourselves.*

b. The Reflexive pronoun of the *third* person has a special form used only in this sense, the same for both singular and plural. It is thus declined:—

Gen.	**suī**, *of himself, herself, itself, themselves*
Dat.	**sibi**, *to himself, herself, itself, themselves*
Acc.	**sē** (**sēsē**), *himself, herself, itself, themselves*
Abl.	**sē** (**sēsē**), [*by*] *himself, herself, itself, themselves*

Note 1.—Emphatic and reduplicated forms of **sē** are made as in the personals (see § 143. *d*, *e*). The preposition **cum** is added enclitically: as, **sēcum**, *with himself*, etc.

Note 2.—An old form **sēd** occurs in the accusative and ablative.

Possessive Pronouns

145. The Possessive pronouns are: —

FIRST PERSON.	**meus**, *my*	**noster**, *our*
SECOND PERSON.	**tuus**, *thy*, *your*	**vester**, *your*
THIRD PERSON.	**suus**, *his*, *her*, *its*	**suus**, *their*

These are really adjectives of the First and Second Declensions, and are so declined (see §§ 110–112). But **meus** has regularly **mī** (rarely **meus**) in the vocative singular masculine.

NOTE. — **Suus** is used only as a reflexive, referring to the subject. For a possessive pronoun of the third person not referring to the subject, the genitive of a demonstrative must be used. Thus, **patrem suum occīdit**, *he killed his* (own) *father;* but **patrem êius occīdit**, *he killed his* (somebody else's) *father.*

a. Emphatic forms in **-pte** are found in the ablative singular: **suōpte**.

b. A rare possessive **cûius** (**quôius**), **-a**, **-um**, *whose*, is formed from the genitive singular of the relative or interrogative pronoun (**quī**, **quis**). It may be either interrogative or relative in force according to its derivation, but is usually the former.

c. The reciprocals *one another* and *each other* are expressed by **inter sē** or **alter . . . alterum**: —

alter alterīus ōva frangit, *they break each other's eggs* (one . . . of the other).
inter sē amant, *they love one another* (they love among themselves).

Demonstrative Pronouns

146. The Demonstrative Pronouns are used to *point out* or designate a person or thing for special attention, either *with nouns* as Adjectives or *alone* as Pronouns. They are: — **hīc**, *this;* **is**, **ille**, **iste**, *that;* with the Intensive **ipse**, *self*, and **īdem**, *same;*[1] and are thus declined: —

hīc, *this*

	SINGULAR			PLURAL		
	M.	F.	N.	M.	F.	N.
NOM.	hīc	haec	hōc	hī	hae	haec
GEN.	hûius	hûius	hûius	hōrum	hārum	hōrum
DAT.	huic	huic	huic	hīs	hīs	hīs
ACC.	hunc	hanc	hōc	hōs	hās	haec
ABL.	hōc	hāc	hōc	hīs	hīs	hīs

[1] These demonstratives are combinations of **o-** and **i-** stems, which are not clearly distinguishable.

NOTE 1.—**Hīc** is a compound of the stem **ho-** with the demonstrative enclitic **-ce**. In most of the cases final **e** is dropped, in some the whole termination. But in these latter it is sometimes retained for emphasis: as, **hûius-ce**, **hīs-ce**. In early Latin **-c** alone is retained in some of these (**hōrunc**). The vowel in **hīc**, **hōc**, was originally short, and perhaps this quantity was always retained. **Ille** and **iste** are sometimes found with the same enclitic: **illic**, **illaec**, **illuc**; also **illoc**. See *a*, p. 67.

NOTE 2.—For the dative and ablative plural of **hīc** the old form **hībus** is sometimes found; **haec** occurs (rarely) for **hae**.

is, *that*

	SINGULAR			PLURAL		
	M.	F.	N.	M.	F.	N.
NOM.	**is**	**ea**	**id**	**eī, iī (ī)**	**eae**	**ea**
GEN.	**êius**	**êius**	**êius**	**eōrum**	**eārum**	**eōrum**
DAT.	**eī**	**eī**	**eī**	**eīs, iīs (īs)**	**eīs, iīs (īs)**	**eīs, iīs (īs)**
ACC.	**eum**	**eam**	**id**	**eōs**	**eās**	**ea**
ABL.	**eō**	**eā**	**eō**	**eīs, iīs (īs)**	**eīs, iīs (īs)**	**eīs, iīs (īs)**

NOTE 3.—Obsolete forms are **eae** (dat. fem.), and **eābus** or **ībus** (dat. plur.). For dative **eī** are found also **êī** and **eî** (monosyllabic); **eî**, **eôs**, etc., also occur in the plural.

ille, *that*

	SINGULAR			PLURAL		
	M.	F.	N.	M.	F.	N.
NOM.	**ille**	**illa**	**illud**	**illī**	**illae**	**illa**
GEN.	**illīus**	**illīus**	**illīus**	**illōrum**	**illārum**	**illōrum**
DAT.	**illī**	**illī**	**illī**	**illīs**	**illīs**	**illīs**
ACC.	**illum**	**illam**	**illud**	**illōs**	**illās**	**illa**
ABL.	**illō**	**illā**	**illō**	**illīs**	**illīs**	**illīs**

Iste, ista, istud, *that* (yonder), is declined like **ille**.

NOTE 4.—**Ille** replaces an earlier **ollus** (**olle**), of which several forms occur.

NOTE 5.—**Iste** is sometimes found in early writers in the form **ste** etc. The first syllable of **ille** and **ipse** is very often used as short in early poetry.

NOTE 6.—The forms **illī**, **istī** (gen.), and **illae**, **istae** (dat.), are sometimes found; also the nominative plural **istaece**, **illaece** (for **istae**, **illae**). See *a*, p. 67.

ipse, *self*

	SINGULAR			PLURAL		
	M.	F.	N.	M.	F.	N.
NOM.	**ipse**	**ipsa**	**ipsum**	**ipsī**	**ipsae**	**ipsa**
GEN.	**ipsīus**	**ipsīus**	**ipsīus**	**ipsōrum**	**ipsārum**	**ipsōrum**
DAT.	**ipsī**	**ipsī**	**ipsī**	**ipsīs**	**ipsīs**	**ipsīs**
ACC.	**ipsum**	**ipsam**	**ipsum**	**ipsōs**	**ipsās**	**ipsa**
ABL.	**ipsō**	**ipsā**	**ipsō**	**ipsīs**	**ipsīs**	**ipsīs**

Note 7.—**Ipse** is compounded of **is** and **-pse** (a pronominal particle of uncertain origin: cf. § 145. *a*), meaning *self*. The former part was originally declined, as in **reāpse** (for **rē eāpse**), *in fact*. An old form **ipsus** occurs, with superlative **ipsissimus**, *own self*, used for comic effect.

Note 8.—The intensive **-pse** is found in the forms **eapse** (nominative), **eumpse**, **eampse**, **eōpse**, **eāpse** (ablative).

īdem, *the same*

	Singular			Plural		
	M.	F.	N.	M.	F.	N.
Nom.	**īdem**	**eădem**	**ĭdem**	**īdem** (**eī-**)	**eaedem**	**eădem**
Gen.	**êiusdem**	**êiusdem**	**êiusdem**	**eōrundem**	**eārundem**	**eōrundem**
Dat.	**eīdem**	**eīdem**	**eīdem**		**eīsdem** or **īsdem**	
Acc.	**eundem**	**eandem**	**ĭdem**	**eōsdem**	**eāsdem**	**eădem**
Abl.	**eōdem**	**eādem**	**eōdem**		**eīsdem** or **īsdem**	

Note 9.—**Īdem** is the demonstrative **is** with the indeclinable suffix **-dem**. The masculine **īdem** is for †**isdem**; the neuter **idem**, however, is not for †**iddem**, but is a relic of an older formation. A final **m** of **is** is changed to **n** before **d**: as, **eundem** for **eumdem**, etc. The plural forms **īdem**, **īsdem**, are often written **iīdem**, **iīsdem**.

a. **Ille** and **iste** appear in combination with the demonstrative particle **-c**, shortened from **-ce**, in the following forms:—

Singular

	M.	F.	N.	M.	F.	N.
Nom.	**illic**	**illaec**	**illuc** (**illoc**)	**istic**	**istaec**	**istuc** (**istoc**)
Acc.	**illunc**	**illanc**	**illuc** (**illoc**)	**istunc**	**istanc**	**istuc** (**istoc**)
Abl.	**illōc**	**illāc**	**illōc**	**istōc**	**istāc**	**istōc**

Plural

N., Acc.	——	——	**illaec**	——	——	**istaec**

Note 1.—The appended **-ce** is also found with pronouns in numerous combinations: as, **hûiusce**, **hunce**, **hōrunce**, **hārunce**, **hōsce**, **hīsce** (cf. § 146. n. 1), **illīusce**, **īsce**; also with the interrogative **-ne**, in **hōcine**, **hōscine**, **istucine**, **illicine**, etc.

Note 2.—By composition with **ecce** or **em**, *behold!* are formed **eccum** (for **ecce eum**), **eccam**, **eccōs**, **eccās**; **eccillum** (for **ecce illum**); **ellum** (for **em illum**), **ellam**, **ellōs**, **ellās**; **eccistam**. These forms are dramatic and colloquial.

b. The combinations **hûiusmodī** (**hûiuscemodī**), **êiusmodī**, etc., are used as indeclinable adjectives, equivalent to **tālis**, *such*: as, **rēs êiusmodī**, *such a thing* (a thing of that sort: cf. § 345. *a*).

For uses of the Demonstrative Pronouns, see §§ 296 ff.

Relative Pronouns

147. The Relative Pronoun **quī**, *who, which*, is thus declined:—

	Singular			Plural		
	M.	F.	N.	M.	F.	N.
Nom.	**quī**	**quae**	**quod**	**quī**	**quae**	**quae**
Gen.	**cûius**	**cûius**	**cûius**	**quōrum**	**quārum**	**quōrum**
Dat.	**cui**	**cui**	**cui**	**quibus**	**quibus**	**quibus**
Acc.	**quem**	**quam**	**quod**	**quōs**	**quās**	**quae**
Abl.	**quō**	**quā**	**quō**	**quibus**	**quibus**	**quibus**

Interrogative and Indefinite Pronouns

148. The Substantive Interrogative Pronoun **quis**, *who?* **quid**, *what?* is declined in the Singular as follows: —

	M., F.	N.
Nom.	**quis**	**quid**
Gen.	**cûius**	**cûius**
Dat.	**cui**	**cui**
Acc.	**quem**	**quid**
Abl.	**quō**	**quō**

The Plural is the same as that of the Relative, **quī, quae, quae**.

a. The singular **quis** is either masculine or of indeterminate gender, but in old writers it is sometimes distinctly feminine.

b. The Adjective Interrogative Pronoun, **quī, quae, quod**, *what kind of? what? which?* is declined throughout like the Relative: —

Substantive	Adjective
quis vocat, *who calls?*	**quī homō vocat**, *what man calls?*
quid vidēs, *what do you see?*	**quod templum vidēs**, *what temple do you see?*

Note. — But **quī** is often used without any apparent adjective force; and **quis** is very common as an adjective, especially with words denoting a person: as, **quī nōminat mē?** *who calls my name?* **quis diēs fuit?** *what day was it?* **quis homō?** *what man?* but often **quī homō?** *what kind of man?* **nesciō quī sīs**, *I know not who you are.*

c. **Quisnam**, *pray, who?* is an emphatic interrogative. It has both substantive and adjective forms like **quis, quī**.

149. The Indefinite Pronouns **quis**, *any one*, and **quī**, *any*, are declined like the corresponding Interrogatives, but **qua** is commonly used for **quae** except in the nominative plural feminine:—

Substantive: **quis**, *any one*; **quid**, *anything*.
Adjective: **quī, qua (quae), quod**, *any*.

a. The feminine forms **qua** and **quae** are sometimes used substantively.

b. The indefinites **quis** and **quī** are rare except after **sī, nisi, nē,** and **num,** and in compounds (see § 310. *a, b*).

Note.—After these particles **quī** is often used as a substantive and **quis** as an adjective (cf. § 148. *b.* n.).

Case-Forms of *quī* and *quis*

150. The Relative, Interrogative, and Indefinite Pronouns are originally of the same stem, and most of the forms are the same (compare § 147 with § 148). The stem has two forms in the masculine and neuter, **quo-, qui-,** and one for the feminine, **quā-.** The interrogative sense is doubtless the original one.

a. Old forms for the genitive and dative singular are **quôius, quoi.**

b. The form **quī** is used for the ablative of both numbers and all genders; but especially as an adverb (*how, by which way, in any way*), and in the combination **quīcum**, *with whom*, as an interrogative or an indefinite relative.

c. A nominative plural **quēs** (stem **qui-**) is found in early Latin. A dative and ablative **quīs** (stem **quo-**) is not infrequent, even in classic Latin.

d. The preposition **cum** is joined enclitically to all forms of the ablative, as with the personal pronouns (§ 143. *f*): as, **quōcum, quīcum, quibuscum.**

Note.—But occasionally **cum** precedes: as, **cum quō** (Iuv. iv. 9).

Compounds of *quis* and *quī*

151. The pronouns **quis** and **quī** appear in various combinations.

a. The adverb **-cumque (-cunque)** (cf. **quisque**) added to the relative makes an indefinite relative, which is declined like the simple word: as, **quīcumque, quaecumque, quodcumque**, *whoever, whatever*; **cûiuscumque**, etc.

Note.—This suffix, with the same meaning, may be used with any relative: as, **quāliscumque**, *of whatever sort*; **quandōcumque** (also rarely **quandōque**), *whenever*; **ubicumque**, *wherever*.

b. In **quisquis**, *whoever*, both parts are declined, but the only forms in common use are **quisquis, quidquid (quicquid)** and **quōquō.**

Note 1.—Rare forms are **quemquem** and **quibusquibus**; an ablative **quīquī** is sometimes found in early Latin; the ablative feminine **quāquā** is both late and rare. **Cuicui** occurs as a genitive in the phrase **cuicui modī**, *of whatever kind*. Other cases are cited, but have no authority. In early Latin **quisquis** is occasionally feminine.

Note 2.—**Quisquis** is usually substantive, except in the ablative **quōquō**, which is more commonly an adjective.

c. The indefinite pronouns **quīdam**, *a certain* (*one*); **quīvīs, quīlibet,** *any you please*, are used both as substantives and as adjectives. The first part is declined like the relative **quī**, but the neuter has both **quid-** (substantive) and **quod-** (adjective): —

quīdam	**quaedam**	**quiddam (quoddam)**
quīvīs	**quaevīs**	**quidvīs (quodvīs)**

Quīdam changes **m** to **n** before **d** in the accusative singular (**quendam**, M.; **quandam**, F.) and the genitive plural (**quōrundam**, M., N.; **quārundam**, F.).

d. The indefinite pronouns **quispiam**, *some, any*, and **quisquam**, *any at all*, are used both as substantives and as adjectives. **Quispiam** has feminine **quaepiam** (adjective), neuter **quidpiam** (substantive) and **quodpiam** (adjective); the plural is very rare. **Quisquam** is both masculine and feminine; the neuter is **quidquam (quicquam)**, substantive only; there is no plural. **Ūllus, -a, -um,** is commonly used as the adjective corresponding to **quisquam.**

e. The indefinite pronoun **aliquis** (substantive), *some one*, **aliquī** (adjective), *some*, is declined like **quis** and **quī**, but **aliqua** is used instead of **aliquae** except in the nominative plural feminine: —

SINGULAR

	M.	F.	N.
NOM.	**aliquis (aliquī)**	**aliqua**	**aliquid (aliquod)**
GEN.	**alicûius**	**alicûius**	**alicûius**
DAT.	**alicui**	**alicui**	**alicui**
ACC.	**aliquem**	**aliquam**	**aliquid (aliquod)**
ABL.	**aliquō**	**aliquā**	**aliquō**

PLURAL

NOM.	**aliquī**	**aliquae**	**aliqua**
GEN.	**aliquōrum**	**aliquārum**	**aliquōrum**
DAT.	**aliquibus**	**aliquibus**	**aliquibus**
ACC.	**aliquōs**	**aliquās**	**aliqua**
ABL.	**aliquibus**	**aliquibus**	**aliquibus**

NOTE. — **Aliquī** is sometimes used substantively and **aliquis** as an adjective.

f. The indefinite pronoun **ecquis** (substantive), *whether any one*, **ecquī** (adjective), *whether any*, is declined like **aliquis**, but has either **ecquae** or **ecqua** in the nominative singular feminine of the adjective form.

NOTE. — **Ecquis (ecquī)** has no genitive singular, and in the plural occurs in the nominative and accusative only.

g. The enclitic particle **-que** added to the interrogative gives a *universal*: as, **quisque**, *every one*; **uterque**, *each* of two, or *both*. **Quisque** is declined like the interrogative **quis, quī**: — substantive, **quisque, quidque**; adjective, **quīque, quaeque, quodque.**

In the compound **ūnusquisque**, *every single one*, both parts are declined (genitive **unīuscûiusque**), and they are sometimes written separately and even separated by other words: —

nē in ūnō quidem **quōque** (Lael. 92), *not even in a single one.*

h. The relative and interrogative have rarely a possessive adjective **cûius** (**-a, -um**), older **quôius**, *whose;* and a patrial **cûiās** (**cûiāt-**), *of what country.*

i. **Quantus**, *how great*, **quālis**, *of what sort*, are derivative adjectives from the interrogative. They are either interrogative or relative, corresponding respectively to the demonstratives **tantus, tālis** (§ 152). Indefinite compounds are **quantuscumque** and **quāliscumque** (see § 151. *a*).

Correlatives

152. Many Pronouns, Pronominal Adjectives, and Adverbs have corresponding *demonstrative*, *relative*, *interrogative*, and *indefinite* forms. Such parallel forms are called Correlatives. They are shown in the following table: —

DEMON.	REL.	INTERROG.	INDEF. REL.	INDEF.
is	**quī**	**quis?**	**quisquis**	**aliquis**
that	*who*	*who?*	*whoever*	*some one*
tantus	**quantus**	**quantus?**	**quantuscumque**	**aliquantus**
so great	*how (as) great*	*how great?*	*however great*	*some*
tālis	**quālis**	**quālis?**	**quāliscumque**	——
such	*as*	*of what sort?*	*of whatever kind*	
ibi	**ubi**	**ubi?**	**ubiubi**	**alicubi**
there	*where*	*where?*	*wherever*	*somewhere*
eō	**quō**	**quō?**	**quōquō**	**aliquō**
thither	*whither*	*whither?*	*whithersoever*	*(to) somewhere*
eā	**quā**	**quā?**	**quāquā**	**aliquā**
that way	*which way*	*which way?*	*whithersoever*	*somewhere*
inde	**unde**	**unde?**	**undecumque**	**alicunde**
thence	*whence*	*whence?*	*whencesoever*	*from somewhere*
tum	**cum**	**quandō?**	**quandōcumque**	**aliquandō**
then	*when*	*when?*	*whenever*	*at some time*
tot	**quot**	**quot?**	**quotquot**	**aliquot**
so many	*as*	*how many?*	*however many*	*some, several*
totiēns	**quotiēns**	**quotiēns?**	**quotiēnscumque**	**aliquotiēns**
so often	*as*	*how often?*	*however often*	*at several times*

VERBS

CONJUGATION OF THE VERB

153. The inflection of the Verb is called its Conjugation.

Voice, Mood, Tense, Person, Number

154. Through its conjugation the Verb expresses Voice, Mood, Tense, Person, and Number.

a. The Voices are two: Active and Passive.

b. The Moods are four: Indicative, Subjunctive, Imperative, and Infinitive.[1]

NOTE.—The Indicative, Subjunctive, and Imperative are called *Finite Moods* in distinction from the Infinitive.

c. The Tenses are six, viz.:—

1. For continued action, Present, Imperfect, Future.
2. For completed action, Perfect, Pluperfect, Future Perfect.

The Indicative Mood has all six tenses, but the Subjunctive has no future or future perfect, and the Imperative has only the present and the future. The Infinitive has the present, perfect, and future.

d. The Persons are three: First, Second, and Third.

e. The Numbers are two: Singular and Plural.

Noun and Adjective Forms

155. The following Noun and Adjective forms are also included in the inflection of the Latin Verb:—

a. Four Participles,[2] viz.:—

Active: the Present and Future Participles.

Passive: the Perfect Participle and the Gerundive.[3]

b. The Gerund: this is in form a neuter noun of the second declension, used only in the oblique cases of the singular.

c. The Supine: this is in form a verbal noun of the fourth declension in the accusative (**-um**) and dative or ablative (-ū)[4] singular.

[1] The Infinitive is strictly the locative case of an abstract noun, expressing the action of the verb (§ 451).

[2] The Participles are adjectives in inflection and meaning, but have the power of verbs in construction and in distinguishing time.

[3] The Gerundive is also used as an adjective of *necessity*, *duty*, etc. (§ 158. *d*). In late use it became a Future Passive Participle.

[4] Originally locative.

Signification of the Forms of the Verb

Voices

156. The Active and Passive Voices in Latin generally correspond to the active and passive in English; but —

a. The passive voice often has a reflexive meaning: —

ferrō accingor, *I gird myself with my sword.*
Turnus vertitur, *Turnus turns* (himself).
induitur vestem, *he puts on his* (own) *clothes.*

NOTE. — This use corresponds very nearly to the Greek Middle voice, and is doubtless a survival of the original meaning of the passive (p. 76, footnote 2).

b. Many verbs are passive in form, but active or reflexive in meaning. These are called Deponents (§ 190):[1] as, **hortor**, *I exhort;* **sequor**, *I follow.*

c. Some verbs with active meaning have the passive form in the perfect tenses; these are called Semi-Deponents: as, **audeō, audēre, ausus sum**, *dare.*

Moods

157. The Moods are used as follows: —

a. The Indicative Mood is used for most *direct assertions* and *interrogations:* as, — **valēsne?** **valeō**, *are you well? I am well.*

b. The Subjunctive Mood has many idiomatic uses, as in *commands, conditions*, and various *dependent clauses.* It is often translated by the English Indicative; frequently by means of the auxiliaries *may, might, would, should;*[2] sometimes by the (rare) Subjunctive; sometimes by the Infinitive; and often by the Imperative, especially in *prohibitions.* A few characteristic examples of its use are the following: —

eāmus, *let us go;* **nē abeat**, *let him not depart.*
adsum ut videam, *I am here to see* (that I may see).
tū nē quaesieris, *do not thou inquire.*
beātus sīs, *may you be blessed.*
quid morer, *why should I delay?*
nesciō quid scrībam, *I know not what to write.*
sī moneam, audiat, *if I should warn, he would hear.*

[1] That is, verbs which have laid aside (*dēpōnere*) the passive meaning.

[2] The Latin uses the subjunctive in many cases where we use the indicative; and we use a colorless auxiliary in many cases where the Latin employs a separate verb with more definite meaning. Thus, *I may write* is often not **scrībam** (subjunctive), but **licet mihi scrībere**; *I can write* is **possum scrībere**; *I would write* is **scrībam, scrīberem**, or **scrībere velim (vellem)**; *I should write,* (*if*, etc.), **scrīberem (sī) . . .**, or (implying duty) **oportet mē scrībere.**

c. The Imperative is used for *exhortation, entreaty,* or *command;* but the Subjunctive is often used instead (§§ 439, 450): —

līber estō, *he shall be free.*
nē ossa legitō, *do not gather the bones.*

d. The Infinitive is used chiefly as an indeclinable noun, as the subject or complement of another verb (§§ 452, 456. N.). In special constructions it takes the place of the Indicative, and may be translated by that mood in English (see Indirect Discourse, § 580 ff.).

NOTE. — For the Syntax of the Moods, see § 436 ff.

Participles

158. The Participles are used as follows: —

a. The Present Participle (ending in **-ns**) has commonly the same meaning and use as the English participle in *-ing*; as, **vocāns**, *calling;* **legentēs**, *reading.* (For its inflection, see **egēns**, § 118.)

b. The Future Participle (ending in **-ūrus**) is oftenest used to express what is *likely* or *about* to happen: as, **rēctūrus**, *about to rule;* **audītūrus**, *about to hear.*

NOTE. — With the tenses of **esse**, *to be*, it forms the First Periphrastic Conjugation (see § 195): as, **urbs est cāsūra**, *the city is about to fall;* **mānsūrus eram**, *I was going to stay.*

c. The Perfect Participle (ending in **-tus**, **-sus**) has two uses: —

1. It is sometimes equivalent to the English perfect passive participle: as, **tēctus**, *sheltered;* **acceptus**, *accepted;* **ictus**, *having been struck;* and often has simply an adjective meaning: as, **acceptus**, *acceptable.*

2. It is used with the verb *to be* (**esse**) to form certain tenses of the passive: as, **vocātus est**, *he was (has been) called.*

NOTE. — There is no Perfect Active or Present Passive Participle in Latin. For substitutes see §§ 492, 493.

d. The Gerundive (ending in **-ndus**), has two uses: —

1. It is often used as an adjective implying obligation, necessity, or propriety (*ought* or *must*): as, **audiendus est**, *he must be heard.*

NOTE. — When thus used with the tenses of the verb *to be* (**esse**) it forms the Second Periphrastic Conjugation: **dēligendus erat**, *he ought to have been chosen* (§ 196).

2. In the oblique cases the Gerundive commonly has the same meaning as the Gerund (cf. § 159. *a*), though its construction is different. (For examples, see § 503 ff.)

Gerund and Supine

159. The Gerund and Supine are used as follows: —

a. The Gerund is a verbal noun, corresponding in meaning to the English verbal noun in *-ing* (§ 502): as, **loquendī causā**, *for the sake of speaking.*

NOTE. — The Gerund is found only in the oblique cases. A corresponding nominative is supplied by the Infinitive: thus, **scrībere est ūtile**, *writing* (to write) *is useful;* but, **ars scrībendī**, *the art of writing.*

b. The Supine is in form a noun of the fourth declension (§ 94. *b*), found only in the accusative ending in **-tum**, **-sum**, and the dative or ablative ending in **-tū**, **-sū**.

The Supine in **-um** is used after verbs and the Supine in **-ū** after adjectives (§§ 509, 510): —

vēnit **spectātum**, *he came to see;* mīrābile **dictū**, *wonderful to tell.*

Tenses of the Finite Verb

160. The Tenses of the Indicative have, in general, the same meaning as the corresponding tenses in English: —

a. Of continued action,

1. PRESENT: **scrībō**, *I write, I am writing, I do write.*
2. IMPERFECT: **scrībēbam**, *I wrote, I was writing, I did write.*
3. FUTURE: **scrībam**, *I shall write.*

b. Of completed action,

4. PERFECT: **scrīpsī**, *I have written, I wrote.*
5. PLUPERFECT: **scrīpseram**, *I had written.*
6. FUTURE PERFECT: **scrīpserō**, *I shall have written.*

161. The Perfect Indicative has two separate uses, — the Perfect Definite and the Perfect Historical (or Indefinite).

1. The Perfect Definite represents the action of the verb as completed in present time, and corresponds to the English perfect with *have:* as, **scrīpsī**, *I have written.*

2. The Perfect Historical *narrates* a simple act or state in past time without representing it as in progress or continuing. It corresponds to the English past or preterite and the Greek aorist: as, **scrīpsit**, *he wrote.*

162. The Tenses of the Subjunctive are chiefly used in dependent clauses, following the rule for the Sequence of Tenses; but have also special idiomatic uses (see Syntax).

For the use of Tenses in the Imperative, see §§ 448, 449.

PERSONAL ENDINGS

163. Verbs have regular terminations[1] for each of the three Persons, both singular and plural, active and passive.[2] These are:

	ACTIVE		PASSIVE
	SINGULAR		
1. -m (-ō):	am-ō, *I love.*	-r (-or):	amo-r, *I am loved.*
2. -s:	amā-s, *thou lovest.*	-ris (-re):	amā-ris, *thou art loved.*
3. -t:	ama-t, *he loves.*	-tur:	amā-tur, *he is loved.*
	PLURAL		
1. -mus:	amā-mus, *we love.*	-mur:	amā-mur, *we are loved.*
2. -tis:	amā-tis, *you love.*	-minī:	amā-minī, *you are loved.*
3. -nt:	ama-nt, *they love.*	-ntur:	ama-ntur, *they are loved.*

a. The Perfect Indicative active has the special terminations[3]:—

SING.	1. -ī:	amāv-ī, *I loved.*
	2. -is-tī	amāv-is-tī, *thou lovedst.*
	3. -i-t:	amāv-i-t, *he loved.*
PLUR.	1. -i-mus:	amāv-i-mus, *we loved.*
	2. -is-tis:	amāv-is-tis, *you loved.*
	3. -ērunt (-ēre):	amāv-ērunt (-ēre), *they loved.*

b. The Imperative has the following terminations:—

PRESENT ACTIVE

	Singular		*Plural*
2. —:	amā, *love thou.*	-te:	amā-te, *love ye.*

FUTURE ACTIVE

2. -tō:	amā-tō, *thou shalt love.*	-tōte:	amā-tōte, *ye shall love.*
3. -tō:	amā-tō, *he shall love.*	-ntō:	ama-ntō, *they shall love.*

[1] Most of these seem to be fragments of old pronouns, whose signification is thus added to that of the verb-stem (cf. § 36). But the ending -minī in the second person plural of the passive is perhaps a remnant of the participial form found in the Greek -μενος, and has supplanted the proper form, which does not appear in Latin. The personal ending -nt is probably connected with the participial nt- (nominative -ns).

[2] The Passive is an old Middle Voice, peculiar to the Italic and Celtic languages, and of uncertain origin.

[3] Of these terminations -ī is not a personal ending, but appears to represent an Indo-European tense-sign -ai of the Perfect Middle. In -is-tī and -is-tis, -tī and -tis are personal endings; for -is-, see § 169. *c.* N. In -i-t and -i-mus, -t and -mus are personal endings, and i is of uncertain origin. Both -ērunt and -ēre are also of doubtful origin, but the former contains the personal ending -nt.

	Singular	Present Passive	Plural
2. -re:	amā-re, *be thou loved.*	-minī:	amā-minī, *be ye loved.*
		Future Passive	
2. -tor:	amā-tor, *thou shalt be loved.*	——	——
3. -tor:	amā-tor, *he shall be loved.*	-ntor:	ama-ntor, *they shall be loved.*

Forms of the Verb

The Three Stems

164. The forms of the verb may be referred to three stems, called (1) the Present, (2) the Perfect, and (3) the Supine stem.

1. On the Present stem are formed —

The Present, Imperfect, and Future Indicative, Active and Passive.
The Present and Imperfect Subjunctive, Active and Passive.
The Imperative, Active and Passive.
The Present Infinitive, Active and Passive.
The Present Participle, the Gerundive, and the Gerund.

2. On the Perfect stem are formed —

The Perfect, Pluperfect, and Future Perfect Indicative Active.
The Perfect and Pluperfect Subjunctive Active.
The Perfect Infinitive Active.

3. On the Supine stem are formed[1] —

a. The Perfect Passive Participle, which combines with the forms of the verb **sum**, *be*, to make —

The Perfect, Pluperfect, and Future Perfect Indicative Passive.
The Perfect and Pluperfect Subjunctive Passive.
The Perfect Infinitive Passive.

b. The Future Active Participle, which combines with **esse** to make the Future Active Infinitive.

c. The Supine in **-um** and **-ū**. The Supine in **-um** combines with **īrī** to make the Future Passive Infinitive (§ 203. *a*).

Note. — The Perfect Participle with **fore** also makes a Future Passive Infinitive (as, **amātus fore**). For **fore (futūrum esse) ut** with the subjunctive, see § 569. 3. *a*.

[1] The Perfect Passive and Future Active Participles and the Supine, though strictly noun-forms, each with its own suffix, agree in having the first letter of the suffix (**t**) the same and in suffering the same phonetic change (**t** to **s**, see § 15. 5). Hence these forms, along with several sets of derivatives (in **-tor**, **-tūra**, etc., see § 238. *b*. n.[1]), were felt by the Romans as belonging to one system, and are conveniently associated with the Supine Stem. Thus, from **pingō**, we have **pictum**, **pictus**, **pictūrus**, **pictor**, **pictūra**; from **rīdeō**, **rīsum** (for †**rīd-tum**), **rīsus** (part.), **rīsus** (noun), **rīsūrus**, **rīsiō**, **rīsor**, **rīsibilis**.

VERB-ENDINGS

165. Every form of the finite verb is made up of two parts:

1. The STEM (see § 24). This is either the root or a modification or development of it.

2. The ENDING, consisting of —

   1. the Signs of Mood and Tense (see §§ 168, 169).
   2. the Personal Ending (see § 163).

Thus in the verb **vocā-bā-s**, *you were calling*, the root is **voc**, modified into the verb-stem **vocā-**, which by the addition of the ending **-bās** becomes the imperfect tense **vocābās**; and this ending consists of the tense-sign **bā-** and the personal ending (**-s**) of the second person singular.

166. The Verb-endings, as they are formed by the signs for mood and tense combined with personal endings, are —

		ACTIVE		PASSIVE	
		INDICATIVE	SUBJUNCTIVE	INDICATIVE	SUBJUNCTIVE
		PRESENT		PRESENT	
SING.	1.	-ō	-m	-or	-r
	2.	-s	-s	-ris (-re)	-ris (-re)
	3.	-t	-t	-tur	-tur
PLUR.	1.	-mus	-mus	-mur	-mur
	2.	-tis	-tis	-minī	-minī
	3.	-nt	-nt	-ntur	-ntur
		IMPERFECT		IMPERFECT	
SING.	1.	-ba-m	-re-m	-ba-r	-re-r
	2.	-bā-s	-rē-s	-bā-ris (-re)	-rē-ris (-re)
	3.	-ba-t	-re-t	-bā-tur	-rē-tur
PLUR.	1.	-bā-mus	-rē-mus	-bā-mur	-rē-mur
	2.	-bā-tis	-rē-tis	-bā-minī	-rē-minī
	3.	-ba-nt	-re-nt	-ba-ntur	-re-ntur

Present Subjunctive Active — *Vowel-Change:* I,[1] to ē; II, to eā; III, to ā; IV, to iā.
Present Subjunctive Passive — *Vowel-Change:* as in Active.

		ACTIVE INDICATIVE FUTURE		PASSIVE INDICATIVE FUTURE	
		I, II[1]	III, IV	I, II	III, IV[1]
SING.	1.	-b-ō	-*a*-m	-bo-r	-*a*-r
	2.	-bi-s	-*ē*-s	-be-ris (-re)	-*ē*-ris (-re)
	3.	-bi-t	-*e*-t	-bi-tur	-*ē*-tur
PLUR.	1.	-bi-mus	-*ē*-mus	-bi-mur	-*ē*-mur
	2.	-bi-tis	-*ē*-tis	-bi-minī	-*ē*-minī
	3.	-bu-nt	-*e*-nt	-bu-ntur	-*e*-ntur

Future III, IV Active — *Vowel-Change:* as indicated in italics; verbs in -*iō* retaining *i* before these vowels.
Future III, IV Passive — *Vowel-Change:* as in Active.

[1] These numerals refer to the four conjugations given later (see § 171).

	Active			*Passive*	
	INDICATIVE	SUBJUNCTIVE		INDICATIVE	SUBJUNCTIVE
	PERFECT			PERFECT	
SING. 1.	-ī	-eri-m	-tus (-ta, -tum)	sum	sim
2.	-is-tī	-eri-s		es	sīs
3.	-i-t	-eri-t		est	sit
PLUR. 1.	-i-mus	-eri-mus	-tī (-tae, -ta)	sumus	sīmus
2.	-is-tis	-eri-tis		estis	sītis
3.	-ēru-nt (-ēre)	-eri-nt		sunt	sint
	PLUPERFECT			PLUPERFECT	
SING. 1.	-era-m	-isse-m	-tus(-ta, -tum)	eram	essem
2.	-erā-s	-issē-s		erās	essēs
3.	-era-t	-isse-t		erat	esset
PLUR. 1.	-erā-mus	-issē-mus	-tī (-tae, -ta)	erāmus	essēmus
2.	-erā-tis	-issē-tis		erātis	essētis
3.	-era-nt	-isse-nt		erant	essent
	FUTURE PERFECT			FUTURE PERFECT	
SING. 1.	-er-ō		-tus (-ta, -tum)	erō	
2.	-eri-s			eris	
3.	-eri-t			erit	
PLUR. 1.	-eri-mus		-tī (-tae, -ta)	erimus	
2.	-eri-tis			eritis	
3.	-eri-nt			erunt	

IMPERATIVE

Active		Passive	
PRESENT		PRESENT	
SING. 2. ——	PLUR. 2. -te	SING. 2. -re	PLUR. 2. -minī
FUTURE		FUTURE	
2. -tō	2. -tōte	2. -tor	
3. -tō	3. -ntō	3. -tor	3. -ntor

For convenience a table of the Noun and Adjective forms of the verb is here added.

INFINITIVE

	Active	Passive
PRES.	-re (Pres. stem)	I, II, IV. -rī ; III. -ī
PERF.	-isse (Perf. stem)	-tus (-ta, -tum) esse
FUT.	-tūrus (-a, -um) esse	-tum īrī

PARTICIPLES

PRES.	-ns, -ntis	PERF.	-tus, -ta, -tum
FUT.	-tūrus, -a, -um	GER.	-ndus, -nda, -ndum

GERUND	SUPINE
-ndī, -ndō, -ndum, -ndō	-tum, -tū

167. A long vowel is shortened before the personal endings **-m** (-r), **-t**, **-nt** (-ntur): as, **ame-t** (for older **amē-t**), **habe-t** (for **habē-t**), **mone-nt, mone-ntur.**

168. The tenses of the Present System are made from the Present Stem as follows: —[1]

a. In the Present Indicative the personal endings are added directly to the present stem. Thus, — present stem **arā-**: **arā-s, arā-mus, arā-tis.**

b. In the Imperfect Indicative the suffix **-bam, -bās**, etc. (originally a complete verb) is added to the present stem: as, **arā-bam, arā-bās, arā-bāmus.**

NOTE. — The form †**bam** was apparently an aorist of the Indo-European root BHU (cf. **fuī, futūrus**, *φύω*, English *be, been*), and meant *I was.* This was added to a complete word, originally a case of a verbal noun, as in *I was a-seeing;* hence **vidē-bam.** The form probably began in the Second or Third Conjugation and was extended to the others. The **a** was at first long, but was shortened in certain forms (§ 167).

c. In the Future Indicative of the First and Second Conjugations a similar suffix, **-bō, -bis**, etc., is added to the present stem: as, **arā-bō, arā-bis, monē-bō.**

NOTE. — The form †**bō** was probably a present tense of the root BHU, with a future meaning, and was affixed to a noun-form as described in *b.* N.

d. In the Future Indicative of the Third and Fourth Conjugations the terminations **-am, -ēs**, etc. (as, **teg-am, teg-ēs, audi-am, audi-ēs**) are really subjunctive endings used in a future sense (see *e*). The vowel was originally long throughout. For shortening, see § 167.

e. In the Present Subjunctive the personal endings were added to a form of the present stem ending in **ē-** or **ā-**, which was shortened in certain forms (§ 167). Thus, **ame-m, amē-s, tegā-mus, tega-nt.**

NOTE 1. — The vowel **ē** (seen in the First Conjugation: as, **am-ē-s**) is an inherited subjunctive mood-sign. It appears to be the thematic vowel **e** (§ 174. 1) lengthened. The **ā** of the other conjugations (**mone-ā-s, reg-ā-s, audi-ā-s**) is of uncertain origin.

NOTE 2. — In a few irregular verbs a Present Subjunctive in **-im, -īs**, etc. occurs: as, **sim, sīs, sīmus, velim, velīs**, etc. This is an old optative, **ī** being a form of the Indo-European optative mood-sign **yē-** (cf. **siem, siēs, siet**, § 170. *b.* N.). The vowel has been shortened in the first and third persons singular and the third person plural.

f. In the Imperfect Subjunctive the suffix **-rem, -rēs**, etc. is added to the present stem: as, **amā-rem, amā-rēs, monē-rem, tege-rem, audī-rem.**

NOTE. — The stem element **-rē-** is of uncertain origin and is not found outside of Italic. The **r** is doubtless the aorist sign **s** (cf. **es-se-m, es-sē-s**) changed to **r** between two vowels (§ 15. 4). The **ē** is probably the subjunctive mood-sign (see *e*).

[1] The conjugation of a verb consists of separate formations from a root, gradually grouped together, systematized, and supplemented by new formations made on old lines to supply deficiencies. Some of the forms were inherited from the parent speech; others were developed in the course of the history of the Italic dialects or of the Latin language itself.

169. The tenses of the Perfect System in the active voice are made from the Perfect Stem as follows: —

a. In the Perfect Indicative the endings **-ī**, **-istī**, etc. are added directly to the perfect stem: as, **amāv-istī**, **tēx-istis**.

b. In the Pluperfect Indicative the suffix **-eram**, **-erās**, etc. is added to the perfect stem: as, **amāv-eram**, **monu-erās**, **tēx-erat**.

NOTE. — This seems to represent an older †-is-ām etc. formed on the analogy of the Future Perfect in -erō (older †-is-ō: see *c* below) and influenced by eram (imperfect of sum) in comparison with erō (future of sum).

c. In the Future Perfect the suffix **-erō**, **-eris**, etc. is added to the perfect stem: as, **amāv-erō**, **monu-eris**, **tēx-erit**.

NOTE. — This formation was originally a subjunctive of the s-aorist, ending probably in †-is-ō. The -is- is doubtless the same as that seen in the second person singular of the perfect indicative (vīd-is-tī), in the perfect infinitive (vīd-is-se), and in the pluperfect subjunctive (vīd-is-sem), s being the aorist sign and i probably an old stem vowel.

d. In the Perfect Subjunctive the suffix **-erim**, **-eris**, etc. is added to the perfect stem: as, **amāv-erim**, **monu-eris**, **tēx-erit**.

NOTE. — This formation was originally an optative of the s-aorist (-er- for older -is-, as in the future perfect, see *c* above). The i after r is the optative mood-sign ī shortened (see § 168. *e*. N. 2). Forms in -īs, -īt, -īmus, -ītis, are sometimes found. The shortening in -ĭs, -ĭmus, -ĭtis, is due to confusion with the future perfect.

e. In the Pluperfect Subjunctive the suffix **-issem**, **-issēs**, etc. is added to the perfect stem: as, **amāv-issem**, **monu-issēs**, **tēx-isset**.

NOTE. — Apparently this tense was formed on the analogy of the pluperfect indicative in †-is-ām (later -er-am, see *b*), and influenced by essem (earlier †essēm) in its relation to eram (earlier †esām).[1]

The Verb *Sum*

170. The verb **sum**, *be*, is both irregular and defective, having no gerund or supine, and no participle but the future.

Its conjugation is given at the outset, on account of its importance for the inflection of other verbs.

[1] The signs of mood and tense are often said to be inserted between the root (or verb-stem) and the personal ending. No such insertion is possible in a language developed like the Latin. All true verb-forms are the result, as shown above, of *composition;* that is, of adding to the root or the stem either personal endings or fully developed auxiliaries (themselves containing the personal terminations), or of imitation of such processes. Thus **vidēbāmus** is made by adding to **vidē-**, originally a significant word or a form conceived as such, a full verbal form †**bāmus**, not by inserting **-bā-** between **vidē-** and **-mus** (§ 168. *b*).

PRINCIPAL PARTS: Present Indicative **sum**, Present Infinitive **esse**, Perfect Indicative **fuī**, Future Participle **futūrus**.

PRESENT STEM **es-** PERFECT STEM **fu-** SUPINE STEM **fut-**

		INDICATIVE	SUBJUNCTIVE
		PRESENT	
SING.	1.	**sum**, *I am*	**sim**[1]
	2.	**ĕs**, *thou art (you are)*	**sīs**
	3.	**est**, *he (she, it) is*	**sit**
PLUR.	1.	**sumus**, *we are*	**sīmus**
	2.	**estis**, *you are*	**sītis**
	3.	**sunt**, *they are*	**sint**
		IMPERFECT	
SING.	1.	**eram**, *I was*	**essem**
	2.	**erās**, *you were*	**essēs**
	3.	**erat**, *he (she, it) was*	**esset**
PLUR.	1.	**erāmus**, *we were*	**essēmus**
	2.	**erātis**, *you were*	**essētis**
	3.	**erant**, *they were*	**essent**
		FUTURE	
SING.	1.	**erō**, *I shall be*	
	2.	**eris**, *you will be*	
	3.	**erit**, *he will be*	
PLUR.	1.	**erimus**, *we shall be*	
	2.	**eritis**, *you will be*	
	3.	**erunt**, *they will be*	
		PERFECT	
SING.	1.	**fuī**, *I was (have been)*	**fuerim**
	2.	**fuistī**, *you were*	**fueris**
	3.	**fuit**, *he was*	**fuerit**
PLUR.	1.	**fuimus**, *we were*	**fuerimus**
	2.	**fuistis**, *you were*	**fueritis**
	3.	**fuērunt**, **fuēre**, *they were*	**fuerint**
		PLUPERFECT	
SING.	1.	**fueram**, *I had been*	**fuissem**
	2.	**fuerās**, *you had been*	**fuissēs**
	3.	**fuerat**, *he had been*	**fuisset**

[1] All translations of the Subjunctive are misleading, and hence none is given; see § 157. *b*.

PLUR.	1. **fuerāmus**, *we had been*	**fuissēmus**
	2. **fuerātis**, *you had been*	**fuissētis**
	3. **fuerant**, *they had been*	**fuissent**

FUTURE PERFECT

SING.	1. **fuerō**, *I shall have been*	PLUR.	1. **fuerimus**, *we shall have been*
	2. **fueris**, *you will have been*		2. **fueritis**, *you will have been*
	3. **fuerit**, *he will have been*		3. **fuerint**, *they will have been*

IMPERATIVE

PRESENT	SING.	2. **ĕs**, *be thou*	PLUR.	2. **este**, *be ye*
FUTURE		2. **estō**, *thou shalt be*		2. **estōte**, *ye shall be*
		3. **estō**, *he shall be*		3. **suntō**, *they shall be*

INFINITIVE

PRESENT	**esse**, *to be*
PERFECT	**fuisse**, *to have been*
FUTURE	**futūrus esse** or **fore**, *to be about to be*

PARTICIPLE

FUTURE	**futūrus, -a, -um**, *about to be*

a. For **essem, essēs**, etc., **forem, forēs, foret, forent**, are often used; so **fore** for **futūrus esse**.

b. The Present Participle, which would regularly be †**sōns**,[1] appears in the adjective **īn-sōns**, *innocent*, and in a modified form in **ab-sēns, prae-sēns**. The simple form **ēns** is sometimes found in late or philosophical Latin as a participle or abstract noun, in the forms **ēns**, *being;* **entia**, *things which are*.

NOTE.—Old forms are:—Indicative: Future, **escit, escunt** (strictly an inchoative present, see § 263. 1).

Subjunctive: Present, **siem, siēs, siet, sient; fuam, fuās, fuat, fuant**; Perfect, **fūvimus**; Pluperfect, **fūvisset**.

The root of the verb **sum** is ES, which in the imperfect is changed to ER (see § 15. 4), and in many forms is shortened to S. Some of its modifications, as found in several languages more or less closely related to Latin, may be seen in the following table,—the Sanskrit *syām* corresponding to the Latin **sim (siem)**:—

SANSKRIT		GREEK	LATIN		LITHUANIAN
as-mi	*syām* (optative)	ἔμμι[2]	s-um	*sim (siem)*	es-mi
as-i	*syās*	ἐσσί[2]	es	*sīs (siēs)*	es-i
as-ti	*syāt*	ἐστί	es-t	*sit (siet)*	es-ti
s-mas	*syāma*	ἐσμέν	s-umus	*sīmus*	es-me
s-tha	*syāta*	ἐστέ	es-tis	*sītis*	es-te
s-anti	*syus*	ἐντί[2]	s-unt	*sint (sient)*	es-ti

The Perfect and Supine stems, **fu-, fut-**, are kindred with the Greek ἔφυ, and with the English *be*.

[1] Compare Sankrit *sant*, Greek ὤν. [2] Old form.

The Four Conjugations

171. Verbs are classed in Four Regular Conjugations, distinguished by the stem-vowel which appears before **-re** in the Present Infinitive Active: —

Conjugation	Infinitive Ending	Stem
First	**-āre** (**amāre**)	**ā**
Second	**-ēre** (**monēre**)	**ē**
Third	**-ĕre** (**regĕre**)	**ĕ**
Fourth	**-īre** (**audīre**)	**ī**

The Principal Parts

172. The Principal Parts of a verb, showing the three stems which determine its conjugation throughout, are —

1. The Present Indicative (as, **amō**) } showing the Present Stem.
2. The Present Infinitive (as, **amā-re**) } showing the Present Stem.
3. The Perfect Indicative (as, **amāv-ī**), showing the Perfect Stem.
4. The neuter of the Perfect Participle (as, **amāt-um**), or, if that form is not in use, the Future Active Participle (**amāt-ūrus**), showing the Supine Stem.

173. The regular forms of the Four Conjugations are seen in the following: —

First Conjugation : —

Active, **amō, amāre, amāvī, amātum,** *love.*
Passive, **amor, amārī, amātus.**
Present Stem **amā-**, Perfect Stem **amāv-**, Supine Stem **amāt-**.

Second Conjugation: —

Active, **dēleō, dēlēre, dēlēvī, dēlētum,** *blot out.*
Passive, **dēleor, dēlērī, dēlētus.**
Present Stem **dēlē-**, Perfect Stem **dēlēv-**, Supine Stem **dēlēt-**.

In the Second conjugation, however, the characteristic **ē-** rarely appears in the perfect and perfect participle. The common type is, therefore: —

Active, **moneō, monēre, monuī, monitum,** *warn.*
Passive, **moneor, monērī, monitus.**
Present Stem **monē-**, Perfect Stem **monu-**, Supine Stem **monit-**.

Third Conjugation: —

Active, **tegō, tegĕre, tēxī, tēctum**, *cover*.
Passive, **tegor, tegī, tēctus.**
Present Stem **tegĕ-**, Perfect Stem **tēx-**, Supine Stem **tēct-**.

Fourth Conjugation: —

Active, **audiō, audīre, audīvī, audītum**, *hear*.
Passive, **audior, audīrī, audītus.**
Present Stem **audī-**, Perfect Stem **audīv-**, Supine Stem **audīt-**.

a. In many verbs the principal parts take forms belonging to two or more different conjugations (cf. § 189): —

1, 2, **domō, domāre, domuī, domitum**, *subdue*.
2, 3, **maneō, manēre, mānsī, mānsum**, *remain*.
3, 4, **petō, petĕre, petīvī, petītum**, *seek*.
4, 3, **vinciō, vincīre, vīnxī, vīnctum**, *bind*.

Such verbs are referred to the conjugation to which the Present stem conforms.

Present Stem

174. The parent (Indo-European) speech from which Latin comes had two main classes of verbs: —

1. Thematic Verbs, in which a so-called *thematic vowel* ($^{e}/_{o}$, in Latin $^{i}/_{u}$) appeared between the root and the personal ending: as, **leg-i-tis** (for †**leg-e-tes**), **leg-u-nt** (for †**leg-o-nti**).[1]

2. Athematic Verbs, in which the personal endings were added directly to the root: as, **es-t, es-tis** (root ES)[2], **dă-mus** (**dō**, root DA), **fer-t** (**ferō**, root FER).

Of the Athematic Verbs few survive in Latin, and these are counted as irregular, except such as have been forced into one of the four "regular" conjugations. Even the irregular verbs have admitted many forms of the thematic type.

Of the Thematic Verbs a large number remain. These may be divided into two classes: —

1. Verbs which preserve the thematic vowel **e** or **o** (in Latin **i** or **u**) before the personal endings. — These make up the Third Conjugation. The present stem is formed in various ways (§ 176), but always ends in a short vowel $^{e}/_{o}$ (Latin $^{i}/_{u}$). Examples are **tegō** (stem **teg**$^{e}/_{o}$-), **sternimus** (stem **stern**$^{e}/_{o}$-) for †**ster-no-mos**, **plectunt** (stem **plect**$^{e}/_{o}$-) for †**plec-to-nti**. So **nōscō** (stem **gnōsc**$^{e}/_{o}$-) for **gnō-sc-ō**. Verbs like **nōscō** became the type for a large number of verbs in **-scō**, called *inceptives* (§ 263. 1).

2. Verbs which form the present stem by means of the suffix **y**$^{e}/_{o}$-, which already contained the thematic vowel $^{e}/_{o}$. — Verbs of this class in which any vowel (except **u**) came in contact with the suffix **y**$^{e}/_{o}$- suffered contraction so as to present a long vowel **ā-, ē-, ī-**, at the end of the stem. In this contraction the thematic $^{e}/_{o}$ disappeared. These became the types of the First, Second, and Fourth conjugations respectively. In imitation of these long vowel-stems numerous verbs were formed by the Romans themselves (after the mode of formation had been entirely forgotten) from noun- and

[1] Cf. λέγ-ε-τε, λέγ-ο-μεν; Doric λέγ-ο-ντι.
[2] Cf. ἐσ-τί, ἐσ-τέ (see p. 83, note).

adjective-stems. This came to be the regular way of forming new verbs, just as in English the borrowed suffix *-ize* can be added to nouns and adjectives to make verbs: as, *macadamize*, *modernize*.

Thematic verbs of the second class in which a consonant or u came into contact with the suffix y^e/$_o$- suffered various phonetic changes. Such verbs fall partly into the Third Conjugation, giving rise to an irregular form of it, and partly into the Fourth, and some have forms of both. Examples are: — (cōn)spiciō (-spicĕre) for †spekyō; veniō (venīre) for †(g)vem-yō; cupiō, cupĕre, but cupīvī; orior, orĭtur, but orīrī. Note, however, pluō (pluere) for †plu-yō; and hence, by analogy, acuō (acuere) for †acu-yō.

In all these cases many cross-analogies and errors as well as phonetic changes have been at work to produce irregularities. Hence has arisen the traditional system which is practically represented in §§ 175, 176.

175. The Present Stem may be found by dropping **-re** in the Present Infinitive: —

> **amā-re**, stem **amā-**; **monē-re**, stem **monē-**; **tegĕ-re**, stem **tegĕ-**; **audī-re**, stem **audī-**.

176. The Present Stem is formed from the Root in all regular verbs in one of the following ways: —

a. In the First, Second, and Fourth conjugations, by adding a *long vowel* (ā-, ē-, ī-) to the root, whose vowel is sometimes changed: as, **vocā-re** (VOC), **monē-re** (MEN, cf. **meminī**), **sopī-re** (SOP).[1]

NOTE. — Verb-stems of these conjugations are almost all really formed from noun-stems on the pattern of older formations (see § 174).

b. In the Third Conjugation, by adding a *short vowel* $^e/_o$[2] to the root. In Latin this $^e/_o$ usually appears as $^i/_u$, but e is preserved in some forms. Thus, **tegi-s** (root TEG), **ali-tis** (AL), **regu-nt** (REG); but **tegĕ-ris** (**tegĕ-re**), **alĕ-ris**.

1. The stem-vowel $^e/_o$ ($^i/_u$) may be preceded by **n**, **t**, or **sc**:[3] as, **tem-ni-tis**, **tem-nu-nt**, **tem-nĕ-ris** (TEM); **plec-ti-s** (PLEC); **crē-sci-tis** (CRĒ).

2. Verbs in **-iō** of the Third Conjugation (as, **capiō**, **capĕre**) show in some forms an **i** before the final vowel of the stem: as, **cap-i-unt** (CAP), **fug-i-unt** (FUG).

c. The root may be changed —

1. By the repetition of a part of it (*reduplication*): as, **gi-gn-e-re** (GEN).
2. By the insertion of a nasal (**m** or **n**): as, **find-e-re** (FID), **tang-e-re** (TAG).

[1] Most verbs of the First, Second, and Fourth Conjugations form the present stem by adding the suffix -y^e/$_o$- to a noun-stem. The ā of the First Conjugation is the stem-ending of the noun (as, **plantā-re**, from **plantā-**, stem of **planta**). The ē of the Second and the ī of the Fourth Conjugation are due to contraction of the short vowel of the noun-stem with the ending -y^e/$_o$-. Thus **albēre** is from **alb**^{o}/$_e$-, stem of **albus**; **fīnīre** is from **fīni-**, stem of **fīnis**. Some verbs of these classes, however, come from roots ending in a vowel.

[2] This is the so-called "thematic vowel."

[3] In these verbs the stem-ending added to the root is respectively **-n**^{e}/$_o$-, **-t**^{e}/$_o$-, **sc**^{e}/$_o$-.

d. In some verbs the present stem is formed from a noun-stem in **u-**: as, **statu-e-re** (statu-s), **aestu-ā-re** (aestu-s); cf. **acuō, acuere.**[1]

NOTE 1.—A few isolated forms use the simple root as a present stem: as, **fer-re, fer-t; es-se; vel-le, vul-t.** These are counted as irregular.

NOTE 2.—In some verbs the final consonant of the root is doubled before the stem-vowel: as, **pell-i-tis** (PEL), **mitt-i-tis** (MIT).

e. Some verbs have roots ending in a vowel. In these the present stem is generally identical with the root: as, **da-mus** (DA), **flē-mus** (stem **flē-**, root form unknown).[2] But others, as **rui-mus** (RU), are formed with an additional vowel according to the analogy of the verbs described in *d.*

NOTE.—Some verbs of this class reduplicate the root: as, **si-st-e-re** (STA, cf. **stāre**).

Perfect Stem

177. The Perfect Stem is formed as follows:—

a. The suffix **v** (**u**) is added to the verb-stem: as, **vocā-v-ī, audī-v-ī**; or to the root: as, **son-u-ī** (**sonā-re**, root SON), **mon-u-ī** (**monē-re**, MON treated as a root).[3]

NOTE.—In a few verbs the vowel of the root is transposed and lengthened: as, **strā-v-ī** (**sternō**, STAR), **sprē-v-ī** (**spernō**, SPAR).

b. The suffix **s** is added to the root: as, **carp-s-ī** (CARP), **tēx-ī** (for **tēg-s-ī**, TEG).[4]

NOTE.—The modifications of the present stem sometimes appear in the perfect: as, **finx-ī** (FIG, present stem **fingĕ-**), **sānx-ī** (SAC, present stem **sancī-**).

c. The root is *reduplicated* by prefixing the first consonant—generally with **ĕ**, sometimes with the root-vowel: as, **ce-cid-ī** (**cadō**, CAD), **to-tond-ī** (**tondeō**, TOND).

NOTE.—In **fid-ī** (for †**fe-fid-ī, find-ō**), **scid-ī** (for †**sci-scid-ī, scindō**), the reduplication has been lost, leaving merely the root.

d. The root vowel is lengthened, sometimes with vowel change: as, **lēg-ī** (**lĕg-ō**), **ēm-ī** (**ĕm-ō**), **vīd-ī** (**vĭd-e-ō**), **fūg-ī** (**fŭg-i-ō**), **ēg-ī** (**ăg-ō**).

e. Sometimes the perfect stem has the same formation that appears in the present tense: as, **vert-ī** (**vert-ō**), **solv-ī** (**solv-ō**).

f. Sometimes the perfect is formed from a lost or imaginary stem: as, **petī-v-ī** (as if from †**peti-ō**, †**petī-re**, PET).

1 These are either old formations in **-y^e/$_o$-** in which the **y** has disappeared after the **u** (as, **statuō** for †**statu-yō**) or later imitations of such forms.

2 In some of the verbs of this class the present stem was originally identical with the root; in others the ending **-y^e/$_o$-** was added, but has been absorbed by contraction.

3 The **v**-perfect is a form of uncertain origin peculiar to the Latin.

4 The **s**-perfect is in origin an aorist. Thus, **dīx-ī** (for †**dīcs-ī**) corresponds to the Greek aorist ἔ-δειξ-α (for †ἔ-δεικσ-α).

Supine Stem

178. The Supine Stem may be found by dropping **-um** from the Supine. It is formed by adding **t** (or, by a phonetic change, **s**)—

a. To the present stem: as, **amā-t-um, dēlē-t-um, audī-t-um.**

b. To the root, with or without **ĭ**: as, **cap-t-um** (**capiō**, CAP), **moni-t-um** (**moneō**, MON used as root), **cās-um** (for **†cad-t-um**, CAD), **lēc-t-um** (LEG).

NOTE 1.—By phonetic change **dt** and **tt** become **s** (**dēfēnsum, versum** for **†dē-fend-t-um, †vert-t-um**); **bt** becomes **pt** (**scrīp-t-um** for **†scrīb-t-um**); **gt** becomes **ct** (**rēc-t-um** for **†reg-t-um**).[1]

NOTE 2.—The modifications of the present stem sometimes appear in the supine: as, **tīnc-t-um** (**tingō**, TIG), **tēn-s-um** for **†tend-t-um** (**ten-d-ō**, TEN).

NOTE 3.—The supine is sometimes from a lost or imaginary verb-stem: as, **petī-t-um** (as if from **†peti-ō, †petī-re**, PET).

NOTE 4.—A few verbs form the supine stem in **s** after the analogy of verbs in **d** and **t**: as, **fal-s-um** (**fallō**), **pul-s-um** (**pellō**).

Forms of Conjugation

179. The forms of the several conjugations from which, by adding the verb-endings in § 166, all the moods and tenses can be made are as follows:—

a. The First Conjugation includes all verbs which add **ā-** to the root to form the present stem:[2] as, **amā-re**; with a few whose root ends in **a** (**†for, fā-rī; flō, flā-re; nō, nā-re; stō, stā-re**).

1. The stem-vowel **ā-** is lost before **-ō**: as, **amō** = **†amā-(y)ō**; and in the present subjunctive it is changed to **ē**: as, **amē-s, amē-mus.**

2. The perfect stem regularly adds **v**, the supine stem **t**, to the present stem: as, **amā-v-ī, amā-t-um.** For exceptions, see § 209. *a.*

b. The Second Conjugation includes all verbs which add **ē-** to the root to form the present stem: as, **monē-re**; with a few whose root ends in **ē**; as, **fle-ō, flē-re; ne-ō, nē-re; re-or, rē-rī** (cf. § 176. *e*).

1. In the present subjunctive **ā** is added to the verb-stem: as, **mone-ā-s, mone-ā-mus** (cf. § 168. *e*).

2. A few verbs form the perfect stem by adding **v** (**u**), and the supine stem by adding **t**, to the present stem: as, **dēlē-v-ī, dēlē-t-um.** But most form the perfect stem by adding **v** (**u**) to the root, and the supine stem by adding **t** to a weaker form of the present stem, ending in **ĭ**: as, **mon-u-ī, monĭ-t-um.** For lists, see § 210.

[1] For these modifications of the supine stem, see § 15. 5, 6, 10.

[2] The present stem is thus the verb-stem. For exceptions, see § 209. *a.*

c. The Third Conjugation includes all verbs (not irregular, see § 197) which add **ĕ-** to the root to form the present stem: as, **tegĕ-re, capĕ-re**; with a few whose root ends in **e**: as, **se-rĕ-re** for †**se-se-re** (reduplicated from SE, cf. **sătum**).

1. The stem-vowel **ĕ** is regularly lost before **-ō**, and becomes **u**[1] before **-nt** and **ĭ** before the other endings of the indicative and imperative: as, **teg-ō, tegi-t, tegu-nt**; in the imperfect indicative it becomes **ē**: as, **tegē-bam, tegē-bās**, etc.; in the future, **ē**: as, **tegē-s** (except in the first person singular, **tega-m, tega-r**); in the present subjunctive, **ā**: as, **tegā-s.**

Verbs in **-iō** lose the **i** before a consonant and also before **ĭ, ī**, and **ĕ** (except in the future, the participle, the gerund, and the gerundive). Thus,—**capi-at, capi-unt, capi-ēbat, capi-ēs, capi-et, capi-ent**; but, **cap-it** (not †**capi-it**), **cap-eret.**

2. All varieties of perfect and supine stems are found in this conjugation. See lists, § 211. The perfect is not formed from the present stem, but from the root.

d. The Fourth Conjugation includes all verbs which add **ī-** to the root to form the present stem: as, **audī-re.**[2] In these the perfect and supine stems regularly add **v, t**, to the verb-stem: as, **audī-v-ī, audī-t-um.**[3] Endings like those of the third conjugation are added in the third person plural of the present (indicative and imperative), in the imperfect and future indicative, and in the present subjunctive: as, **audi-unt, audi-ēbat, audi-ētis, audi-at**, the **i** being regularly short before a vowel.

e. The Present Imperative Active (second person singular) is the same as the present stem: as, **amā, monē, tegĕ, audī.** But verbs in **-iō** of the third conjugation omit **i**: as, **capĕ** (not †**capie**).

f. The tenses of *completed action* in the Active voice are all regularly formed by adding the tense-endings (given in § 166) to the perfect stem: as, **amāv-ī, amāv-eram, amāv-erō, amāv-erim, amāv-issem, amāv-isse.**

g. The tenses of *completed action* in the Passive voice are formed by adding to the perfect participle the corresponding tenses of *continued action* of the verb **esse**: as, perfect **amātus sum**; pluperfect **amātus eram**, etc.

[1] The gerundive varies between **-endus** and **-undus.**

[2] A few are formed from noun-stems, as **fīnī-re** (from **fīni-s**), and a few roots perhaps end in **i**; but these are not distinguishable in form.

[3] For exceptions, see § 212. *b.*

Synopsis of the Verb

180. The following synopsis shows the forms of the verb arranged according to the three stems (§ 164). **Amō**, a regular verb of the first conjugation, is taken as a type.

PRINCIPAL PARTS: *Active*, **amō, amāre, amāvī, amātum.**
Passive, **amor, amārī, amātus sum.**

PRESENT STEM **amā-** PERFECT STEM **amāv-** SUPINE STEM **amāt-**

	ACTIVE		PASSIVE
		Present stem, amā-	
		INDICATIVE	
PRES.	amō		amo-**r**
IMPERF.	amā-**bam**		amā-**bar**
FUT.	amā-**bō**		amā-**bor**
		SUBJUNCTIVE	
PRES.	ame-**m**		ame-**r**
IMPERF.	amā-**rem**		amā-**rer**
		IMPERATIVE	
PRES.	amā		amā-**re**
FUT.	amā-**tō**		amā-**tor**
		INFINITIVE	
PRES.	amā-**re**		amā-**rī**
		PARTICIPLE	
PRES.	amā-**ns**		GERUNDIVE ama-**ndus**
GERUND	ama-**ndī**		
	Perfect stem, amāv-		**Supine stem, amāt-**
		INDICATIVE	
PERF.	amāv-**ī**		amāt-**us sum**
PLUPERF.	amāv-**eram**		amāt-**us eram**
FUT. PERF.	amāv-**erō**		amāt-**us erō**
		SUBJUNCTIVE	
PERF.	amāv-**erim**		amāt-**us sim**
PLUPERF.	amāv-**issem**		amāt-**us essem**
		INFINITIVE	
PERF.	amāv-**isse**		
		Supine stem, amāt-	
		INFINITIVE	
PERF.			amāt-**us esse**
FUT.	amāt-**ūrus esse**		amāt-**um īrī**
		PARTICIPLE	
FUT.	amāt-**ūrus**		PERF. amāt-**us**
SUPINE	amāt-**um** amāt-**ū**		

Peculiarities of Conjugation

181. In tenses formed upon the Perfect Stem, **v** between two vowels is often lost and contraction takes place.

a. Perfects in **-āvī**, **-ēvī**, **-ōvī**, often contract the two vowels into **ā**, **ē**, **ō**, respectively: as, **amāsse** for **amāvisse**; **amārim** for **amāverim**; **amāssem** for **amāvissem**; **cōnsuērat** for **cōnsuēverat**; **flēstis** for **flēvistis**; **nōsse** for **nōvisse**. So in perfects in **-vī**, where the **v** is a part of the present stem: as, **commōrat** for **commōverat**.

NOTE.—The first person of the perfect indicative (as, **amāvī**) is never contracted, the third very rarely.

b. Perfects in **-īvī** regularly omit **v**, but rarely contract the vowels except before **st** and **ss**, and very rarely in the third person perfect:—

> **audieram** for **audīveram**; **audīsse** for **audīvisse**; **audīstī** for **audīvistī**; **abiit** for **abīvit**; **abiērunt** for **abīvērunt**.

NOTE 1.—The forms **sīris**, **sīrit**, **sīrītis**, **sīrint**, for **sīveris** etc. (from **sīverō** or **sīverim**), are archaic.

NOTE 2.—In many forms from the perfect stem **is**, **iss**, **sis**, are lost in like manner, when **s** would be repeated if they were retained: as, **dīxtī** for **dīxistī** (**x** = **cs**); **trāxe** for **trāxisse**; **ēvāstī** for **ēvāsistī**; **vīxet** for **vīxisset**; **ērēpsēmus** for **ērēpsissēmus**; **dēcēsse** for **dēcessisse**. These forms belong to archaic and colloquial usage.

182. Four verbs,—**dīcō**, **dūcō**, **faciō**, **ferō**,—with their compounds, drop the vowel-termination of the Imperative, making **dīc**, **dūc**, **făc**, **fĕr**; but compounds in **-ficiō** retain it, as, **cōnfice**.

NOTE.—The imperative forms **dīce**, **dūce**, **face** (never **fere**), occur in early Latin.

a. For the imperative of **sciō**, the future form **scītō** is always used in the singular, and **scītōte** usually in the plural.

183. The following ancient forms are found chiefly in poetry:

1. In the fourth conjugation, **-ībam**, **-ībō**, for **-iēbam**, **-iam** (future). These forms are regular in **eō**, *go* (§ 203).

2. In the present subjunctive, **-im**: as in **duim**, **perduim**, retained in religious formulas and often in comedy. This form is regular in **sum** and **volō** and their compounds (§§ 170, 199).

3. In the perfect subjunctive and future perfect indicative, **-sim**, **-sō**: as, **faxim**, **faxō**, **iussō**, **recēpsō** (= **fēcerim** etc.); **ausim** (= **ausus sim**).

4. In the passive infinitive, **-ier**: as, **vocārier** for **vocārī**; **agier** for **agī**.

5. A form in **-āssō**, **-āssere** is found used as a future perfect: as, **amāssis**, from **amō**; **levāssō**, from **levō**; **impetrāssere**, from **impetrō**; **iūdicāssit**, from **iūdicō** (cf. § 263. 2. *b*. N.).

FIRST CONJUGATION (*ā*-STEMS) — ACTIVE VOICE

184. The First Conjugation includes all verbs which add **ā-** to the root to form the present stem, with a few whose root ends in **a-**. The verb **amō**, *love*, is conjugated as follows: —

Principal Parts: Present Indicative **amō**, Present Infinitive **amāre**, Perfect Indicative **amāvī**, Supine **amātum**.

Present stem **amā-** Perfect stem **amāv-** Supine stem **amāt-**

INDICATIVE	SUBJUNCTIVE
Present	
amō,[1] *I love, am loving, do love*	**amem**[2]
amās, *thou lovest* (*you love*)	**amēs**
amat, *he* (*she, it*) *loves*	**amet**
amāmus, *we love*	**amēmus**
amātis, *you love*	**amētis**
amant, *they love*	**ament**
Imperfect	
amābam, *I loved, was loving, did love*	**amārem**
amābās, *you loved*	**amārēs**
amābat, *he loved*	**amāret**
amābāmus, *we loved*	**amārēmus**
amābātis, *you loved*	**amārētis**
amābant, *they loved*	**amārent**
Future	
amābō, *I shall love*	
amābis, *you will love*	
amābit, *he will love*	
amābimus, *we shall love*	
amābitis, *you will love*	
amābunt, *they will love*	

[1] The stem-vowel ā- is lost before -ō, and in the Present Subjunctive becomes ē-.

[2] The translation of the Subjunctive varies widely according to the construction. Hence no translation of this mood is given in the paradigms.

INDICATIVE		SUBJUNCTIVE
	PERFECT	
amāvī, *I loved, have loved*		amāverim
amāvistī, *you loved*		amāveris
amāvit, *he loved*		amāverit
amāvimus, *we loved*		amāverimus
amāvistis, *you loved*		amāveritis
amāvērunt (-ēre), *they loved*		amāverint
	PLUPERFECT	
amāveram, *I had loved*		amāvissem
amāverās, *you had loved*		amāvissēs
amāverat, *he had loved*		amāvisset
amāverāmus, *we had loved*		amāvissēmus
amāverātis, *you had loved*		amāvissētis
amāverant, *they had loved*		amāvissent

FUTURE PERFECT

Singular	*Plural*
amāverō, *I shall have loved*	amāverimus, *we shall have loved*
amāveris, *you will have loved*	amāveritis, *you will have loved*
amāverit, *he will have loved*	amāverint, *they will have loved*

IMPERATIVE

PRESENT	amā, *love thou*	amāte, *love ye*
FUTURE	amātō, *thou shalt love*	amātōte, *ye shall love*
	amātō, *he shall love*	amantō, *they shall love*

INFINITIVE

PRESENT amāre, *to love*
PERFECT amāvisse or amāsse, *to have loved*
FUTURE amātūrus esse, *to be about to love*

PARTICIPLES

PRESENT amāns, -antis, *loving*
FUTURE amātūrus, -a, -um, *about to love*

GERUND

GENITIVE	amandī, *of loving*	ACCUSATIVE	amandum, *loving*
DATIVE	amandō, *for loving*	ABLATIVE	amandō, *by loving*

SUPINE

amātum, *to love* amātū, *to love*

FIRST CONJUGATION (*ā*-STEMS)—PASSIVE VOICE

PRINCIPAL PARTS: Present Indicative **amor**, Present Infinitive **amārī**, Perfect Indicative **amātus sum**.[1]

PRESENT STEM **amā-**	SUPINE STEM **amāt-**
INDICATIVE	SUBJUNCTIVE
PRESENT	
am**or**,[2] *I am loved, being loved*	am**er**[3]
amā**ris** (-**re**), *you are loved*	amē**ris** (-**re**)
amā**tur**, *he is loved*	amē**tur**
amā**mur**, *we are loved*	amē**mur**
amā**minī**, *you are loved*	amē**minī**
ama**ntur**, *they are loved*	ame**ntur**
IMPERFECT	
amā**bar**, *I was loved, being loved*	amā**rer**
amā**bāris** (-**re**), *you were loved*	amā**rēris** (-**re**)
amā**bātur**, *he was loved*	amā**rētur**
amā**bāmur**, *we were loved*	amā**rēmur**
amā**bāminī**, *you were loved*	amā**rēminī**
amā**bantur**, *they were loved*	amā**rentur**
FUTURE	
amā**bor**, *I shall be loved*	
amā**beris** (-**re**), *you will be loved*	
amā**bitur**, *he will be loved*	
amā**bimur**, *we shall be loved*	
amā**biminī**, *you will be loved*	
amā**buntur**, *they will be loved*	

[1] **Fuī**, **fuistī**, etc., are sometimes used instead of **sum**, **es**, etc.; so also **fueram** instead of **eram** and **fuerō** instead of **erō**. Similarly in the Perfect and Pluperfect Subjunctive **fuerim**, **fueris**, etc. are sometimes used instead of **sim**, **sīs**, etc., and **fuissem** instead of **essem**.

[2] The stem-vowel **ā-** is lost before **-or**, and in the Present Subjunctive becomes **ē-**.

[3] The translation of the Subjunctive varies widely according to the construction. Hence no translation of this mood is given in the paradigms.

Perfect

INDICATIVE	SUBJUNCTIVE
amātus **sum**,[1] *I was loved*	amātus **sim**[1]
amātus **es**, *you were loved*	amātus **sīs**
amātus **est**, *he was loved*	amātus **sit**
amātī **sumus**, *we were loved*	amātī **sīmus**
amātī **estis**, *you were loved*	amātī **sītis**
amātī **sunt**, *they were loved*	amātī **sint**

Pluperfect

INDICATIVE	SUBJUNCTIVE
amātus **eram**,[1] *I had been loved*	amātus **essem**[1]
amātus **erās**, *you had been loved*	amātus **essēs**
amātus **erat**, *he had been loved*	amātus **esset**
amātī **erāmus**, *we had been loved*	amātī **essēmus**
amātī **erātis**, *you had been loved*	amātī **essētis**
amātī **erant**, *they had been loved*	amātī **essent**

Future Perfect

Singular	*Plural*
amātus **erō**,[1] *I shall have been loved*	amātī **erimus**, *we shall have*, etc.
amātus **eris**, *you will have*, etc.	amātī **eritis**, *you will have*, etc.
amātus **erit**, *he will have*, etc.	amātī **erunt**, *they will have*, etc.

IMPERATIVE

Present	am**āre**, *be thou loved*	am**āminī**, *be ye loved*
Future	am**ātor**, *thou shalt be loved*	———
	am**ātor**, *he shall be loved*	am**antor**, *they shall be loved*

INFINITIVE

Present	am**ārī**, *to be loved*
Perfect	amātus **esse**, *to have been loved*
Future	amātum **īrī**, *to be about to be loved*

PARTICIPLES

Perfect	am**ātus, -a, -um**, *loved* (*beloved*, or *having been loved*)
Future (Gerundive)	am**andus, -a, -um**, *to-be-loved* (*lovely*)

[1] See page 94, footnote 1.

SECOND CONJUGATION (*ē*-STEMS)

185. The Second Conjugation includes all verbs which add **ē-** to the root to form the present stem, with a few whose root ends in **ē-**.

PRINCIPAL PARTS: *Active*, **moneō, monēre, monuī, monitum**; *Passive*, **moneor, monērī, monitus sum.**

PRESENT STEM **monē-** PERFECT STEM **monu-** SUPINE STEM **monit-**

ACTIVE VOICE		PASSIVE VOICE	
INDICATIVE	SUBJUNCTIVE	INDICATIVE	SUBJUNCTIVE
PRESENT		PRESENT	
mon**eō**, *I warn*	mon**eam**[1]	mon**eor**	mon**ear**[1]
mon**ēs**, *you warn*	mon**eās**	mon**ēris (-re)**	mon**eāris (-re)**
mon**et**, *he warns*	mon**eat**	mon**ētur**	mon**eātur**
mon**ēmus**	mon**eāmus**	mon**ēmur**	mon**eāmur**
mon**ētis**	mon**eātis**	mon**ēminī**	mon**eāminī**
mon**ent**	mon**eant**	mon**entur**	mon**eantur**
IMPERFECT		IMPERFECT	
mon**ēbam**	mon**ērem**	mon**ēbar**	mon**ērer**
mon**ēbās**	mon**ērēs**	mon**ēbāris (-re)**	mon**ērēris (-re)**
mon**ēbat**	mon**ēret**	mon**ēbātur**	mon**ērētur**
mon**ēbāmus**	mon**ērēmus**	mon**ēbāmur**	mon**ērēmur**
mon**ēbātis**	mon**ērētis**	mon**ēbāminī**	mon**ērēminī**
mon**ēbant**	mon**ērent**	mon**ēbantur**	mon**ērentur**
FUTURE		FUTURE	
mon**ēbō**		mon**ēbor**	
mon**ēbis**		mon**ēberis (-re)**	
mon**ēbit**		mon**ēbitur**	
mon**ēbimus**		mon**ēbimur**	
mon**ēbitis**		mon**ēbiminī**	
mon**ēbunt**		mon**ēbuntur**	

[1] See § 179. *b*. 1.

Active Voice		*Passive Voice*	
INDICATIVE	SUBJUNCTIVE	INDICATIVE	SUBJUNCTIVE
PERFECT		PERFECT	
monuī	monuerim	monitus sum [1]	monitus sim [1]
monuistī	monueris	monitus es	monitus sīs
monuit	monuerit	monitus est	monitus sit
monuimus	monuerimus	monitī sumus	monitī sīmus
monuistis	monueritis	monitī estis	monitī sītis
monuērunt (-re)	monuerint	monitī sunt	monitī sint
PLUPERFECT		PLUPERFECT	
monueram	monuissem	monitus eram [1]	monitus essem [1]
monuerās	monuissēs	monitus erās	monitus essēs
monuerat	monuisset	monitus erat	monitus esset
monuerāmus	monuissēmus	monitī erāmus	monitī essēmus
monuerātis	monuissētis	monitī erātis	monitī essētis
monuerant	monuissent	monitī erant	monitī essent
FUTURE PERFECT		FUTURE PERFECT	
monuerō		monitus erō [1]	
monueris		monitus eris	
monuerit		monitus erit	
monuerimus		monitī erimus	
monueritis		monitī eritis	
monuerint		monitī erunt	

IMPERATIVE

	Singular	*Plural*		*Singular*	*Plural*
PRESENT	monē	monēte	PRESENT	monēre	monēminī
FUTURE	monētō	monētōte	FUTURE	monētor	———
	monētō	monentō		monētor	monentor

INFINITIVE

	Active	Passive
PRESENT	monēre	monērī
PERFECT	monuisse	monitus esse
FUTURE	monitūrus esse	monitum īrī

PARTICIPLES

PRESENT	monēns, -entis	PERFECT	monitus, -a, -um
FUTURE	monitūrus, -a, -um	GERUNDIVE	monendus, -a,-um

GERUND	SUPINE
monendī, -dō, -dum, -dō	monitum, monitū

[1] See footnote 1 on page 94.

THIRD CONJUGATION (*ĕ*-STEMS)

186. The Third Conjugation includes all verbs (not irregular, see § 197) which add **ĕ-** to the root to form the present stem, with a few whose root ends in **ĕ-**.

PRINCIPAL PARTS: *Active*, **tegō, tegĕre, tēxī, tēctum**; *Passive*, **tegor, tegī, tēctus sum.**

PRESENT STEM **tege-** PERFECT STEM **tēx-**[1] SUPINE STEM **tēct-**

ACTIVE VOICE		PASSIVE VOICE	
INDICATIVE	SUBJUNCTIVE	INDICATIVE	SUBJUNCTIVE
PRESENT		PRESENT	
tegō,[2] *I cover*	**tegam**[2]	**tegor**[2]	**tegar**[2]
tegis, *you cover*	**tegās**	**tegeris (-re)**	**tegāris (-re)**
tegit, *he covers*	**tegat**	**tegitur**	**tegātur**
tegimus	**tegāmus**	**tegimur**	**tegāmur**
tegitis	**tegātis**	**tegiminī**	**tegāminī**
tegunt	**tegant**	**teguntur**	**tegantur**
IMPERFECT		IMPERFECT	
tegēbam	**tegerem**	**tegēbar**	**tegerer**
tegēbās	**tegerēs**	**tegēbāris (-re)**	**tegerēris (-re)**
tegēbat	**tegeret**	**tegēbātur**	**tegerētur**
tegēbāmus	**tegerēmus**	**tegēbāmur**	**tegerēmur**
tegēbātis	**tegerētis**	**tegēbāminī**	**tegerēminī**
tegēbant	**tegerent**	**tegēbantur**	**tegerentur**
FUTURE		FUTURE	
tegam[2]		**tegar**[2]	
tegēs		**tegēris (-re)**	
teget		**tegētur**	
tegēmus		**tegēmur**	
tegētis		**tegēminī**	
tegent		**tegentur**	

[1] The perfect stem in this conjugation is always formed from the root; **tēx-** is for **tēg-s-** (see § 15. 9).

[2] See § 179. *c*. 1.

Active Voice		*Passive Voice*	
INDICATIVE	SUBJUNCTIVE	INDICATIVE	SUBJUNCTIVE
PERFECT		PERFECT	
tēxī	tēxerim	tēctus sum [1]	tēctus sim [1]
tēxistī	tēxeris	tēctus es	tēctus sīs
tēxit	tēxerit	tēctus est	tēctus sit
tēximus	tēxerimus	tēctī sumus	tēctī sīmus
tēxistis	tēxeritis	tēctī estis	tēctī sītis
tēxērunt (-re)	tēxerint	tēctī sunt	tēctī sint
PLUPERFECT		PLUPERFECT	
tēxeram	tēxissem	tēctus eram [1]	tēctus essem [1]
tēxerās	tēxissēs	tēctus erās	tēctus essēs
tēxerat	tēxisset	tēctus erat	tēctus esset
tēxerāmus	tēxissēmus	tēctī erāmus	tēctī essēmus
tēxerātis	tēxissētis	tēctī erātis	tēctī essētis
tēxerant	tēxissent	tēctī erant	tēctī essent
FUTURE PERFECT		FUTURE PERFECT	
tēxerō		tēctus erō [1]	
tēxeris		tēctus eris	
tēxerit		tēctus erit	
tēxerimus		tēctī erimus	
tēxeritis		tēctī eritis	
tēxerint		tēctī erunt	

IMPERATIVE

	Singular	*Plural*	*Singular*	*Plural*
PRESENT	tege	tegite	tegere	tegiminī
FUTURE	tegitō	tegitōte	tegitor	———
	tegitō	teguntō	tegitor	teguntor

INFINITIVE

PRESENT	tegere	tegī
PERFECT	tēxisse	tēctus esse
FUTURE	tēctūrus esse	tēctum īrī

PARTICIPLES

PRESENT	tegēns, -entis	PERFECT	tēctus, -a, -um
FUTURE	tēctūrus, -a, -um	GERUNDIVE	tegendus (-undus)

GERUND	SUPINE
tegendī, -dō, -dum, -dō	tēctum, tēctū

[1] See footnote 1 on page 94.

FOURTH CONJUGATION (ī-STEMS)

187. The Fourth Conjugation includes all verbs which add **ī-** to the root to form the present stem.

PRINCIPAL PARTS: *Active*, **audiō, audīre, audīvī, audītum**; *Passive*, **audior, audīrī, audītus sum.**

PRESENT STEM **audī-** PERFECT STEM **audīv-** SUPINE STEM **audīt-**

ACTIVE VOICE		PASSIVE VOICE	
INDICATIVE	SUBJUNCTIVE	INDICATIVE	SUBJUNCTIVE
PRESENT		PRESENT	
audiō, *I hear*	audiam [1]	audior	audiar [1]
audīs, *you hear*	audiās	audīris (-re)	audiāris (-re)
audit, *he hears*	audiat	audītur	audiātur
audīmus	audiāmus	audīmur	audiāmur
audītis	audiātis	audīminī	audiāminī
audiunt	audiant	audiuntur	audiantur
IMPERFECT		IMPERFECT	
audiēbam [1]	audīrem	audiēbar [1]	audīrer
audiēbās	audīrēs	audiēbāris (-re)	audīrēris (-re)
audiēbat	audīret	audiēbātur	audīrētur
audiēbāmus	audīrēmus	audiēbāmur	audīrēmur
audiēbātis	audīrētis	audiēbāminī	audīrēminī
audiēbant	audīrent	audiēbantur	audīrentur
FUTURE		FUTURE	
audiam [1]		audiar [1]	
audiēs		audiēris (-re)	
audiet		audiētur	
audiēmus		audiēmur	
audiētis		audiēminī	
audient		audientur	

[1] See § 179. *d*.

Active Voice		*Passive Voice*	
INDICATIVE	SUBJUNCTIVE	INDICATIVE	SUBJUNCTIVE
PERFECT		PERFECT	
audīvī	audīverim	audītus sum [1]	audītus sim [1]
audīvistī	audīveris	audītus es	audītus sīs
audīvit	audīverit	audītus est	audītus sit
audīvimus	audīverimus	audītī sumus	audītī sīmus
audīvistis	audīveritis	audītī estis	audītī sītis
audīvērunt (-re)	audīverint	audītī sunt	audītī sint
PLUPERFECT		PLUPERFECT	
audīveram	audīvissem	audītus eram [1]	audītus essem [1]
audīverās	audīvissēs	audītus erās	audītus essēs
audīverat	audīvisset	audītus erat	audītus esset
audīverāmus	audīvissēmus	audītī erāmus	audītī essēmus
audīverātis	audīvissētis	audītī erātis	audītī essētis
audīverant	audīvissent	audītī erant	audītī essent
FUTURE PERFECT		FUTURE PERFECT	
audīverō		audītus erō [1]	
audīveris		audītus eris	
audīverit		audītus erit	
audīverimus		audītī erimus	
audīveritis		audītī eritis	
audīverint		audītī erunt	

IMPERATIVE

	Singular	*Plural*	*Singular*	*Plural*
PRESENT	audī	audīte	audīre	audīminī
FUTURE	audītō	audītōte	audītor	———
	audītō	audiuntō	audītor	audiuntor

INFINITIVE

PRESENT	audīre	audīrī
PERFECT	audīvisse	audītus esse
FUTURE	audītūrus esse	audītum īrī

PARTICIPLES

PRESENT	audiēns, -ientis	PERFECT	audītus, -a, -um
FUTURE	audītūrus, -a, -um	GERUNDIVE	audiendus, -a, -um

GERUND	SUPINE
audiendī, -dō, -dum, -dō	audītum, audītū

[1] See footnote 1. p. 94.

VERBS IN *-iō* OF THE THIRD CONJUGATION

188. Verbs of the Third Conjugation in **-iō** have certain forms of the present stem like the fourth conjugation. They lose the **i** of the stem before a consonant and also before **ĭ**, **ī**, and **ĕ** (except in the future, the participle, the gerund, and the gerundive).[1] Verbs of this class are conjugated as follows:—

PRINCIPAL PARTS: *Active*, **capiō, capĕre, cēpī, captum**;
Passive, **capior, capī, captus sum.**

PRESENT STEM **capie- (cape-)** PERFECT STEM **cēp-** SUPINE STEM **capt-**

ACTIVE VOICE		PASSIVE VOICE	
INDICATIVE	SUBJUNCTIVE	INDICATIVE	SUBJUNCTIVE
PRESENT		PRESENT	
capiō, *I take*	capiam	capior	capiar
capis, *you take*	capiās	caperis (-re)	capiāris (-re)
capit, *he takes*	capiat	capitur	capiātur
capimus	capiāmus	capimur	capiāmur
capitis	capiātis	capiminī	capiāminī
capiunt	capiant	capiuntur	capiantur
IMPERFECT		IMPERFECT	
capiēbam	caperem	capiēbar	caperer
FUTURE		FUTURE	
capiam		capiar	
capiēs		capiēris (-re)	
capiet, etc.		capiētur, etc.	
PERFECT		PERFECT	
cēpī	cēperim	captus sum	captus sim
PLUPERFECT		PLUPERFECT	
cēperam	cēpissem	captus eram	captus essem
FUTURE PERFECT		FUTURE PERFECT	
cēperō		captus erō	

[1] This is a practical working rule. The actual explanation of the forms of such verbs is not fully understood.

IMPERATIVE

Active Voice		*Passive Voice*	
PRESENT		PRESENT	
Singular	*Plural*	*Singular*	*Plural*
cape	capite	capere	capiminī
FUTURE		FUTURE	
capitō	capitōte	capitor	———
capitō	capiunto	capitor	capiuntor

INFINITIVE

	Active	Passive
PRESENT	capere	capī
PERFECT	cēpisse	captus esse
FUTURE	captūrus esse	captum īrī

PARTICIPLES

PRESENT	capiēns, -ientis	PERFECT	captus, -a, -um
FUTURE	captūrus, -a, -um	GERUNDIVE	capiendus, -a, -um

GERUND	SUPINE
capiendī, -dō, -dum, -dō	captum, -tū

Parallel Forms

189. Many verbs have more than one set of forms, of which only one is generally found in classic use: —

> **lavō, lavāre** or **lavĕre**, *wash* (see § 211. *e*).
> **scateō, scatēre** or **scatĕre**, *gush forth.*
> **lūdificō, -āre,** or **lūdificor, -ārī,** *mock.*
> **fulgō, fulgĕre,** or **fulgeō, fulgēre,** *shine.*

DEPONENT VERBS

190. Deponent Verbs have the forms of the Passive Voice, with an active or reflexive signification: —

PRINCIPAL PARTS	First conjugation:	**mīror, mīrārī, mīrātus,** *admire.*
	Second conjugation:	**vereor, verērī, veritus,** *fear.*
	Third conjugation:	**sequor, sequī, secūtus,** *follow.*
	Fourth conjugation:	**partior, partīrī, partītus,** *share.*

INDICATIVE

PRES.	mīror	vereor	sequor	partior
	mīrāris (-re)	verēris (-re)	sequeris (-re)	partīris (-re)
	mīrātur	verētur	sequitur	partītur
	mīrāmur	verēmur	sequimur	partīmur
	mīrāminī	verēminī	sequiminī	partīminī
	mīrantur	verentur	sequuntur	partiuntur
IMPF.	mīrābar	verēbar	sequēbar	partiēbar
FUT.	mīrābor	verēbor	sequar	partiar
PERF.	mīrātus sum	veritus sum	secūtus sum	partītus sum
PLUP.	mīrātus eram	veritus eram	secūtus eram	partītus eram
F. P.	mīrātus erō	veritus erō	secūtus erō	partītus erō

SUBJUNCTIVE

PRES.	mīrer	verear	sequar	partiar
IMPF.	mīrārer	verērer	sequerer	partīrer
PERF.	mīrātus sim	veritus sim	secūtus sim	partītus sim
PLUP.	mīrātus essem	veritus essem	secūtus essem	partītus essem

IMPERATIVE

PRES.	mīrāre	verēre	sequere	partīre
FUT.	mīrātor	verētor	sequitor	partītor

INFINITIVE

PRES.	mīrārī	verērī	sequī	partīrī
PERF.	mīrātus esse	veritus esse	secūtus esse	partītus esse
FUT.	mīrātūrus esse	veritūrus esse	secūtūrus esse	partītūrus esse

PARTICIPLES

PRES.	mīrāns	verēns	sequēns	partiēns
FUT.	mīrātūrus	veritūrus	secūtūrus	partītūrus
PERF.	mīrātus	veritus	secūtus	partītus
GER.	mīrandus	verendus	sequendus	partiendus

GERUND

mīrandī, -ō, etc.	verendī, etc.	sequendī, etc.	partiendī, etc.

SUPINE

mīrātum, -tū	veritum, -tū	secūtum, -tū	partītum, -tū

a. Deponents have the participles of both voices: —

sequēns, *following*.	**secūtūrus**, *about to follow*.
secūtus, *having followed*.	**sequendus**, *to be followed*.

b. The perfect participle generally has an active sense, but in verbs otherwise deponent it is often passive: as, **mercātus**, *bought*; **adeptus**, *gained* (or *having gained*).

c. The future infinitive is always in the active form: thus, **sequor** has **secūtūrus (-a, -um) esse** (not **secūtum īrī**).

d. The gerundive, being passive in meaning, is found only in transitive verbs, or intransitive verbs used impersonally: —

hōc cōnfitendum est, *this must be acknowledged*.
moriendum est omnibus, *all must die*.

e. Most deponents are intransitive or reflexive in meaning, corresponding to what in Greek is called the Middle Voice (§ 156. *a.* N.).

f. Some deponents are occasionally used in a passive sense: as, **crīminor**, *I accuse*, or *I am accused*.

g. About twenty verbs have an active meaning in both active and passive forms: as, **mereō** or **mereor**, *I deserve*.

191. More than half of all deponents are of the First Conjugation, and all of these are regular. The following deponents are irregular: —

adsentior, -īrī, adsēnsus, *assent*.
apīscor, (-ip-), -ī, aptus (-eptus), *get*.
dēfetīscor, -ī, -fessus, *faint*.
expergīscor, -ī, -perrēctus, *rouse*.
experior, -īrī, expertus, *try*.
fateor, -ērī, fassus, *confess*.
fruor, -ī, frūctus (fruitus), *enjoy*.
fungor, -ī, fūnctus, *fulfil*.
gradior (-gredior), -ī, gressus, *step*.
īrāscor, -ī, īrātus, *be angry*.
lābor, -ī, lāpsus, *fall*.
loquor, -ī, locūtus, *speak*.
mētior, -īrī, mēnsus, *measure*.
-minīscor, -ī, -mentus, *think*.
morior, -ī (-īrī), mortuus (moritūrus), *die*.
nancīscor, -ī, nactus (nānctus), *find*.
nāscor, -ī, nātus, *be born*.
nītor, -ī, nīsus (nīxus), *strive*.
oblīvīscor, -ī, oblītus, *forget*.
opperior, -īrī, oppertus, *await*.
ōrdior, -īrī, ōrsus, *begin*.
orior, -īrī, ortus (oritūrus), *rise* (3d conjugation in most forms).
pacīscor, -ī, pactus, *bargain*.
patior (-petior), -ī, passus (-pessus), *suffer*.
-plector, -ī, -plexus, *clasp*.
proficīscor, -ī, profectus, *set out*.
queror, -ī, questus, *complain*.
reor, rērī, ratus, *think*.
revertor, -ī, reversus, *return*.
ringor, -ī, rictus, *snarl*.
sequor, -ī, secūtus, *follow*.
tueor, -ērī, tuitus (tūtus), *defend*.
ulcīscor, -ī, ultus, *avenge*.
ūtor, -ī, ūsus, *use, employ*.

NOTE. — The deponent **comperior, -īrī, compertus**, is rarely found for **comperiō, -īre. Revertor**, until the time of Augustus, had regularly the active forms in the perfect system, **revertī, reverteram**, etc.

a. The following deponents have no supine stem: —

dēvertor, -tī, *turn aside* (to lodge).
diffiteor, -ērī, *deny*.
fatīscor, -ī, *gape*.
līquor, -ī, *melt* (intrans.).
medeor, -ērī, *heal*.
reminīscor, -ī, *call to mind*.
vescor, -ī, *feed upon*.

NOTE. — Deponents are really passive (or middle) verbs whose active voice has disappeared. There is hardly one that does not show signs of having been used in the active at some period of the language.

Semi-Deponents

192. A few verbs having no perfect stem are regular in the present, but appear in the tenses of completed action as deponents. These are called Semi-deponents. They are: —

audeō, audēre, ausus, *dare*.
fīdō, fīdere, fīsus, *trust*.
gaudeō, gaudēre, gāvīsus, *rejoice*.
soleō, solēre, solitus, *be wont*.

a. From **audeō** there is an old perfect subjunctive **ausim**. The form **sōdēs** (for **sī audēs**), *an thou wilt*, is frequent in the dramatists and rare elsewhere.

b. The active forms **vāpulō, vāpulāre**, *be flogged*, and **vēneō, vēnīre**, *be sold* (contracted from **vēnum īre**, *go to sale*), have a passive meaning, and are sometimes called *neutral passives*. To these may be added **fierī**, *to be made* (§ 204), and **exsulāre**, *to be banished* (live in exile); cf. **accēdere**, *to be added*.

NOTE. — The following verbs are sometimes found as semi-deponents: **iūrō, iūrāre, iūrātus**, *swear*; **nūbō, nūbere, nūpta**, *marry*; **placeō, placēre, placitus**, *please*.

THE PERIPHRASTIC CONJUGATIONS

193. A Periphrastic form, as the name indicates, is a "roundabout way of speaking." In the widest sense, all verb-phrases consisting of participles and **sum** are Periphrastic Forms. The Present Participle is, however, rarely so used, and the Perfect Participle with **sum** is included in the regular conjugation (**amātus sum, eram**, etc.). Hence the term Periphrastic Conjugation is usually restricted to verb-phrases consisting of the Future Active Participle or the Gerundive with **sum**.

NOTE. — The Future Passive Infinitive, as **amātum īrī**, formed from the infinitive passive of **eō**, *go*, used impersonally with the supine in **-um**, may also be classed as a periphrastic form (§ 203. *a*).

194. There are two Periphrastic Conjugations, known respectively as the First (or Active) and the Second (or Passive).

a. The First Periphrastic Conjugation combines the Future Active Participle with the forms of **sum**, and denotes a *future* or *intended* action.

b. The Second Periphrastic Conjugation combines the Gerundive with the forms of **sum**, and denotes *obligation, necessity*, or *propriety*.

c. The periphrastic forms are inflected regularly throughout the Indicative and Subjunctive and in the Present and Perfect Infinitive.

195. The First Periphrastic Conjugation: —

INDICATIVE

Present	amātūrus sum, *I am about to love*
Imperfect	amātūrus eram, *I was about to love*
Future	amātūrus erō, *I shall be about to love*
Perfect	amātūrus fuī, *I have been, was, about to love*
Pluperfect	amātūrus fueram, *I had been about to love*
Future Perfect	amātūrus fuerō, *I shall have been about to love*

SUBJUNCTIVE

Present	amātūrus sim
Imperfect	amātūrus essem
Perfect	amātūrus fuerim
Pluperfect	amātūrus fuissem

INFINITIVE

Present	amātūrus esse, *to be about to love*
Perfect	amātūrus fuisse, *to have been about to love*

So in the other conjugations: —

Second: **monitūrus sum**, *I am about to advise.*
Third: **tēctūrus sum**, *I am about to cover.*
Fourth: **audītūrus sum**, *I am about to hear.*
Third (in -iō): **captūrus sum**, *I am about to take.*

196. The Second Periphrastic Conjugation: —

INDICATIVE

Present	amandus sum, *I am to be, must be, loved*
Imperfect	amandus eram, *I was to be, had to be, loved*
Future	amandus erō, *I shall have to be loved*
Perfect	amandus fuī, *I was to be, had to be, loved*
Pluperfect	amandus fueram, *I had had to be loved*
Future Perfect	amandus fuerō, *I shall have had to be loved*

SUBJUNCTIVE

Present	amandus sim
Imperfect	amandus essem
Perfect	amandus fuerim
Pluperfect	amandus fuissem

INFINITIVE

Present	amandus esse, *to have to be loved*
Perfect	amandus fuisse, *to have had to be loved*

So in the other conjugations: —

> Second: **monendus sum**, *I am to be, must be, advised.*
> Third: **tegendus sum**, *I am to be, must be, covered.*
> Fourth: **audiendus sum**, *I am to be, must be, heard.*
> Third (in -iō): **capiendus sum**, *I am to be, must be, taken.*

IRREGULAR VERBS

197. Several verbs add some of the personal endings of the present system directly to the root,[1] or combine two verbs in their inflection. These are called Irregular Verbs. They are **sum, volō, ferō, edō, dō, eō, queō, fīō,** and their compounds.

Sum has already been inflected in § 170.

198. **Sum** is compounded without any change of inflection with the prepositions **ab, ad, dē, in, inter, ob, prae, prō** (earlier form **prōd**), **sub, super.**

a. In the compound **prōsum** (*help*), **prō** retains its original **d** before **e**:

Principal Parts: **prōsum, prōdesse, prōfuī, prōfutūrus**

	INDICATIVE		SUBJUNCTIVE	
	Singular	*Plural*	*Singular*	*Plural*
Present	prōsum	prōsumus	prōsim	prōsīmus
	prōdes	prōdestis	prōsīs	prōsītis
	prōdest	prōsunt	prōsit	prōsint
Imperfect	prōderam	prōderāmus	prōdessem	prōdessēmus
Future	prōderō	prōderimus	——	——
Perfect	prōfuī	prōfuimus	prōfuerim	prōfuerimus
Pluperfect	prōfueram	prōfuerāmus	prōfuissem	prōfuissēmus
Fut. Perf.	prōfuerō	prōfuerimus	——	——

IMPERATIVE

Present prōdes, prōdeste Future prōdestō, prōdestōte

INFINITIVE

Present prōdesse Perfect prōfuisse
Future prōfutūrus esse

PARTICIPLE

Future prōfutūrus

[1] These are athematic verbs, see § 174. 2.

b. **Sum** is also compounded with the adjective **potis**, or **pote**, *able*, making the verb **possum** (*be able, can*). **Possum** is inflected as follows:—[1]

PRINCIPAL PARTS: **possum, posse, potuī**[2]

	INDICATIVE		SUBJUNCTIVE	
	Singular	*Plural*	*Singular*	*Plural*
PRESENT	possum	possumus	possim	possīmus
	potes	potestis	possīs	possītis
	potest	possunt	possit	possint
IMPERFECT	poteram	poterāmus	possem	possēmus
FUTURE	poterō	poterimus	——	——
PERFECT	potuī	potuimus	potuerim	potuerimus
PLUPERFECT	potueram	potuerāmus	potuissem	potuissēmus
FUT. PERF.	potuerō	potuerimus	——	——

INFINITIVE

PRES. posse PERF. potuisse

PARTICIPLE

PRES. potēns (adjective), *powerful*

199. **volō, nōlō, mālō**

PRINCIPAL PARTS:
- **volō, velle, voluī,** ——, *be willing, will, wish*
- **nōlō, nōlle, nōluī,** ——, *be unwilling, will not*
- **mālō, mālle, māluī,** ——, *be more willing, prefer*

NOTE.—**Nōlō** and **mālō** are compounds of **volō**. **Nōlō** is for **ne-volō**, and **mālō** for **mā-volō** from **mage-volō**.

INDICATIVE

PRESENT	volō	nōlō	mālō
	vīs[3]	nōn vīs	māvīs
	vult (volt)	nōn vult	māvult
	volumus	nōlumus	mālumus
	vultis (voltis)	nōn vultis	māvultis
	volunt	nōlunt	mālunt
IMPERFECT	volēbam	nōlēbam	mālēbam
FUTURE	volam, volēs, etc.	nōlam, nōlēs, etc.	mālam, mālēs, etc.
PERFECT	voluī	nōluī	māluī
PLUPERFECT	volueram	nōlueram	mālueram
FUT. PERF.	voluerō	nōluerō	māluerō

[1] The forms **potis sum, pote sum**, etc. occur in early writers. Other early forms are **potesse**; **possiem, -ēs, -et**; **poterint, potisit** (for **possit**); **potestur** and **possitur** (used with a passive infinitive, cf. § 205. *a*).

[2] **Potuī** is from an obsolete †**potēre**.

[3] **Vīs** is from a different root.

		SUBJUNCTIVE	
PRESENT	velim, -īs, -it,	nōlim	mālim
	velīmus, -ītis, -int		
IMPERFECT	vellem,[1] -ēs, -et,	nōllem	māllem
	vellēmus, -ētis, -ent		
PERFECT	voluerim	nōluerim	māluerim
PLUPERFECT	voluissem	nōluissem	māluissem
		IMPERATIVE	
PRESENT	——	nōlī, nōlīte	——
FUTURE	——	nōlītō, etc.	——
		INFINITIVE	
PRESENT	velle[1]	nōlle	mālle
PERFECT	voluisse	nōluisse	māluisse
		PARTICIPLES	
PRESENT	volēns, -entis	nōlēns, -entis	——

NOTE.—The forms **sīs** for **sī vīs**, **sūltis** for **sī vultis**, and the forms **nĕvīs** (**nĕ-vīs**), **nĕvolt**, **māvolō**, **māvolunt**, **māvelim**, **māvellem**, etc., occur in early writers.

200. **Ferō**, *bear, carry, endure*[2]

PRINCIPAL PARTS: **ferō, ferre,**[3] **tulī, lātum**

PRESENT STEM **fer-** PERFECT STEM **tul-** SUPINE STEM **lāt-**

	ACTIVE		PASSIVE	
		INDICATIVE		
PRESENT	ferō	ferimus	feror	ferimur
	fers	fertis	ferris (-re)	feriminī
	fert	ferunt	fertur	feruntur
IMPERFECT	ferēbam		ferēbar	
FUTURE	feram		ferar	
PERFECT	tulī		lātus sum	
PLUPERFECT	tuleram		lātus eram	
FUTURE PERFECT	tulerō		lātus erō	

[1] **Vellem** is for †**vel-sēm**, and **velle** for †**vel-se** (cf. **es-se**), the **s** being assimilated to the **l** preceding.

[2] **Ferō** has two independent stems: **fer-** in the present system, and **tul-** (for **tol-**) in the perfect from TOL, root of **tollō**. The perfect **tetulī** occurs in Plautus. In the participle the root is weakened to **tl-**, **lātum** standing for †**tlātum** (cf. τλητός).

[3] **Ferre, ferrem**, are for †**fer-se**, †**fer-sēm** (cf. **es-se, es-sem**), **s** being assimilated to preceding **r**; or **ferre, ferrem**, may be for †**ferese**, †**feresēm** (see § 15. 4).

	Active		*Passive*	
	SUBJUNCTIVE			
PRESENT	feram		ferar	
IMPERFECT	ferrem[1]		ferrer	
PERFECT	tulerim		lātus sim	
PLUPERFECT	tulissem		lātus essem	
	IMPERATIVE			
PRESENT	fer	ferte	ferre	feriminī
FUTURE	fertō	fertōte	fertor	
	fertō	feruntō	fertor	feruntor
	INFINITIVE			
PRESENT	ferre		ferrī	
PERFECT	tulisse		lātus esse	
FUTURE	lātūrus esse		lātum īrī	

PARTICIPLES

PRESENT	ferēns, -entis	PERFECT	lātus
FUTURE	lātūrus	GERUNDIVE	ferendus

GERUND	SUPINE
ferendī, -dō, -dum, -dō	lātum, lātū

a. The compounds of **ferō**, conjugated like the simple verb, are the following: —

ad-	adferō	adferre	attulī	allātum
au-, ab-	auferō	auferre	abstulī	ablātum
con-	cōnferō	cōnferre	contulī	collātum
dis-, dī-	differō	differre	distulī	dīlātum
ex-, ē-	efferō	efferre	extulī	ēlātum
in-	īnferō	īnferre	intulī	illātum
ob-	offerō	offerre	obtulī	oblātum
re-	referō	referre	rettulī	relātum
sub-	sufferō	sufferre	sustulī[2]	sublātum[2]

NOTE. — In these compounds the phonetic changes in the preposition are especially to be noted. **ab-** and **au-** are two distinct prepositions with the same meaning.

[1] See note 3, page 110.

[2] **Sustulī** and **sublātum** also supply the perfect and participle of the verb **tollō**.

201. **Edō, edere, ēdī, ēsum,** *eat*, is regular of the third conjugation, but has also an archaic present subjunctive and some alternative forms directly from the root (ED), without the thematic vowel. These are in full-faced type.

ACTIVE

INDICATIVE

PRESENT	edō, edis (**ēs**[1]), edit (**ēst**)
	edimus, editis (**ēstis**), edunt
IMPERFECT	edēbam, edēbās, etc.

SUBJUNCTIVE

PRESENT	edam (**edim**), edās (**edīs**), edat (**edit**)
	edāmus (**edīmus**), edātis (**edītis**), edant (**edint**)
IMPERFECT	ederem, ederēs (**ēssēs**), ederet (**ēsset**)
	ederēmus (**ēssēmus**), ederētis (**ēssētis**), ederent (**ēssent**)

IMPERATIVE

	Singular	*Plural*
PRESENT	ede (**ēs**)	edite (**ēste**)
FUTURE	editō (**ēstō**)	editōte (**ēstōte**)
	editō (**ēstō**)	eduntō

INFINITIVE

PRESENT	edere (**ēsse**)
PERFECT	ēdisse
FUTURE	ēsūrus esse

PARTICIPLES

PRESENT	edēns, -entis
FUTURE	ēsūrus [2]

GERUND

edendī, -dō, -dum, -dō

SUPINE

ēsum, ēsū [2]

a. In the Passive the following irregular forms occur in the third person singular: Present Indicative **ēstur**, Imperfect Subjunctive **ēssētur**.

[1] In **ēs** etc. the **e** is long. In the corresponding forms of **sum**, **e** is short. The difference in quantity between **ĕdō** and **ēs** etc. depends upon inherited vowel variation (§ 17. *a*).

[2] Old forms are **ēssūrus** and supine **ēssum**.

202. The irregular verb **dō**, *give*, is conjugated as follows:—

PRINCIPAL PARTS: **dō, dăre, dedī, datum**

PRESENT STEM **dă-** PERFECT STEM **ded-** SUPINE STEM **dat-**

	ACTIVE		PASSIVE	
	INDICATIVE			
PRESENT	dō	damus	——	damur
	dās	datis	daris (-re)	daminī
	dat	dant	datur	dantur
IMPERFECT	dabam		dabar	
FUTURE	dabō		dabor	
PERFECT	dedī		datus sum	
PLUPERFECT	dederam		datus eram	
FUTURE PERFECT	dederō		datus erō	
	SUBJUNCTIVE			
PRESENT	dem, dēs, det, etc.		——, dēris (-re), dētur, etc.	
IMPERFECT	darem		darer	
PERFECT	dederim		datus sim	
PLUPERFECT	dedissem		datus essem	
	IMPERATIVE			
PRESENT	dā	date	dare	daminī
FUTURE	datō	datōte	dator	——
	datō	dantō	dator	dantor
	INFINITIVE			
PRESENT	dare		darī	
PERFECT	dedisse		datus esse	
FUTURE	datūrus esse		datum īrī	
	PARTICIPLES			
PRESENT	dāns, dantis	PERFECT	datus	
FUTURE	datūrus	GERUNDIVE	dandus	

GERUND

dandī, -dō, -dum, -dō

SUPINE

datum, datū

For compounds of **dō**, see § 209. *a.* N.

203. **Eō**, *go.*[1] Principal Parts: **eō, īre, iī (īvī), ĭtum**

	INDICATIVE	SUBJUNCTIVE
Present	eō, īs, it	eam, eās, eat
	īmus, ītis, eunt	eāmus, eātis, eant
Imperfect	ībam, ībās, ībat	īrem, īrēs, īret
	ībāmus, ībātis, ībant	īrēmus, īrētis, īrent
Future	ībō, ībis, ībit	
	ībimus, ībitis, ībunt	
Perfect	iī (īvī)	ierim (īverim)
Pluperfect	ieram (īveram)	īssem (īvissem)
Future Perfect	ierō (īverō)	

IMPERATIVE

Present	ī	Future	ītō, ītōte
	īte		ītō, euntō

INFINITIVE

Present īre Perfect īsse (īvisse) Future itūrus esse

PARTICIPLES

Present iēns, *gen.* euntis Future itūrus Gerundive eundum

GERUND eundī, -dō, -dum, -dō SUPINE itum, itū

a. The compounds **adeō**, *approach*, **ineō**, *enter*, and some others, are transitive. They are inflected as follows in the passive: —

INDICATIVE				SUBJUNCTIVE	
Pres.	adeor	Impf.	adībar	Pres.	adear
	adīris	Fut.	adībor	Impf.	adīrer
	adītur	Perf.	aditus sum	Perf.	aditus sim
	adīmur	Plup.	aditus eram	Plup.	aditus essem
	adīminī	F. P.	aditus erō		
	adeuntur				

INFIN. adīrī aditus esse PART. aditus adeundus

Thus inflected, the forms of **eō** are used impersonally in the third person singular of the passive: as, **itum est** (§ 208. *d*). The infinitive **īrī** is used with the supine in **-um** to make the future infinitive passive (§ 193. N.). The verb **vēneō**, *be sold* (i.e. **vēnum eō**, *go to sale*), has also several forms in the passive.

b. In the perfect system of **eō** the forms with **v** are very rare in the simple verb and unusual in the compounds.

c. **ii** before **s** is regularly contracted to **ī**: as, **īsse.**

[1] The root of **eō** is EI (weak form I). This **ei** becomes **ī** except before **a**, **o**, and **u**, where it becomes **e** (cf. **eō, eam, eunt**). The strong form of the root, **ī**, is shortened before **a** vowel or final **-t**; the weak form, **ĭ**, appears in **itum** and **itūrus.**

d. The compound **ambiō** is inflected regularly like a verb of the fourth conjugation. But it has also **ambībat** in the imperfect indicative.

e. **Prō** with **eō** retains its original **d**: as, **prōdeō, prōdīs, prōdit.**

204. **Faciō, facere, fēcī, factum,** *make*, is regular. But it has imperative **fac** in the active, and, besides the regular forms, the future perfect **faxō**, perfect subjunctive **faxim.** The passive of **faciō** is —

fīō, fĭĕrī, factus sum, *be made* or *become.*

The present system of **fīō** is regular of the fourth conjugation, but the subjunctive imperfect is **fierem**, and the infinitive **fierī.**

NOTE. — The forms in brackets are not used in good prose.

	INDICATIVE	SUBJUNCTIVE
PRESENT	fīō, fīs, fit	fīam, fīās, fīat
	[fīmus], [fītis], fīunt	fīāmus, fīātis, fīant
IMPERFECT	fīēbam, fīēbās, etc.	fierem, fierēs, etc.
FUTURE	fīam, fīēs, etc.	
PERFECT	factus sum	factus sim
PLUPERFECT	factus eram	factus essem
FUTURE PERFECT	factus erō	

IMPERATIVE

[fī, fīte, fītō, ——][1]

INFINITIVE

PRESENT fierī PERFECT factus esse FUTURE factum īrī

PARTICIPLES

PERFECT factus GERUNDIVE faciendus

a. Most compounds of **faciō** with prepositions weaken **ă** to **ĭ** in the present stem and to **ĕ** in the supine stem, and are inflected regularly like verbs in **-iō**: —

cōnficiō, cōnficĕre, cōnfēcī, cōnfectum, *finish.*
cōnficior, cōnficī, cōnfectus.

b. Other compounds retain **a**, and have **-fīō** in the passive: as, **benefaciō, -facere, -fēcī, -factum**; passive **benefīō, -fierī, -factus,** *benefit.* These retain the accent of the simple verb: as, **bene-fă′cis** (§ 12. *a*, *Exc.*).

c. A few isolated forms of **fīo** occur in other compounds: —

cōnfit, *it happens,* **cōnfīunt; cōnfīat; cōnfieret, cōnfierent; cōnfierī.**
dēfit, *it lacks,* **dēfīunt; dēfīet; dēfīat; dēfierī.**
effierī, *to be effected.*
īnfīō, *begin* (to speak), **īnfit.**
interfīat, *let him perish;* **interfierī,** *to perish.*
superfit, *it remains over;* **superfīat, superfierī.**

[1] The imperative is rarely found, and then only in early writers.

DEFECTIVE VERBS

205. Some verbs have lost the Present System, and use only tenses of the Perfect, in which they are inflected regularly. These are —

	coepī,[1] *I began*	**ōdī**,[2] *I hate*	**meminī**,[3] *I remember*
	INDICATIVE		
PERFECT	coepī	ōdī	meminī
PLUPERFECT	coeperam	ōderam	memineram
FUTURE PERFECT	coeperō	ōderō	meminerō
	SUBJUNCTIVE		
PERFECT	coeperim	ōderim	meminerim
PLUPERFECT	coepissem	ōdissem	meminissem
	IMPERATIVE		
			mementō
			mementōte
	INFINITIVE		
PERFECT	coepisse	ōdisse	meminisse
FUTURE	coeptūrus esse	ōsūrus esse	
	PARTICIPLES		
PERFECT	coeptus, *begun*	ōsus, *hating* or *hated*	
FUTURE	coeptūrus	ōsūrus, *likely to hate*	

a. The passive of **coepī** is often used with the passive infinitive: as, **coeptus sum vocārī**, *I began to be called*, but **coepī vocāre**, *I began to call*. For the present system **incipiō** is used.

NOTE. — Early and rare forms are **coepiō, coepiam, coeperet, coepere.**

b. The Perfect, Pluperfect, and Future Perfect of **ōdī** and **meminī** have the meanings of a Present, Imperfect, and Future respectively: —

ōdī, *I hate;* **ōderam**, *I hated* (*was hating*); **ōderō**, *I shall hate.*

NOTE 1. — A present participle **meminēns** is early and late.

NOTE 2. — **Nōvī** and **cōnsuēvī** (usually referred to **nōscō** and **cōnsuēscō**) are often used in the sense of *I know* (have learned) and *I am accustomed* (have become accustomed) as preteritive verbs. Many other verbs are occasionally used in the same way (see 476. N.).

[1] Root AP (as in apīscor) with co(n-).

[2] Root OD, as in ŏdium.

[3] Root MEN, as in mēns.

206. Many verbs are found only in the Present System. Such are **maereō, -ēre,** *be sorrowful* (cf. **maestus,** *sad*); **feriō, -īre,** *strike.*

In many the simple verb is incomplete, but the missing parts occur in its compounds: as, **vādō, vādere, in-vāsī, in-vāsum.**

Some verbs occur very commonly, but only in a few forms:—

a. **Âiō,** *I say*:—

INDIC.	PRES.	âiō, ais,[1] ait; ——, ——, âiunt
	IMPF.	âiēbam,[2] âiēbās, etc.
SUBJV.	PRES.	——, âiās, âiat; ——, ——, âiant
IMPER.		aī (rare)
PART.		âiēns

The vowels **a** and **i** are pronounced separately (**a-is, a-it**) except sometimes in old or colloquial Latin. Before a vowel, one **i** stands for two (see § 6. *c*):—thus **âiō** was pronounced **a͡ī-yō** and was sometimes written **aiiō.**

b. **Inquam,** *I say,* except in poetry, is used only in direct quotations (cf. the English *quoth*).

INDIC.	PRES.	inquam, inquis, inquit; inquimus, inquitis (late), inquiunt
	IMPF.	——, ——, inquiēbat; ——, ——, ——
	FUT.	——, inquiēs, inquiet; ——, ——, ——
	PERF.	inquiī, inquīstī, ——; ——, ——, ——
IMPER.	PRES.	inque
	FUT.	inquitō

The only common forms are **inquam, inquis, inquit, inquiunt,** and the future **inquiēs, inquiet.**

c. The deponent **fārī,** *to speak,* has the following forms:—

INDIC.	PRES.	——, ——, fātur; ——, ——, fantur
	FUT.	fābor, ——, fābitur; ——, ——, ——
	PERF.	——, ——, fātus est; ——, ——, fātī sunt
	PLUP.	fātus eram, ——, fātus erat; ——, ——, ——
IMPER.	PRES.	fāre
INFIN.	PRES.	fārī
PART.	PRES.	fāns, fantis, etc. (in singular)
	PERF.	fātus (*having spoken*)
	GER.	fandus (*to be spoken of*)
GERUND, *gen.*		fandī, *abl.* fandō SUPINE fātū

Several forms compounded with the prepositions **ex, prae, prō, inter,** occur: as, **praefātur, praefāmur, affārī, prōfātus, interfātur,** etc. The compound **īnfāns** is regularly used as a noun (*child*). **Īnfandus, nefandus,** are used as adjectives, *unspeakable, abominable.*

[1] The second singular **ais** with the interrogative **-ne** is often written **ain.**

[2] An old imperfect **aibam, aibās,** etc. (dissyllabic) is sometimes found.

d. **Queō**, *I can*, **nequeō**, *I cannot*, are conjugated like **eō**. They are rarely used except in the present. **Queō** is regularly accompanied by a negative. The forms given below occur, those in full-faced type in classic prose. The Imperative, Gerund, and Supine are wanting.

INDICATIVE	SUBJUNCTIVE	INDICATIVE	SUBJUNCTIVE
PRESENT		PRESENT	
queō	**queam**	**nequeō (nōn queō)**	**nequeam**
quīs	**queās**	nequīs	**nequeās**
quit	**queat**	nequit	nequeat
quīmus	**queāmus**	nequīmus	**nequeāmus**
quītis	——	**nequītis**	——
queunt	**queant**	**nequeunt**	**nequeant**
IMPERFECT		IMPERFECT	
quībam	——	——	**nequīrem**
quībat	**quīret**	**nequībat**	**nequīret**
——	quīrent	nequībant	nequīrent
FUTURE		FUTURE	
quībō		nequībit	
quībunt		nequībunt	
PERFECT		PERFECT	
quīvī	——	nequīvī	**nequīverim**
——	——	nequīstī	——
quīvit	quīverit (-ierit)	nequīvit (nequiit)	**nequīverit**
quīvērunt (-ēre)	quierint	nequīvērunt (-quiēre)	**nequīverint**
PLUPERFECT		PLUPERFECT	
——	——	**nequīverat** (-ierat)	**nequīvisset** (-quīsset)
——	quīvissent	**nequīverant** (-ierant)	nequīssent
INFINITIVE			
quīre	quīsse	**nequīre**	**nequīvisse** (-quīsse)
PARTICIPLES			
quiēns		**nequiēns, nequeuntēs**	

NOTE. — A few passive forms are used with passive infinitives: as, **quītur, queuntur, quitus sum, queātur, queantur, nequītur, nequitum**; but none of these occurs in classic prose.

e. **Quaesō**, *I ask, beg* (original form of **quaerō**), has —

INDIC.	PRES.	quaesō, quaesŭmus

NOTE. — Other forms of **quaesō** are found occasionally in early Latin. For the perfect system (**quaesīvī**, etc.), see **quaerō** (§ 211. *d*).

f. **Ovāre**, *to triumph*, has the following: —

INDIC.	PRES.	ovās, ovat
SUBJV.	PRES.	ovet
	IMPF.	ovāret
PART.		ovāns, ovātūrus, ovātus
GER.		ovandī

g. A few verbs are found chiefly in the Imperative: —

PRES. singular **salvē**, plural **salvēte**, FUT. **salvētō**, *hail!* (from **salvus**, *safe and sound*). An infinitive **salvēre** and the indicative forms **salveō**, **salvētis**, **salvēbis**, are rare.

PRES. singular **avē** (or **havē**), plural **avēte**, FUT. **avētō**, *hail* or *farewell*. An infinitive **avēre** also occurs.

PRES. singular **cĕdo**, plural **cĕdite** (**cette**), *give, tell.*

PRES. singular **apage**, *begone* (properly a Greek word).

IMPERSONAL VERBS

207. Many verbs, from their meaning, appear only in the *third person singular*, the *infinitive*, and the *gerund*. These are called Impersonal Verbs, as having no personal subject.[1] The passive of many intransitive verbs is used in the same way.

CONJ. I	II	III	IV	PASS. CONJ. I
it is plain	*it is allowed*	*it chances*	*it results*	*it is fought*
cōnstat	licet	accidit	ēvenit	pūgnātur
cōnstābat	licēbat	accidēbat	ēveniēbat	pūgnābātur
cōnstābit	licēbit	accidet	ēveniet	pūgnābitur
cōnstitit	licuit, -itum est	accidit	ēvēnit	pūgnātum est
cōnstiterat	licuerat	acciderat	ēvēnerat	pūgnātum erat
cōnstiterit	licuerit	acciderit	ēvēnerit	pūgnātum erit
cōnstet	liceat	accidat	ēveniat	pūgnētur
cōnstāret	licēret	accideret	ēvenīret	pūgnārētur
cōnstiterit	licuerit	acciderit	ēvēnerit	pūgnātum sit
cōnstitisset	licuisset	accidisset	ēvēnisset	pūgnātum esset
cōnstāre	licēre	accidĕre	ēvenīre	pūgnārī
cōnstitisse	licuisse	accidisse	ēvēnisse	pūgnātum esse
-stātūrum esse	-itūrum esse	——	-tūrum esse	pūgnātum īrī

[1] With impersonal verbs the word *it* is used in English, having usually no representative in Latin, though **id**, **hōc**, **illud**, are often used nearly in the same way.

208. Impersonal Verbs may be classified as follows: —

a. Verbs expressing the *operations of nature* and the *time of day*: —

vesperāscit (inceptive, § 263. 1), *it grows late.*
lūcīscit hōc, *it is getting light.*
grandinat, *it hails.*
pluit, *it rains.*
ningit, *it snows.*
fulgurat, *it lightens.*
tonat, *it thunders.*
rōrat, *the dew falls.*

NOTE. — In these no subject is distinctly thought of. Sometimes, however, the verb is used personally with the name of a divinity as the subject: as, **Iuppiter tonat,** *Jupiter thunders.* In poetry other subjects are occasionally used: as, **fundae saxa pluunt,** *the slings rain stones.*

b. Verbs of *feeling*, where the person who is the proper subject becomes the object, as being himself affected by the feeling expressed in the verb (§ 354. *b*): —

miseret, *it grieves.*
piget, *it disgusts.*
taedet, *it wearies.*
paenitet (poenitet), *it repents.*
pudet, *it shames.*
miseret mē, *I pity* (it distresses me); **pudet mē,** *I am ashamed.*

NOTE. — Such verbs often have also a passive form: as, **misereor,** *I pity* (am moved to pity); and occasionally other parts: as, **paenitūrus** (as from †**paeniō**), **paenitendus, pudendus, pertaesum est, pigitum est.**

c. Verbs which have a *phrase* or *clause* as their subject (cf. §§ 454, 569. 2): —

accidit, contingit, ēvenit, obtingit, obvenit, fit, *it happens.*
libet, *it pleases.*
licet, *it is permitted.*
certum est, *it is resolved.*
cōnstat, *it is clear.*
placet, *it seems good* (pleases).
vidētur, *it seems, seems good.*
decet, *it is becoming.*
dēlectat, iuvat, *it delights.*
oportet, *it is fitting, ought.*
necesse est, *it is needful.*
praestat, *it is better.*
interest, rēfert, *it concerns.*
vacat, *there is leisure.*
restat, superest, *it remains.*

NOTE. — Many of these verbs may be used personally; as, **vacō,** *I have leisure.* **Libet** and **licet** have also the passive forms **libitum (licitum) est** etc. The participles **libēns** and **licēns** are used as adjectives.

d. The *passive of intransitive verbs* is very often used impersonally (see synopsis in § 207): —

ventum est, *they came* (there was coming).
pūgnātur, *there is fighting* (it is fought).
ītur, *some one goes* (it is gone).
parcitur mihi, *I am spared* (it is spared to me, see § 372).

NOTE. — The impersonal use of the passive proceeds from its original *reflexive* (or *middle*) meaning, the action being regarded as *accomplishing itself* (compare the French *cela se fait*).

Classified Lists of Verbs

First Conjugation

209. There are about 360 simple verbs of the First Conjugation, most of them formed directly on a noun- or adjective-stem:

armō, *arm* (arma, *arms*); caecō, *to blind* (caecus, *blind*); exsulō, *be an exile* (exsul, *an exile*) (§ 259).

Their conjugation is usually regular, like amō; though of many only a few forms are found in use.

a. The following verbs form their Perfect and Supine stems irregularly. Those marked * have also regular forms.

crepō, crepuī (-crepāvī), -crepit-, *resound.*
cubō, *cubuī, -cubit-, *lie down.*
dō, dăre, dedī, dăt-, *give* (DA).
domō, domuī, domit-, *subdue.*
fricō, fricuī, *frict-, *rub.*
iuvō (ad-iuvō), iūvī, iūt-,[1] *help.*
micō, micuī, ——, *glitter.*
necō, *necuī, necāt- (-nect-), *kill.*[2]
plicō, *-plicuī, *-plicit-, *fold.*
pōtō, pōtāvī, *pōt-, *drink.*
secō, secuī, sect-, *cut.*
sonō, sonuī, sonit-,[1] *sound.*
stō, stetī, -stat- (-stit-), *stand.*
tonō, tonuī, *-tonit-, *thunder.*
vetō, vetuī, vetit-, *forbid.*

NOTE.—Compounds of these verbs have the following forms:—

crepō: *con-crepuī, dis-crepuī* or *-crepāvī; in-crepuī* or *-crepāvī.*

dō: *circum-, inter-, pessum-, satis-, super-, vēnum-dō, -dedī, -dat-,* of the first conjugation. Other compounds belong to the root DHA, *put,* and are of the third conjugation: as, *condō, condĕre, condidī, conditum.*

micō: *dī-micāvī, -micāt-; ē-micuī, -micāt-.*

plicō: *re-, sub- (sup-), multi-plicō, -plicāvī, -plicāt-; ex-plicō* (unfold), *-uī, -it-;* (explain), *-āvī, -āt-; im-plicō, -āvī (-uī), -ātum (-itum).*

stō: *cōn-stō, -stitī, (-stātūrus); ad-, re-stō, -stitī, ——; ante- (anti-), inter-, super-stō, -stetī, ——; circum-stō, -stetī (-stitī), ——; prae-stō, -stitī, -stit- (-stāt-); dī-stō, ex-stō,* no perfect or supine (future participle *ex-stātūrus*).

Second Conjugation

210. There are nearly 120 simple verbs of the Second Conjugation, most of them denominative verbs of condition, having a corresponding noun and adjective from the same root, and an inceptive in -scō (§ 263. 1):—

caleō, *be warm;* calor, *warmth;* calidus, *warm;* calēscō, *grow warm.*
timeō, *fear;* timor, *fear;* timidus, *timid;* per-timēsco, *to take fright.*

[1] Future Participle also in -ātūrus (either in the simple verb or in composition).

[2] Necō has regularly necāvī, necātum, except in composition.

a. Most verbs of the second conjugation are inflected like **moneō**, but many lack the supine (as, **arceō**, *ward off;* **careō**, *lack;* **egeō**, *need;* **timeō**, *fear*), and a number have neither perfect nor supine (as, **maereō**, *be sad*).

b. The following keep ē in all the systems: —

dēleō, *destroy*	**dēlēre**	**dēlēvī**	**dēlētum**
fleō, *weep*	**flēre**	**flēvī**	**flētum**
neō, *sew*	**nēre**	**nēvī**	[**nētum**]
vieō, *plait*	**viēre**	[**viēvī**]	**viētum**
com-pleō, *fill up*[1]	**-plēre**	**-plēvī**	**-plētum**

c. The following show special irregularities: —

algeō, alsī, *be cold.*
ārdeō, ārsī, ārsūrus, *burn.*
audeō, ausus sum, *dare.*
augeō, auxī, auct-, *increase.*
caveō, cāvī, caut-, *care.*
cēnseō, cēnsuī, cēns-, *value.*
cieō, cīvī, cit-, *excite.*
doceō, docuī, doct-, *teach.*
faveō, fāvī, faut-, *favor.*
ferveō, fervī (ferbuī), ——, *glow.*
foveō, fōvī, fōt-, *cherish.*
fulgeō, fulsī, ——, *shine.*
gaudeō, gāvīsus sum, *rejoice.*
haereō, haesī, haes-, *cling.*
indulgeō, indulsī, indult-, *indulge.*
iubeō, iussī, iuss-, *order.*
liqueō, licuī (līquī), ——, *melt.*
lūceō, lūxī, ——, *shine.*
lūgeō, lūxī, ——, *mourn.*
maneō, mānsī, māns-, *wait.*
misceō, -cuī, mixt- (mist-), *mix.*
mordeō, momordī, mors-, *bite.*
moveō, mōvī, mōt-, *move.*
mulceō, mulsī, muls-, *soothe.*
mulgeō, mulsī, muls-, *milk.*
(cō)nīveō, -nīvī (-nīxī), ——, *wink.*
(ab)oleō, -olēvī, -olit-, *destroy.*
pendeō, pependī, -pēns-, *hang.*
prandeō, prandī, prāns-, *dine.*
rīdeō, rīsī, -rīs-, *laugh.*
sedeō, sēdī, sess-, *sit.*
soleō, solitus sum, *be wont.*
sorbeō, sorbuī (sorpsī), ——, *suck.*
spondeō, spopondī, spōns-, *pledge.*
strīdeō, strīdī, ——, *whiz.*
suādeō, suāsī, suās-, *urge.*
teneō (-tineō), tenuī, -tent-, *hold.*
tergeō, tersī, ters-, *wipe.*
tondeō, -totondī (-tondī), tōns-, *shear.*
torqueō, torsī, tort-, *twist.*
torreō, torruī, tost-, *roast.*
turgeō, tursī, ——, *swell.*
urgeō, ursī, ——, *urge.*
videō, vīdī, vīs-, *see.*
voveō, vōvī, vōt-, *vow.*

Third Conjugation

211. The following lists include most simple verbs of the Third Conjugation, classed according to the formation of the Perfect Stem: —

a. Forming the perfect stem in **s (x)** (§ 177. *b* and note): —

angō, ānxī, ——, *choke.*
carpō, carpsī, carpt-, *pluck.*
cēdō, cessī, cess-, *yield.*
cingō, cīnxī, cīnct-, *bind.*
claudō, clausī, claus-, *shut.*
cōmō, cōmpsī, cōmpt-, *comb, deck.*
coquō, coxī, coct-, *cook.*
-cutiō, -cussī, -cuss-, *shake.*

[1] And other compounds of **-pleō**.

dēmō, dēmpsī, dēmpt-, *take away.*
dīcō, dīxī, dict-, *say.*
dīvidō, dīvīsī, dīvīs-, *divide.*
dūcō, dūxī, duct-, *guide.*
ēmungō, -mūnxī, -mūnct-, *clean out.*
fīgō, fīxī, fīx-, *fix.*
fingō [FIG], fīnxī, fict-, *fashion.*
flectō, flexī, flex-, *bend.*
-flīgō, -flīxī, -flīct-, ——, *smite.*
fluō, flūxī, flux-, *flow.*
frendō, ——, frēs- (fress-), *gnash.*
frīgō, frīxī, frīct-, *fry.*
gerō, gessī, gest-, *carry.*
iungō, iūnxī, iūnct-, *join.*
laedō, laesī, laes-, *hurt.*
-liciō, -lexī, -lect-, *entice* (ēlicuī, -licit-).
lūdo, lūsī, lūs-, *play.*
mergō, mersī, mers-, *plunge.*
mittō, mīsī, miss-, *send.*
nectō [NEC], nexī (nexuī), nex-, *weave.*
nūbō, nūpsi, nūpt-, *marry.*
pectō, pexī, pex-, *comb.*
pergō, perrēxī, perrēct-, *go on.*
pingō [PIG], pīnxī, pict-, *paint.*
plangō [PLAG], plānxī, plānct-, *beat.*
plaudō, plausī, plaus-, *applaud.*
plectō, plexī, plex-, *braid.*
premō, pressī, press-, *press.*
prōmō, -mpsī, -mpt-, *bring out.*
quatiō, (-cussī), quass-, *shake.*
rādō, rāsī, rās-, *scrape.*
regō, rēxī, rēct-, *rule.*
rēpō, rēpsī, ——, *creep.*
rōdō, rōsī, rōs-, *gnaw.*
scalpō, scalpsī, scalpt-, *scrape.*
scrībō, scrīpsī, scrīpt-, *write.*
sculpō, sculpsī, sculpt-, *carve.*
serpō, serpsī, ——, *crawl.*
spargō, sparsī, spars-, *scatter.*
-spiciō, -spexī, -spect-, *view.*
-stinguō, -stīnxī, -stīnct-, *quench.*
stringō, strīnxī, strict-, *bind.*
struō, strūxī, strūct-, *build.*
sūgō, sūxī, sūct-, *suck.*
sūmō, sūmpsī, sūmpt-, *take.*
surgō, surrēxī, surrēct-, *rise.*
tegō, tēxī, tēct-, *shelter.*
temnō, -tempsī, -tempt-, *despise.*
tergō, tersī, ters-, *wipe.*
tingō, tīnxī, tīnct-, *stain.*
trahō, trāxī, trāct-, *drag.*
trūdō, trūsī, trūs-, *thrust.*
unguō (ungō), ūnxī, ūnct-, *anoint.*
ūrō, ussī, ust-, *burn.*
vādō, -vāsī, -vās-, *go.*
vehō, vēxī, vect-, *draw.*
vīvō, vīxī, vīct-, *live.*

b. Reduplicated in the perfect (§ 177. *c*): —

cadō, cecīdī, cās-, *fall.*
caedō, cecīdī, caes-, *cut.*
canō, cecinī, ——, *sing.*
currō, cucurrī, curs-, *run.*
discō [DIC], didicī, ——, *learn.*
-dō [DHA], -didī, -dit- (as in ab-dō, etc., with crēdō, vēndō), *put.*
fallō, fefellī, fals-, *deceive.*
pangō [PAG], pepigī (-pēgī), pāct-, *fasten, fix, bargain.*
parcō, pepercī (parsī), (parsūrus), *spare.*
pariō, peperī, part- (paritūrus), *bring forth.*
pellō, pepulī, puls-, *drive.*
pendō, pependī, pēns-, *weigh.*
poscō, poposcī, ——, *demand.*
pungō [PUG], pupugī (-pūnxī), pūnct-, *prick.*
sistō [STA], stitī, stat-, *stop.*
tangō [TAG], tetigī, tāct-, *touch.*
tendō [TEN], tetendī (-tendī), tent-, *stretch.*
tundō [TUD], tutudī, tūns- (-tūs-), *beat.*

c. Adding **u** (**v**) to the verb-root (§ 177. *a*): —

alō, aluī, alt- (alit-), *nourish.*
cernō, crēvī, -crēt-, *decree.*
colō, coluī, cult-, *dwell, till.*
compēscō, compēscuī, ——, *restrain.*
cōnsulō, -luī, cōnsult-, *consult.*
crēscō, crēvī, crēt-, *increase.*

-cumbō [CUB], **-cubuī, -cubit-**, *lie down.*
depsō, depsuī, depst-, *knead.*
fremō, fremuī, ——, *roar.*
gemō, gemuī, ——, *groan.*
gignō [GEN], **genuī, genit-**, *beget.*
metō, messuī, -mess-, *reap.*
molō, moluī, molit-, *grind.*
occulō, occuluī, occult-, *hide.*
(ad)olēscō, -ēvī, -ult-, *grow up.*
pāscō, pāvī, pāst-, *feed.*
percellō, -culī, -culs-, *upset.*
pōnō [POS], **posuī, posit-**, *put.*
quiēscō, quiēvī, quiēt-, *rest.*
rapiō, rapuī, rapt-, *seize.*
scīscō, scīvī, scīt-, *decree.*
serō, sēvī, sat-, *sow.*
serō, seruī, sert-, *entwine.*
sinō, sīvī, sit-, *permit.*
spernō, sprēvī, sprēt-, *scorn.*
sternō, strāvī, strāt-, *strew.*
stertō, -stertuī, ——, *snore.*
strepō, strepuī, ——, *sound.*
suēscō, suēvī, suēt-, *be wont.*
texō, texuī, text-, *weave.*
tremō, tremuī, ——, *tremble.*
vomō, vomuī, ——, *vomit.*

d. Adding **iv** to the verb-root (§ 177. *f*): —

arcessō,[1] **-īvī, arcessīt-**, *summon.*
capessō, capessīvī, ——, *undertake.*
cupiō, cupīvī, cupīt-, *desire.*
incessō, incessīvī, ——, *attack.*
lacessō, lacessīvī, lacessīt-, *provoke.*
petō, petīvī, petīt-, *seek.*
quaerō, quaesīvī, quaesīt-, *seek.*
rudō, rudīvī, ——, *bray.*
sapiō, sapīvī, ——, *be wise.*
terō, trīvī, trīt-, *rub.*

e. Lengthening the vowel of the root (cf. § 177. *d*): —

agō, ēgī, āct-, *drive.*
capiō, cēpī, capt-, *take.*
edō, ēdī, ēsum, *eat* (see § 201).
emō, ēmī, ēmpt-, *buy.*
faciō, fēcī, fact-, *make* (see § 204).
fodiō, fōdī, foss-, *dig.*
frangō [FRAG], **frēgī, frāct-**, *break.*
fugiō, fūgī, (fugitūrus), *flee.*
fundō [FUD], **fūdī, fūs-**, *pour.*
iaciō, iēcī, iact-, *throw* (**-iciō, -iect-**).
lavō, lāvī, lōt- (laut-), wash (also regular of first conjugation).
legō,[2] **lēgī, lēct-**, *gather.*
linō [LI], **lēvī (līvī), lit-**, *smear.*
linquō [LIC], **-līquī, -lict-**, *leave.*
nōscō [GNO], **nōvī, nōt- (cō-gnit-, ā-gnit-, ad-gnit-)**, *know.*
rumpō [RUP], **rūpī, rupt-**, *burst.*
scabō, scābī, ——, *scratch.*
vincō [VIC], **vīcī, vict-**, *conquer.*

f. Retaining the present stem or verb-root (cf. § 177. *e*): —

acuō, -uī, -ūt-, *sharpen.*
arguō, -uī, -ūt-, *accuse.*
bibō, bibī, (pōtus), *drink.*
-cendō, -cendī, -cēns-, *kindle.*
(con)gruō, -uī, ——, *agree.*
cūdō, -cūdī, -cūs-, *forge.*
facessō, -iī (facessī), facessīt-, *execute*
-fendō, -fendī, -fēns-, *ward off.*
findō [FID], **fidī,**[3] **fiss-**, *split.*
īcō, īcī, ict-, *hit.*
imbuō, -uī, -ūt-, *give a taste of.*
luō, luī, -lūt-, *wash.*
mandō, mandī, māns-, *chew.*
metuō, -uī, -ūt-, *fear.*
minuō, -uī, -ūt-, *lessen.*
-nuō, -nuī, ——, *nod.*
pandō, pandī, pāns- (pass-), *open.*
pīnsō, -sī, pīns- (pīnst-, pīst-), *bruise.*
prehendō, -hendī, -hēns-, *seize.*
ruō, ruī, rut- (ruitūrus), *fall.*

[1] Sometimes **accersō**, etc.
[2] The following compounds of **legō** have **-lēxī**: **dīligō, intellegō, neglegō.**
[3] In this the perfect stem is the same as the verb-root, having lost the reduplication (§ 177. *c.* N.).

scandō, -scendī, -scēnsus, *climb.*
scindō [SCID], scidī,[1] sciss-, *tear.*
sīdō, sīdī (-sēdī), -sess-, *settle.*
solvō, solvī, solūt-, *loose, pay.*
spuō, -uī, ——, *spit.*
statuō, -uī, -ūt-, *establish.*
sternuo, -uī, ——, *sneeze.*
strīdō, strīdī, ——, *whiz.*
suō, suī, sūt-, *sew.*
(ex)uō, -uī, -ūt-, *put off.*
tribuō, -uī, -ūt-, *assign.*
vellō, vellī (-vulsī), vuls-, *pluck.*
verrō, -verrī, vers-, *sweep.*
vertō, vertī, vers-, *turn.*
vīsō [VID], vīsī, vīs-, *visit.*
volvō, volvī, volūt-, *turn.*

NOTE.—Several have no perfect or supine: as, claudō, *limp;* fatīscō, *gape;* hīscō, *yawn;* tollō (sustulī, sublātum, supplied from sufferō), *raise;* vergō, *incline.*

Fourth Conjugation

212. There are—besides a few deponents and some regular derivatives in -ŭriō, as, ēsuriō, *be hungry* (cf. § 263. 4)—about 60 verbs of this conjugation, a large proportion of them being *descriptive* verbs: like—

crōciō, *croak;* mūgiō, *bellow;* tinniō, *tinkle.*

a. Most verbs of the Fourth Conjugation are conjugated regularly, like audiō, though a number lack the supine.

b. The following verbs show special peculiarities:—

amiciō, amixī (-cuī), amict-, *clothe.*
aperiō, aperuī, apert-, *open.*
comperiō, -perī, compert-, *find.*
farciō, farsī, fartum, *stuff.*
feriō, ——, ——, *strike.*
fulciō, fulsī, fult-, *prop.*
hauriō, hausī, haust- (hausūrus), *drain.*
operiō, operuī, opert-, *cover.*
reperiō, repperī, repert-, *find.*
saepiō, saepsī, saept-, *hedge in.*
saliō (-siliō), saluī (saliī), [salt- (-sult-)], *leap.*
sanciō [SAC], sānxī, sānct-, *sanction.*
sarciō, sarsī, sart-, *patch.*
sentiō, sēnsī, sēns-, *feel.*
sepeliō, sepelīvī, sepult-, *bury.*
veniō, vēnī, vent-, *come.*
vinciō, vīnxī, vīnct-, *bind.*

For Index of Verbs, see pp. 436 ff.

[1] See footnote 3, page 124.

PARTICLES

213. Adverbs, Prepositions, Conjunctions, and Interjections are called Particles.

In their origin Adverbs, Prepositions, and Conjunctions are either (1) *case-forms*, actual or extinct, or (2) *compounds* and *phrases*.

Particles cannot always be distinctly classified, for many adverbs are used also as prepositions and many as conjunctions (§§ 219 and 222).

ADVERBS

Derivation of Adverbs

214. Adverbs are regularly formed from Adjectives as follows:

a. From adjectives of the *first and second declensions* by changing the characteristic vowel of the stem to **-ē**: as, **cārē**, *dearly*, from **cārus**, *dear* (stem **cāro-**); **amīcē**, *like a friend*, from **amīcus**, *friendly* (stem **amīco-**).

NOTE.—The ending **-ē** is a relic of an old ablative in **-ēd** (cf. § 43. N. 1).

b. From adjectives of the *third declension* by adding **-ter** to the stem. Stems in **nt-** (nom. **-ns**) lose the **t-**. All others are treated as **i**-stems:—

fortiter, *bravely*, from **fortis** (stem **forti-**), *brave*.
ācriter, *eagerly*, from **ācer** (stem **ācri-**), *eager*.
vigilanter, *watchfully*, from **vigilāns** (stem **vigilant-**).
prūdenter, *prudently*, from **prūdēns** (stem **prūdent-**).
aliter, *otherwise*, from **alius** (old stem **ali-**).

NOTE.—This suffix is perhaps the same as **-ter** in the Greek -τερος and in **uter**, **alter**. If so, these adverbs are in origin either neuter accusatives (cf. *d*) or masculine nominatives.

c. Some adjectives of the first and second declensions have adverbs of both forms (**-ē** and **-ter**). Thus **dūrus**, *hard*, has both **dūrē** and **dūriter**; **miser**, *wretched*, has both **miserē** and **miseriter**.

d. The *neuter accusative* of adjectives and pronouns is often used as an adverb: as, **multum**, *much*; **facilĕ**, *easily*; **quid**, *why*.

This is the origin of the ending **-ius** in the comparative degree of adverbs (§ 218): as, **ācrius**, *more keenly* (positive **ācriter**); **facilius**, *more easily* (positive **facilĕ**).

NOTE.—These adverbs are strictly cognate accusatives (§ 390).

e. The *ablative singular neuter* or (less commonly) *feminine* of adjectives, pronouns, and nouns may be used adverbially: as, **falsō**, *falsely*; **citŏ**, *quickly* (with shortened o); **rēctā** (**viā**), *straight* (*straightway*); **crēbrō**, *frequently*; **volgō**, *commonly*; **fortĕ**, *by chance*; **spontĕ**, *of one's own accord.*

NOTE. — Some adverbs are derived from adjectives not in use: as, **abundē**, *plentifully* (as if from †**abundus**; cf. **abundō**, *abound*); **saepĕ**, *often* (as if from †**saepis**, *dense, close-packed*; cf. **saepēs**, *hedge*, and **saepiō**, *hedge in*).

215. Further examples of Adverbs and other Particles which are in origin case-forms of nouns or pronouns are given below. In some the case is not obvious, and in some it is doubtful.

1. Neuter Accusative forms: **nōn** (for **nē-oinom**, later **ūnum**), *not*; **iterum** (comparative of **i-**, stem of **is**), *a second time*; **dēmum** (superlative of **dē**, *down*), *at last.*

2. Feminine Accusatives: **partim**, *partly*. So **statim**, *on the spot*; **saltim**, *at least* (generally **saltem**), from lost nouns in **-tis** (genitive **-tis**). Thus **-tim** became a regular adverbial termination; and by means of it adverbs were made from many noun- and verb-stems immediately, without the intervention of any form which could have an accusative in **-tim**: as, **sēparātim**, *separately*, from **sēparātus**, *separate*. Some adverbs that appear to be feminine accusative are possibly instrumental: as, **palam**, *openly*; **perperam**, *wrongly*; **tam**, *so*; **quam**, *as.*

3. Plural Accusatives: as, **aliās**, *elsewhere*; **forās**, *out of doors* (as end of motion). So perhaps **quia**, *because.*

4. Ablative or Instrumental forms: **quā**, *where*; **intrā**, *within*; **extrā**, *outside*; **quī**, *how*; **aliquī**, *somehow*; **forīs**, *out of doors*; **quō**, *whither*; **adeō**, *to that degree*; **ultrō**, *beyond*; **citrō**, *this side* (as end of motion); **retrō**, *back*; **illōc** (for †**illō-ce**), weakened to **illūc**, *thither*. Those in **-trō** are from comparative stems (cf. **ūls**, **cis**, **re-**).

5. Locative forms: **ibi**, *there*; **ubi**, *where*; **illī**, **illī-c**, *there*; **peregrī** (**peregrē**), *abroad*; **hīc** (for †**hī-ce**), *here*. Also the compounds **hodiē** (probably for †**hōdiē**), *to-day*; **perendiē**, *day after to-morrow.*

6. Of uncertain formation: (1) those in **-tus** (usually preceded by **i**), with an ablative meaning: as, **funditus**, *from the bottom, utterly*; **dīvīnitus**, *from above, providentially*; **intus**, *within*; **penitus**, *within*; (2) those in **-dem**, **-dam**, **-dō**: as, **quidem**, *indeed*; **quondam**, *once*; **quandō** (cf. **dōnec**), *when*; (3) **dum** (probably accusative of time), *while*; **iam**, *now.*

216. A phrase or short sentence has sometimes grown together into an adverb (cf. *notwithstanding, nevertheless, besides*): —

> **postmodo**, *presently* (a short time after).
> **dēnuō** (for **dē novō**), *anew.*
> **vidēlicet** (for **vidē licet**), *to wit* (see, you may).
> **nihilōminus**, *nevertheless* (by nothing the less).

NOTE. — Other examples are: — **anteā**, old **antideā**, *before* (**ante eā**, probably ablative or instrumental); **īlicō** (**in locō**), *on the spot, immediately*; **prōrsus**, *absolutely* (**prō vorsus**, *straight ahead*); **rūrsus** (**re-vorsus**), *again*; **quotannīs**, *yearly* (**quot annīs**, *as many years as there are*); **quam-ob-rem**, *wherefore*; **cōminus**, *hand to hand* (**con manus**); **ēminus**, *at long range* (**ex manus**); **nīmīrum**, *without doubt* (**nī mīrum**); **ob-viam** (as in **īre obviam**, *to go to meet*); **prīdem** (cf. **prae** and **-dem** in **i-dem**), *for some time*; **forsan** (**fors an**), *perhaps* (it's a chance whether); **forsitan** (**fors sit an**), *perhaps* (it would be a chance whether); **scīlicet** (†**scī**, **licet**), *that is to say* (know, you may; cf. **ī-licet**, *you may go*); **āctūtum** (**āctū**, *on the act*, and **tum**, *then*).

Classification of Adverbs

217. The classes of Adverbs, with examples, are as follows: —

a. Adverbs of Place[1]

hīc, *here.*	**hūc**, *hither.*	**hinc**, *hence.*	**hāc**, *by this way.*
ibi, *there.*	**eō**, *thither.*	**inde**, *thence.*	**eā**, *by that way.*
istīc, *there.*	**istūc**, *thither.*	**istinc**, *thence.*	**istā**, *by that way.*
illīc, *there.*	**illūc**, *thither.*	**illinc**, *thence.*	**illā** (**illāc**), " "
ubi, *where.*	**quō**, *whither.*	**unde**, *whence.*	**quā**, *by what way.*
alicubi, *somewhere.*	**aliquō**, *somewhither, (to) somewhere.*	**alicunde**, *from somewhere.*	**aliquā**, *by some way.*
ibīdem, *in the same place.*	**eōdem**, *to the same place.*	**indidem**, *from the same place.*	**eādem**, *by the same way.*
alibī, *elsewhere, in another place.*	**aliō**, *elsewhere, to another place.*	**aliunde**, *from another place.*	**aliā**, *in another way.*
ubiubi, *wherever.*	**quōquō**, *whithersoever.*	**undecunque**, *whencesoever.*	**quāquā**, *in whatever way.*
ubivīs, *anywhere, where you will.*	**quōvīs**, *anywhere, whither you will.*	**undique**, *from every quarter.*	**quāvīs**, *by whatever way.*
sīcubi, *if anywhere.*	**sīquō**, *if anywhere (anywhither).*	**sīcunde**, *if from anywhere.*	**sīquā**, *if anywhere.*
nēcubi, *lest anywhere.*	**nēquō**, *lest anywhither.*	**nēcunde**, *lest from anywhere.*	**nēquā**, *lest anywhere.*

Note. — The demonstrative adverbs **hīc**, **ibi**, **istīc**, **illī**, **illīc**, and their correlatives, correspond in signification with the pronouns **hīc**, **is**, **iste**, **ille** (see § 146), and are often equivalent to these pronouns with a preposition: as, **inde** = **ab eō**, etc. So the relative or interrogative **ubi** corresponds with **quī** (**quis**), **ali-cubi** with **aliquis**, **ubiubi** with **quisquis**, **sī-cubi** with **sīquis** (see §§ 147–151, with the table of correlatives in § 152).

ūsque, *all the way to;* **usquam**, *anywhere;* **nusquam**, *nowhere;* **citrō**, *to this side;* **intrō**, *inwardly;* **ultrō**, *beyond* (or *freely*, i.e. beyond what is required); **porrō**, *further on.*

quōrsum (for **quō vorsum**, *whither turned?*), *to what end?* **hōrsum**, *this way;* **prōrsum**, *forward* (**prōrsus**, *utterly*); **intrōrsum**, *inwardly;* **retrōrsum**, *backward;* **sūrsum**, *upward;* **deorsum**, *downward;* **seorsum**, *apart;* **aliōrsum**, *another way.*

b. Adverbs of Time

quandō, *when?* (interrogative); **cum** (**quom**), *when* (relative); **ut**, *when, as;* **nunc**, *now;* **tunc** (**tum**), *then;* **mox**, *presently;* **iam**, *already;* **dum**, *while;* **iam diū**, **iam dūdum**, **iam prīdem**, *long ago, long since.*

[1] All these adverbs were originally case-forms of pronouns. The forms in **-bi** and **-īc** are locative, those in **-ō** and **-ūc**, **-ā** and **-āc**, ablative (see § 215); those in **-inc** are from **-im** (of uncertain origin) with the particle **-ce** added (thus **illim**, **illin-c**).

prīmum (**prīmō**), *first;* **deinde** (**posteā**), *next after;* **postrēmum** (**postrēmō**), *finally;* **posteāquam, postquam,** *when* (*after that, as soon as*).
umquam (**unquam**), *ever;* **numquam** (**nunquam**), *never;* **semper,** *always.*
aliquandō, *at some time, at length;* **quandōque** (**quandōcumque**), *whenever;* **dēnique,** *at last.*
quotiēns (**quotiēs**), *how often;* **totiēns,** *so often;* **aliquotiēns,** *a number of times.*
cotīdiē, *every day;* **hodiē,** *to-day;* **herī,** *yesterday;* **crās,** *to-morrow;* **prīdiē,** *the day before;* **postrīdiē,** *the day after;* **in diēs,** *from day to day.*
nōndum, *not yet;* **necdum,** *nor yet;* **vixdum,** *scarce yet;* **quam prīmum,** *as soon as possible;* **saepe,** *often;* **crēbrō,** *frequently;* **iam nōn,** *no longer.*

c. Adverbs of Manner, Degree, or Cause

quam, *how, as;* **tam,** *so;* **quamvīs,** *however much, although;* **paene,** *almost;* **magis,** *more;* **valdē,** *greatly;* **vix,** *hardly.*
cūr, quārē, *why;* **ideō, idcircō, propterea,** *on this account, because;* **eō,** *therefore;* **ergō, itaque, igitur,** *therefore.*
ita, sīc, *so;* **ut** (**utī**), *as, how;* **utut, utcumque,** *however.*

d. Interrogative Particles

an, -ne, anne, utrum, utrumne, num, *whether.*
nōnne, annōn, *whether not;* **numquid, ecquid,** *whether at all.*

On the use of the Interrogative Particles, see §§ 332, 335.

e. Negative Particles

nōn, *not* (in simple denial); **haud, minimē,** *not* (in contradiction); **nē,** *not* (in prohibition); **nēve, neu,** *nor;* **nēdum,** *much less.*
nē, *lest;* **neque, nec,** *nor;* **nē . . . quidem,** *not even.*
nōn modo . . . vērum (**sed**) **etiam,** *not only . . . but also.*
nōn modo . . . sed nē . . . quidem, *not only* NOT . . . *but not even.*
sī minus, *if not;* **quō minus** (**quōminus**), *so as not.*
quīn (relative), *but that;* (interrogative), *why not?*
nē, nec (in composition), *not;* so in **nesciō,** *I know not;* **negō,** *I say no* (**âiō,** *I say yes*); **negōtium,** *business* (†**nec-ōtium**); **nēmō** (**nē-** and **hemō,** old form of **homō**), *no one;* **nē quis,** *lest any one;* **neque enim,** *for . . . not.*

For the use of Negative Particles, see § 325 ff.
For the Syntax and Peculiar uses of Adverbs, see § 320 ff.

Comparison of Adverbs

218. The Comparative of Adverbs is the neuter accusative of the comparative of the corresponding adjective; the Superlative is the Adverb in **-ē** formed regularly from the superlative of the Adjective: —

cārē, *dearly* (from **cārus**, *dear*); **cārius**, **cārissimē**.
miserē (**miseriter**), *wretchedly* (from **miser**, *wretched*); **miserius**, **miserrimē**.
leviter (from **levis**, *light*); **levius**, **levissimē**.
audācter (**audāciter**) (from **audāx**, *bold*); **audācius**, **audācissimē**.
benĕ, *well* (from **bonus**, *good*); **melius**, **optimē**.
malĕ, *ill* (from **malus**, *bad*); **pêius**, **pessimē**.

a. The following are irregular or defective:—

diū, *long* (in time); **diūtius**, **diūtissimē**.
potius, *rather;* **potissimum**, *first of all, in preference to all.*
saepe, *often;* **saepius**, *oftener, again;* **saepissimē**.
satis, *enough;* **satius**, *preferable.*
secus, *otherwise;* **sētius**, *worse.*
multum (**multō**), **magis**, **maximē**, *much, more, most.*
parum, *not enough;* **minus**, *less;* **minimē**, *least.*
nūper, *newly;* **nūperrimē**.
temperē, *seasonably;* **temperius**.

NOTE.—In poetry the comparative **mage** is sometimes used instead of **magis**.

PREPOSITIONS

219. Prepositions were not originally distinguished from Adverbs in form or meaning, but have become specialized in use. They developed comparatively late in the history of language. In the early stages of language development the cases alone were sufficient to indicate the sense, but, as the force of the case-endings weakened, adverbs were used for greater precision (cf. § 338). These adverbs, from their habitual association with particular cases, became Prepositions; but many retained also their independent function as adverbs.

Most prepositions are true case-forms: as, the comparative ablatives **extrā**, **īnfrā**, **suprā** (for †**exterā**, †**īnferā**, †**superā**), and the accusatives **circum**, **cōram**, **cum** (cf. § 215). **Circiter** is an adverbial formation from **circum** (cf. § 214. *b.* N.); **praeter** is the comparative of **prae**, **propter** of **prope**.[1] Of the remainder, **versus** is a petrified nominative (participle of **vertō**); **adversus** is a compound of **versus**; **trāns** is probably an old present participle (cf. **in-trā-re**); while the origin of the brief forms **ab**, **ad**, **dē**, **ex**, **ob**, is obscure and doubtful.

220. Prepositions are regularly used either with the Accusative or with the Ablative.

a. The following prepositions are used with the Accusative:—

ad, *to.*	**circiter**, *about.*	**intrā**, *inside.*
adversus, *against.*	**cis**, **citrā**, *this side.*	**iūxtā**, *near.*
adversum, *towards.*	**contrā**, *against.*	**ob**, *on account of.*
ante, *before.*	**ergā**, *towards.*	**penes**, *in the power of.*
apud, *at, near.*	**extrā**, *outside.*	**per**, *through.*
circā, *around.*	**īnfrā**, *below.*	**pōne**, *behind.*
circum, *around.*	**inter**, *among.*	**post**, *after.*

[1] The case-form of these prepositions in **-ter** is doubtful.

praeter, *beyond*.
prope, *near*.
propter, *on account of*.
secundum, *next to*.
suprā, *above*.
trāns, *across*.
ultrā, *on the further side*.
versus, *towards*.

b. The following prepositions are used with the Ablative: —[1]

ā, ăb, abs, *away from, by*.
absque, *without, but for*.
cōram, *in presence of*.
cum, *with*.
dē, *from*.
ē, ex, *out of*.
prae, *in comparison with*.
prō, *in front of, for*.
sine, *without*.
tenus, *up to, as far as*.

c. The following may be used with either the Accusative or the Ablative, but with a difference in meaning: —

in, *into, in*.
subter, *beneath*.
sub, *under*.
super, *above*.

In and **sub**, when followed by the accusative, indicate *motion to*, when by the ablative, *rest in*, a place:

vēnit **in aedīs**, *he came into the house;* erat **in aedibus**, *he was in the house.*
disciplīna **in Britanniā** reperta atque inde **in Galliam** trānslāta esse exīstimātur, *the system is thought to have been discovered in Great Britain and thence brought over to Gaul.*
sub īlice cōnsēderat, *he had seated himself under an ilex.*
sub lēgēs mittere orbem, *to subject the world to laws* (to send the world under laws).

221. The uses of the Prepositions are as follows: —

1. **Ā, ab**, *away from*,[2] *from, off from*, with the ablative.

a. Of place: as, — ab urbe profectus est, *he set out from the city.*

b. Of time: (1) *from:* as, — ab hōrā tertiā ad vesperam, *from the third hour till evening;* (2) *just after:* as, — ab eō magistrātū, *after* [holding] *that office.*

c. Idiomatic uses: ā reliquīs differunt, *they differ from the others;* ā parvulīs, *from early childhood;* prope ab urbe, *near* (not far from) *the city;* līberāre ab, *to set free from;* occīsus ab hoste (periit ab hoste), *slain by an enemy;* ab hāc parte, *on this side;* ab rē êius, *to his advantage;* ā rē pūblicā, *for the interest of the state.*

2. **Ad**, *to, towards, at, near*, with the accusative (cf. **in**, *into*).

a. Of place: as, — ad urbem vēnit, *he came to the city;* ad merīdiem, *towards the south;* ad exercitum, *to the army;* ad hostem, *toward the enemy;* ad urbem, *near the city.*

b. Of time: as, — ad nōnam hōram, *till the ninth hour.*

c. With persons: as, — ad eum vēnit, *he came to him.*

[1] For **palam** etc., see § 432.

[2] **Ab** signifies direction *from* the object, but often *towards* the speaker; compare **dē**, *down from*, and **ex**, *out of*.

d. Idiomatic uses: ad supplicia dēscendunt, *they resort to punishment;* ad haec respondit, *to this he answered;* ad tempus, *at the* [fit] *time;* adīre ad rem pūblicam, *to go into public life;* ad petendam pācem, *to seek peace;* ad latera, *on the flank;* ad arma, *to arms;* ad hunc modum, *in this way;* quem ad modum, *how, as;* ad centum, *nearly a hundred;* ad hōc, *besides;* omnēs ad ūnum, *all to a man;* ad diem, *on the day.*

3. **Ante,** *in front of, before,* with the accusative (cf. **post,** *after*).

a. Of place: as,—ante portam, *in front of the gate;* ante exercitum, *in advance of the army.*

b. Of time: as,—ante bellum, *before the war.*

c. Idiomatic uses: ante urbem captam, *before the city was taken;* ante diem quīntum (a.d.v.) Kal., *the fifth day before the Calends;* ante quadriennium, *four years before* or *ago;* ante tempus, *too soon* (before the time).

4. **Apud,** *at, by, among,* with the accusative.

a. Of place (rare and archaic): as,—apud forum, *at the forum* (in the market-place).

b. With reference to persons or communities: as,—apud Helvētiōs, *among the Helvetians;* apud populum, *before the people;* apud aliquem, *at one's house;* apud sē, *at home* or *in his senses;* apud Cicerōnem, *in* [the works of] *Cicero.*

5. **Circā,** *about, around,* with the accusative (cf. **circum, circiter**).

a. Of place: templa circā forum, *the temples about the forum;* circā sē habet, *he has with him* (of persons).

b. Of time or number (in poetry and later writers): circā eandem hōram, *about the same hour;* circā īdūs Octōbrīs, *about the fifteenth of October;* circā decem mīlia, *about ten thousand.*

c. Figuratively (in later writers), *about, in regard to* (cf. dē): circā quem pūgna est, *with regard to whom,* etc.; circā deōs neglegentior, *rather neglectful of* (i.e. in worshipping) *the gods.*

6. **Circiter,** *about,* with the accusative.

a. Of time or number: circiter īdūs Novembrīs, *about the thirteenth of November;* circiter merīdiem, *about noon.*

7. **Circum,** *about, around,* with the accusative.

a. Of place: circum haec loca, *hereabout;* circum Capuam, *round Capua;* circum illum, *with him;* lēgātiō circum īnsulās missa, *an embassy sent to the islands round about;* circum amīcōs, *to his friends round about.*

8. **Contrā,** *opposite, against,* with the accusative.

contrā Ītaliam, *over against Italy;* contrā haec, *in answer to this.*

a. Often as adverb: as,—haec contrā, *this in reply;* contrā autem, *but on the other hand;* quod contrā, *whereas, on the other hand.*

9. **Cum,** *with, together with,* with the ablative.

a. Of place: as, — vāde mēcum, *go with me;* cum omnibus impedīmentīs, *with all* [their] *baggage.*

b. Of time: as, — prīmā cum lūce, *at early dawn* (with first light).

c. Idiomatic uses: māgnō cum dolōre, *with great sorrow;* commūnicāre aliquid cum aliquō, *share something with some one;* cum malō suō, *to his own hurt;* cōnflīgere cum hoste, *to fight with the enemy;* esse cum tēlō, *to go armed;* cum silentiō, *in silence.*

10. **Dē**, *down from*, *from*, with the ablative (cf. **ab**, *away from;* **ex**, *out of*).

a. Of place: as, — dē caelō dēmissus, *sent down from heaven;* dē nāvibus dēsilīre, *to jump down from the ships.*

b. Figuratively, *concerning*, *about*, *of:*[1] as, — cōgnōscit dē Clōdī caede, *he learns of the murder of Clodius;* cōnsilia dē bellō, *plans of war.*

c. In a partitive sense (compare ex), *out of*, *of:* as, — ūnus dē plēbe, *one of the people.*

d. Idiomatic uses: multīs dē causīs, *for many reasons;* quā dē causā, *for which reason;* dē imprōvīsō, *of a sudden;* dē industriā, *on purpose;* dē integrō, *anew;* dē tertiā vigiliā, *just at midnight* (starting at the third watch); dē mēnse Decembrī nāvigāre, *to sail as early as December.*

11. **Ex**, **ē**, *from* (the midst, opposed to **in**), *out of*, with the ablative (cf. **ab** and **dē**).

a. Of place: as, — ex omnibus partibus silvae ēvolāvērunt, *they flew out from all parts of the forest;* ex Hispāniā, [a man] *from Spain.*

b. Of time: as, — ex eō diē quīntus, *the fifth day from that* (four days after); ex hōc diē, *from this day forth.*

c. Idiomatically or less exactly: ex cōnsulātū, *right after his consulship;* ex ēius sententiā, *according to his opinion;* ex aequō, *justly;* ex imprōvīsō, *unexpectedly;* ex tuā rē, *to your advantage;* māgnā ex parte, *in a great degree;* ex equō pūgnāre, *to fight on horseback;* ex ūsū, *expedient;* ē regiōne, *opposite;* quaerere ex aliquō, *to ask of some one;* ex senātūs cōnsultō, *according to the decree of the senate;* ex fugā, *in* [their] *flight* (proceeding immediately from it); ūnus ē fīliīs, *one of the sons.*

12. **In**, with the accusative or the ablative.

1. With the accusative, *into* (opposed to **ex**).

a. Of place: as, — in Ītaliam contendit, *he hastens into Italy.*

b. Of time, *till*, *until:* as, — in lūcem, *till daylight.*

c. Idiomatically or less exactly: in merīdiem, *towards the south;* amor in (ergā, adversus) patrem, *love for his father;* in āram cōnfūgit, *he fled to the altar* (on the steps, or merely *to*); in diēs, *from day to day;* in longitūdinem, *lengthwise;* in lātitūdinem patēbat, *extended in width;* in haec verba iūrāre, *to swear to these words;* hunc in modum, *in this way;* ōrātiō in Catilīnam, *a speech against*

[1] *Of* originally meant *from* (cf. *off*).

Catiline; in perpetuum, *forever;* in pêius, *for the worse;* in diem vīvere, *to live from hand to mouth* (for the day).

2. With the ablative, *in, on, among.*

In very various connections: as,—in castrīs, *in the camp* (cf. ad castra, *to, at,* or *near the camp*); in marī, *on the sea;* in urbe esse, *to be in town;* in tempore, *in season;* in scrībendō, *while writing;* est mihi in animō, *I have it in mind, I intend;* in ancorīs, *at anchor;* in hōc homine, *in the case of this man;* in dubiō esse, *to be in doubt.*

13. **Īnfrā**, *below,* with the accusative.

a. Of place: as,—ad mare īnfrā oppidum, *by the sea below the town;* īnfrā caelum, *under the sky.*

b. Figuratively or less exactly: as,—īnfrā Homērum, *later than Homer;* īnfrā trēs pedēs, *less than three feet;* īnfrā elephantōs, *smaller than elephants;* īnfrā īnfimōs omnīs, *the lowest of the low.*

14. **Inter**, *between, among,* with the accusative.

inter mē et Scīpiōnem, *between myself and Scipio;* inter ōs et offam, *between the cup and the lip* (the mouth and the morsel); inter hostium tēla, *amid the weapons of the enemy;* inter omnīs prīmus, *first of all;* inter bibendum, *while drinking;* inter sē loquuntur, *they talk together.*

15. **Ob**, *towards, on account of,* with the accusative.

a. Literally: (1) of motion (archaic): as,—ob Rōmam, *towards Rome* (Ennius); ob viam, *to the road* (preserved as adverb, *in the way of*). (2) Of place in which, *before,* in a few phrases: as,—ob oculōs, *before the eyes.*

b. Figuratively, *in return for* (mostly archaic, probably a word of account, balancing one thing *against* another): as,—ob mulierem, *in pay for the woman;* ob rem, *for gain.* Hence applied to reason, cause, and the like, *on account of* (a similar mercantile idea), *for:* as,—ob eam causam, *for that reason;* quam ob rem (quamobrem), *wherefore, why.*

16. **Per**, *through, over,* with the accusative.

a. Of motion: as,—per urbem īre, *to go through the city;* per mūrōs, *over the walls.*

b. Of time: as,—per hiemem, *throughout the winter.*

c. Figuratively, of persons as means or instruments: as,—per hominēs idōneōs, *through the instrumentality of suitable persons;* licet per mē, *you* (etc.) *may for all me.* Hence, stat per mē, *it is through my instrumentality;* so, per sē, *in and of itself.*

d. Weakened, in many adverbial expressions: as,—per iocum, *in jest;* per speciem, *in show, ostentatiously.*

17. **Prae**, *in front of,* with the ablative.

a. Literally, of place (in a few connections): as,—prae sē portāre, *to carry in one's arms;* prae sē ferre, *to carry before one,* (hence figuratively) *exhibit, proclaim ostentatiously, make known.*

b. Figuratively, of hindrance, as by an obstacle in front (compare English *for*): as, —prae gaudiō conticuit, *he was silent for joy.*

c. Of comparison: as, —prae māgnitūdine corporum suōrum, *in comparison with their own great size.*

18. **Praeter,** *along by, by,* with the accusative.

a. Literally: as, —praeter castra, *by the camp* (along by, in front of); praeter oculōs, *before the eyes.*

b. Figuratively, *beyond, besides, more than, in addition to, except:* as, —praeter spem, *beyond hope;* praeter aliōs, *more than others;* praeter paucōs, *with the exception of a few.*

19. **Prō,** *in front of,* with the ablative.

sedēns prō aede Castoris, *sitting in front of the temple of Castor;* prō populō, *in presence of the people.* So prō rōstrīs, *on* [the front of] *the rostra;* prō contiōne, *before the assembly* (in a speech).

a. In various idiomatic uses: prō lēge, *in defence of the law;* prō vitulā, *instead of a heifer;* prō centum mīlibus, *as good as a hundred thousand;* prō ratā parte, *in due proportion;* prō hāc vice, *for this once;* prō cōnsule, *in place of consul;* prō vīribus, *considering his strength;* prō virīlī parte, *to the best of one's ability;* prō tuā prūdentiā, *in accordance with your wisdom.*

20. **Propter,** *near, by,* with the accusative.

propter tē sedet, *he sits next you.* Hence, *on account of* (cf. *all along of*): as, —propter metum, *through fear.*

21. **Secundum,**[1] *just behind, following,* with the accusative.

a. Literally: as, —īte secundum mē (Plaut.), *go behind me;* secundum lītus, *near the shore;* secundum flūmen, *along the stream* (cf. secundō flūmine, *down stream*).

b. Figuratively, *according to:* as, —secundum nātūram, *according to nature.*

22. **Sub,** *under, up to,* with the accusative or the ablative.

1. Of motion, with the accusative: as, —sub montem succēdere, *to come close to the hill.*

a. Idiomatically: sub noctem, *towards night;* sub lūcem, *near daylight;* sub haec dicta, *at* (following) *these words.*

2. Of rest, with the ablative: as, —sub Iove, *in the open air* (under the heaven, personified as Jove); sub monte, *at the foot of the hill.*

a. Idiomatically: sub eōdem tempore, *about the same time* (just after it).

23. **Subter,** *under, below,* with the accusative (sometimes, in poetry, the ablative).

subter togam (Liv.), *under his mantle;* but, —subter lītore (Catull.), *below the shore.*

24. **Super,**[2] with the accusative or the ablative.

[1] Old participle of **sequor.**

[2] Comparative of **sub.**

1. With the accusative, *above, over, on, beyond, upon.*

a. Of place: super vāllum praecipitārī (Iug. 58), *to be hurled over the rampart;* super laterēs coria indūcuntur (B.C. ii. 10), *hides are drawn over the bricks;* super terrae tumulum statuī (Legg. ii. 65), *to be placed on the mound of earth;* super Numidiam (Iug. 19), *beyond Numidia.*

b. Idiomatically or less exactly: vulnus super vulnus, *wound upon wound;* super vīnum (Q. C. viii. 4), *over his wine.*

2. With the ablative, *concerning, about* (the only use with this case in prose).

hāc super rē, *concerning this thing;* super tālī rē, *about such an affair;* litterās super tantā rē exspectāre, *to wait for a letter in a matter of such importance.*

a. Poetically, in other senses: līgna super focō largē repōnēns (Hor. Od. i. 9. 5), *piling logs generously on the fire;* nocte super mediā (Aen. ix. 61), *after midnight.*

25. **Suprā,** *on top of, above,* with the accusative.

suprā terram, *on the surface of the earth.* So also figuratively: as,—suprā hanc memoriam, *before our remembrance;* suprā mōrem, *more than usual;* suprā quod, *besides.*

26. **Tenus** (postpositive), *as far as, up to,* regularly with the ablative, sometimes with the genitive (cf. § 359. *b*).

1. With the ablative: Taurō tenus, *as far as Taurus;* capulō tenus, *up to the hilt.*

2. With the genitive: Cumārum tenus (Fam. viii. 1. 2), *as far as Cumae.*

NOTE 1.—Tenus is frequently connected with the feminine of an adjective pronoun, making an adverbial phrase: as, hāctenus, *hitherto;* quātenus, *so far as;* dē hāc rē hāctenus, *so much for that* (about this matter so far).

NOTE 2.—Tenus was originally a neuter noun, meaning *line* or *extent.* In its use with the genitive (mostly poetical) it may be regarded as an adverbial accusative (§ 397. *a*).

27. **Trans,** *across, over, through, by,* with the accusative.

a. Of motion: as,—trāns mare currunt, *they run across the sea;* trāns flūmen ferre, *to carry over a river;* trāns aethera, *through the sky;* trāns caput iace, *throw over your head.*

b. Of rest: as,—trāns Rhēnum incolunt, *they live across the Rhine.*

28. **Ultrā,** *beyond* (on the further side), with the accusative.

cis Padum ultrāque, *on this side of the Po and beyond;* ultrā eum numerum, *more than that number;* ultrā fidem, *incredible;* ultrā modum, *immoderate.*

NOTE.—Some adverbs appear as prepositions: as, intus, īnsuper (see § 219). For Prepositions in Compounds, see § 267.

CONJUNCTIONS

222. Conjunctions, like prepositions (cf. § 219), are closely related to adverbs, and are either petrified cases of nouns, pronouns, and adjectives, or obscured phrases: as, **quod**, an old accusative; **dum**, probably an old accusative (cf. **tum, cum**); **vērō**, an old neuter ablative of **vērus**; **nihilōminus**, *none the less;* **proinde**, lit. *forward from there.* Most conjunctions are connected with *pronominal* adverbs, which cannot always be referred to their original case-forms.

223. Conjunctions connect words, phrases, or sentences. They are of two classes, Coördinate and Subordinate: —

a. Coördinate, connecting coördinate or similar constructions (see § 278. 2. *a*). These are: —

1. Copulative or disjunctive, implying a *connection* or *separation* of thought as well as of words: as, **et**, *and;* **aut**, *or;* **neque**, *nor.*
2. Adversative, implying a connection of words, but a contrast in thought: as, **sed**, *but.*
3. Causal, introducing a cause or reason: as, **nam**, *for.*
4. Illative, denoting an inference: as, **igitur**, *therefore.*

b. Subordinate, connecting a subordinate or independent clause with that on which it depends (see § 278. 2. *b*). These are: —

1. Conditional, denoting a condition or hypothesis: as, **sī**, *if;* **nisi**, *unless.*
2. Comparative, implying comparison as well as condition: as, **ac sī**, *as if.*
3. Concessive, denoting a concession or admission: as, **quamquam**, *although* (lit. *however* much it may be true that, etc.).
4. Temporal: as, **postquam**, *after.*
5. Consecutive, expressing result: as, **ut**, *so that.*
6. Final, expressing purpose: as, **ut**, *in order that;* **nē**, *that not.*
7. Causal, expressing cause: as, **quia**, *because.*

224. Conjunctions are more numerous and more accurately distinguished in Latin than in English. The following list includes the common conjunctions[1] and conjunctive phrases: —

Coördinate

a. Copulative and Disjunctive

et, -que, atque (ac), *and.*
et . . . et; et . . . -que (atque); -que . . . et; -que . . . -que (poetical), *both . . . and.*
etiam, quoque, neque nōn (necnōn), quīn etiam, itidem (item), *also.*
cum . . . tum; tum . . . tum, *both . . . and; not only . . . but also.*

[1] Some of these have been included in the classification of adverbs. See also list of Correlatives, § 152.

quā . . . quā, *on the one hand . . . on the other hand.*
modo . . . modo, *now . . . now.*
aut . . . aut; vel . . . vel (-ve), *either . . . or.*
sīve (seu) . . . sīve, *whether . . . or.*
nec (neque) . . . nec (neque); neque . . . nec; nec . . . neque (rare), *neither . . . nor.*
et . . . neque, *both . . . and not.*
nec . . . et; nec (neque) . . . -que, *neither (both not) . . . and.*

b. Adversative

sed, autem, vērum, vērō, at, atquī, *but.*
tamen, attamen, sed tamen, vērum tamen, *but yet, nevertheless.*
nihilōminus, *none the less.*
at vērō, *but in truth;* **enimvērō**, *for in truth.*
cēterum, *on the other hand, but.*

c. Causal

nam, namque, enim, etenim, *for.*
quāpropter, quārē, quamobrem, quōcircā, unde, *wherefore, whence.*

d. Illative

ergō, igitur, itaque, ideō, idcircō, inde, proinde, *therefore, accordingly.*

Subordinate

a. Conditional

sī, *if;* **sīn**, *but if;* **nisi (nī)**, *unless, if not;* **quod sī**, *but if.*
modo, dum, dummodo, sī modo, *if only, provided.*
dummodo nē (dum nē, modo nē), *provided only not.*

b. Comparative

ut, utī, sīcut, *just as;* **velut**, *as, so as;* **prout, praeut, ceu**, *like as, according as.*
tamquam (tanquam), quasi, ut sī, ac sī, velut, velutī, velut sī, *as if.*
quam, atque (ac), *as, than.*

c. Concessive

etsī, etiamsī, tametsī, *even if;* **quamquam (quanquam)**, *although.*
quamvīs, quantumvīs, quamlibet, quantumlibet, *however much.*
licet (properly a verb), **ut, cum (quom)**, *though, suppose, whereas.*

d. Temporal

cum (quom), quandō, *when;* **ubi, ut**, *when, as;* **cum prīmum, ut prīmum, ubi prīmum, simul, simul ac, simul atque**, *as soon as;* **postquam (posteāquam)**, *after.*
prius . . . quam, ante . . . quam, *before;* **nōn ante . . . quam**, *not . . . until.*
dum, ūsque dum, dōnec, quoad, *until, as long as, while.*

e. Consecutive and Final

ut (**utī**), **quō**, *so that, in order that.*
nē, **ut nē**, *lest* (*that . . . not, in order that not*); **nēve** (**neu**), *that not, nor.*
quīn (after negatives), **quōminus**, *but that* (so as to prevent), *that not.*

f. Causal

quia, **quod**, **quoniam** (†**quom-iam**), **quandō**, *because.*
cum (**quom**), *since.*
quandōquidem, **sī quidem**, **quippe**, **ut pote**, *since indeed, inasmuch as.*
proptereā . . . quod, *for this reason . . . that.*

On the use of Conjunctions, see §§ 323, 324.

INTERJECTIONS

225. Some Interjections are mere natural exclamations of feeling; others are derived from inflected parts of speech, e.g. the imperatives **em**, *lo* (probably for **eme**, *take*); **age**, *come*, etc. Names of deities occur in **herclē**, **pol** (from **Pollux**), etc. Many Latin interjections are borrowed from the Greek, as **euge**, **euhoe**, etc.

226. The following list comprises most of the Interjections in common use: —

ō, **ēn**, **ecce**, **ehem**, **papae**, **vāh** (of *astonishment*).
iō, **ēvae**, **ēvoe**, **euhoe** (of *joy*).
heu, **ĕheu**, **vae**, *alas* (of *sorrow*).
heus, **eho**, **ehodum**, *ho* (of *calling*); **st**, *hist.*
êia, **euge** (of *praise*).
prō (of *attestation*): as, **prō pudor**, *shame!*

FORMATION OF WORDS

227. All formation of words is originally a process of composition. An element significant in itself is added to another significant element, and thus the meaning of the two is combined. No other combination is possible for the formation either of inflections or of stems. Thus, in fact, *words* (since roots and stems are significant elements, and so words) are first placed side by side, then brought under one accent, and finally felt as one word. The gradual process is seen in *sea voyage*, *sea-nymph*, *seaside*. But as all derivation, properly so called, appears as a combination of uninflected stems, every type of formation in use must antedate inflection. Hence words were not in strictness derived either from nouns or from verbs, but from *stems* which were neither, because they were in fact both; for the distinction between noun-stems and verb-stems had not yet been made.

After the development of Inflection, however, that one of several kindred words which seemed the simplest was regarded as the *primitive* form, and from this the other words of the group were thought to be *derived*. Such supposed processes of formation were then imitated, often erroneously, and in this way *new modes of derivation* arose. Thus new adjectives were formed from nouns, new nouns from adjectives, new adjectives from verbs, and new verbs from adjectives and nouns.

In course of time the real or apparent relations of many words became confused, so that nouns and adjectives once supposed to come from nouns were often assigned to verbs, and others once supposed to come from verbs were assigned to nouns.

Further, since the language was constantly changing, many words went out of use, and do not occur in the literature as we have it. Thus many Derivatives survive of which the Primitive is lost.

Finally, since all conscious word-formation is imitative, intermediate steps in derivation were sometimes omitted, and occasionally apparent Derivatives occur for which no proper Primitive ever existed.

ROOTS AND STEMS

228. Roots[1] are of two kinds: —

1. *Verbal*, expressing ideas of action or condition (sensible phenomena).
2. *Pronominal*, expressing ideas of position and direction.

From verbal roots come all parts of speech except pronouns and certain particles derived from pronominal roots.

229. Stems are either identical with roots or derived from them. They are of two classes: (1) Noun-stems (including Adjective-stems) and (2) Verb-stems.

NOTE. — Noun-stems and verb-stems were not originally different (see p. 163), and in the consciousness of the Romans were often confounded; but in general they were treated as distinct.

230. Words are formed by inflection: (1) from roots inflected as stems; (2) from derived stems (see § 232).

[1] For the distinction between Roots and Stems, see §§ 24, 25.

231. A root used as a stem may appear —

a. With a short vowel: as, **duc-is** (**dux**), DUC; **nec-is** (**nex**); **i-s, i-d.** So in verbs: as, **es-t, fer-t** (cf. § 174. 2).

b. With a long vowel[1]: as, **lūc-is** (**lūx**), LUC; **pāc-is** (**pāx**). So in verbs: **dūc-ō, ī-s** for †**eis**, from **eō, īre**; **fātur** from **fārī**.

c. With reduplication: as, **fur-fur, mar-mor, mur-mur.** So in verbs: as, **gi-gnō** (root GEN), **si-stō** (root STA).

DERIVED STEMS AND SUFFIXES

232. Derived Stems are formed from roots or from other stems by means of *suffixes*. These are: —

1. Primary: added to the root, or (in later times by analogy) to verb-stems.

2. Secondary: added to a noun-stem or an adjective-stem.

Both primary and secondary suffixes are for the most part pronominal roots (§ 228. 2), but a few are of doubtful origin.

NOTE 1. — The distinction between primary and secondary suffixes, not being original (see § 227), is continually lost sight of in the development of a language. Suffixes once primary are used as secondary, and those once secondary are used as primary. Thus in **hosticus** (**hosti** + **cus**) the suffix **-cus**, originally ko- (see § 234. II. 12) primary, as in **paucus**, has become secondary, and is thus regularly used to form derivatives; but in **pudīcus, aprīcus**, it is treated as primary again, because these words were really or apparently connected with verbs. So in English *-able* was borrowed as a primary suffix (*tolerable, eatable*), but also makes forms like *clubbable, salable*; *-some* is properly a secondary suffix, as in *toilsome, lonesome*, but makes also such words as *meddlesome, venturesome*.

NOTE 2. — It is the *stem* of the word, not the *nominative*, that is formed by the derivative suffix. For convenience, however, the nominative will usually be given.

Primary Suffixes

233. The words in Latin formed immediately from the root by means of Primary Suffixes, are few. For —

1. Inherited words so formed were mostly further developed by the addition of other suffixes, as we might make an adjective *lone-ly-some-ish*, meaning nothing more than *lone*, *lonely*, or *lonesome*.

2. By such accumulation of suffixes, new compound suffixes were formed which crowded out even the old types of derivation. Thus, —

[1] The difference in vowel-quantity in the same root (as DŬC) depends on inherited variations (see § 17. *a*).

A word like **mēns, mentis**, by the suffix **ōn-** (nom. **-ō**), gave **mentiō**, and this, being divided into **men** + **tiō**, gave rise to a new type of abstract nouns in **-tiō**: as, **lēgā-tiō**, *embassy*.

A word like **audītor**, by the suffix **io-** (nom. **-ius**), gave rise to adjectives like **audītōr-ius**, of which the neuter (**audītōrium**) is used to denote the *place where* the action of the verb is performed. Hence **tōrio-** (nom. **-tōrium**), N., becomes a regular noun-suffix (§ 250. *a*).

So in English such a word as *suffocation* gives a suffix *-ation*, and with this is made *starvation*, though there is no such word as *starvate*.

234. Examples of primary stem-suffixes are: —

I. Vowel suffixes: —

1. **o-** (M., N.), **ā-** (F.), found in nouns and adjectives of the first two declensions: as, **sonus, lūdus, vagus, toga** (root TEG).

2. **i-**, as in **ovis, avis**; in Latin frequently changed, as in **rūpēs**, or lost, as in **scobs** (**scobis**, root SCAB).

3. **u-**, disguised in most adjectives by an additional **i**, as in **suā-vis** (for †**suād-vis**, instead of †**suā-dus**, cf. ἡδύς), **ten-uis** (root TEN in **tendō**), and remaining alone only in nouns of the fourth declension, as **acus** (root AK, *sharp*, in **ācer, aciēs**, ὠκύς), **pecū, genū**.

II. Suffixes with a consonant: —

1. **to-** (M., N.), **tā-** (F.), in the regular perfect passive participle, as **tēctus, tēctum**; sometimes with an active sense, as in **pōtus, prānsus**; and found in a few words not recognized as participles, as **pūtus** (cf. **pūrus**), **altus** (**alō**).

2. **ti-** in abstracts and rarely in nouns of agency, as **messis, vestis, pars, mēns**. But in many the **i** is lost.

3. **tu-** in abstracts (including supines), sometimes becoming concretes, as **āctus, lūctus**.

4. **no-** (M., N.), **nā-** (F.), forming perfect participles in other languages, and in Latin making adjectives of like participial meaning, which often become nouns, as **māgnus, plēnus, rēgnum**.

5. **ni-**, in nouns of agency and adjectives, as **īgnis, sēgnis**.

6. **nu-**, rare, as in **manus, pīnus, cornū**.

7. **mo-** (**mā-**), with various meanings, as in **animus, almus, fīrmus, forma**.

8. **vo-** (**vā-**) (commonly **uo-, uā-**), with an active or passive meaning, as in **equus** (**equos**), **arvum, cōnspicuus, exiguus, vacīvus** (**vacuus**).

9. **ro-** (**rā-**), as in **ager** (stem **ag-ro-**), **integer** (cf. **intāctus**), **sacer, plērī-que** (cf. **plēnus, plētus**).

10. **lo-** (**lā-**), as in **caelum** (for †**caed-lum**), *chisel*, **exemplum, sella** (for †**sedla**).

11. **yo-** (**yā-**), forming gerundives in other languages, and in Latin making adjectives and abstracts, including many of the first and fifth declensions, as **eximius, audācia, Flōrentia, perniciēs**.

12. **ko-** (**kā-**), sometimes primary, as in **paucī** (cf. παῦρος), **locus** (for **stlocus**). In many cases the vowel of this termination is lost, leaving a consonant stem: as, **apex, cortex, loquāx**.

13. **en-** (**on-**, **ēn-**, **ōn-**), in nouns of agency and abstracts: as, **aspergō**, **compāgō** (**-ĭnis**), **gerō** (**-ōnis**).

14. **men-**, expressing *means*, often passing into the action itself: as, **agmen**, **flūmen**, **fulmen**.

15. **ter-** (**tor-**, **tĕr-**, **tōr-**, **tr-**), forming nouns of *agency:* as, **pater** (i.e. *protector*), **frāter** (i.e. *supporter*), **ōrātor**.

16. **tro-**, forming nouns of *means:* as, **claustrum** (CLAUD), **mūlctrum** (MULG).

17. **es-** (**os-**), forming names of actions, passing into concretes: as, **genus** (**generis**), **tempus** (see § 15. 4). The infinitive in **-ere** (as in **reg-ere**) is a locative of this stem (**-er-e** for †**-es-i**).

18. **nt-** (**ont-**, **ent-**), forming present active *participles:* as, **legēns**, with some adjectives from roots unknown: as, **frequēns**, **recēns**.

The above, with some suffixes given below, belong to the Indo-European parent speech, and most of them were not felt as living formations in the Latin.

Significant Endings

235. Both primary and secondary suffixes, especially in the form of compound suffixes, were used in Latin with more or less consciousness of their meaning. They may therefore be called Significant Endings.

They form: (1) Nouns of Agency; (2) Abstract Nouns (including Names of Actions); (3) Adjectives (active or passive).

NOTE.—There is really no difference in etymology between an adjective and a noun, except that some formations are habitually used as adjectives and others as nouns (§ 20. *b*. N. 2).

DERIVATION OF NOUNS

Nouns of Agency

236. Nouns of Agency properly denote the *agent* or *doer* of an action. But they include many words in which the idea of agency has entirely faded out, and also many words used as adjectives.

a. Nouns denoting the *agent* or *doer of an action* are formed from roots or verb-stems by means of the suffixes—

-tor (**-sor**), M.; **-trīx**, F.

can-tor, **can-trīx**, *singer;*	**can-ere** (root CAN), *to sing.*
vic-tor, **vic-trīx**, *conqueror* (*victorious*);	**vinc-ere** (VIC), *to conquer.*
tōn-sor (for †**tond-tor**), **tōns-trīx** (for †**tond-trīx**), *hair-cutter;*	**tond-ēre** (TOND as root), *to shear.*
petī-tor, *candidate;*	**pet-ĕre** (PET; **petī-** as stem), *to seek.*

By analogy **-tor** is sometimes added to noun-stems, but these may be stems of lost verbs: as, **viā-tor**, *traveller*, from **via**, *way* (but cf. the verb **inviō**).

NOTE 1.—The termination **-tor** (**-sor**) has the same phonetic change as the supine ending **-tum** (**-sum**), and is added to the same form of root or verb-stem as that ending. The stem-ending is **tōr-** (§ 234. II. 15), which is shortened in the nominative.

NOTE 2.—The feminine form is always **-trīx**. Masculines in **-sor** lack the feminine, except **expulsor** (**expultrīx**) and **tōnsor** (**tōnstrīx**).

b. **t-**, M. or F., added to verb-stems makes nouns in **-es** (**-itis**, **-etis**; stem **it-**, **et-**) descriptive of a character:—

> **prae-stes**, **-stitis**, (verb-stem from root STA, **stāre**, *stand*), *guardian*.
> **teges**, **-etis** (verb-stem **tege-**, cf. **tegō**, *cover*), *a coverer*, *a mat*.
> **pedes**, **-itis** (**pēs**, **ped-is**, *foot*, and I, root of **īre**, *go*), *foot-soldier*.

c. **-ō** (genitive **-ōnis**, stem **ōn-**), M., added to verb-stems[1] indicates a person employed in some specific art or trade:—

> **com-bibō** (BIB as root in **bibō**, **bibere**, *drink*), *a pot-companion*.
> **gerō**, **-ōnis** (GES in **gerō**, **gerere**, *carry*), *a carrier*.

NOTE.—This termination is also used to form many nouns descriptive of personal characteristics (cf. § 255).

Names of Actions and Abstract Nouns

237. Names of Actions are confused, through their terminations, with real abstract nouns (names of *qualities*), and with concrete nouns denoting *means* and *instrument*.

They are also used to express the *concrete result* of an action (as often in English).

Thus **legiō** is literally *the act of collecting*, but comes to mean *legion* (the body of soldiers collected); cf. *levy* in English.

238. Abstract Nouns and Names of Actions are formed from roots and verb-stems by means of the endings—

a. Added to roots or forms conceived as roots—

NOM.	**-or**, M.	**-ēs**, F.	**-us**, N.
GEN.	**-ōris**	**-is**	**-eris** or **-oris**
STEM	**ōr-** (earlier **ōs-**)	**i-**	**er-** (earlier **$^e/_o$s-**)

tim-or, *fear*;	**timēre**, *to fear*.
am-or, *love*;	**amāre**, *to love*.
sēd-ēs, *seat*;	**sedēre**, *to sit*.
caed-ēs, *slaughter*;	**caedere**, *to kill*.
genus, *birth*, *race*;	GEN, *to be born* (root of **gignō**, *bear*).

[1] So conceived, but perhaps this termination was originally added to noun-stems.

NOTE.—Many nouns of this class are formed by analogy from imaginary roots: as facinus from a supposed root FACIN.

b. Apparently added to roots or verb-stems—

NOM.	**-iō**, F.	**-tiō (-siō)**, F.	**-tūra (-sūra)**, F.	**-tus**, M.
GEN.	**-iōnis**	**-tiōnis (-siōnis)**	**-tūrae (-sūrae)**	**-tūs (-sūs)**
STEM	**iōn-**	**tiōn- (siōn-)**	**tūrā- (sūrā-)**	**tu- (su-)**

leg-iō, *a collecting* (*levy*), *a legion;*	legere, *to collect.*
reg-iō, *a direction, a region;*	regere, *to direct.*
vocā-tiō, *a calling;*	vocāre, *to call.*
mōlī-tiō, *a toiling;*	mōlīrī, *to toil.*
scrīp-tūra, *a writing;*	scrībere, *to write.*
sēn-sus (for †sent-tus), *feeling;*	sentīre, *to feel.*

NOTE 1.—-tiō, -tūra, -tus are added to roots or verb-stems precisely as -tor, with the same phonetic change (cf. § 236. *a.* N. [1]). Hence they are conveniently associated with the supine stem (see § 178). They sometimes form nouns when there is no corresponding verb in use: as, senātus, *senate* (cf. senex); mentiō, *mention* (cf. mēns); fētūra, *offspring* (cf. fētus); litterātūra, *literature* (cf. litterae); cōnsulātus, *consulship* (cf. cōnsul).

NOTE 2.—Of these endings, -tus was originally primary (cf. § 234. II. 3.); -iō is a compound formed by adding ōn- to a stem ending in a vowel (originally i): as, diciō (cf. -dicus and dicis); -tiō is a compound formed by adding ōn- to stems in ti-: as, gradātiō (cf. gradātim); -tūra is formed by adding -ra, feminine of -rus, to stems in tu-: as, nātūra from nātus; statūra from status (cf. figūra, of like meaning, from a simple u-stem, †figu-s; and mātūrus, Mātūta).

239. Nouns denoting *acts*, or *means* and *results* of acts, are formed from roots or verb-stems by the use of the suffixes—

-men, N.; **-mentum**, N.; **-mōnium**, N.; **-mōnia**, F.

ag-men, *line of march, band;*	AG, root of agere, *to lead.*
regi-men, *rule;* / regi-mentum, *rule;*	regi- (rege-), stem of regere, *to direct.*
certā-men, *contest, battle;*	certā-, stem of certāre, *to contend.*

So colu-men, *pillar;* mō-men, *movement;* nō-men, *name;* flū-men, *stream.*

testi-mōnium, *testimony;*	testārī, *to witness.*
queri-mōnia, *complaint;*	querī, *to complain.*

-mōnium and **-mōnia** are also used as secondary, forming nouns from other nouns and from adjectives: as, **sāncti-mōnia**, *sanctity* (**sānctus**, *holy*); **mātri-mōnium**, *marriage* (**māter**, *mother*).

NOTE.—Of these endings, -men is primary (cf. § 234. II. 14); -mentum is a compound of men- and to-, and appears for the most part later in the language than -men: as, mōmen, *movement* (Lucr.); mōmentum (later). So elementum is a development from L-M-N-a, *l-m-n's* (letters of the alphabet), changed to elementa along with other nouns in -men. -mōnium and -mōnia were originally compound secondary suffixes formed from mōn- (a by-form of men-), which was early associated with mo-. Thus almus (stem **almo-**), *fostering;* **Almōn**, a river near Rome; **alimōnia**, *support.* But the last was formed directly from **alō** when **-mōnia** had become established as a supposed primary suffix.

240. Nouns denoting *means* or *instrument* are formed from roots and verb-stems (rarely from noun-stems) by means of the neuter suffixes —

-bulum, -culum, -brum, -crum, -trum

pā-bulum, *fodder;*	**pāscere**, *to feed.*
sta-bulum, *stall;*	**stāre**, *to stand.*
vehi-culum, *wagon;*	**vehere**, *to carry.*
candēlā-brum, *candlestick;*	**candēla**, *candle* (a secondary formation).
sepul-crum, *tomb;*	**sepelīre**, *to bury.*
claus-trum (†**claud-trum**), *bar;*	**claudere**, *to shut.*
arā-trum, *plough;*	**arāre**, *to plough.*

NOTE. — **-trum** (stem **tro-**) was an old formation from **tor-** (§ 234. II. 15), with the stem suffix **o-**, and **-clum** (stem **clo-** for **tlo-**) appears to be related; **-culum** is the same as **-clum**; **-bulum** contains **lo-** (§ 234. II. 9, 10) and **-brum** is closely related.

a. A few masculines and feminines of the same formation occur as nouns and adjectives: —

fā-bula, *tale;*	**fārī**, *to speak.*
rīdi-culus, *laughable;*	**rīdēre**, *to laugh.*
fa-ber, *smith;*	**facere**, *to make.*
late-bra, *hiding-place;*	**latēre**, *to hide.*
tere-bra, *auger;*	**terere**, *to bore.*
mulc-tra, *milk-pail;*	**mulgēre**, *to milk.*

241. Abstract Nouns, mostly from adjective-stems, rarely from noun-stems, are formed by means of the secondary feminine suffixes —

-ia (-iēs), -tia (-tiēs), -tās, -tūs, -tūdō

audāc-ia, *boldness;*	**audāx**, *bold.*
pauper-iēs, *poverty;*	**pauper**, *poor.*
trīsti-tia, *sadness;*	**trīstis**, *sad.*
sēgni-tiēs, *laziness;*	**sēgnis**, *lazy.*
boni-tās, *goodness;*	**bonus**, *good.*
senec-tūs, *age;*	**senex**, *old.*
māgni-tūdō, *greatness;*	**māgnus**, *great.*

1. In stems ending in **o-** or **ā-** the stem-vowel is lost before **-ia** (as **superb-ia**) and appears as **i** before **-tās**, **-tūs**, **-tia** (as in **boni-tās**, above).

2. Consonant stems often insert **i** before **-tās**: as, **loquāx** (stem **loquāc-**), **loquāci-tās**; but **hones-tās**, **mâies-tās** (as if from old adjectives in **-es**), **ūber-tās**, **volup-tās**. **o** after **i** is changed to **e**: as, **pius** (stem **pio-**), **pie-tās**; **socius**, **socie-tās**.

a. In like manner **-dō** and **-gō** (F.) form abstract nouns, but are associated with verbs and apparently added to verb-stems: —

cupī-dō, *desire*, from **cupere**, *to desire* (as if from stem **cupī-**).
dulcē-dō, *sweetness* (cf. **dulcis**, *sweet*), as if from a stem **dulcē-**, cf. **dulcē-scō**.
lumbā-gō, *lumbago* (cf. **lumbus**, *loin*), as if from †**lumbō**, **-āre**.

NOTE. — Of these, **-ia** is inherited as secondary (cf. § 234. II. 11). **-tia** is formed by adding **-ia** to stems with a t-suffix: as, **mīlitia**, from **mīles** (stem **mīlit-**); **molestia** from **molestus**; **clēmentia** from **clēmēns**; whence by analogy, **mali-tia**, **avāri-tia**. **-tās** is inherited, but its component parts, **tā-** + **ti-**, are found as suffixes in the same sense: as, **senecta** from **senex**; **sēmen-tis** from **sēmen**. **-tūs** is **tū-** + **ti-**, cf. **servitū-dō**. **-dō** and **-gō** appear only with long vowels, as from verb-stems, by a false analogy; but **-dō** is **do-** + **ōn-**: as, **cupidus**, **cupīdō**; **gravidus**, **gravēdō** (cf. **gravē-scō**); **albidus**, **albēdō** (cf. **albēscō**); **formidus**, *hot*, **formīdō** (cf. **formīdulōsus**), (*hot flash?*) *fear*; **-gō** is possibly **co-** + **ōn-**; cf. **vorāx**, **vorāgō**, but cf. **Cethēgus**. **-tūdō** is compounded of **-dō** with **tu**-stems, which acquire a long vowel from association with verb-stems in **u-** (cf. **volūmen**, from **volvō**): as, **cōnsuētū-dō**, **valētū-dō**, **habitū-dō**, **sollicitū-dō**; whence **servitūdō** (cf. **servitūs**, **-tūtis**).

b. Neuter Abstracts, which easily pass into concretes denoting *offices* and *groups*, are formed from noun-stems and perhaps from verb-stems by means of the suffixes —

-ium, -tium

hospit-ium, *hospitality*, *an inn*;[1]	**hospes** (gen. **hospit-is**), *a guest*.
collēg-ium, *colleagueship*, *a college*;	**collēga**, *a colleague*.
auspic-ium, *soothsaying*, *an omen*;	**auspex** (gen. **auspic-is**), *a soothsayer*.
gaud-ium, *joy*;	**gaudēre**, *to rejoice*.
effug-ium, *escape*;	**effugere**, *to escape*.
benefic-ium, *a kindness*;	**benefacere**, *to benefit*; cf. **beneficus**.
dēsīder-ium, *longing*;	**dēsīderāre**, *to miss*, from †**dē-sīdēs**, *out of place*, of missing soldiers.
adverb-ium, *adverb*;	**ad verbum**, [added] *to a verb*.
interlūn-ium, *time of new moon*;	**inter lūnās**, *between moons*.
rēgifug-ium, *flight of the kings*;	**rēgis fuga**, *flight of a king*.
servi-tium, *slavery*, *the slave class*;	**servus**, *a slave*.

Vowel stems lose their vowel before **-ium**: as, **collēg-ium**, from **collēga**.

NOTE. — **-ium** is the neuter of the adjective suffix **-ius**. It is an inherited primary suffix, but is used with great freedom as secondary. **-tium** is formed like **-tia**, by adding **-ium** to stems with **t**: as, **exit-ium**, **equit-ium** (cf. **exitus**, **equitēs**); so, by analogy, **calvitium**, **servitium** (from **calvus**, **servus**).

c. Less commonly, abstract nouns (which usually become concrete) are formed from noun-stems (confused with verb-stems) by means of the suffixes —

[1] The abstract meaning is put first.

-nia, F.; **-nium**, **-lium**, **-cinium**, N.

pecū-nia, *money* (*chattels*);	**pecū**, *cattle*.
contici-nium, *the hush of night*;	**conticēscere**, *to become still*.
auxi-lium, *help*;	**augēre**, *to increase*.
lātrō-cinium, *robbery*;	**latrō**, *robber* (cf. **latrōcinor**, *rob*, implying an adjective †**latrōcinus**).

For Diminutives and Patronymics, see §§ 243, 244.

DERIVATION OF ADJECTIVES

242. Derivative Adjectives, which often become nouns, are either *Nominal* (from nouns or adjectives) or *Verbal* (as from roots or verb-stems).

Nominal Adjectives

243. Diminutive Adjectives are usually confined to one gender, that of the primitive, and are used as *Diminutive Nouns*.

They are formed by means of the suffixes —

-ulus (-a, -um), **-olus** (after a vowel), **-culus**, **-ellus**, **-illus**

rīv-ulus, *a streamlet*;	**rīvus**, *a brook*.
gladi-olus, *a small sword*;	**gladius**, *a sword*.
fīli-olus, *a little son*;	**fīlius**, *a son*.
fīli-ola, *a little daughter*;	**fīlia**, *a daughter*.
ātri-olum, *a little hall*;	**ātrium**, *a hall*.
homun-culus, *a dwarf*;	**homō**, *a man*.
auri-cula, *a little ear*;	**auris**, *an ear*.
mūnus-culum, *a little gift*;	**mūnus**, N., *a gift*.
cōdic-illī, *writing-tablets*;	**cōdex**, *a block*.
mis-ellus, *rather wretched*;	**miser**, *wretched*.
lib-ellus, *a little book*;	**liber**, *a book*.
aure-olus (-a, -um), *golden*;	**aureus** (-a, -um), *golden*.
parv-olus (later **parv-ulus**), *very small*;	**parvus** (-a, -um), *little*.
mâius-culus, *somewhat larger*;	**mâior** (old **mâiōs**), *greater*.

NOTE 1.—These diminutive endings are all formed by adding **-lus** to various stems. The formation is the same as that of **-ulus** in § 251. But these words became settled as diminutives, and retained their connection with nouns. So in English the diminutives *whitish*, *reddish*, are of the same formation as *bookish* and *snappish*. **-culus** comes from **-lus** added to adjectives in **-cus** formed from stems in **n-** and **s-**: as, **iuven-cus**, **Aurun-cus** (cf. **Aurunculêius**), **prīs-cus**, whence the **cu** becomes a part of the termination, and the whole ending (**-culus**) is used elsewhere, but mostly with **n-** and **s-** stems, in accordance with its origin.

NOTE 2.—Diminutives are often used to express affection, pity, or contempt: as, **dēliciolae**, *little pet*; **muliercula**, *a poor* (weak) *woman*; **Graeculus**, *a miserable Greek*.

a. -ciō, added to stems in n-, has the same diminutive force, but is used with masculines only: as, **homun-ciō**, *a dwarf* (from **homō**, *a man*).

244. Patronymics, indicating *descent* or *relationship*, are formed by adding to proper names the suffixes —

-adēs, -idēs, -īdēs, -eus, M.; **-ās, -is, -ēis**, F.

These words, originally Greek adjectives, have almost all become nouns in Latin: —

Atlās: **Atlanti-adēs**, *Mercury*; **Atlant-idĕs** (Gr. plur.), *the Pleiads*.
Scīpiō: **Scīpi-adēs**, *son of Scipio*.
Tyndareus: **Tyndar-idēs**, *Castor* or *Pollux*, *son of Tyndarus*; **Tyndar-is**, *Helen, daughter of Tyndarus*.
Anchīsēs: **Anchīsi-adēs**, *Æneas, son of Anchises*.
Thēseus: **Thēs-īdēs**, *son of Theseus*.
Tȳdeus: **Tȳd-īdēs**, *Diomedes, son of Tydeus*.
Oīleus: **Âiāx Oīl-eus**, *son of Oileus*.
Cisseus: **Cissē-is**, *Hecuba, daughter of Cisseus*.
Thaumās: **Thaumant-iās**, *Iris, daughter of Thaumas*.
Hesperus: **Hesper-ides** (from **Hesper-is, -idis**), plur., *the daughters of Hesperus, the Hesperides*.

245. Adjectives meaning *full of*, *prone to*, are formed from noun-stems with the suffixes —

-ōsus, -lēns, -lentus

fluctu-ōsus, *billowy*;	**fluctus**, *a billow*.
form-ōsus, *beautiful*;	**forma**, *beauty*.
perīcul-ōsus, *dangerous*;	**perīculum**, *danger*.
pesti-lēns, pesti-lentus, *pestilent*;	**pestis**, *pest*.
vīno-lentus, vīn-ōsus, *given to drink*;	**vīnum**, *wine*.

246. Adjectives meaning *provided with* are formed from nouns by means of the regular participial endings —

-tus, -ātus, -ītus, -ūtus

fūnes-tus, *deadly*;	**fūnus** (st. **fūner-**, older **fūn^{e}/$_{o}$s-**), *death*.
hones-tus, *honorable*;	**honor**, *honor*.
faus-tus (for †**faves-tus**), *favorable*;	**favor**, *favor*.
barb-ātus, *bearded*;	**barba**, *a beard*.
turr-ītus, *turreted*;	**turris**, *a tower*.
corn-ūtus, *horned*;	**cornū**, *a horn*.

NOTE. — **-ātus, -ītus, -ūtus**, imply reference to an imaginary verb-stem; **-tus** is added directly to nouns without any such reference.

247. Adjectives of various meanings, but signifying in general *made of* or *belonging to*, are formed from nouns by means of the suffixes —

-eus, -ius, -āceus, -īcius, -āneus (-neus), -ticus

aur-eus, *golden;*	**aurum**, *gold.*
patr-ius, *paternal;*	**pater**, *a father.*
uxōr-ius, *uxorious;*	**uxor**, *a wife.*
ros-āceus, *of roses;*	**rosa**, *a rose.*
later-īcius, *of brick;*	**later**, *a brick.*
praesent-āneus, *operating instantly;*	**praesēns**, *present.*
extr-āneus, *external;*	**extrā**, *without.*
subterr-āneus, *subterranean;*	**sub terrā**, *underground.*
salīg-neus, *of willow;*	**salix**, *willow.*
volā-ticus, *winged* (**volātus**, *a flight*);	**volāre**, *to fly.*
domes-ticus, *of the house, domestic;*	**domus**, *a house.*
silvā-ticus, *sylvan;*	**silva**, *a wood.*

NOTE. — -ius is originally primitive (§ 234. II. 11); -eus corresponds to Greek -ειος, -εος, and has lost a y-sound (cf. yo-, § 234. II. 11); -īcius and -āceus are formed by adding -ius and -eus to stems in ī-c-, ā-c- (suffix ko-, § 234. II. 12); -neus is no- + -eus (§ 234. II. 4); -āneus is formed by adding -neus to ā-stems; -ticus is a formation with -cus (cf. hosti-cus with silvā-ticus), and has been affected by the analogy of participial stems in to- (nominative -tus).

248. Adjectives denoting *pertaining to* are formed from noun-stems with the suffixes —

-ālis, -āris, -ēlis, -īlis, -ūlis

nātūr-ālis, *natural;*	**nātūra**, *nature.*
popul-āris, *fellow-countryman;*	**populus**, *a people.*
patru-ēlis, *cousin;*	**patruus**, *uncle.*
host-īlis, *hostile;*	**hostis**, *an enemy.*
cur-ūlis, *curule;*	**currus**, *a chariot.*

NOTE. — The suffixes arise from adding -lis (stem li-) to various vowel stems. The long vowels are due partly to confusion between stem and suffix (cf. vītā-lis, from vītā-, with rēg-ālis), partly to confusion with verb-stems: cf. Aprīlis (aperīre), edūlis (edere), with senīlis (senex). -ris is an inherited suffix, but in most of these formations -āris arises by differentiation for -ālis in words containing an l (as mīlit-āris).

249. Adjectives with the sense of *belonging to* are formed by means of the suffixes —

-ānus, -ēnus, -īnus; -ās, -ēnsis; -cus, -acus (-ācus), -icus; -eus, -êius, -icius

1. So from common nouns: —

mont-ānus, *of the mountains;*	**mōns** (stem **monti-**), *mountain.*
veter-ānus, *veteran;*	**vetus** (stem **veter-**), *old.*
antelūc-ānus, *before daylight;*	**ante lūcem**, *before light.*

terr-ēnus, *earthly;*	**terra**, *earth.*
ser-ēnus, *calm* (of evening stillness);	**sērus**, *late.*
coll-īnus, *of a hill;*	**collis**, *hill.*
dīv-īnus, *divine;*	**dīvus**, *god.*
lībert-īnus, *of the class of freedmen;*	**lībertus**, *one's freedman.*
cûi-ās, *of what country?*	**quis**, *who?*
īnfim-ās, *of the lowest rank;*	**īnfimus**, *lowest.*
for-ēnsis, *of a market-place, or the Forum;*	**forum**, *a market-place.*
cīvi-cus, *civic, of a citizen;*	**cīvis**, *a citizen.*
fullōn-icus, *of a fuller;*	**fullō**, *a fuller.*
mer-ācus, *pure;*	**merum**, *pure wine.*
fēmin-eus, *of a woman, feminine;*	**fēmina**, *a woman.*
lact-eus, *milky;*	**lac**, *milk* (stem **lacti-**).
plēb-ēius, *of the commons, plebeian;*	**plēbēs**, *the commons.*
patr-icius, *patrician;*	**pater**, *father.*

2. But especially from proper nouns to denote *belonging to* or *coming from:*

Rōm-ānus, *Roman;*	**Rōma**, *Rome.*
Sull-ānī, *Sulla's veterans;*	**Sulla.**
Cyzic-ēnī, *Cyzicenes, people of Cyzicus;*	**Cyzicus.**
Ligur-īnus, *of Liguria;*	**Liguria.**
Arpīn-ās, *of Arpinum;*	**Arpīnum.**
Sicili-ēnsis, *Sicilian;*	**Sicilia**, *Sicily.*
Īli-acus, *Trojan* (a Greek form);	**Īlium**, *Troy.*
Platōn-icus, *Platonic;*	**Platō.**
Aquil-êius, a Roman name; **Aquil-êia**, a town in Italy;	**Aquila.**

a. Many derivative adjectives with these endings have by usage become nouns: —

Silv-ānus, M., *a god of the woods;*	**silva**, *a wood.*
membr-āna, F., *skin;*	**membrum**, *limb.*
Aemili-ānus, M., name of Scipio Africanus;	**Aemilia** (**gēns**).
lani-ēna, F., *a butcher's stall;*	**lanius**, *butcher.*
Aufidi-ēnus, M., a Roman name;	†**Aufidius** (**Aufidus**).
inquil-īnus, M., *a lodger;*	**incola**, *an inhabitant.*
Caec-īna, used as M., a Roman name;	**caecus**, *blind.*
ru-īna, F., *a fall;*	**ruō**, *fall* (no noun existing).
doctr-īna, F., *learning;*	**doctor**, *teacher.*

NOTE. — Of these terminations, **-ānus**, **-ēnus**, **-īnus** are compounded from **-nus** added to a stem-vowel: as, **arca**, **arcānus**; **collis**, **collīnus**. The long vowels come from a confusion with verb-stems (as in **plē-nus**, **fīnī-tus**, **tribū-tus**), and from the noun-stem in **ā-**: as, **arcānus**. A few nouns occur of similar formation, as if from verb-stems in **ō-** and **ū-**: as, **colōnus** (**colō**, cf. **incola**), **patrōnus** (cf. **patrō**, **-āre**), **tribūnus** (cf. **tribuō**, **tribus**), **Portūnus** (cf. **portus**), **Vacūna** (cf. **vacō**, **vacuus**).

250. Other adjectives meaning in a general way *belonging to* (especially of *places* and *times*) are formed with the suffixes —

-ter (-tris), -ester (-estris), -timus, -nus, -ernus, -urnus, -ternus (-turnus)

palūs-ter, *of the marshes;*	**palūs**, *a marsh.*
pedes-ter, *of the foot-soldiers;*	**pedes**, *a footman.*
sēmēs-tris, *lasting six months;*	**sex mēnsēs**, *six months.*
silv-ester, silv-estris, *woody;*	**silva**, *a wood.*
fīni-timus, *neighboring, on the borders;*	**fīnis**, *an end.*
mari-timus, *of the sea;*	**mare**, *sea.*
vēr-nus, *vernal;*	**vēr**, *spring.*
hodi-ernus, *of to-day;*	**hodiē**, *to-day.*
di-urnus, *daily;*	**diēs**, *day.*
hes-ternus, *of yesterday;*	**herī** (old **hesī**), *yesterday.*
diū-turnus, *lasting;*	**diū**, *long* (in time).

Note.—Of these, **-ester** is formed by adding **tri-** (cf. **tro-**, § 234. II. 16) to stems in **t-** or **d-**. Thus †**pedet-tri-** becomes **pedestri-**, and others follow the analogy. **-nus** is an inherited suffix (§ 234. II. 4). **-ernus** and **-urnus** are formed by adding **-nus** to **s**-stems: as, **diur-nus** (for †**dius-nus**), and hence, by analogy, **hodiernus** (**hodiē**). By an extension of the same principle were formed the suffixes **-ternus** and **-turnus** from words like **paternus** and **nocturnus**.

a. Adjectives meaning *belonging to* are formed from nouns by means of the suffixes—

-ārius, -tōrius (-sōrius)

ōrdin-ārius, *regular;*	**ōrdō**, *rank, order.*
argent-ārius, *of silver* or *money;*	**argentum**, *silver.*
extr-ārius, *stranger;*	**extrā**, *outside.*
meri-tōrius, *profitable;*	**meritus**, *earned.*
dēvor-sōrius, *of an inn* (cf. § 254. 5);	**dēvorsus**, *turned aside.*

Note 1.—Here **-ius** (§ 234. II. 11) is added to shorter forms in **-āris** and **-or**: as, **pecūliārius** (from **pecūliāris**), **bellātōrius** (from **bellātor**).

Note 2.—These adjectives are often fixed as nouns (see § 254).

Verbal Adjectives

251. Adjectives expressing the action of the verb as a *quality* or *tendency* are formed from real or apparent verb-stems with the suffixes—

-āx, -idus, -ulus, -vus (-uus, -īvus, -tīvus)

-āx denotes a *faulty* or *aggressive* tendency; **-tīvus** is oftener passive.

pūgn-āx, *pugnacious;*	**pūgnāre**, *to fight.*
aud-āx, *bold;*	**audēre**, *to dare.*
cup-idus, *eager;*	**cupere**, *to desire.*
bib-ulus, *thirsty* (as dry earth etc.);	**bibere**, *to drink.*
proter-vus, *violent, wanton;*	**prōterere**, *to trample.*

noc-uus (**noc-īvus**), *hurtful, injurious;*	**nocēre**, *to do harm.*
recid-īvus, *restored;*	**recidere**, *to fall back.*
cap-tīvus, *captive;* M., *a prisoner of war;*	**capere**, *to take.*

NOTE. — Of these, **-āx** is a reduction of **-ācus** (stem-vowel **ā-** + **-cus**), become independent and used with verb-stems. Similar forms in **-ĕx**, **-ōx**, **-īx**, and **-ūx** are found or employed in derivatives: as, **imbrex**, M., *a rain-tile* (from **imber**); **senex**, *old* (from **seni-s**); **ferōx**, *fierce* (from **ferus**); **atrōx**, *savage* (from **āter**, *black*); **celōx**, F., *a yacht* (cf. **cellō**); **fēlīx**, *happy*, originally *fertile* (cf. **fēlō**, *suck*); **fīdūcia**, F., *confidence* (as from †**fīdūx**); cf. also **victrīx** (from **victor**). So **mandūcus**, *chewing* (from **mandō**).

-idus is no doubt denominative, as in **herbidus**, *grassy* (from **herba**, *herb*); **tumidus**, *swollen* (cf. **tumu-lus**, *hill;* **tumul-tus**, *uproar*); **callidus**, *tough, cunning* (cf. **callum**, *tough flesh*); **mūcidus**, *slimy* (cf. **mūcus**, *slime*); **tābidus**, *wasting* (cf. **tābēs**, *wasting disease*). But later it was used to form adjectives directly from verb-stems.

-ulus is the same suffix as in diminutives, but attached to verb-stems. Cf. **aemulus**, *rivalling* (cf. **imitor** and **imāgō**); **sēdulus**, *sitting by, attentive* (cf. **domi-seda**, *home-staying*, and **sēdō**, *set, settle*, hence *calm*); **pendulus**, *hanging* (cf. **pondō**, ablative, *in weight;* **perpendiculum**, *a plummet;* **appendix**, *an addition*); **strāgulus**, *covering* (cf. **strāgēs**); **legulus**, *a picker* (cf. **sacri-legus**, *a picker up of things sacred*).

-vus seems originally primary (cf. § 234. II. 8), but **-īvus** and **-tīvus** have become secondary and are used with nouns: as, **aestīvus**, *of summer* (from **aestus**, *heat*); **tempestīvus**, *timely* (from **tempus**); cf. **domes-ticus** (from **domus**).

252. Adjectives expressing *passive qualities*, but occasionally active, are formed by means of the suffixes —

-ilis, -bilis, -ius, -tilis (-silis)

frag-ilis, *frail;*	**frangere** (FRAG), *to break.*
nō-bilis, *well known, famous;*	**nōscere** (GNO), *to know.*
exim-ius, *choice, rare* (cf. **ē-greg-ius**);	**eximere**, *to take out, select.*
ag-ilis, *active;*	**agere**, *to drive.*
hab-ilis, *handy;*	**habēre**, *to hold.*
al-tilis, *fattened* (see note);	**alere**, *to nourish.*

NOTE. — Of these, **-ius** is primary, but is also used as secondary (cf. § 241. *b*. N.). **-ilis** is both primary (as in **agilis**, **fragilis**) and secondary (as in **similis**, *like*, cf. ὅμος, ὁμαλος, English *same*); **-bilis** is in some way related to **-bulum** and **-brum** (§ 240. N.); in **-tilis** and **-silis**, **-lis** is added to **to-** (**so-**), stem of the perfect participle: as, **fossilis**, *dug up* (from **fossus**, *dug*); **volātilis**, *winged* (from **volātus**, *flight*).

253. Verbal Adjectives that are Participial in meaning are formed with the suffixes —

-ndus, -bundus, -cundus

a. **-ndus** (the same as the gerundive ending) forms a few active or reflexive adjectives: —

secu-ndus, *second* (the following), *favorable;*	**sequī**, *to follow.*
rotu-ndus, *round* (whirling)[1];	**rotāre**, *to whirl.*

[1] Cf. **volvendīs mēnsibus** (Aen. i. 269), *in the revolving months;* cf. **oriundī ab Sabīnīs** (Liv. i. 17), *sprung from the Sabines*, where **oriundī** = **ortī**.

b. **-bundus, -cundus**, denote a continuance of the *act* or *quality* expressed by the verb: —

vītā-bundus, *avoiding;*	**vītāre**, *to shun.*
treme-bundus, *trembling;*	**tremere**, *to tremble.*
mori-bundus, *dying, at the point of death;*	**morīrī**, *to die.*
fā-cundus, *eloquent;*	**fārī**, *to speak.*
fē-cundus, *fruitful;*	root FĒ, *nourish.*
īrā-cundus, *irascible;*	cf. **īrāscī**, *to be angry.*

NOTE. — These must have been originally nominal: as in the series, **rubus**, *red bush;* **rubidus** (but no †**rubicus**), *ruddy;* **Rubicōn**, *Red River* (cf. **Miniō**, a river of Etruria; **Minius**, a river of Lusitania); **rubicundus** (as in **averruncus**, **homun-culus**). So **turba**, *commotion;* **turbō**, *a top;* **turbidus**, *roily*, etc. Cf. **apexabō**, **longabō**, **gravēdō**, **dulcēdō**.

c. Here belong also the participial suffixes **-minus**, **-mnus** (cf. Greek -μενος), from which are formed a few nouns in which the participial force is still discernible: —[1]

fē-mina, *woman* (the nourisher);	root FĒ, *nourish.*
alu-mnus, *a foster-child, nursling;*	**alere**, *to nourish.*

Nouns with Adjective Suffixes

254. Many fixed forms of the Nominal Adjective suffixes mentioned in the preceding sections, make Nouns more or less regularly used in particular senses: —

1. **-ārius**, *person employed about* anything: —

argent-ārius, M., *silversmith, broker*, from **argentum**, *silver.*
Corinthi-ārius, M., *worker in Corinthian bronze* (sarcastic nickname of Augustus), from (**aes**) **Corinthium**, *Corinthian bronze.*
centōn-ārius, M., *ragman*, from **centō**, *patchwork.*

2. **-āria**, *thing connected with* something: —

argent-āria, F., *bank*, from **argentum**, *silver.*
arēn-āriae, F. plural, *sandpits*, from **arēna**, *sand.*
Asin-āria, F., name of a play, from **asinus**, *ass.*[2]

3. **-ārium**, *place of* a thing (with a few of more general meaning): —

aer-ārium, N., *treasury*, from **aes**, *copper.*
tepid-ārium, N., *warm bath*, from **tepidus**, *warm.*
sūd-ārium, N., *a towel*, cf. **sūdō**, **-āre**, *sweat.*
sal-ārium, N., *salt money, salary*, from **sāl**, *salt.*
calend-ārium, N., *a note-book*, from **calendae**, *calends.*

[1] Cf. § 163. footnote 1.
[2] Probably an adjective with **fābula**, *play*, understood.

4. **-tōria** (**-sōria**): —

Agitā-tōria, F., a play of Plautus, *The Carter*, from **agitātor**.
vor-sōria, F., *a tack* (nautical), from **vorsus**, *a turn*.

5. **-tōrium** (**-sōrium**), *place of action* (with a few of more general meaning):

dēvor-sōrium, N., *an inn*, as from **dēvortō**, *turn aside*.
audī-tōrium, N., *a lecture-room*, as from **audiō**, *hear*.
ten-tōrium, N., *a tent*, as from **tendō**, *stretch*.
tēc-tōrium, N., *plaster*, as from **tegō**, **tēctus**, *cover*.
por-tōrium, N., *toll*, cf. **portō**, *carry*, and **portus**, *harbor*.

6. **-īle**, *animal-stall*: —

bov-īle, N., *cattle-stall*, from **bōs**, **bŏvis**, *ox*, *cow*.
ov-īle, N., *sheepfold*, from **ovis**, stem **ovi-**, *sheep*.

7. **-al** for **-āle**, *thing connected with* the primitive: —

capit-al, N., *headdress*, *capital crime*, from **caput**, *head*.
penetr-āle (especially in plural), N., *inner apartment*, cf. **penetrō**, *enter*.
Sāturn-ālia, N. plural (the regular form for *names of festivals*), *feast of Saturn*, from **Sāturnus**.

8. **-ētum**, N. (cf. **-ātus**, **-ūtus**, see § 246. N.), **-tum**, *place of* a thing, especially with names of trees and plants to designate where these *grow*: —

querc-ētum, N., *oak grove*, from **quercus**, *oak*.
olīv-ētum, N., *olive grove*, from **olīva**, *an olive tree*.
salic-tum, N., *a willow thicket*, from **salix**, *a willow tree*.
Argil-ētum, N., *The Clay Pit*, from **argilla**, *clay*.

9. **-cus** (sometimes with inserted **i**, **-icus**), **-īcus**, in any one of the genders, with various meanings: —

vīli-cus, M., *a steward*, **vīli-ca**, F., *a stewardess*, from **vīlla**, *farm-house*.
fabr-ica, F., *a workshop*, from **faber**, *workman*.
am-īcus, M., **am-īca**, F., *friend*, cf. **amāre**, *to love*.
būbul-cus, M., *ox-tender*, from **būb-ulus**, diminutive, cf. **bōs**, *ox*.
cant-icum, N., *song*, from **cantus**, *act of singing*.
rubr-īca, F., *red paint*, from **ruber**, *red*.

10. **-eus**, **-ea**, **-eum**, with various meanings: —

alv-eus, M., *a trough*, from **alvus**, *the belly*.
capr-ea, F., *a wild she-goat*, from **caper**, *he-goat*.
flamm-eum, N., *a bridal veil*, from **flamma**, *flame*, from its color.

11. **-ter** (stem **tri-**), **-aster**, **-ester**: —

eques-ter, M., *knight*, for †**equet-ter**.
sequ-ester, M., *a stake-holder*, from derivative of **sequor**, *follow*.
ole-aster, M., *wild olive*, from **olea**, *an olive tree*.

IRREGULAR DERIVATIVES

255. The suffix **-ō** (genitive **-ōnis**, stem **ōn-**), usually added to verb-stems (see § 236. *c*), is sometimes used with noun-stems to form nouns denoting *possessed of*. These were originally adjectives expressing *quality* or *character*, and hence often appear as *proper names*: —

> **epulae**, *a feast;* **epul-ō**, *a feaster.*
> **nāsus**, *a nose;* **nās-ō**, *with a large nose* (also as a proper name).
> **volus** (in **bene-volus**), *wishing;* **vol-ōnēs** (plural), *volunteers.*
> **frōns**, *forehead;* **front-ō**, *big-head* (also as a proper name).
> **cūria**, *a curia;* **cūri-ō**, *head of a curia* (also as a proper name).
> **restis**, *a rope;* **resti-ō**, *a rope-maker.*

a. Rarely suffixes are added to *compound* stems imagined, but not used in their compound form: —

> **ad-verb-ium**, *adverb;* **ad**, *to*, and **verbum**, *verb*, but without the intervening †**adverbus**.
> **lāti-fund-ium**, *large estate;* **lātus**, *wide*, **fundus**, *estate*, but without the intervening †**lātifundus**.
> **su-ove-taur-īlia**, *a sacrifice of a swine, a sheep, and a bull;* **sūs**, *swine*, **ovis**, *sheep*, **taurus**, *bull*, where the primitive would be impossible in Latin, though such formations are common in Sanskrit.

DERIVATION OF VERBS

256. Verbs may be classed as *Primitive* or *Derivative.*

1. Primitive Verbs are those inherited by the Latin from the parent speech.
2. Derivative Verbs are those formed in the development of the Latin as a separate language.

257. Derivative Verbs are of two main classes: —

1. Denominative Verbs, formed from nouns or adjectives.
2. Verbs apparently derived from the stems of other verbs.

Denominative Verbs

258. Verbs were formed in Latin from almost every form of noun-stem and adjective-stem.

259. 1. Verbs of the First Conjugation are formed directly from **ā**-stems, regularly with a transitive meaning: as, **fuga**, *flight;* **fugāre**, *put to flight.*

2. Many verbs of the First Conjugation are formed from o-stems, changing the o- into ā-. These are more commonly transitive: —

stimulō, -āre, *to incite*, from stimulus, *a goad* (stem stimulo-).
aequō, -āre, *to make even*, from aequus, *even* (stem aequo-).
hībernō, -āre, *to pass the winter*, from hībernus, *of the winter* (stem hīberno-).
albō, -āre, *to whiten*, from albus, *white* (stem albo-).
piō, -āre, *to expiate*, from pius, *pure* (stem pio-).
novō, -āre, *to renew*, from novus, *new* (stem novo-).
armō, -āre, *to arm*, from arma, *arms* (stem armo-).
damnō, -āre, *to injure*, from damnum, *injury* (stem damno-).

3. A few verbs, generally intransitive, are formed by analogy from consonant and i- or u-stems, adding ā to the stem: —[1]

vigilō, -āre, *to watch*, from vigil, *awake*.
exsulō, -āre, *to be in exile*, from exsul, *an exile*.
auspicor, -ārī, *to take the auspices*, from auspex (stem auspic-), *augur*.
pulverō, -āre, *to turn* (anything) *to dust*, from pulvis (stem pulver- for pulvis-), *dust*.
aestuō, -āre, *to surge*, *boil*, from aestus (stem aestu-), *tide*, *seething*.
levō, -āre, *to lighten*, from levis (stem levi-), *light*.

260. A few verbs of the Second Conjugation (generally intransitive) are recognizable as formed from noun-stems; but most are inherited, or the primitive noun-stem is lost: —

albeō, -ēre, *to be white*, from albus (stem alb$^{o}/_{e}$-), *white*.
cāneo, -ēre, *to be hoary*, from cānus (stem cān$^{o}/_{e}$-), *hoary*.
clāreō, -ēre, *to shine*, from clārus, *bright*.
claudeō, -ēre, *to be lame*, from claudus, *lame*.
algeō, -ēre, *to be cold*, cf. algidus, *cold*.

261. Some verbs of the Third Conjugation in -uō, -uere, are formed from noun-stems in u- and have lost a consonant i: —

statuō (for †statu-yō), -ere, *to set up*, from status, *position*.
metuō, -ere, *to fear*, from metus, *fear*.
acuō, -ere, *to sharpen*, from acus, *needle*.
arguō, -ere, *to clear up*, from inherited stem †argu-, *bright* (cf. ἄργυρος).

NOTE. — Many verbs in u are inherited, being formed from roots in u: as, fluō, fluere, *flow*; so-lvō (for †sē-luō, cf. λύω), solvere, *dissolve*. Some roots have a parasitic u: as, loquor, locūtus, *speak*.

[1] The type of all or most of the denominative formations in §§ 259–262 was inherited, but the process went on in the development of Latin as a separate language.

262. Many ī-verbs or verbs of the Fourth Conjugation are formed from **i**-stems: —

mōlior, -īrī, *to toil*, from **mōlēs (-is)**, *mass.*
fīniō, -īre, *to bound*, from **fīnis**, *end.*
sitiō, -īre, *to thirst*, from **sitis**, *thirst.*
stabiliō, -īre, *to establish*, from **stabilis**, *stable.*

a. Some arise by confusion from other stems treated as **i**-stems: —

bulliō, -īre, *to boil*, from **bulla** (stem **bullā-**), *bubble.*
condiō, -īre, *to preserve*, from **condus** (stem **condo-**), *storekeeper.*
īnsāniō, -īre, *to rave*, from **īnsānus** (stem **īnsāno-**), *mad.*
gestiō, -īre, *to show wild longing*, from **gestus** (stem **gestu-**), *gesture.*

NOTE. — Some of this form are of doubtful origin: as, **ōrdior**, *begin*, cf. **ōrdō** and **exōrdium**. The formation is closely akin to that of verbs in **-iō** of the third conjugation (p. 102).

b. Some are formed with **-iō** from consonant stems: —

cūstōdiō, -īre, *to guard*, from **cūstōs** (stem **cūstōd-**), *guardian.*
fulguriō, -īre, *to lighten*, from **fulgur**, *lightning.*

NOTE. — Here probably belong the so-called *desideratives* in **-uriō** (see § 263. 4. N.).

Verbs from Other Verbs

263. The following four classes of verbs regularly derived from other verbs have special meanings connected with their terminations.

NOTE. — These classes are all really denominative in their origin, but the formations had become so associated with actual verbs that new derivatives were often formed directly from verbs without the intervention of a noun-stem.

1. Inceptives or Inchoatives add **-scō** [1] to the present stem of verbs. They denote the *beginning* of an action and are of the Third Conjugation. Of some there is no simple verb in existence: —

calē-scō, *grow warm*, from **caleō**, *be warm.*
labā-scō, *begin to totter*, from **labō**, *totter.*
scī-scō, *determine*, from **sciō**, *know.*
con-cupī-scō, *conceive a desire for*, from **cupiō**, *desire.*
alē-scō, *grow*, from **alō**, *feed.*
So **īrā-scor,** *get angry;* cf. **īrā-tus.**
iuvenē-scō, *grow young;* cf. **iuvenis**, *young man.*
mītē-scō, *grow mild;* cf. **mītis**, *mild.*
vesperā-scit, *it is getting late;* cf. **vesper**, *evening.*

[1] For **-scō** in primary formation, see § 176. *b.* 1.

NOTE.—Inceptives properly have only the present stem, but many use the perfect and supine systems of simple verbs: as, **calēscō**, *grow warm*, **caluī**; **ārdēscō**, *blaze forth*, **ārsī**; **proficīscor**, *set out*, **profectus**.

2. Intensives or Iteratives are formed from the Supine stem and end in **-tō** or **-itō** (rarely **-sō**). They denote a *forcible* or *repeated* action, but this special sense often disappears. Those derived from verbs of the First Conjugation end in **-itō** (not **-ātō**).

iac-tō, *hurl*, from **iaciō**, *throw*.
dormī-tō, *be sleepy*, from **dormiō**, *sleep*.
vol-itō, *flit*, from **volō**, *fly*.
vēndi-tō, *try to sell*, from **vēndō**, *sell*.
quas-sō, *shatter*, from **quatiō**, *shake*.

They are of the first conjugation, and are properly denominative.

a. Compound suffixes **-titō**, **-sitō**, are formed with a few verbs. These are probably derived from other Iteratives; thus, **cantitō** may come from **cantō**, iterative of **canō**, *sing*.

b. Another form of Intensives—sometimes called Meditatives, or verbs of *practice*—ends in **-essō** (rarely **-issō**). These denote a certain *energy* or *eagerness* of action rather than its repetition:—

cap-essō, *lay hold on*, from **capiō**, *take*.
fac-essō, *do* (with energy), from **faciō**, *do*.
pet-esso, **pet-issō**, *seek* (eagerly), from **petō**, *seek*.

These are of the third conjugation, usually having the perfect and supine of the fourth:—

arcessō, arcessĕre, arcessīvī, arcessītum, *summon*.
lacessō, lacessĕre, lacessīvī, lacessītum, *provoke*.

NOTE.—The verbs in **-essō**, **-issō**, show the same formation as **levāssō**, **impetrāssere**, **iūdicāssit**, etc. (§ 183. 5), but its origin is not fully explained.

3. Diminutives end in **-illō**, and denote a *feeble* or *petty* action:—

cav-illor, *jest*, cf. **cavilla**, *raillery*.
cant-illō, *chirp* or *warble*, from **cantō**, *sing*.

NOTE.—Diminutives are formed from verb-stems derived from real or supposed diminutive nouns.

4. Desideratives end in **-turiō** (**-suriō**), and express *longing* or *wishing*. They are of the fourth conjugation, and only two are in common use:—

par-turiō, *be in labor*, from **pariō**, *bring forth*.
ē-suriō (for †**ed-turiō**), *be hungry*, from **edō**, *eat*.

Others are used by the dramatists.

NOTE.—Desideratives are probably derived from some noun of agency: as, **ēmpturiō**, *wish to buy*, from **ēmptor**, *buyer*. **Vīsō**, *go to see*, is an inherited desiderative of a different formation.

COMPOUND WORDS

264. A Compound Word is one whose stem is made up of two or more simple stems.

a. A final stem-vowel of the first member of the compound usually disappears before a vowel, and usually takes the form of **i** before a consonant. Only the second member receives inflection.[1]

b. Only noun-stems can be thus compounded. A preposition, however, often becomes attached to a verb.

265. New stems are formed by Composition in three ways:—

1. The second part is simply added to the first:—

su-ove-taurīlia (**sūs, ovis, taurus**), *the sacrifice of a swine, a sheep, and a bull* (cf. § 255. *a*).
septen-decim (**septem, decem**), *seventeen.*

2. The first part modifies the second as an adjective or adverb (*Determinative Compounds*):—

lāti-fundium (**lātus, fundus**), *a large landed estate.*
omni-potēns (**omnis, potēns**), *omnipotent.*

3. The first part has the force of a case, and the second a verbal force (*Objective Compounds*):—

agri-cola (**ager,** *field,* †**cola** akin to **colō,** *cultivate*), *a farmer.*
armi-ger (**arma,** *arms,* †**ger** akin to **gerō,** *carry*), *armor-bearer.*
corni-cen (**cornū,** *horn,* †**cen** akin to **canō,** *sing*), *horn-blower.*
carni-fex (**carō,** *flesh,* †**fex** akin to **faciō,** *make*), *executioner.*

a. Compounds of the above kinds, in which the last word is a noun, may become adjectives, meaning *possessed of* the quality denoted:—

āli-pēs (**āla,** *wing,* **pēs,** *foot*), *wing-footed.*
māgn-animus (**māgnus,** *great,* **animus,** *soul*), *great-souled.*
an-ceps (**amb-,** *at both ends,* **caput,** *head*), *double.*

NOTE.—Many compounds of the above classes appear only in the form of some further derivative, the proper compound not being found in Latin.

[1] The second part generally has its usual inflection; but, as this kind of composition is in fact older than inflection, the compounded stem sometimes has an inflection of its own (as, **cornicen, -cinis; lūcifer, -ferī; iūdex, -dicis**), from stems not occurring in Latin. Especially do compound adjectives in Latin take the form of **i**-stems: as, **animus, exanimis; nōrma, abnōrmis** (see § 73). In composition, stems regularly have their uninflected form: as, **īgni-spicium,** *divining by fire.* But in **o**- and **ā**-stems the final vowel of the stem appears as **i**-, as in **āli-pēs** (from **āla,** stem **ālā-**); and **i**- is so common a termination of compounded stems, that it is often added to stems which do not properly have it: as, **flōri-comus,** *flower-crowned* (from **flōs, flōr-is,** and **coma,** *hair*).

Syntactic Compounds

266. In many apparent compounds, complete words — not stems — have grown together in speech. These are not strictly compounds in the etymological sense. They are called Syntactic Compounds. Examples are: —

a. Compounds of **faciō, factō**, with an actual or formerly existing noun-stem confounded with a verbal stem in ē-. These are *causative* in force:

cōnsuē-faciō, *habituate* (cf. **cōnsuē-scō**, *become accustomed*).
cale-faciō, cale-factō, *to heat* (cf. **calē-scō**, *grow warm*).

b. An adverb or noun combined with a verb: —

bene-dīcō (**bene**, *well*, **dīcō**, *speak*), *to bless.*
satis-faciō (**satis**, *enough*, **faciō**, *do*), *to do enough* (for).

c. Many apparent compounds of stems: —

fide-iubeō (**fide**, *surety*, **iubeō**, *command*), *to give surety.*
mān-suētus (**manuī**, *to the hand*, **suētus**, *accustomed*), *tame.*
Mārci-por (**Mārcī puer**), *slave of Marcus.*
Iuppiter (†**Iū**, old vocative, and **pater**), *father Jove.*
anim-advertō (**animum advertō**), *attend to, punish.*

d. A few phrases forced into the ordinary inflections of nouns: —

prō-cōnsul, *proconsul* (for **prō cōnsule**, *instead of a consul*).
trium-vir, *triumvir* (singular from **trium virōrum**).
septen-triō, *the Bear*, a constellation (supposed singular of **septem triōnēs**, *the Seven Plough-Oxen*).

In all these cases it is to be observed that *words*, not *stems*, are united.

267. Many syntactic compounds are formed by prefixing a Particle to some other part of speech.

a. Prepositions are often prefixed to Verbs. In these compounds the prepositions retain their original adverbial sense: —

ā, ab, AWAY: **ā-mittere**, *to send away.*
ad, TO, TOWARDS: **af-ferre** (**ad-ferō**), *to bring.*
ante, BEFORE: **ante-ferre**, *to prefer;* **ante-cellere**, *to excel.*
circum, AROUND: **circum-mūnīre**, *to fortify completely.*
com-, con- (**cum**), TOGETHER or FORCIBLY: **cōn-ferre**, *to bring together;* **col-locāre**, *to set firm.*
dē, DOWN, UTTERLY: **dē-spicere**, *despise;* **dē-struere**, *destroy.*
ē, ex, OUT: **ef-ferre** (**ec-ferō**), *to carry forth, uplift.*
in (with verbs), IN, ON, AGAINST: **īn-ferre**, *to bear against.*
inter, BETWEEN, TO PIECES: **inter-rumpere**, *to interrupt.*
ob, TOWARDS, TO MEET: **of-ferre**, *to offer;* **ob-venīre**, *to meet.*
sub, UNDER, UP FROM UNDER: **sub-struere**, *to build beneath;* **sub-dūcere**, *to lead up.*
super, UPON, OVER AND ABOVE: **super-fluere**, *to overflow.*

NOTE 1.—In such compounds, however, the prepositions sometimes have their ordinary force as prepositions, especially **ad**, **in**, **circum**, **trāns**, and govern the case of a noun: as, **trānsīre flūmen**, *to cross a river* (see § 388. *b*).

NOTE 2.—Short **a** of the root is weakened to **i** before one consonant, to **e** before two: as, **faciō**, **cōnficiō**, **cōnfectus**; **iaciō**, **ēiciō**, **ēiectus**. But long **a** is retained: as, **perāctus**.

b. VERBS are also compounded with the following *inseparable particles*, which do not appear as prepositions in Latin:—

amb- (**am-**, **an-**), AROUND: **amb-īre**, *to go about* (cf. ἀμφί, *about*).

dis-, **dī-**, ASUNDER, APART: **dis-cēdere**, *to depart* (cf. **duo**, *two*); **dī-vidĕre**, *to divide.*

por-, FORWARD: **por-tendere**, *to hold forth*, *predict* (cf. **porrō**, *forth*).

red-, **re-**, BACK, AGAIN: **red-īre**, *to return*; **re-clūdere**, *to open* (from **claudō**, *shut*); **re-ficere**, *to repair* (make again).

sēd-, **sē-**, APART: **sē-cernō**, *to separate*; cf. **sēd-itiō**, *a going apart*, *secession* (**eō**, **īre**, *to go*).

c. Many Verbals are found compounded with a preposition, like the verbs to which they correspond:—

per-fuga, *deserter*; cf. **per-fugiō**.
trā-dux, *vine-branch*; cf. **trā-dūcō** (**trāns-dūcō**).
ad-vena, *stranger*; cf. **ad-veniō**.
con-iux (**con-iūnx**), *spouse*; cf. **con-iungō**.
in-dex, *pointer out*; cf. **in-dīcō**.
prae-ses, *guardian*; cf. **prae-sideō**.
com-bibō, *boon companion*; cf. **com-bibō**, **-ĕre**.

d. An Adjective is sometimes modified by an adverbial prefix.

1. Of these, **per-** (less commonly **prae-**), *very*; **sub-**, *somewhat*; **in-**, *not*, are regular, and are very freely prefixed to adjectives:—

per-māgnus, *very large.*
per-paucī, *very few.*
sub-rūsticus, *rather clownish.*
sub-fuscus, *darkish.*
prae-longus, *very long.*
in-nocuus, *harmless.*
in-imīcus, *unfriendly.*
īn-sānus, *insane.*
īn-fīnītus, *boundless.*
im-pūrus, *impure.*

NOTE.—**Per** and **sub**, in these senses, are also prefixed to verbs: as, **per-terreō**, *terrify*; **sub-rīdeō**, *smile*. In **īgnōscō**, *pardon*, **in-** appears to be the negative prefix.

2. The negative **in-** sometimes appears in combination with an adjective that does not occur alone:—

in-ermis, *unarmed* (cf. **arma**, *arms*).
im-bellis, *unwarlike* (cf. **bellum**, *war*).
im-pūnis, *without punishment* (cf. **poena**, *punishment*).
in-teger, *untouched*, *whole* (cf. **tangō**, *to touch*, root TAG).
in-vītus, *unwilling* (probably from root seen in **vī-s**, *thou wishest*).

PART SECOND—SYNTAX

INTRODUCTORY NOTE

268. The study of formal grammar arose at a late period in the history of language, and dealt with language as a fully developed product. Accordingly the terms of Syntax correspond to the logical habits of thought and forms of expression that had grown up at such a period, and have a *logical* as well as a merely *grammatical* meaning. But a developed syntactical structure is not essential to the expression of thought. A form of words—like **ō puerum pulchrum!** *oh! beautiful boy*—expresses a thought and might even be called a sentence; though it does not logically declare anything, and does not, strictly speaking, make what is usually called a sentence at all.

At a very early period of spoken language, word-forms were no doubt significant in themselves, without inflections, and constituted the whole of language,—just as to a child the name of some familiar object will stand for all he can say about it. At a somewhat later stage, such uninflected words put side by side made a rudimentary form of proposition: as a child might say *fire bright; horse run.* With this began the first form of logical distinction, that of Subject and Predicate; but as yet there was no distinction in form between noun and verb, and no fixed distinction in function. At a later stage forms were differentiated in function and—by various processes of composition which cannot be fully traced—Inflections were developed. These served to express *person, tense, case,* and other grammatical relations, and we have true Parts of Speech.

Not until language reached this last stage was there any fixed limit to the association of words, or any rule prescribing the manner in which they should be combined. But gradually, by usage, particular forms came to be limited to special functions (as nouns, verbs, adjectives), and fixed customs arose of combining words into what we now call Sentences. These customs are in part the result of general laws or modes of thought (logic), resulting from our habits of mind (*General Grammar*); and in part are what may be called By-Laws, established by custom in a given language (*Particular Grammar*), and making what is called the Syntax of that language.

In the fully developed methods of expression to which we are almost exclusively accustomed, the unit of expression is the *Sentence:* that is, the completed statement, with its distinct Subject and Predicate. Originally sentences were simple. But two simple sentence-forms may be used together, without the grammatical subordination of either, to express a more complex form of thought than could be denoted by one alone. This is *parataxis* (arrangement side by side). Since, however, the two sentences, independent in form, were in fact used to express parts of a complex whole and were therefore mutually dependent, the sense of unity found expression in conjunctions, which denoted the grammatical subordination of the one to the other. This is *hypotaxis* (arrangement under, subordination). In this way, through various stages of development, which correspond to our habitual modes of thought, there were produced various forms of *complex sentences.* Thus, to express the complex idea *I beseech you to pardon me,* the two simple sentence-forms **quaesō** and **ignōscās** were used side by side, **quaesō ignōscās**; then the feeling of grammatical subordination found expression in a conjunction, **quaesō ut ignōscās**, forming a complex sentence. The results of these processes constitute the subject-matter of Syntax.

THE SENTENCE

Kinds of Sentences

269. A Sentence is a form of words which contains a Statement, a Question, an Exclamation, or a Command.

a. A sentence in the form of a Statement is called a Declarative Sentence: as,—**canis currit**, *the dog runs.*

b. A sentence in the form of a Question is called an Interrogative Sentence: as,—**canisne currit?** *does the dog run?*

c. A sentence in the form of an Exclamation is called an Exclamatory Sentence: as,—**quam celeriter currit canis!** *how fast the dog runs!*

d. A sentence in the form of a Command, an Exhortation, or an Entreaty is called an Imperative Sentence: as,—**ī, curre per Alpīs**, *go, run across the Alps;* **currat canis**, *let the dog run.*

Subject and Predicate

270. Every sentence consists of a Subject and a Predicate. The Subject of a sentence is the *person or thing spoken of.* The Predicate is *that which is said* of the Subject.

Thus in **canis currit**, *the dog runs*, **canis** is the subject, and **currit** the predicate.

271. The Subject of a sentence is usually a Noun or Pronoun, or some word or group of words used as a Noun:—

> **equitēs ad Caesarem vēnērunt**, *the cavalry came to Cæsar.*
> **hūmānum est errāre**, *to err is human.*
> **quaeritur num mors malum sit**, *the question is whether death is an evil.*

a. But in Latin the subject is often implied in the termination of the verb:—

> **sedē-mus**, *we sit.* **curri-tis**, *you run.* **inqui-t**, *says he.*

272. The Predicate of a sentence may be a Verb (as in **canis currit**, *the dog runs*), or it may consist of some form of **sum** and a Noun or Adjective which *describes* or *defines* the subject (as in **Caesar cōnsul erat**, *Cæsar was consul*).

Such a noun or adjective is called a Predicate Noun or Adjective, and the verb **sum** is called the Copula (i.e. the *connective*).

Thus in the example given, **Caesar** is the subject, **cōnsul** the predicate noun, and **erat** the copula (see § 283).

Transitive and Intransitive Verbs

273. Verbs are either Transitive or Intransitive.

1. A Transitive Verb has or requires a direct object to complete its sense (see § 274): as,— **frātrem cecīdit**, *he slew his brother*.

2. An Intransitive Verb admits of no direct object to complete its sense:—

cadō, *I fall* (or *am falling*). sōl lūcet, *the sun shines* (or *is shining*).

NOTE 1.—Among transitive verbs Factitive Verbs are sometimes distinguished as a separate class. These state an act which *produces* the thing expressed by the word which completes their sense. Thus mēnsam fēcit, *he made a table* (which was not in existence before), is distinguished from mēnsam percussit, *he struck a table* (which already existed).

NOTE 2.—A transitive verb may often be used *absolutely*, i.e. without any object expressed: as,—arat, *he is ploughing*, where the verb does not cease to be transitive because the object is left indefinite, as we see by adding,—quid, *what?* agrum suum, *his land*.

NOTE 3.—Transitive and Intransitive Verbs are often called Active and Neuter Verbs respectively.

Object

274. The person or thing immediately affected by the action of a verb is called the Direct Object.

A person or thing indirectly affected by the action of a verb is called the Indirect Object.

Only transitive verbs can have a Direct Object; but an Indirect Object may be used with both transitive and intransitive verbs (§§ 362, 366):—

pater vocat fīlium (direct object), *the father calls his son.*
mihi (ind. obj.) agrum (dir. obj.) ostendit, *he showed me a field.*
mihi (ind. obj.) placet, *it is pleasing to me.*

NOTE.—The distinction between transitive and intransitive verbs is not a fixed distinction, for most transitive verbs may be used intransitively, and many verbs usually intransitive may take a direct object and so become transitive (§ 388. *a*).

a. With certain verbs, the Genitive, Dative, or Ablative is used where the English, from a difference in meaning, requires the direct object (Objective):—

hominem videō, *I see the man* (Accusative).
hominī serviō, *I serve the man* (Dative, see § 367).
hominis misereor, *I pity the man* (Genitive, see § 354. *a*).
homine amīcō ūtor, *I treat the man as a friend* (Ablative, see § 410).

b. Many verbs transitive in Latin are rendered into English by an intransitive verb with a preposition:—

petit **aprum**, *he aims at the boar.*
laudem affectat, *he strives after praise.*
cūrat **valētūdinem**, *he takes care of his health.*
meum **cāsum** doluērunt, *they grieved at my misfortune.*
rīdet nostram **āmentiam** (Quinct. 55), *he laughs at our stupidity.*

275. When a transitive verb is changed from the Active to the Passive voice, the Direct Object becomes the Subject and is put in the Nominative case: —

Active: pater **fīlium** vocat, *the father calls his son.*
Passive: **fīlius** ā patre vocātur, *the son is called by his father.*
Active: **lūnam** et **stellās** vidēmus, *we see the moon and the stars.*
Passive: **lūna** et **stellae** videntur, *the moon and stars are seen* (appear).

Modification

276. A Subject or a Predicate may be *modified* by a single word, or by a group of words (a *phrase* or a *clause*).

The modifying word or group of words may itself be modified in the same way.

a. A single modifying word may be an adjective, an adverb, an appositive (§ 282), or the oblique case of a noun.

Thus in the sentence **vir fortis patienter fert**, *a brave man endures patiently*, the adjective **fortis**, *brave*, modifies the subject **vir**, *man*, and the adverb **patienter**, *patiently*, modifies the predicate **fert**, *endures.*

b. The modifying word is in some cases said to *limit* the word to which it belongs.

Thus in the sentence **puerī patrem videō**, *I see the boy's father*, the genitive **puerī** limits **patrem** (by excluding any other father).

277. A Phrase is a group of words, without subject or predicate of its own, which may be used as an Adjective or an Adverb.

Thus in the sentence **vir fuit summā nōbilitāte**, *he was a man of the highest nobility*, the words **summā nōbilitāte**, *of the highest nobility*, are used for the adjective **nōbilis**, *noble* (or **nōbilissimus**, *very noble*), and are called an Adjective Phrase.

So in the sentence **māgnā celeritāte vēnit**, *he came with great speed*, the words **māgnā celeritāte**, *with great speed*, are used for the adverb **celeriter**, *quickly* (or **celerrimē**, *very quickly*), and are called an Adverbial Phrase.

Clauses and Sentences

278. Sentences are either Simple or Compound.

1. A sentence containing a single statement is called a Simple Sentence.

2. A sentence containing more than one statement is called a Compound Sentence, and each single statement in it is called a Clause.

a. If one statement is simply added to another, the clauses are said to be Coördinate. They are usually connected by a Coördinate Conjunction (§ 223. *a*); but this is sometimes omitted: —

dīvide **et** imperā, *divide and control.* But, —
vēnī, vīdī, vīcī, *I came, I saw, I conquered.*

b. If one statement modifies another in any way, the modifying clause is said to be Subordinate, and the clause modified is called the Main Clause.

This subordination is indicated by some connecting word, either a Subordinate Conjunction (§ 223. *b*) or a Relative: —

ōderint **dum** metuant, *let them hate so long as they fear.*
servum mīsit **quem** sēcum habēbat, *he sent the slave whom he had with him.*

A sentence containing one or more subordinate clauses is sometimes called Complex.

NOTE. — A subordinate clause may itself be modified by other subordinate clauses.

279. Subordinate Clauses are of various kinds.

a. A clause introduced by a Relative Pronoun or Relative Adverb is called a Relative Clause: —

Mosa prōfluit ex monte Vosegō, **quī est in fīnibus Lingonum** (B. G. iv. 10), *the Meuse rises in the Vosges mountains, which are on the borders of the Lingones.*

For Relative Pronouns (or Relative Adverbs) serving to connect independent sentences, see § 308. *f*.

b. A clause introduced by an Adverb of Time is called a Temporal Clause: —

cum tacent, clāmant (Cat. i. 21), *while they are silent, they cry aloud.*
hominēs aegrī morbō gravī, **cum iactantur aestū febrīque,** sī aquam gelidam biberint, prīmō relevārī videntur (id. i. 31), *men suffering with a severe sickness, when they are tossing with the heat of fever, if they drink cold water, seem at first to be relieved.*

c. A clause containing a Condition, introduced by **sī**, *if* (or some equivalent expression), is called a Conditional Clause. A sentence containing a conditional clause is called a Conditional Sentence.

Thus, **sī aquam gelidam biberint, prīmō relevārī videntur** (in *b*, above) is a Conditional Sentence, and **sī . . . biberint** is a Conditional Clause.

d. A clause expressing the Purpose of an action is called a Final Clause: —

edō ut vīvam, *I eat to live* (that I may live).
mīsit lēgātōs quī dīcerent, *he sent ambassadors to say* (who should say).

e. A clause expressing the Result of an action is called a Consecutive Clause: —[1]

tam longē aberam ut nōn vidērem, *I was too far away to see* (so far away that I did not see).

AGREEMENT

280. A word is said to *agree* with another when it is required by usage to be in the same Gender, Number, Case, or Person.

The following are the general forms of agreement, sometimes called the Four Concords: —

1. The agreement of the Noun in Apposition or as Predicate (§§ 281–284).
2. The agreement of the Adjective with its Noun (§ 286).
3. The agreement of the Relative with its Antecedent (§ 305).
4. The agreement of the Finite Verb with its Subject (§ 316).

a. A word sometimes takes the gender or number, not of the word with which it should regularly agree, but of some other word *implied* in that word.

This use is called Synesis, or *cōnstrūctiō ad sēnsum* (construction according to sense).

AGREEMENT OF NOUNS

281. A noun used to *describe* another, and denoting the same person or thing, agrees with it in Case.

The descriptive noun may be either an Appositive (§ 282) or a Predicate noun (§ 283).

[1] Observe that the classes defined in *a–e* are not mutually exclusive, but that a single clause may belong to several of them at once. Thus a relative clause is usually subordinate, and may be at the same time temporal or conditional: and subordinate clauses may be coördinate with each other.

Apposition

282. A noun used to *describe* another, and standing in the same part of the sentence with the noun described, is called an Appositive, and is said to be *in apposition:* —

externus timor, maximum concordiae **vinculum**, iungēbat animōs (Liv. ii. 39), *fear of the foreigner, the chief bond of harmony, united their hearts.* [Here the appositive belongs to the *subject.*]

quattuor hīc prīmum **ōmen** equōs vīdī (Aen. iii. 537), *I saw here four horses, the first omen.* [Here both nouns are in the *predicate.*]

litterās Graecās **senex** didicī (Cat. M. 26), *I learned Greek when an old man.* [Here **senex**, though in apposition with the subject of **didicī**, really states something further: viz., the *time, condition*, etc., of the act (*Predicate Apposition*).]

a. Words expressing *parts* may be in apposition with a word including the parts, or vice versa (*Partitive Apposition*): —

Nec P. Popilius neque Q. Metellus, clārissimī **virī** atque amplissimī, vim tribūnīciam sustinēre potuērunt (Clu. 95), *neither Publius Popilius nor Quintus Metellus,* [both of them] *distinguished and honorable men, could withstand the power of the tribunes.*

Gnaeus et Pūblius **Scīpiōnēs**, *Cneius and Publius Scipio* (the Scipios).

b. An Adjective may be used as an appositive: —

ea Sex. Rōscium **inopem** recēpit (Rosc. Am. 27), *she received Sextus Roscius in his poverty* (needy).

c. An appositive generally agrees with its noun in Gender and Number when it can: —

sequuntur nātūram, **optimam ducem** (Lael. 19), *they follow nature, the best guide.*

omnium doctrīnārum **inventrīcēs** Athēnās (De Or. i. 13), *Athens, discoverer of all learning.*

NOTE. — But such agreement is often impossible: as, — **ōlim truncus eram fīculnus, inūtile līgnum** (Hor. S. i. 8. 1), *I once was a fig-tree trunk, a useless log.*

d. A common noun in apposition with a Locative (§ 427) is put in the Ablative, with or without the preposition **in**: —

Antiochīae, celebrī quondam **urbe** (Arch. 4), *at Antioch, once a famous city.*

Albae cōnstitērunt, **in urbe** mūnītā (Phil. iv. 6), *they halted at Alba, a fortified town.*

For a Genitive in apposition with a Possessive Pronoun or an Adjective, see § 302. *e.*
For the so-called Appositional Genitive, see § 343. *d.*
For the construction with **nōmen est**, see § 373. *a.*

Predicate Noun or Adjective

283. With **sum** and a few other intransitive or passive verbs, a noun or an adjective *describing* or *defining* the subject may stand in the predicate. This is called a Predicate Noun or Adjective.

The verb **sum** is especially common in this construction, and when so used is called the *copula* (i.e. connective).

Other verbs which take a predicate noun or adjective are the so-called *copulative verbs* signifying *to become, to be made, to be named, to appear,* and the like.

284. A Predicate Noun or Adjective after the copula **sum** or a copulative verb is in the same case as the Subject:—

pācis semper **auctor** fuī (Lig. 28), *I have always been an adviser of peace.*
quae **pertinācia** quibusdam, eadem aliīs **cōnstantia** vidērī potest (Marc. 31), *what may seem obstinacy to some, may seem to others consistency.*
êius mortis sedētis **ultōrēs** (Mil. 79), *you sit as avengers of his death.*
habeātur vir ēgregius Paulus (Cat. iv. 21), *let Paulus be regarded as an extraordinary man.*
ego **patrōnus** exstitī (Rosc. Am. 5), *I have come forward as an advocate.*
dīcit nōn omnīs bonōs esse **beātōs**, *he says that not all good men are happy.*

a. A predicate noun referring to two or more singular nouns is in the plural:—

cōnsulēs creantur Caesar et Servīlius (B. C. iii. 1), *Cæsar and Servilius are elected consuls.*

b. **Sum** in the sense of *exist* makes a complete predicate without a predicate noun or adjective. It is then called the *substantive verb:*—

sunt virī fortēs, *there are* (exist) *brave men.* [Cf. vīxēre fortēs ante Agamemnona (Hor. Od. iv. 9. 25), *brave men lived before Agamemnon.*]

For Predicate Accusative and Predicate Ablative, see §§ 392, 415. N.

AGREEMENT OF ADJECTIVES

Attributive and Predicate Adjectives

285. Adjectives are either Attributive or Predicate.

1. An Attributive Adjective simply qualifies its noun without the intervention of a verb or participle, expressed or implied: as,—**bonus imperātor**, *a good commander;* **stellae lūcidae**, *bright stars;* **verbum Graecum**, *a Greek word.*

2. All other adjectives are called Predicate Adjectives: —

stellae **lūcidae** erant, *the stars were bright.*
sit Scīpiō **clārus** (Cat. iv. 21), *let Scipio be illustrious.*
hominēs **mītīs** reddidit (Inv. i. 2), *has rendered men mild.*
tria praedia Capitōnī **propria** trāduntur (Rosc. Am. 21), *three farms are handed over to Capito as his own.*
cōnsilium cēpērunt **plēnum** sceleris (id. 28), *they formed a plan full of villany.*

NOTE. — A predicate adjective may be used with **sum** or a copulative verb (§ 283); it may have the construction of a predicate accusative after a verb of *naming, calling,* or the like (§ 393. N.); or it may be used in apposition like a noun (§ 282. *b*).

Rules of Agreement

286. Adjectives, Adjective Pronouns, and Participles agree with their nouns in *Gender, Number,* and *Case:* —

vir **fortis**, *a brave man.*
illa mulier, *that woman.*
urbium **māgnārum**, *of great cities.*
cum **ducentīs** mīlitibus, *with two hundred soldiers.*
imperātor **victus est**, *the general was beaten.*
secūtae sunt tempestātēs, *storms followed.*

NOTE. — All rules for the agreement of adjectives apply also to adjective pronouns and to participles.

a. With two or more nouns the adjective is regularly plural, but often agrees with the nearest (especially when attributive): —

Nīsus et Euryalus **prīmī** (Aen. v. 294), *Nisus and Euryalus first.*
Caesaris **omnī** et grātiā et opibus fruor (Fam. i. 9. 21), *I enjoy all Cæsar's favor and resources.*

NOTE. — An adjective referring to two nouns connected by the preposition **cum** is occasionally plural (*synesis,* § 280. *a*): as, — **Iuba cum Labiēnō captī** (B. Afr. 52), *Juba and Labienus were taken.*

b. A collective noun may take an adjective of a different gender and number agreeing with the gender and number of the individuals implied (*synesis,* § 280. *a*): —

pars certāre **parātī** (Aen. v. 108), *a part ready to contend.*
colōniae aliquot dēductae, Prīscī Latīnī **appellātī** (Liv. i. 3), *several colonies were planted* (led out) [of men] *called Old Latins.*
multitūdō **convictī** sunt (Tac. Ann. xv. 44), *a multitude were convicted.*
māgna pars **raptae** (id. i. 9), *a large part* [of the women] *were seized.*

NOTE. — A superlative in the predicate rarely takes the gender of a partitive genitive by which it is limited: as, — **vēlōcissimum animālium delphīnus est** (Plin. N. H. ix. 20), *the dolphin is the swiftest* [creature] *of creatures.*

287. One adjective may belong in sense to two or more nouns of different genders. In such cases, —

1. An Attributive Adjective agrees with the nearest noun: —

multae operae ac labōris, *of much trouble and toil.*
vīta mōrēsque **meī**, *my life and character.*
sī rēs, sī vir, sī tempus **ūllum** dīgnum fuit (Mil. 19), *if any thing, if any man, if any time was fit.*

2. A Predicate Adjective may agree with the nearest noun, if the nouns form one connected idea: —

factus est strepitus et admurmurātiō (Verr. i. 45), *a noise of assent was made* (noise and murmur).

NOTE. — This is only when the copula agrees with the nearest subject (§ 317. c).

3. But generally, a Predicate Adjective will be masculine, if nouns of different genders mean *living beings;* neuter, if *things without life:* —

uxor deinde ac līberī **amplexī** (Liv. ii. 40), *then his wife and children embraced him.*
labor (M.) **voluptāsque** (F.) societāte quādam inter sē nātūrālī sunt **iūncta** (N.) (id. v. 4), *labor and delight are bound together by a certain natural alliance.*

4. If nouns of different genders include both living beings and things without life, a Predicate Adjective is sometimes masculine (or feminine), sometimes neuter, and sometimes agrees in gender with the nearest if that is plural: —

rēx rēgiaque classis ūnā **profectī** (Liv. xxi. 50), *the king and the royal fleet set out together.*
nātūrā **inimīca** sunt lībera cīvitās et rēx (id. xliv. 24), *by nature a free state and a king are hostile.*
lēgātōs sortēsque ōrāculī **exspectandās** (id. v. 15), *that the ambassadors and the replies of the oracle should be waited for.*

a. Two or more abstract nouns of the same gender may have a Predicate Adjective in the neuter plural (cf. § 289. *c*): —

stultitia et temeritās et iniūstitia . . . sunt **fugienda** (Fin. iii. 39), *folly, rashness, and injustice are* [things] *to be shunned.*

Adjectives used Substantively

288. Adjectives are often used as Nouns (*substantively*), the masculine usually to denote *men* or *people in general* of that kind, the feminine *women*, and the neuter *things:* —

omnēs, *all men* (everybody).
omnia, *all things* (everything).
mâiōrēs, *ancestors.*
minōrēs, *descendants.*
Rōmānī, *Romans.*
barbarī, *barbarians.*
līberta, *a freedwoman.*
Sabīnae, *the Sabine wives.*
sapiēns, *a sage* (philosopher).
amīcus, *a friend.*
bonī, *the good* (good people).
bona, *goods, property.*

NOTE. — The plural of adjectives, pronouns, and participles is very common in this use. The singular is comparatively rare except in the neuter (§ 289. *a, c*) and in words that have become practically nouns.

a. Certain adjectives have become practically nouns, and are often modified by other adjectives or by the possessive genitive: —

tuus **vīcīnus** proximus, *your next-door neighbor.*
propinquī cēterī, *his other relatives.*
meus **aequālis**, *a man of my own age.*
êius **familiāris** Catilīna (Har. Resp. 5), *his intimate friend Catiline.*
Leptae nostrī **familiārissimus** (Fam. ix. 13. 2), *a very close friend of our friend Lepta.*

b. When ambiguity would arise from the substantive use of an adjective, a noun must be added: —

bonī, *the good;* omnia, *everything* (all things); but, —
potentia **omnium rērum**, *power over everything.*

c. Many adjectives are used substantively either in the singular or the plural, with the added meaning of some noun which is understood from constant association: —

Āfricus [ventus], *the southwest wind;* Iānuārius [mēnsis], *January;* vitulīna [carō], *veal* (calf's flesh); fera [bēstia], *a wild beast;* patria [terra], *the fatherland;* Gallia [terra], *Gaul* (the land of the Gallī); hīberna [castra], *winter quarters;* trirēmis [nāvis], *a three-banked galley, trireme;* argentārius [faber], *a silversmith;* rēgia [domus], *the palace;* Latīnae [fēriae], *the Latin festival.*

NOTE. — These adjectives are *specific* in meaning, not *generic* like those in § 288. They include the names of winds and months (§ 31).
For Nouns used as Adjectives, see § 321. *c.*
For Adverbs used like Adjectives, see § 321. *d.*

289. Neuter Adjectives are used substantively in the following special senses: —

a. The neuter *singular* may denote either a single object or an abstract quality: —

raptō vīvere, *to live by plunder.*
in **āridō**, *on dry ground.*
honestum, *an honorable act*, or *virtue* (as a quality).
opus est **mātūrātō**, *there is need of haste.* [Cf. impersonal passives, § 208. *d.*]

b. The neuter *plural* is used to signify *objects in general* having the quality denoted, and hence may stand for the abstract idea: —

honesta, *honorable deeds* (in general). praeterita, *the past* (lit., bygones).
omnēs **fortia** laudant, *all men praise bravery* (brave things).

c. A neuter adjective may be used as an appositive or predicate noun with a noun of different gender (cf. § 287. *a*): —

trīste lupus stabulīs (Ecl. iii. 80), *the wolf* [is] *a grievous thing for the fold.*
varium et **mūtābile** semper fēmina (Aen. iv. 569), *woman is ever a changing and fickle thing.*
malum mihi vidētur esse mors (Tusc. i. 9), *death seems to me to be an evil.*

d. A neuter adjective may be used as an attributive or a predicate adjective with an infinitive or a substantive clause: —

istuc ipsum nōn esse (Tusc. i. 12), *that very "not to be."*
hūmānum est errāre, *to err is human.*
aliud est errāre Caesarem nōlle, **aliud** nōlle miserērī (Lig. 16), *it is one thing to be unwilling that Cæsar should err, another to be unwilling that he should pity.*

Adjectives with Adverbial Force

290. An adjective, agreeing with the subject or object, is often used to qualify the action of the verb, and so has the force of an adverb: —

prīmus vēnit, *he was the first to come* (came first).
nūllus dubitō, *I no way doubt.*
laetī audiēre, *they were glad to hear.*
erat Rōmae **frequēns** (Rosc. Am. 16), *he was often at Rome.*
sērus in caelum redeās (Hor. Od. i. 2. 45), *mayst thou return late to heaven.*

Comparatives and Superlatives

291. Besides their regular signification (as in English), the forms of comparison are used as follows: —

a. The Comparative denotes a *considerable* or *excessive* degree of a quality: as, — **brevior**, *rather short;* **audācior**, *too bold.*

b. The Superlative (*of eminence*) often denotes a *very high* degree of a quality without implying a distinct comparison: as, — **mōns altissimus**, *a very high mountain.*

NOTE. — The Superlative of Eminence is much used in complimentary references to persons and may often be translated by the simple positive.

c. With **quam, vel,** or **ūnus** the Superlative denotes the *highest possible* degree: —

> **quam plūrimī**, *as many as possible.*
> **quam maximē** potest (**maximē quam** potest), *as much as can be.*
> **vel minimus**, *the very least.*
> vir **ūnus doctissimus**, *the one most learned man.*

NOTE 1. — A high degree of a quality is also denoted by such adverbs as **admodum, valdē**, *very*, or by **per** or **prae** in composition (§ 267. *d*. 1): as, — **valdē malus**, *very bad* = **pessimus**; **permāgnus**, *very great*; **praealtus**, *very high* (or *deep*).

NOTE 2. — A low degree of a quality is indicated by **sub** in composition: as, — **subrūsticus**, *rather clownish*, or by **minus**, *not very*; **minimē**, *not at all*; **parum**, *not enough*; **nōn satis**, *not much*.

NOTE 3. — The comparative **māiōrēs** (for **māiōrēs nātū**, *greater by birth*) has the special signification of *ancestors*; so **minōrēs** often means *descendants*.

For the Superlative with **quisque**, see § 313. *b*. For the construction of a substantive after a Comparative, see §§ 406, 407; for that of a clause, see § 535. *c*, 571. *a*. For the Ablative of Degree of Difference with a Comparative (**multō** etc.), see § 414.

292. When two qualities of an object are compared, both adjectives are in the Comparative: —

> **longior** quam **lātior** aciēs erat (Liv. xxvii. 48), *the line was longer than it was broad* (or, *rather long than broad*).
> **vērior** quam **grātior** (id. xxii. 38), *more true than agreeable.*

NOTE. — So also with adverbs: as, — **libentius quam vērius** (Mil. 78), *with more freedom than truth.*

a. Where **magis** is used, both adjectives are in the positive: —

> **disertus** magis quam **sapiēns** (Att. x. 1. 4), *eloquent rather than wise.*
> **clārī** magis quam **honestī** (Iug. 8), *more renowned than honorable.*

NOTE. — A comparative and a positive, or even two positives, are sometimes connected by **quam**. This use is rarer and less elegant than those before noticed: —

> **clāris māiōribus** quam **vetustīs** (Tac. Ann. iv. 61), *of a family more famous than old.*
> **vehementius** quam **cautē** (Tac. Agr. 4), *with more fury than good heed.*

293. Superlatives (and more rarely Comparatives) denoting order and succession — also **medius**, [**cēterus**], **reliquus** — usually designate not *what object*, but *what part of it*, is meant: —

> **summus** mōns, *the top of the hill.*
> in **ultimā** plateā, *at the end of the place.*
> **prior** āctiō, *the earlier part of an action.*
> **reliquī** captīvī, *the rest of the prisoners.*
> in colle **mediō** (B. G. i. 24), *half way up the hill* (on the middle of the hill).
> inter **cēteram** plānitiem (Iug. 92), *in a region elsewhere level.*

NOTE. — A similar use is found in **sērā** (**multā**) **nocte**, *late at night*, and the like. But **medium viae**, *the middle of the way*; **multum diēī**, *much of the day*, also occur.

PRONOUNS

294. A Pronoun indicates some person or thing without either naming or describing it. Pronouns are derived from a distinct class of roots, which seem to have denoted only ideas of place and direction (§ 228. 2), and from which nouns or verbs can very rarely be formed. They may therefore stand for Nouns when the person or thing, being already present to the senses or imagination, needs only to be *pointed out*, not *named*.

Some pronouns indicate the object in itself, without reference to its class, and have no distinction of gender. These are Personal Pronouns. They stand syntactically for Nouns, and have the same construction as nouns.

Other pronouns designate a particular object of a class, and take the gender of the individuals of that class. These are called Adjective Pronouns. They stand for Adjectives, and have the same construction as adjectives.

Others are used in both ways; and, though called adjective pronouns, may also be treated as personal, taking, however, the gender of the object indicated.

In accordance with their meanings and uses, Pronouns are classified as follows: —

Personal Pronouns (§ 295).
Demonstrative Pronouns (§ 296).
Reflexive Pronouns (§ 299).
Possessive Pronouns (§ 302).
Interrogative Pronouns (§ 333).
Relative Pronouns (§ 303).
Indefinite Pronouns (§ 309).

Personal Pronouns

295. The Personal Pronouns have, in general, the same constructions as nouns.

a. The personal pronouns are not expressed as subjects, except for distinction or emphasis: —

tē vocō, *I call you.* But, —
quis mē vocat? **ego** tē vocō, *who is calling me? I* (emphatic) *am calling you.*

b. The personal pronouns have two forms for the genitive plural, that in **-um** being used *partitively* (§ 346), and that in -ī oftenest *objectively* (§ 348): —

mâior **vestrum**, *the elder of you.*
habētis ducem memorem **vestrī**, oblītum suī (Cat. iv. 19), *you have a leader who thinks* (is mindful) *of you and forgets* (is forgetful of) *himself.*
pars **nostrum**, *a part* (i.e. some) *of us.*

NOTE 1.— The genitives **nostrum, vestrum**, are occasionally used objectively (§ 348): as, — **cupidus vestrum** (Verr. iii. 224), *fond of you*; **cūstōs vestrum** (Cat. iii. 29), *the guardian of you* (your guardian).

NOTE 2.— "One of themselves" is expressed by **ūnus ex suīs** or **ipsīs** (rarely **ex sē**), or **ūnus suōrum**.

c. The Latin has no personal pronouns of the third person except the reflexive **sē**. The want is supplied by a Demonstrative or Relative (§§ 296. 2, 308. *f*).

Demonstrative Pronouns

296. Demonstrative Pronouns are used either adjectively or substantively.

1. As adjectives, they follow the rules for the agreement of adjectives and are called Adjective Pronouns or Pronominal Adjectives (§§ 286, 287): —

hōc proeliō factō, *after this battle was fought* (this battle having been fought).
eōdem proeliō, *in the same battle.*
ex **eīs** aedificiīs, *out of those buildings.*

2. As substantives, they are equivalent to personal pronouns. This use is regular in the oblique cases, especially of **is**: —

Caesar et exercitus **êius**, *Cæsar and his army* (not **suus**). [But, Caesar exercitum **suum** dīmīsit, *Cæsar disbanded his* [own] *army.*]
sī obsidēs ab **eīs** dentur (B. G. i. 14), *if hostages should be given by them* (persons just spoken of).
hī sunt extrā prōvinciam trāns Rhodanum prīmī (id. i. 10), *they* (those just mentioned) *are the first* [inhabitants] *across the Rhone.*
ille minimum propter adulēscentiam poterat (id. i. 20), *he* (emphatic) *had very little power, on account of his youth.*

a. An adjective pronoun usually agrees with an appositive or predicate noun, if there be one, rather than with the word to which it refers (cf. § 306): —

hīc locus est ūnus quō perfugiant; **hīc** portus, **haec** arx, **haec** āra sociōrum (Verr. v. 126), *this is the only place to which they can flee for refuge; this is the haven, this the citadel, this the altar of the allies.*
rērum caput **hōc** erat, **hīc** fōns (Hor. Ep. i. 17. 45), *this was the head of things, this the source.*
eam sapientiam interpretantur **quam** adhūc mortālis nēmō est cōnsecūtus [for **id** . . . **quod**] (Lael. 18), *they explain that* [thing] *to be wisdom which no man ever yet attained.*

297. The main uses of **hīc, ille, iste,** and **is** are the following: —

a. **Hīc** is used of what is *near the speaker* (in time, place, or thought). It is hence called the *demonstrative of the first person.*

It is sometimes used of the speaker himself; sometimes for "the latter" of two persons or things mentioned in speech or writing; more rarely for "the former," when that, though more remote *on the written page*, is nearer the speaker in *time, place*, or *thought.* Often it refers to that which has *just been mentioned.*

b. **Ille** is used of what is *remote* (in time, etc.); and is hence called the *demonstrative of the third person.*

It is sometimes used to mean "the former"; also (usually following its noun) of what is *famous* or *well-known;* often (especially the neuter **illud**) to mean "the following."

c. **Iste** is used of what is *between the two others* in remoteness: often in allusion to the person addressed,—hence called the *demonstrative of the second person.*

It especially refers to one's opponent (in court, etc.), and frequently implies antagonism or contempt.

d. **Is** is a weaker demonstrative than the others and is especially common as a personal pronoun. It does not denote any special object, but refers to one just mentioned, or to be afterwards explained by a relative. Often it is merely a correlative to the relative **quī**:—

> vēnit mihi obviam tuus puer, **is** mihi litterās abs tē reddidit (Att. ii. 1. 1), *your boy met me, he delivered to me a letter from you.*
>
> **eum** quem, *one whom.*
>
> **eum** cōnsulem quī nōn dubitet (Cat. iv. 24), *a consul who will not hesitate.*

e. The pronouns **hīc**, **ille**, and **is** are used to point in either direction, back to something just mentioned or forward to something about to be mentioned.

The neuter forms often refer to a clause, phrase, or idea:—

> est **illud** quidem vel maximum, animum vidēre (Tusc. i. 52), *that is in truth a very great thing,—to see the soul.*

f. The demonstratives are sometimes used as *pronouns of reference,* to indicate with emphasis a noun or phrase just mentioned:—

> nūllam virtūs aliam mercēdem dēsīderat praeter **hanc** laudis (Arch. 28), *virtue wants no other reward except that* [just mentioned] *of praise.*

NOTE.—But the ordinary English use of *that of* is hardly known in Latin. Commonly the genitive construction is continued without a pronoun, or some other construction is preferred:—

> cum eī Simōnidēs artem memoriae pollicērētur: **oblīviōnis**, inquit, māllem (Fin. ii. 104), *when Simonides promised him the art of memory, "I should prefer," said he,* "[that] *of forgetfulness."*
>
> Caesaris exercitus **Pompêiānōs** ad Pharsālum vīcit, *the army of Cæsar defeated that of Pompey* (the Pompeians) *at Pharsalus.*

298. The main uses of **īdem** and **ipse** are as follows:—

a. When a quality or act is ascribed with emphasis to a person or thing already named, **is** or **īdem** (often with the concessive **quidem**) is used to indicate that person or thing:—

per ūnum servum et **eum** ex gladiātōriō lūdō (Att. i. 16. 5), *by means of a single slave, and that too one from the gladiatorial school.*

vincula, et **ea** sempiterna (Cat. iv. 7), *imprisonment, and that perpetual.*

Ti. Gracchus rēgnum occupāre cōnātus est, vel rēgnāvit **is quidem** paucōs mēnsīs (Lael. 41), *Tiberius Gracchus tried to usurp royal power, or rather he actually reigned a few months.*

Note.—So rarely with ille: as,—nunc dextrā ingemināns ictūs, nunc **ille** sinistrā (Aen. v. 457), *now dealing redoubled blows with his right hand, now* (he) *with his left.* [In imitation of the Homeric ὅ γε: cf. Aen. v. 334; ix. 796.]

b. **Īdem**, *the same*, is often used where the English requires an adverb or adverbial phrase (*also, too, yet, at the same time*):—

ōrātiō splendida et grandis et **eadem** in prīmīs facēta (Brut. 273), *an oration, brilliant, able, and very witty too.*

cum [haec] dīcat, negat **īdem** esse in Deō grātiam (N. D. i. 121), *when he says this, he denies also that there is mercy with God* (he, the same man).

Note.—This is really the same use as in *a* above, but in this case the pronoun cannot be represented by a pronoun in English.

c. The intensive **ipse**, *self*, is used with any of the other pronouns, with a noun, or with a temporal adverb for the sake of emphasis:—

turpe mihi **ipsī** vidēbātur (Phil. i. 9), *even to me* (to me myself) *it seemed disgraceful.*

id **ipsum**, *that very thing;* quod **ipsum**, *which of itself alone.*

in eum **ipsum** locum, *to that very place.*

tum **ipsum** (Off. ii. 60), *at that very time.*

Note 1.—The emphasis of ipse is often expressed in English by *just, very, mere*, etc.

Note 2.—In English, the pronouns *himself* etc. are used both intensively (as, *he will come himself*) and reflexively (as, *he will kill himself*): in Latin the former would be translated by ipse, the latter by sē or sēsē.

d. **Ipse** is often used alone, substantively, as follows:—

1. As an emphatic pronoun of the third person:—

idque reī pūblicae praeclārum, **ipsīs** glōriōsum (Phil. ii. 27), *and this was splendid for the state, glorious for themselves.*

omnēs bonī quantum in **ipsīs** fuit (id. ii. 29), *all good men so far as was in their power* (in themselves).

dī capitī **ipsīus** generīque reservent (Aen. viii. 484), *may the gods hold in reserve* [such a fate] *to fall on his own and his son-in-law's head.*

2. To emphasize an omitted subject of the first or second person:—

vōbīscum **ipsī** recordāminī (Phil. ii. 1), *remember in your own minds* (yourselves with yourselves).

3. To distinguish the principal personage from subordinate persons:—

ipse dīxit (cf. αὐτὸς ἔφα), *he* (the Master) *said it.*

Nōmentānus erat super **ipsum** (Hor. S. ii. 8. 23), *Nomentanus was above* [the host] *himself* [at table].

e. **Ipse** is often (**is** rarely) used instead of a reflexive (see § 300. *b*).

f. **Ipse** usually agrees with the subject, even when the real emphasis in English is on a reflexive in the predicate: —

> **mē ipse** cōnsōlor (Lael. 10), *I console myself.* [Not **mē ipsum,** as the English would lead us to expect.]

Reflexive Pronouns

299. The Reflexive Pronoun (**sē**), and usually its corresponding possessive (**suus**), are used in the predicate to refer to the subject of the sentence or clause: —

> **sē** ex nāvī prōiēcit (B. G. iv. 25), *he threw himself from the ship.*
> Dumnorīgem ad **sē** vocat (id. i. 20), *he calls Dumnorix to him.*
> **sēsē** castrīs tenēbant (id. iii. 24), *they kept themselves in camp.*
> contemnī **sē** putant (Cat. M. 65), *they think they are despised.*
> Caesar **suās** cōpiās subdūcit (B. G. i. 22), *Cæsar leads up his troops.*
> Caesar statuit **sibi** Rhēnum esse trānseundum (id. iv. 16), *Cæsar decided that he must cross the Rhine* (the Rhine must be crossed by himself).

a. For reflexives of the first and second persons the oblique cases of the personal pronouns (**meī, tuī,** etc.) and the corresponding possessives (**meus, tuus,** etc.) are used: —

> mortī **mē** obtulī (Mil. 94), *I have exposed myself to death.*
> hinc **tē** rēgīnae ad līmina perfer (Aen. i. 389), *do you go* (bear yourself) *hence to the queen's threshold.*
> quid est quod tantīs **nōs** in labōribus exerceāmus (Arch. 28), *what reason is there why we should exert ourselves in so great toils?*
> singulīs **vōbīs** novēnōs ex turmīs manipulīsque **vestrī** similēs ēligite (Liv. xxi. 54), *for each of you pick out from the squadrons and maniples nine like yourselves.*

300. In a subordinate clause of a complex sentence there is a double use of Reflexives.

1. The reflexive may always be used to refer to the subject of its own clause (*Direct Reflexive*): —

> iūdicārī potest quantum habeat in **sē** bonī cōnstantia (B. G. i. 40), *it can be determined how much good firmness possesses* (has in itself).
> [Caesar] nōluit eum locum vacāre, nē Germānī ē **suīs** fīnibus trānsīrent (id. i. 28), *Cæsar did not wish this place to lie vacant, for fear the Germans would cross over from their territories.*
> sī qua sīgnificātiō virtūtis ēlūceat ad quam **sē** similis animus adplicet et adiungat (Lael. 48), *if any sign of virtue shine forth to which a similar disposition may attach itself.*

2. If the subordinate clause expresses the words or thought of the subject of the main clause, the reflexive is regularly used to refer to that subject (*Indirect Reflexive*): —

petiērunt ut **sibi** licēret (B. G. i. 30), *they begged that it might be allowed them* (the petitioners).

Iccius nūntium mittit, nisi subsidium **sibi** submittātur (id. ii. 6), *Iccius sends a message that unless relief be furnished him*, etc.

decima legiō eī grātiās ēgit, quod dē **sē** optimum iūdicium fēcisset (id. i. 41), *the tenth legion thanked him because* [they said] *he had expressed a high opinion of them.*

sī obsidēs ab **eīs** (the Helvetians) **sibi** (Cæsar, who is the speaker) dentur, sē (Cæsar) cum eīs pācem esse factūrum (id. i. 14), [Cæsar said that] *if hostages were given him by them he would make peace with them.*

NOTE. — Sometimes the person or thing to which the reflexive refers is not the grammatical subject of the main clause, though it is in effect the subject of discourse: Thus, — cum ipsī **deō** nihil minus grātum futūrum sit quam nōn omnibus patēre ad **sē** plācandum viam (Legg. ii. 25), *since to God himself nothing will be less pleasing than that the way to appease him should not be open to all men.*

a. If the subordinate clause does not express the words or thought of the main subject, the reflexive is not regularly used, though it is occasionally found: —

sunt ita multī ut **eōs** carcer capere nōn possit (Cat. ii. 22), *they are so many that the prison cannot hold them.* [Here **sē** could not be used; so also in the example following.]

ibi in proximīs vīllīs ita bipartītō fuērunt, ut Tiberis **inter eōs** et pōns interesset (id. iii. 5), *there they stationed themselves in the nearest farmhouses, in two divisions, in such a manner that the Tiber and the bridge were between them* (the divisions).

nōn fuit eō contentus quod eī praeter spem acciderat (Manil. 25), *he was not content with that which had happened to him beyond his hope.*

Compare: quī fit, Maecēnās, ut nēmō, quam **sibi** sortem seu ratiō dederit seu fors obiēcerit, illā contentus vīvat (Hor. S. i. 1. 1), *how comes it, Mæcenas, that nobody lives contented with that lot which choice has assigned him or chance has thrown in his way?* [Here **sibi** is used to put the thought into the mind of the discontented man.]

b. **Ipse** is often (is rarely) used instead of an *indirect reflexive*, either to avoid ambiguity or from carelessness; and in later writers is sometimes found instead of the *direct reflexive*: —

cūr dē suā virtūte aut dē **ipsīus** dīligentiā dēspērārent (B. G. i. 40), *why* (he asked) *should they despair of their own courage or his diligence?*

omnia aut **ipsōs** aut hostēs populātōs (Q. C. iii. 5. 6), [they said that] *either they themselves or the enemy had laid all waste.* [Direct reflexive.]

qui sē ex hīs minus timidōs exīstimārī volēbant, nōn **sē** hostem verērī, sed angustiās itineris et māgnitūdinem silvārum quae intercēderent inter **ipsōs** (the persons referred to by **sē** above) atque Ariovistum . . . timēre dīcēbant (B. G. i. 39), *those of them who wished to be thought less timid said they did not fear the enemy, but were afraid of the narrows and the vast extent of the forests which were between themselves and Ariovistus.*

audīstis nūper dīcere lēgātōs Tyndaritānōs Mercurium quī sacrīs anniversāriīs **apud eōs** colerētur esse sublātum (Verr. iv. 84), *you have just heard the ambassadors from Tyndaris say that the statue of Mercury which was worshipped with annual rites among them was taken away.* [Here Cicero wavers between **apud eōs colēbātur,** a remark of his own, and **apud sē colerētur,** the words of the ambassadors. **eōs** does not strictly refer to the ambassadors, but to the people — the *Tyndaritani.*]

301. Special uses of the Reflexive are the following: —

a. The reflexive in a subordinate clause sometimes refers to the subject of a suppressed main clause: —

Paetus omnīs librōs quōs frāter **suus** relīquisset mihi dōnāvit (Att. ii. 1), *Pœtus gave me all the books which* (as he said in the act of donation) *his brother had left him.*

b. The reflexive may refer to any noun or pronoun in its own clause which is so emphasized as to become the *subject of discourse:* —

Sōcratem cīvēs **suī** interfēcērunt, *Socrates was put to death by his own fellow-citizens.*

quī poterat salūs **sua cuiquam** nōn probārī (Mil. 81), *how can any one fail to approve his own safety?* [In this and the preceding example the emphasis is preserved in English by the change of voice.]

hunc sī secūtī erunt **suī** comitēs (Cat. ii. 10), *this man, if his companions follow him.*

NOTE. — Occasionally the clause to which the reflexive really belongs is absorbed: as, — studeō sānāre **sibi ipsōs** (Cat. ii. 17), *I am anxious to cure these men for their own benefit* (i.e. **ut sānī sibi sint**).

c. **Suus** is used for *one's own* as emphatically opposed to *that of others,* in any part of the sentence and with reference to any word in it: —

suīs flammīs dēlēte Fīdēnās (Liv. iv. 33), *destroy Fidenœ with its own fires* (the fires kindled by that city, figuratively). [Cf. Cat. i. 32.]

d. The reflexive may depend upon a verbal noun or adjective: —

suī laus, *self-praise.*

habētis ducem memorem vestrī, oblītum **suī** (Cat. iv. 19), *you have a leader mindful of you, forgetful of himself.*

perditī hominēs cum **suī** similibus servīs (Phil. i. 5), *abandoned men with slaves like themselves.*

e. The reflexive may refer to the subject implied in an infinitive or verbal abstract used indefinitely: —

contentum **suīs** rēbus esse maximae sunt dīvitiae (Par. 51), *the greatest wealth is to be content with one's own.*

cui prōposita sit cōnservātiō **suī** (Fin. v. 37), *one whose aim is self-preservation.*

f. **Inter sē** (**nōs**, **vōs**), *among themselves* (*ourselves, yourselves*), is regularly used to express reciprocal action or relation: —

inter sē cōnflīgunt (Cat. i. 25), *contend with each other.*

inter sē continentur (Arch. 2), *are joined to each other.*

Possessive Pronouns

302. The Possessive Pronouns are derivative adjectives, which take the gender, number, and case of the noun *to which they belong*, not those of the *possessor*: —

haec ōrnāmenta sunt **mea** (Val. iv. 4), *these are my jewels.* [**mea** is neuter plural, though the speaker is a woman.]

meī sunt ōrdinēs, **mea** dīscrīptiō (Cat. M. 59), *mine are the rows, mine the arrangement.* [**mea** is feminine, though the speaker is Cyrus.]

multa in **nostrō** collēgiō praeclāra (id. 64), [there are] *many fine things in our college.* [**nostrō** is neuter singular, though *men* are referred to.]

Germānī **suās** cōpiās castrīs ēdūxērunt (B. G. i. 51), *the Germans led their troops out of the camp.*

a. To express possession and similar ideas the possessive pronouns are regularly used, not the genitive of the personal or reflexive pronouns (§ 343. *a*): —

domus **mea**, *my house.* [Not **domus meī.**]

pater **noster**, *our father.* [Not **pater nostrī.**]

patrimōnium **tuum**, *your inheritance.* [Not **tuī.**]

NOTE 1. — Exceptions are rare in classic Latin, common in later writers. For the use of a possessive pronoun instead of an Objective Genitive, see § 348. *a.*

NOTE 2. — The Interrogative Possessive **cûius**, **-a**, **-um**, occurs in poetry and early Latin: as, — **cûium pecus** (Ecl. iii. 1), *whose flock?* The genitive **cûius** is generally used instead.

b. The possessives have often the acquired meaning of *peculiar to, favorable* or *propitious towards*, the person or thing spoken of: —

[petere] ut **suā** clēmentiā ac mānsuētūdine ūtātur (B. G. ii. 14), *they asked* (they said) *that he would show his* [wonted] *clemency and humanity.*

īgnōrantī quem portum petat nūllus **suus** ventus est (Sen. Ep. 71. 3), *to him who knows not what port he is bound to, no wind is fair* (his own).

tempore **tuō** pūgnāstī (Liv. xxxviii. 45. 10), *did you fight at a fit time?*

NOTE. — This use is merely a natural development of the meaning of the possessive, and the pronoun may often be rendered literally.

c. The possessives are regularly omitted (like other pronouns) when they are plainly implied in the context:—

> **socium fraudāvit**, *he cheated his partner.* [**socium suum** would be distinctive, *his partner* (and not another's); **suum socium**, emphatic, *his own partner.*]

d. Possessive pronouns and adjectives implying possession are often used substantively to denote some special class or relation:—

> **nostrī**, *our countrymen*, or *men of our party.*
> **suōs continēbat** (B. G. i. 15), *he held his men in check.*
> **flamma extrēma meōrum** (Aen. ii. 431), *last flames of my countrymen.*
> **Sullānī**, *the veterans of Sulla's army;* **Pompêiānī**, *the partisans of Pompey.*

NOTE.—There is no reason to suppose an ellipsis here. The adjective becomes a noun like other adjectives (see § 288).

e. A possessive pronoun or an adjective implying possession may take an appositive in the genitive case agreeing in gender, number, and case with an implied noun or pronoun:—

> **meā sōlīus causā** (Ter. Heaut. 129), *for my sake only.*
> **in nostrō omnium flētū** (Mil. 92), *amid the tears of us all.*
> **ex Anniānā Milōnis domō** (Att. iv. 3. 3), *out of Annius Milo's house.* [Equivalent to **ex Annī Milōnis domō.**]
> **nostra omnium patria**, *the country of us all.*
> **suum ipsīus rēgnum**, *his own kingdom.*

For the special reflexive use of the possessive **suus**, see §§ 299, 300.

Relative Pronouns

303. A Relative Pronoun agrees with some word expressed or implied either in its own clause, or (often) in the antecedent (demonstrative) clause. In the fullest construction the antecedent is expressed in both clauses, with more commonly a corresponding *demonstrative* to which the relative refers: as,—**iter in ea loca facere coepit, quibus in locīs esse Germānōs audiēbat** (B. G. iv. 7), *he began to march into those* PLACES *in which* PLACES *he heard the Germans were.* But one of these nouns is commonly omitted.

The antecedent is in Latin very frequently (rarely in English) found in the relative clause, but more commonly in the antecedent clause.

Thus relatives serve two uses at the same time:—

1. As Nouns (or Adjectives) in their own clause: as,—**eī quī Alesiae obsīdēbantur** (B. G. vii. 77), *those who were besieged at Alesia.*

2. As Connectives: as,—**T. Balventius, quī superiōre annō prīmum pīlum dūxerat** (id. v. 35), *Titus Balventius, who the year before had been a centurion of the first rank.*

When the antecedent is in a different sentence, the relative is often equivalent to a demonstrative with a conjunction: as,—**quae cum ita sint** (=**et cum ea ita sint**), [and] *since this is so.*

The subordinating force did not belong to the relative originally, but was developed from an interrogative or indefinite meaning specialized by use. But the subordinating and the later connective force were acquired by **quī** at such an early period that the steps of the process cannot now be traced.

304. A Relative Pronoun indicates a relation between its own clause and some substantive. This substantive is called the Antecedent of the relative.

Thus, in the sentence —

eum **nihil** dēlectābat **quod** fās esset (Mil. 43), *nothing pleased him which was right*,

the relative **quod** connects its antecedent **nihil** with the predicate **fās esset**, indicating a relation between the two.

305. A Relative agrees with its Antecedent in *Gender* and *Number;* but its *Case* depends on its construction in the clause in which it stands: —

ea diēs **quam** cōnstituerat vēnit (B. G. i. 8), *that day which he had appointed came.*

pontem **quī** erat ad Genāvam iubet rescindī (id. i. 7), *he orders the bridge which was near Geneva to be cut down.*

Aduatucī, dē **quibus** suprā dīximus, domum revertērunt (id. ii. 29), *the Aduatuci, of whom we have spoken above, returned home.*

NOTE. — This rule applies to all relative words so far as they are variable in form: as, **quālis**, **quantus**, **quīcumque**, etc.

a. If a relative has two or more antecedents, it follows the rules for the agreement of predicate adjectives (§§ 286, 287): —

fīlium et fīliam, **quōs** valdē dīlēxit, unō tempore āmīsit, *he lost at the same time a son and a daughter whom he dearly loved.*

grandēs nātū mātrēs et parvulī līberī, **quōrum** utrōrumque aetās misericordiam nostram requīrit (Verr. v. 129), *aged matrons and little children, whose time of life in each case demands our compassion.*

ōtium atque dīvitiae, **quae** prīma mortālēs putant (Sall. Cat. 36), *idleness and wealth, which men count the first* (objects of desire).

eae frūgēs et frūctūs **quōs** terra gignit (N. D. ii. 37), *those fruits and crops which the earth produces.*

For the Person of the verb agreeing with the Relative, see § 316. *a*.

306. A Relative generally agrees in gender and number with an appositive or predicate noun in its own clause, rather than with an antecedent of different gender or number (cf. § 296. *a*): —

mare etiam **quem** Neptūnum esse dīcēbās (N. D. iii. 52), *the sea, too, which you said was Neptune.* [Not **quod**.]

Thēbae ipsae, **quod** Boeōtiae caput est (Liv. xlii. 44), *even Thebes, which is the chief city of Bœotia.* [Not **quae**.]

NOTE. — This rule is occasionally violated: as, — flūmen **quod** appellātur Tamesis (B. G. v. 11), *a river which is called the Thames.*

a. A relative occasionally agrees with its antecedent in case (by *attraction*): —

sī aliquid agās **eōrum quōrum** cōnsuēstī (Fam. v. 14), *if you should do something of what you are used to do.* [For **eōrum quae.**]

Note. — Occasionally the antecedent is attracted into the case of the relative: —

urbem quam statuō vestra est (Aen. i. 573), *the city which I am founding is yours.*

Naucratem, quem convenīre voluī, in nāvī nōn erat (Pl. Am. 1009), *Naucrates, whom I wished to meet, was not on board the ship.*

b. A relative may agree in gender and number with an *implied* antecedent: —

quārtum genus . . . **quī** in vetere aere aliēnō vacillant (Cat. ii. 21), *a fourth class, who are staggering under old debts.*

ūnus ex eō numerō **quī** parātī erant (Iug. 35), *one of the number* [of those] *who were ready.*

coniūrāvēre paucī, dē **quā** [i.e. coniūrātiōne] dīcam (Sall. Cat. 18), *a few have conspired, of which* [conspiracy] *I will speak.*

Note. — So regularly when the antecedent is implied in a possessive pronoun: as, — nostra ācta, **quōs** tyrannōs vocās (Vat. 29), *the deeds of us, whom you call tyrants.* [Here **quōs** agrees with the **nostrum** (genitive plural) implied in **nostra.**]

Antecedent of the Relative

307. The Antecedent Noun sometimes appears in both clauses, but usually only in the one that precedes. Sometimes it is wholly omitted.

a. The antecedent noun may be repeated in the relative clause: —

locī nātūra erat haec quem **locum** nostrī dēlēgerant (B. G. ii. 18), *the nature of the ground which our men had chosen was this.*

b. The antecedent noun may appear only in the relative clause, agreeing with the relative in case: —

quās **rēs** in cōnsulātū nostrō gessimus attigit hīc versibus (Arch. 28), *he has touched in verse the things which I did in my consulship.*

quae prīma innocentis mihi **dēfēnsiō** est oblāta suscēpī (Sull. 92), *I undertook the first defence of an innocent man that was offered me.*

Note. — In this case the relative clause usually comes first (cf. § 308. *d*) and a demonstrative usually stands in the antecedent clause: —

quae pars cīvitātis calamitātem populō Rōmānō intulerat, **ea** prīnceps poenās persolvit (B. G. i. 12), *that part of the state which had brought disaster on the Roman people was the first to pay the penalty.*

quae grātia currum fuit vīvīs, **eadem** sequitur (Aen. vi. 653), *the same pleasure that they took in chariots in their lifetime follows them* (after death).

quī fit ut nēmō, **quam** sibi **sortem** ratiō dederit, **illā** contentus vīvat (cf. Hor. S. i. 1. 1), *how does it happen that no one lives contented with the lot which choice has assigned him?*

c. The antecedent may be omitted, especially if it is indefinite: —

quī decimae legiōnis aquilam ferēbat (B. G. iv. 25), [the man] *who bore the eagle of the tenth legion.*

quī cōgnōscerent mīsit (id. i. 21), *he sent* [men] *to reconnoitre.*

d. The phrase **id quod** or **quae rēs** may be used (instead of **quod** alone) to refer to a group of words or an idea: —

[obtrectātum est] Gabīniō dīcam anne Pompêiō? an utrīque — **id quod** est vērius? (Manil. 57), *an affront has been offered — shall I say to Gabinius or to Pompey? or — which is truer — to both?*

multum sunt in vēnātiōnibus, **quae rēs** vīrēs alit (B. G. iv. 1), *they spend much time in hunting, which* [practice] *increases their strength.*

Note. — But **quod** alone often occurs: as, — Cassius noster, **quod** mihi māgnae voluptātī fuit, hostem rêiēcerat (Fam. ii. 10), *our friend Cassius — which was a great satisfaction to me — had driven back the enemy.*

e. The antecedent noun, when in apposition with the main clause, or with some word of it, is put in the relative clause: —

fīrmī [amīcī], cûius **generis** est māgna pēnūria (Lael. 62), *steadfast friends, a class of which there is great lack* (of which class there is, etc.).

f. A predicate adjective (especially a superlative) belonging to the antecedent may stand in the relative clause: —

vāsa ea quae **pulcherrima** apud eum vīderat (Verr. iv. 63), *those most beautiful vessels which he had seen at his house.* [Nearly equivalent to *the vessels of which he had seen some very beautiful ones.*]

Special Uses of the Relative

308. In the use of Relatives, the following points are to be observed: —

a. The relative is never omitted in Latin, as it often is in English: —

liber **quem** mihi dedistī, *the book you gave me.*

is sum **quī** semper fuī, *I am the same man I always was.*

eō in locō est dē **quō** tibi locūtus sum, *he is in the place I told you of.*

b. When two relative clauses are connected by a copulative conjunction, a relative pronoun sometimes stands in the first and a demonstrative in the last: —

erat profectus obviam legiōnibus Macedonicīs quattuor, **quās** sibi conciliāre pecūniā cōgitābat **eāsque** ad urbem addūcere (Fam. xii. 23. 2), *he had set out to meet four legions from Macedonia, which he thought to win over to himself by a gift of money and to lead* (them) *to the city.*

c. A relative clause in Latin often takes the place of some other construction in English, — particularly of a participle, an appositive, or a noun of agency: —

lēgēs quae nunc sunt, *the existing laws* (the laws which now exist).
Caesar quī Galliam vīcit, *Cæsar the conqueror of Gaul.*
iūsta glōria quī est frūctus virtūtis (Pison. 57), *true glory* [which is] *the fruit of virtue.*
ille quī petit, *the plaintiff* (he who sues).
quī legit, *a reader* (one who reads).

d. In formal or emphatic discourse, the relative clause usually comes first, often containing the antecedent noun (cf. § 307. *b*): —

quae pars cīvitātis Helvētiae īnsīgnem calamitātem populō Rōmānō intulerat, **ea** prīnceps poenās persolvit (B. G. i. 12), *the portion of the Helvetian state which had brought a serious disaster on the Roman people was the first to pay the penalty.*

Note. — In colloquial language, the relative clause in such cases often contains a redundant demonstrative pronoun which logically belongs in the antecedent clause: as, — **ille** quī cōnsultē cavet, diūtinē ūtī bene licet partum bene (Plaut. Rud. 1240), *he who is on his guard, he may long enjoy what he has well obtained.*

e. The relative with an abstract noun may be used in a parenthetical clause to *characterize a person,* like the English *such*: —

quae vestra prūdentia est (Cael. 45), *such is your wisdom.* [Equivalent to **prō vestrā prūdentiā.**]
audīssēs cōmoedōs vel lēctōrem vel lyristēn, vel, **quae mea līberālitās**, omnēs (Plin. Ep. i. 15), *you would have listened to comedians, or a reader, or a lyre-player, or — such is my liberality — to all of them.*

f. A relative pronoun (or adverb) often stands at the beginning of an independent sentence or clause, serving to connect it with the sentence or clause that precedes: —

Caesar statuit exspectandam classem; **quae** ubi convēnit (B. G. iii. 14), *Cæsar decided that he must wait for the fleet; and when this had come together,* etc.
quae quī audiēbant, *and those who heard this* (which things).
quae cum ita sint, *and since this is so.*
quōrum quod simile factum (Cat. iv. 13), *what deed of theirs like this?*
quō cum vēnisset, *and when he had come there* (whither when he had come).

Note. — This arrangement is common even when another relative or an interrogative follows. The relative may usually be translated by an English demonstrative, with or without *and.*

g. A relative adverb is regularly used in referring to an antecedent in the Locative case; so, often, to express any relation of place instead of the formal relative pronoun: —

mortuus Cūmīs **quō** sē contulerat (Liv. ii. 21), *having died at Cumæ, whither he had retired.* [Here **in quam urbem** might be used, but not **in quās.**]

locus **quō** aditus nōn erat, *a place to which* (whither) *there was no access.*

rēgna **unde** genus dūcis (Aen. v. 801), *the kingdom from which you derive your race.*

unde petitur, *the defendant* (he from whom something is demanded).

h. The relatives **quī, quālis, quantus, quot**, etc. are often rendered simply by *as* in English: —

idem **quod** semper, *the same as always.*

cum esset tālis **quālem** tē esse videō (Mur. 32), *since he was such a man as I see you are.*

tanta dīmicātiō **quanta** numquam fuit (Att. vii. 1. 2), *such a fight as never was before.*

tot mala **quot** sīdera (Ov. Tr. i. 5. 47), *as many troubles as stars in the sky.*

i. The general construction of relatives is found in clauses introduced by relative adverbs: **as, ubi, quō, unde, cum, quārē.**

Indefinite Pronouns

309. The Indefinite Pronouns are used to indicate that *some* person or thing is meant, without designating *what one.*

310. Quis, quispiam, aliquis, quīdam, are *particular indefinites*, meaning *some, a certain, any.* Of these, **quis**, *any one*, is least definite, and **quīdam**, *a certain one*, most definite; **aliquis** and **quispiam**, *some one*, stand between the two: —

dīxerit **quis (quispiam)**, *some one may say.*

aliquī philosophī ita putant, *some philosophers think so.* [**quīdam** would mean *certain persons* defined to the speaker's mind, though not named.]

habitant hīc **quaedam** mulierēs pauperculae (Ter. Ad. 647), *some poor women live here* [i.e. some women he knows of; *some women or other* would be **aliquae** or **nesciō quae**].

a. The indefinite **quis** is rare except in the combinations **sī quis**, *if any;* **nisi quis**, *if any . . . not;* **nē quis**, *lest any, in order that none;* **num quis** (**ecquis**), *whether any;* and in relative clauses.

b. The compounds **quispiam** and **aliquis** are often used instead of **quis** after **sī, nisi, nē**, and **num**, and are rather more emphatic: —

quid sī hōc **quispiam** voluit deus (Ter. Eun. 875), *what if some god had desired this?*

nisi **alicui** suōrum negōtium daret (Nep. Dion. 8. 2), *unless he should employ some one of his friends.*

cavēbat Pompēius omnia, nē **aliquid** vōs timērētis (Mil. 66), *Pompey took every precaution, so that you might have no fear.*

311. In a *particular* negative **aliquis (aliquī)**, *some one (some)*, is regularly used, where in a *universal* negative **quisquam**, *any one*, or **ūllus**, *any*, would be required: —

iūstitia numquam nocet **cuiquam** (Fin. i. 50), *justice never does harm to anybody.* [**alicui** would mean *to somebody who possesses it.*]

nōn sine **aliquō** metū, *not without some fear.* But, — sine **ūllō** metū, *without any fear.*

cum **aliquid** nōn habeās (Tusc. i. 88), *when there is something you have not.*

NOTE. — The same distinction holds between **quis** and **aliquis** on the one hand, and **quisquam (ūllus)** on the other, in conditional and other sentences when a negative is expressed or suggested: —

sī **quisquam**, ille sapiēns fuit (Lael. 9), *if any man was* (ever) *a sage, he was.*

dum praesidia **ūlla** fuērunt (Rosc. Am. 126), *while there were any armed forces.*

sī **quid** in tē peccāvī (Att. iii. 15. 4), *if I have done wrong towards you* [in any particular case (see § 310)].

312. Quīvīs or **quīlibet** (*any one you will*), **quisquam**, and the corresponding adjective **ūllus**, *any at all*, are *general indefinites*.

Quīvīs and **quīlibet** are used chiefly in *affirmative* clauses, **quisquam** and **ūllus** in clauses where a *universal negative* is expressed or suggested: —

nōn **cuivīs** hominī contingit adīre Corinthum (Hor. Ep. i. 17. 36), *it is not every man's luck to go to Corinth.* [**nōn cuiquam** would mean *not any man's.*]

quemlibet modo **aliquem** (Acad. ii. 132), *anybody you will, provided it be somebody.*

sī **quisquam** est timidus, is ego sum (Fam. vi. 14. 1), *if any man is timorous, I am he.*

sī tempus est **ūllum** iūre hominis necandī (Mil. 9), *if there is any occasion whatever when homicide is justifiable.*

NOTE. — The use of the indefinites is very various, and must be learned from the Lexicon and from practice. The choice among them may depend merely on the point of view of the speaker, so that they are often practically interchangeable. The differences are (with few exceptions) those of logic, not of syntax.

313. The distributives **quisque** (*every*), **uterque** (*each* of two), and **ūnus quisque** (*every single one*) are used in general assertions: —

bonus liber melior est **quisque** quō mâior (Plin. Ep. i. 20. 4), *the larger a good book is, the better* (each good book is better in proportion, etc.).

ambō exercitūs suās **quisque** abeunt domōs (Liv. ii. 7. 1), *both armies go away, every man to his home.*

uterque utrīque erat exercitus in cōnspectū (B. G. vii. 35), *each army was in sight of the other* (each to each).

pōnite ante oculōs **ūnum quemque** rēgum (Par. i. 11), *set before your eyes each of the kings.*

a. **Quisque** regularly stands in a dependent clause, if there is one:—

quō **quisque** est sollertior, hōc docet īrācundius (Rosc. Com. 31), *the keener-witted a man is, the more impatiently he teaches.*

NOTE.—**Quisque** is generally postpositive[1]: as, **suum cuique**, *to every man his own.*

b. **Quisque** is idiomatically used with superlatives and with ordinal numerals:—

nōbilissimus **quisque**, *all the noblest* (one after the other in the order of their nobility).[2]
prīmō **quōque** tempore (Rosc. Am. 36), *at the very first opportunity.*
antīquissimum **quodque** tempus (B. G. i. 45), *the most ancient times.*
decimus **quisque** (id. v. 52), *one in ten.*

NOTE 1.—Two superlatives with **quisque** imply a proportion: as,—sapientissimus quisque aequissimō animō moritur (Cat. M. 83), *the wisest men die with the greatest equanimity.*

NOTE 2.—**Quotus quisque** has the signification of *how many, pray?* often in a disparaging sense (*how few*):—

quotus enim **quisque** disertus? **quotus quisque** iūris perītus est (Planc. 62), *for how few are eloquent! how few are learned in the law!*
quotus enim istud **quisque** fēcisset (Lig. 26), *for how many would have done this?* [i.e. scarcely anybody would have done it].

314. **Nēmō**, *no one*, is used of persons only—

1. As a substantive:—

nēminem accūsat, *he accuses no one.*

2. As an adjective pronoun instead of **nūllus**:—

vir **nēmō** bonus (Legg. ii. 41), *no good man.*

NOTE.—Even when used as a substantive, **nēmō** may take a noun in apposition: as,—**nēmō scrīptor**, *nobody* [who is] *a writer.*

a. **Nūllus**, *no*, is commonly an adjective; but in the genitive and ablative singular it is regularly used instead of the corresponding cases of **nēmō**, and in the plural it may be either an adjective or a substantive:—

nūllum mittitur tēlum (B. C. ii. 13), *not a missile is thrown.*
nūllō hoste prohibente (B. G. iii. 6), *without opposition from the enemy.*
nūllīus īnsector calamitātem (Phil. ii. 98), *I persecute the misfortune of no one.*
nūllō adiuvante (id. x. 4), *with the help of no one* (no one helping).
nūllī erant praedōnēs (Flacc. 28), *there were no pirates.*
nūllī eximentur (Pison. 94), *none shall be taken away.*

For **nōn nēmō**, **nōn nūllus** (**nōn nūllī**), see § 326. *a.*

[1] That is, it does not stand first in its clause.

[2] As, in taking things one by one off a pile, each thing is uppermost when you take it.

Alius and *Alter*

315. **Alius** means simply *other*, *another* (of an indefinite number); **alter**, *the other* (of two), often the *second* in a series; **cēterī** and **reliquī**, *all the rest*, *the others*; **alteruter**, *one of the two*: —

> propterea quod **aliud** iter habērent nūllum (B. G. i. 7), *because* (as they said) *they had no other way*.
>
> ūnī epistulae respondī, veniō ad **alteram** (Fam. ii. 17. 6), *one letter I have answered, I come to the other*.
>
> **alterum** genus (Cat. ii. 19), *the second class*.
>
> iēcissem ipse mē potius in profundum ut **cēterōs** cōnservārem (Sest. 45), *I should have rather thrown myself into the deep to save the rest*.
>
> Servīlius cōnsul, **reliquīque** magistrātūs (B. C. iii. 21), *Servilius the consul and the rest of the magistrates*.
>
> cum sit necesse **alterum utrum** vincere (Fam. vi. 3), *since it must be that one of the two should prevail*.

NOTE. — Alter is often used, especially with negatives, in reference to an indefinite number where *one* is opposed to *all the rest* taken singly: —

> dum nē sit tē dītior **alter** (Hor. S. i. 1. 40), *so long as another is not richer than you* (lit. *the other*, there being at the moment only *two persons* considered).
>
> nōn ut magis **alter**, amīcus (id. i. 5. 33), *a friend such that no other is more so*.

a. The expressions **alter . . . alter**, *the one . . . the other*, **alius . . . alius**, *one . . . another*, may be used in pairs to denote either *division* of a group or *reciprocity* of action: —

> **alterī** dīmicant, **alterī** victōrem timent (Fam. vi. 3), *one party fights, the other fears the victor*.
>
> **alteram alterī** praesidiō esse iusserat (B. C. iii. 89), *he had ordered each* (of the two legions) *to support the other*.
>
> **aliī** gladiīs adoriuntur, **aliī** fragmentīs saeptōrum (Sest. 79), *some make an attack with swords, others with fragments of the railings*.
>
> **alius** ex **aliō** causam quaerit (B. G. vi. 37), *they ask each other the reason*.
>
> **alius alium** percontāmur (Pl. Stich. 370), *we keep asking each other*.

b. **Alius** and **alter** are often used to express *one* as well as *another* (*the other*) of the objects referred to: —

> **alter** cōnsulum, *one of the* [two] *consuls*.
>
> **aliud** est maledīcere, **aliud** accūsāre (Cael. 6), *it is one thing to slander, another to accuse*.

c. **Alius** repeated in another case, or with an adverb from the same stem, expresses briefly a double statement: —

> **alius aliud** petit, *one man seeks one thing, another another* (another seeks another thing).
>
> iussit **aliōs alibī** fodere (Liv. xliv. 33), *he ordered different persons to dig in different places*.
>
> **aliī aliō** locō resistēbant (B. C. ii. 39), *some halted in one place, some in another*.

VERBS

Agreement of Verb and Subject

316. A Finite Verb agrees with its Subject in Number and Person: —

ego statuō, *I resolve.* senātus dēcrēvit, *the senate ordered.*
silent lēgēs inter arma (Mil. 11), *the laws are dumb in time of war.*

NOTE. — In verb-forms containing a participle, the participle agrees with the subject in gender and number (§ 286): —

ōrātiō est **habita**, *the plea was delivered.* bellum **exortum** est, *a war arose.*

a. A verb having a relative as its subject takes the person of the expressed or implied antecedent: —

adsum quī **fēcī** (Aen. ix. 427), *here am I who did it.*
tū, quī **scīs**, omnem dīligentiam adhibēbis (Att. v. 2. 3), *you, who know, will use all diligence.*
vidēte quam dēspiciāmur omnēs quī **sumus** ē mūnicipiīs (Phil. iii. 15), *see how all of us are scorned who are from the free towns.*

b. A verb sometimes agrees in number (and a participle in the verb-form in number and gender) with an appositive or predicate noun: —

amantium īrae amōris integrātiō **est** (Ter. And. 555), *the quarrels of lovers are the renewal of love.*
nōn omnis error stultitia **dīcenda** est (Div. ii. 90), *not every error should be called folly.*
Corinthus lūmen Graeciae **exstīnctum** est (cf. Manil. 11), *Corinth, the light of Greece, is put out.*

Double or Collective Subject

317. Two or more Singular Subjects take a verb in the Plural:

pater et avus **mortuī sunt**, *his father and grandfather are dead.*

NOTE. — So rarely (by *synesis*, § 280. *a*) when to a singular subject is attached an ablative with **cum**: as, — dux cum aliquot prīncipibus **capiuntur** (Liv. xxi. 60), *the general and several leading men are taken.*

a. When subjects are of different *persons*, the verb is usually in the *first* person rather than the *second*, and in the *second* rather than the *third*: —

sī tū et Tullia **valētis** ego et Cicerō **valēmus** (Fam. xiv. 5), *if you and Tullia are well, Cicero and I are well.* [Notice that the first person is also *first in order*, not last, as by courtesy in English.]

NOTE. — In case of different genders a participle in a verb-form follows the rule for predicate adjectives (see § 287. 2–4).

b. If the subjects are connected by disjunctives (§ 223. *a*), or if they are considered as a single whole, the verb is usually singular: —

quem **neque** fidēs **neque** iūs iūrandum **neque** illum misericordia **repressit** (Ter. Ad. 306), *not faith, nor oath, nay, nor mercy, checked him.*

senātus populusque Rōmānus **intellegit** (Fam. v. 8), *the Roman senate and people understand.* [But, neque Caesar neque ego **habitī essēmus** (id. xi. 20), *neither Cæsar nor I should have been considered.*]

fāma et vīta innocentis **dēfenditur** (Rosc. Am. 15), *the reputation and life of an innocent man are defended.*

est in eō virtūs et probitās et summum officium summaque observantia (Fam. xiii. 28 A. 2), *in him are to be found worth, uprightness, the highest sense of duty, and the greatest devotion.*

NOTE. — So almost always when the subjects are abstract nouns.

c. When a verb belongs to two or more subjects *separately*, it often agrees with one and is understood with the others: —

intercēdit M. Antōnius Q. Cassius tribūnī plēbis (B. C. i. 2), *Mark Antony and Quintus Cassius, tribunes of the people, interpose.*

hōc mihi et Peripatēticī et vetus Acadēmia **concēdit** (Acad. ii. 113), *this both the Peripatetic philosophers and the Old Academy grant me.*

d. A collective noun commonly takes a verb in the singular; but the plural is often found with collective nouns when *individuals* are thought of (§ 280. *a*): —

(1) senātus haec **intellegit** (Cat. i. 2), *the senate is aware of this.*

ad hīberna exercitus **redit** (Liv. xxi. 22), *the army returns to winter-quarters.*

plēbēs ā patribus **sēcessit** (Sall. Cat. 33), *the plebs seceded from the patricians.*

(2) **pars** praedās **agēbant** (Iug. 32), *a part brought in booty.*

cum tanta **multitūdō** lapidēs **conicerent** (B. G. ii. 6), *when such a crowd were throwing stones.*

NOTE 1. — The point of view may change in the course of a sentence: as, — equitātum omnem . . . **quem** habēbat praemittit, **quī videant** (B. G. i. 15), *he sent ahead all the cavalry he had, to see* (who should see).

NOTE 2. — The singular of a noun regularly denoting an individual is sometimes used collectively to denote a group: as, **Poenus**, *the Carthaginians;* **mīles**, *the soldiery;* **eques**, *the cavalry.*

e. **Quisque**, *each*, and **ūnus quisque**, *every single one*, have very often a plural verb, but may be considered as in partitive apposition with a plural subject implied (cf. § 282. *a*): —

sibi quisque habeant quod suum est (Pl. Curc. 180), *let every one keep his own* (let them keep every man his own).

NOTE. — So also **uterque**, *each* (*of two*), and the reciprocal phrases **alius . . . alium**, **alter . . . alterum** (§ 315. *a*).

Omission of Subject or Verb

318. The Subject of the Verb is sometimes omitted: —

a. A Personal pronoun, as subject, is usually omitted unless emphatic: —

loquor, *I speak.* But, ego loquor, *it is I that speak.*

b. An *indefinite* subject is often omitted: — **crēderēs,** *you would have supposed;* **putāmus,** *we* (people) *think;* **dīcunt, ferunt, perhibent,** *they say.*

c. A passive verb is often used impersonally without a subject expressed or understood (§ 208. *d*): —

diū atque ācriter **pūgnātum est** (B. G. i. 26), *they fought long and vigorously.*

319. The verb is sometimes omitted: —

a. **Dīcō, faciō, agō,** and other common verbs are often omitted in familiar phrases: —

quōrsum haec [spectant], *what does this aim at?*
ex ungue leōnem [cōgnōscēs], *you will know a lion by his claw.*
quid multa, *what need of many words?* (why should I say much?)
quid? quod, *what of this, that . . .?* (what shall I say of this, that . . .?) [A form of transition.]
Aeolus haec contrā (Aen. i. 76), *Æolus thus* [spoke] *in reply.*
tum Cotta [inquit], *then said Cotta.*
dī meliōra [duint]! (Cat. M. 47), *Heaven forfend* (may the gods grant better things)!
unde [venīs] et quō [tendis]? (Hor. S. ii. 4. 1), *where from and whither bound?* [Cf. id. i. 9. 62 for the full form.]

b. The copula **sum** is very commonly omitted in the present indicative and present infinitive, rarely (except by late authors) in the subjunctive: —

tū coniūnx (Aen. iv. 113), *you* [are] *his wife.*
quid ergō? audācissimus ego ex omnibus (Rosc. Am. 2), *what then? am I the boldest of all?*
omnia praeclāra rāra (Lael. 79), *all the best things are rare.*
potest incidere saepe contentiō et comparātiō dē duōbus honestīs utrum honestius (Off. i. 152), *there may often occur a comparison of two honorable actions, as to which is the more honorable.* [Here, if any copula were expressed, it would be sit, but the direct question would be complete without any.]
accipe quae peragenda prius (Aen. vi. 136), *hear what is first to be accomplished.* [Direct: **quae peragenda prius?**]

Particles

Adverbs

320. The proper function of Adverbs, as petrified case-forms, is to modify Verbs: as,—**celeriter īre**, *to go with speed*. It is from this use that they derive their name (**adverbium**, from **ad**, *to*, and **verbum**, *verb*; see § 241. *b*). They also modify adjectives, showing in what manner or degree the quality described is manifested: as, **splendidē mendāx**, *gloriously false*. More rarely they modify other adverbs: as, **nimis graviter**, *too severely*. Many adverbs, especially relative adverbs, serve as connectives, and are hardly to be distinguished from conjunctions (see § 20. *g*. N.).[1]

321. Adverbs are used to modify Verbs, Adjectives, and other Adverbs.

a. A Demonstrative or Relative adverb is often equivalent to the corresponding Pronoun with a preposition (see § 308. *g*):—

eō [= **in ea**] impōnit vāsa (Iug. 75), *upon them* (thither, thereon, on the beasts) *he puts the camp-utensils*.

eō mīlitēs impōnere (B. G. i. 42), *to put soldiers upon them* (the horses).

apud eōs **quō** [= **ad quōs**] sē contulit (Verr. iv. 38), *among those to whom* (whither) *he resorted*.

quī eum necāsset **unde** [= **quō**] ipse nātus esset (Rosc. Am. 71), *one who should have killed his own father* (him whence he had his birth).

ō condiciōnēs miserās administrandārum prōvinciārum **ubi** [= **in quibus**] sevēritās perīculōsa est (Flacc. 87), *O! wretched terms of managing the provinces, where strictness is dangerous*.

b. The participles **dictum** and **factum**, when used as nouns, are regularly modified by adverbs rather than by adjectives; so occasionally other perfect participles:—

praeclārē facta (Nep. Timoth. 1), *glorious deeds* (things gloriously done).

multa **facētē** dicta (Off. i. 104), *many witty sayings*.

c. A noun is sometimes used as an adjective, and may then be modified by an adverb:—

victor exercitus, *the victorious army*.

admodum puer, *quite a boy* (young).

magis vir, *more of a man* (more manly).

populum **lātē** rēgem (Aen. i. 21), *a people ruling far and wide*.

NOTE.—Very rarely adverbs are used with nouns which have no adjective force but which contain a verbal idea:—

hinc abitiō (Plaut. Rud. 503), *a going away from here*.

quid cōgitem dē **obviam** itiōne (Att. xiii. 50), *what I think about going to meet* (him). [Perhaps felt as a compound.]

[1] For the derivation and classification of adverbs, see §§ 214–217.

d. A few adverbs appear to be used like adjectives. Such are **obviam, palam,** sometimes **contrā,** and occasionally others: —

fit **obviam** Clōdiō (Mil. 29), *he falls in with* (becomes in the way of) *Clodius*. [Cf. the adjective **obvius**: as, — sī ille **obvius** eī futūrus nōn erat (id. 47), *if he was not likely to fall in with him.*]

haec commemorō quae sunt **palam** (Pison. 11), *I mention these facts, which are well-known.*

alia probābilia, **contrā** alia dīcimus (Off. ii. 7), *we call some things probable, others the opposite* (not probable). [In this use, **contrā** contradicts a previous adjective, and so in a manner repeats it.]

erī **semper** lēnitās (Ter. And. 175), *my master's constant* (always) *gentleness*. [An imitation of a Greek construction.]

NOTE. — In some cases one can hardly say whether the adverb is treated as an adjective modifying the noun, or the noun modified is treated as an adjective (as in c above).

For propius, prīdiē, palam, and other adverbs used as prepositions, see § 432.

322. The following adverbs require special notice: —

a. **Etiam** (**et iam**), *also, even,* is stronger than **quoque**, *also,* and usually precedes the emphatic word, while **quoque** follows it: —

nōn verbīs sōlum sed **etiam** vī (Verr. ii. 64), *not only by words, but also by force.*

hōc **quoque** maleficium (Rosc. Am. 117), *this crime too.*

b. **Nunc**[1] means definitely *now, in the immediate present,* and is rarely used of the immediate past.

Iam means *now, already, at length, presently,* and includes a reference to previous time through which the state of things described has been or will be reached. It may be used of *any* time. With negatives **iam** means *(no) longer.*

Tum, *then,* is correlative to **cum**, *when,* and may be used of any time. **Tunc**, *then, at that time,* is a strengthened form of **tum** (†**tum-ce**, cf. **nunc**): —

ut **iam** anteā dīxī, *as I have already said before.*

sī **iam** satis aetātis atque rōboris habēret (Rosc. Am. 149), *if he had attained a suitable age and strength* (lit. *if he now had,* as he will have by and by).

nōn est **iam** lēnitātī locus, *there is no longer room for mercy.*

quod **iam** erat īnstitūtum, *which had come to be a practice* (had now been established).

nunc quidem dēlēta est, **tunc** flōrēbat (Lael. 13), *now* ('t is true) *she* [Greece] *is ruined, then she was in her glory.*

tum cum rēgnābat, *at the time when he reigned.*

[1] For †**num-ce**; cf. **tunc** (for †**tum-ce**).

c. **Certō** means *certainly*, **certē** (usually) *at least, at any rate:* —

certō sciō, *I know for a certainty;* ego **certē**, *I at least.*

d. **Prīmum** means *first* (*first in order*, or *for the first time*), and implies a *series* of events or acts. **Prīmō** means *at first*, as opposed to *afterwards*, giving prominence merely to the difference of time: —

hōc **prīmum** sentiō, *this I hold in the first place.*
aedīs **prīmō** ruere rēbāmur, *at first we thought the house was falling.*

NOTE. — In enumerations, **prīmum** (or **prīmō**) is often followed by **deinde**, *secondly, in the next place*, or by **tum**, *then*, or by both in succession. **Deinde** may be several times repeated (*secondly, thirdly*, etc.). The series is often closed by **dēnique** or **postrēmō**, *lastly, finally*. Thus, — **prīmum** dē genere bellī, **deinde** dē māgnitūdine, **tum** dē imperātōre dēligendō (Manil. 6), *first of the kind of war, next of its magnitude, then of the choice of a commander.*

e. **Quidem**, *indeed*, gives emphasis, and often has a *concessive* meaning, especially when followed by **sed, autem**, etc.: —

hōc **quidem** vidēre licet (Lael. 54), THIS *surely one may see.* [Emphatic.]
[sēcūritās] speciē **quidem** blanda, **sed** reāpse multīs locīs repudianda (id. 47), (*tranquillity*) *in appearance, 't is true, attractive, but in reality to be rejected for many reasons.* [Concessive.]

f. **Nē . . . quidem** means *not even* or *not . . . either*. The emphatic word or words must stand between **nē** and **quidem**: —

sed **nē** Iugurtha **quidem** quiētus erat (Iug. 51), *but Jugurtha was not quiet either.*
ego autem **nē** īrāscī possum **quidem** iīs quōs valdē amō (Att. ii. 19. 1), *but I cannot even get angry with those whom I love very much.*

NOTE. — **Equidem** has the same senses as **quidem**, but is in Cicero confined to the first person. Thus, — **equidem** adprobābō (Fam. ii. 3. 2), *I for my part shall approve.*

CONJUNCTIONS[1]

323. Copulative and Disjunctive Conjunctions connect similar constructions, and are regularly followed by the same case or mood that precedes them: —

scrīptum senātuī **et** populō (Cat. iii. 10), *written to the senate and people.*
ut eās [partīs] sānārēs **et** cōnfīrmārēs (Mil. 68), *that you might cure and strengthen those parts.*
neque meā prūdentiā **neque** hūmānīs cōnsiliīs frētus (Cat. ii. 29), *relying neither on my own foresight nor on human wisdom.*

[1] For the classification of conjunctions, see §§ 223, 224.

a. Conjunctions of Comparison (as **ut, quam, tamquam, quasi**) also commonly connect similar constructions: —

> hīs igitur **quam** physicīs potius crēdendum exīstimās (Div. ii. 37), *do you think these are more to be trusted than the natural philosophers?*
> hominem callidiōrem vīdī nēminem **quam** Phormiōnem (Ter. Ph. 591), *a shrewder man I never saw than Phormio* (cf. § 407).
> **ut** nōn omne vīnum sīc nōn omnis nātūra vetustāte coacēscit (Cat. M. 65), *as every wine does not sour with age, so* [does] *not every nature.*
> in mē **quasi** in tyrannum (Phil. xiv. 15), *against me as against a tyrant.*

b. Two or more coördinate words, phrases, or sentences are often put together without the use of conjunctions (*Asyndeton*, § 601. *c*):

> omnēs dī, hominēs, *all gods and men.*
> summī, mediī, īnfimī, *the highest, the middle class, and the lowest.*
> iūra, lēgēs, agrōs, lībertātem nōbīs relīquērunt (B. G. vii. 77), *they have left us our rights, our laws, our fields, our liberty.*

c. 1. Where there are more than two coördinate words etc., a conjunction, if used, is ordinarily used with all (or all except the first): —

> **aut** aere aliēnō **aut** māgnitūdine tribūtōrum **aut** iniūriā potentiōrum (B. G. vi. 13), *by debt, excessive taxation, or oppression on the part of the powerful.*
> at sunt mōrōsī **et** anxiī **et** īrācundī **et** difficilēs senēs (Cat. M. 65), *but* (you say) *old men are capricious, solicitous, choleric, and fussy.*

2. But words are often so divided into groups that the members of the groups omit the conjunction (or express it), while the groups themselves express the conjunction (or omit it): —

> propudium illud **et** portentum, L. Antōnius īnsīgne odium omnium hominum (Phil. xiv. 8), *that wretch and monster, Lucius Antonius, the abomination of all men.*
> utrumque ēgit graviter, auctōritāte **et** offēnsiōne animī nōn acerbā (Lael. 77), *he acted in both cases with dignity, without loss of authority and with no bitterness of feeling.*

3. The enclitic **-que** is sometimes used with the last member of a series, even when there is no grouping apparent: —

> vōce voltū mōtūque (Brut. 110), *by voice, expression, and gesture.*
> cūram cōnsilium vigilantiamque (Phil. vii. 20), *care, wisdom, and vigilance.*
> quōrum auctōritātem dīgnitātem voluntātemque dēfenderās (Fam. i. 7. 2), *whose dignity, honor, and wishes you had defended.*

d. Two adjectives belonging to the same noun are regularly connected by a conjunction: —

> multae **et** gravēs causae, *many weighty reasons.*
> vir līber **ac** fortis (Rep. ii. 34), *a free and brave man.*

e. Often the same conjunction is repeated in two coördinate clauses:

et . . . **et** (**-que** . . . **-que**), *both . . . and.*
aut . . . **aut**, *either . . . or.*
vel . . . **vel**, *either . . . or.* [Examples in § 324. *e.*]
sīve (**seu**) . . . **sīve** (**seu**), *whether . . . or.* [Examples in § 324. *f.*]

f. Many adverbs are similarly used in pairs, as conjunctions, partly or wholly losing their adverbial force: —

nunc . . . **nunc**, **tum** . . . **tum**, **iam** . . . **iam**, *now . . . now.*
modo . . . **modo**, *now . . . now.*
simul . . . **simul**, *at the same time . . . at the same time.*
quā . . . **quā**, *now . . . now, both . . . and, alike* [this] *and* [that].
modo ait **modo** negat (Ter. Eun. 714), *now he says yes, now no.*
simul grātiās agit, **simul** grātulātur (Q. C. vi. 7. 15), *he thanks him and at the same time congratulates him.*
ērumpunt saepe vitia amīcōrum **tum** in ipsōs amīcōs **tum** in aliēnōs (Lael. 76), *the faults of friends sometimes break out, now against their friends themselves, now against strangers.*
quā marīs **quā** fēminās (Pl. Mil. 1113), *both males and females.*

g. Certain relative and demonstrative adverbs are used correlatively as conjunctions: —

ut (rel.) . . . **ita**, **sīc** (dem.), *as* (*while*) . . . *so* (*yet*).
tam (dem.) . . . **quam** (rel.), *so* (*as*) . . . *as.*
cum (rel.) . . . **tum** (dem.), *while . . . so also; not only . . . but also.*

324. The following Conjunctions require notice: —

a. **Et**, *and*, simply *connects* words or clauses; **-que** *combines* more closely into one connected whole. **-que** is always enclitic to the word connected or to the first or second of two or more words connected:

cum coniugibus **et** līberīs, *with* [their] *wives and children.*
ferrō īgnī**que**, *with fire and sword.* [Not as separate things, but as the combined means of devastation.]
aquā **et** īgnī interdictus, *forbidden the use of water and fire.* [In a legal formula, where they are considered separately.]

b. **Atque** (**ac**), *and*, adds with some emphasis or with some implied reflection on the word added. Hence it is often equivalent to *and so, and yet, and besides, and then.* But these distinctions depend very much upon the feeling of the speaker, and are often untranslatable: —

omnia honesta **atque** inhonesta, *everything honorable and dishonorable* (too, without the slightest distinction).
ūsus **atque** disciplīna, *practice and theory beside* (the more important or less expected).
atque ego crēdō, *and yet I believe* (for my part).

c. **Atque (ac)**, in the sense of *as*, *than*, is also used after words of comparison and likeness: —

simul **atque**, *as soon as.*
nōn secus (nōn aliter) **ac** sī, *not otherwise than if.*
prō eō **ac** dēbuī, *as was my duty* (in accordance as I ought).
aequē **ac** tū, *as much as you.*
haud minus **ac** iussī faciunt, *they do just as they are ordered.*

For *and not*, see § 328. *a.*

d. **Sed** and the more emphatic **vērum** or **vērō**, *but*, are used to introduce something in opposition to what precedes, especially after negatives (*not this . . . but something else*). **At** (old form **ast**) introduces with emphasis a new point in an argument, but is also used like the others; sometimes it means *at least.* **At enim** is almost always used to introduce a supposed objection which is presently to be overthrown. **At** is more rarely used alone in this sense.

Autem, *however*, *now*, is the weakest of the adversatives, and often marks a mere transition and has hardly any adversative force perceptible. **Atquī**, *however*, *now*, sometimes introduces an objection and sometimes a fresh step in the reasoning. **Quod sī**, *but if*, *and if*, *now if*, is used to continue an argument.

NOTE. — **Et**, **-que**, and **atque (ac)** are sometimes used where the English idiom would suggest *but*, especially when a negative clause is followed by an affirmative clause continuing the same thought: as, — impetum hostēs ferre nōn potuērunt **ac** terga vertērunt (B. G. iv. 35), *the enemy could not stand the onset, but turned their backs.*

e. **Aut**, *or*, excludes the alternative; **vel** (an old imperative of **volō**) and **-ve** give a choice between two alternatives. But this distinction is not always observed: —

sed quis ego sum **aut** quae est in mē facultās (Lael. 17), *but who am I or what special capacity have I?* [Here **vel** could not be used, because in fact a negative is implied and both alternatives are excluded.]

aut bibat **aut** abeat (Tusc. v. 118), *let him drink or* (if he won't do that, then let him) *quit.* [Here **vel** would mean, let him do either as he chooses.]

vīta tālis fuit **vel** fortūnā **vel** glōriā (Lael. 12), *his life was such either in respect to fortune or fame* (whichever way you look at it).

sī propinquōs habeant imbēcilliōrēs **vel** animō **vel** fortūnā (id. 70), *if they have relatives beneath them either in spirit or in fortune* (in either respect, for example, or in both).

aut deōrum **aut** rēgum fīliī (id. 70), *sons either of gods or of kings.* [Here one case would exclude the other.]

implicātī **vel** ūsū diūturnō **vel** etiam officiīs (id. 85), *entangled either by close intimacy or even by obligations.* [Here the second case might exclude the first.]

f. **Sīve** (**seu**) is properly used in disjunctive conditions (*if either . . . or if*), but also with alternative words and clauses, especially with two names for the same thing: —

> **sīve** inrīdēns **sīve** quod ita putāret (De Or. i. 91), *either laughingly or because he really thought so.*
>
> **sīve** deae **seu** sint volucrēs (Aen. iii. 262), *whether they* (the Harpies) *are goddesses or birds.*

g. **Vel**, *even, for instance*, is often used as an intensive particle with no alternative force: as, — **vel minimus**, *the very least.*

h. **Nam** and **namque**, *for*, usually introduce a real reason, formally expressed, for a previous statement; **enim** (always postpositive), a less important explanatory circumstance put in by the way; **etenim** (*for, you see; for, you know; for, mind you*) and its negative **neque enim** introduce something self-evident or needing no proof.

> (ea vīta) quae est sōla vīta nōminanda. **nam** dum sumus inclūsī in hīs compāgibus corporis, mūnere quōdam necessitātis et gravī opere perfungimur; est **enim** animus caelestis, etc. (Cat. M. 77), (that life) *which alone deserves to be called life; for so long as we are confined by the body's frame, we perform a sort of necessary function and heavy task. For the soul is from heaven.*
>
> hārum trium sententiārum nūllī prōrsus adsentior. nec **enim** illa prīma vēra est (Lael. 57), *for of course that first one is n't true.*

i. **Ergō**, *therefore*, is used of things proved formally, but often has a weakened force. **Igitur**, *then, accordingly*, is weaker than **ergō** and is used in passing from one stage of an argument to another. **Itaque**, *therefore, accordingly, and so*, is used in proofs or inferences from the nature of things rather than in formal logical proof. All of these are often used merely to resume a train of thought broken by a digression or parenthesis. **Idcircō**, *for this reason, on this account*, is regularly followed (or preceded) by a correlative (as, **quia, quod, sī, ut, nē**), and refers to the special point introduced by the correlative.

> malum mihi vidētur esse mors. est miserum **igitur**, quoniam malum. certē. **ergō** et eī quibus ēvēnit iam ut morerentur et eī quibus ēventūrum est miserī. mihi ita vidētur. nēmō **ergō** nōn miser. (Tusc. i. 9.) *Death seems to me to be an evil. 'It is wretched, then, since it is an evil.' Certainly. 'Therefore, all those who have already died and who are to die hereafter are wretched.' So it appears to me. 'There is no one, therefore, who is not wretched.'*
>
> **quia** nātūra mūtārī nōn potest, **idcircō** vērae amīcitiae sempiternae sunt (Lael. 32), *because nature cannot be changed, for this reason true friendships are eternal.*

j. **Autem**, **enim**, and **vērō** are *postpositive*[1]; so generally **igitur** and often **tamen**.

k. Two conjunctions of similar meaning are often used together for the sake of emphasis or to bind a sentence more closely to what precedes: as, **at vērō**, *but in truth, but surely, still, however;* **itaque ergō**, *accordingly then;* **namque**, *for;* **et-enim**, *for, you see, for of course* (§ 324. *h*).

For Conjunctions introducing Subordinate Clauses, see Syntax.

Negative Particles[2]

325. In the use of the Negative Particles, the following points are to be observed: —

326. Two negatives are equivalent to an affirmative: —

nēmō nōn audiet, *every one will hear* (nobody will not hear).
nōn possum nōn cōnfitērī (Fam. ix. 14. 1), *I must confess.*
ut . . . nē nōn timēre quidem sine aliquō timōre possīmus (Mil. 2), *so that we cannot even be relieved of fear without some fear.*

a. Many compounds or phrases of which **nōn** is the first part express an *indefinite* affirmative: —

nōn nūllus, *some;* nōn nūllī (= aliquī), *some few.*
nōn nihil (= aliquid), *something.*
nōn nēmō (= aliquot), *sundry persons.*
nōn numquam (= aliquotiēns), *sometimes.*

b. Two negatives of which the second is **nōn** (belonging to the predicate) express a *universal* affirmative: —

nēmō nōn, nūllus nōn, *nobody* [does] *not*, i.e. *everybody* [does]. [Cf. nōn nēmō, *not nobody*, i.e. *somebody.*]
nihil nōn, *everything.* [Cf. nōn nihil, *something.*]
numquam nōn, *never not*, i.e. *always.* [Cf. nōn numquam, *sometimes.*]

c. A statement is often made emphatic by denying its contrary (*Litotes*, § 641): —

nōn semel (= saepissimē), *often enough* (not once only).
nōn haec sine nūmine dīvom ēveniunt (Aen. ii. 777), *these things do not occur without the will of the gods.*
haec nōn nimis exquīrō (Att. vii. 18. 3), *not very much*, i.e. *very little.*

NOTE. — Compare **nōn nūllus**, **nōn nēmō**, etc., in *a* above.

[1] That is, they do not stand first in their clause.
[2] For a list of Negative Particles, see § 217. *e*.

327. A *general* negation is not destroyed —

1. By a following **nē . . . quidem**, *not even*, or **nōn modo**, *not only*: —

numquam tū nōn modo ōtium, sed nē bellum quidem nisi nefārium concupīstī (Cat. i. 25), *not only have you never desired repose, but you have never desired any war except one which was infamous.*

2. By succeeding negatives each introducing a separate subordinate member: —

eaque **nesciēbant nec** ubi **nec** quālia essent (Tusc. iii. 4), *they knew not where or of what kind these things were.*

3. By **neque** introducing a coördinate member: —

nequeō satis mīrārī **neque** conicere (Ter. Eun. 547), *I cannot wonder enough nor conjecture.*

328. The negative is frequently joined with a conjunction or with an indefinite pronoun or adverb. Hence the forms of negation in Latin differ from those in English in many expressions: —

nūllī (neutrī) crēdō (not **nōn crēdō ūllī**), *I do not believe either* (I believe neither).

sine ūllō perīculō (less commonly **cum nūllō**), *with no danger* (without any danger).

nihil umquam audīvī iūcundius, *I never heard anything more amusing.*

Cf. **negō** haec esse vēra (not **dīcō nōn esse**), *I say this is not true* (I deny, etc.).

a. In the second of two connected ideas, *and not* is regularly expressed by **neque (nec)**, not by **et nōn**: —

hostēs terga vertērunt, **neque** prius fugere dēstitērunt (B. G. i. 53), *the enemy turned and fled, and did not stop fleeing until*, etc.

NOTE. — Similarly **nec quisquam** is regularly used for **et nēmō**; **neque ūllus** for **et nūllus**; **nec umquam** for **et numquam**; **nēve (neu)**, for **et nē**.

329. The particle **immo**, *nay*, is used to contradict some part of a preceding statement or question, or its form; in the latter case, the same statement is often repeated in a stronger form, so that **immo** becomes nearly equivalent to *yes* (*nay but*, *nay rather*): —

causa igitur nōn bona est? **immo** optima (Att. ix. 7. 4), *is the cause then not a good one? on the contrary, the best.*

a. **Minus**, *less* (especially with **sī**, *if*, **quō**, *in order that*), and **minimē**, *least*, often have a negative force: —

sī minus possunt, *if they cannot.* [For **quō minus**, see § 558. *b.*]

audācissimus ego ex omnibus? **minimē** (Rosc. Am. 2), *am I the boldest of them all? by no means* (not at all).

QUESTIONS

Forms of Interrogation

330. Questions are either Direct or Indirect.

1. A Direct Question gives the exact words of the speaker: —

quid est? *what is it?* ubi sum? *where am I?*

2. An Indirect Question gives the substance of the question, adapted to the form of the sentence in which it is quoted. It depends on a verb or other expression of *asking, doubting, knowing,* or the like: —

rogāvit **quid esset,** *he asked what it was.* [Direct: **quid est,** *what is it?*]
nesciō **ubi sim,** *I know not where I am.* [Direct: **ubi sum,** *where am I?*]

331. Questions in Latin are introduced by special interrogative words, and are not distinguished by the order of words, as in English.[1]

Note. — The form of Indirect Questions (in English introduced by *whether*, or by an interrogative pronoun or adverb) is in Latin the same as that of Direct; the difference being only in the verb, which in indirect questions is regularly in the Subjunctive (§ 574).

332. A question of *simple fact*, requiring the answer *yes* or *no*, is formed by adding the enclitic **-ne** to the emphatic word: —

tūne id veritus es (Q. Fr. i. 3. 1), *did* YOU *fear that?*
hīcine vir usquam nisi in patriā moriētur (Mil. 104), *shall* THIS *man die anywhere but in his native land?*
is tibi **mortemne** vidētur aut dolōrem timēre (Tusc. v. 88), *does he seem to you to fear death or pain?*

a. The interrogative particle **-ne** is sometimes omitted: —

patēre tua cōnsilia nōn sentīs (Cat. i. 1), *do you not see that your schemes are manifest?* (you do not see, eh?)

Note. — In such cases, as no sign of interrogation appears, it is often doubtful whether the sentence is a question or an ironical statement.

b. When the enclitic **-ne** is added to a negative word, as in **nōnne**, an *affirmative* answer is expected. The particle **num** suggests a *negative* answer: —

nōnne animadvertis (N. D. iii. 89), *do you not observe?*
num dubium est (Rosc. Am. 107), *there is no doubt, is there?*

Note. — In Indirect Questions **num** commonly loses its peculiar force and means simply *whether*.

[1] For a list of Interrogative Particles, see § 217. *d*.

c. The particle **-ne** often when added to the verb, less commonly when added to some other word, has the force of **nōnne**: —

> **meministīne** mē in senātū dīcere (Cat. i. 7), *don't you remember my saying in the Senate?*
>
> **rēctēne** interpretor sententiam tuam (Tusc. iii. 37), *do I not rightly interpret your meaning?*

NOTE 1. — This was evidently the original meaning of **-ne**; but in most cases the negative force was lost and **-ne** was used merely to express a question. So the English interrogative *no?* shades off into *eh?*

NOTE 2. — The enclitic **-ne** is sometimes added to other interrogative words: as, **utrumne**, *whether?* **anne**, *or;* **quantane** (Hor. S. ii. 3. 317), *how big?* **quōne malō** (id. ii. 3. 295), *by what curse?*

333. A question concerning *some special circumstance* is formed by prefixing to the sentence an interrogative pronoun or adverb as in English (§ 152): —

> **quid** exspectās (Cat. ii. 18), *what are you looking forward to?*
>
> **quō** igitur haec spectant (Fam. vi. 6. 11), *whither then is all this tending?*
>
> Īcare, **ubi** es (Ov. M. viii. 232), *Icarus, where are you?*
>
> **quod** vectīgal vōbīs tūtum fuit? **quem** socium dēfendistis? **cui** praesidiō classibus vestrīs fuistis? (Manil. 32), *what revenue has been safe for you? what ally have you defended? whom have you guarded with your fleets?*

NOTE. — A question of this form becomes an exclamation by changing the tone of the voice: as, —

> **quālis** vir erat! *what a man he was!*
>
> **quot** calamitātēs passī sumus! *how many misfortunes we have suffered!*
>
> **quō** studiō cōnsentiunt (Cat. iv. 15), *with what zeal they unite!*

a. The particles **-nam** (enclitic) and **tandem** may be added to interrogative pronouns and adverbs for the sake of emphasis: —

> **quisnam** est, *pray who is it?* [**quis tandem est**? would be stronger.]
>
> **ubinam** gentium sumus (Cat. i. 9), *where in the world are we?*
>
> in **quā tandem** urbe hōc disputant (Mil. 7), *in what city, pray, do they maintain this?*

NOTE — **Tandem** is sometimes added to verbs: —

> **ain tandem** (Fam. ix. 21), *you don't say so!* (say you so, pray?)
>
> **itane tandem** uxōrem dūxit Antiphō (Ter. Ph. 231), *so then, eh? Antipho's got married.*

Double Questions

334. A Double or Alternative Question is an inquiry as to which of two or more supposed cases is the true one.

335. In Double or Alternative Questions, **utrum** or **-ne**, *whether*, stands in the first member; **an, anne**, *or*, **annōn, necne**, *or not*, in the second; and usually **an** in the third, if there be one: —

utrum nescīs, **an** prō nihilō id putās (Fam. x. 26), *is it that you don't know, or do you think nothing of it?*

vōs**ne** L. Domitium **an** vōs Domitius dēseruit (B. C. ii. 32), *did you desert Lucius Domitius, or did Domitius desert you?*

quaerō servōs**ne** **an** līberōs (Rosc. Am. 74), *I ask whether slaves or free.*

utrum hostem **an** vōs **an** fortūnam utrīusque populī īgnōrātis (Liv. xxi. 10), *is it the enemy, or yourselves, or the fortune of the two peoples, that you do not know?*

NOTE. — **Anne** for **an** is rare. **Necne** is rare in direct questions, but in indirect questions it is commoner than **annōn**. In poetry **-ne** . . . **-ne** sometimes occurs.

a. The interrogative particle is often omitted in the first member; in which case **an** or **-ne** (**anne, necne**) may stand in the second: —

Gabīniō dīcam **anne** Pompêiō **an** utrīque (Manil. 57), *shall I say to Gabinius, or to Pompey, or to both?*

sunt haec tua verba **necne** (Tusc. iii. 41), *are these your words or not?*

quaesīvī ā Catilīnā in conventū apud M. Laecam fuisset **necne** (Cat. ii. 13), *I asked Catiline whether he had been at the meeting at Marcus Læca's or not.*

b. Sometimes the first member is omitted or implied, and **an** (**anne**) alone asks the question, — usually with indignation or surprise: —

an tū miserōs putās illōs (Tusc. i. 13), *what! do you think those men wretched?*

an iste umquam dē sē bonam spem habuisset, nisi dē vōbīs malam opīniōnem animō imbibisset (Verr. i. 42), *would he ever have had good hopes about himself unless he had conceived an evil opinion of you?*

c. Sometimes the second member is omitted or implied, and **utrum** may ask a question to which there is no alternative: —

utrum est in clārissimīs cīvibus is, quem . . . (Flacc. 45), *is he among the noblest citizens, whom, etc.?*

d. The following table exhibits the various forms of alternative questions: —

utrum	. . .	**an** . . . **an**
utrum	. . .	**annōn** (**necne**, see § 335. N.)
——	. . .	**an** (**anne**)
-ne	. . .	**an**
——	. . .	**-ne, necne**
-ne	. . .	**necne**
-ne	. . .	**-ne**

NOTE. — From double (*alternative*) questions must be distinguished those which are in themselves single, but of which *some detail* is alternative. These have the common disjunctive particles **aut** or **vel** (**-ve**). Thus, — quaerō num iniūstē **aut** improbē fēcerit (Off. iii. 54), *I ask whether he acted unjustly or even dishonestly.* Here there is no double question. The only inquiry is whether the man did *either* of the two things supposed, not *which* of the two he did.

Question and Answer

336. There is no one Latin word in common use meaning simply *yes* or *no*. In answering a question *affirmatively*, the verb or some other emphatic word is generally repeated; in answering *negatively*, the verb, etc., with **nōn** or a similar negative: —

valetne, *is he well?* **valet**, *yes* (he is well).
eratne tēcum, *was he with you?* **nōn erat**, *no* (he was not).
num quidnam novī? *there is nothing new, is there?* **nihil sānē**, *oh! nothing.*

a. An intensive or negative particle, a phrase, or a clause is sometimes used to answer a direct question: —

1. For YES: —

vērō, *in truth, true, no doubt, yes.*
etiam, *even so, yes*, etc.
ita, *so, true*, etc.
sānē, *surely, no doubt, doubtless*, etc.
certē, *certainly, unquestionably*, etc.
factum, *true, it's a fact, you're right*, etc. (lit., it was done).
ita vērō, *certainly* (so in truth), etc.
sānē quidem, *yes, no doubt*, etc.
ita est, *it is so, true*, etc.

2. For NO: —

nōn, *not so.*
nūllō modō, *by no means.*
minimē, *not at all* (lit., in the smallest degree, cf. § 329. *a*).
minimē vērō, *no, not by any means; oh! no*, etc.
nōn quidem, *why, no; certainly not*, etc.
nōn hercle vērō, *why, gracious, no!* (certainly not, by Hercules!)

Examples are: —

quidnam? an laudātiōnēs? **ita**, *why, what? is it eulogies? just so.*
aut **etiam** aut **nōn** respondēre (Acad. ii. 104), *to answer* (categorically) *yes or no.*
estne ut fertur forma? **sānē** (Ter. Eun. 361), *is she as handsome as they say she is?* (is her beauty as it is said?) *oh! yes.*
miser ergō Archelāus? **certē** sī iniūstus (Tusc. v. 35), *was Archelaus wretched then? certainly, if he was unjust.*
an haec contemnitis? **minimē** (De Or. ii. 295), *do you despise these things? not at all.*
volucribusne et ferīs? **minimē vērō** (Tusc. i. 104), *to the birds and beasts? why, of course not.*
ex tuī animī sententiā tū uxōrem habēs? **nōn hercle**, ex meī animī sententiā (De Or. ii. 260), *Lord! no*, etc.

337. In answering a double question, one member of the alternative, or some part of it, must be repeated: —

vīdistī an dē audītō nūntiās? — egomet vīdī (Plaut. Merc. 902), *did you see it or are you repeating something you have heard? — I saw it myself.*

CONSTRUCTION OF CASES

338. The Cases of nouns express their relations to other words in the sentence. The most primitive way of expressing such relations was by mere juxtaposition of uninflected forms. From this arose in time composition, i.e. the growing together of stems, by means of which a complex expression arises with its parts mutually dependent. Thus such a complex as **armi-gero-** came to mean *arm-bearing;* **fidi-cen-**, *playing on the lyre.* Later, Cases were formed by means of suffixes expressing more definitely such relations, and Syntax began. But the primitive method of composition still continues to hold an important place even in the most highly developed languages.

Originally the Indo-European family of languages, to which Latin belongs, had at least seven case-forms, besides the Vocative. But in Latin the Locative and the Instrumental were lost[1] except in a few words (where they remained without being recognized as cases), and their functions were divided among the other cases.

The Nominative, Accusative, and Vocative express the simplest and perhaps the earliest case-relations. The Nominative is the case of the Subject, and generally ends in **-s**. The Vocative, usually without a termination, or like the Nominative (§ 38. *a*), perhaps never had a suffix of its own.[2] The Accusative, most frequently formed by the suffix **-m**, originally connected the noun loosely with the verb-idea, not necessarily expressed by a verb proper, but as well by a noun or an adjective (see § 386).

The Genitive appears to have expressed a great variety of relations and to have had no single primitive meaning ; and the same may be true of the Dative.

The other cases perhaps at first expressed relations of place or direction (TO, FROM, AT, WITH), though this is not clear in all instances. The earlier meanings, however, have become confused with each other, and in many instances the cases are no longer distinguishable in meaning or in form. Thus the Locative was for the most part lost from its confusion with the Dative and Ablative; and its function was often performed by the Ablative, which is freely used to express the *place where* (§ 421). To indicate the case-relations — especially those of place — more precisely, Prepositions (originally adverbs) gradually came into use. The case-endings, thus losing something of their significance, were less distinctly pronounced as time went on (see § 36, *phonetic decay*), and prepositions have finally superseded them in the modern languages derived from Latin. But in Latin a large and various body of relations was still expressed by case-forms. It is to be noticed that in their *literal* use cases tended to adopt the preposition, and in their *figurative* uses to retain the old construction. (See Ablative of Separation, §§ 402–404; Ablative of Place and Time, § 421 ff.)

The word **cāsus**, *case*, is a translation of the Greek πτῶσις, *a falling away* (from the erect position). The term πτῶσις was originally applied to the Oblique Cases (§ 35. *g*), to mark them as variations from the Nominative, which was called ὀρθή, *erect* (*cāsus rēctus*). The later name *Nominative* (*cāsus nōminātīvus*) is from **nōminō**, and means the *naming* case. The other case-names (except *Ablative*) are of Greek origin. The name *Genitive* (*cāsus genetīvus*) is a translation of γενική [πτῶσις], from γένος (*class*), and refers to the *class* to which a thing belongs. *Dative* (*cāsus datīvus*, from **dō**) is translated from δοτική, and means the case of *giving*. *Accusative* (*accūsātīvus*, from **accūsō**) is a mistranslation of αἰτιατική (the case of *causing*), from αἰτία, *cause*, and meant to the Romans the case of *accusing*. The name *Vocative* (*vocātīvus*, from **vocō**) is translated from κλητική (the case of *calling*). The name *Ablative* (*ablātīvus*, from **ablātus, auferō**) means *taking from*. This case the Greek had lost.

[1] Some of the endings, however, which in Latin are assigned to the dative and ablative are doubtless of locative or instrumental origin (see p. 34, footnote).

[2] The **e**-vocative of the second declension is a form of the stem (§ 45. *c*).

NOMINATIVE CASE

339. The Subject of a finite verb is in the Nominative: —

Caesar Rhēnum trānsīre dēcrēverat (B. G. iv. 17), *Cæsar had determined to cross the Rhine.*

For the omission of a pronominal subject, see § 295. *a*.

a. The nominative may be used in exclamations: —

ēn dextra fidēsque (Aen. iv. 597), *lo, the faith and plighted word!*
ecce tuae litterae dē Varrōne (Att. xiii. 16), *lo and behold, your letters about Varro!*

NOTE. — But the accusative is more common (§ 397. *d*).

VOCATIVE CASE

340. The Vocative is the case of direct address: —

Tiberīne pater, tē, **sāncte**, precor (Liv. ii. 10), *O father Tiber, thee, holy one, I pray.*
rēs omnis mihi tēcum erit, **Hortēnsī** (Verr. i. 33), *my whole attention will be devoted to you, Hortensius.*

a. A noun in the nominative in apposition with the subject of the imperative mood is sometimes used instead of the vocative: —

audī tū, **populus Albānus** (Liv. i. 24), *hear, thou people of Alba.*

b. The vocative of an adjective is sometimes used in poetry instead of the nominative, where the verb is in the second person: —

quō **moritūre** ruis (Aen. x. 811), *whither art thou rushing to thy doom?*
cēnsōrem **trabeāte** salūtās (Pers. iii. 29), *robed you salute the censor.*

c. The vocative **macte** is used as a predicate in the phrase **macte estō (virtūte)**, *success attend your* (valor): —

iubērem tē **macte** virtūte esse (Liv. ii. 12), *I should bid you go on and prosper in your valor.*
macte novā virtūte puer (Aen. ix. 641), *success attend your valor, boy!*

NOTE. — As the original quantity of the final e in macte is not determinable, it may be that the word was an adverb, as in bene est and the like.

GENITIVE CASE

341. The Genitive is regularly used to express the relation of one noun to another. Hence it is sometimes called the *adjective* case, to distinguish it from the Dative and the Ablative, which may be called *adverbial* cases.

The uses of the Genitive may be classified as follows: —

I. **Genitive with Nouns:**	1. Of Possession (§ 343). 2. Of Material (§ 344). 3. Of Quality (§ 345). 4. Of the Whole, after words designating a Part (Partitive, § 346). 5. With Nouns of Action and Feeling (§ 348).
II. **Genitive with Adjectives:**	1. After Relative Adjectives (or Verbals) (§ 349). 2. Of Specification (later use) (§ 349. *d*).
III. **Genitive with Verbs:**	1. Of Memory, Feeling, etc. (§§ 350, 351, 354). 2. Of Accusing, etc. (Charge or Penalty) (§ 352).

GENITIVE WITH NOUNS

342. A noun used to limit or define another, and *not* meaning the same person or thing, is put in the Genitive.

This relation is most frequently expressed in English by the preposition *of*, sometimes by the English genitive (or possessive) case: —

librī **Cicerōnis**, *the books of Cicero*, or *Cicero's books*.
inimīcī **Caesaris**, *Cæsar's enemies*, or *the enemies of Cæsar*.
talentum **aurī**, *a talent of gold*.
vir summae **virtūtis**, *a man of the greatest courage*.

But observe the following equivalents: —

vacātiō **labōris**, *a respite* FROM *toil*.
petītiō **cōnsulātūs**, *candidacy* FOR *the consulship*.
rēgnum **cīvitātis**, *royal power* OVER *the state*.

Possessive Genitive

343. The Possessive Genitive denotes the person or thing to which an object, quality, feeling, or action belongs: —

Alexandrī canis, *Alexander's dog*.
potentia **Pompêī** (Sall. Cat. 19), *Pompey's power*.
Ariovistī mors (B. G. v. 29), *the death of Ariovistus*.
perditōrum temeritās (Mil. 22), *the recklessness of desperate men*.

NOTE 1. — The Possessive Genitive may denote (1) the actual *owner* (as in *Alexander's dog*) or *author* (as in *Cicero's writings*), or (2) the person or thing that possesses some *feeling* or *quality* or does some *act* (as in *Cicero's eloquence, the strength of the bridge, Catiline's evil deeds*). In the latter use it is sometimes called the Subjective Genitive; but this term properly includes the possessive genitive and several other genitive constructions (nearly all, in fact, except the Objective Genitive, § 347).

NOTE 2. — The noun limited is understood in a few expressions: —

ad Castoris [aedēs] (Quinct. 17), *at the* [temple] *of Castor*. [Cf. *St. Paul's*.]
Flaccus Claudī, *Flaccus* [slave] *of Claudius*.
Hectoris Andromachē (Aen. iii. 319), *Hector's* [wife] *Andromache*.

a. For the genitive of possession a possessive or derivative adjective is often used, — regularly for the possessive genitive of the personal pronouns (§ 302. *a*): —

liber **meus**, *my book*. [Not **liber meī**.]
aliēna perīcula, *other men's dangers.* [But also **aliōrum**.]
Sullāna tempora, *the times of Sulla.* [Oftener **Sullae**.]

b. The possessive genitive often stands in the predicate, connected with its noun by a verb (*Predicate Genitive*): —

haec domus est **patris meī**, *this house is my father's.*
iam mē **Pompêī** tōtum esse scīs (Fam. ii. 13), *you know I am now all for Pompey* (all Pompey's).
summa laus et tua et **Brūtī** est (Fam. xii. 4. 2), *the highest praise is due both to you and to Brutus* (is both yours and Brutus's).
compendī facere, *to save* (make of saving).
lucrī facere, *to get the benefit of* (make of profit).

NOTE. — These genitives bear the same relation to the examples in § 343 that a predicate noun bears to an appositive (§§ 282, 283).

c. An infinitive or a clause, when used as a noun, is often limited by a genitive in the predicate: —

neque **suī iūdicī** [erat] discernere (B. C. i. 35), *nor was it for his judgment to decide* (nor did it belong to his judgment).
cûiusvīs hominis est errāre (Phil. xii. 5), *it is any man's* [liability] *to err.*
negāvit **mōris** esse Graecōrum, ut in convīviō virōrum accumberent mulierēs (Verr. ii. 1. 66), *he said it was not the custom of the Greeks for women to appear as guests* (recline) *at the banquets of men.*
sed **timidī** est optāre necem (Ov. M. iv. 115), *but 't is the coward's part to wish for death.*
stultī erat spērāre, suādēre **impudentis** (Phil. ii. 23), *it was folly* (the part of a fool) *to hope, effrontery to urge.*
sapientis est pauca loquī, *it is wise* (the part of a wise man) *to say little.* [Not **sapiēns** (*neuter*) est, etc.]

NOTE 1. — This construction is regular with adjectives of the third declension instead of the neuter nominative (see the last two examples).

NOTE 2. — A derivative or possessive adjective may be used for the genitive in this construction, and *must* be used for the genitive of a personal pronoun: —

mentīrī nōn est **meum** [not **meī**], *it is not for me to lie.*
hūmānum [for **hominis**] est errāre, *it is man's nature to err* (to err is human).

d. A limiting genitive is sometimes used instead of a noun in apposition (*Appositional Genitive*) (§ 282): —

nōmen **īnsāniae** (for **nōmen īnsānia**), *the word madness.*
oppidum **Antiochīae** (for **oppidum Antiochīa**, the regular form), *the city of Antioch.*

Genitive of Material

344. The Genitive may denote the Substance or Material of which a thing consists (cf. § 403): —

talentum **aurī**, *a talent of gold.* flūmina **lactis**, *rivers of milk.*

Genitive of Quality

345. The Genitive is used to denote Quality, but only when the quality is modified by an adjective: —

vir **summae virtūtis**, *a man of the highest courage.* [But not **vir virtūtis.**]
māgnae est **dēlīberātiōnis**, *it is an affair of great deliberation.*
māgnī formīca **labōris** (Hor. S. i. 1. 33), *the ant* [a creature] *of great toil.*
ille autem **suī iūdicī** (Nep. Att. 9), *but he* [a man] *of independent* (his own) *judgment.*

NOTE. — Compare Ablative of Quality (§ 415). In expressions of quality, the genitive or the ablative may often be used indifferently: as, **praestantī prūdentiā vir**, *a man of surpassing wisdom;* **maximī animī homō**, *a man of the greatest courage.* In classic prose, however, the genitive of quality is much less common than the ablative; it is practically confined to expressions of measure or number, to a phrase with **êius**, and to nouns modified by **māgnus, maximus, summus,** or **tantus.** In general the Genitive is used rather of *essential*, the Ablative of *special* or *incidental* characteristics.

a. The genitive of quality is found in the adjective phrases **êius modī, cûius modī** (equivalent to **tālis**, *such;* **quālis**, *of what sort*): —

êius modī sunt tempestātēs cōnsecūtae, utī (B. G. iii. 29), *such storms followed, that*, etc.

b. The genitive of quality, with numerals, is used to define measures of *length, depth*, etc. (*Genitive of Measure*): —

fossa **trium pedum**, *a trench of three feet* [in depth].
mūrus **sēdecim pedum**, *a wall of sixteen feet* [high].

For the Genitive of Quality used to express *indefinite value*, see § 417.

Partitive Genitive

346. Words denoting a Part are followed by the Genitive of the Whole to which the part belongs.

a. Partitive words, followed by the genitive, are —

1. Nouns or Pronouns (cf. also 3 below): —

pars **mīlitum**, *part of the soldiers.* quis **nostrum**, *which of us?*
nihil erat **reliquī**, *there was nothing left.*
nēmō **eōrum** (B. G. vii. 66), *not a man of them.*
māgnam partem **eōrum** interfēcērunt (id. ii. 23), *they killed a large part of them.*

2. Numerals, Comparatives, Superlatives, and Pronominal words like **alius**, **alter**, **nūllus**, etc.: —

ūnus **tribūnōrum**, *one of the tribunes* (see *c* below).
sapientum octāvus (Hor. S. ii. 3. 296), *the eighth of the wise men.*
mīlia **passuum** sescenta (B. G. iv. 3), *six hundred miles* (thousands of paces).
mâior **frātrum**, *the elder of the brothers.*
animālium fortiōra, *the stronger* [of] *animals.*
Suēbōrum gēns est longē maxima et bellicōsissima **Germānōrum omnium** (B. G. iv. 1), *the tribe of the Suevi is far the largest and most warlike of all the Germans.*
alter **cōnsulum**, *one of the* [two] *consuls.*
nūlla **eārum** (B.G. iv. 28), *not one of them* (the ships).

3. Neuter Adjectives and Pronouns, used as nouns: —

tantum **spatī**, *so much* [of] *space.*
aliquid **nummōrum**, *a few pence* (something of coins).
id **locī** (or **locōrum**), *that spot of ground;* id **temporis**, *at that time* (§ 397. *a*).
plāna **urbis**, *the level parts of the town.*
quid **novī**, *what news?* (what of new?)
paulum **frūmentī** (B. C. i. 78), *a little grain.*
plūs **dolōris** (B. G. i. 20), *more grief.*
suī aliquid **timōris** (B. C. ii. 29), *some fear of his own* (something of his own fear).

NOTE 1. — In classic prose neuter adjectives (not pronominal) seldom take a partitive genitive, except **multum**, **tantum**, **quantum**, and similar words.

NOTE 2. — The genitive of adjectives of the *third declension* is rarely used partitively: — **nihil novī** (genitive), *nothing new;* but, — **nihil memorābile** (nominative), *nothing worth mention* (not **nihil memorābilis**).

4. Adverbs, especially those of Quantity and of Place: —

parum **ōtī**, *not much ease* (too little of ease).
satis **pecūniae**, *money enough* (enough of money).
plūrimum **tōtīus Galliae** equitātū valet (B. G. v. 3), *is strongest of all Gaul in cavalry.*
ubinam **gentium** sumus (Cat. i. 9), *where in the world are we* (where of nations)?
ubicumque **terrārum** et **gentium** (Verr. v. 143), *wherever in the whole world.*
rēs erat eō iam **locī** ut (Sest. 68), *the business had now reached such a point that*, etc.
eō **miseriārum** (Iug. 14. 3), *to that* [pitch] *of misery.*
inde **locī**, *next in order* (thence of place). [Poetical.]

b. The poets and later writers often use the partitive genitive after adjectives, instead of a noun in its proper case: —

sequimur tē, sāncte **deōrum** (Aen. iv. 576), *we follow thee, O holy deity.* [For **sāncte deus** (§ 49. *g.* N.)]
nigrae **lānārum** (Plin. H. N. viii. 193), *black wools.* [For **nigrae lānae.**]
expedītī **mīlitum** (Liv. xxx. 9), *light-armed soldiers.* [For **expedītī mīlitēs.**]
hominum cūnctōs (Ov. M. iv. 631), *all men.* [For **cūnctōs hominēs**; cf. *e.*]

c. Cardinal numerals (except **mīlia**) regularly take the Ablative with **ē** (**ex**) or **dē** instead of the Partitive Genitive. So also **quīdam**, *a certain one*, commonly, and other words occasionally: —

> ūnus **ex tribūnīs**, *one of the tribunes.* [But also, ūnus **tribūnōrum** (cf. *a.* 2).]
> minumus **ex illīs** (Iug. 11), *the youngest of them.*
> medius **ex tribus** (ib.), *the middle one of the three.*
> quīdam **ex mīlitibus**, *certain of the soldiers.*
> ūnus **dē multīs** (Fin. ii. 66), *one of the many.*
> paucī **dē nostrīs** cadunt (B. G. i. 15), *a few of our men fall.*
> hominem **dē comitibus meīs**, *a man of my companions.*

d. **Uterque**, *both* (properly *each*), and **quisque**, *each*, with Nouns are regularly used as adjectives in agreement, but with Pronouns take a partitive genitive: —

> uterque **cōnsul**, *both the consuls;* but, uterque **nostrum**, *both of us.*
> ūnus quisque **vestrum**, *each one of you.*
> utraque **castra**, *both camps.*

e. Numbers and words of quantity including the *whole* of any thing take a case in agreement, and not the partitive genitive. So also words denoting a part when *only that part* is thought of: —

> **nōs** omnēs, *all of us* (we all). [Not **omnēs nostrum.**]
> quot sunt **hostēs**, *how many of the enemy are there?*
> cavē inimīcōs, quī multī sunt, *beware of your enemies, who are many.*
> multī **mīlitēs**, *many of the soldiers.*
> nēmō **Rōmānus**, *not one Roman.*

Objective Genitive

347. The Objective Genitive is used with Nouns, Adjectives, and Verbs.

348. Nouns of *action*, *agency*, and *feeling* govern the Genitive of the Object: —

> cāritās **tuī**, *affection for you.*
> vacātiō **mūneris**, *relief from duty.*
> fuga **malōrum**, *refuge from disaster.*
> contentiō **honōrum**, *struggle for office.*
> dēsīderium **ōtī**, *longing for rest.*
> grātia **beneficī**, *gratitude for kindness.*
> precātiō **deōrum**, *prayer to the gods.*
> opīniō **virtūtis**, *reputation for valor.*

Note. — This usage is an extension of the idea of *belonging to* (Possessive Genitive). Thus in the phrase **odium Caesaris**, *hate of Cæsar*, the hate in a passive sense *belongs* to Cæsar, as *odium*, though in its active sense he is the *object* of it, as *hate* (cf. *a*). The distinction between the Possessive (subjective) and the Objective Genitive is very unstable and is often lost sight of. It is illustrated by the following example: the phrase **amor patris**, *love of a father*, may mean *love felt by a father*, *a father's love* (subjective genitive), or *love towards a father* (objective genitive).

a. The objective genitive is sometimes replaced by a possessive pronoun or other derivative adjective: —

mea invidia, *my unpopularity* (the dislike of which I am the object). [Cf. odium meī (Har. Resp. 5), *hatred of me.*]
laudātor **meus** (Att. i. 16. 5), *my eulogist* (one who praises me). [Cf. **nostrī** laudātor (id. i. 14. 6).]
Clōdiānum crīmen (Mil. 72), *the murder of Clodius* (the Clodian charge). [As we say, *the Nathan murder.*]
metus **hostīlis** (Iug. 41), *fear of the enemy* (hostile fear).
ea quae faciēbat, **tuā** sē fīdūciā facere dīcēbat (Verr. v. 176), *what he was doing, he said he did relying on you* (with your reliance).
neque neglegentiā **tuā**, neque id odiō fēcit **tuō** (Ter. Ph. 1016), *he did this neither from neglect nor from hatred of you.*

b. Rarely the objective genitive is used with a noun already limited by another genitive: —

animī multārum **rērum** percursiō (Tusc. iv. 31), *the mind's traversing of many things.*

c. A noun with a preposition is often used instead of the objective genitive: —

odium **in Antōnium** (Fam. x. 5. 3), *hate of Antony.*
merita **ergā mē** (id. i. 1. 1), *services to me.*
meam **in tē** pietātem (id. i. 9. 1), *my devotion to you.*
impetus **in urbem** (Phil. xii. 29), *an attack on the city.*
excessus **ē vītā** (Fin. iii. 60), *departure from life.* [Also, **excessus vītae**, Tusc. i. 27.]
adoptiō **in Domitium** (Tac. Ann. xii. 25), *the adoption of Domitius.* [A late and bold extension of this construction.]

NOTE. — So also in late writers the dative of reference (cf. § 366. *b*): as, — **longō bellō** māteria (Tac. H. i. 89), *resources for a long war.*

GENITIVE WITH ADJECTIVES

349. Adjectives requiring an object of reference govern the Objective Genitive.

a. Adjectives denoting *desire, knowledge, memory, fulness, power, sharing, guilt,* and their opposites govern the genitive: —

avidī **laudis** (Manil. 7), *greedy of praise.*
fastīdiōsus **litterārum**, *disdaining letters.*
iūris perītus, *skilled in law.* [So also the ablative, **iūre**, cf. § 418.]
memorem **vestrī**, oblītum **suī** (Cat. iv. 19), *mindful of you, forgetful of himself.*
ratiōnis et ōrātiōnis expertēs (Off. i. 50), *devoid of sense and speech.*
nostrae **cōnsuētūdinis** imperītī (B.G. iv. 22), *unacquainted with our customs.*

plēnus fideī, *full of good faith.*
omnis **speī** egēnam (Tac. Ann. i. 53), *destitute of all hope.*
tempestātum potentem (Aen. i. 80), *having sway over the storms.*
impotēns **īrae** (Liv. xxix. 9. 9), *ungovernable in anger.*
coniūrātiōnis participēs (Cat. iii. 14), *sharing in the conspiracy.*
affīnis **reī capitālis** (Verr. ii. 2. 94), *involved in a capital crime.*
īnsōns **culpae** (Liv. xxii. 49), *innocent of guilt.*

b. Participles in **-ns** govern the genitive when they are used as adjectives, i.e. when they denote a *constant disposition* and not a *particular act:* —

sī quem **tuī** amantiōrem cōgnōvistī (Q. Fr. i. 1. 15), *if you have become acquainted with any one more fond of you.*
multitūdō īnsolēns **bellī** (B. C. ii. 36), *a crowd unused to war.*
erat Iugurtha appetēns **glōriae** mīlitāris (Iug. 7), *Jugurtha was eager for military glory.*

NOTE 1. — Participles in -ns, when used *as participles*, take the case regularly governed by the verb to which they belong: as, — Sp. Maelium **rēgnum** appetentem interēmit (Cat. M. 56), *he put to death Spurius Mælius, who was aspiring to royal power.*

NOTE 2. — Occasionally participial forms in -ns are treated as participles (see note 1) even when they express a *disposition* or *character:* as, — virtūs quam aliī ipsam temperantiam dīcunt esse, aliī obtemperantem temperantiae praeceptīs et eam subsequentem (Tusc. iv. 30), *observant of the teachings of temperance and obedient to her.*

c. Verbals in **-āx** (§ 251) govern the genitive in poetry and later Latin: —

iūstum et tenācem **prōpositī** virum (Hor. Od. iii. 3), *a man just and steadfast to his purpose.*
circus capāx **populī** (Ov. A. A. i. 136), *a circus big enough to hold the people.*
cibī **vīnīque** capācissimus (Liv. ix. 16. 13), *a very great eater and drinker* (very able to contain food and wine).

d. The poets and later writers use the genitive with almost any adjective, to denote that *with reference to which* the quality exists (*Genitive of Specification*): —

callidus **reī mīlitāris** (Tac. H. ii. 32), *skilled in soldiership.*
pauper **aquae** (Hor. Od. iii. 30. 11), *scant of water.*
nōtus **animī paternī** (id. ii. 2. 6), *famed for a paternal spirit.*
fessī **rērum** (Aen. i. 178), *weary of toil.*
integer **vītae scelerisque** pūrus (Hor. Od. i. 22. 1), *upright in life, and unstained by guilt.*

NOTE. — The Genitive of Specification is only an extension of the construction with adjectives requiring an object of reference (§ 349). Thus callidus denotes *knowledge;* pauper, *want;* pūrus, *innocence;* and so these words in a manner belong to the classes under *a.*

For the Ablative of Specification, the prose construction, see § 418. For Adjectives of *likeness* etc. with the Genitive, apparently Objective, see § 385. *c.* For Adjectives with animī (locative in origin), see § 358.

GENITIVE WITH VERBS

Verbs of Remembering and Forgetting

350. Verbs of *remembering* and *forgetting* take either the Accusative or the Genitive of the object: —

a. **Meminī** takes the Accusative when it has the literal sense of *retaining in the mind* what one has seen, heard, or learned. Hence the accusative is used of *persons* whom one remembers as acquaintances, or of *things* which one has experienced.

So **oblīvīscor** in the opposite sense, — to *forget* literally, to *lose all memory of* a thing (very rarely, of a person).

Cinnam meminī (Phil. v. 17), *I remember Cinna.*

utinam **avum** tuum meminissēs (id. i. 34), *oh! that you could remember your grandfather!* (but he died before you were born).

Postumium, cûius **statuam** in Isthmō meminisse tē dīcis (Att. xiii. 32), *Postumius, whose statue you say you remember* (to have seen) *on the Isthmus.*

omnia meminit Sīron Epicūrī **dogmata** (Acad. ii. 106), *Siron remembers all the doctrines of Epicurus.*

multa ab aliīs audīta meminērunt (De Or. ii. 355), *they remember many things that they have heard from others.*

tōtam **causam** oblītus est (Brut. 217), *he forgot the whole case.*

hinc iam oblīvīscere **Grâiōs** (Aen. ii. 148), *from henceforth forget the Greeks* (i.e. not merely *disregard* them, but *banish them from your mind*, as if you had never known them).

b. **Meminī** takes the Genitive when it means to *be mindful* or *regardful of* a person or thing, to *think of* somebody or something (often with special interest or warmth of feeling).

So **oblīvīscor** in the opposite sense, — to *disregard*, or *dismiss from the mind*, — and the adjective **oblītus**, *careless* or *regardless.*

ipse **suī** meminerat (Verr. ii. 136), *he was mindful of himself* (of his own interests).

faciam ut hûius **locī diēīque mēīque** semper memineris (Ter. Eun. 801), *I will make you remember this place and this day and me as long as you live.*

nec mē meminisse pigēbit **Elissae**, dum memor ipse meī (Aen. iv. 335), *nor shall I feel regret at the thought of Elissa, so long as I remember myself.*

meminerint **verēcundiae** (Off. i. 122), *let them cherish modesty.*

hūmānae **īnfirmitātis** meminī (Liv. xxx. 31. 6), *I remember human weakness.*

oblīvīscī **temporum** meōrum, meminisse **āctiōnum** (Fam. i. 9. 8), *to disregard my own interests, to be mindful of the matters at issue.*

nec tamen **Epicūrī** licet oblīvīscī (Fin. v. 3), *and yet I must not forget Epicurus.*

oblīvīscere **caedis** atque **incendiōrum** (Cat. i. 6), *turn your mind from slaughter and conflagrations* (dismiss them from your thoughts).

NOTE 1. — With both **meminī** and **oblīvīscor** the personal and reflexive pronouns are regularly in the Genitive; neuter pronouns and adjectives used substantively are regularly in the Accusative; abstract nouns are often in the Genitive. These uses come in each instance from the natural meaning of the verbs (as defined above).

NOTE 2. — **Meminī** in the sense of *mention* takes the Genitive: as, — eundem Achillam cûius suprā meminimus (B. C. iii. 108), *that same Achillas whom I mentioned above.*

c. **Reminīscor** is rare. It takes the Accusative in the literal sense of *call to mind, recollect;* the Genitive in the more figurative sense of *be mindful of:* —

dulcīs moriēns reminīscitur **Argōs** (Aen. x. 782), *as he dies he calls to mind his beloved Argos.*

reminīscerētur et veteris **incommodī** populī Rōmānī et prīstinae **virtūtis** Helvētiōrum (B. G. i. 13), *let him remember both the former discomfiture of the Roman people and the ancient valor of the Helvetians.* [A warning, — *let him bear it in mind* (and beware)!]

d. **Recordor**, *recollect, recall,* regularly takes the Accusative: —

recordāre **cōnsēnsum** illum theātrī (Phil. i. 30), *recall that unanimous agreement of the* [audience in the] *theatre.*

recordāminī omnīs cīvīlīs **dissēnsiōnēs** (Cat. iii. 24), *call to mind all the civil wars.*

NOTE. — **Recordor** takes the genitive once (Pison. 12); it is never used with a personal object, but may be followed by **dē** with the ablative of the person or thing (cf. § 351. N.): —

dē tē recordor (Scaur. 49), *I remember about you.*

dē illīs (lacrimīs) recordor (Planc. 104), *I am reminded of those tears.*

Verbs of Reminding

351. Verbs of *reminding* take with the Accusative of the person a Genitive of the thing; except in the case of a neuter pronoun, which is put in the accusative (cf. § 390. *c*).

So **admoneō, commoneō, commonefaciō, commonefīō**. But **moneō** with the genitive is found in late writers only.

Catilīna admonēbat **alium egestātis, alium cupiditātis** suae (Sall. Cat. 21), *Catiline reminded one of his poverty, another of his cupidity.*

eōs hōc moneō (Cat. ii. 20), *I give them this warning.*

quod vōs lēx commonet (Verr. iii. 40), *that which the law reminds you of.*

NOTE. — All these verbs often take **dē** with the ablative, and the accusative of nouns as well as of pronouns is sometimes used with them: —

saepius tē admoneō **dē syngraphā** Sittiānā (Fam. viii. 4. 5) *I remind you again and again of Sittius's bond.*

officium vostrum ut vōs malō cōgātis commonērier (Plaut. Ps. 150), *that you may by misfortune force yourselves to be reminded of your duty.*

Verbs of Accusing, Condemning, and Acquitting

352. Verbs of *accusing*, *condemning*, and *acquitting*, take the Genitive of the Charge or Penalty: —

> arguit mē **furtī**, *he accuses me of theft.*
>
> **pecūlātūs** damnātus (**pecūniae** pūblicae damnātus) (Flacc. 43), *condemned for embezzlement.*
>
> videō nōn tē absolūtum esse **improbitātis**, sed illōs damnātōs esse **caedis** (Verr. ii. 1. 72), *I see, not that you were acquitted of outrage, but that they were condemned for homicide.*

a. Peculiar genitives, under this construction, are —

> **capitis**, as in **damnāre capitis**, *to sentence to death.*
>
> **mâiestātis** [laesae], *treason* (crime against the dignity of the state).
>
> **repetundārum** [rērum], *extortion* (lit. of an action for *reclaiming* money).
>
> **vōtī damnātus** (or **reus**), *bound* [to the payment] *of one's vow*, i.e. *successful* in one's effort.
>
> **pecūniae** (damnāre, iūdicāre, see note).
>
> **duplī** etc., as in **duplī condemnāre**, *condemn to pay twofold.*

Note. — The origin of these genitive constructions is pointed at by **pecūniae damnāre** (Gell. xx. 1. 38), *to condemn to pay money*, in a case of injury to the person; **quantae pecūniae iūdicātī essent** (id. xx. 1. 47), *how much money they were adjudged to pay*, in a mere suit for debt; **cōnfessī aeris ac dēbitī iūdicātī** (id. xx. 1. 42), *adjudged to owe an admitted sum due.* These expressions show that the genitive of the penalty comes from the use of the genitive of value to express a *sum of money due* either as a debt or as a fine. Since in early civilizations all offences could be compounded by the payment of fines, the genitive came to be used of other punishments, not pecuniary. From this to the genitive of the actual crime is an easy transition, inasmuch as there is always a confusion between crime and penalty (cf. Eng. *guilty of death*). It is quite unnecessary to assume an ellipsis of **crīmine** or **iūdiciō**.

353. Other constructions for the Charge or Penalty are —

1. The Ablative of Price: regularly of a *definite amount* of fine, and often of indefinite penalties (cf. § 416): —

> Frusinātēs **tertiā parte** agrī damnātī (Liv. x. 1), *the people of Frusino condemned* [to forfeit] *a third part of their land.*

2. The Ablative with **dē**, or the Accusative with **inter**, in idiomatic expressions: —

> dē aleā, *for gambling;* dē ambitū, *for bribery.*
>
> dē pecūniīs repetundīs, *of extortion* (cf. § 352. *a*).
>
> inter sīcāriōs (Rosc. Am. 90), *as an assassin* (among the assassins).
>
> dē vī et mâiestātis damnātī (Phil. i. 21), *convicted of assault and treason.*

Note. — The accusative with **ad** and **in** occurs in later writers to express the *penalty:* as, — **ad mortem** (Tac. Ann. xvi. 21), *to death;* **ad** (**in**) **metalla**, *to the mines.*

Verbs of Feeling

354. Many verbs of *feeling* take the Genitive of the object which excites the feeling.

a. Verbs of *pity*, as **misereor** and **miserēscō**, take the genitive: —

miserēminī **familiae**, iūdicēs, miserēminī **patris**, miserēminī **fīlī** (Flacc. 106), *have pity on the family*, etc.

miserēre **animī** nōn dīgna ferentis (Aen. ii. 144), *pity a soul that endures unworthy things.*

miserēscite **rēgis** (id. viii. 573), *pity the king.* [Poetical.]

NOTE. — But **miseror, commiseror**, *bewail*, take the accusative: as, — **commūnem condiciōnem** miserārī (Mur. 55), *bewail the common lot.*

b. As impersonals, **miseret, paenitet, piget, pudet, taedet** (or **pertaesum est**), take the genitive of the *cause of the feeling* and the accusative of the *person affected*: —

quōs **īnfāmiae** suae neque pudet neque taedet (Verr. i. 35), *who are neither ashamed nor weary of their dishonor.*

mē miseret **parietum** ipsōrum (Phil. ii. 69), *I pity the very walls.*

mē cīvitātis **mōrum** piget taedetque (Iug. 4), *I am sick and tired of the ways of the state.*

decemvirōrum **vōs** pertaesum est (Liv. iii. 67), *you became tired of the decemvirs.*

c. With **miseret, paenitet**, etc., the *cause of the feeling* may be expressed by an infinitive or a clause: —

neque mē paenitet **mortālīs inimīcitiās habēre** (Rab. Post. 32), *nor am I sorry to have deadly enmities.*

nōn dedisse istunc pudet; mē **quia nōn accēpī** piget (Pl. Pseud. 282), *he is ashamed not to have given; I am sorry because I have not received.*

NOTE. — **Miseret** etc. are sometimes used personally with a neuter pronoun as subject: as, — nōn tē **haec** pudent (Ter. Ad. 754), *do not these things shame you?*

Interest and *Rēfert*

355. The impersonals **interest** and **rēfert** take the Genitive of the person (rarely of the thing) affected.

The subject of the verb is a neuter pronoun or a substantive clause: —

Clōdī intererat Milōnem perīre (cf. Mil. 56), *it was the interest of Clodius that Milo should die.*

aliquid quod **illōrum** magis quam suā rētulisse vidērētur (Iug. 111), *something which seemed to be more for their interest than his own.*

videō enim quid meā intersit, quid **utrīusque** nostrum (Fam. vii. 23. 4), *for I see what is for my good and for the good of us both.*

a. Instead of the genitive of a personal pronoun the corresponding possessive is used in the ablative singular feminine after **interest** or **rēfert**: —

> quid **tuā** id rēfert? māgnī (Ter. Ph. 723), *how does that concern you? much.* [See also the last two examples above.]
>
> vehementer intererat **vestrā** quī patrēs estis (Plin. Ep. iv. 13. 4), *it would be very much to your advantage, you who are fathers.*

NOTE. — This is the only construction with **rēfert** in classic prose, except in one passage in Sallust (see example above).

b. The accusative with **ad** is used with **interest** and **rēfert** to express the thing *with reference to which* one is interested: —

> māgnī **ad honōrem** nostrum interest (Fam. xvi. 1), *it is of great consequence to our honor.*
>
> rēfert etiam **ad frūctūs** (Varr. R. R. i. 16. 6), *it makes a difference as to the crop.*

NOTE 1. — Very rarely the *person* is expressed by **ad** and the accusative, or (with **rēfert**) by the dative (probably a popular corruption): —

> quid id **ad mē** aut **ad meam rem** rēfert (Pl. Pers. 513), *what difference does that make to me or to my interests?*
>
> quid rēferat intrā nātūrae fīnīs **vīventī** (Hor. S. i. 1. 49), *what difference does it make to me who live within the limits of natural desire?*
>
> nōn rēferre **dēdecorī** (Tac. Ann. xv. 65), *that it makes no difference as to the disgrace.*

NOTE 2. — The degree of interest is expressed by a genitive of value, an adverb, or an adverbial accusative.

Verbs of Plenty and Want

356. Verbs of Plenty and Want sometimes govern the genitive (cf. § 409. *a.* N.): —

> convīvium **vīcīnōrum** compleō (Cat. M. 46, in the mouth of Cato), *I fill up the banquet with my neighbors.*
>
> implentur veteris **Bacchī** pinguisque **ferīnae** (Aen. i. 215), *they fill themselves with old wine and fat venison.*
>
> nē quis **auxilī** egeat (B. G. vi. 11), *lest any require aid.*
>
> quid est quod **dēfēnsiōnis** indigeat (Rosc. Am. 34), *what is there that needs defence?*
>
> quae ad cōnsōlandum mâiōris **ingenī** et ad ferendum singulāris **virtūtis** indigent (Fam. vi. 4. 2), [sorrows] *which for their comforting need more ability, and for endurance unusual courage.*

NOTE. — Verbs of plenty and want more commonly take the ablative (see §§ 409. *a*, 401), except **egeō**, which takes either case, and **indigeō**. But the genitive is by a Greek idiom often used in poetry instead of the ablative with all words denoting *separation* and *want* (cf. § 357. *b*. 3): —

> abstinētō **īrārum** (Hor. Od. iii. 27. 69), *refrain from wrath.*
>
> **operum** solūtīs (id. iii. 17. 16), *free from toils.*
>
> dēsine mollium **querellārum** (id. ii. 9. 17), *have done with weak complaints.*

Genitive with Special Verbs

357. The Genitive is used with certain special verbs.

a. The genitive sometimes follows **potior**, *get possession of;* as always in the phrase **potīrī rērum**, *to be master of affairs:* —

illīus **rēgnī** potīrī (Fam. i. 7. 5), *to become master of that kingdom.*
Cleanthēs sōlem dominārī et **rērum** potīrī putat (Acad. ii. 126), *Cleanthes thinks the sun holds sway and is lord of the universe.*

NOTE.—But **potior** usually takes the ablative (see § 410).

b. Some other verbs rarely take the genitive—

1. By analogy with those mentioned in § 354: —

neque hûius sīs veritus **fēminae** prīmāriae (Ter. Ph. 971), *and you had no respect for this high-born lady.*

2. As akin to adjectives which take the genitive: —

fastīdit **meī** (Plaut. Aul. 245), *he disdains me.* [Cf. fastīdiōsus.]
studet **tuī** (quoted N. D. iii. 72), *he is zealous for you.* [Cf. studiōsus.]

3. In imitation of the Greek: —

iūstitiaene prius mīrer, bellīne **labōrum** (Aen. xi. 126), *shall I rather admire his justice or his toils in war?*
neque ille sēpositī **ciceris** nec longae invīdit **avēnae** (Hor. S. ii. 6. 84), *nor did he grudge his garnered peas,* etc. [But cf. invidus, parcus.]
labōrum dēcipitur (Hor. Od. ii. 13. 38), *he is beguiled of his woes.*
mē **labōrum** levās (Pl. Rud. 247), *you relieve me of my troubles.*

358. The apparent Genitive **animī** (really Locative) is used with a few verbs and adjectives of *feeling* and the like: —

Antiphō mē excruciat **animī** (Ter. Ph. 187), *Antipho tortures my mind* (me in my mind).
quī pendet **animī** (Tusc. iv. 35), *who is in suspense.*
mē **animī** fallit (Lucr. i. 922), *my mind deceives me.*
So, by analogy, dēsipiēbam **mentis** (Pl. Epid. 138), *I was out of my head.*
aeger **animī**, *sick at heart;* cōnfūsus **animī**, *disturbed in spirit.*
sānus **mentis** aut **animī** (Pl. Trin. 454), *sound in mind or heart.*

PECULIAR GENITIVES

359. Peculiar Genitive constructions are the following: —

a. A poetical genitive occurs rarely in exclamations, in imitation of the Greek (*Genitive of Exclamation*): —

dī immortālēs, **mercimōnī** lepidī (Pl. Most. 912), *good heavens! what a charming bargain!*
foederis heu **tacitī** (Prop. iv. 7. 21), *alas for the unspoken agreement!*

b. The genitive is often used with the ablatives **causā**, **grātiā**, *for the sake of;* **ergō**, *because of;* and the indeclinable **īnstar**, *like;* also with **prīdiē**, *the day before;* **postrīdiē**, *the day after;* **tenus**, *as far as:*

honōris causā, *with due respect* (for the sake of honor).
verbī grātiā, *for example.*
ēius lēgis ergō, *on account of this law.*
equus īnstar montis (Aen. ii. 15), *a horse huge as a mountain* (the image of a mountain).
laterum tenus (id. x. 210), *as far as the sides.*

NOTE 1.—Of these the genitive with **causā** is a development from the possessive genitive and resembles that in **nōmen īnsāniae** (§ 343.*d*). The others are of various origin.

NOTE 2.—In prose of the Republican Period **prīdiē** and **postrīdiē** are thus used only in the expressions **prīdiē (postrīdiē) ēius diēī**, *the day before (after) that* (cf. "the eve, the morrow of that day"). Tacitus uses the construction with other words: as,—**postrīdiē īnsidiārum**, *the day after the plot.* For the accusative, see § 432. *a.* **Tenus** takes also the ablative (p. 136).

DATIVE CASE

360. The Dative is probably, like the Genitive, a grammatical case, that is, it is a form appropriated to the expression of a variety of relations other than that of the direct object. But it is held by some to be a Locative with the primary meaning of *to* or *towards*, and the poetic uses (like it **clāmor caelō**, Aen. v. 451) are regarded as survivals of the original use.

In Latin the Dative has two classes of meanings:—

1. The Dative denotes an object not as *caused* by the action, or *directly affected* by it (like the Accusative), but as reciprocally *sharing* in the action or *receiving it consciously* or actively. Thus in **dedit puerō librum**, *he gave the boy a book*, or **fēcit mihi iniūriam**, *he did me a wrong*, there is an idea of *the boy's receiving the book*, and of *my feeling the wrong*. Hence expressions denoting *persons*, or *things with personal attributes*, are more likely to be in the dative than those denoting mere *things*. So in Spanish the dative is used whenever a *person* is the object of an action; *yo veo al hombre*, *I see* [to] *the man*. This difference between the Accusative and the Dative (i.e. between the Direct and the Indirect Object) depends upon the point of view implied in the verb or existing in the mind of the writer. Hence Latin verbs of similar meaning (to an English mind) often differ in the case of their object (see § 367. *a*).

2. The Dative is used to express the *purpose* of an action or that for which it *serves* (see § 382). This construction is especially used with abstract expressions, or those implying an action.

These two classes of Datives approach each other in some cases and are occasionally confounded, as in §§ 383, 384.

The uses of the Dative are the following:—

1. **Indirect Object** (general use):
   1. With Transitives (§ 362).
   2. With Intransitives (§§ 366–372).

2. **Special or Idiomatic Uses**:
   1. Of Possession (with **esse**) (§ 373).
   2. Of Agency (with Gerundive) (§ 374).
   3. Of Reference (*datīvus commodī*) (§§ 376–381).
   4. Of Purpose or End (predicate use) (§ 382).
   5. Of Fitness etc. (with Adjectives) (§§ 383, 384).

INDIRECT OBJECT

361. The Dative is used to denote the object *indirectly affected* by an action.

This is called the Indirect Object (§ 274). It is usually denoted in English by the objective with *to*: —

cēdite **temporī**, *yield to the occasion.*
prōvincia **Cicerōnī** obtigit, *the province fell by lot to Cicero.*
inimīcīs nōn crēdimus, *we do not trust* [to] *our enemies.*

Indirect Object with Transitives

362. The Dative of the Indirect Object with the Accusative of the Direct may be used with any transitive verb whose meaning allows (see § 274): —

dō **tibi** librum, *I give you a book.*
illud **tibi** affīrmō (Fam. i. 7. 5), *this I assure you.*
commendō **tibi** ēius omnia negōtia (id. i. 3), *I put all his affairs in your hands* (commit them to you).
dabis profectō **misericordiae** quod **īrācundiae** negāvistī (Deiot. 40), *you will surely grant to mercy what you refused to wrath.*
litterās ā tē **mihi** stator tuus reddidit (Fam. ii. 17), *your messenger delivered to me a letter from you.*

a. Many verbs have both a transitive and an intransitive use, and take either the Accusative with the Dative, or the Dative alone: —

mihi id **aurum** crēdidit (cf. Plaut. Aul. 15), *he trusted that gold to me.*
equō nē crēdite (Aen. ii. 48), *put not your trust in the horse.*
concessit senātus **postulātiōnī** tuae (Mur. 47), *the senate yielded to your demand.*
concēdere **amīcīs quidquid velint** (Lael. 38), *to grant to friends all they may wish.*

363. Certain verbs implying motion vary in their construction between the Dative of the Indirect Object and the Accusative of the End of Motion (§§ 426, 427): —

1. Some verbs implying motion take the Accusative (usually with **ad** or **in**) instead of the Indirect Object, when the idea of *motion* prevails: —

litterās quās **ad Pompêium** scrīpsī (Att. iii. 8. 4), *the letter which I have written* [and sent] *to Pompey.* [Cf. nōn quō habērem quod **tibi** scrīberem (id. iv. 4 A), *not that I had anything to write to you.*]

litterae extemplō **Rōmam** scrīptae (Liv. xli. 16), *a letter was immediately written* [and sent] *to Rome.*

hostīs **in fugam** dat (B. G. v. 51), *he puts the enemy to flight.* [Cf. ut mē dem **fugae** (Att. vii. 23), *to take to flight.*]

omnēs rem **ad Pompêium** dēferrī volunt (Fam. i. 1), *all wish the matter to be put in the hands of Pompey* (referred to Pompey).

2. On the other hand, many verbs of motion usually followed by the Accusative with **ad** or **in**, take the Dative when the idea of *motion* is merged in some other idea: —

mihi litterās mittere (Fam. vii. 12), *to send me a letter.*

eum librum **tibi** mīsī (id. vii. 19), *I sent you that book.*

nec quicquam quod nōn **mihi** Caesar dētulerit (id. iv. 13), *and nothing which Cæsar did not communicate to me.*

cūrēs ut **mihi** vehantur (id. viii. 4. 5), *take care that they be conveyed to me.*

cum alius **aliī** subsidium ferrent (B. G. ii. 26), *while one lent aid to another.*

364. Certain verbs may take either the Dative of the person and the Accusative of the thing, or (in a different sense) the Accusative of the person and the Ablative of the thing[1]: —

dōnat **corōnās suīs**, *he presents wreaths to his men;* or,

dōnat **suōs corōnīs**, *he presents his men with wreaths.*

vincula exuere **sibi** (Ov. M. vii. 772), *to shake off the leash* (from himself).

omnīs armīs exuit (B. G. v. 51), *he stripped them all of their arms.*

Note 1. — **Interdīcō**, *forbid*, takes either (1) the Dative of the person and the Ablative of the thing, or (2) in later writers, the Dative of the person and the Accusative of the thing: —

aquā et **īgnī alicui** interdīcere, *to forbid one the use of fire and water.* [The regular formula for banishment.]

interdīxit **histriōnibus scaenam** (Suet. Dom. 7), *he forbade the actors* [to appear on] *the stage* (he prohibited the stage to the actors).

fēminīs (dat.) purpurae **ūsū** interdīcēmus (Liv. xxxiv. 7), *shall we forbid women the wearing of purple?*

Note 2. — The Dative with the Accusative is used in poetry with many verbs of *preventing, protecting,* and the like, which usually take the Accusative and Ablative. **Interclūdō** and **prohibeō** sometimes take the Dative and Accusative, even in prose: —

hīsce omnīs **aditūs** ad Sullam interclūdere (Rosc. Am. 110), *to shut these men off from all access to Sulla* (close to them every approach). [Cf. utī **commeātū Caesarem** interclūderet (B. G. i. 48), *to shut Cæsar off from supplies.*]

hunc (oestrum) arcēbis **pecorī** (Georg. iii. 154), *you shall keep this away from the flock.* [Cf. **illum** arcuit **Galliā** (Phil. v. 37), *he excluded him from Gaul.*]

sōlstitium pecorī dēfendite (Ecl. vii. 47), *keep the summer heat from the flock.* [Cf. utī **sē ā contumēliīs** inimīcōrum dēfenderet (B. C. i. 22), *to defend himself from the slanders of his enemies.*]

[1] Such are **dōnō, impertiō, induō, exuō, adspergō, īnspergō, circumdō,** and in poetry **accingō, implicō,** and similar verbs.

365. Verbs which in the active voice take the Accusative and Dative retain the Dative when used in the passive: —

nūntiābantur haec eadem **Cūriōnī** (B. C. ii. 37), *these same things were announced to Curio.* [Active: **nūntiābant (quīdam) haec eadem Cūriōnī**]

nec docendī Caesaris **propinquīs** êius spatium datur, nec **tribūnīs** plēbis suī perīculī dēprecandī facultās tribuitur (id. i. 5), *no time is given Cæsar's relatives to inform him, and no opportunity is granted to the tribunes of the plebs to avert danger from themselves.*

prōvinciae **prīvātīs** dēcernuntur (id. i. 6), *provinces are voted to private citizens.*

Indirect Object with Intransitives

366. The Dative of the Indirect Object may be used with any Intransitive verb whose meaning allows: —

cēdant arma **togae** (Phil. ii. 20), *let arms give place to the gown.*

Caesarī respondet, *he replies to Cæsar.*

Caesarī respondētur, *a reply is given to Cæsar* (Cæsar is replied to). [Cf. § 372.]

respondī maximīs **crīminibus** (Phil. ii. 36), *I have answered the heaviest charges.*

ut ita **cuique** ēveniat (id. ii. 119), *that it may so turn out to each.*

Note 1. — Intransitive verbs have no Direct Object. The Indirect Object, therefore, in these cases stands alone as in the second example (but cf. § 362. *a*).

Note 2. — **Cēdō**, *yield*, sometimes takes the Ablative of the thing along with the Dative of the person: as, — cēdere **alicui possessiōne** hortōrum (cf. Mil. 75), *to give up to one the possession of a garden.*

a. Many phrases consisting of a noun with the copula **sum** or a copulative verb are equivalent to an intransitive verb and take a kind of indirect object (cf. § 367. *a.* N.[2]): —

auctor esse **alicui**, *to advise* or *instigate one* (cf. **persuādeō**).

quis **huic reī** testis est (Quinct. 37), *who testifies* (is witness) *to this fact?*

is fīnis **populātiōnibus** fuit (Liv. ii. 30. 9), *this put an end to the raids.*

b. The dative is sometimes used without a copulative verb in a sense approaching that of the genitive (cf. §§ 367. *d*, 377): —

lēgātus **frātrī** (Mur. 32), *a lieutenant to his brother* (i.e. a man assigned to his brother).

ministrī **sceleribus** (Tac. Ann. vi. 36), *agents of crime.* [Cf. **sēditiōnis** ministrī (id. i. 17), *agents of sedition.*]

miseriīs suīs remedium mortem exspectāre (Sall. Cat. 40), *to look for death as a cure for their miseries.* [Cf. sōlus **meārum miseriārum**st remedium (Ter. Ad. 294).]

Note. — The cases in *a* and *b* differ from the constructions of § 367. *a.* N.[2] and § 377 in that the dative is more closely connected in idea with some single word to which it serves as an indirect object.

Indirect Object with Special Verbs

367. Many verbs signifying to *favor*, *help*, *please*, *trust*, and their contraries; also to *believe*, *persuade*, *command*, *obey*, *serve*, *resist*, *envy*, *threaten*, *pardon*, and *spare*,[1] take the Dative: —

cūr **mihi** invidēs, *why do you envy me?*
mihi parcit atque īgnōscit, *he spares and pardons me.*
īgnōsce patriō **dolōrī** (Liv. iii. 48), *excuse a father's grief.*
subvenī **patriae**, opitulāre **conlēgae** (Fam. x. 10. 2), *come to the aid of your country, help your colleague.*
mihi nōn displicet (Clu. 144), *it does not displease me.*
nōn **omnibus** serviō (Att. xiii. 49), *I am not a servant to every man.*
nōn parcam **operae** (Fam. xiii. 27), *I will spare no pains.*
sīc **mihi** persuāsī (Cat. M. 78), *so I have persuaded myself.*
mihi Fabius dēbēbit īgnōscere sī minus êius **fāmae** parcere vidēbor quam anteā cōnsuluī (Tull. 3), *Fabius will have to pardon me if I seem to spare his reputation less than I have heretofore regarded it.*
huic **legiōnī** Caesar cōnfīdēbat maximē (B. G. i. 40. 15), *in this legion Cæsar trusted most.*

In these verbs the Latin retains an original intransitive meaning. Thus: **invidēre**, *to envy*, is literally *to look askance at*; **servīre** is *to be a slave to*; **suādēre** is *to make a thing pleasant* (sweet) *to.*

a. Some verbs apparently of the same meanings take the Accusative.

Such are **iuvō, adiuvō**, *help*; **laedō**, *injure*; **iubeō**, *order*; **dēficiō**, *fail*; **dēlectō**, *please*: —

hīc pulvis **oculum** meum **laedit**, *this dust hurts my eye.* [Cf. multa **oculīs nocent**, *many things are injurious to the eyes.*]

NOTE 1. — **Fīdō** and **cōnfīdō** take also the Ablative (§ 431): as, — multum **nātūrā** **locī** cōnfīdēbant (B. G. iii. 9), *they had great confidence in the strength of their position.*

NOTE 2. — Some common phrases regularly take the dative precisely like verbs of similar meaning. Such are — praestō esse, *be on hand* (cf. **adesse**); mōrem gerere, *humor* (cf. **mōrigerārī**); grātum facere, *do a favor* (cf. **grātificārī**); dictō audiēns esse, *be obedient* (cf. **oboedīre**); cui fidem habēbat (B. G. i. 19), *in whom he had confidence* (cf. **cōnfīdēbat**).

So also many phrases where no corresponding verb exists. Such are — bene (male, pulchrē, aegrē, etc.) esse, *be well* (*ill*, etc.) *off*; iniūriam facere, *do injustice to*; diem dīcere, *bring to trial* (name a day for, etc.); agere grātiās, *express one's thanks*; habēre grātiam, *feel thankful*; referre grātiam, *repay a favor*; opus esse, *be necessary*; damnum dare, *inflict an injury*; acceptum (expēnsum) ferre (esse), *credit* (*charge*); honōrem habēre, *to pay honor to.*

[1] These include, among others, the following: **adversor, cēdō, crēdō, faveō, fīdō, īgnōscō, imperō, indulgeō, invideō, īrāscor, minitor, noceō, parcō, pāreō, placeō, resistō, serviō, studeō, suādeō (persuādeō), suscēnseō, temperō (obtemperō).**

b. Some verbs are used *transitively* with the Accusative or *intransitively* with the Dative without perceptible difference of meaning.

Such are **adūlor, aemulor, dēspērō, praestōlor, medeor**: —

adūlātus est **Antōniō** (Nep. Att. 8), *he flattered Antony.*
adūlārī **Nerōnem** (Tac. Ann. xvi. 19), *to flatter Nero.*
pācem nōn dēspērās (Att. viii. 15. 3), *you do not despair of peace.*
salūtī dēspērāre vetuit (Clu. 68), *he forbade him to despair of safety.*

c. Some verbs are used *transitively* with the Accusative or *intransitively* with the Dative with a difference of meaning: —[1]

partī cīvium cōnsulunt (Off. i. 85), *they consult for a part of the citizens.*
cum **tē** cōnsuluissem (Fam. xi. 29), *when I had consulted you.*
metuēns **puerīs** (Plaut. Am. 1113), *anxious for the children.*
nec metuunt **deōs** (Ter. Hec. 772), *they fear not even the gods.* [So also **timeō**.]
prōspicite **patriae** (Cat. iv. 3), *have regard for the state.*
prōspicere **sēdem** senectūtī (Liv. iv. 49. 14), *to provide a habitation for old age.* [So also **prōvideō**.]

d. A few verbal nouns (as **īnsidiae**, *ambush;* **obtemperātiō**, *obedience*) rarely take the dative like the corresponding verbs: —

īnsidiae **cōnsulī** (Sall. Cat. 32), *the plot against the consul* (cf. **īnsidior**).
obtemperātiō **lēgibus** (Legg. i. 42), *obedience to the laws* (cf. **obtemperō**).
sibi ipsī respōnsiō (De Or. iii. 207), *an answer to himself* (cf. **respondeō**).

NOTE. — In these cases the dative depends immediately upon the verbal force of the noun and not on any complex idea (cf. § 366. *a, b*).

368. The Dative is used —

1. With the impersonals **libet (lubet)**, *it pleases,* and **licet**, *it is allowed:* —

quod **mihi** maximē lubet (Fam. i. 8. 3), *what most pleases me.*
quasi **tibi** nōn licēret (id. vi. 8), *as if you were not permitted.*

2. With verbs compounded with **satis, bene,** and **male**: —

mihi ipse numquam satisfaciō (Fam. i. 1), *I never satisfy myself.*
optimō **virō** maledīcere (Deiot. 28), *to speak ill of a most excellent man.*
pulchrum est benefacere **reī pūblicae** (Sall. Cat. 3), *it is a glorious thing to benefit the state.*

NOTE. — These are not real compounds, but phrases, and were apparently felt as such by the Romans. Thus, — satis officiō meō, satis illōrum voluntātī quī ā mē hōc petīvērunt factum esse arbitrābor (Verr. v. 130), *I shall consider that enough has been done for my duty, enough for the wishes of those who asked this of me.*

[1] See the Lexicon under **caveō, conveniō, cupiō, īnsistō, maneō, praevertō, recipiō, renūntiō, solvō, succēdō.**

3. With **grātificor, grātulor, nūbō, permittō, plaudō, probō, studeō, supplicō, excellō**:—

Pompêiō sē grātificārī putant (Fam. i. 1), *they suppose they are doing Pompey a service.*
grātulor **tibi**, mī Balbe (id. vi. 12), *I congratulate you, my dear Balbus.*
tibi permittō respondēre (N. D. iii. 4), *I give you leave to answer.*
mihi plaudō ipse domī (Hor. S. i. 1. 66), *I applaud myself at home.*
cum inimīcī M. Fontêī vōbīs ac populō Rōmānō minentur, amīcī ac propinquī supplicent **vōbīs** (Font. 35), *while the enemies of Marcus Fonteius are threatening you and the Roman people too, while his friends and relatives are beseeching you.*

NOTE.—**Misceō** and **iungō** sometimes take the dative (see § 413. *a.* N.). **Haereō** usually takes the ablative, with or without **in**, rarely the dative: as,—haerentem **capitī** corōnam (Hor. S. i. 10. 49), *a wreath clinging to the head.*

a. The dative is often used by the poets in constructions which would in prose require a noun with a preposition. So especially with verbs of *contending* (§ 413. *b*):—

contendis **Homērō** (Prop. i. 7. 3), *you vie with Homer.* [In prose: **cum Homērō**.]
placitōne etiam pūgnābis **amōrī** (Aen. iv. 38), *will you struggle even against a love that pleases you?*
tibi certat (Ecl. v. 8), *vies with you.* [**tēcum**.]
differt **sermōnī** (Hor. S. i. 4. 48), *differs from prose.* [**ā sermōne**, § 401.]
laterī abdidit ēnsem (Aen. ii. 553), *buried the sword in his side.* [**in latere**, § 430.]

For the Dative instead of **ad** with the Accusative, see § 428. *h.*

369. Some verbs ordinarily intransitive may have an Accusative of the direct object along with the Dative of the indirect (cf. § 362. *a*):—

cui cum rēx **crucem** minārētur (Tusc. i. 102), *and when the king threatened him with the cross.*
Crētēnsibus obsidēs imperāvīt (Manil. 35), *he exacted hostages of the Cretans.*
omnia sibi īgnōscere (Vell. ii. 30), *to pardon one's self everything.*
Ascaniōne pater Rōmānās invidet **arcēs** (Aen. iv. 234), *does the father envy Ascanius his Roman citadels?* [With **invideō** this construction is poetic or late.]

a. With the passive voice this dative may be retained:—

quī iam nunc sanguinem meum **sibi** indulgērī aequum cēnset (Liv. xl. 15. 16), *who even now thinks it right that my blood should be granted to him as a favor.*
singulīs **cēnsōribus** dēnāriī trecentī imperātī sunt (Verr. ii. 137), *three hundred denarii were exacted of each censor.*
Scaevolae concessa est fācundiae virtūs (Quint. xii. 3. 9), *to Scaevola has been granted excellence in oratory.*

Indirect Object with Compounds

370. Many verbs compounded with **ad, ante, con, in, inter, ob, post, prae, prō, sub, super,** and some with **circum,** admit the Dative of the indirect object: —

neque enim adsentior **eīs** (Lael. 13), *for I do not agree with them.*
quantum nātūra hominis **pecudibus** antecēdit (Off. i. 105), *so far as man's nature is superior to brutes.*
sī **sibi** ipse cōnsentit (id. i. 5), *if he is in accord with himself.*
virtūtēs semper **voluptātibus** inhaerent (Fin. i. 68), *virtues are always connected with pleasures.*
omnibus **negōtiīs** nōn interfuit sōlum sed praefuit (id. i. 6), *he not only had a hand in all matters, but took the lead in them.*
tempestātī obsequī artis est (Fam. i. 9. 21), *it is a point of skill to yield to the weather.*
nec umquam succumbet **inimīcīs** (Deiot. 36), *and he will never yield to his foes.*
cum et Brūtus **cuilibet** ducum praeferendus vidērētur et Vatīnius **nūllī** nōn esset postferendus (Vell. ii. 69), *since Brutus seemed worthy of being put before any of the generals and Vatinius deserved to be put after all of them.*

a. In these cases the dative depends not on the preposition, but on the compound verb in its acquired meaning. Hence, if the acquired meaning is not suited to an indirect object, the original construction of the simple verb remains.

Thus in **convocat suōs**, *he calls his men together*, the idea of *calling* is not so modified as to make an indirect object appropriate. So **hominem interficere**, *to make way with a man* (kill him). But in **praeficere imperātōrem bellō**, *to put a man as commander-in-chief in charge of a war*, the idea resulting from the composition is suited to an indirect object (see also *b*, §§ 371, 388. *b*).

NOTE 1. — Some of these verbs, being originally transitive, take also a direct object: as, — nē offerāmus nōs perīculīs (Off. i. 83), *that we may not expose ourselves to perils.*

NOTE 2. — The construction of § 370 is not different in its nature from that of §§ 362, 366, and 367; but the compound verbs make a convenient group.

b. Some compounds of **ad, ante, ob,** with a few others, have acquired a transitive meaning, and take the accusative (cf. § 388. *b*): —[1]

nōs oppūgnat (Fam. i. 1), *he opposes us.*
quis audeat bene **comitātum** aggredī (Phil. xii. 25), *who would dare encounter a man well attended?*
mūnus obīre (Lael. 7), *to attend to a duty.*

[1] Such verbs are **aggredior, adeō, antecēdō, anteeō, antegredior, conveniō, ineō, obeō, offendō, oppūgnō, praecēdō, subeō.**

c. The adjective **obvius** and the adverb **obviam** with a verb take the dative: —

sī ille obvius **eī** futūrus nōn erat (Mil. 47), *if he was not intending to get in his way.*

mihi obviam vēnistī (Fam. ii. 16. 3), *you came to meet me.*

371. When *place* or *motion* is distinctly thought of, the verbs mentioned in § 370 regularly take a noun with a preposition:

inhaeret **in visceribus** (Tusc. iv. 24), *it remains fixed in the vitals.*

homine coniūnctō **mēcum** (Tull. 4), *a man united to me.*

cum hōc concurrit ipse Eumenēs (Nep. Eum. 4. 1), *with him Eumenes himself engages in combat* (runs together).

īnserite oculōs **in cūriam** (Font. 43), *fix your eyes on the senate-house.*

īgnis quī est **ob ōs** offūsus (Tim. 14), *the fire which is diffused before the sight.*

obicitur **contrā** istōrum **impetūs** Macedonia (Font. 44), *Macedonia is set to withstand their attacks.* [Cf. sī quis **vōbīs** error obiectus (Caec. 5), *if any mistake has been caused you.*]

in segetem flamma incidit (Aen. ii. 304), *the fire falls upon the standing corn.*

Note.—But the usage varies in different authors, in different words, and often in the same word and the same sense. The Lexicon must be consulted for each verb.

372. Intransitive verbs that govern the dative are used *impersonally* in the passive (§ 208. *d*). The dative is retained (cf. § 365):

cui parcī potuit (Liv. xxi. 14), *who could be spared?*

nōn modo nōn invidētur **illī aetātī** vērum etiam favētur (Off. ii. 45), *that age* (youth) *not only is not envied, but is even favored.*

temporī serviendum est (Fam. ix. 7), *we must serve the exigency of the occasion.*

Note.—In poetry the personal construction is sometimes found: as,—**cūr invideor** (Hor. A. P. 56), *why am I envied?*

Dative of Possession

373. The Dative is used with **esse** and similar words to denote Possession: —

est **mihi** domī pater (Ecl. iii. 33), *I have a father at home* (there is to me).

hominī cum deō similitūdō est (Legg. i. 25), *man has a likeness to God.*

quibus opēs nūllae sunt (Sall. Cat. 37), [those] *who have no wealth.*

Note.—The Genitive or a Possessive with **esse** emphasizes the *possessor;* the Dative, the fact of *possession:* as,—**liber est meus**, *the book is* MINE (and no one's else); **est mihi liber**, *I* HAVE *a book* (among other things).

a. With **nōmen est**, and similar expressions, the *name* is often put in the Dative by a kind of apposition with the *person;* but the Nominative is also common: —

(1) cui **Āfricānō** fuit cōgnōmen (Liv. xxv. 2), *whose* (to whom) *surname was Africanus.*

puerō ab inopiā **Egeriō** inditum nōmen (id. i. 34), *the name Egerius was given the boy from his poverty.*

(2) puerō nōmen est **Mārcus**, *the boy's name is Marcus* (to the boy is, etc.).

cui nōmen **Arethūsa** (Verr. iv. 118), [a fount] *called Arethusa.*

NOTE. — In early Latin the dative is usual; Cicero prefers the nominative, Livy the dative; Sallust uses the dative only. In later Latin the genitive also occurs (cf. § 343. *d*): as, — Q. Metellō **Macedonicī** nōmen inditum est (Vell. i. 11), *to Quintus Metellus the name of Macedonicus was given.*

b. **Dēsum** takes the dative; so occasionally **absum** (which regularly has the ablative): —

hōc ūnum **Caesarī** dēfuit (B.G. iv. 26), *this only was lacking to Cæsar.*

quid **huic** abesse poterit (De Or. i. 48), *what can be wanting to him?*

Dative of the Agent

374. The Dative of the Agent is used with the Gerundive to denote the person on whom the necessity rests: —

haec **vōbīs** prōvincia est dēfendenda (Manil. 14), *this province is for you to defend* (to be defended by you).

mihi est pūgnandum, *I have to fight* (i.e. the need of fighting is to me: cf. **mihi est liber,** *I have a book*, § 373. N.).

a. This is the regular way of expressing the *agent* with the Second or Passive Periphrastic Conjugation (§ 196).

NOTE 1. — The Ablative of the Agent with **ab** (§ 405) is sometimes used with the Second Periphrastic Conjugation when the Dative would be ambiguous or when a stronger expression is desired: —

quibus est **ā vōbīs** cōnsulendum (Manil. 6), *for whom you must consult.* [Here two datives, **quibus** and **vōbīs**, would have been ambiguous.]

rem **ab omnibus vōbīs** prōvidendam (Rabir. 4), *that the matter must be attended to by all of you.* [The dative might mean *for all of you.*]

NOTE 2. — The Dative of the Agent is either a special use of the Dative of Possession or a development of the Dative of Reference (§ 376).

375. The Dative of the Agent is common with *perfect participles* (especially when used in an adjective sense), but rare with other parts of the verb: —

mihi dēlīberātum et cōnstitūtum est (Leg. Agr. i. 25), *I have deliberated and resolved* (it has been deliberated by me).

mihi rēs prōvīsa est (Verr. iv. 91), *the matter has been provided for by me.*

sīc dissimillimīs **bēstiolīs** commūniter cibus quaeritur (N. D. ii. 123), *so by very different creatures food is sought in common.*

a. The Dative of the Agent is used by the poets and later writers with almost any passive verb:—

neque cernitur **ūllī** (Aen. i. 440), *nor is seen by any.*

fēlīx est dicta **sorōrī** (Ov. Fast. iii. 1. 597), *she was called happy by her sister.*

Aelia Paetina **Narcissō** fovēbātur (Tac. Ann. xii. 1), *Ælia Pœtina was favored by Narcissus.*

b. The dative of the person who *sees* or *thinks* is regularly used after **videor,** *seem*:—

vidētur **mihi,** *it seems* (or *seems good*) *to me.*

dīs aliter vīsum [est] (Aen. ii. 428), *it seemed otherwise to the gods.*

videor **mihi** perspicere ipsīus animum (Fam. iv. 13. 5), *I seem* (to myself) *to see the soul of the man himself.*

Note.—The verb **probāre,** *approve* (originally a mercantile word), takes a Dative of Reference (§ 376), which has become so firmly attached that it is often retained with the passive, seemingly as Dative of Agent:—

haec sententia et **illī** et **nōbīs** probābātur (Fam. i. 7. 5), *this view met both his approval and mine* (was made acceptable both to him and to me).

hōc cōnsilium **plērīsque** nōn probābātur (B. C. i. 72), *this plan was not approved by the majority.* [But also, cōnsilium **ā cūnctīs** probābātur (id. i. 74).]

Dative of Reference

376. The Dative often depends, not on any *particular word,* but on the *general meaning* of the sentence (*Dative of Reference*).

The dative in this construction is often called the Dative of Advantage or Disadvantage,[1] as denoting the person or thing for whose benefit or to whose prejudice the action is performed.

tibi arās (Plaut. Merc. 71), *you plough for yourself.*

tuās rēs **tibi** habētō (Plaut. Trin. 266), *keep your goods to yourself* (formula of divorce).

laudāvit **mihi** frātrem, *he praised my brother* (out of regard for me; **laudāvit frātrem meum** would imply no such motive).

meritōs mactāvit honōrēs, taurum **Neptūnō,** taurum **tibi,** pulcher Apollō (Aen. iii. 118), *he offered the sacrifices due, a bull to Neptune, a bull to thee, beautiful Apollo.*

Note.—In this construction the meaning of the sentence is complete without the dative, which is not, as in the preceding constructions, closely connected with any single word. Thus the Dative of Reference is easily distinguishable in most instances even when the sentence consists of only two words, as in the first example.

377. The Dative of Reference is often used to qualify a whole idea, instead of the Possessive Genitive modifying a single word:

[1] *Datīvus commodī aut incommodī.*

iter **Poenīs** vel corporibus suīs obstruere (Cat. M. 75), *to block the march of the Carthaginians even with their own bodies* (to block, etc., for the disadvantage of, etc.).
sē in cōnspectum **nautīs** dedit (Verr. v. 86), *he put himself in sight of the sailors* (he put himself to the sailors into sight).
versātur **mihi** ante oculōs (id. v. 123), *it comes before my eyes* (it comes to me before the eyes).

378. The Dative is used of the person from whose *point of view* an opinion is stated or a situation or a direction is defined.

This is often called the Dative of the Person Judging,[1] but is merely a weakened variety of the Dative of Reference. It is used —

1. Of the mental point of view (*in my opinion, according to me,* etc.): —

Platō **mihi** ūnus īnstar est centum mīlium (Brut. 191), *in my opinion* (to me) *Plato alone is worth a hundred thousand.*
erit ille **mihi** semper deus (Ecl. i. 7), *he will always be a god to me* (in my regard).
quae est ista servitūs tam clārō **hominī** (Par. 41), *what is that slavery according to the view of this distinguished man?*

2. Of the local point of view (*as you go in* etc.). In this use the person is commonly denoted indefinitely by a participle in the dative plural: —

oppidum prīmum Thessaliae **venientibus** ab Ēpīrō (B. C. iii. 80), *the first town of Thessaly as you come from Epirus* (to those coming, etc.).
laevā parte sinum **intrantī** (Liv. xxvi. 26), *on the left as you sail up the gulf* (to one entering).
est urbe **ēgressīs** tumulus (Aen. ii. 713), *there is, as you come out of the city, a mound* (to those having come out).

Note. — The Dative of the Person Judging is (by a Greek idiom) rarely modified by **nōlēns, volēns** (participles of **nōlō, volō**), or by some similar word: —

ut **quibusque** bellum **invītīs** aut **cupientibus** erat (Tac. Ann. i. 59), *as each might receive the war reluctantly or gladly.*
ut **mīlitibus** labōs **volentibus** esset (Iug. 100), *that the soldiers might assume the task willingly.*

379. The Dative of Reference is used idiomatically without any verb in colloquial questions and exclamations: —

quō **mihi** fortūnam (Hor. Ep. i. 5. 12), *of what use to me is fortune?*
unde **mihī** lapidem (Hor. S. ii. 7. 116), *where can I get a stone?*
quō **tibi**, Tillī (id. i. 6. 24), *what use for you, Tillius?*

[1] *Datīvus iūdicantis.*

a. The dative of reference is sometimes used after interjections:

ei (hei) **mihi** (Aen. ii. 274), *ah me!*
vae **victīs** (Liv. v. 48), *woe to the conquered.*
em **tibi**, *there, take that* (there for you)! [Cf. § 380.]

NOTE.—To express FOR—meaning *instead of, in defence of, in behalf of*—the ablative with **prō** is used:—

prō patriā morī (Hor. Od. iii. 2. 13), *to die for one's country.*
ego ībō **prō tē** (Plaut. Most. 1131), *I will go instead of you.*

Ethical Dative

380. The Dative of the Personal Pronouns is used to show a certain interest felt by the person indicated.[1]

This construction is called the Ethical Dative.[2] It is really a faded variety of the Dative of Reference.

quid **mihi** Celsus agit (Hor. Ep. i. 3. 15), *pray what is Celsus doing?*
suō **sibi** servit patrī (Plaut. Capt. 5), *he serves his own father.*
at **tibi** repente venit mihi Canīnius (Fam. ix. 2), *but, look you, of a sudden comes to me Caninius.*
hem **tibi** talentum argentī (Pl. Truc. 60), *hark ye, a talent of silver.*
quid **tibi** vīs, *what would you have* (what do you wish for yourself)?

Dative of Separation

381. Many verbs of *taking away* and the like take the Dative (especially of a *person*) instead of the Ablative of Separation (§ 401).

Such are compounds of **ab, dē, ex,** and a few of **ad**:—

aureum **eī** dētrāxit amiculum (N. D. iii. 83), *he took from him his cloak of gold.*
hunc **mihi** terrōrem ēripe (Cat. i. 18), *take from me this terror.*
vītam **adulēscentibus** vīs aufert (Cat. M. 71), *violence deprives young men of life.*
nihil enim **tibi** dētrāxit senātus (Fam. i. 5 B), *for the senate has taken nothing from you.*
nec **mihi** hunc errōrem extorquērī volō (Cat. M. 85), *nor do I wish this error wrested from me.*

NOTE.—The Dative of Separation is a variety of the Dative of Reference. It represents the action as *done to* the person or thing, and is thus more vivid than the Ablative.

1 Compare "I'll rhyme *you* so eight years together."—*As You Like It,* iii. 2.
2 *Datīvus ēthicus.*

a. The distinct idea of *motion* requires the ablative with a preposition — thus generally with names of *things* (§ 426. 1): —

illum **ex perīculō** ēripuit (B. G. iv. 12), *he dragged him out of danger.*

Note. — Sometimes the dative of the person and the ablative of the thing with a preposition are both used with the same verb: as, — **mihi** praeda **dē manibus** ēripitur (Verr. ii. 1. 142), *the booty is wrested from my hands.*

Dative of the Purpose or End

382. The Dative is used to denote the Purpose or End, often with another Dative of the person or thing affected.

This use of the dative, once apparently general, remains in only a few constructions, as follows: —

1. The dative of an abstract noun is used to show that *for which a thing serves* or *which it accomplishes*, often with another dative of the person or thing affected: —

rei pūblicae **clādī** sunt (Iug. 85. 43), *they are ruin to the state* (they are for a disaster to the state).

māgnō **ūsuī** nostrīs fuit (B. G. iv. 25), *it was of great service to our men* (to our men for great use).

tertiam aciem nostrīs **subsidiō** mīsit (id. i. 52), *he sent the third line as a relief to our men.*

suīs **salūtī** fuit (id. vii. 50), *he was the salvation of his men.*

ēvēnit facile quod dīs **cordī** esset (Liv. i. 39), *that came to pass easily which was desired by the gods* (was for a pleasure [lit. heart] to the gods).

Note 1. — This construction is often called the Dative of Service, or the Double Dative construction. The verb is usually **sum**. The noun expressing the *end for which* is regularly abstract and singular in number and is never modified by an adjective, except one of degree (**māgnus**, **minor**, etc.), or by a genitive.

Note 2. — The word **frūgī** used as an adjective is a dative of this kind: —

cōgis mē dīcere inimīcum **Frūgī** (Font. 39), *you compel me to call my enemy Honest.*

hominēs satis fortēs et plānē **frūgī** (Verr. iii. 67), *men brave enough and thoroughly honest.* Cf. erō **frūgī bonae** (Plaut. Pseud. 468), *I will be good for something.* [See § 122. *b.*]

2. The Dative of Purpose of concrete nouns is used in prose in a few military expressions, and with freedom in poetry: —

locum **castrīs** dēligit (B. G. vii. 16), *he selects a site for a camp.*

receptuī canere, *to sound a retreat* (for a retreat).

receptuī sīgnum (Phil. xiii. 15), *the signal for retreat.*

optāvit locum **rēgnō** (Aen. iii. 109), *he chose a place for a kingdom.*

locum **īnsidiīs** circumspectāre (Liv. xxi. 53), *to look about for a place for an ambush.* [Cf. locum **sēditiōnis** quaerere (id. iii. 46).]

For the Dative of the Gerundive denoting Purpose, see § 505. *b.*

Dative with Adjectives

383. The Dative is used after Adjectives or Adverbs, to denote that *to which the given quality is directed, for which it exists*, or *towards which it tends*.

NOTE.—The dative with certain adjectives is in origin a Dative of Purpose or End.

384. The Dative is used with adjectives (and a few Adverbs) of *fitness, nearness, likeness, service, inclination*, and their opposites:[1]

nihil est tam **nātūrae** aptum (Lael. 17), *nothing is so fitted to nature.*
nihil difficile **amantī** putō (Or. 33), *I think nothing hard to a lover.*
castrīs idōneum locum dēlēgit (B. G. i. 49), *he selected a place suitable for a camp.*
tribūnī **nōbīs** sunt amīcī (Q. Fr. i. 2. 16), *the tribunes are friendly to us.*
esse propitius potest **nēminī** (N. D. i. 124), *he can be gracious to nobody.*
māgnīs autem **virīs** prosperae semper omnēs rēs (id. ii. 167), *but to great men everything is always favorable.*
sēdēs huic nostrō nōn importūna **sermōnī** (De Or. iii. 18), *a place not unsuitable for this conversation of ours.*
cui **fundō** erat affīnis M. Tullius (Tull. 14), *to which estate Marcus Tullius was next neighbor.*
convenienter **nātūrae** vīvere (Off. iii. 13), *to live in accordance with nature* (ὁμολογουμένως τῇ φύσει).

NOTE 1.—So, also, in poetic and colloquial use, with **īdem**: as,—**invītum quī servat idem facit occīdentī** (Hor. A. P. 467), *he who saves a man against his will does the same as one who kills him.*

NOTE 2.—Adjectives of *likeness* are often followed by **atque** (**ac**), *as.* So also the adverbs **aequē, pariter, similiter**, etc. The pronoun **īdem** has regularly **atque** or a relative:—

sī parem sapientiam habet **ac** formam (Plaut. Mil. 1251), *if he has sense equal to his beauty* (like as his beauty).
tē suspicor **eīsdem** rēbus **quibus** mē ipsum commovērī (Cat. M. 1), *I suspect you are disturbed by the same things by which I am.*

385. Other constructions are sometimes found where the dative might be expected:—

a. Adjectives of *fitness* or *use* take oftener the Accusative with **ad** to denote the purpose or end; but regularly the Dative of *persons*:—

aptus **ad rem** mīlitārem, *fit for a soldier's duty.*
locus **ad īnsidiās** aptior (Mil. 53), *a place fitter for lying in wait.*
nōbīs ūtile est **ad hanc rem** (cf. Ter. And. 287), *it is of use to us for this thing.*

[1] Adjectives of this kind are **accommodātus, aptus; amīcus, inimīcus, īnfestus, invīsus, molestus; idōneus, opportūnus, proprius; ūtilis, inūtilis; affīnis, fīnitimus, propinquus, vīcīnus; pār, dispār, similis, dissimilis; iūcundus, grātus; nōtus, īgnōtus**, and others.

b. Adjectives and nouns of *inclination* and the like may take the Accusative with **in** or **ergā**: —

cōmis **in uxōrem** (Hor. Ep. ii. 2. 133), *kind to his wife.*
dīvīna bonitās **ergā hominēs** (N. D. ii. 60), *the divine goodness towards men.*
dē benevolentiā quam quisque habeat **ergā nōs** (Off. i. 47), *in regard to each man's good will which he has towards us.*
grātiōrem mē esse **in tē** (Fam. xi. 10), *that I am more grateful to you.*

c. Some adjectives of *likeness, nearness, belonging,* and a few others, ordinarily requiring the Dative, often take the Possessive Genitive: —[1]

quod ut **illī** proprium ac perpetuum sit . . . optāre dēbētis (Manil. 48), *which you ought to pray may be secure* (his own) *and lasting to him.* [Dative.]
fuit hōc quondam proprium **populī Rōmānī** (id. 32), *this was once the peculiar characteristic of the Roman people.* [Genitive.]
cum **utrīque** sīs maximē necessārius (Att. ix. 7 A), *since you are especially bound to both.* [Dative.]
prōcūrātor aequē **utrīusque** necessārius (Quinct. 86), *an agent alike closely connected with both.* [Genitive.]

1. The genitive is especially used with these adjectives when they are used wholly or approximately as nouns: —

amīcus **Cicerōnī**, *friendly to Cicero.* But, **Cicerōnis** amīcus, *a friend of Cicero*; and even, **Cicerōnis** amīcissimus, *a very great friend of Cicero.*
crēticus et êius aequālis paean (Or. 215), *the cretic and its equivalent the pæan.*
hī erant affīnēs **istīus** (Verr. ii. 36), *these were this man's fellows.*

2. After **similis**, *like*, the genitive is more common in early writers. Cicero regularly uses the genitive of *persons*, and either the genitive or the dative of *things*. With personal pronouns the genitive is regular (**meī, tuī,** etc.), and also in **vērī similis**, *probable*: —

dominī similis es (Ter. Eun. 496), *you're like your master* (your master's like).
ut essēmus similēs **deōrum** (N. D. i. 91), *that we might be like the gods.*
est similis **mâiōrum** suom (Ter. Ad. 411), *he's like his ancestors.*
patris similis esse (Off. i. 121), *to be like his father.*
sīmia quam similis turpissima bēstia **nōbīs** (N. D. i. 97, quoted from Enn.), *how like us is that wretched beast the ape!*
sī enim hōc **illī** simile sit, est illud **huic** (id. i. 90), *for if this is like that, that is like this.*

NOTE. — The genitive in this construction is not objective like those in § 349, but possessive (cf. § 343).

For the Dative or Accusative with **propior, proximus, propius, proximē,** see § 432. *a.*

[1] Such are **aequālis, affīnis, aliēnus, amīcus, cōgnātus, commūnis, cōnsanguineus, contrārius, dispār, familiāris, fīnitimus, inimīcus, necessārius, pār, pecūliāris, propinquus, proprius** (regularly genitive), **sacer, similis, superstes, vīcīnus.**

ACCUSATIVE CASE

386. The Accusative originally served to connect the noun more or less loosely with the verb-idea, whether expressed by a verb proper or by a verbal noun or adjective. Its earliest use was perhaps to repeat the verb-idea as in the Cognate Accusative (*run a race, fight a battle*, see § 390). From this it would be a short step to the Factitive Accusative (denoting the result of an act, as in *make a table, drill a hole*, cf. § 273. N.[1]). From this last could easily come the common accusative (of Affecting, *break a table, plug a hole*, see § 387. *a*). Traces of all these uses appear in the language, and the loose connection of noun with verb-idea is seen in the use of stems in composition (cf. § 265. 3).[1] It is impossible, however, to derive the various constructions of the accusative with certainty from any single function of that case.

The uses of the accusative may be classified as follows:

I. **Primary Object:**	1. Directly affected by the Action (§ 387. *a*). 2. Effect of the Action { Thing produced (§ 387. *a*). / Cognate Accusative (§ 390).
II. **Two Accusatives:**	1. Predicate Accusative (Of Naming etc.) (§ 393). 2. Of Asking or Teaching (§ 396). 3. Of Concealing (§ 396. *c*).
III. **Idiomatic Uses:**	1. Adverbial (§ 397. *a*). 2. Of Specification (Greek Accusative) (§ 397. *b*). 3. Of Extent and Duration (§§ 423, 425). 4. Of Exclamation (§ 397. *d*). 5. Subject of Infinitive (§ 397. *e*).

Direct Object

387. The Direct Object of a transitive verb is put in the Accusative (§ 274).

a. The Accusative of the Direct Object denotes (1) that which is *directly affected*, or (2) that which is *caused* or *produced* by the action of the verb: —

(1) Brūtus **Caesarem** interfēcit, *Brutus killed Cæsar.*

(2) **aedem** facere, *to make a temple.* [Cf. **proelium pūgnāre**, *to fight a battle*, § 390.]

Note. — There is no definite line by which transitive verbs can be distinguished from intransitive. Verbs which usually take a direct object (expressed or implied) are called transitive, but many of these are often used *intransitively* or *absolutely*. Thus **timeō**, *I fear*, is transitive in the sentence **inimīcum timeō**, *I fear my enemy*, but intransitive (*absolute*) in **nōlī timēre**, *don't be afraid*. Again, many verbs are transitive in one sense and intransitive in another: as, — **Helvētiōs superāvērunt Rōmānī**, *the Romans overcame the Helvetians;* but **nihil superābat**, *nothing remained* (was left over). So also many verbs commonly intransitive may be used transitively with a slight change of meaning: as, — **rīdēs**, *you are laughing;* but **mē rīdēs**, *you 're laughing at me.*

[1] Compare **armiger**, *armor-bearer*, with **arma gerere**, *to bear arms;* **fidicen**, *lyre-player*, with **fidibus canere**, *to* (play on) *sing to the lyre.* Compare also **istanc tāctiō** (Plaut.), *the* [act of] *touching her*, with **istanc tangere**, *to touch her* (§ 388. *d*. N.[2]).

b. The object of a transitive verb in the active voice becomes its subject in the passive, and is put in the nominative (§ 275): —

Brūtus Caesarem interfēcit, *Brutus killed Cæsar.*
Caesar ā Brūtō interfectus est, *Cæsar was killed by Brutus.*
domum aedificat, *he builds a house.*
domus aedificātur, *the house is building* (being built).

388. Certain special verbs require notice.

a. Many verbs apparently intransitive, expressing *feeling*, take an accusative, and may be used in the passive: —

meum **cāsum lūctumque** doluērunt (Sest. 145), *they grieved at my calamity and sorrow.*
sī nōn **Acrisium** rīsissent Iuppiter et Venus (Hor. Od. iii. 16. 5), *if Jupiter and Venus had not laughed at Acrisius.*
rīdētur ab omnī conventū (Hor. S. i. 7. 22), *he is laughed at by the whole assembly.*

For the Cognate Accusative with verbs of *taste, smell*, and the like, see § 390. *a.*

Note. — Some verbs commonly intransitive may be used transitively (especially in poetry) from a similarity of meaning with other verbs that take the accusative: —

gemēns īgnōminiam (Georg. iii. 226), *groaning at the disgrace.* [Cf. **doleō**.]
festīnāre fugam (Aen. iv. 575), *to hasten their flight.* [Cf. **accelerō**.]
cōmptōs ārsit crīnīs (Hor. Od. iv. 9. 13), *she burned with love for his well-combed locks.* [Cf. **adamō**.]

b. Verbs of motion, compounds of **circum, trāns**, and **praeter**, and a few others, frequently become transitive, and take the accusative (cf. § 370. *b*): —

mortem obīre, *to die* (to meet death).
cōnsulātum ineunt (Liv. ii. 28), *they enter upon the consulship.*
nēminem convēnī (Fam. ix. 14), *I met no one.*
sī **īnsulam** adīsset (B. G. iv. 20), *if he should go to the island.*
trānsīre **flūmen** (id. ii. 23), *to cross the river* (cf. § 395).
cīvēs quī circumstant **senātum** (Cat. i. 21), *the citizens who stand about the senate.*

Note. — Among such verbs are some compounds of **ad, in, per**, and **sub**.

c. The accusative is used after the impersonals **decet, dēdecet, dēlectat, iuvat, oportet, fallit, fugit, praeterit**: —

ita ut **vōs** decet (Plaut. Most. 729), *so as befits you.*
mē pedibus dēlectat claudere verba (Hor. S. ii. 1. 28), *my delight is* (it pleases me) *to arrange words in measure.*
nisi **mē** fallit, *unless I am mistaken* (unless it deceives me).
iūvit **mē** tibi tuās litterās prōfuisse (Fam. v. 21. 3), *it pleased me that your literary studies had profited you.*
tē nōn praeterit (Fam. i. 8. 2), *it does not escape your notice.*

NOTE 1.—So after **latet** in poetry and post-classical prose: as,—**latet plērōsque** (Plin. N. H. ii. 82), *it is unknown to most persons.*

NOTE 2.—These verbs are merely ordinary transitives with an idiomatic signification. Hence most of them are also used personally.

NOTE 3.—**Decet** and **latet** sometimes take the dative:—

ita **nōbīs** decet (Ter. Ad. 928), *thus it befits us.*
hostīque Rōma latet (Sil. It. xii. 614), *and Rome lies hidden from the foe.*

d. A few verbs in isolated expressions take the accusative from a forcing of their meaning. Such expressions are:—

ferīre **foedus**, *to strike a treaty* (i.e. to sanction by striking down a victim).
vincere **iūdicium** (**spōnsiōnem, rem, hōc**), *to prevail on a trial, etc.* [As if the case were a difficulty to overcome; cf. **vincere iter**, Aen. vi. 688.]
aequor nāvigāre (Aen. i. 67), *to sail the sea.* [As if it were **trānsīre**, § 388. *b.*]
maria aspera iūrō (id. vi. 351), *I swear by the rough seas* (cf. id. vi. 324). [The accusative with verbs of *swearing* is chiefly poetic.]
noctīs dormīre, *to sleep* [whole] *nights* (to spend in sleep).

NOTE 1.—These accusatives are of various kinds. The last example approaches the cognate construction (cf. the second example under § 390).

NOTE 2.—In early and popular usage some nouns and adjectives derived from transitive verbs retain verbal force sufficient to govern the accusative:—

quid tibi **istanc** tāctiō est (Plaut. Poen. 1308), *what business have you to touch her?* [Cf. **tangō**.]
mīrābundī **bēstiam** (Ap. Met. iv. 16), *full of wonder at the creature.* [Cf. **mīror**.]
vītābundus **castra** (Liv. xxv. 13), *trying to avoid the camp.* [Cf. **vītō**.]

389. Many verbs ordinarily transitive may be used *absolutely*, having their natural object in the ablative with **dē** (§ 273. N. 2): —

priusquam Pompōnius **dē** ēius **adventū** cōgnōsceret (B. C. iii. 101), *before Pomponius could learn of his coming.* [Cf. **ēius adventū cōgnitō**, *his arrival being discovered.*]

For Accusative and Genitive after Impersonals, see § 354. *b.* For the Accusative after the impersonal Gerundive with **esse**, see § 500. 3.

Cognate Accusative

390. An intransitive verb often takes the Accusative of a noun of kindred meaning, usually modified by an adjective or in some other manner.

This construction is called the *Cognate Accusative* or *Accusative of Kindred Signification*: —

tūtiōrem **vītam** vīvere (Verr. ii. 118), *to live a safer life.*
tertiam iam **aetātem** hominum vīvēbat (Cat. M. 31), *he was now living the third generation of men.*
servitūtem servīre, *to be in slavery.*
coīre **societātem**, *to* [go together and] *form an alliance.*

a. Verbs of *taste, smell,* and the like take a cognate accusative of the quality: —

vīnum redolēns (Phil. ii. 63), *smelling* [of] *wine.*
herbam mella sapiunt (Plin. H. N. xi. 18), *the honey tastes* [of] *grass.*
olēre **malitiam** (Rosc. Com. 20), *to have the odor of malice.*
Cordubae nātīs poētīs, pingue **quiddam** sonantibus atque **peregrīnum** (Arch. 26), *to poets born at Cordova, whose speech had a somewhat thick and foreign accent.*

b. The cognate accusative is often loosely used by the poets: —

huic errōrī similem [**errōrem**] īnsānīre (Hor. S. ii. 3. 62), *to suffer a delusion like this.*
saltāre **Cyclōpa** (id. i. 5. 63), *to dance the Cyclops* (represent in dancing).
Bacchānālia vīvere (Iuv. ii. 3), *to live in revellings.*
Amaryllida resonāre (Ecl. i. 5), *to reëcho* [the name of] *Amaryllis.*
intonuit **laevum** (Aen. ii. 693), *it thundered on the left.*
dulce rīdentem, dulce loquentem (Hor. Od. i. 22. 23), *sweetly smiling, sweetly prattling.*
acerba tuēns (Aen. ix. 794), *looking fiercely.* [Cf. Eng. "to look daggers."]
torvum clāmat (id. vii. 399), *he cries harshly.*

c. A neuter pronoun or an adjective of indefinite meaning is very common as cognate accusative (cf. §§ 214. *d*, 397. *a*): —

Empedoclēs **multa alia** peccat (N. D. i. 29), *Empedocles commits many other errors.*
ego **illud** adsentior Theophrastō (De Or. iii. 184), *in this I agree with Theophrastus.*
multum tē ista fefellit opīniō (Verr. ii. 1. 88), *you were much deceived in this expectation* (this expectation deceived you much).
plūs valeō, *I have more strength.*
plūrimum potest, *he is strongest.*
quid mē ista laedunt (Leg. Agr. ii. 32), *what harm do those things do me?*
hōc tē moneō, *I give you this warning* (cf. *d.* N.[1]).
id laetor, *I rejoice at this* (cf. *d.* N.[1]).
quid moror, *why do I delay?*
quae hominēs arant, nāvigant, aedificant (Sall. Cat. ii. 7), *what men do in ploughing, sailing, and building.*

d. So in many common phrases: —

sī **quid** ille sē velit (B. G. i. 34), *if he should want anything of him* (if he should want him in anything).
numquid, Geta, aliud mē vīs (Ter. Ph. 151), *can I do anything more for you, Geta* (there is nothing you want of me, is there)? [A common form of leave-taking.]
quid est quod, etc., *why is it that,* etc.? [Cf. **hōc erat quod** (Aen. ii. 664), *was it for this that,* etc.?]

NOTE 1.—In these cases substantives *with a definite meaning* would be in some other construction:—

in hōc eōdem peccat, *he errs in this same point.*
bonīs rēbus laetārī, *to rejoice at prosperity.* [Also: in, dē, or ex.]
dē testāmentō monēre, *to remind one of the will.* [Later: genitive, § 351.]
officī admonēre, *to remind one of his duty.* [Also: dē officiō.]

NOTE 2.—In some of these cases the connection of the accusative with the verb has so faded out that the words have become real adverbs: as,—**multum, plūs, plūrimum; plērumque,** *for the most part, generally;* **cēterum, cētera,** *for the rest, otherwise, but;* **prīmum,** *first;* **nihil,** *by no means, not at all;* **aliquid,** *somewhat;* **quid,** *why;* **facile,** *easily.* So in the comparative of adverbs (§ 218). But the line cannot be sharply drawn, and some of the examples under *b* may be classed as adverbial.

Two Accusatives

391. Some transitive verbs take a second accusative in addition to their Direct Object.

This second accusative is either (1) a Predicate Accusative or (2) a Secondary Object.

Predicate Accusative

392. An accusative in the Predicate referring to the same person or thing as the Direct Object, but not in apposition with it, is called a Predicate Accusative.

393. Verbs of *naming, choosing, appointing, making, esteeming, showing,* and the like, may take a Predicate Accusative along with the direct object:—

ō Spartace, **quem** enim tē potius appellem (Phil. xiii. 22), *O Spartacus, for what else shall I call you* (than Spartacus)?
Cicerōnem **cōnsulem** creāre, *to elect Cicero consul.*
mē **augurem** nōmināvērunt (Phil. ii. 4), *they nominated me for augur.*
cum grātiās ageret quod sē **cōnsulem** fēcisset (De Or. ii. 268), *when he thanked him because he had made him consul* (supported his candidacy).
hominem prae sē nēminem putāvit (Rosc. Am. 135), *he thought nobody a man in comparison with himself.*
ducem sē praebuit (Vat. 33), *he offered himself as a leader.*

NOTE.—The predicate accusative may be an adjective: as,—hominēs **mītīs** reddidit et **mānsuētōs** (Inv. i. 2), *has made men mild and gentle.*

a. In changing from the active voice to the passive, the Predicate Accusative becomes Predicate Nominative (§ 284):—

rēx ab suīs appellātur (B. G. viii. 4), *he is called king by his subjects.* [Active: suī eum **rēgem** appellant.]

Secondary Object

394. The Accusative of the Secondary Object is used (along with the direct object) to denote something more remotely affected by the action of the verb.

395. Transitive verbs compounded with prepositions sometimes take (in addition to the direct object) a Secondary Object, originally governed by the preposition: —

Caesar Germānōs **flūmen** trāicit (B. C. i. 83), *Cæsar throws the Germans across the river.*

idem iūs iūrandum adigit **Afrānium** (id. i. 76), *he exacts the same oath from Afranius.*

quōs Pompêius omnia sua **praesidia** circumdūxit (id. iii. 61), *whom Pompey conducted through all his garrison.*

Note 1.—This construction is common only with **trādūcō**, **trāiciō**, and **trānsportō**. The preposition is sometimes repeated with compounds of **trāns**, and usually with compounds of the other prepositions. The ablative is also used: —

dōnec rēs suās trāns **Halyn** flūmen trāicerent (Liv. xxxviii. 25), *till they should get their possessions across the river Halys.*

(exercitus) **Padō** trāiectus Cremōnam (id. xxi. 56), *the army was conveyed across the Po to Cremona* (by way of the Po, § 429. *a*).

Note 2.—The secondary object may be retained with a passive verb: as,—Belgae **Rhēnum** trāductī sunt (B. G. ii. 4), *the Belgians were led over the Rhine.*

Note 3.—The double construction indicated in § 395 is possible only when the force of the preposition and the force of the verb are each distinctly felt in the compound, the verb governing the direct, and the preposition the secondary object.

But often the two parts of the compound become closely united to form a transitive verb of simple meaning. In this case the compound verb is transitive solely by virtue of its prepositional part and can have but one accusative,—the same which was formerly the secondary object, but which now becomes the direct. So **trāiciō** comes to mean either (1) *to pierce* (anybody) [by hurling] or (2) *to cross* (a river etc.): —

gladiō hominem trāiēcit, *he pierced the man with a sword.* [Here **iaciō** has lost all transitive force, and serves simply to give the force of a verb to the meaning of **trāns**, and to tell the *manner* of the act.]

Rhodanum trāiēcit, *he crossed the Rhone.* [Here **iaciō** has become simply a verb of motion, and **trāiciō** is hardly distinguishable from **trānseō**.]

In these examples **hominem** and **Rhodanum**, which would be secondary objects if **trāiēcit** were used in its primary signification, have become the direct objects. Hence in the passive construction they become the subjects and are put in the nominative: —

homō trāiectus est gladiō, *the man was pierced with a sword.*

Rhodanus trāiectus est, *the Rhone was crossed.*

The poetical **trāiectus lōra** (Aen. ii. 273), *pierced with thongs*, comes from a mixture of two constructions: (1) eum trāiēcit lōra, *he rove thongs through him,*[1] and (2) eum trāiēcit lōrīs, *he pierced him with thongs.* In putting the sentence into a passive form, the direct object of the former (**lōra**) is irregularly kept, and the direct object of the latter (**eum**) is made the subject.

[1] Perhaps not found in the active, but cf. **trāiectō fūne** (Aen. v. 488).

396. Some verbs of *asking* and *teaching* may take two accusatives, one of the Person (*direct object*), and the other of the Thing (*secondary object*): —

> **mē sententiam** rogāvit, *he asked me my opinion.*
> **ōtium dīvōs** rogat (Hor. Od. ii. 16. 1), *he prays the gods for rest.*
> **haec praetōrem** postulābās (Tull. 39), *you demanded this of the prætor.*
> **aedīlīs populum** rogāre (Liv. vi. 42), *to ask the people* [to elect] *ædiles.*
> docēre **puerōs elementa**, *to teach children their A B C's.*

Note. — This construction is found in classical authors with **ōrō, poscō, reposcō, rogō, interrogō, flāgitō, doceō.**

a. Some verbs of *asking* take the ablative of the person with a preposition instead of the accusative. So, always, **petō** (**ab**), **quaerō** (**ex, ab, dē**); usually **poscō** (**ab**), **flāgitō** (**ab**), **postulō** (**ab**), and occasionally others: —

> **pācem ab Rōmānīs** petiērunt (B. G. ii. 13), *they sought peace from the Romans.*
> quod quaesīvit **ex mē** P. Apulêius (Phil. vi. 1), *what Publius Apuleius asked of me.*

b. With the passive of some verbs of asking or teaching, the *person* or the *thing* may be used as subject (cf. *c.* N. 2): —

> **Caesar** sententiam rogātus est, *Cæsar was asked his opinion.*
> **id** ab eō flāgitābātur (B. C. i. 71), *this was urgently demanded of him.*

Note. — The accusative of the *thing* may be retained with the passive of **rogō**, and of verbs of teaching, and occasionally with a few other verbs: —

> fuerant **hōc** rogātī (Cael. 64), *they had been asked this.*
> poscor **meum Laelapa** (Ov. M. vii. 771), *I am asked for my Lælaps.*
> Cicerō **cūncta** ēdoctus (Sall. Cat. 45), *Cicero, being informed of everything.*

But with most verbs of asking in prose the accusative of the thing becomes the subject nominative, and the accusative of the person is put in the ablative with a preposition: as, — nē postulantur quidem vīrēs **ā senectūte** (Cat. M. 34), *strength is not even expected of an old man* (asked from old age).

c. The verb **cēlō**, *conceal*, may take two accusatives, and the usually intransitive **lateō**, *lie hid*, an accusative of the person: —

> nōn **tē** cēlāvī **sermōnem** T. Ampī (Fam. ii. 16. 3), *I did not conceal from you the talk of Titus Ampius.*
> nec latuēre dolī **frātrem** Iūnōnis (Aen. i. 130), *nor did the wiles of Juno escape the notice of her brother.*

Note 1. — The accusative of the person with **lateō** is late or poetical (§ 388. *c.* N. 1).

Note 2. — All the double constructions indicated in § 396 arise from the wavering meaning of the verbs. Thus **doceō** means both to *show* a thing, and to *instruct* a person; **cēlō**, to *keep* a person *in the dark*, and to *hide* a thing; **rogō**, to *question* a person, and to *ask* a *question* or a *thing*. Thus either accusative may be regarded as the direct object, and so become the subject of the passive (cf. *b* above), but for convenience the accusative of the thing is usually called secondary.

Idiomatic Uses

397. The Accusative has the following special uses: —

a. The accusative is found in a few adverbial phrases (*Adverbial Accusative*): —

id temporis, *at that time;* id (istuc) aetātis, *at that age.*
id (quod) genus, *of that* (*what*) *sort* (perhaps originally nominative).
meam vicem, *on my part.*
bonam partem, *in a great measure;* maximam partem, *for the most part.*
virīle (muliebre) secus, *of the male* (*female*) *sex* (probably originally in apposition).
quod sī, *but if* (as to which, if); quod nisi, *if not.*

b. The so-called *synecdochical* or Greek Accusative, found in poetry and later Latin, is used to denote the part affected: —

caput nectentur (Aen. v. 309), *their heads shall be bound* (they shall be bound about the head).
ārdentīs **oculōs** suffectī sanguine et īgnī (id. ii. 210), *their glaring eyes bloodshot and blazing with fire* (suffused as to their eyes with blood and fire).
nūda **genū** (id. i. 320), *with her knee bare* (bare as to the knee).
femur trāgulā ictus (Liv. xxi. 7. 10), *wounded in the thigh by a dart.*

NOTE. — This construction is also called the Accusative of Specification.

c. In many apparently similar expressions the accusative may be regarded as the direct object of a verb in the middle voice (§ 156. *a*):

inūtile **ferrum** cingitur (Aen. ii. 510), *he girds on the useless steel.*
nodō **sinūs** collēcta fluentīs (id. i. 320), *having her flowing folds gathered in a knot.*
umerōs īnsternor pelle leōnis (id. ii. 722), *I cover my shoulders with a lion's skin.*
prōtinus induitur **faciem cultum**que Diānae (Ov. M. ii. 425), *forthwith she assumes the shape and garb of Diana.*

d. The Accusative is used in Exclamations: —

ō fortūnātam rem pūblicam, *O fortunate republic!* [Cf. ō fortūnāta mors (Phil. xiv. 31), *oh, happy death!* (§ 339. *a*).]
ō mē īnfēlīcem (Mil. 102), *oh, unhappy I!*
mē miserum, *ah, wretched me!*
ēn quattuor ārās (Ecl. v. 65), *lo, four altars!*
ellum (= em illum), *there he is!* [Cf. § 146. *a.* N. 2.]
eccōs (= ecce eōs), *there they are, look at them!*
prō deum fidem, *good heavens* (O protection of the gods)!
hōcine saeclum (Ter. Ad. 304), *O this generation!*
huncine hominem (Verr. v. 62), *this man, good heavens!*

Note 1.—Such expressions usually depend upon some long-forgotten verb. The substantive is commonly accompanied by an adjective. The use of -ne in some cases suggests an original question, as in quid? *what? why? tell me.*

Note 2.—The omission of the verb has given rise to some other idiomatic accusatives. Such are:—

> salūtem (sc. dīcit) (in addressing a letter), *greeting.*
> mē dīus fidius (sc. adiuvet), *so help me heaven* (the god of faith).
> unde mihī lapidem (Hor. S. ii. 7. 116), *where can I get a stone?*
> quō mihi fortūnam (Hor. Ep. i. 5. 12), *of what use to me is fortune?* [No verb thought of.]

e. The subject of an infinitive is in the accusative:—

> intellegō tē sapere (Fam. vii. 32. 3), *I perceive that you are wise.*
> eās rēs iactārī nōlēbat (B. G. i. 18), *he was unwilling that these matters should be discussed.*

Note.—This construction is especially common with verbs of *knowing, thinking, telling,* and *perceiving* (§ 580).

f. The accusative in later writers is sometimes used in apposition with a clause:—

> dēserunt tribūnal . . . manūs intentantēs, causam discordiae et initium armōrum (Tac. Ann. i. 27), *they abandon the tribunal shaking their fists,—a cause of dissension and the beginning of war.*

Note.—This construction is an extension (under Greek influence) of a usage more nearly within the ordinary rules, such as,—Eumenem prōdidēre Antiochō, pācis mercēdem (Sall. Ep. Mith. 8), *they betrayed Eumenes to Antiochus, the price of peace.* [Here Eumenes may be regarded as the price, although the real price is the betrayal.]

For the Accusative of the End of Motion, see § 427. 2; for the Accusative of Duration of Time and Extent of Space, see §§ 423, 425; for the Accusative with Prepositions, see § 220.

ABLATIVE CASE

398. Under the name Ablative are included the meanings and, in part, the forms of three cases,—the Ablative proper, expressing the relation FROM; the Locative, IN; and the Instrumental, WITH or BY. These three cases were originally not wholly distinct in meaning, and their confusion was rendered more certain (1) by the development of meanings that approached each other and (2) by phonetic decay, by means of which these cases have become largely identical in form. Compare, for the first, the phrases ā parte dexterā, ON *the right;* quam ob causam, FROM *which cause;* ad fāmam, AT (in consequence of) *the report;* and, for the second, the like forms of the dative and ablative plural, the old dative in -ē of the fifth declension (§ 96), and the loss of the original -d of the ablative (§ 49. *e;* cf. §§ 43. N. 1, 92. *f*, 214. *a*. N.).

The relation of FROM includes *separation, source, cause, agent,* and *comparison;* that of WITH or BY, *accompaniment, instrument, means, manner, quality,* and *price;* that of IN or AT, *place, time, circumstance.* This classification according to the original cases (to which, however, too great a degree of certainty should not be attached)[1] is set forth in the following table:—

[1] Thus the Ablative of Cause may be, at least in part, of Instrumental origin, and the Ablative Absolute appears to combine the Instrumental and the Locative.

I. **Ablative Proper** (*from*) (*Separative*):	1. Of Separation, Privation, and Want (§ 400). 2. Of Source (participles of origin etc.) (§ 403). 3. Of Cause (**labōrō, exsiliō**, etc.) (§ 404). 4. Of Agent (with **ab** after Passives) (§ 405). 5. Of Comparison (THAN) (§ 406).
II. **Instrumental Ablative** (*with*):	1. Of Manner, Means, and Instrument (§ 408 ff.). 2. Of Object of the Deponents **ūtor** etc. (§ 410). 3. Of Accompaniment (with **cum**) (§ 413). 4. Of Degree of Difference (§ 414). 5. Of Quality (with Adjectives) (§ 415). 6. Of Price and Exchange (§ 416). 7. Of Specification (§ 418). 8. Ablative Absolute (§ 419).
III. **Locative Ablative** (*in, on, at*):	1. Of Place *where* (commonly with **in**) (§ 421). 2. Of Time and Circumstance (§ 423).

399. The Ablative is used to denote the relations expressed in English by the prepositions *from; in, at; with, by*:—

līberāre **metū**, *to deliver from fear.*
excultus **doctrīnā**, *trained in learning.*
hōc ipsō **tempore**, *at this very time.*
caecus **avāritiā**, *blind with avarice.*
occīsus **gladiō**, *slain by the sword.*

USES OF THE ABLATIVE PROPER

Ablative of Separation

400. Words signifying Separation or Privation are followed by the ablative.

401. Verbs meaning to *remove, set free, be absent, deprive,* and *want,* take the Ablative (sometimes with **ab** or **ex**):—

oculīs sē prīvāvit (Fin. v. 87), *he deprived himself of eyes.*
omnī Galliā Rōmānīs interdīcit (B. G. i. 46), *he* (Ariovistus) *bars the Romans from the whole of Gaul.*
eī **aquā** et **īgnī** interdīcitur (Vell. ii. 45), *he is debarred the use of fire and water.* [The regular formula of banishment.]
voluptātibus carēre (Cat. M. 7), *to lack enjoyments.*
nōn egeō **medicīnā** (Lael. 10), *I want no physic.*
levāmur **superstitiōne**, līberāmur mortis **metū** (Fin. i. 63), *we are relieved from superstition, we are freed from fear of death.*
solūtī **ā cupiditātibus** (Leg. Agr. i. 27), *freed from desires.*
multōs **ex hīs incommodīs** pecūniā sē līberāsse (Verr. v. 23), *that many have freed themselves by money from these inconveniences.*

For the Genitive with verbs of *separation* and *want,* see § 356. N.

402. Verbs compounded with **ā, ab, dē, ex,** (1) take the simple Ablative when used *figuratively;* but (2) when used literally to denote actual *separation* or *motion,* they usually require a preposition (§ 426. 1): —

(1) **cōnātū** dēsistere (B. G. i. 8), *to desist from the attempt.*
dēsine commūnibus **locīs** (Acad. ii. 80), *quit commonplaces.*
abīre **magistrātū,** *to leave one's office.*
abstinēre **iniūriā,** *to refrain from wrong.*
(2) **ā prōpositō** aberrāre (Fin. v. 83), *to wander from the point.*
dē prōvinciā dēcēdere (Verr. ii. 48), *to withdraw from one's province.*
ab iūre abīre (id. ii. 114), *to go outside of the law.*
ex cīvitāte excessēre (B. G. vi. 8), *they departed from the state.* [But cf. **fīnibus** suīs excesserant (id. iv. 18), *they had left their own territory.*]
ā māgnō dēmissum nōmen **Iūlō** (Aen. i. 288), *a name descended* (sent down) *from great Iulus.*

For the Dative used instead of the Ablative of Separation, see § 381. For the Ablative of the actual *place whence* in idiomatic expressions, see §§ 427. 1, 428. *f.*

a. Adjectives denoting *freedom* and *want* are followed by the ablative: —

urbs nūda **praesidiō** (Att. vii. 13), *the city naked of defence.*
immūnis **mīlitiā** (Liv. i. 43), *free of military service.*
plēbs orba **tribūnīs** (Leg. iii. 9), *the people deprived of tribunes.*

NOTE. — A preposition sometimes occurs: —
ā culpā vacuus (Sall. Cat. 14), *free from blame.*
līberī **ā dēliciīs** (Leg. Agr. i. 27), *free from luxuries.*
Messāna **ab hīs rēbus** vacua atque nūda est (Verr. iv. 3), *Messana is empty and bare of these things.*

For the Genitive with adjectives of want, see § 349. *a.*

Ablative of Source and Material

403. The Ablative (usually with a preposition) is used to denote the Source from which anything is derived, or the Material of which it consists: —

1. Source: —

Rhēnus oritur **ex Lepontiīs** (B. G. iv. 10), *the Rhine rises in* (from) *the country of the Lepontii.*
ab hīs sermō oritur (Lael. 5), *the conversation is begun by* (arises from) *them.*
cûius ratiōnis vim atque ūtilitātem ex illō caelestī Epicūrī **volūmine** accēpimus (N. D. i. 43), *of this reasoning we have learned the power and advantage from that divine book of Epicurus.*
suāvitātem odōrum quī afflārentur **ē flōribus** (Cat. M. 59), *the sweetness of the odors which breathed from the flowers.*

2. Material:-

erat tōtus **ex fraude et mendāciō** factus (Clu. 72), *he was entirely made up of fraud and falsehood.*

valvās māgnificentiōrēs, **ex aurō** atque **ebore** perfectiōrēs (Verr. iv. 124), *more splendid doors, more finely wrought of gold and ivory.*

factum dē **cautibus** antrum (Ov. M. i. 575), *a cave formed of rocks.*

templum dē **marmore** pōnam (Georg. iii. 13), *I'll build a temple of marble.*

NOTE 1.—In poetry the preposition is often omitted.

NOTE 2.—The Ablative of Material is a development of the Ablative of Source. For the Genitive of Material, see § 344.

a. Participles denoting *birth* or *origin* are followed by the Ablative of Source, generally without a preposition:—[1]

Iove nātus et **Mâiā** (N. D. iii. 56), *son of Jupiter and Maia.*

ēdite **rēgibus** (Hor. Od. i. 1. 1), *descendant of kings.*

quō **sanguine** crētus (Aen. ii. 74), *born of what blood.*

genitae **Pandīone** (Ov. M. vi. 666), *daughters of Pandion.*

NOTE 1.—A preposition (ab, dē, ex) is usually expressed with pronouns, with the name of the mother, and often with that of other ancestors:—

ex mē hīc nātus nōn est sed **ex frātre** meō (Ter. Ad. 40), *this is not my son, but my brother's* (not born from me, etc.).

cum **ex utrāque** [uxōre] fīlius nātus esset (De Or. i. 183), *each wife having had a son* (when a son had been born of each wife).

Bēlus et omnēs **ā Bēlō** (Aen. i. 730), *Belus and all his descendants.*

NOTE 2.—Rarely, the place of birth is expressed by the ablative of source: as,—dēsīderāvit C. Flegīnātem **Placentiā**, A. Grānium **Puteolīs** (B. C. iii. 71), *he lost Caius Fleginas of Placentia, Aulus Granius of Puteoli.*

NOTE 3.—The Roman tribe is regularly expressed by the ablative alone: as,—Q. Verrem **Rōmiliā** (Verr. i. 23), *Quintus Verres of the Romilian tribe.*

b. Some verbs may take the Ablative of Material without a preposition. Such are **cōnstāre, cōnsistere,** and **continērī**.[2] But with **cōnstāre, ex** is more common:—

domūs amoenitās nōn **aedificiō** sed **silvā** cōnstābat (Nep. Att. 13), *the charm of the house consisted not in the buildings but in the woods.*

ex animō cōnstāmus et **corpore** (Fin. iv. 19), *we consist of soul and body.*

vīta **corpore** et **spīritū** continētur (Marc. 28), *life consists of body and spirit.*

c. The Ablative of Material without a preposition is used with **facere, fierī,** and similar words, in the sense of *do with, become of*:—

quid hōc **homine** faciātis (Verr. ii. 1. 42), *what are you going to do with this man?*

quid **Tulliolā** meā fīet (Fam. xiv. 4. 3), *what will become of my dear Tullia?*

quid **tē** futūrum est (Verr. ii. 155), *what will become of you?*

1 As nātus, satus, ēditus, genitus, ortus, prōgnātus, generātus, crētus, creātus, oriundus.

2 The ablative with cōnsistere and continērī is probably locative in origin (cf. § 431).

d. The Ablative of Material with **ex**, and in poetry without a preposition, sometimes depends directly on a noun: —

nōn pauca pōcula **ex aurō** (Verr. iv. 62), *not a few cups of gold.*
scopulīs pendentibus antrum (Aen. i. 166), *a cave of hanging rocks.*

For Ablative of Source instead of Partitive Genitive, see § 346. *c.*

Ablative of Cause

404. The Ablative (with or without a preposition) is used to express Cause: —[1]

neglegentiā plectimur (Lael. 85), *we are chastised for negligence.*
gubernātōris ars **ūtilitāte** nōn **arte** laudātur (Fin. i. 42), *the pilot's skill is praised for its service, not its skill.*
certīs **dē causīs**, *for cogent reasons.*
ex vulnere aeger (Rep. ii. 38), *disabled by* (from) *a wound.*
mare **ā sōle** lucet (Acad. ii. 105), *the sea gleams in the sun* (from the sun).

a. The Ablative of Cause without a preposition is used with **labōrō** (also with **ex**), **exsiliō**, **exsultō**, **triumphō**, **lacrimō**, **ārdeō**: —

doleō tē **aliīs malīs** labōrāre (Fam. iv. 3), *I am sorry that you suffer with other ills.* [Cf. **ex aere aliēnō** labōrāre (B. C. iii. 22), *to labor under debt* (from another's money).]
exsultāre **laetitiā**, triumphāre **gaudiō** coepit (Clu. 14), *she began to exult in gladness, and triumph in joy.*
exsiluī **gaudiō** (Fam. xvi. 16), *I jumped for joy.* [Cf. lacrimō **gaudiō** (Ter. Ad. 409), *I weep for joy.*]
ārdēre **dolōre** et **īrā** (Att. ii. 19. 5), *to be on fire with pain and anger.*

For **gaudeō** and **glōrior**, see § 431.

b. The *motive* which influences the mind of the person acting is expressed by the ablative of cause; the *object* exciting the emotion often by **ob**[2] or **propter** with the accusative: —

nōn **ob praedam** aut spoliandī **cupīdine** (Tac. H. i. 63), *not for booty or through lust of plunder.*
amīcitia **ex sē** et **propter sē** expetenda (Fin. ii. 83), *friendship must be sought of and for itself.*

NOTE. — But these constructions are often confused: as, — pārēre lēgibus **propter metum** (Par. 34), *to obey the laws on account of fear.* [Here **metum** is almost equivalent to "the terrors of the law," and hence **propter** is used, though the ablative would be more natural.]

[1] The *cause*, in the ablative, is originally *source*, as is shown by the use of **ab**, **dē**, **ex**; but when the accusative with **ad**, **ob**, is used, the idea of cause arises from *nearness*. Occasionally it is difficult to distinguish between *cause* and *means* (which is the old Instrumental case) or *circumstance* (which is either the Locative or the Instrumental).

[2] Originally a mercantile use: cf. **ob decem minās**, *for the price of ten minæ.*

c. The ablatives **causā** and **grātiā**, *for the sake of*, are used with a genitive preceding, or with a pronoun in agreement: —

> eā causā, *on account of this;* quā grātiā (Ter. Eun. 99), *for what purpose?*
> meā causā, *for my sake;* meā grātiā (Plaut.), *for my sake.*
> ex meā et reī pūblicae causā, *for my own sake and the republic's.*
> praedictiōnis causā (N. D. iii. 5), *by way of prophecy.*
> exemplī grātiā (verbī grātiā), *for example.*
> suī pūrgāndī grātiā, *for the sake of clearing themselves.*

NOTE.—But grātiā with possessives in this use is rare.

Ablative of Agent

405. The Voluntary Agent after a passive verb is expressed by the Ablative with **ā** or **ab**: —

> laudātur **ab hīs**, culpātur **ab illīs** (Hor. S. i. 2. 11), *he is praised by these, blamed by those.*
> **ab animō** tuō quidquid agitur id agitur **ā tē** (Tusc. i. 52), *whatever is done by your soul is done by yourself.*
> **ā fīliīs** in iūdicium vocātus est (Cat. M. 22), *he was brought to trial by his sons.*
> cum **ā** cūnctō **cōnsessū** plausus esset multiplex datus (id. 64), *when great applause had been given by the whole audience.*
> nē virtūs **ab audāciā** vincerētur (Sest. 92), *that valor might not be overborne by audacity.* [**Audācia** is in a manner *personified.*]

NOTE 1.—This construction is developed from the Ablative of Source. The *agent* is conceived as the *source* or *author* of the action.

NOTE 2.—The ablative of the *agent* (which requires **ā** or **ab**) must be carefully distinguished from the ablative of *instrument*, which has no preposition (§ 409). Thus—occīsus **gladiō**, *slain by a sword;* but, occīsus **ab hoste**, *slain by an enemy.*

NOTE 3.—The ablative of the agent is commonest with nouns denoting *persons*, but it occurs also with names of things or qualities when these are conceived as performing an action and so are partly or wholly *personified*, as in the last example under the rule.

a. The ablative of the agent with **ab** is sometimes used after intransitive verbs that have a passive sense: —

> perīre **ab hoste**, *to be slain by an enemy.*

b. The personal agent, when considered as instrument or means, is often expressed by **per** with the accusative, or by **operā** with a genitive or possessive: —

> **ab explōrātōribus** certior factus est (B. G. i. 21), *he was informed by scouts* (in person). But, —
> **per explōrātōrēs** Caesar certior factus est (id. i. 12), *Cæsar was informed by* (means of) *scouts.*
> ēlautae **operā Neptūnī** (Plaut. Rud. 699), *washed clean by the services of Neptune.*
> nōn **meā operā** ēvēnit (Ter. Hec. 228), *it hasn't happened through me* (by my exertions). [Cf. ēius operā, B. G. v. 27.]

NOTE 1.—The ablative of means or instrument is often used instead of the ablative of agent, especially in military phrases: as,—**haec excubitōribus tenēbantur** (B. G. vii. 69), *these* (redoubts) *were held by means of sentinels.*

NOTE 2.—An animal is sometimes regarded as the *means* or *instrument*, sometimes as the *agent*. Hence both the simple ablative and the ablative with **ab** occur:—

equō vehī, *to ride on horseback* (be conveyed by means of a horse). [Not **ab equō**.]
clipeōs **ā mūribus** esse dērōsōs (Div. i. 99), *that the shields were gnawed by mice.*

For the Dative of the Agent with the Gerundive, see § 374.

Ablative of Comparison

406. The Comparative degree is often followed by the Ablative[1] signifying *than*:—

Catō est **Cicerōne** ēloquentior, *Cato is more eloquent than Cicero.*
quid **nōbīs duōbus** labōriōsius est (Mil. 5), *what more burdened with toil than we two?*
vīlius argentum est **aurō**, **virtūtibus** aurum (Hor. Ep. i. 1. 52), *silver is less precious than gold, gold than virtue.*

a. The idiomatic ablatives **opīniōne, spē, solitō, dictō, aequō, crēdibilī**, and **iūstō** are used after comparatives instead of a clause:—

celerius **opīniōne** (Fam. xiv. 23), *faster than one would think.*
sērius **spē** omnium (Liv. xxvi. 26), *later than all hoped* (than the hope of all).
amnis **solitō** citātior (id. xxiii. 19. 11), *a stream swifter than its wont.*
gravius **aequō** (Sall. Cat. 51), *more seriously than was right.*

407. The comparative may be followed by **quam**, *than*. When **quam** is used, the two things compared are put in the same case:

nōn callidior es quam **hīc** (Rosc. Am. 49), *you are not more cunning than he.*
cōntiōnibus accommodātior est quam **iūdiciīs** (Clu. 2), *fitter for popular assemblies than for courts.*
misericordiā dīgnior quam **contumēliā** (Pison. 32), *more worthy of pity than of disgrace.*

a. The construction with **quam** is required when the first of the things compared is not in the Nominative or Accusative.

NOTE 1.—There are several limitations on the use of the ablative of comparison, even when the first of the things compared is in the nominative or accusative. Thus the **quam** construction is regularly used (1) when the comparative is in agreement with a genitive, dative, or ablative: as,—senex est eō meliōre condiciōne **quam** adulēscēns (Cat. M. 68), *an old man is in this respect in a better position than a young man*; and (2) when the second member of the comparison is modified by a clause: as,—minor fuit aliquantō is quī prīmus fābulam dedit **quam** eī quī, etc. (Brut. 73), *he who first presented a play was somewhat younger than those who*, etc.

[1] This is a branch of the Ablative of Separation. The object with which anything is compared is the starting-point *from which* we reckon. Thus, "Cicero is eloquent"; but, starting *from him*, we come to Cato, who is "more so than he."

NOTE 2.—The poets sometimes use the ablative of comparison where the prose construction requires **quam**: as,—pāne egeō iam **mellītīs** potiōre **placentīs** (Hor. Ep. i. 10. 11), *I now want bread better than honey-cakes.*

NOTE 3.—Relative pronouns having a definite antecedent never take **quam** in this construction, but always the ablative: as,—rēx erat Aenēās nōbīs, **quō** iūstior alter nec, etc. (Aen. i. 544), *Æneas was our king, than whom no other* [was] *more righteous.*

b. In sentences expressing or implying a *general negative* the ablative (rather than **quam**) is the regular construction when the first member of the comparison is in the nominative or accusative:—

nihil dētestābilius **dēdecore**, nihil foedius **servitūte** (Phil. iii. 36), *nothing is more dreadful than disgrace, nothing viler than slavery.*

nēminem esse cāriōrem **tē** (Att. x. 8 A. 1), *that no one is dearer than you.*

c. After the comparatives **plūs**, **minus**, **amplius**, **longius**, without **quam**, a word of *measure* or *number* is often used with no change in its case:—

plūs **septingentī** captī (Liv. xli. 12), *more than seven hundred were taken.* [Nominative.]

plūs **tertiā parte** interfectā (B. G. iii. 6), *more than a third part being slain.* [Ablative Absolute.]

aditus in lātitūdinem nōn amplius **ducentōrum pedum** relinquēbātur (id. ii. 29), *an approach of not more than two hundred feet in width was left.* [Genitive of Measure: § 345. *b.*]

NOTE.—The noun takes the case required by the context, without reference to the comparative, which is in a sort of apposition: "seven hundred were taken [and] more."

d. **Alius** is sometimes followed by the ablative in poetic and colloquial use; in formal prose it is followed by **ac** (**atque**), **et**, more rarely by **nisi**, **quam**:—

nec quicquam **aliud lībertāte** commūnī (Fam. xi. 2), *nothing else than the common liberty.*

alius Lȳsippō (Hor. Ep. ii. 1. 240), *another than Lysippus.*

num **aliud** vidētur esse **ac** meōrum bonōrum dīreptiō (Dom. 51), *does it seem anything different from the plundering of my property?*

erat historia nihil **aliud nisi** annālium cōnfectiō (De Or. ii. 52), *history was nothing else but a compiling of records.*

e. The comparative of an adverb is usually followed by **quam**, rarely by the ablative except in poetry:—

tempus tē citius **quam** ōrātiō dēficeret (Rosc. Am. 89), *time would fail you sooner than words.* But,—

cur olīvum **sanguine vīperīnō** cautius vītat (Hor. Od. i. 8. 9), *why does he shun oil more carefully than viper's blood?*

NOTE.—Prepositions meaning *before* or *beyond* (as **ante**, **prae**, **praeter**, **suprā**) are sometimes used with a comparative: as,—scelere **ante aliōs** immānior omnīs (Aen. i. 347), *more monstrous in crime than all other men.*

USES OF THE ABLATIVE AS INSTRUMENTAL

408. Means, Instrument, Manner, and Accompaniment are denoted by the Instrumental Ablative (see § 398), but some of these uses more commonly require a preposition. As they all come from one source (the old *Instrumental Case*) no sharp line can be drawn between them, and indeed the Romans themselves can hardly have thought of any distinction. Thus, in **omnibus precibus ōrābant**, *they entreated with every* [kind of] *prayer*, the ablative, properly that of *means*, cannot be distinguished from that of *manner*.

Ablative of Means or Instrument

409. The Ablative is used to denote the *means* or *instrument* of an action: —

certantēs **pūgnīs, calcibus, unguibus, morsū** dēnique (Tusc. v. 77), *fighting with fists, heels, nails, and even teeth.*

cum **pūgnīs** et **calcibus** concīsus esset (Verr. iii. 56), *when he had been pummelled with their fists and heels.*

meīs **labōribus** interitū rem pūblicam līberāvī (Sull. 33), *by my toils I have saved the state from ruin.*

multae istārum arborum meā **manū** sunt satae (Cat. M. 59), *many of those trees were set out with my own hands.*

vī victa vīs, vel potius oppressa **virtūte** audācia est (Mil. 30), *violence was overcome by violence, or rather, boldness was put down by courage.*

a. The Ablative of Means is used with verbs and adjectives of *filling*, *abounding*, and the like: —

Deus **bonīs omnibus** explēvit mundum (Tim. 3), *God has filled the world with all good things.*

aggere et **crātibus** fossās explent (B. G. vii. 86), *they fill up the ditches with earth and fascines.*

tōtum montem **hominibus** complēvit (id. i. 24), *he filled the whole mountain with men.*

opīmus **praedā** (Verr. ii. 1. 132), *rich with spoils.*

vīta plēna et cōnferta **voluptātibus** (Sest. 23), *life filled and crowded with delights.*

Forum Appī differtum **nautīs** (Hor. S. i. 5. 4), *Forum Appii crammed with bargemen.*

Note.—In poetry the Genitive is often used with these words. **Compleō** and **impleō** sometimes take the genitive in prose (cf. § 356); so regularly **plēnus** and (with personal nouns) **complētus** and **refertus** (§ 349. *a*): —

omnia plēna **lūctūs** et **maerōris** fuērunt (Sest. 128), *everything was full of grief and mourning.*

ōllam **dēnāriōrum** implēre (Fam. ix. 18), *to fill a pot with money.* [Here evidently colloquial, otherwise rare in Cicero.]

convīvium **vīcīnōrum** compleō (Cat. M. 46, in the mouth of Cato), *I fill up the banquet with my neighbors.*

cum complētus **mercātōrum** carcer esset (Verr. v. 147), *when the prison was full of traders.*

410. The deponents **ūtor, fruor, fungor, potior, vescor,** with several of their compounds,[1] govern the Ablative: —

ūtar vestrā **benīgnitāte** (Arch. 18), *I will avail myself of your kindness.*
ita mihi salvā **rē pūblicā** vōbīscum perfruī liceat (Cat. iv. 11), *so may I enjoy with you the state secure and prosperous.*
fungī inānī **mūnere** (Aen. vi. 885), *to perform an idle service.*
aurō hērōs potitur (Ov. M. vii. 156), *the hero takes the gold.*
lacte et ferīnā **carne** vescēbantur (Iug. 89), *they fed on milk and game.*

NOTE. — This is properly an Ablative of Means (*instrumental*) and the verbs are really in the middle voice (§ 156. *a*). Thus **ūtor** with the ablative signifies *I employ myself* (or *avail myself*) by *means* of, etc. But these earlier meanings disappeared from the language, leaving the construction as we find it.

a. **Potior** sometimes takes the Genitive, as always in the phrase **potīrī rērum,** *to get control* or *be master of affairs* (§ 357. *a*): —

tōtīus Galliae sēsē potīrī posse spērant (B. G. i. 3), *they hope they can get possession of the whole of Gaul.*

NOTE 1. — In early Latin, these verbs are sometimes transitive and take the accusative: —

fūnctus est **officium** (Ter. Ph. 281), *he performed the part,* etc.
ille patria potitur **commoda** (Ter. Ad. 871), *he enjoys his ancestral estate.*

NOTE 2. — The Gerundive of these verbs is used personally in the passive as if the verb were transitive (but cf. § 500. 3): as, — Hēracliō omnia **ūtenda** ac possidenda trādiderat (Verr. ii. 46), *he had given over everything to Heraclius for his use and possession* (to be used and possessed).

411. **Opus** and **ūsus,** signifying *need,* take the Ablative: —[2]

magistrātibus opus est (Leg. iii. 5), *there is need of magistrates.*
nunc **vīribus** ūsus (Aen. viii. 441), *now there is need of strength.*

NOTE. — The ablative with **ūsus** is not common in classic prose.

a. With **opus** the ablative of a perfect participle is often found, either agreeing with a noun or used as a neuter abstract noun: —

opus est tuā **exprōmptā** malitiā atque astūtiā (Ter. And. 723), *I must have your best cunning and cleverness set to work.*
properātō opus erat (cf. Mil. 49), *there was need of haste.*

NOTE 1. — So rarely with **ūsus** in comedy: as, — quid istīs ūsust **cōnscrīptīs** (Pl. Bacch. 749), *what's the good of having them in writing?*

NOTE 2. — The omission of the noun gives rise to complex constructions: as, — quid opus factōst (cf. B. G. i. 42), *what must be done?* [Cf. **quid opus est fierī?** with **quō factō opus est?**]

[1] These are **abūtor, deūtor** (very rare), **dēfungor, dēfruor, perfruor, perfungor.**

[2] This construction is properly an instrumental one, in which **opus** and **ūsus** mean *work* and *service,* and the ablative expresses that *with which* the work is performed or the service rendered. The noun **ūsus** follows the analogy of the verb **ūtor,** and the ablative with **opus est** appears to be an extension of that with **ūsus est.**

b. **Opus** is often found in the predicate, with the *thing needed* in the nominative as subject:—

dux nōbīs et **auctor** opus est (Fam. ii. 6. 4), *we need a chief and responsible adviser* (a chief, etc., is necessary for us).

sī **quid** ipsī opus esset (B. G. i. 34), *if he himself wanted anything* (if anything should be necessary for him).

quae opus sunt (Cato R. R. 14. 3), *things which are required.*

Ablative of Manner

412. The Manner of an action is denoted by the Ablative; usually with **cum**, unless a limiting adjective is used with the noun:

cum celeritāte vēnit, *he came with speed.* But,—

summā celeritāte vēnit, *he came with the greatest speed.*

quid rēfert **quā** mē **ratiōne** cōgātis (Lael. 26), *what difference does it make in what way you compel me?*

a. But **cum** is often used even when the ablative has a limiting adjective:—

quantō id **cum perīculō** fēcerit (B. G. i. 17), *at what risk he did this.*

nōn **minōre cum taediō** recubant (Plin. Ep. ix. 17. 3), *they recline with no less weariness.*

b. With such words of manner as **modō, pactō, ratiōne, rītū, vī, viā,** and with stock expressions which have become virtually adverbs (as **silentiō, iūre, iniūriā**), **cum** is not used:—

apis Matīnae **mōre modōque** carmina fingō (Hor. Od. iv. 2. 28), *in the style and manner of a Matinian bee I fashion songs.*

Note.—So in poetry the ablative of manner often omits **cum**: as,—īnsequitur **cumulō** aquae mōns (Aen. i. 105), *a mountain of water follows in a mass.* [Cf. **murmure** (id. i. 124); **rīmīs** (id. i. 123).]

Ablative of Accompaniment

413. Accompaniment is denoted by the Ablative, regularly with **cum**:—

cum coniugibus ac **līberīs** (Att. viii. 2. 3), *with wives and children.*

cum funditōribus sagittāriīsque flūmen trānsgressī (B. G. ii. 19), *having crossed the river with the archers and slingers.*

quae supplicātiō sī **cum cēterīs** cōnferātur (Cat. iii. 15), *if this thanksgiving be compared with others.*

quae [lēx] esse **cum tēlō** vetat (Mil. 11), *the law which forbids* [one] *to go armed* (be with a weapon).

sī **sēcum** suōs ēdūxerit (Cat. i. 30), *if he leads out with him his associates.* [For **sēcum**, see § 144. *b.* n.[1].]

a. The ablative is used without **cum** in some military phrases, and here and there by early writers: —

subsequēbātur **omnibus cōpiīs** (B. G. ii. 19), *he followed close with all his forces.* [But also **cum omnibus cōpiīs**, id. i. 26.]

hōc praesidiō profectus est (Verr. ii. 1. 86), *with this force he set out.*

NOTE. — **Misceō** and **iungō**, with some of their compounds, and **cōnfundō** take either (1) the Ablative of Accompaniment with or without **cum**, or (2) sometimes the Dative (mostly poetical or late): —

mixta **dolōre** voluptās (B. Al. 56), *pleasure mingled with pain.*

cûius animum **cum suō** misceat (Lael. 81), *whose soul he may mingle with his own.*

flētumque **cruōrī** miscuit (Ov. M. iv. 140), *and mingled tears with blood.*

Caesar eās cohortīs **cum exercitū suō** coniūnxit (B. C. i. 18), *Cæsar united those cohorts with his own army.*

āēr coniūnctus **terrīs** (Lucr. v. 562), *air united with earth.*

hūmānō **capitī** cervīcem equīnam iungere (Hor. A. P. 1), *to join to a human head a horse's neck.*

b. Words of Contention and the like require **cum**: —

armīs **cum hoste** certāre (Off. iii. 87), *to fight with the enemy in arms.*

libenter haec **cum Q. Catulō** disputārem (Manil. 66), *I should gladly discuss these matters with Quintus Catulus.*

NOTE. — But words of contention may take the Dative in poetry (see § 368. *a*).

Ablative of Degree of Difference

414. With Comparatives and words implying comparison the ablative is used to denote the Degree of Difference: —

quīnque **mīlibus** passuum distat, *it is five miles distant.*

ā **mīlibus** passuum circiter duōbus (B. G. v. 32), *at a distance of about two miles.* [For ā as an adverb, see § 433. 3.]

aliquot ante **annīs** (Tusc. i. 4), *several years before.*

aliquantō post suspexit (Rep. vi. 9), *a while after, he looked up.*

multō mē vigilāre ācrius (Cat. i. 8), *that I watch much more sharply.*

nihilō erat ipse Cyclōps quam ariēs prūdentior (Tusc. v. 115), *the Cyclops himself was not a whit wiser than the ram.*

a. The ablatives **quō . . . eō (hōc)**, and **quantō . . . tantō**, are used correlatively with comparatives, like the English *the . . . the*[1]: —

quō minus cupiditātis, **eō** plūs auctōritātis (Liv. xxiv. 28), *the less greed, the more weight* (by what the less, by that the more).

quantō erat gravior oppūgnātiō, **tantō** crēbriōrēs litterae mittēbantur (B. G. v. 45), *the severer the siege was, the more frequently letters were sent.*

[1] In this phrase *the* is not the definite article but a pronominal adverb, being the Anglo-Saxon *thȳ*, the instrumental case of the pronoun *thæt, that.* This pronoun is used both as relative (*by which, by how much*) and as demonstrative (*by that, by so much*). Thus *the . . . the* corresponds exactly to **quō . . . eō**.

NOTE.—To this construction are doubtless to be referred all cases of **quō** and **eō** (**hōc**) with a comparative, even when they have ceased to be distinctly felt as degree of difference and approach the Ablative of Cause:—

eōque mē minus paenitet (N. D. i. 8), *and for that reason I regret less*, etc. (by so much the less I regret).

haec **eō** facilius faciēbant, quod (B. G. iii. 12), *this they did the more easily for this reason, because*, etc. [Cf. hōc mâiōre spē, quod (id. iii. 9).]

b. The Ablative of Comparison (§ 406) and the Ablative of Degree of Difference are sometimes used together with the same adjective:—

paulō minus **ducentīs** (B. C. iii. 28), *a little less than two hundred.*

patria, quae mihi **vītā meā multō** est cārior (Cat. i. 27), *my country, which is much dearer to me than life.*

But the construction with **quam** is more common.

Ablative of Quality

415. The *quality* of a thing is denoted by the Ablative with an adjective or genitive modifier.

This is called the *Descriptive Ablative* or *Ablative of Quality*:—[1]

animō meliōre sunt gladiātōrēs (Cat. ii. 26), *the gladiators are of a better mind.*

quae cum esset cīvitās **aequissimō iūre ac foedere** (Arch. 6), *as this was a city with perfectly equal constitutional rights.*

mulierem **eximiā pulchritūdine** (Verr. ii. 1. 64), *a woman of rare beauty.*

Aristotelēs, vir **summō ingeniō, scientiā, cōpiā** (Tusc. i. 7), *Aristotle, a man of the greatest genius, learning, and gift of expression.*

dē Domitiō dīxit versum Graecum **eādem sententiā** (Deiot. 25), *concerning Domitius he recited a Greek line of the same tenor.*

NOTE.—The Ablative of Quality (like the Genitive of Quality, § 345) modifies a substantive by *describing* it. It is therefore equivalent to an adjective, and may be either attributive or predicate. In this it differs from other ablatives, which are equivalent to adverbs.

a. In expressions of quality the Genitive or the Ablative may often be used indifferently; but *physical* qualities are oftener denoted by the Ablative (cf. § 345. N.):—

capillō sunt **prōmissō** (B. G. v. 14), *they have long hair.*

ut **capite opertō** sit (Cat. M. 34), *to have his head covered* (to be with covered head).

quam fuit inbēcillus P. Āfricānī fīlius, quam **tenuī** aut **nūllā** potius **valētūdine** (id. 35), *how weak was the son of Africanus, of what feeble health, or rather none at all!*

[1] It was originally instrumental and appears to have developed from *accompaniment* (§ 413) and *manner* (§ 412).

Ablative of Price

416. The *price* of a thing is put in the Ablative: —

agrum vēndidit sēstertium **sex mīlibus**, *he sold the land for* 6000 *sesterces.*
Antōnius rēgna addīxit **pecūniā** (Phil. vii. 15), *Antony sold thrones for money.*
logōs rīdiculōs: quis **cēnā** poscit (Pl. Stich. 221), *jokes: who wants them for* (at the price of) *a dinner?*
māgnō illī ea cūnctātiō stetit (Liv. ii. 36), *that hesitation cost him dear.*

NOTE. — To this head is to be referred the Ablative of the Penalty (§ 353. 1).

417. Certain adjectives of quantity are used in the Genitive to denote *indefinite value.* Such are **māgnī, parvī, tantī, quantī, plūris, minōris**: —

meā **māgnī** interest, *it is of great consequence to me.*
illud **parvī** rēfert (Manil. 18), *this is of small account.*
est mihi **tantī** (Cat. ii. 15), *it is worth the price* (it is of so much).
Verrēsne tibi **tantī** fuit (Verr. ii. 1. 77), *was Verres of so much account to you?*
tantōne **minōris** decumae vēniērunt (id. iii. 106), *were the tithes sold for so much less?*
ut tē redimās captum quam queās **minimō**: sī nequeās **paululō**, at **quantī** queās (Ter. Eun. 74), *to ransom yourself, when captured, at the cheapest rate you can; if you can't for a small sum, then at any rate for what you can.*

NOTE. — These are really Genitives of Quality (§ 345. *b*).

a. The genitive of certain colorless nouns is used to denote indefinite value. Such are **nihilī (nīlī)**, *nothing;* **assis**, *a farthing* (rare); **floccī** (a lock of wool), *a straw:* —

nōn **floccī** faciō (Att. xiii. 50), *I care not a straw.* [Colloquial.]
utinam ego istuc abs tē factum **nīlī** penderem (Ter. Eun. 94), *O that I cared nothing for this being done by you!* [Colloquial.]

b. With verbs of *exchanging*, either the *thing taken* or the *thing given* in exchange may be in the Ablative of Price. Such are **mūtō, commūtō, permūtō, vertō**: —

fidem suam et religiōnem **pecūniā** commūtāre (Clu. 129), *to barter his faith and conscience for money.*
exsilium patriā **sēde** mūtāvit (Q. C. iii. 7. 11), *he exchanged his native land for exile* (he took exile in exchange for his native land).
vēlōx saepe Lucrētilem mūtat **Lycaeō** Faunus (Hor. Od. i. 17. 1), *nimble Faunus often changes Lycæus for Lucretilis.* [He takes Lucretilis *at the price of* Lycæus, i.e. he goes *from* Lycæus *to* Lucretilis.]
vertere **fūneribus** triumphōs (id. i. 35. 4), *to change the triumph to the funeral train* (exchange triumphs for funerals). [Poetical.]

NOTE. — With verbs of exchanging **cum** is often used, perhaps with a different conception of the action: as, — ariēs . . . **cum** croceō mūtābit vellera **lūtō** (Ecl. iv. 44), *the ram shall change his fleece for* [one dyed with] *the yellow saffron.*

c. With verbs of *buying* and *selling* the simple Ablative of Price must be used, except in the case of **tantī, quantī, plūris, minōris**: —

quantī eam ēmit? **vīlī** . . . quot **minīs**? quadrāgintā **minīs** (Pl. Epid. 51), *what did he buy her for? Cheap. For how many minæ? Forty.*

Ablative of Specification

418. The Ablative of Specification denotes that *in respect to which* anything *is* or *is done*: —

virtūte praecēdunt (B. G. i. 1), *they excel in courage.*
claudus alterō **pede** (Nep. Ages. 8), *lame of one foot.*
linguā haesitantēs, **vōce** absonī (De Or. i. 115), *hesitating in speech, harsh in voice.*
sunt enim hominēs nōn **rē** sed **nōmine** (Off. i. 105), *for they are men not in fact, but in name.*
mâior **nātū**, *older;* minor **nātū**, *younger* (cf. § 131. *c*).
paulum **aetāte** prōgressī (Cat. M. 33), *somewhat advanced in age.*
corpore senex esse poterit, **animō** numquam erit (id. 38), *he may be an old man in body, he never will be* [old] *at heart.*

a. To this head are to be referred many expressions where the ablative expresses that *in accordance with* which anything is or is done: —

meō iūre, *with perfect right;* but, **meō modō**, *in my fashion.*
meā sententiā, *in my opinion;* but also more formally, **ex meā sententiā**. [Here the sense is the same, but the first ablative is *specification*, the second *source.*]
propinquitāte coniūnctōs atque **nātūrā** (Lael. 50), *closely allied by kindred and nature.* [Here the ablative is not different in sense from those above, but no doubt is a development of *means.*]
quī vincit **vīribus** (id. 55), *who surpasses in strength.* [Here it is impossible to tell whether **vīribus** is the *means* of the superiority or that *in respect to which* one is superior.]

NOTE. — As the Romans had no such categories as we make, it is impossible to classify all uses of the ablative. The ablative of *specification* (originally *instrumental*) is closely akin to that of *manner*, and shows some resemblance to *means* and *cause*.

For the Supine in **-ū** as an Ablative of Specification, see § 510.

b. The adjectives **dīgnus** and **indīgnus** take the ablative: —

vir **patre, avō, mâiōribus** suīs dīgnissimus (Phil. iii. 25), *a man most worthy of his father, grandfather, and ancestors.*
tē omnī **honōre** indīgnissimum iūdicāvit (Vat. 39), *he judged you entirely unworthy of every honor.*

NOTE 1. — So the verb **dīgnor** in poetry and later prose: as, — haud equidem tālī mē **dīgnor honōre** (Aen. i. 335), *I do not deem myself worthy of such an honor.*

NOTE 2. — **Dīgnus** and **indīgnus** sometimes take the genitive in colloquial usage and in poetry: —

cūram dīgnissimam tuae **virtūtis** (Balbus in Att. viii. 15), *care most worthy of your noble character.*

dīgnus **salūtis** (Plaut. Trin. 1153), *worthy of safety.*

māgnōrum haud umquam indīgnus **avōrum** (Aen. xii. 649), *never unworthy of my great ancestors.*

Ablative Absolute

419. A noun or pronoun, with a participle in agreement, may be put in the Ablative to define the *time* or *circumstances* of an action. This construction is called the Ablative Absolute: —[1]

Caesar, **acceptīs litterīs**, nūntium mittit (B. G. v. 46), *having received the letter, Cæsar sends a messenger* (the letter having been received).

quibus **rēbus cōgnitīs** Caesar apud mīlitēs cōntiōnātur (B. C. i. 7), *having learned this, Cæsar makes a speech to the soldiers.*

fugātō omnī **equitātū** (B. G. vii. 68), *all the cavalry being put to flight.*

interfectō Indūtiomārō (id. vi. 2), *upon the death of Indutiomarus.*

nōndum **hieme cōnfectā** in fīnīs Nerviōrum contendit (id. vi. 3), *though the winter was not yet over, he hastened into the territory of the Nervii.*

compressī [sunt] cōnātūs nūllō **tumultū** pūblicē **concitātō** (Cat. i. 11), *the attempts were put down without exciting any general alarm.*

nē vōbīs quidem omnibus **rē** etiam tum **probātā** (id. ii. 4), *since at that time the facts were not yet proved even to all of you.*

NOTE. — The ablative absolute is an *adverbial modifier* of the predicate. It is, however, not grammatically dependent on any word in the sentence: hence its name *absolute* (**absolūtus**, i.e. *free* or *unconnected*). A substantive in the ablative absolute very seldom denotes a person or thing elsewhere mentioned in the same clause.

a. An adjective, or a second noun, may take the place of the participle in the Ablative Absolute construction: —[2]

exiguā **parte** aestātis **reliquā** (B. G. iv. 20), *when but a small part of the summer was left* (a small part of the summer remaining).

L. Domitiō Ap. Claudiō cōnsulibus (id. v. 1), *in the consulship of Lucius Domitius and Appius Claudius* (Lucius Domitius and Appius Claudius [being] consuls). [The regular way of expressing a date, see § 424. *g.*]

nīl dēspērandum **Teucrō duce** et **auspice Teucrō** (Hor. Od. i. 7. 27), *there should be no despair under Teucer's leadership and auspices* (Teucer being leader, etc.).

[1] The Ablative Absolute is perhaps of *instrumental* origin. It is, however, sometimes explained as an outgrowth of the *locative*, and in any event certain locative constructions (of *place* and *time*) must have contributed to its development.

[2] The present participle of esse, wanting in Latin (§ 170. *b*), is used in Sanskrit and Greek as in English.

b. A phrase or clause, used substantively, sometimes occurs as ablative absolute with a participle or an adjective: —

incertō quid peterent (Liv. xxviii. 36), *as it was uncertain what they should aim at* (it being uncertain, etc.).

compertō vānum esse formīdinem (Tac. Ann. i. 66), *when it was found that the alarm was groundless.*

cūr praetereātur **dēmōnstrātō** (Inv. ii. 34), *when the reason for omitting it has been explained* (why it is passed by being explained).

NOTE. — This construction is very rare except in later Latin.

c. A participle or an adjective is sometimes used adverbially in the ablative absolute without a substantive: —

cōnsultō (Off. i. 27), *on purpose* (the matter having been deliberated on).

mihi **optātō** vēneris (Att. xiii. 28. 3), *you will come in accordance with my wish.*

serēnō (Liv. xxxi. 12), *under a clear sky* (it [being] clear).

nec **auspicātō** nec **lītātō** (id. v. 38), *with no auspices or favorable sacrifice.*

tranquillō, ut âiunt, quīlibet gubernātor est (Sen. Ep. 85. 34), *in good weather, as they say, any man's a pilot.*

420. The Ablative Absolute often takes the place of a Subordinate Clause.

Thus it may replace —

1. A Temporal Clause (§ 541 ff.): —

patre interfectō, [his] *father having been killed.* [This corresponds to **cum pater interfectus esset**, *when his father had been killed.*]

recentibus sceleris êius **vestīgiīs** (Q. C. vii. 1. 1), *while the traces of the crime were fresh.* [Cf. **dum recentia sunt vestīgia.**]

2. A Causal Clause (§ 540): —

at eī quī Alesiae obsidēbantur **praeteritā diē** quā auxilia suōrum exspectāverant, **cōnsūmptō** omnī **frūmentō**, conciliō coāctō cōnsultābant (B. G. vii. 77), *but those who were under siege at Alesia, since the time,* etc., *had expired, and their grain had been exhausted, calling a council* (see 5 below), *consulted together.* [Cf. **cum diēs praeterīsset**, etc.]

Dārēus, **dēspērātā pāce**, ad reparandās vīrīs intendit animum (Q. C. iv. 6. 1), *Darius, since he despaired of peace, devoted his energies to recruiting his forces.* [Cf. **cum pācem dēspērāret.**]

3. A Concessive Clause (§ 527): —

at **eō repūgnante** fīēbat (cōnsul), immo vērō eō fīēbat magis (Mil. 34), *but though he* (Clodius) *opposed, he* (Milo) *was likely to be elected consul; nay, rather,* etc.

turribus excitātīs, tamen hās altitūdō puppium ex barbarīs nāvibus superābat (B. G. iii. 14), *although towers had been built up, still the high sterns of the enemy's ships rose above them.*

4. A Conditional Clause (§ 521): —

occurrēbat eī, mancam et dēbilem praetūram futūram suam, **cōnsule Milōne** (Mil. 25), *it occurred to him that his prætorship would be maimed and feeble, if Milo were consul.* [**sī Milō cōnsul esset.**]

quā (regiōne) **subāctā** licēbit dēcurrere in illud mare (Q. C. ix. 3. 13), *if this region is subdued, we shall be free to run down into that sea.*

quā quidem **dētrāctā** (Arch. 28), *if this be taken away.*

5. A Clause of Accompanying Circumstance: —

ego haec ā Chrȳsogonō meā sponte, **remōtō Sex. Rōsciō**, quaerō (Rosc. Am. 130), *of my own accord, without reference to Sextus Roscius* (Sextus Roscius being put aside), *I ask these questions of Chrysogonus.*

nec **imperante** nec **sciente** nec **praesente dominō** (Mil. 29), *without their master's giving orders, or knowing it, or being present.*

Note. — As the English Nominative Absolute is far less common than the Ablative Absolute in Latin, a change of form is generally required in translation. Thus the present participle is oftenest to be rendered in English by a relative clause with *when* or *while;* and the perfect passive participle by the perfect active participle. These changes may be seen in the following example: —

At illī, *intermissō spatiō, imprūdentibus nostrīs* atque *occupātīs* in mūnītiōne castrōrum, subitō sē ex silvīs ēiēcērunt; *impetū*que in eōs *factō* quī erant in statiōne prō castrīs conlocātī, ācriter pūgnāvērunt; *duābusque missīs* subsidiō *cohortibus* ā Caesare, cum hae (*perexiguō intermissō* locī *spatiō* inter sē) cōnstitissent, novō genere pūgnae *perterritīs nostrīs*, per mediōs audācissimē perrūpērunt sēque inde incolumīs recēpērunt. — Caesar, B. G. v. 15.

But they, *having paused a space, while our men* were *unaware* and *busied* in fortifying the camp, suddenly threw themselves out of the woods; then, *making an attack* upon those who were on guard in front of the camp, they fought fiercely; and, *though two cohorts had been sent* by Cæsar as reinforcements, after these had taken their position (*leaving very little space* of ground between them), *as our men were alarmed* by the strange kind of fighting, they dashed most daringly through the midst of them and got off safe.

For the Ablative with Prepositions, see § 220.

THE ABLATIVE AS LOCATIVE

Ablative of Place

421. The *Locative Case* was originally used (literally) to denote the *place where* and (figuratively) to denote the *time when* (a development from the idea of place). But this case was preserved only in names of towns and a few other words, and the *place where* is usually denoted by the Ablative. In this construction the Ablative was, no doubt, used at first without a preposition, but afterwards it became associated in most instances with the preposition in.

422. In expressions of Time and Place the Latin shows a variety of idiomatic constructions (Ablative, Accusative, and Locative), which are systematically treated in § 423 ff.

TIME AND PLACE

Time

423. Time *when*, or *within which*, is expressed by the Ablative; time *how long* by the Accusative.

1. Ablative: —

cōnstitūtā diē, *on the appointed day;* prīmā lūce, *at daybreak.*
quotā hōrā, *at what o'clock?* tertiā vigiliā, *in the third watch.*
tribus proximīs annīs (Iug. 11), *within the last three years.*
diēbus vīgintī quīnque aggerem exstrūxērunt (B. G. vii. 24), *within twenty-five days they finished building a mound.*

2. Accusative: —

diēs continuōs trīgintā, *for thirty days together.*
cum **trīduum** iter fēcisset (B. G. ii. 16), *when he had marched three days.*

NOTE. — The Ablative of Time is *locative* in its origin (§ 421); the Accusative is the same as that of the *extent of space* (§ 425).

424. Special constructions of *time* are the following: —

a. The Ablative of time *within which* sometimes takes **in**, and the Accusative of time *how long* **per**, for greater precision: —

in diēbus proximīs decem (Iug. 28), *within the next ten days.*
lūdī **per** decem diēs (Cat. iii. 20), *games for ten days.*

b. Duration of time is occasionally expressed by the Ablative: —

mīlitēs quīnque **hōrīs** proelium sustinuerant (B. C. i. 47), *the men had sustained the fight five hours.*

NOTE. — In this use the period of time is regarded as that *within which* the act is done, and it is only implied that the act lasted *through* the period. Cf. inter annōs quattuordecim (B. G. i. 36), *for fourteen years.*

c. Time *during which* or *within which* may be expressed by the Accusative or Ablative of a noun in the singular, with an ordinal numeral: —

quīntō diē, *within* [just] *four days* (lit. on the fifth day). [The Romans counted both ends, see § 631. *d.*]
rēgnat iam **sextum annum**, *he has reigned going on six years.*

d. Many expressions have in Latin the construction of *time when*, where in English the main idea is rather of *place:* —

pūgnā Cannēnsī (or, apud Cannās), *in the fight at Cannæ.*
lūdīs Rōmānīs, *at the Roman games.*
omnibus Gallicīs bellīs, *in all the Gallic wars.*

e. In many idiomatic expressions of time, the Accusative with **ad**, **in**, or **sub** is used. Such are the following: —

supplicātiō dēcrēta est **in Kalendās Iānuāriās**, *a thanksgiving was voted for the first of January.*

convēnērunt **ad diem**, *they assembled on the* [appointed] *day.*

ad vesperum, *till evening;* sub vesperum, *towards evening.*

sub idem tempus, *about the same time;* sub noctem, *at nightfall.*

f. Distance of time *before* or *after* anything is variously expressed:

post (ante) trēs annōs, post tertium annum, trēs post annōs, tertium post annum, tribus post annīs, tertiō post annō (§ 414), *three years after.*

tribus annīs (tertiō annō) post exsilium (postquam ēiectus est), *three years after his exile.*

hīs tribus proximīs annīs, *within the last three years.*

paucīs annīs, *a few years hence.*

abhinc annōs trēs (tribus annīs), ante hōs trēs annōs, *three years ago.*

triennium est cum (trēs annī sunt cum), *it is three years since.*

octāvō mēnse quam, *the eighth month after* (see § 434. N.).

g. In Dates the phrase **ante diem** (**a. d.**) with an ordinal, or the ordinal alone, is followed by an accusative, like a preposition; and the phrase itself may also be governed by a preposition.

The year is expressed by the names of the consuls in the ablative absolute, usually without a conjunction (§ 419. *a*): —

is diēs erat a. d. v. Kal. Apr. (quīntum Kalendās Aprīlīs) L. Pīsōne A. Gabīniō cōnsulibus (B. G. i. 6), *that day was the 5th before the calends of April* (March 28), *in the consulship of Piso and Gabinius.*

in a. d. v. Kal. Nov. (Cat. i. 7), *to the 5th day before the calends of November* (Oct. 28).

xv. Kal. Sextīlīs, *the 15th day before the calends of August* (July 18). [Full form: **quīntō decimō diē ante Kalendās.**]

For the Roman Calendar, see § 631.

Extent of Space

425. Extent of Space is expressed by the Accusative: —

fossās quīndecim **pedēs** lātās (B. G. vii. 72), *trenches fifteen feet broad.*

prōgressus **mīlia** passuum circiter duodecim (id. v. 9), *having advanced about twelve miles.*

in omnī vītā suā quemque ā rēctā cōnscientiā **trānsversum unguem** nōn oportet discēdere (quoted in Att. xiii. 20), *in all one's life, one should not depart a nail's breadth from straightforward conscience.*

NOTE. — This Accusative denotes the object *through* or *over which* the action takes place, and is kindred with the Accusative of the End of Motion (§ 427. 2).

a. Measure is often expressed by the Genitive of Quality (§ 345. *b*):

vāllum duodecim **pedum** (B. G. vii. 72), *a rampart of twelve feet* (in height).

b. Distance when considered as *extent of space* is put in the Accusative; when considered as *degree of difference*, in the Ablative (§ 414): —

mīlia passuum tria ab eōrum castrīs castra pōnit (B. G. i. 22), *he pitches his camp three miles from their camp.*

quīnque diērum **iter** abest (Liv. xxx. 29), *it is distant five days' march.*

trīgintā **mīlibus** passuum īnfrā eum locum (B. G. vi. 35), *thirty miles below that place* (below by thirty miles).

Relations of Place

426. Relations of Place[1] are expressed as follows: —

1. The *place from which*, by the Ablative with **ab**, **dē**, or **ex**.

2. The *place to which* (or *end of motion*), by the Accusative with **ad** or **in**.

3. The *place where*, by the Ablative with **in** (*Locative Ablative*).

Examples are: —

1. Place *from which*: —

ā septentriōne, *from the north.*

cum **ā vōbīs** discesserō (Cat. M. 79), *when I leave you.*

dē prōvinciā dēcēdere, *to come away from one's province.*

dē monte, *down from the mountain.*

negōtiātor **ex Āfricā** (Verr. ii. 1. 14), *a merchant from Africa.*

ex Britanniā obsidēs mīsērunt (B. G. iv. 38), *they sent hostages from Britain.*

Mōsa prōfluit **ex monte** Vosegō (id. iv. 10), *the Meuse* (flows from) *rises in the Vosges mountains.*

2. Place *to which* (*end of motion*): —

nocte **ad Nerviōs** pervēnērunt (B. G. ii. 17), *they came by night to the Nervii.*

adībam **ad istum fundum** (Caec. 82), *I was going to that estate.*

in Āfricam nāvigāvit, *he sailed to Africa*; **in Ītaliam** profectus, *gone to Italy.*

lēgātum **in Treverōs** mittit (B. G. iii. 11), *he sends his lieutenant into the* [country of the] *Treveri.*

[1] Originally all these relations were expressed by the cases alone. The accusative, in one of its oldest functions, denoted the *end of motion*; the ablative, in its proper meaning of separation, denoted the *place from which*, and, in its locative function, the *place where*. The prepositions, originally adverbs, were afterwards added to define more exactly the direction of motion (as in *to usward, toward us*), and by long association became indispensable except as indicated below.

3. Place *where*: —

in hāc urbe vītam dēgit, *he passed his life in this city.*
sī **in Galliā** remanērent (B. G. iv. 8), *if they remained in Gaul.*
dum haec **in Venetīs** geruntur (id. iii. 17), *while this was going on among the Veneti.*
oppidum **in īnsulā** positum (id. vii. 58), *a town situated on an island.*

427. With names of *towns* and *small islands*, and with **domus** and **rūs**, the Relations of Place are expressed as follows: —

1. The *place from which*, by the Ablative without a preposition.
2. The *place to which*, by the Accusative without a preposition.
3. The *place where*, by the Locative.[1]

Examples are: —

1. Place *from which*: —

Rōmā profectus, *having set out from Rome;* **Rōmā** abesse, *to be absent from Rome.*
domō abīre, *to leave home;* **rūre** reversus, *having returned from the country.*

2. Place *to which*: —

cum **Rōmam** sextō diē Mutinā vēnisset (Fam. xi. 6. 1), *when he had come to Rome from Modena in five days* (on the sixth day).
Dēlō **Rhodum** nāvigāre, *to sail from Delos to Rhodes.*
rūs ībō, *I shall go into the country.*
domum iit, *he went home.*[2] [So, suās **domōs** abīre, *to go to their homes.*]

3. Place *where* (or *at which*): —

Rōmae, *at Rome* (Rōma).	**Athēnīs**, *at Athens* (Athēnae).
Rhodī, *at Rhodes* (Rhodus).	**Lānuvī**, *at Lanuvium.*
Samī, *at Samos.*	**Cyprī**, *at Cyprus.*
Tīburī or **Tībure**, *at Tibur.*	**Cūribus**, *at Cures.*
Philippīs, *at Philippi.*	**Capreīs**, *at Capri* (Capreae).
domī (rarely **domuī**), *at home.*	**rūrī**, *in the country.*

a. The Locative Case is also preserved in the following nouns, which are used (like names of towns) without a preposition: —

bellī, **mīlitiae** (in contrast to **domī**), *abroad, in military service.*

humī, *on the ground.*	**vesperī** (-e), *in the evening.*
forīs, *out of doors.*	**animī** (see § 358).
herī (-e), *yesterday.*	**temperī**, *betimes.*

Cf. **īnfēlīcī arborī** (Liv. i. 26), *on the ill-omened* (barren) *tree;* **terrā marīque**, *by land and sea.*

[1] The Locative has in the singular of the first and second declensions the same form as the Genitive, in the plural and in the third declension the same form as the Dative or Ablative. (See p. 34, footnote.)

[2] The English *home* in this construction is, like **domum**, an old accusative of the *end of motion.*

428. Special uses of place *from which, to which,* and *where* are the following: —

a. With names of towns and small islands **ab** is often used to denote *from the vicinity of,* and **ad** to denote *towards, to the neighborhood of:* —

ut ā **Mutinā** discēderet (Phil. xiv. 4), *that he should retire from Modena* (which he was besieging).

erat ā **Gergoviā** dēspectus in castra (B. G. vii. 45), *there was from about Gergovia a view into the camp.*

ad Alesiam proficīscuntur (id. vii. 76), *they set out for Alesia.*

ad Alesiam perveniunt (id. vii. 79), *they arrive at Alesia* (i.e. in the neighborhood of the town).

D. Laelius cum classe **ad Brundisium** vēnit (B. C. iii. 100), *Decimus Lælius came to Brundisium with a fleet* (arriving in the harbor).

b. The general words **urbs, oppidum, īnsula** require a preposition to express the place *from which, to which,* or *where:* —

ab (ex) urbe, *from the city.*
ad urbem, *to the city.*
in urbem, *into the city.*
in urbe, *in the city.*
Rōmae in urbe, *in the city of Rome.*
Rōmā ex urbe, *from the city of Rome.*
ad urbem Rōmam (Rōmam ad urbem), *to the city of Rome.*

c. With the name of a country, **ad** denotes *to the borders;* **in** with the accusative, *into* the country itself. Similarly **ab** denotes *away from the outside;* **ex,** *out of the interior.*

Thus **ad Ītaliam pervēnit** would mean *he came* to the frontier, regardless of the destination; **in Ītaliam,** *he went to Italy,* i.e. to a place within it, to Rome, for instance.

So **ab Ītaliā profectus est** would mean *he came away from the frontier,* regardless of the original starting-point; **ex Ītaliā,** *he came from Italy,* from within, as from Rome, for instance.

d. With all names of places *at,* meaning *near* (not *in*), is expressed by **ad** or **apud** with the accusative.

pūgna ad Cannās, *the fight at Cannae.*
conchās ad Cāiētam legunt (De Or. ii. 22), *at Caieta* (along the shore).
ad (apud) īnferōs, *in the world below* (near, or among, those below).
ad forīs, *at the doors.*
ad iānuam, *at the door.*

NOTE 1. — *In the neighborhood of* may be expressed by **circā** with the accusative; *among,* by **apud** with the accusative: —

apud Graecōs, *among the Greeks.*
apud Solēnsīs (Leg. ii. 41), *at Soli.*
apud mē, *at my house.*
circā Capuam, *round about Capua.*

NOTE 2. — In citing an *author,* **apud** is regularly used; in citing a particular *work,* **in.** Thus, — apud Xenophōntem, *in Xenophon;* but, in Xenophōntis Oeconomicō, *in Xenophon's Œconomicus.*

e. Large islands, and all places when thought of as a *territory* and not as a *locality*, are treated like names of countries: —

in Siciliā, *in Sicily.*
in Ithacā leporēs illātī moriuntur (Plin. H. N. viii. 226), *in Ithaca hares, when carried there, die.* [*Ulysses lived at Ithaca* would require **Ithacae.**]

f. The Ablative without a preposition is used to denote the *place from which* in certain idiomatic expressions: —

cessisset **patriā** (Mil. 68), *he would have left his country.*
patriā pellere, *to drive out of the country.*
manū mittere, *to emancipate* (let go from the hand).

g. The poets and later writers often omit the preposition with the place *from which* or *to which* when it would be required in classical prose: —

mānīs **Acheronte** remissōs (Aen. v. 99), *the spirits returned from Acheron.*
Scythiā profectī (Q. C. iv. 12. 11), *setting out fr m Scythia.*
Ītaliam Lāvīniaque vēnit **lītora** (Aen. i. 2), *he came to Italy and the Lavinian shores.*
terram Hesperiam veniēs (id. ii. 781), *you shall come to the Hesperian land.*
Aegyptum proficīscitur (Tac. Ann. ii. 59), *he sets out for Egypt.*

h. In poetry the place *to which* is often expressed by the Dative, occasionally also in later prose: —

it clāmor **caelō** (Aen. v. 451), *a shout goes up to the sky.*
facilis dēscēnsus **Avernō** (id. vi. 126), *easy is the descent to Avernus.*
diadēma **capitī** repōnere iussit (Val. Max. v. 1. 9), *he ordered him to put back the diadem on his head.*

i. The preposition is not used with the supine in **-um** (§ 509) and in the following old phrases: —

exsequiās īre, *to go to the funeral.*
īnfitiās īre, *to resort to denial.*
pessum īre, *to go to ruin.*
pessum dare, *to ruin* (cf. **perdō**).
vēnum dare, *to sell* (give to sale). [Hence **vēndere.**]
vēnum īre, *to be sold* (go to sale). [Hence **vēnīre.**]
forās (used as adverb), *out:* as, — forās ēgredī, *to go out of doors.*
suppetiās advenīre, *to come to one's assistance.*

j. When two or more names of place are used with a verb of motion, each must be under its own construction: —

quadriduō quō haec gesta sunt rēs **ad Chrȳsogonum in castra** L. Sullae **Volāterrās** dēfertur (Rosc. Am. 20), *within four days after this was done, the matter was reported* TO *Chrysogonus* IN *Sulla's camp* AT *Volaterræ.*

NOTE. — The accusative with or without a preposition is often used in Latin when *motion to* a place is implied but not expressed in English (see *k*, N.).

k. **Domum** denoting the place *to which*, and the locative **domī**, may be modified by a possessive pronoun or a genitive: —

domum **rēgis** (Deiot. 17), *to the king's house.* [But also **in M. Laecae domum** (Cat. i. 8), *to Marcus Læca's house.*]
domī **meae**, *at my house;* domī **Caesaris**, *at Cæsar's house.*
domī **suae** vel **aliēnae**, *at his own or another's house.*

NOTE. — At times when thus modified, and regularly when otherwise modified, **in domum** or **in domō** is used: —

in domum prīvātam conveniunt (Tac. H. iv. 55), *they come together in a private house.*
in Mārcī Crassī **castissimā domō** (Cael. 9), *in the chaste home of Marcus Crassus.* [Cf. ex Anniānā Milōnis domō, § 302. *e.*]

429. The *place where* is denoted by the Ablative without a preposition in the following instances: —

1. Often in indefinite words, such as **locō**, **parte**, etc.: —

quibus **locō** positīs (De Or. iii. 153), *when these are set in position.*
quā parte bellī vīcerant (Liv. xxi. 22), *the branch of warfare in which they were victorious.*
locīs certīs horrea cōnstituit (B. C. iii. 32), *he established granaries in particular places.*

2. Frequently with nouns which are qualified by adjectives (regularly when **tōtus** is used): —

mediā **urbe** (Liv. i. 33), *in the middle of the city.*
tōtā **Siciliā** (Verr. iv. 51), *throughout Sicily* (in the whole of Sicily).
tōtā **Tarracīnā** (De Or. ii. 240), *in all Tarracina.*
cūnctā **Asiā** atque **Graeciā** (Manil. 12), *throughout the whole of Asia and Greece too.*

3. In many idiomatic expressions which have lost the idea of place:

pendēmus **animīs** (Tusc. i. 96), *we are in suspense of mind* (in our minds).
socius **perīculīs** vōbīscum aderō (Iug. 85. 47), *I will be present with you, a companion in dangers.*

4. Freely in poetry: —

lītore curvō (Aen. iii. 16), *on the winding shore.*
antrō sēclūsa relinquit (id. iii. 446), *she leaves them shut up in the cave.*
Ēpīrō, **Hesperiā** (id. iii. 503), *in Epirus, in Hesperia.*
premit altum **corde** dolōrem (id. i. 209), *he keeps down the pain deep in his heart.*

a. The *way by which* is put in the Ablative without a preposition:

viā breviōre equitēs praemīsī (Fam. x. 9), *I sent forward the cavalry by a shorter road.*
Aegaeō **marī** trāiēcit (Liv. xxxvii. 14), *he crossed by way of the Ægean Sea.*
prōvehimur **pelagō** (Aen. iii. 506), *we sail forth over the sea.*

NOTE. — In this use the *way by which* is conceived as the *means* of passage.

b. Position is frequently expressed by the Ablative with **ab** (rarely **ex**), properly meaning *from:* —[1]

ā tergō, *in the rear;* ā sinistrā, *on the left hand.* [Cf. hinc, *on this side.*]
ā parte Pompêiānā, *on the side of Pompey.*
ex alterā parte, *on the other side.*
māgnā ex parte, *in a great degree* (*from*, i.e. *in*, a great part).

430. Verbs of *placing*, though implying motion, take the construction of the place *where:* —

Such are **pōnō, locō, collocō, statuō, cōnstituō**, etc.: —

quī **in sēde** ac **domō** collocāvit (Par. 25), *who put* [one] *into his place and home.*
statuitur eques Rōmānus **in** Aprōnī **convīviō** (Verr. iii. 62), *a Roman knight is brought into a banquet of Apronius.*
īnsula Dēlos **in** Aegaeō **marī** posita (Manil. 55), *the island of Delos, situated in the Ægean Sea.*
sī in ūnō **Pompêiō** omnia pōnerētis (id. 59), *if you made everything depend on Pompey alone.*

Note. — Compounds of **pōnō** take various constructions (see the Lexicon under each word).

431. Several verbs are followed by the Ablative.

These are **acquiēscō, dēlector, laetor, gaudeō, glōrior, nītor, stō, maneō, fīdō, cōnfīdō, cōnsistō, contineor.**

nōminibus veterum glōriantur (Or. 169), *they glory in the names of the ancients.* [Also, dē dīvitiīs (in virtūte, circā rem, aliquid, haec) glōriārī.]
spē nītī (Att. iii. 9), *to rely on hope.*
prūdentiā fīdēns (Off. i. 81), *trusting in prudence.*

Note. — The ablative with these verbs sometimes takes the preposition **in** (but **fīdō in** is late), and the ablative with them is probably locative. Thus, — **in quibus** causa nītitur (Cael. 25), *on whom the case depends.*

With several of these verbs the neuter Accusative of pronouns is often found. For **fīdō** and **cōnfīdō** with the Dative, see § 367.

a. The verbals **frētus, contentus,** and **laetus** take the Locative Ablative: —

frētus **grātiā** Brūtī (Att. v. 21. 12), *relying on the favor of Brutus.*
laetus **praedā**, *rejoicing in the booty.*
contentus **sorte**, *content with his lot.* [Possibly Ablative of Cause.]
nōn fuit contentus **glōriā** (Dom. 101), *he was not content with the glory.*

Note. — So **intentus**, rarely: as, — aliquō **negōtiō** intentus (Sall. Cat. 2), *intent on some occupation.*

[1] Apparently the direction whence the sensuous impression comes.

SPECIAL USES OF PREPOSITIONS[1]

Adverbs and Prepositions

432. Certain Adverbs and Adjectives are sometimes used as Prepositions: —

a. The adverbs **prīdiē, postrīdiē, propius, proximē,** less frequently the adjectives **propior** and **proximus,** may be followed by the Accusative: —

> prīdiē **Nōnās** Māiās (Att. ii. 11), *the day before the Nones of May* (see § 631).
> postrīdiē **lūdōs** (Att. xvi. 4), *the day after the games.*
> propius **perīculum** (Liv. xxi. 1), *nearer to danger.*
> propior **montem** (Iug. 49), *nearer the hill.*
> proximus **mare** ōceanum (B. G. iii. 7), *nearest the ocean.*

NOTE.—**Prīdiē** and **postrīdiē** take also the Genitive (§ 359. *b*). **Propior, propius, proximus,** and **proximē,** take also the Dative, or the Ablative with **ab**: —

> propius **Tiberī** quam **Thermopylīs** (Nep. Hann. 8), *nearer to the Tiber than to Thermopylæ.*
> Sugambrī quī sunt proximī **Rhēnō** (B. G. vi. 35), *the Sugambri, who are nearest to the Rhine.*
> proximus **ā postrēmō** (Or. 217), *next to the last.*

b. **Ūsque** sometimes takes the Accusative, but **ūsque ad** is much more common: —

> **terminōs** ūsque Libyae (Iust. i. 1. 5), *to the bounds of Libya.*
> ūsque **ad castra** hostium (B. G. i. 51), *to the enemy's camp.*

c. The adverbs **palam, procul, simul,** may be used as prepositions and take the Ablative: —

> rem crēditōrī palam **populō** solvit (Liv. vi. 14), *he paid the debt to his creditor in the presence of the people.*
> haud procul **castrīs** in modum mūnicipī exstrūcta (Tac. H. iv. 22), *not far from the camp, built up like a town.*
> simul **nōbīs** habitat barbarus (Ov. Tr. v. 10. 29), *close among us dwells the barbarian.*

NOTE.—But **simul** regularly takes **cum**; **procul** is usually followed by **ab** in classic writers; and the use of **palam** as a preposition is comparatively late.

d. The adverb **clam** is found in early Latin with the Accusative, also once with the Genitive and once in classical Latin with the Ablative: —

> clam **mātrem** suam (Pl. Mil. 112), *unknown to his mother.*
> clam **patris** (id. Merc. 43), *without his father's knowledge.*
> clam **vōbīs** (B. C. ii. 32. 8), *without your knowledge.*

[1] For a list of Prepositions with their ordinary uses, see § 221.

433. Prepositions often retain their original meaning as Adverbs:—

1. **Ante** and **post** in relations of time:—

quōs paulō **ante** dīximus (Brut. 32), *whom I mentioned a little while ago.*
post tribus diēbus, *three days after* (cf. § 424. *f*).

2. **Adversus, circiter, prope**:—

nēmō **adversus** ībat (Liv. xxxvii. 13. 8), *no one went out in opposition.*
circiter pars quārta (Sall. Cat. 56), *about the fourth part.*
prope exanimātus, *nearly lifeless.*

3. **Ā** or **ab**, *off*, in expressions of *distance*, with the Ablative of Degree of Difference (§ 414):—

ā mīlibus passuum circiter duōbus Rōmānōrum adventum exspectābant (B. G. v. 32), *at a distance of about two miles* (about two miles off) *they awaited the approach of the Romans.*

4. In general, prepositions ending in **-ā**:—

Aeolus haec **contrā** (Aen. i. 76), *thus Æolus in reply.*
forte fuit **iūxtā** tumulus (id. iii. 22), *there happened to be a mound close by.*

434. Some Prepositions and Adverbs which imply *comparison* are followed, like comparatives, by **quam**, which may be separated by several words, or even clauses.

Such words are **ante, prius, post, posteā, prīdiē, postrīdiē**; also **magis** and **prae** in compounds:—

neque **ante** dīmīsit eum **quam** fidem dedit (Liv. xxxix. 10), *nor did he let him go until he gave a pledge.*
post diem tertium **quam** dīxerat (Mil. 44), *the third day after he said it.*
Catō ipse iam servīre **quam** pūgnāre **māvult** (Att. vii. 15), *Cato himself by this time had rather be a slave than fight.*
Gallōrum **quam** Rōmānōrum imperia **praeferre** (B. G. i. 17), [they] *prefer the rule of Gauls to that of Romans.*

NOTE.—The ablative of time is sometimes followed by **quam** in the same way (§ 424. *f*): as,—octāvō mēnse **quam** (Liv. xxi. 15), *within eight months after*, etc.

435. The following Prepositions sometimes come after their nouns: **ad, citrā, circum, contrā, dē, ē (ex), inter, iūxtā, penes, propter, ultrā**; so regularly **tenus** and **versus**, and occasionally others:—

[ūsus] **quem penes** arbitrium est et iūs et norma loquendī (Hor. A. P. 72), *custom, under whose control is the choice, right, and rule of speech.*
cûius ā mē corpus est cremātum, **quod contrā** decuit ab illō meum (Cat. M. 84), *whose body I burned* [on the funeral pile], *while on the contrary* (contrary to which) *mine should have been burned by him.*

SYNTAX OF THE VERB

MOODS AND TENSES

436. The Syntax of the Verb relates chiefly to the use of the Moods (which express the *manner* in which the action is conceived) and the Tenses (which express the *time* of the action). There is no difference in origin between mood and tense; and hence the uses of mood and tense frequently cross each other. Thus the tenses sometimes have modal significations (compare indicative in apodosis, § 517. *c*; future for imperative, § 449. *b*); and the moods sometimes express time (compare subjunctive in future conditions, § 516. *b*, and notice the want of a future subjunctive).

The parent language had, besides the Imperative mood, two or more forms with modal signification. Of these, the Subjunctive appears with two sets of terminations, **-ā-m**, **-ā-s**, in the present tense (**moneam**, **dīcam**), and **-ē-m**, **-ē-s**, in the present (**amem**) or other tenses (**essem**, **dīxissem**). The Optative was formed by **iē-**, **ī-**, with the present stem (**sim**, **duim**) or the perfect (**dīxerim**). (See details in §§ 168, 169.)

Each mood has two general classes or ranges of meaning. The uses of the Subjunctive may all be classed under the general ideas of *will* or *desire* and of action *vividly conceived;* and the uses of the Optative under the general ideas of *wish* and of action *vaguely conceived.*

It must not be supposed, however, that in any given construction either the subjunctive or the optative was deliberately used *because* it denoted conception or possibility. On the contrary, each construction has had its own line of development from more tangible and literal forms of thought to more vague and ideal; and by this process the mood used came to have in each case a special meaning, which was afterwards habitually associated with it in that construction. Similar developments have taken place in English. Thus, the expression *I would do this* has become equivalent to a mild command, while by analysis it is seen to be the apodosis of a present condition contrary to fact (§ 517): *if I were you*, etc. By further analysis, *I would do* is seen to have meant, originally, *I should have wished* (or *I did wish*) *to do.*

In Latin, the original Subjunctive and the Optative became confounded in meaning and in form, and were merged in the Subjunctive, at first in the present tense. Then new tense-forms of the subjunctive were formed,[1] and to these the original as well as the derived meanings of both moods became attached (see § 438). All the *independent* uses of the Latin subjunctive are thus to be accounted for.

The *dependent* uses of the subjunctive have arisen from the employment of some *independent* subjunctive construction in connection with a main statement. Most frequently the main statement is prefixed to a sentence containing a subjunctive, as a more complete expression of a complex idea (§ 268). Thus a question implying a general negative (**quīn rogem?** *why should n't I ask?*) might have the general negative expressed in a prefixed statement (**nūlla causa est**, *there is no reason*); or **abeat**, *let him go away*, may be expanded into **sine abeat**. When such a combination comes into habitual use, the original meaning of the subjunctive partially or wholly disappears and a new meaning arises by implication. Thus, in **mīsit lēgātōs quī dīcerent**, *he sent ambassadors to say* (i.e. who *should say*), the original hortatory sense of the subjunctive is partially lost, and the mood becomes in part an expression of purpose. Similar processes may be seen in the growth of Apodosis. Thus, **tolle hanc opīniōnem, lūctum sustuleris**, *remove this notion, you will have done away with grief* (i.e. *if you remove*, etc.).

[1] For the signification of the tense-endings, see §§ 168, 169.

The Infinitive is originally a verbal noun (§ 451), modifying a verb like other nouns: **volō vidēre**, lit. "I wish for-seeing": compare English "what went ye out for to see?" But in Latin it has been surprisingly developed, so as to have forms for tense, and some proper modal characteristics, and to be used as a substitute for finite moods.

The other noun and adjective forms of the verb have been developed in various ways, which are treated under their respective heads below.

The proper Verbal Constructions may be thus classified: —

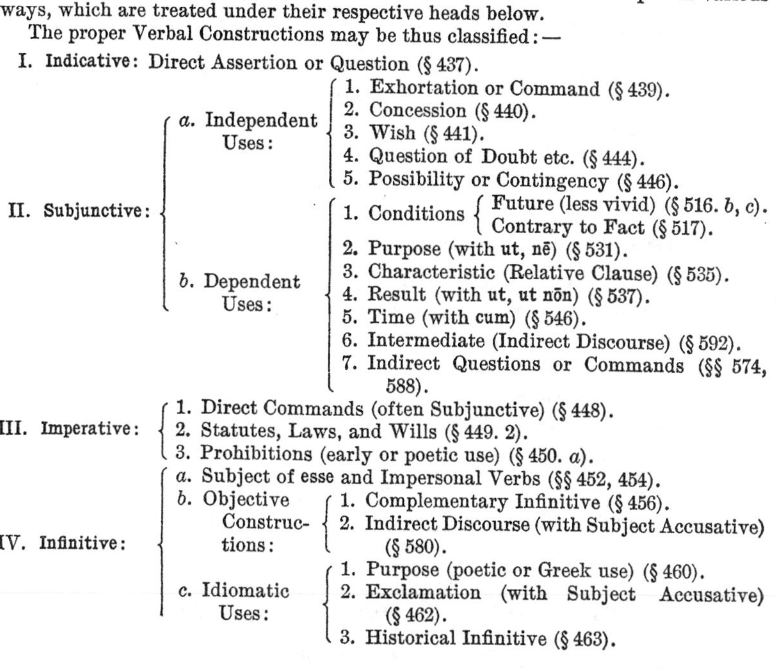

I. **Indicative**: Direct Assertion or Question (§ 437).

II. **Subjunctive**:
- *a.* Independent Uses:
  1. Exhortation or Command (§ 439).
  2. Concession (§ 440).
  3. Wish (§ 441).
  4. Question of Doubt etc. (§ 444).
  5. Possibility or Contingency (§ 446).
- *b.* Dependent Uses:
  1. Conditions: Future (less vivid) (§ 516. *b*, *c*); Contrary to Fact (§ 517).
  2. Purpose (with **ut, nē**) (§ 531).
  3. Characteristic (Relative Clause) (§ 535).
  4. Result (with **ut, ut nōn**) (§ 537).
  5. Time (with **cum**) (§ 546).
  6. Intermediate (Indirect Discourse) (§ 592).
  7. Indirect Questions or Commands (§§ 574, 588).

III. **Imperative**:
1. Direct Commands (often Subjunctive) (§ 448).
2. Statutes, Laws, and Wills (§ 449. 2).
3. Prohibitions (early or poetic use) (§ 450. *a*).

IV. **Infinitive**:
- *a.* Subject of **esse** and Impersonal Verbs (§§ 452, 454).
- *b.* Objective Constructions:
  1. Complementary Infinitive (§ 456).
  2. Indirect Discourse (with Subject Accusative) (§ 580).
- *c.* Idiomatic Uses:
  1. Purpose (poetic or Greek use) (§ 460).
  2. Exclamation (with Subject Accusative) (§ 462).
  3. Historical Infinitive (§ 463).

MOODS

INDICATIVE MOOD

437. The Indicative is the mood of direct assertions or questions when there is no modification of the verbal idea except that of time.

a. The Indicative is sometimes used where the English idiom would suggest the Subjunctive: —

> longum est, *it would be tedious* [if, etc.]; satius erat, *it would have been better* [if, etc.]; persequī possum, *I might follow up* [in detail].

NOTE. — Substitutes for the Indicative are (1) the Historical Infinitive (§ 463), and (2) the Infinitive in Indirect Discourse (§ 580).

For the Indicative in Conditions, see §§ 515, 516; for the Indicative in implied Commands, see § 449. *b*.

SUBJUNCTIVE MOOD

438. The Subjunctive in general expresses the verbal idea with some modification[1] such as is expressed in English by auxiliaries, by the infinitive, or by the rare subjunctive (§ 157. *b*).

a. The Subjunctive is used *independently* to express —

1. An Exhortation or Command (*Hortatory Subjunctive:* § 439).
2. A Concession (*Concessive Subjunctive:* § 440).
3. A Wish (*Optative Subjunctive:* § 441).
4. A Question of Doubt etc. (*Deliberative Subjunctive:* § 444).
5. A Possibility or Contingency (*Potential Subjunctive:* § 446).

For the special idiomatic uses of the Subjunctive in Apodosis, see § 514.

b. The Subjunctive is used in *dependent* clauses to express —

1. Condition: future or contrary to fact (§§ 516. *b*, *c*, 517).
2. Purpose (*Final*, § 531).
3. Characteristic (§ 535).
4. Result (*Consecutive*, § 537).
5. Time (*Temporal*, § 546).
6. Indirect Question (§ 574).

c. The Subjunctive is also used with Conditional Particles of Comparison (§ 524), and in subordinate clauses in the Indirect Discourse (§ 580).

Subjunctive in Independent Sentences

Hortatory Subjunctive

439. The Hortatory Subjunctive is used in the present tense to express an *exhortation* or a *command*. The negative is **nē**.

hōs latrōnēs **interficiāmus** (B. G. vii. 38), *let us kill these robbers.*

caveant intemperantiam, **meminerint** verēcundiae (Off. i. 122), *let them shun excess and cherish modesty.*

Note 1.—The hortatory subjunctive occurs rarely in the perfect (except in prohibitions: § 450): as,—Epicūrus hōc **vīderit** (Acad. ii. 19), *let Epicurus look to this.*

Note 2.—The term *hortatory subjunctive* is sometimes restricted to the first person plural, the second and third persons being designated as the *jussive subjunctive;* but the constructions are substantially identical.

[1] These modifications are of various kinds, each of which has had its own special development (cf. § 436). The subjunctive in Latin has also many idiomatic uses (as in clauses of Result and Time) where the English does not modify the verbal idea at all, but expresses it directly. In such cases the Latin merely takes a different view of the action and has developed the construction differently from the English.

NOTE 3.—Once in Cicero and occasionally in the poets and later writers the negative with the hortatory subjunctive is **nōn**: as,—ā lēgibus **nōn recēdāmus** (Clu. 155), *let us not abandon the laws.*

a. The Second Person of the hortatory subjunctive is used only of an *indefinite subject,* except in prohibitions, in early Latin, and in poetry:—

iniūriās fortūnae, quās ferre nequeās, dēfugiendō **relinquās** (Tusc. v. 118), *the wrongs of fortune, which you cannot bear, leave behind by flight.*

exoriāre aliquis ultor (Aen. iv. 625), *rise, some avenger.*

istō bonō **ūtāre** dum adsit, cum absit nē **requīrās** (Cat. M. 33), *use this blessing while it is present; when it is wanting do not regret it.*

doceās iter et sacra ōstia **pandās** (Aen. vi. 109), *show us the way and lay open the sacred portals.*

For Negative Commands (*prohibitions*), see § 450.

b. The Imperfect and Pluperfect of the hortatory subjunctive denote an *unfulfilled obligation* in past time:—

morerētur, inquiēs (Rab. Post. 29), *he should have died, you will say.*

potius **docēret** (Off. iii. 88), *he should rather have taught.*

nē **poposcissēs** (Att. ii. 1. 3), *you should not have asked.*

saltem aliquid dē pondere **dētrāxisset** (Fin. iv. 57), *at least he should have taken something from the weight.*

NOTE 1.—In this construction the Pluperfect usually differs from the Imperfect only in more clearly representing the time for action as *momentary* or as *past.*

NOTE 2.—This use of the subjunctive is carefully to be distinguished from the *potential* use (§ 446). The difference is indicated by the translation, *should* or *ought* (not *would* or *might*).

440. The Hortatory Subjunctive is used to express a *concession.*[1] The Present is used for present time, the Perfect for past. The negative is **nē.**

sit fūr, **sit** sacrilegus: at est bonus imperātor (Verr. v. 4), *grant he is a thief, a godless wretch: yet he is a good general.*

fuerit aliīs; tibi quandō esse coepit (Verr. ii. 1. 37), *suppose he was* [so] *to others; when did he begin to be to you?*

nēmō is umquam fuit: **nē fuerit** (Or. 101), *there never was such a one* [you will say]: *granted* (let there not have been).

nē sit summum malum dolor, malum certē est (Tusc. ii. 14), *granted that pain is not the greatest evil, at least it is an evil.*

NOTE.—The concessive subjunctive with **quamvīs** and **licet** is originally hortatory (§ 527. *a, b*).

For other methods of expressing Concession, see § 527.

For the Hortatory Subjunctive denoting a Proviso, see § 528. *a.*

[1] Many scholars regard the concessive subjunctive as a development of the Optative Subjunctive in a wish.

Optative Subjunctive

441. The Optative Subjunctive is used to express a Wish. The present tense denotes the wish as *possible*, the imperfect as *unaccomplished* in present time, the pluperfect as *unaccomplished* in past time. The negative is **nē**: —

ita **vīvam** (Att. v. 15), *as true as I live, so may I live.*
ne **vīvam** sī sciō (id. iv. 16. 8), *I wish I may not live if I know.*
dī tē **perduint** (Deiot. 21), *the gods confound thee!*
valeant, valeant cīvēs meī; **sint** incolumēs (Mil. 93), *farewell, farewell to my fellow-citizens; may they be secure from harm.*
dī **facerent** sine patre forem (Ov. M. viii. 72), *would that the gods allowed me to be without a father* (but they do not)!

a. The perfect subjunctive in a wish is archaic: —

dī **faxint** (Fam. xiv. 3. 3), *may the gods grant.*
quod dī ōmen **āverterint** (Phil. xii. 14, in a religious formula), *and may the gods avert this omen.*

442. The Optative Subjunctive is often preceded by the particle **utinam**; so regularly in the imperfect and pluperfect: —

falsus **utinam** vātēs **sim** (Liv. xxi. 10. 10), *I wish I may be a false prophet.*
utinam Clōdius **vīveret** (Mil. 103), *would that Clodius were now alive.*
utinam mē mortuum **vīdissēs** (Q. Fr. i. 3. 1), *would you had seen me dead.*
utinam nē vērē **scrīberem** (Fam. v. 17. 3), *would that I were not writing the truth.*

NOTE. — **Utinam nōn** is occasionally used instead of **utinam nē**: as, — **utinam susceptus nōn essem** (Att. ix. 9. 3), *would that I had not been born.*

a. In poetry and old Latin **utī** or **ut** often introduces the optative subjunctive; and in poetry **sī** or **ō sī** with the subjunctive sometimes expresses a wish: —

ut pereat positum rōbīgine tēlum (Hor. S. ii. 1. 43), *may the weapon unused perish with rust.*
ō sī angulus ille **accēdat** (id. ii. 6. 8), *O if that corner might only be added!*
sī nunc sē nōbīs ille aureus rāmus **ostendat** (Aen. vi. 187), *if now that golden branch would only show itself to us!*

NOTE 1. — The subjunctive with **utī** (**ut**) or **utinam** was originally deliberative, meaning *how may I*, etc. (§ 444). The subjunctive with sī or ō sī is a protasis (§ 512. *a*), the apodosis not being expressed.

NOTE 2. — The subjunctive of wish without a particle is seldom found in the imperfect or pluperfect except by sequence of tenses in Indirect Discourse (§ 585): as, — ac venerāta Cerēs, ita culmō surgeret altō (Hor. S. ii. 2. 124), *and Ceres worshipped* [with libations] *that so she might rise with tall stalk.* [In addressing the goddess directly the prayer would be: ita surgās.]

b. **Velim** and **vellem**, and their compounds, with a subjunctive or infinitive, are often equivalent to an optative subjunctive: —

> **velim** tibi **persuādeās** (Fam. ix. 13. 2), *I should like to have you believe* (I should wish that you would persuade yourself).
>
> dē Menedēmō **vellem** vērum **fuisset**, dē rēgīnā **velim** vērum **sit** (Att. xv. 4. 4), *about Menedemus I wish it had been true; about the queen I wish it may be.*
>
> **nōllem accidisset** tempus (Fam. iii. 10. 2), *I wish the time never had come.*
>
> **māllem** Cerberum **metuerēs** (Tusc. i. 12), *I had rather have had you afraid of Cerberus* (I should have preferred that you feared Cerberus).

NOTE. — Velim etc., in this use, are either potential subjunctives, or apodoses with the protasis omitted (§ 447. 1. N.). The *thing wished* may be regarded as a substantive clause used as object of the verb of wishing (§ 565. N.[1]).

Deliberative Subjunctive

443. The Subjunctive was used in sentences of interrogative form, at first when the speaker wished information in regard to the will or desire of the person addressed. The mood was therefore *hortatory* in origin. But such questions when addressed by the speaker to himself, as if asking his own advice, become *deliberative* or, not infrequently, merely *exclamatory*. In such cases the mood often approaches the meaning of the Potential (see § 445). In these uses the subjunctive is often called *Deliberative* or *Dubitative*.

444. The Subjunctive is used in questions implying (1) *doubt*, *indignation*, or (2) an *impossibility* of the thing's being done. The negative is **nōn**.

> quid **agam**, iūdicēs? quō mē **vertam** (Verr. v. 2), *what am I to do, judges? whither shall I turn?*
>
> etiamne eam **salūtem** (Pl. Rud. 1275), *shall I greet her?*
>
> quid hōc homine **faciās**? quod supplicium dīgnum libīdinī êius **inveniās** (Verr. ii. 40), *what are you to do with this man? what fit penalty can you devise for his wantonness?*
>
> an ego nōn **venīrem** (Phil. ii. 3), *what, should I not have come?*
>
> quid **dīcerem** (Att. vi. 3. 9), *what was I to say?*
>
> quis enim **cēlāverit** īgnem (Ov. H. xv. 7), *who could conceal the flame?*

NOTE. — The hortatory origin of some of these questions is obvious. Thus, — **quid faciāmus?** = **faciāmus** [**aliquid**], **quid?** *let us do — what?* (Compare the expanded form **quid vīs faciāmus?** *what do you wish us to do?*) Once established, it was readily transferred to the past: **quid faciam?** *what* AM *I to do?* **quid facerem?** *what* WAS *I to do?* Questions implying impossibility, however, cannot be distinguished from Apodosis (cf. § 517).

a. In many cases the question has become a mere exclamation, rejecting a suggested possibility:

> mihi umquam bonōrum praesidium dēfutūrum **putārem** (Mil. 94), *could I think that the defence of good men would ever fail me!*

NOTE. — The indicative is sometimes used in deliberative questions: as, — **quid agō,** *what am I to do?*

Potential Subjunctive

445. Of the two principal uses of the Subjunctive in independent sentences (cf. § 436), the second, or Potential Subjunctive,[1] is found in a variety of sentence-forms having as their common element the fact that the mood represents the action as merely *conceived* or *possible*, not as desired (*hortatory, optative*) or real (*indicative*). Some of these uses are very old and may go back to the Indo-European parent speech, but no satisfactory connection between the Potential and the Hortatory and Optative Subjunctive has been traced. There is no single English equivalent for the Potential Subjunctive; the mood must be rendered, according to circumstances, by the auxiliaries *would, should, may, might, can, could.*

446. The Potential Subjunctive is used to suggest an action as *possible* or *conceivable.* The negative is **nōn.**

In this use the Present and the Perfect refer without distinction to the immediate *future;* the Imperfect (occasionally the Perfect) to *past* time; the Pluperfect (which is rare) to what *might have* happened.

447. The Potential Subjunctive has the following uses: —

1. In cautious or modest assertions in the first person singular of expressions of *saying, thinking,* or *wishing* (present or perfect): —

pāce tuā **dīxerim** (Mil. 103), *I would say by your leave.*
haud **sciam** an (Lael. 51), *I should incline to think.*
tū **velim** sīc exīstimēs (Fam. xii. 6), *I should like you to think so.*
certum affīrmāre nōn **ausim** (Liv. iii. 23), *I should not dare to assert as sure.*

NOTE. — **Vellem, nōllem,** or **māllem** expressing an unfulfilled wish in present time may be classed as independent potential subjunctive or as the apodosis of an unexpressed condition (§ 521): as — **vellem** adesset M. Antōnius (Phil. i. 16), *I could wish Antony were here.*

2. In the indefinite second person singular of verbs of *saying, thinking,* and the like (present or imperfect): —

crēdās nōn dē puerō scrīptum sed ā puerō (Plin. Ep. iv. 7. 7), *you would think that it was written not about a boy but by a boy.*
crēderēs victōs (Liv. ii. 43. 9), *you would have thought them conquered.*
reōs **dīcerēs** (id. ii. 35. 5), *you would have said they were culprits.*
vidērēs susurrōs (Hor. S. ii. 8. 77), *you might have seen them whispering* (lit. whispers).
fretō assimilāre **possīs** (Ov. M. v. 6), *you might compare it to a sea.*

3. With other verbs, in all persons, when some word or phrase in the context implies that the action is expressed as merely possible or conceivable: —

[1] The name *Potential Subjunctive* is not precisely descriptive, but is fixed in grammatical usage.

nīl ego **contulerim** iūcundō sānus amīcō (Hor. S. i. 5. 44), *when in my senses I should compare nothing with an interesting friend.*

fortūnam citius **reperiās** quam **retineās** (Pub. Syr. 168), *you may sooner find fortune than keep it.*

aliquis **dīcat** (Ter. And. 640), *somebody may say.*

NOTE.—In this use the subjunctive may be regarded as the apodosis of an undeveloped protasis. When the conditional idea becomes clearer, it finds expression in a formal protasis, and a conditional sentence is developed.

a. **Forsitan**, *perhaps*, regularly takes the Potential Subjunctive except in later Latin and in poetry, where the Indicative is also common:—

forsitan **quaerātis** quī iste terror sit (Rosc. Am. 5), *you may perhaps inquire what this alarm is.*

forsitan temerē **fēcerim** (id. 31), *perhaps I have acted rashly.*

NOTE.—The subjunctive clause with **forsitan** (= **fors sit an**) was originally an Indirect Question: *it would be a chance whether*, etc.

b. **Fortasse**, *perhaps*, is regularly followed by the Indicative; sometimes, however, by the Subjunctive, but chiefly in later Latin:—

quaerēs fortasse (Fam. xv. 4. 13), *perhaps you will ask.*

NOTE.—Other expressions for *perhaps* are (1) **forsan** (chiefly poetical; construed with the indicative or the subjunctive, more commonly the indicative), **fors** (rare and poetical; construed with either the indicative or the subjunctive). **Forsit** (or **fors sit**) occurs once (Hor. S. i. 6. 49) and takes the subjunctive. **Fortasse** is sometimes followed by the infinitive with subject accusative in Plautus and Terence. **Fortassis** (rare; construed like **fortasse**) and **fortasse an** (very rare; construed with the subjunctive) are also found.

IMPERATIVE MOOD

448. The Imperative is used in Commands and Entreaties:—

cōnsulite vōbīs, **prōspicite** patriae, **cōnservāte** vōs (Cat. iv. 3), *have a care for yourselves, guard the country, preserve yourselves.*

dīc, Mārce Tullī, sententiam, *Marcus Tullius, state your opinion.*

tē ipsum **concute** (Hor. S. i. 3. 35), *examine yourself.*

vīve, **valēque** (id. ii. 5. 110), *farewell, bless you* (live and be well)!

miserēre animī nōn dīgna ferentis (Aen. ii. 144), *pity a soul bearing undeserved misfortune.*

a. The *third person* of the imperative is antiquated or poetic:—

ollīs salūs populī suprēma lēx **estō** (Legg. iii. 8), *the safety of the people shall be their first law.*

iūsta imperia **suntō**, eīsque cīvēs modestē **pārentō** (id. iii. 6), *let there be lawful authorities, and let the citizens strictly obey them.*

NOTE.—In prose the Hortatory Subjunctive is commonly used instead (§ 439).

449. The Future Imperative is used in commands, etc., where there is a distinct reference to *future time*: —

1. In connection with some adverb or other expression that indicates at what time in the future the action of the imperative *shall take place*. So especially with a future, a future perfect indicative, or (in poetry and early Latin) with a present imperative: —

crās **petitō**, dabitur (Pl. Merc. 769), *ask to-morrow* [and] *it shall be given.*
cum valētūdinī cōnsulueris, tum **cōnsulitō** nāvigātiōnī (Fam. xvi. 4. 3), *when you have attended to your health, then look to your sailing.*
Phyllida mitte mihī, meus est nātālis, Iollā; cum faciam vitulā prō frūgibus, ipse **venītō** (Ecl. iii. 76), *send Phyllis to me, it is my birthday, Iollas; when I* [shall] *sacrifice a heifer for the harvest, come yourself.*
dīc quibus in terrīs, etc., et Phyllida sōlus **habētō** (id. iii. 107), *tell in what lands*, etc., *and have Phyllis for yourself.*

2. In *general directions* serving for all time, as Precepts, Statutes, and Wills: —

is iūris cīvīlis cūstōs **estō** (Legg. iii. 8), *let him* (the prætor) *be the guardian of civil right.*
Boreā flante, nē **arātō**, sēmen nē **iacitō** (Plin. H. N. xviii. 334), *when the north wind blows, plough not nor sow your seed.*

a. The verbs **sciō, meminī,** and **habeō** (in the sense of *consider*) regularly use the Future Imperative instead of the Present: —

filiolō mē auctum **scītō** (Att. i. 2), *learn that I am blessed with a little boy.*
sīc **habētō**, mī Tirō (Fam. xvi. 4. 4), *so understand it, my good Tiro.*
dē pallā **mementō**, amābō (Pl. Asin. 939), *remember, dear, about the gown.*

b. The Future Indicative is sometimes used for the imperative; and **quīn** (*why not?*) with the Present Indicative may have the force of a command: —

sī quid acciderit novī, **faciēs** ut sciam (Fam. xiv. 8), *you will let me know if anything new happens.*
quīn accipis (Ter. Haut. 832), *here, take it* (why not take it?).

c. Instead of the simple Imperative, **cūrā ut, fac** (**fac ut**), or **velim**, followed by the subjunctive (§ 565), is often used, especially in colloquial language: —

cūrā ut Rōmae sīs (Att. i. 2), *take care to be at Rome.*
fac ut valētūdinem cūrēs (Fam. xiv. 17), *see that you take care of your health.*
domī adsītis **facite** (Ter. Eun. 506), *be at home, do.*
eum mihi **velim** mittās (Att. viii. 11), *I wish you would send it to me.*

For commands in Indirect Discourse, see § 588.
For the Imperative with the force of a Conditional Clause, see § 521. *b*.

Prohibition (Negative Command)

450. Prohibition is regularly expressed in classic prose (1) by **nōlī** with the Infinitive, (2) by **cavē** with the Present Subjunctive, or (3) by **nē** with the Perfect Subjunctive: —[1]

(1) **nōlī** putāre (Lig. 33), *do not suppose* (be unwilling to suppose).
nōlī impudēns esse (Fam. xii. 30. 1), *don't be shameless.*
nōlīte cōgere sociōs (Verr. ii. 1. 82), *do not compel the allies.*
(2) **cavē** putēs (Att. vii. 20), *don't suppose* (take care lest you suppose).
cavē īgnōscās (Lig. 14), *do not pardon.*
cavē festīnēs (Fam. xvi. 12. 6), *do not be in haste.*
(3) **nē** necesse **habueris** (Att. xvi. 2. 5), *do not regard it as necessary.*
nē sīs admīrātus (Fam. vii. 18. 3), *do not be surprised.*
hōc facitō; hōc **nē fēceris** (Div. ii. 127), *thou shalt do this, thou shalt not do that.*
nē Apellae quidem **dīxeris** (Fam. vii. 25. 2), *do not tell Apella even.*
nē vōs quidem mortem **timueritis** (Tusc. i. 98), *nor must you fear death.*

All three of these constructions are well established in classic prose. The first, which is the most ceremonious, occurs oftenest; the third, though not discourteous, is usually less formal and more peremptory than the others.

NOTE 1.—Instead of **nōlī** the poets sometimes use other imperatives of similar meaning (cf. § 457. *a*): —

parce piās scelerāre manūs (Aen. iii. 42), *forbear to defile your pious hands.*
cētera **mitte** loquī (Hor. Epod. 13. 7), *forbear to say the rest.*
fuge quaerere (Hor. Od. i. 9. 13), *do not inquire.*

NOTE 2.—**Cavē nē** is sometimes used in prohibitions; also **vidē nē** and (colloquially) **fac nē**: as,—**fac nē** quid aliud cūrēs (Fam. xvi. 11), *see that you attend to nothing else.*

NOTE 3.—The present subjunctive with **nē** and the perfect with **cavē** are found in old writers; **nē** with the present is common in poetry at all periods: —

nē exspectētis (Pl. Ps. 1234), *do not wait.*
nē metuās (Mart. Ep. i. 70. 13), *do not fear.*
cave quicquam **responderis** (Pl. Am. 608), *do not make any reply.*

NOTE 4.—Other negatives sometimes take the place of **nē**: —

nihil īgnōveris (Mur. 65), *grant no pardon* (pardon nothing).
nec mihi illud dīxeris (Fin. i. 25), *and do not say this to me.*

NOTE 5.—The regular connective, *and do not*, is **nēve**.

a. The Present Imperative with **nē** is used in prohibitions by early writers and the poets: —

nē **timē** (Pl. Curc. 520), *don't be afraid.*
nimium nē **crēde** colōrī (Ecl. ii. 17), *trust not too much to complexion.*
equō nē **crēdite** (Aen. ii. 48), *trust not the horse.*

b. The Future Imperative with **nē** is used in prohibitions in laws and formal precepts (see § 449. 2).

[1] In prohibitions the subjunctive with **nē** is hortatory; that with **cavē** is an object clause (cf. §§ 450. N.[2], 565. N.[1]).

INFINITIVE MOOD

451. The Infinitive is properly a noun denoting the action of the verb abstractly. It differs, however, from other abstract nouns in the following points: (1) it often admits the distinction of tense; (2) it is modified by *adverbs*, not by *adjectives;* (3) it governs the same case as its verb; (4) it is limited to special constructions.

The Latin Infinitive is the dative or locative case of such a noun[1] and was originally used to denote Purpose; but it has in many constructions developed into a substitute for a finite verb. Hence the variety of its use.

In its use as a verb, the Infinitive may take a Subject Accusative (§ 397. *e*), originally the object of another verb on which the Infinitive depended. Thus **iubeō tē valēre** is literally *I command you for being well* (cf. substantive clauses, § 562. N.).

Infinitive as Noun

452. The Infinitive, with or without a subject accusative, may be used with **est** and similar verbs (1) as the Subject, (2) in Apposition with the subject, or (3) as a Predicate Nominative.[2]

1. As Subject: —

dolēre malum est (Fin. v. 84), *to suffer pain is an evil.*

bellum est sua vitia **nōsse** (Att. ii. 17), *it's a fine thing to know one's own faults.*

praestat **compōnere** fluctūs (Aen. i. 135), *it is better to calm the waves.*

2. In Apposition with the Subject: —

proinde quasi iniūriam **facere** id dēmum esset imperiō ūtī (Sall. Cat. 12), *just as if this and this alone, to commit injustice, were to use power.* [Here **facere** is in apposition with **id.**]

3. As Predicate Nominative: —

id est convenienter nātūrae **vīvere** (Fin. iv. 41), *that is to live in conformity with nature.* [Cf. ūtī in the last example.]

NOTE 1. — An infinitive may be used as Direct Object in connection with a Predicate Accusative (§ 393), or as Appositive with such Direct Object: —

istuc ipsum **nōn esse** cum fueris miserrimum putō (Tusc. i. 12), *for I think this very thing most wretched, not to be when one has been.* [Here **istuc ipsum** belongs to the *noun* **nōn esse.**]

miserārī, invidēre, gestīre, laetārī, haec omnia morbōs Graecī appellant (id. iii. 7), *to feel pity, envy, desire, joy, — all these things the Greeks call diseases.* [Here the infinitives are in apposition with **haec.**]

[1] The ending **-ĕ** (**amāre, monēre, regere, audīre**) was apparently locative, the ending **-ī** (**amārī, monērī, regī, audīrī**) apparently dative; but this difference of case had no significance for Latin syntax. The general Latin restriction of the ī-infinitives to the passive was not a primitive distinction, but grew up in the course of time.

[2] In these constructions the abstract idea expressed by the infinitive is represented as *having some quality* or *belonging to some thing.*

NOTE 2. — An Appositive or Predicate noun or adjective used with an infinitive in any of these constructions is put in the Accusative, whether the infinitive has a subject expressed or not. Thus, — nōn esse **cupidum** pecūnia est (Par. 51), *to be free from desires* (not to be desirous) *is money in hand.* [No Subject Accusative.]

a. The infinitive as subject is not common except with **est** and similar verbs. But sometimes, especially in poetry, it is used as the subject of verbs which are apparently more active in meaning: —

quōs omnīs eadem **cupere**, eadem **ōdisse**, eadem **metuere**, in ūnum **coēgit** (Iug. 31), *all of whom the fact of desiring, hating, and fearing the same things has united into one.*

ingenuās **didicisse** fidēliter artīs **ēmollit** mōrēs (Ov. P. ii. 9. 48), *faithfully to have learned liberal arts softens the manners.*

posse loquī **ēripitur** (Ov. M. ii. 483), *the power of speech is taken away.*

453. Rarely the Infinitive is used exactly like the Accusative of a noun: —

beātē **vīvere** aliī in aliō, vōs in voluptāte pōnitis (Fin. ii. 86), *a happy life different* [philosophers] *base on different things, you on pleasure.*

quam multa . . . facimus causā amīcōrum, **precārī** ab indīgnō, **supplicāre**, etc. (Lael. 57), *how many things we do for our friends' sake, ask favors from an unworthy person, resort to entreaty,* etc.

nihil explōrātum habeās, nē **amāre** quidem aut **amārī** (id. 97), *you have nothing assured, not even loving and being loved.*

NOTE. — Many complementary and other constructions approach a proper accusative use of the infinitive, but their development has been different from that of the examples above. Thus, — avāritia . . . superbiam, crūdēlitātem, deōs **neglegere**, omnia vēnālia **habēre** ēdocuit (Sall. Cat. 10), *avarice taught pride, cruelty, to neglect the gods, and to hold everything at a price.*

Infinitive as Apparent Subject of Impersonals

454. The Infinitive is used as the apparent Subject with many impersonal verbs and expressions:

Such are **libet, licet, oportet, decet, placet, vīsum est, pudet, piget, necesse est, opus est,** etc.: —

libet mihi **cōnsīderāre** (Quinct. 48), *it suits me to consider.*

necesse est **morī** (Tusc. ii. 2), *it is necessary to die.*

quid attinet glōriōsē **loquī** nisi cōnstanter loquāre (Fin. ii. 89), *what good does it do to talk boastfully unless you speak consistently?*

neque mē **vīxisse** paenitet (id. 84), *I do not feel sorry to have lived.*

gubernāre mē taedēbat (Att. ii. 7. 4), *I was tired of being pilot.*

NOTE. — This use is a development of the Complementary Infinitive (§ 456); but the infinitives approach the subject construction and may be conveniently regarded as the subjects of the impersonals.

455. With impersonal verbs and expressions that take the Infinitive as an apparent subject, the personal subject of the action may be expressed —

1. By a Dative, depending on the verb or verbal phrase: —

rogant ut id **sibi** facere liceat (B. G. i. 7), *they ask that it be allowed them to do this.*

nōn lubet enim **mihi** dēplōrāre vītam (Cat. M. 84), *for it does not please me to lament my life.*

vīsum est **mihi** dē senectūte aliquid cōnscrībere (id. 1), *it seemed good to me to write something about old age.*

quid est tam secundum nātūram quam **senibus** ēmorī (id. 71), *what is so much in accordance with nature as for old men to die?*

exstinguī **hominī** suō tempore optābile est (id. 85), *for a man to die at the appointed time is desirable.*

2. By an Accusative expressed as the subject of the infinitive or the object of the impersonal: —

sī licet vīvere **eum** quem Sex. Naevius nōn volt (Quinct. 94), *if it is allowed a man to live against the will of Sextus Nævius.*

nōnne oportuit praescīsse **mē** ante (Ter. And. 239), *ought I not to have known beforehand?*

ōrātōrem īrāscī minimē decet (Tusc. iv. 54), *it is particularly unbecoming for an orator to lose his temper.*

pudēret **mē** dīcere (N. D. i. 109), *I should be ashamed to say.*

cōnsilia ineunt quōrum **eōs** in vestīgiō paenitēre necesse est (B. G. iv. 5), *they form plans for which they must at once be sorry.*

Note.—**Libet, placet,** and **vīsum est** take the dative only; **oportet, pudet, piget,** and generally **decet,** the accusative only; **licet** and **necesse est** take either case.

a. A predicate noun or adjective is commonly in the Accusative; but with **licet** regularly, and with other verbs occasionally, the Dative is used: —

expedit **bonās** esse vōbīs (Ter. Haut. 388), *it is for your advantage to be good.*

licuit esse **ōtiōsō** Themistoclī (Tusc. i. 33), *Themistocles might have been inactive* (it was allowed to Themistocles to be inactive).

mihi **neglegentī** esse nōn licet (Att. i. 17. 6), *I must not be negligent.* [But also **neglegentem.**]

cūr hīs esse **līberōs** nōn licet (Flacc. 71), *why is it not allowed these men to be free?*

nōn est omnibus **stantibus** necesse dīcere (Marc. 33), *it is not necessary for all to speak standing.*

Note.—When the subject is not expressed, as being indefinite (*one, anybody*), a predicate noun or adjective is regularly in the accusative (cf. § 452. 3. n.[2]): as,—vel pāce vel bellō **clārum** fierī licet (Sall. Cat. 3), *one can become illustrious either in peace or in war.*

Complementary Infinitive

456. Verbs which imply *another action of the same subject* to complete their meaning take the Infinitive without a subject accusative.

Such are verbs denoting *to be able, dare, undertake, remember, forget, be accustomed, begin, continue, cease, hesitate, learn, know how, fear*, and the like: —

hōc queō **dīcere** (Cat. M. 32), *this I can say.*
mittō **quaerere** (Rosc. Am. 53), *I omit to ask.*
vereor **laudāre** praesentem (N. D. i. 58), *I fear to praise a man to his face.*
ōrō ut mātūrēs **venīre** (Att. iv. 1), *I beg you will make haste to come.*
oblīvīscī nōn possum quae volō (Fin. ii. 104), *I cannot forget that which I wish.*
dēsine id mē **docēre** (Tusc. ii. 29), *cease to teach me that.*
dīcere solēbat, *he used to say.*
audeō **dīcere,** *I venture to say.*
loquī posse coepī, *I began to be able to speak.*

NOTE. — The peculiarity of the Complementary Infinitive construction is that no Subject Accusative is in general admissible or conceivable. But some infinitives usually regarded as *objects* can hardly be distinguished from this construction when they have no subject expressed. Thus **volō dīcere** and **volō mē dīcere** mean the same thing, *I wish to speak,* but the latter is object-infinitive, while the former is not apparently different in origin and construction from **queō dīcere** (complementary infinitive), and again **volō eum dīcere,** *I wish him to speak,* is essentially different from either (cf. § 563. *b*).

457. Many verbs take either a Subjunctive Clause or a Complementary Infinitive, without difference of meaning.

Such are verbs signifying *willingness, necessity, propriety, resolve, command, prohibition, effort,* and the like (cf. § 563): —

dēcernere optābat (Q. C. iii. 11. 1), *he was eager to decide.*
optāvit **ut tollerētur** (Off. iii. 94), *he was eager to be taken up.*
oppūgnāre contendit (B. G. v. 21), *he strove to take by storm.*
contendit **ut caperet** (id. v. 8), *he strove to take.*
bellum **gerere** cōnstituit (id. iv. 6), *he decided to carry on war.*
cōnstitueram **ut manērem** (Att. xvi. 10. 1), *I had decided to remain.*

NOTE 1. — For the infinitive with subject accusative used with some of these verbs instead of a *complementary* infinitive, see § 563.

NOTE 2. — Some verbs of these classes never take the subjunctive, but are identical in meaning with others which do: —

eōs quōs **tūtārī** dēbent dēserunt (Off. i. 28), *they forsake those whom they ought to protect.*
aveō **pūgnāre** (Att. ii. 18. 3), *I'm anxious to fight.*

a. In poetry and later writers many verbs may have the infinitive, after the analogy of verbs of more literal meaning that take it in prose: —

furit tē **reperīre** (Hor. Od. i. 15. 27), *he rages to find thee.* [A forcible way of saying **cupit** (§§ 457, 563. *b*).]
saevit **exstinguere** nōmen (Ov. M. i. 200), *he rages to blot out the name.*
fuge **quaerere** (Hor. Od. i. 9. 13), *forbear to ask* (cf. § 450. N. [1]).
parce piās **scelerāre** manūs (Aen. iii. 42), *forbear to defile your pious hands.*

458. A Predicate Noun or Adjective after a complementary infinitive takes the case of the subject of the main verb: —

fierīque studēbam êius prūdentiā **doctior** (Lael. 1), *I was eager to become more wise through his wisdom.*
sciō quam soleās esse **occupātus** (Fam. xvi. 21. 7), *I know how busy you usually are* (are wont to be).
brevis esse labōrō, **obscūrus** fīō (Hor. A. P. 25), *I struggle to be brief, I become obscure.*

Infinitive with Subject Accusative

459. The Infinitive with Subject Accusative is used with verbs and other expressions of *knowing*, *thinking*, *telling*, and *perceiving* (*Indirect Discourse*, § 579): —

dīcit **montem** ab hostibus **tenērī** (B. G. i. 22), *he says that the hill is held by the enemy.* [Direct: **mōns** ab hostibus **tenētur.**]

Infinitive of Purpose

460. In a few cases the Infinitive retains its original meaning of Purpose.

a. The infinitive is used in isolated passages instead of a subjunctive clause after **habeō, dō, ministrō**: —

tantum habeō **pollicērī** (Fam. i. 5 A. 3), *so much I have to promise.* [Here the more formal construction would be **quod pollicear.**]
ut Iovī **bibere** ministrāret (Tusc. i. 65), *to serve Jove with wine* (to drink).
merīdiē **bibere** datō (Cato R. R. 89), *give* (to) *drink at noonday.*

b. **Parātus, suētus,** and their compounds, and a few other participles (used as adjectives), take the infinitive like the verbs from which they come: —

id quod parātī sunt **facere** (Quint. 8), *that which they are ready to do.*
adsuēfactī **superārī** (B. G. vi. 24), *used to being conquered.*
currū **succēdere** suētī (Aen. iii. 541), *used to being harnessed to the chariot.*
cōpiās **bellāre** cōnsuētās (B. Afr. 73), *forces accustomed to fighting.*

NOTE.—In prose these words more commonly take the Gerund or Gerundive construction (§ 503 ff.) either in the genitive, the dative, or the accusative with **ad**:—

īnsuētus **nāvigandī** (B. G. v. 6), *unused to making voyages.*
alendīs līberīs suētī (Tac. Ann. xiv. 27), *accustomed to supporting children.*
corpora īnsuēta **ad onera portanda** (B. C. i. 78), *bodies unused to carry burdens.*

c. The poets and early writers often use the infinitive to express purpose when there is no analogy with any prose construction:—

fīlius intrō iit **vidēre** quid agat (Ter. Hec. 345), *your son has gone in to see what he is doing.* [In prose: the supine **vīsum.**]

nōn ferrō Libycōs **populāre** Penātīs vēnimus (Aen. i. 527), *we have not come to lay waste with the sword the Libyan homes.*

lōrīcam dōnat **habēre** virō (id. v. 262), *he gives the hero a breastplate to wear.* [In prose: **habendam.**]

NOTE.—So rarely in prose writers of the classic period.

For the Infinitive used instead of a Substantive Clause of Purpose, see § 457.
For **tempus est abīre**, see § 504. N.[2].

Peculiar Infinitives

461. Many Adjectives take the Infinitive in poetry, following a Greek idiom:—

dūrus **compōnere** versūs (Hor. S. i. 4. 8), *harsh in composing verse.*
cantārī dīgnus (Ecl. v. 54), *worthy to be sung.* [In prose: **quī cantētur.**]
fortis **trāctāre** serpentīs (Hor. Od. i. 37. 26), *brave to handle serpents.*
cantāre perītī (Ecl. x. 32), *skilled in song.*
facilēs aurem **praebēre** (Prop. iii. 14. 15), *ready to lend an ear.*
nescia **vincī** pectora (Aen. xii. 527), *hearts not knowing how to yield.*
tē **vidēre** aegrōtī (Plaut. Trin. 75), *sick of seeing you.*

a. Rarely in poetry the infinitive is used to express *result*:—

fingit equum docilem magister **īre** viam quā mōnstret eques (Hor. Ep. i. 2. 64), *the trainer makes the horse gentle so as to go in the road the rider points out.*

hīc **levāre** . . . pauperem labōribus vocātus audit (Hor. Od. ii. 18. 38), *he, when called, hears, so as to relieve the poor man of his troubles.*

NOTE.—These poetic constructions were originally regular and belong to the Infinitive as a noun in the Dative or Locative case (§ 451). They had been supplanted, however, by other more formal constructions, and were afterwards restored in part through Greek influence.

b. The infinitive occasionally occurs as a pure noun limited by a demonstrative, a possessive, or some other adjective:—

hōc **nōn dolēre** (Fin. ii. 18), *this freedom from pain.* [Cf. tōtum hōc beātē **vīvere** (Tusc. v. 33), *this whole matter of the happy life.*]
nostrum **vīvere** (Pers. i. 9), *our life* (to live).
scīre tuum (id. i. 27), *your knowledge* (to know).

Exclamatory Infinitive

462. The Infinitive, with Subject Accusative,[1] may be used in Exclamations (cf. § 397. *d*): —

tē in tantās aerumnās propter mē **incidisse** (Fam. xiv. 1), *alas, that you should have fallen into such grief for me!*

mēne inceptō **dēsistere** victam (Aen. i. 37), *what! I beaten desist from my purpose?*

NOTE 1. — The interrogative particle **-ne** is often attached to the emphatic word (as in the second example).

NOTE 2. — The Present and the Perfect Infinitive are used in this construction with their ordinary distinction of time (§ 486).

a. A subjunctive clause, with or without **ut**, is often used elliptically in exclamatory questions. The question may be introduced by the interrogative **-ne**: —

quamquam quid loquor? tē **ut** ūlla rēs **frangat** (Cat. i. 22), *yet why do I speak?* [the idea] *that anything should bend you!*

egone **ut** tē **interpellem** (Tusc. ii. 42), *what, I interrupt you?*

ego tibi **īrāscerer** (Q. Fr. i. 3), *I angry with you?*

NOTE. — The Infinitive in exclamations usually refers to something actually occurring; the Subjunctive, to something contemplated.

Historical Infinitive

463. The Infinitive is often used for the Imperfect Indicative in narration, and takes a subject in the Nominative: —

tum Catilīna **pollicērī** novās tabulās (Sall. Cat. 21), *then Catiline promised abolition of debts* (clean ledgers).

ego **īnstāre** ut mihi responderet (Verr. ii. 188), *I kept urging him to answer me.*

pars **cēdere**, aliī **īnsequī**; neque sīgna neque ōrdinēs **observāre**; ubi quemque perīculum cēperat, ibi **resistere** ac **prōpulsāre**; arma, tēla, equī, virī, hostēs atque cīvēs permixtī; nihil cōnsiliō neque imperiō **agī**; fors omnia **regere** (Iug. 51), *a part give way, others press on; they hold neither to standards nor ranks; where danger overtook them, there each would stand and fight; arms, weapons, horses, men, foe and friend, mingled in confusion; nothing went by counsel or command; chance ruled all.*

NOTE. — This construction is not strictly *historical*, but rather *descriptive*, and is never used to state a mere historical fact. It is rarely found in subordinate clauses. Though occurring in most of the writers of all periods, it is most frequent in the historians Sallust, Livy, Tacitus. It does not occur in Suetonius.

[1] This construction is elliptical; that is, the thought is quoted in Indirect Discourse, though no verb of *saying* etc. is expressed or even, perhaps, implied (compare the French *dire que*). Passages like **hancine ego ad rem nātam miseram mē memorābō?** (Plaut. Rud. 188) point to the origin of the construction.

TENSES

464. The number of possible Tenses is very great. For in each of the three times, Present, Past, and Future, an action may be represented as *going on*, *completed*, or *beginning*; as *habitual* or *isolated*; as *defined* in time or *indefinite* (*aoristic*); as *determined* with reference to the time of the speaker, or as not itself so determined but as *relative* to some time which is determined; and the past and future times may be near or remote. Thus a scheme of thirty or more tenses might be devised.

But, in the development of forms, which always takes place gradually, no language finds occasion for more than a small part of these. The most obvious distinctions, according to our habits of thought, appear in the following scheme:—

	1. Definite (fixing the time of the action)		2. Indefinite
	INCOMPLETE	COMPLETE	NARRATIVE
Present:	a. *I am writing.*	d. *I have written.*	g. *I write.*
Past:	b. *I was writing.*	e. *I had written.*	h. *I wrote.*
Future:	c. *I shall be writing.*	f. *I shall have written.*	i. *I shall write.*

Most languages disregard some of these distinctions, and some make other distinctions not here given. The Indo-European parent speech had a Present tense to express *a* and *g*, a Perfect to express *d*, an Aorist to express *h*, a Future to express *c* and *i*, and an Imperfect to express *b*. The Latin, however, confounded the Perfect and Aorist in a single form (the Perfect **scrīpsī**), thus losing all distinction of form between *d* and *h*, and probably in a great degree the distinction of meaning. The nature of this confusion may be seen by comparing **dīxī**, **dicāvī**, and **didicī** (all Perfects derived from the same root, DIC), with ἔδειξα, Skr. *adiksham*, δέδειχα, Skr. *dideça*. Latin also developed two new forms, those for *e* (**scrīpseram**) and *f* (**scrīpserō**), and thus possessed six tenses, as seen in § 154. *c*.

The lines between these six tenses in Latin are not hard and fast, nor are they precisely the same that we draw in English. Thus in many verbs the form corresponding to *I have written* (*d*) is used for those corresponding to *I am writing* (*a*) and *I write* (*g*) in a slightly different sense, and the form corresponding to *I had written* (*e*) is used in like manner for that corresponding to *I was writing* (*b*). Again, the Latin often uses the form for *I shall have written* (*f*) instead of that for *I shall write* (*i*). Thus, **nōvī**, *I have learned*, is used for *I know;* **cōnstiterat**, *he had taken his position*, for *he stood;* **cōgnōverō**, *I shall have learned*, for *I shall be aware*. In general a writer may take his own point of view.

TENSES OF THE INDICATIVE

Incomplete Action

PRESENT TENSE

465. The Present Tense denotes an action or state (1) as *now taking place* or *existing*, and so (2) as *incomplete* in present time, or (3) as *indefinite*, referring to no particular time, but denoting a *general truth:*—

senātus haec **intellegit**, cōnsul **videt**, hīc tamen **vīvit** (Cat. i. 2), *the senate knows this, the consul sees it, yet this man lives.*

tibi **concēdō** meās sēdīs (Div. i. 104), *I give you my seat* (an offer which may or may not be accepted).

exspectō quid velīs (Ter. And. 34), *I await your pleasure* (what you wish).

tū āctiōnem **īnstituis**, ille aciem **īnstruit** (Mur. 22), *you arrange a case, he arrays an army.* [The present is here used of *regular employment.*]

minōra dī **neglegunt** (N. D. iii. 86), *the gods disregard trifles.* [General truth.]

obsequium amīcōs, vēritās odium **parit** (Ter. And. 68), *flattery gains friends, truth hatred.* [General truth.]

NOTE.—The present of a *general truth* is sometimes called the Gnomic Present.

a. The present is regularly used in quoting writers whose works are extant:—

Epicūrus vērō ea **dīcit** (Tusc. ii. 17), *but Epicurus says such things.*

apud illum Ulixēs **lāmentātur** in volnere (id. ii. 49), *in him* (Sophocles) *Ulysses laments over his wound.*

Polyphēmum Homērus cum ariete colloquentem **facit** (id. v. 115), *Homer brings in* (makes) *Polyphemus talking with his ram.*

Present with *iam diū* etc.

466. The Present with expressions of *duration of time* (especially **iam diū, iam dūdum**) denotes an action continuing in the present, but begun in the past (cf. § 471. *b*).

In this use the present is commonly to be rendered by the perfect in English:—

iam diū **īgnōrō** quid agās (Fam. vii. 9), *for a long time I have not known what you were doing.*

tē iam dūdum **hortor** (Cat. i. 12), *I have long been urging you.*

patimur multōs iam annōs (Verr. v. 126), *we suffer now these many years.* [The Latin perfect would imply that *we no longer suffer.*]

annī sunt octō cum ista causa **versātur** (cf. Clu. 82), *it is now eight years that this case has been in hand.*

annum iam **audīs** Cratippum (Off. i. 1), *for a year you have been a hearer of Cratippus.*

adhūc Plancius mē **retinet** (Fam. xiv. 1. 3), *so far Plancius has kept me here.*

NOTE 1.—The difference in the two idioms is that the English states the beginning and leaves the continuance to be inferred, while the Latin states the continuance and leaves the beginning to be inferred. Compare *he has long suffered* (*and still suffers*) with *he still suffers* (*and has suffered long*).

NOTE 2.—Similarly the Present Imperative with **iam dūdum** indicates that the action commanded *ought to have been done* or *was wished for* long ago (cf. the Perfect Imperative in Greek): as,—iam dūdum **sūmite** poenās (Aen. ii. 103), *exact the penalty long delayed.*

Conative Present

467. The Present sometimes denotes an action *attempted* or *begun* in present time, but never completed at all (*Conative Present*, cf. § 471. *c*): —

iam iamque manū **tenet** (Aen. ii. 530), *and now, even now, he attempts to grasp him.*

dēnsōs **fertur** in hostīs (id. ii. 511), *he starts to rush into the thickest of the foe.*

dēcernō quīnquāgintā diērum supplicātiōnēs (Phil. xiv. 29), *I move for fifty days' thanksgiving.* [Cf. **senātus dēcrēvit,** *the senate ordained.*]

Present for Future

468. The Present, especially in colloquial language and poetry, is often used for the Future: —

īmusne sessum (De Or. iii. 17), *shall we take a seat?* (are we going to sit?)

hodiē uxōrem **dūcis** (Ter. And. 321), *are you to be married to-day?*

quod sī **fit,** pereō funditus (id. 244), *if this happens, I am utterly undone.*

ecquid mē **adiuvās** (Clu. 71), *won't you give me a little help?*

in iūs vocō tē. nōn **eō.** nōn **īs** (Pl. Asin. 480), *I summon you to the court. I won't go. You won't?*

NOTE. — **Eō** and its compounds are especially frequent in this use (cf. *where are you going to-morrow?* and the Greek εἶμι in a future sense). Verbs of *necessity, possibility, wish,* and the like (as **possum, volō,** etc.) also have reference to the future.

For other uses of the Present in a future sense, see under Conditions (§ 516. *a.* N.), **antequam** and **priusquam** (§ 551. *c*), **dum** (§ 553. N.[2]), and § 444. *a.* N.

Historical Present

469. The Present in lively narrative is often used for the Historical Perfect: —

affertur nūntius Syrācūsās; **curritur** ad praetōrium; Cleomenēs in pūblicō esse nōn **audet**; **inclūdit** sē domī (Verr. v. 92), *the news is brought to Syracuse; they run to headquarters; Cleomenes does not venture to be abroad; he shuts himself up at home.*

NOTE. — This usage, common in all languages, comes from imagining past events as going on before our eyes (*repraesentātiō*, § 585. *b.* N.).

For the Present Indicative with **dum,** *while,* see § 556.

a. The present may be used for the perfect in a summary enumeration of past events (*Annalistic Present*): —

Rōma interim crēscit Albae ruīnīs: **duplicātur** cīvium numerus; Caelius **additur** urbī mōns (Liv. i. 30), *Rome meanwhile grows as a result of the fall of Alba: the number of citizens is doubled; the Cælian hill is added to the town.*

IMPERFECT TENSE

470. The Imperfect denotes an action or a state as *continued* or *repeated* in past time:—

hunc **audiēbant** anteā (Manil. 13), *they used to hear of him before.*

[Sōcratēs] ita **cēnsēbat** itaque disseruit (Tusc. i. 72), *Socrates thought so* (habitually), *and so he spoke* (then).

prūdēns esse **putābātur** (Lael. 6), *he was* (generally) *thought wise.* [The perfect would refer to some particular case, and not to a state of things.]

iamque **rubēscēbat** Aurōra (Aen. iii. 521), *and now the dawn was blushing.*

āra vetus **stābat** (Ov. M. vi. 326), *an old altar stood there.*

NOTE.—The Imperfect is a *descriptive* tense and denotes an action conceived as *in progress* or a state of things as *actually observed.* Hence in many verbs it does not differ in meaning from the Perfect. Thus **rēx erat** and **rēx fuit** may often be used indifferently; but the former *describes* the condition while the latter only *states* it. The English is less exact in distinguishing these two modes of statement. Hence the Latin Imperfect is often translated by the English Preterite:—

Haeduī graviter **ferēbant**, neque lēgātōs ad Caesarem mittere **audēbant** (B. G. v. 6), *the Hædui were displeased, and did not dare to send envoys to Cæsar.* [Here the Imperfects describe the state of things.] But,—

id **tulit** factum graviter Indūtiomārus (id. v. 4), *Indutiomarus was displeased at this action.* [Here the Perfect merely states the fact.]

aedificia vīcōsque **habēbant** (id. iv. 4), *they had buildings and villages.*

471. The Imperfect represents a present tense transferred to past time. Hence all the meanings which the Present has derived from the *continuance of the action* belong also to the Imperfect in reference to past time.

a. The Imperfect is used in *descriptions:*—

erant omnīnō itinera duo . . . mōns altissimus **impendēbat** (B. G. i. 6), *there were in all two ways . . . a very high mountain overhung.*

b. With **iam diū**, **iam dūdum**, and other expressions of duration of time, the Imperfect denotes an action continuing in the past but begun at some previous time (cf. § 466).

In this construction the Imperfect is rendered by the English Pluperfect:—

iam dūdum flēbam (Ov. M. iii. 656), *I had been weeping for a long time.*

cōpiās quās **diū comparābant** (Fam. xi. 13. 5), *the forces which they had long been getting ready.*

c. The Imperfect sometimes denotes an action as begun (*Inceptive Imperfect*), or as attempted or only intended (*Conative Imperfect;* cf. § 467):—

in exsilium **ēiciēbam** quem iam ingressum esse in bellum vidēbam (Cat. ii. 14), *was I trying to send into exile one who I saw had already gone into war?*

hunc igitur diem sibi prōpōnēns Milō, cruentīs manibus ad illa augusta centuriārum auspicia **veniēbat** (Mil. 43), *was Milo coming* (i.e. was it likely that he would come), etc.?

sī licitum esset **veniēbant** (Verr. v. 129), *they were coming if it had been allowed* (they were on the point of coming, and would have done so if, etc.).

NOTE.—To this head may be referred the imperfect with **iam**, denoting the *beginning* of an action or state: as,—iamque arva **tenēbant** ultima (Aen. vi. 477), *and now they were just getting to the farthest fields.*

d. The Imperfect is sometimes used to express a surprise at the *present* discovery of a fact already existing:—

ō tū quoque **aderās** (Ter. Ph. 858), *oh, you are here too!*

ehem, tūn hīc **erās**, mī Phaedria (Ter. Eun. 86), *what! you here, Phædria?*

ā miser! quantā **labōrābās** Charybdī (Hor. Od. i. 27. 19), *unhappy boy, what a whirlpool you are struggling in* [and I never knew it]!

e. The Imperfect is often used in dialogue by the comic poets where later writers would employ the Perfect:—

ad amīcum Calliclem quoi rem **aībat** mandāsse hīc suam (Pl. Trin. 956), *to his friend Callicles, to whom, he said, he had intrusted his property.*

praesāgībat mī animus frūstrā mē īre quom **exībam** domō (Pl. Aul. 178), *my mind mistrusted when I went from home that I went in vain.*

NOTE.—So, in conversation the imperfect of verbs of saying (cf. *as I was a-saying*) is common in classic prose:—

at medicī quoque, ita enim **dīcēbās**, saepe falluntur (N. D. iii. 15), *but physicians also,—for that is what you were saying just now,—are often mistaken.*

haec mihi ferē in mentem **veniēbant** (id. ii. 67, 168), *this is about what occurred to me*, etc. [In a straightforward narration this would be **vēnērunt.**]

f. The Imperfect with negative words often has the force of the English auxiliary *could* or *would:*—

itaque (Dāmoclēs) nec pulchrōs illōs ministrātōrēs **aspiciēbat** (Tusc. v. 62), *therefore he could not look upon those beautiful slaves.* [In this case *did not* would not express the idea of *continued prevention* of enjoyment by the overhanging sword.]

nec enim dum eram vōbīscum animum meum **vidēbātis** (Cat. M. 79), *for, you know, while I was with you, you could not see my soul.* [Here the Perfect would refer only to *one moment.*]

Lentulus satis erat fortis ōrātōr, sed cōgitandī nōn **ferēbat** labōrem (Brut. 268), *Lentulus was bold enough as an orator, but could not endure the exertion of thinking hard.*

For the Epistolary Imperfect, see § 479; for the Imperfect Indicative in apodosis *contrary to fact*, see § 517. *b. c.*

FUTURE TENSE

472. The Future denotes an action or state that will occur hereafter.

a. The Future may have the force of an Imperative (§ 449. *b*).

b. The Future is often required in a subordinate clause in Latin where in English futurity is sufficiently expressed by the main clause:

cum **aderit** vidēbit, *when he is there he will see* (cf. § 547).
sānābimur sī **volēmus** (Tusc. iii. 13), *we shall be healed if we wish* (cf. § 516. *a*).

NOTE.—But the Present is common in future protases (§ 516. *a.* N.).

COMPLETED ACTION

PERFECT TENSE

Perfect Definite and Historical Perfect

473. The Perfect denotes an action either as *now completed* (*Perfect Definite*), or as *having taken place* at some undefined point of past time (*Historical* or *Aoristic Perfect*).

The Perfect Definite corresponds in general to the English Perfect with *have;* the Historical Perfect to the English Preterite (or Past):

(1) ut ego **fēcī**, quī Graecās litterās senex **didicī** (Cat. M. 26), *as I have done, who have learned Greek in my old age.*
diūturnī silentī fīnem hodiernus diēs **attulit** (Marc. 1), *this day has put an end to my long-continued silence.*
(2) tantum bellum extrēmā hieme **apparāvit**, ineunte vēre **suscēpit**, mediā aestāte **cōnfēcit** (Manil. 35), *so great a war he made ready for at the end of winter, undertook in early spring, and finished by midsummer.*

NOTE.—The distinction between these two uses is represented by two forms in most other Indo-European languages, but was almost if not wholly lost to the minds of the Romans. It must be noticed, however, on account of the marked distinction in English and also because of certain differences in the sequence of tenses.

a. The Indefinite Present, denoting a *customary action* or a *general truth* (§ 465), often has the Perfect in a subordinate clause referring to time antecedent to that of the main clause:—

quī in compedibus corporis semper **fuērunt**, etiam cum **solūtī sunt** tardius **ingrediuntur** (Tusc. i. 75), *they who have always been in the fetters of the body, even when released move more slowly.*
simul ac mihi **collibitum est**, praestō est imāgō (N. D. i. 108), *as soon as I have taken a fancy, the image is before my eyes.*

haec morte **effugiuntur**, etiam sī nōn **ēvēnērunt**, tamen quia **possunt** ēvenīre (Tusc. i. 86), *these things are escaped by death even if they have not* [yet] *happened, because they still may happen.*

NOTE.—This use of the perfect is especially common in the protasis of General Conditions in present time (§ 518. *b*).

474. The Perfect is sometimes used emphatically to denote that a thing or condition of things that once existed no longer exists:

fuit ista quondam in hāc rē pūblicā virtūs (Cat. i. 3), *there was once such virtue in this commonwealth.*
habuit, nōn habet (Tusc. i. 87), *he had, he has no longer.*
fīlium habeō . . . immo **habuī**; nunc habeam necne incertumst (Ter. Haut. 93), *I have a son, no, I had one; whether I have now or not is uncertain.*
fuimus Trōes, **fuit** Īlium (Aen. ii. 325), *we have ceased to be Trojans, Troy is no more.*

Special Uses of the Perfect

475. The Perfect is sometimes used of a *general truth*, especially with negatives (*Gnomic Perfect*):—

quī studet contingere mētam multa **tulit fēcit**que (Hor. A. P. 412), *he who aims to reach the goal, first bears and does many things.*
nōn aeris acervus et aurī **dēdūxit** corpore febrīs (id. Ep. i. 2. 47), *the pile of brass and gold removes not fever from the frame.*

NOTE.—The gnomic perfect strictly refers to past time; but its use implies that something which never *did* happen in any known case never *does* happen, and never *will* (cf. the English "*Faint heart never* won *fair lady*"); or, without a negative, that what *has once* happened will *always* happen under similar circumstances.

a. The Perfect is often used in expressions containing or implying a *negation*, where in affirmation the Imperfect would be preferred:—

dīcēbat melius quam **scrīpsit** Hortēnsius (Or. 132), *Hortensius spoke better than he wrote.* [Here the negative is implied in the comparison: compare the use of **quisquam**, **ūllus**, etc. (§§ 311, 312), and the French *ne* after comparatives and superlatives.]

476. The completed tenses of some verbs are equivalent to the incomplete tenses of verbs of kindred meaning.

Such are the preteritive verbs **ōdī**, *I hate;* **meminī**, *I remember;* **nōvī**, *I know;* **cōnsuēvī**, *I am accustomed*,[1] with others used preteritively, as **vēnerat** (= **aderat**, *he was at hand*, etc.), **cōnstitērunt**, *they stand firm* (have taken their stand), and many inceptives (see § 263. 1):—

[1] Cf. **dētestor**, **reminīscor**, **sciō**, **soleō**.

quī diēs aestūs maximōs efficere **cōnsuēvit** (B. G. iv. 29), *which day generally makes the highest tides* (is accustomed to make).

cûius splendor **obsolēvit** (Quinct. 59), *whose splendor is now all faded.*

NOTE.—Many other verbs are occasionally so used: as,—dum oculōs certāmen **āverterat** (Liv. xxxii. 24), *while the contest had turned their eyes* (kept them turned). [Here **āverterat** = **tenēbat**.]

PLUPERFECT TENSE

477. The Pluperfect is used (1) to denote an action or state *completed* in past time; or (2) sometimes to denote an action in indefinite time, but prior to some past time referred to:—

(1) locī nātūra erat haec, quem locum nostrī castrīs **dēlēgerant** (B. G. ii. 18), *this was the nature of the ground which our men had chosen for a camp.*

Viridovīx summam imperī tenēbat eārum omnium cīvitātum quae **dēfēcerant** (id. iii. 17), *Viridovix held the chief command of all those tribes which had revolted.*

(2) neque vērō cum aliquid **mandāverat** cōnfectum putābat (Cat. iii. 16), *but when he had given a thing in charge he did not look on it as done.*

quae sī quandō adepta est id quod eī **fuerat concupītum**, tum fert alacritātem (Tusc. iv. 15), *if it* (desire) *ever has gained what it had* [previously] *desired, then it produces joy.*

For the Epistolary Pluperfect, see § 479.

FUTURE PERFECT TENSE

478. The Future Perfect denotes an action as completed in the future:—

ut sēmentem **fēceris**, ita metēs (De Or. ii. 261), *as you sow* (shall have sown), *so shall you reap.*

carmina tum melius, cum **vēnerit** ipse, canēmus (Ecl. ix. 67), *then shall we sing our songs better, when he himself has come* (shall have come).

sī illīus īnsidiae clāriōrēs hāc lūce **fuerint**, tum dēnique obsecrābō (Mil. 6), *when the plots of that man have been shown to be as clear as daylight, then, and not till then, shall I conjure you.*

ego certē meum officium **praestiterō** (B. G. iv. 25), *I at least shall have done my duty* (i.e. when the time comes to reckon up the matter, I *shall* be found to have done it, whatever the event).

NOTE.—Latin is far more exact than English in distinguishing between mere future action and action *completed* in the future. Hence the Future Perfect is much commoner in Latin than in English. It may even be used instead of the Future, from the fondness of the Romans for representing an action as completed:—

quid inventum sit paulō post **vīderō** (Acad. ii. 76), *what has been found out I shall see presently.*

quī Antōnium **oppresserit** bellum taeterrimum **cōnfēcerit** (Fam. x. 19), *whoever crushes* (shall have crushed) *Antony will finish* (will have finished) *a most loathsome war.*

EPISTOLARY TENSES

479. In Letters, the Perfect Historical or the Imperfect may be used for the present, and the Pluperfect for any past tense, as if the letter were *dated* at the time it is supposed to be *received*:—

neque tamen, haec cum **scrībēbam**, **eram** nescius quantīs oneribus premerēre (Fam. v. 12. 2), *nor while I write this am I ignorant under what burdens you are weighed down.*

ad tuās omnīs [epistulās] **rescrīpseram** prīdiē (Att. ix. 10. 1), *I answered all your letters yesterday.*

cum quod scrīberem ad tē nihil habērem, tamen hās **dedī** litterās (Att. ix. 16), *though I have nothing to write to you, still I write this letter.*

Note.—In this use these tenses are called the Epistolary Perfect, Imperfect, and Pluperfect. The epistolary tenses are not employed with any uniformity, but only when attention is particularly directed to the *time of writing* (so especially **scrībēbam**, **dabam**, etc.).

TENSES OF THE SUBJUNCTIVE

480. The tenses of the Subjunctive in Independent Clauses denote time in relation to the time of the speaker.

The Present always refers to *future* (or *indefinite*) *time*, the Imperfect to either *past* or *present*, the Perfect to either *future* or *past*, the Pluperfect always to *past*.

481. The tenses of the Subjunctive in Dependent Clauses were habitually used in certain fixed connections with the tenses of the main verb.

These connections were determined by the time of the main verb and the time of the dependent verb together. They are known, collectively, as the *Sequence of Tenses.*

Note.—The so-called Sequence of Tenses is not a mechanical law. Each tense of the subjunctive in dependent clauses (as in independent) originally denoted its own time in relation to the time of the speaker, though less definitely than the corresponding tenses of the indicative. Gradually, however, as the complex sentence was more strongly felt as a unit, certain types in which the tenses of the dependent clause seemed to accord with those of the main clause were almost unconsciously regarded as regular, and others, in which there was no such agreement, as exceptional. Thus a pretty definite system of correspondences grew up, which is codified in the rules for the Sequence of Tenses. These, however, are by no means rigid. They do not apply with equal stringency to all dependent constructions, and they were frequently disregarded, not only when their strict observance would have obscured the sense, but for the sake of emphasis and variety, or merely from carelessness.

Sequence of Tenses

482. The tenses of the Subjunctive in Dependent Clauses follow special rules for the Sequence of Tenses.

With reference to these rules all tenses when used in *independent* clauses are divided into two classes,—*Primary* and *Secondary*.

1. PRIMARY. — The *Primary Tenses* include all forms that express *present* or *future* time. These are the Present, Future, and Future Perfect Indicative, the Present and Perfect Subjunctive, and the Present and Future Imperative.

2. SECONDARY. — The *Secondary Tenses* include all forms that refer to *past* time. These are the Imperfect, Perfect, and Pluperfect Indicative, the Imperfect and Pluperfect Subjunctive, and the Historical Infinitive.

NOTE. — To these may be added certain forms less commonly used in independent clauses: —(1) Primary: Present Infinitive in Exclamations; (2) Secondary: Perfect Infinitive in Exclamations (see §§ 462, 485. *a*. N.).

The Perfect Definite is sometimes treated as primary (see § 485. *a*).

For the Historical Present, see § 485. *e*; for the Imperfect Subjunctive in Apodosis, see § 485. *h*.

483. The following is the general rule for the Sequence of Tenses: —[1]

In complex sentences a Primary tense in the main clause is followed by the Present or Perfect in the dependent clause, and a Secondary tense by the Imperfect or Pluperfect: —

PRIMARY TENSES

rogō,	*I ask, am asking*	**quid faciās,** *what you are doing.*
rogābō,	*I shall ask*	**quid fēceris,** *what you did, were doing, have done, have been doing.*
rogāvī (sometimes),	*I have asked*	
rogāverō,	*I shall have asked*	**quid factūrus sīs,** *what you will do.*
scrībit,	*he writes*	**ut nōs moneat,** *to warn us.*
scrībet,	*he will write*	
scrībe (scrībitō),	*write*	**ut nōs moneās,** *to warn us.*
scrībit,	*he writes*	**quasi oblītus sit,** *as if he had forgotten.*

[1] The term is sometimes extended to certain relations between the tenses of subordinate verbs in the indicative and those of the main verb. These relations do not differ in principle from those which we are considering; but for convenience the term Sequence of Tenses is in this book restricted to subjunctives, in accordance with the usual practice.

SECONDARY TENSES

rogābam,	*I asked, was asking*	**quid facerēs,** *what you were doing.*
rogāvī,	*I asked, have asked*	**quid fēcissēs,** *what you had done, had been doing.*
rogāveram,	*I had asked*	**quid factūrus essēs,** *what you would do.*
scrīpsit,	*he wrote*	**ut nōs monēret,** *to warn us.*
scrīpsit,	*he wrote*	**quasi oblītus esset,** *as if he had forgotten.*

484. In applying the rule for the Sequence of Tenses, observe —

(1) Whether the main verb is (*a*) primary or (*b*) secondary.

(2) Whether the dependent verb is to denote completed action (i.e. past with reference to the main verb) or incomplete action (i.e. present or future with reference to the main verb). Then —

a. If the leading verb is *primary*, the dependent verb must be in the *Present* if it denotes *incomplete action*, in the *Perfect* if it denotes *completed action*.

b. If the leading verb is *secondary*, the dependent verb must be in the *Imperfect* if it denotes *incomplete action*, in the *Pluperfect* if it denotes *completed action*: —

(1) *He writes* [primary] *to warn* [incomplete action] *us*, **scrībit ut nōs moneat.**
I ask [primary] *what you were doing* [now past], **rogō quid fēceris.**

(2) *He wrote* [secondary] *to warn* [incomplete] *us*, **scrīpsit ut nōs monēret.**
I asked [secondary] *what you were doing* [incomplete], **rogāvī quid facerēs.**

c. Notice that the Future Perfect denotes action completed (at the time referred to), and hence is represented in the Subjunctive by the Perfect or Pluperfect: —

He shows that if they come (shall have come), *many will perish*, **dēmōnstrat, sī vēnerint, multōs interitūrōs.**

He showed that if they should come (should have come), *many would perish*, **dēmōnstrāvit, sī vēnissent, multōs interitūrōs.**

485. In the Sequence of Tenses the following special points are to be noted: —

a. The Perfect Indicative is ordinarily a secondary tense, but allows the primary sequence when the present time is clearly in the writer's mind: —

ut satis esset praesidī prōvīsum est (Cat. ii. 26), *provision has been made that there should be ample guard.* [Secondary sequence.]

addūxī hominem in quō satisfacere exterīs nātiōnibus possētis (Verr. i. 2), *I have brought a man in whose person you can make satisfaction to foreign nations.* [Secondary sequence]

est enim rēs iam in eum locum **adducta**, ut quamquam multum intersit inter eōrum causās quī dīmicant, tamen inter victōriās nōn multum interfutūrum **putem** (Fam. v. 21. 3), *for affairs have been brought to such a pass that, though there is a great difference between the causes of those who are fighting, still I do not think there will be much difference between their victories.* [Primary sequence.]

ea adhibita doctrīna **est** quae vel vitiōsissimam nātūram excolere **possit** (Q. Fr. i. 1. 7), *such instruction has been given as can train even the faultiest nature.* [Primary sequence.]

NOTE.—The Perfect Infinitive in exclamations follows the same rule:—

quemquamne **fuisse** tam scelerātum quī hōc **fingeret** (Phil. xiv. 14), *was any one so abandoned as to imagine this?* [Secondary.]

adeōn rem **redīsse** patrem ut **extimēscam** (Ter. Ph. 153), *to think that things have come to such a pass that I should dread my father!* [Primary.]

b. After a primary tense the Perfect Subjunctive is regularly used to denote *any past action.* Thus the Perfect Subjunctive may represent—

1. A Perfect Definite:—

nōn dubitō quīn omnēs tuī **scrīpserint** (Fam. v. 8), *I do not doubt that all your friends have written.* [Direct statement: **scrīpsērunt.**]

quā rē nōn īgnōrō quid accidat in ultimīs terrīs, cum **audierim** in Ītaliā querellās cīvium (Q. Fr. i. 1. 33), *therefore I know well what happens at the ends of the earth, when I have heard in Italy the complaints of citizens.* [Direct statement: **audīvī.**]

2. A Perfect Historical:—

mē autem hīc laudat quod **rettulerim**, nōn quod **patefēcerim** (Att. xii. 21), *me he praises because I brought the matter* [before the senate], *not because I brought it to light.* [Direct statement: **rettulit.**]

3. An Imperfect:—

sī forte cecidērunt, tum intellegitur quam **fuerint** inopēs amīcōrum (Lael. 53), *if perchance they fall* (have fallen), *then one can see how poor they were in friends.* [Direct question: quam inopēs **erant**?]

quī status rērum **fuerit** cum hās litterās dedī, scīre poteris ex C. Titiō Strabōne (Fam. xii. 6), *what the condition of affairs was when I wrote this letter, you can learn from Strabo.* [Direct question: quī status **erat**?]

quam cīvitātī cārus **fuerit** maerōre fūneris indicātum est (Lael. 11), *how dear he was to the state has been shown by the grief at his funeral.* [Direct question: quam cārus **erat**?]

ex epistulīs intellegī licet quam frequēns **fuerit** Platōnis audītor (Or. 15), *it may be understood from his letters how constant a hearer he was of Plato.* [Direct question: quam frequēns **erat**?]

NOTE.—Thus the Perfect Subjunctive may represent, not only a Perfect Definite or a Perfect Historical of a direct statement or question, but an Imperfect as well. This comes from the want of any special tense of the subjunctive for continued past action after a primary tense. Thus, **mīror quid fēcerit** may mean (1) *I wonder what he has done,* (2) *I wonder what he did* (hist. perf.), or (3) *I wonder what he was doing.*

c. In clauses of Result, the Perfect Subjunctive is regularly (the Present rarely) used after secondary tenses: —

Hortēnsius **ārdēbat** dīcendī cupiditāte sīc ut in nūllō umquam flagrantius studium **vīderim** (Brut. 302), *Hortensius was so hot with desire of speaking that I have never seen a more burning ardor in any man.*

[Siciliam Verrēs] per triennium ita **vexāvit** ac **perdidit** ut ea restituī in antīquum statum nūllō modō **possit** (Verr. i. 12), *for three years Verres so racked and ruined Sicily that she can in no way be restored to her former state.* [Here the Present describes a state of things actually existing.]

videor **esse cōnsecūtus** ut nōn **possit** Dolābella in Ītaliam pervenīre (Fam. xii. 14. 2), *I seem to have brought it about that Dolabella cannot come into Italy.*

NOTE 1. — This construction emphasizes the result; the regular sequence of tenses would subordinate it.

NOTE 2. — There is a special fondness for the Perfect Subjunctive to represent a Perfect Indicative: —

Thorius erat ita nōn superstitiōsus ut illa plūrima in suā patriā et sacrificia et fāna **contemneret**; ita nōn timidus ad mortem ut in aciē **sit** ob rem pūblicam **interfectus** (Fin. ii. 63), *Thorius was so little superstitious that he despised* [contemnēbat] *the many sacrifices and shrines in his country; so little timorous about death that he was killed* [interfectus est] *in battle, in defence of the state.*

d. A *general truth* after a past tense follows the sequence of tenses:

ex hīs quae tribuisset, sibi quam mūtābilis **esset** reputābat (Q. C. iii. 8. 20), *from what she* (Fortune) *had bestowed on him, he reflected how inconstant she is.* [Direct: **mūtābilis est.**]

ibi quantam vim ad stimulandōs animōs īra **habēret** appāruit (Liv. xxxiii. 37), *here it appeared what power anger has to goad the mind.* [Direct: **habet.**]

NOTE. — In English the original tense is more commonly kept.

e. The Historical Present (§ 469) is sometimes felt as a *primary*, sometimes as a *secondary* tense, and accordingly it takes either the primary or the secondary sequence: —

rogat ut **cūret** quod **dīxisset** (Quinct. 18), *he asks him to attend to the thing he had spoken of.* [Both primary and secondary sequence.]

NOTE. — After the historical present, the subjunctive with **cum** temporal must follow the secondary sequence: —

quō cum **vēnisset cōgnōscit** (B. C. i. 34), *when he had come there he learns.*

cum **esset pūgnātum** hōrīs quīnque, nostrīque gravius **premerentur**, impetum in cohortīs **faciunt** (id. i. 46), *when they had fought for five hours, and our men were pretty hard pressed, they make an attack on the cohorts.*

f. The Historical Infinitive regularly takes the secondary sequence: —

interim cotīdiē Caesar Haeduōs frūmentum, quod **essent pollicitī**, **flāgitāre** (B. G. i. 16), *meanwhile Cæsar demanded of the Hædui every day the grain which they had promised.*

g. The Imperfect and Pluperfect in conditions contrary to fact (§ 517) and in the Deliberative Subjunctive (§ 444) are not affected by the sequence of tenses: —

quia tāle sit, ut vel sī **ignōrārent** id hominēs vel sī **obmutuissent** (Fin. ii. 49), *because it is such that even if men* WERE *ignorant of it, or* HAD BEEN *silent about it.*

quaerō ā tē cūr C. Cornēlium nōn **dēfenderem** (Vat. 5), *I ask you why I was not to defend Caius Cornelius?* [Direct: **cūr nōn dēfenderem**?]

h. The Imperfect Subjunctive in present conditions contrary to fact (§ 517) is regularly followed by the secondary sequence: —

sī aliī cōnsulēs essent, ad tē potissimum, Paule, **mitterem**, ut eōs mihi quam amīcissimōs **redderēs** (Fam. xv. 13. 3), *if there were other consuls, I should send to you, Paulus, in preference to all, that you might make them as friendly to me as possible.*

sī sōlōs eōs **dīcerēs** miserōs quibus moriendum **esset**, nēminem **exciperēs** (Tusc. i. 9), *if you were to call only those wretched who must die, you would except no one.*

i. The Present is sometimes followed by a secondary sequence, seemingly because the writer is thinking of past time: —

sed sī rēs cōget, **est** quiddam tertium, quod neque Seliciō nec mihi displicēbat: ut neque iacēre rem **paterēmur**, etc. (Fam. i. 5 A. 3), *but if the case shall demand, there is a third* [course] *which neither Selicius nor myself disapproved, that we should not allow,* etc. [Here Cicero is led by the time of **displicēbat**.]

sed tamen ut **scīrēs**, haec tibi **scrībō** (Fam. xiii. 47), *but yet that you may know, I write thus.* [As if he had used the epistolary imperfect **scrībēbam** (§ 479).]

cûius praeceptī tanta vīs **est** ut ea nōn hominī cuipiam sed Delphicō deō **tribuerētur** (Legg. i. 58), *such is the force of this precept, that it was ascribed not to any man, but to the Delphic god.* [The precept was an old one.]

j. When a clause depends upon one already dependent, its sequence may be secondary if the verb of that clause expresses past time, even if the main verb is in a primary tense: —

sed tamen quā rē **acciderit** ut ex meīs superiōribus litterīs id **suspicārēre** nesciō (Fam. ii. 16), *but yet how it happened that you suspected this from my previous letter, I don't know.*

tantum **prōfēcisse** vidēmur ut ā Graecīs nē verbōrum quidem cōpiā **vincerēmur** (N. D. i. 8), *we seem to have advanced so far that even in abundance of words we* ARE *not surpassed by the Greeks.*

NOTE. — So regularly after a Perfect Infinitive which depends on a primary tense (§ 585. *a*).

TENSES OF THE INFINITIVE

486. Except in Indirect Discourse, only the Present and Perfect Infinitives are used.

The Present represents the action of the verb as in progress without distinct reference to time, the Perfect as completed.

For the Tenses of the Infinitive in Indirect Discourse see § 584.

a. With past tenses of verbs of *necessity*, *propriety*, and *possibility* (as **dēbuī, oportuit, potuī**), the Present Infinitive is often used in Latin where the English idiom prefers the Perfect Infinitive: —

numne, sī Coriolānus habuit amīcōs, **ferre** contrā patriam arma illī cum Coriolānō **dēbuērunt** (Lael. 36), *if Coriolanus had friends, ought they to have borne arms with him against their fatherland?*

pecūnia, quam hīs **oportuit** cīvitātibus prō frūmentō **darī** (Verr. iii. 174), *money which ought to have been paid to these states for grain.*

cōnsul **esse** quī **potuī**, nisi eum vītae cursum tenuissem ā pueritiā (Rep. i. 10), *how could I have become consul had I not from boyhood followed that course of life?*

b. With verbs of *necessity*, *propriety*, and *possibility*, the Perfect Infinitive may be used to emphasize the idea of completed action: —

tametsī statim **vīcisse dēbeō** (Rosc. Am. 73), *although I ought to win my case at once* (to be regarded as having won it).

bellum quod **possumus** ante hiemem **perfēcisse** (Liv. xxxvii. 19. 5), *a war which we can have completed before winter.*

nīl ego, sī peccem, **possum nescīsse** (Ov. H. xvi. 47), *if I should go wrong, I cannot have done it in ignorance* (am not able not to have known).

NOTE. — With the past tenses of these verbs the perfect infinitive is apparently due to attraction: —

quod iam prīdem **factum esse oportuit** (Cat. i. 5), (a thing) *which ought to have been done long ago.*

haec **facta** ab illō **oportēbat** (Ter. Haut. 536), *this ought to have been done by him.*

tum **decuit metuisse** (Aen. x. 94), *then was the time to fear* (then you should have feared).

c. In archaic Latin and in legal formulas the Perfect Active Infinitive is often used with **nōlō** or **volō** in prohibitions: —

Chaldaeum nēquem **cōnsuluisse velit** (Cato R. R. v. 4), *let him not venture to have consulted a soothsayer.*

nōlītō dēvellisse (Pl. Poen. 872), *do not have them plucked.*

nēquis **humāsse velit** Āiācem (Hor. S. ii. 3. 187), *let no one venture to have buried Ajax.*

NEIQVIS EORVM BACANAL **HABVISE VELET** (S. C. de Bac. 1), *let no one of them venture to have had a place for Bacchanalian worship.*

d. With verbs of *wishing*[1] the Perfect Passive Infinitive (commonly without **esse**) is often used emphatically instead of the Present:

domesticā cūrā tē **levātum** volō (Q. Fr. iii. 9. 3), *I wish you relieved of private care.*

illōs **monitōs** volō (Cat. ii. 27), *I wish them thoroughly warned.*

quī illam [patriam] **exstīnctam** cupit (Fin. iv. 66), *who is eager for her utter destruction.*

illud tē **esse admonitum** volō (Cael. 8), *I wish you to be well advised of this.*

quī sē ab omnibus **dēsertōs** potius quam abs tē **dēfēnsōs esse** mālunt (Caecil. 21), *who prefer to be deserted by all rather than to be defended by you.*

NOTE.—The participle in this case is rather in predicate agreement (with or without esse) than used to form a strict perfect infinitive, though the full form can hardly be distinguished from that construction.

e. In late Latin, and in poetry (often for metrical convenience), rarely in good prose, the Perfect Active Infinitive is used emphatically instead of the Present, and even after other verbs than those of *wishing*:—

nēmō eōrum est quī nōn **perīsse** tē cupiat (Verr. ii. 149), *there is no one of them who is not eager for your death.*

haud equidem premendō alium mē **extulisse** velim (Liv. xxii. 59. 10), *I would not by crushing another exalt myself.*

sunt quī nōlint **tetigisse** (Hor. S. i. 2. 28), *there are those who would not touch.*

commīsisse cavet (Hor. A. P. 168), *he is cautious of doing.*

nunc quem **tetigisse** timērent, anguis erās (Ov. M. viii. 733), *again you became a serpent which they dreaded to touch.*

frātrēsque tendentēs opācō Pēlion **imposuisse** Olympō (Hor. Od. iii. 4. 51), *and the brothers striving to set Pelion on dark Olympus.*

f. After verbs of *feeling* the Perfect Infinitive is used, especially by the poets, to denote a completed action.

So also with **satis est, satis habeō, melius est, contentus sum**, and in a few other cases where the distinction of time is important:—

nōn paenitēbat intercapēdinem scrībendī **fēcisse** (Fam. xvi. 21), *I was not sorry to have made a respite of writing.*

pudet mē nōn **praestitisse** (id. xiv. 3), *I am ashamed not to have shown.*

sunt quōs pulverem Olympicum **collēgisse** iuvat (Hor. Od. i. 1. 3), *some delight to have stirred up the dust at Olympia.*

quiēsse erit melius (Liv. iii. 48), *it will be better to have kept quiet.*

ac sī quis amet **scrīpsisse** (Hor. S. i. 10. 60), *than if one should choose to have written.*

id sōlum **dīxisse** satis habeō (Vell. ii. 124), *I am content to have said only this.*

[1] **Volō**, and less frequently **nōlō, mālō**, and **cupiō**.

NOUN AND ADJECTIVE FORMS OF THE VERB

487. The several Noun and Adjective forms associated with the verb are employed as follows: —[1]

- I. **Participles:**
  - *a.* Present and Perfect:
    1. Attributive (§ 494).
    2. Simple Predicate (§ 495).
    3. Periphrastic Perfect (passive) (§ 495. N.).
    4. Predicate of Circumstance (§ 496).
    5. Descriptive (Indirect Discourse) (§ 497 *d*).
  - *b.* Future
    1. Periphrastic with **esse** (§ 498. *a*).
    2. Periphrastic with **fuī** (= Pluperfect Subjunctive) (§ 498. *b*).
  - *c.* Gerundive
    1. As Descriptive Adjective (§ 500. 1).
    2. Periphrastic with **esse** (§ 500. 2).
    3. Of Purpose with certain verbs (§ 500. 4).
- II. **Gerund or Gerundive:**
  1. Genitive as Subjective or Objective Genitive (§ 504).
  2. Dative, with Adjectives (of Fitness), Nouns, Verbs (§ 505).
  3. Accusative, with certain Prepositions (§ 506).
  4. Ablative, of Means, Comparison, or with Prepositions (§ 507).
- III. **Supine:**
  1. Accusative Supine (in **-um**), with Verbs of Motion (§ 509).
  2. Ablative Supine (in **-ū**), chiefly with Adjectives (§ 510).

PARTICIPLES

488. The Participle expresses the action of the verb in the form of an Adjective, but has a partial distinction of tense and may govern a case.

NOTE. — Thus the participle combines all the functions of an adjective with some of the functions of a verb. As an Adjective, it limits substantives and agrees with them in gender, number, and case (§ 286). As a Verb, it has distinctions of time (§ 489) and often takes an object.

Distinctions of Tense in Participles

489. Participles denote time as *present*, *past*, or *future* with respect to the time of the verb in their clause.

Thus the Present Participle represents the action as *in progress* at the time indicated by the tense of the verb, the Perfect as *completed*, and the Future as *still to take place*.

490. The Present Participle has several of the special uses of the Present Indicative. Thus it may denote —

1. An action *continued* in the present but *begun* in the past (§ 466):

quaerentī mihi iam diū certa rēs nūlla veniēbat in mentem (Fam. iv. 13), *though I had long sought, no certain thing came to my mind.*

[1] For the Syntax of the Infinitive, see §§ 451 ff., 486.

2. Attempted action (§ 467): —

C. Flāminiō restitit agrum Pīcentem **dīvidentī** (Cat. M. 11), *he resisted Flaminius when attempting to divide the Picene territory.*

3. Rarely (in poetry and later Latin) futurity or purpose, with a verb of motion: —

Eurypylum **scītantem** ōrācula mittimus (Aen. ii. 114), *we send Eurypylus to consult the oracle.* [Cf. § 468.]

491. The Perfect Participle of a few deponent verbs is used nearly in the sense of a Present.

Such are, regularly, **ratus**, **solitus**, **veritus**; commonly, **arbitrātus**, **fīsus**, **ausus**, **secūtus**, and occasionally others, especially in later writers: —

rem incrēdibilem **ratī** (Sall. Cat. 48), *thinking the thing incredible.*
īnsidiās **veritus** (B. G. ii. 11), *fearing an ambuscade.*
cohortātus mīlitēs docuit (B. C. iii. 80), *encouraging the men, he showed.*
īrātus dīxistī (Mur. 62), *you spoke in a passion.*
ad pūgnam **congressī** (Liv. iv. 10), *meeting in fight.*

492. The Latin has no Present Participle in the passive.

The place of such a form is supplied usually by a clause with **dum** or **cum**: —

obiēre **dum calciantur** mātūtīnō duo Caesarēs (Plin. N. H. vii. 181), *two Cæsars died while having their shoes put on in the morning.*

mēque ista dēlectant **cum** Latīnē **dīcuntur** (Acad. i. 18), *those things please me when they are spoken in Latin.*

Note. — These constructions are often used when a participle might be employed: —

dīc, hospes, Spartae nōs tē hīc vīdisse iacentīs, **dum** sānctīs patriae lēgibus **obsequimur** (Tusc. i. 101), *tell it, stranger, at Sparta, that you saw us lying here obedient to our country's sacred laws.* [Here **dum obsequimur** is a translation of the Greek present participle πειθόμενοι.]

dum [Ulixēs] sibi, dum sociīs reditum **parat** (Hor. Ep. i. 2. 21), *Ulysses, while securing the return of himself and his companions.* [In Greek: ἀρνύμενος.]

493. The Latin has no Perfect Participle in the active voice. The deficiency is supplied —

1. In deponents by the perfect passive form with its regular active meaning: —

nam singulās [nāvīs] nostrī **cōnsectātī** expūgnāvērunt (B. G. iii. 15), *for our men, having overtaken them one by one, captured them by boarding.*

Note. — The perfect participle of several deponent verbs may be either active or passive in meaning (§ 190. *b*).

2. In other verbs, either by the perfect passive participle in the ablative absolute (§ 420. N.) or by a temporal clause (especially with **cum** or **postquam**): —

itaque **convocātīs centuriōnibus** mīlitēs certiōrēs facit (B. G. iii. 5), *and so, having called the centurions together, he informs the soldiers* (the centurions having been called together).

cum vēnisset animadvertit collem (id. vii. 44), *having come* (when he had come), *he noticed a hill.*

postquam id **animum advertit** cōpiās suās Caesar in proximum collem subdūcit (B. G. i. 24), *having observed this* (after he had observed this) *Cæsar led his troops to the nearest hill.*

Uses of Participles

494. The Present and Perfect Participles are sometimes used as attributives, nearly like adjectives: —

aeger et **flagrāns** animus (Tac. Ann. iii. 54), *his sick and passionate mind.*

cum antīquissimam sententiam tum **comprobātam** (Div. i. 11), *a view at once most ancient and well approved.*

sīgna numquam ferē **mentientia** (id. i. 15), *signs hardly ever deceitful.*

auspiciīs ūtuntur **coāctīs** (id. i. 27), *they use forced auspices.*

a. Participles often become complete adjectives, and may be compared, or used as nouns: —

quō mulierī esset rēs **cautior** (Caec. 11), *that the matter might be more secure for the woman.*

in illīs artibus **praestantissimus** (De Or. i. 217), *preëminent in those arts.*

sibi **indulgentēs** et corporī **dēservientēs** (Legg. i. 39), *the self-indulgent, and slaves to the body* (indulging themselves and serving the body).

rēctē **facta** paria esse dēbent (Par. 22), *right deeds* (things rightly done) *ought to be like in value* (see § 321. *b*).

male **parta** male dīlābuntur (Phil. ii. 65), *ill got, ill spent* (things ill acquired are ill spent).

cōnsuētūdō **valentis** (De Or. ii. 186), *the habit of a man in health.*

495. Participles are often used as Predicate Adjectives. As such they may be joined to the subject by **esse** or a copulative verb (see § 283): —

Gallia est **dīvīsa** (B. G. i. 1), *Gaul is divided.*

locus quī nunc **saeptus** est (Liv. i. 8), *the place which is now enclosed.*

vidētis ut senectūs sit operōsa et semper **agēns** aliquid et **mōliēns** (Cat. M. 26), *you see how busy old age is, always aiming and trying at something.*

nēmō adhūc convenīre mē voluit cui fuerim **occupātus** (id. 32), *nobody hitherto has* [ever] *wished to converse with me, to whom I have been "engaged."*

NOTE. — From this predicate use arise the compound tenses of the passive, — the participle of *completed action* with the incomplete tenses of esse developing the idea of past time: as, **interfectus est**, *he was* (or *has been*) *killed*, lit. *he is having-been-killed* (i.e. already slain).

The perfect participle used with fuī etc. was perhaps originally an intensified expression in the popular language for the perfect, pluperfect, etc.

At times these forms indicate a state of affairs no longer existing: —

cōtem quoque eōdem locō **sitam fuisse** memorant (Liv. i. 36. 5), *they say that a whetstone was* (once) *deposited in this same place.* [At the time of writing it was no longer there.]

arma quae **fixa** in parietibus **fuerant**, humī inventa sunt (Div. i. 74), *the arms which had been fastened on the walls were found upon the ground.*

But more frequently they are not to be distinguished from the forms with sum etc.

The construction is found occasionally at all periods, but is most common in Livy and later writers.

496. The Present and Perfect Participles are often used as a predicate, where in English a phrase or a subordinate clause would be more natural.

In this use the participles express *time, cause, occasion, condition, concession, characteristic* (or *description*), *manner, means, attendant circumstances*: —

volventēs hostīlia cadāvera amīcum reperiēbant (Sall. Cat. 61), *while rolling over the corpses of the enemy they found a friend.* [Time.]

paululum **commorātus**, sīgna canere iubet (id. 59), *after delaying a little while, he orders them to give the signal.* [Time.]

longius prōsequī **veritus**, ad Cicerōnem pervēnit (B. G. v. 52), *because he feared to follow further, he came to Cicero.* [Cause.]

quī scīret laxās dare **iussus** habēnās (Aen. i. 63), *who might know how to give them loose rein when bidden.* [Occasion.]

damnātum poenam sequī oportēbat (B. G. i. 4), *if condemned, punishment must overtake him.* [Condition.]

salūtem **īnspērantibus** reddidistī (Marc. 21), *you have restored a safety for which we did not hope* (to [us] not hoping). [Concession.]

Dardanius caput ecce puer **dētēctus** (Aen. x. 133), *the Trojan boy with his head uncovered.* [Description.]

nec trepidēs in ūsum **poscentis** aevī pauca (Hor. Od. ii. 11. 5), *be not anxious for the needs of age that demands little.* [Characteristic.]

incitātī fugā montīs altissimōs petēbant (B. C. iii. 93), *in headlong flight they made for the highest mountains.* [Manner.]

mīlitēs **sublevātī** aliī ab aliīs māgnam partem itineris cōnficerent (id. i. 68), *the soldiers, helped up by each other, accomplished a considerable part of the route.* [Means.]

hōc **laudāns**, Pompêius idem iūrāvit (id. iii. 87), *approving this, Pompey took the same oath.* [Attendant Circumstance.]

aut **sedēns** aut **ambulāns** disputābam (Tusc. i. 7), *I conducted the discussion either sitting or walking.* [Attendant Circumstance.]

NOTE 1.—These uses are especially frequent in the Ablative Absolute (§ 420).

NOTE 2.—A coördinate clause is sometimes compressed into a perfect participle:—

> īnstrūctōs ōrdinēs in locum aequum dēdūcit (Sall. Cat. 59), *he draws up the lines, and leads them to level ground.*
>
> ut hōs trāductōs necāret (B. G. v. 6), *that he might carry them over and put them to death.*

NOTE 3.—A participle with a negative often expresses the same idea which in English is given by *without* and a verbal noun: as,—miserum est **nihil prōficientem** angī (N. D. iii. 14), *it is wretched to vex oneself without effecting anything.*

NOTE 4.—Acceptum and expēnsum as predicates with ferre and referre are bookkeeping terms: as,—quās pecūniās **ferēbat** eīs **expēnsās** (Verr. ii. 170), *what sums he charged to them.*

497. A noun and a passive participle are often so united that the participle and not the noun contains the main idea:—[1]

> ante **conditam condendamve** urbem (Liv. Pref.), *before the city was built or building.*
>
> illī lībertātem **imminūtam** cīvium Rōmānōrum nōn tulērunt; vōs **ēreptam** vītam neglegētis (Manil. 11), *they did not endure the infringement of the citizens' liberty; will you disregard the destruction of their lives?*
>
> post **nātōs** hominēs (Brut. 224), *since the creation of man.*
>
> iam ā **conditā** urbe (Phil. iii. 9), *even from the founding of the city.*

a. The perfect participle with a noun in agreement, or in the neuter as an abstract noun, is used in the ablative with **opus**, *need* (cf. § 411. *a*):—

> opus **factō** est **viāticō** (Pl. Trin. 887), *there is need of laying in provision.*
>
> **mātūrātō** opus est (Liv. viii. 13. 17), *there is need of haste.*

b. The perfect participle with **habeō** (rarely with other verbs) has almost the same meaning as a perfect active, but denotes the *continued effect* of the action of the verb:—[2]

> fidem quam **habent spectātam** iam et diū **cōgnitam** (Caecil. 11), *my fidelity, which they have proved and long known.*
>
> cohortīs in aciē LXXX **cōnstitūtās habēbat** (B. C. iii. 89), *he had eighty cohorts stationed in line of battle.*
>
> nefāriōs ducēs **captōs** iam et **comprehēnsōs tenētis** (Cat. iii. 16), *you have now captured the infamous leaders and hold them in custody.*

c. A verb of *effecting* or the like may be used in combination with the perfect participle of a transitive verb to express the action of that verb more forcibly:—

[1] Compare the participle in indirect discourse in Greek (Goodwin's Greek Grammar, § 1588); and the English "'T was at the royal feast *for Persia won*" (Dryden), i.e. *for the conquest of Persia.*

[2] The perfect with *have*, in modern languages of Latin stock, has grown out of this use of **habeō**.

praefectōs suōs multī **missōs fēcērunt** (Verr. iii. 134), *many discharged their officers* (made dismissed).

hīc **trānsāctum reddet** omne (Pl. Capt. 345), *he will get it all done* (restore it finished).

adēmptum tibi iam **faxō** omnem metum (Ter. Haut. 341), *I will relieve you of all fear* (make it taken away).

illam tibi **incēnsam dabō** (Ter. Ph. 974), *I will make her angry with you.*

NOTE.—Similarly **volō** (with its compounds) and **cupiō**, with a perfect participle without **esse** (cf. § 486. *d*).

d. After verbs denoting an *action of the senses* the present participle in agreement with the object is nearly equivalent to the infinitive of indirect discourse (§ 580), but expresses the action more vividly:

ut eum nēmō umquam in equō **sedentem** vīderit (Verr. v. 27), *so that no one ever saw him sitting on a horse.* [Cf. Tusc. iii. 31.]

NOTE.—The same construction is used after **faciō**, **indūcō**, and the like, with the name of an author as subject: as,—Xenophōn facit Sōcratem **disputantem** (N. D. i. 31), *Xenophon represents Socrates disputing.*

Future Participle (Active)

498. The Future Participle (except **futūrus** and **ventūrus**) is rarely used in simple agreement with a noun, except by poets and later writers.

a. The future participle is chiefly used with the forms of **esse** (often omitted in the infinitive) in the Active Periphrastic Conjugation (see § 195):—

morere, Diagorā, nōn enim in caelum **adscēnsūrus es** (Tusc. i. 111), *die, Diagoras, for you are not likely to rise to heaven.*

spērat adulēscēns diū **sē vīctūrum** (Cat. M. 68), *the young man hopes to live long* (that he shall live long).

neque **petītūrus** umquam cōnsulātum **vidērētur** (Off. iii. 79), *and did not seem likely ever to be a candidate for the consulship.*

b. With the past tenses of **esse** in the indicative, the future participle is often equivalent to the pluperfect subjunctive (§ 517. *d*). For **fūturum fuisse**, see § 589. *b*.

499. By later writers and the poets the Future Participle is often used in simple agreement with a substantive to express—

1. Likelihood or certainty:—

rem ausus plūs fāmae **habitūram** (Liv. ii. 10), *having dared a thing which would have more repute.*

2. Purpose, intention, or readiness: —

ēgreditur castrīs Rōmānus vāllum **invāsūrus** (Liv. iii. 60. 8), *the Roman comes out of the camp with the intention of attacking the rampart.*

dispersōs per agrōs mīlitēs equitibus **invāsūrīs** (id. xxxi. 36), *while the horse were ready to attack the soldiers scattered through the fields.*

sī **peritūrus** abīs (Aen. ii. 675), *if you are going away to perish.*

3. Apodosis: —

dedit mihi quantum maximum potuit, **datūrus** amplius sī potuisset (Plin. Ep. iii. 21. 6), *he gave me as much as he could, ready to give me more if he had been able.* [Here **datūrus** is equivalent to **dedisset.**]

Gerundive (Future Passive Participle)

Note. — The participle in **-dus**, commonly called the Gerundive, has two distinct uses: —

(1) Its predicate and attribute use as Participle or Adjective (§ 500).

(2) Its use with the meaning of the Gerund (§ 503). This may be called its *gerundive* use.

500. The Gerundive when used as a Participle or an Adjective is always passive, denoting *necessity, obligation,* or *propriety.*

In this use of the Gerundive the following points are to be observed: —

1. The gerundive is sometimes used, like the present and perfect participles, in simple agreement with a noun: —

fortem et **cōnservandum** virum (Mil. 104), *a brave man, and worthy to be preserved.*

gravis iniūria facta est et nōn **ferenda** (Flacc. 84), *a grave and intolerable wrong has been done.*

2. The most frequent use of the gerundive is with the forms of **esse** in the Second (or *passive*) Periphrastic Conjugation (see § 196): —

nōn **agitanda** rēs **erit** (Verr. v. 179), *will not the thing have to be agitated?*

3. The neuter gerundive of both transitive and intransitive verbs may be used impersonally in the second periphrastic conjugation.

With verbs that take the dative or ablative, an object may be expressed in the appropriate case; with transitive verbs, an object in the accusative is sometimes found: —

temporī **serviendum est** (Fam. ix. 7. 2), *one must obey the time.*

lēgibus **pārendum est**, *the laws must be obeyed.*

ūtendum exercitātiōnibus modicīs (Cat. M. 36), *we must use moderate exercise.*

agitandumst vigiliās (Pl. Trin. 869), *I have got to stand guard.*

via quam nōbīs **ingrediendum** sit (Cat. M. 6), *the way we have to enter.*

4. After verbs signifying *to give, deliver, agree for, have, receive, undertake, demand*,[1] a gerundive in agreement with the object is used to express purpose: —

> redēmptor quī columnam illam condūxerat **faciendam** (Div. ii. 47), *the contractor who had undertaken to make that column.* [The regular construction with this class of verbs.]
>
> aedem Castoris habuit **tuendam** (Verr. ii. 1. 150), *he had the temple of Castor to take care of.*
>
> nāvīs atque onera **adservanda** cūrābat (id. v. 146), *he took care that the ships and cargoes should be kept.*

GERUND

501. The Gerund is the neuter of the Gerundive, used substantively in the Genitive, Dative, Accusative, and Ablative.

502. The Gerund expresses an action of the verb in the form of a verbal noun.

As a *noun* the gerund is itself governed by other words; as a *verb* it may take an object in the proper case: —

> ars bene **disserendī** et vēra ac falsa **diiūdicandī** (De Or. ii. 157), *the art of discoursing well, and distinguishing the true and the false.*

NOTE. — The Nominative of the gerund is supplied by the Infinitive. Thus in the example above, the verbal nouns *discoursing* and *distinguishing*, if used in the nominative, would be expressed by the infinitives **disserere** and **diiūdicāre**.

The Gerund is the neuter of the gerundive used impersonally, but retaining the verbal idea sufficiently to govern an object. It may therefore be regarded as a noun (cf. **mātūrātō opus est**, § 497. *a*) with a verbal force (cf. **istanc tāctiō**, p. 240, footnote).

GERUND AND GERUNDIVE

503. When the Gerund would have an object in the Accusative, the Gerundive[2] is generally used instead. The gerundive agrees with its noun, which takes the case that the gerund would have had: —

> parātiōrēs ad omnia perīcula **subeunda** (B. G. i. 5), *readier to undergo all dangers.* [Here **subeunda** agrees with **perīcula**, which is itself governed by **ad**. The (inadmissible) construction with the gerund would be **ad subeundum perīcula**; **ad** governing the gerund, and the gerund governing the accusative **perīcula**.] For details, see §§ 504–507.

[1] Such verbs are **accipiō, adnōtō, attribuō, condūcō, cūrō, dēnōtō, dēposcō, dō, dīvidō, dōnō, ēdīcō, ēdoceō, ferō, habeō, locō, mandō, obiciō, permittō, petō, pōnō, praebeō, prōpōnō, relinquō, rogō, suscipiō, trādō, voveō.**

[2] The gerundive construction is probably the original one.

NOTE 1.—In this use the gerund and the gerundive are translated in the same way, but have really a different construction. The gerundive is a *passive* participle, and agrees with its noun, though in translation we change the voice, just as we may translate **vigiliae agitandae sunt** (*guard must be kept*) by *I must stand guard.*

NOTE 2.—In the gerundive construction the verbs **ūtor, fruor,** etc., are treated like transitive verbs governing the accusative, as they do in early Latin (§ 410. *a.* N.[1]): as,—**ad perfruendās voluptātēs** (Off. i. 25), *for enjoying pleasures.*

a. The following examples illustrate the parallel constructions of Gerund and Gerundive:—

GEN. cōnsilium	**urbem capiendī** **urbis capiendae**	*a design of taking the city.*	
DAT. dat operam	**agrōs colendō** **agrīs colendīs**	*he attends to tilling the fields.*	
ACC. veniunt ad	**mihi pārendum** **pācem petendam**	*they come*	*to obey me.* *to seek peace.*
ABL. terit tempus	**scrībendō epistulās** **scrībendīs epistulīs**	*he spends time in writing letters.*	

NOTE 1.—The gerund with a direct object is practically limited to the Genitive and the Ablative (without a preposition); even in these cases the gerundive is commoner.

NOTE 2.—The gerund or gerundive is often found coördinated with nominal constructions, and sometimes even in apposition with a noun:—

(1) **in forō, in cūriā, in amīcōrum perīculīs prōpulsandīs** (Phil. vii. 7), *in the forum, in the senate-house, in defending my friends in jeopardy.*

(2) **ad rēs dīversissimās, pārendum atque imperandum** (Liv. xxi. 4), *for the most widely different things, obeying and commanding.*

Genitive of the Gerund and Gerundive

504. The Genitive of the Gerund and Gerundive is used after nouns or adjectives, either as *subjective* or *objective* genitive:—

vīvendī fīnis est optimus (Cat. M. 72), *it is the best end of living.* [Subjective.]

neque **cōnsilī habendī** neque arma **capiendī** spatiō datō (B. G. iv. 14), *time being given neither for forming plans nor for taking arms.* [Objective.]

nōn tam **commūtandārum** quam **ēvertendārum rērum** cupidōs (Off. ii. 3), *desirous not so much of changing as of destroying the state.* [Objective.]

NOTE 1.—In these uses the gerund and the gerundive are about equally common.

NOTE 2.—In a few phrases the Infinitive is used with nouns which ordinarily have the genitive of the gerund or gerundive: as,—**tempus est abīre**, *it is time to go.*

a. The genitive of the gerund sometimes takes a direct object, especially a neuter pronoun or a neuter adjective used substantively:—

nūlla causa iūsta cuiquam esse potest contrā patriam arma capiendī (Phil. ii. 53), *no one can have a just cause for taking up arms against his country.*

artem vēra ac falsa dīiūdicandī (De Or. ii. 157), *the art of distinguishing true from false.*

NOTE 1. — The genitive of the gerund or gerundive is used (especially in later Latin) as a predicate genitive. When so used it often expresses purpose: —

quae postquam glōriōsa modo neque **bellī patrandī** cōgnōvit (Iug. 88), *when he perceived that these were only brilliant deeds and not likely to end the war.*

Aegyptum proficīscitur **cōgnōscendae antīquitātis** (Tac. Ann. ii. 59), *he sets out for Egypt to study old times.*

b. The genitive of the gerund or gerundive with **causā** or **gratiā** expresses purpose (§ 533. *b*): —

pābulandī aut frūmentandī causā prōgressī (B. C. i. 48), *having advanced for the purpose of collecting fodder or supplies.*

vītandae suspīcionis causā (Cat. i. 19), *in order to avoid suspicion.*

simulandī grātiā (Iug. 37), *in order to deceive.*

exercendae memōriae grātiā (Cat. M. 38), *for the sake of training the memory.*

c. The genitive of the gerund is occasionally limited by a noun or pronoun (especially a personal pronoun in the plural) in the objective genitive instead of taking a direct object: —

rêiciendī **trium iūdicum** potestās (Verr. ii. 77), *the power of challenging three jurors* (of the rejecting of three jurors).

suī colligendī facultās (B. G. iii. 6), *the opportunity to recover themselves.*

Dative of the Gerund and Gerundive

505. The Dative of the Gerund and Gerundive is used in a few expressions after verbs: —[1]

diem praestitit **operī faciendō** (Verr. ii. 1. 148), *he appointed a day for doing the work.*

praeesse **agrō colendō** (Rosc. Am. 50), *to take charge of cultivating the land.*

esse **solvendō**, *to be able to pay* (to be for paying).

NOTE. — The dative of the gerund with a direct object is never found in classic Latin, but occurs twice in Plautus.

a. The dative of the gerund and gerundive is used after adjectives,[2] especially those which denote *fitness* or *adaptability:* —

genus armōrum **aptum tegendīs corporibus** (Liv. xxxii. 10), *a sort of armor suited to the defence of the body.*

reliqua tempora **dēmetendīs frūctibus** et **percipiendīs accommodāta** sunt (Cat. M. 70), *the other seasons are fitted to reap and gather in the harvest.*

perferendīs mīlitum **mandātīs idōneus** (Tac. Ann. i. 23), *suitable for carrying out the instructions of the soldiers.*

NOTE. — This construction is very common in Livy and later writers, infrequent in classical prose.

[1] Such are praeesse, operam dare, diem dīcere, locum capere.

[2] Such are accommodātus, aptus, ineptus, bonus, habilis, idōneus, pār, ūtilis, inūtilis. But the accusative with **ad** is common with most of these (cf. § 385. *a*).

b. The dative of the gerund and gerundive is used in certain legal phrases after nouns meaning *officers, offices, elections,* etc., to indicate the function or scope of the office etc.: —

comitia **cōnsulibus rogandīs** (Div. i. 33), *elections for nominating consuls.*
triumvir **colōniīs dēdūcundīs** (Iug. 42), *a triumvir for planting colonies.*
triumvirī **reī pūblicae cōnstituendae** (title of the Triumvirate), *triumvirs* (a commission of three) *for settling the government.*

Accusative of the Gerund and Gerundive

506. The Accusative of the Gerund and Gerundive is used after the preposition **ad,** to denote Purpose (cf. § 533): —

mē vocās **ad scrībendum** (Or. 34), *you summon me to write.*
vīvis nōn **ad dēpōnendam** sed **ad cōnfīrmandam audāciam** (Cat. i. 4), *you live not to put off but to confirm your daring.*
nactus aditūs **ad ea cōnanda** (B. C. i. 31), *having found means to undertake these things.*

Note 1. — Other prepositions appear in this construction; **inter** and **ob** a few times, **circā, in, ante,** and a few others very rarely: as, **inter agendum** (Ecl. ix. 24), *while driving.*

Note 2. — The Accusative of the gerund with a preposition never takes a direct object in classic Latin.

Ablative of the Gerund and Gerundive

507. The Ablative of the Gerund and Gerundive is used (1) to express *manner,*[1] *means, cause,* etc.; (2) after Comparatives; and (3) after the propositions **ab, dē, ex, in,** and (rarely) **prō**: —

(1) multa **pollicendō** persuādet (Iug. 46), *he persuades by large promises.*
Latīnē **loquendō** cuivīs pār (Brut. 128), *equal to any man in speaking Latin.*
hīs ipsīs legendīs (Cat. M. 21), *by reading these very things.*
obscūram atque humilem **conciendō** ad sē multitūdinem (Liv. i. 8), *calling to them a mean and obscure multitude.*
(2) nūllum officium **referendā grātiā** magis necessārium est (Off. i. 47), *no duty is more important than repaying favors.*
(3) **in rē gerendā** versārī (Cat. M. 17), *to be employed in conducting affairs.*

Note 1. — The Ablative of the Gerund and Gerundive is also very rarely used with verbs and adjectives: as, — **nec continuandō abstitit magistrātū** (Liv. ix. 34), *he did not desist from continuing his magistracy.*

Note 2. — The ablative of the gerund rarely takes a direct object in classic prose.

[1] In this use the ablative of the gerund is, in later writers nearly, and in mediæval writers entirely, equivalent to a present participle: as, — **cum ūnā diērum** FLENDŌ sēdisset, quīdam mīles generōsus iūxtā eam EQUITANDŌ vēnit (Gesta Romanorum, 66 [58]), *as one day she sat weeping, a certain knight came riding by* (compare § 507, fourth example). Hence come the Italian and Spanish forms of the present participle (as *mandando, esperando*), the true participial form becoming an adjective in those languages.

SUPINE

508. The Supine is a verbal abstract of the fourth declension (§ 94. *b*), having no distinction of tense or person, and limited to two uses. (1) The form in **-um** is the Accusative of the *end of motion* (§ 428. *i*). (2) The form in **-ū** is usually Dative of *purpose* (§ 382), but the Ablative was early confused with it.

509. The Supine in **-um** is used after verbs of *motion* to express purpose. It may take an object in the proper case:—

quid est, īmusne **sessum**? etsī **admonitum** vēnimus tē, nōn **flāgitātum** (De Or. iii. 17), *how now, shall we be seated? though we have come to remind, not to entreat you.*

nūptum dare (collocāre), *to give in marriage.*

vēnērunt **questum** iniūriās (Liv. iii. 25), *they came to complain of wrongs.*

Note 1.—The supine in **-um** is especially common with **eō**, and with the passive infinitive **īrī** forms the future infinitive passive:—

fuēre cīvēs quī rem pūblicam **perditum īrent** (Sall. Cat. 36), *there were citizens who went about to ruin the republic.*

sī scīret sē **trucīdātum īrī** (Div. ii. 22), *if he* (Pompey) *had known that he was going to be murdered.* [Rare except in Cicero. For the more usual way of expressing the future passive infinitive, see § 569. 3. *a*.]

Note 2.—The supine in **-um** is occasionally used when *motion* is merely implied.

510. The Supine in **-ū**[1] is used with a few adjectives and with the nouns **fās**, **nefās**, and **opus**, to denote an action *in reference to which* the quality is asserted:—

rem nōn modo **vīsū** foedam, sed etiam **audītū** (Phil. ii. 63), *a thing not only shocking to see, but even to hear of.*

quaerunt quid optimum **factū** sit (Verr. ii. 1. 68), *they ask what is best to do.*

sī hōc fās est **dictū** (Tusc. v. 38), *if this is lawful to say.*

vidētis nefās esse **dictū** miseram fuisse tālem senectūtem (Cat. M. 13), *you see it is a sin to say that such an old age was wretched.*

Note 1.—The supine in **-ū** is thus in appearance an Ablative of Specification (§ 418).

Note 2.—The supine in **-ū** is found especially with such adjectives as indicate an effect on the senses or the feelings, and those which denote *ease*, *difficulty*, and the like. But with **facilis**, **difficilis**, and **iūcundus**, **ad** with the gerund is more common:—

nec **vīsū** facilis nec **dictū** adfābilis ūllī (Aen. iii. 621), *he is not pleasant for any man to look at or address.*

difficilis **ad distinguendum** similitūdō (De Or. ii. 212), *a likeness difficult to distinguish.*

Note 3.—With all these adjectives the poets often use the Infinitive in the same sense: as,—facilēs aurem **praebēre** (Prop. ii. 21. 15), *indulgent to lend an ear.*

Note 4.—The supine in **-ū** with a verb is extremely rare: as,—pudet **dictū** (Tac. Agr. 32), *it is a shame to tell.* [On the analogy of **pudendum dictū**.]

[1] The only common supines in **-ū** are **audītū**, **dictū**, **factū**, **inventū**, **memorātū**, **nātū**, **vīsū**. In classic use this supine is found in comparatively few verbs. It is never followed by an object-case.

CONDITIONAL SENTENCES

511. The Conditional Sentence differs from other complex sentences in this, that the form of the main clause (APODOSIS) is determined in some degree by the nature of the subordinate clause (PROTASIS) upon the truth of which the whole statement depends. Like all complex sentences, however, the Conditional Sentence has arisen from the use of two independent sentence-forms to express the parts of a thought which was too complicated to be fully expressed by a simple sentence. But because the thoughts thus expressed are in reality closely related, as parts of a single whole, the sentences which represent them are also felt to be mutually dependent, even though the relation is not expressed by any connecting word. Thus, *Speak the word: my servant shall be healed* is a simpler and an earlier form of expression than *If thou speak the word*, etc.

The Conditional Particles were originally pronouns without conditional meaning: thus, **sī**, *if*, is a weak demonstrative of the same origin as **sīc**, *so* (**sī-ce** like **hī-ce**, see § 215. 5), and had originally the meaning of *in that way*, or *in some way*. Its relative sense (*if*) seems to have come from its use with **sīc** to make a pair of correlatives: *thus . . . thus* (see § 512. *b*).

In its origin the Conditional Sentence assumed one of two forms. The condition was from the first felt to be a condition, not a fact or a command; but, as no special sentence-form for a condition was in use, it employed for its expression either a statement of *fact* (with the Indicative) or a form of *mild command* (the Subjunctive). From the former have come all the uses of the Indicative in protasis; from the latter all the uses of the Subjunctive in protasis. The Apodosis has either (1) the Indicative, expressing the conclusion *as a fact*, and the Present and Perfect Subjunctive, expressing it originally as *future*—and hence more or less *doubtful*—or (2) the Imperfect and Pluperfect Subjunctive expressing it as *futūrum in praeteritō*,[1] and so *unfulfilled* in the present or past. Thus,—**rīdēs, mâiōre cachinnō concutitur**, *you laugh, he shakes with more boisterous laughter*, is the original form for the Indicative in protasis and apodosis; **sī rīdēs** originally means merely *you laugh in some way or other*, and so, later, IF *you laugh*. So **rogēs Aristōnem, neget**, *ask Aristo, he would say no*, is the original form of the subjunctive in protasis and apodosis; **sī rogēs** would mean *ask in some way or other*. In **sī rogārēs, negāret**, the Imperfect **rogārēs** transfers the command of **rogēs** to past time,[2] with the meaning *suppose you had asked*, and **sī** would have the same meaning as before; while **negāret** transfers the future idea of **neget** to past time, and means *he was going to deny*. Now the stating of this supposition at all gives rise to the implication that it is *untrue in point of fact*,—because, if it were true, there would ordinarily be no need to state it as a supposition: for it would then be a simple fact, and as such would be put in the indicative.[3] Such a condition or conclusion

[1] The *futūrum in praeteritō* is a tense *future relatively* to a time *absolutely past*. It denotes a future act *transferred to the point of view of past time*, and hence is naturally expressed by a past tense of the Subjunctive: thus **dīxisset**, *he would have said* = **dictūrus fuit**, *he was about to say* [but did not]. As that which looks towards the future from some point in the past has a natural limit in present time, such a tense (the imperfect subjunctive) came naturally to be used to express a *present* condition purely ideal, that is to say, contrary to fact.

[2] Compare **potius dīceret**, *he should rather have said* (§ 439. *b*).

[3] There are, however, some cases in which this implication does not arise: as,—**deciēns centēna dedissēs, nīl erat in loculīs** (Hor. S. i. 3. 15), *if you'd given him a million, there was nothing in his coffers*.

(originally past, meaning *suppose you had asked* [yesterday], *he was going to deny*) came to express an unfulfilled condition in the present: *suppose* (or *if*) *you were now asking, he would* [now] *deny* — just as in English *ought*, which originally meant *owed*,[1] has come to express a present obligation.

For the classification of Conditional Sentences, see § 513.

PROTASIS AND APODOSIS

512. A complete Conditional Sentence consists of two clauses, the Protasis and the Apodosis.

The clause containing the *condition* is called the PROTASIS; the clause containing the *conclusion* is called the APODOSIS: —

sī quī exīre volunt [PROTASIS], cōnīvēre possum [APODOSIS] (Cat. ii. 27), *if any wish to depart, I can keep my eyes shut.*

sī est in exsiliō [PROTASIS], quid amplius postulātis [APODOSIS] (Lig. 13), *if he is in exile, what more do you ask?*

It should be carefully noted that the Apodosis is the *main* clause and the Protasis the *dependent* clause.

a. The Protasis is regularly introduced by the conditional particle **sī**, *if*, or one of its compounds.

NOTE. — These compounds are **sīn, nisi, etiam sī, etsī, tametsī, tamenetsī** (see Conditional and Concessive Particles, p. 138). An Indefinite Relative, or any relative or concessive word, may also serve to introduce a conditional clause: see Conditional Relative Clauses (§§ 519, 542); Concessive Clauses (§ 527).

b. The Apodosis is often introduced by some correlative word or phrase: as, **ita, tum** (rarely **sīc**), or **eā condiciōne** etc.: —

ita enim senectūs honesta est, sī sē ipsa dēfendit (Cat. M. 38), *on this condition is old age honorable, if it defends itself.*

sī quidem mē amāret, **tum** istuc prōdesset (Ter. Eun. 446), *if he loved me, then this would be profitable.*

sīc scrībēs aliquid, sī vacābis (Att. xii. 38. 2), *if you are* (shall be) *at leisure, then you will write something.*

c. The Apodosis is the principal clause of the conditional sentence, but may at the same time be subordinate to some other clause, and so appear in the form of a Participle, an Infinitive, or a Phrase: —

sepultūrā quoque **prohibitūrī**, nī rēx humārī iussisset (Q. C. viii. 2. 12), *intending also to deprive him of burial, unless the king had ordered him to be interred.*

[1] "There was a certain lender which ought him five hundred pieces." — *Tyndale's New Testament.*

quod sī praetereā nēmō sequātur, tamen sē cum sōlā decimā legiōne itūrum [esse] (B. G. i. 40. 14), *but if no one else should follow, he would go with the tenth legion alone.*

sī quōs adversum proelium commovēret, hōs reperīre posse (id. 40. 8), *if the loss of a battle alarmed any, they might find*, etc.

NOTE. — When the Apodosis itself is in Indirect Discourse, or in any other dependent construction, the verb of the Protasis is regularly in the Subjunctive (as in the above examples, see § 589).

CLASSIFICATION OF CONDITIONS

513. Conditions are either (1) Particular or (2) General.

1. A Particular Condition refers to a definite act or series of acts occurring at some definite time.

2. A General Condition refers to any one of a class of acts which may occur (or may have occurred) at any time.

514. The principal or typical forms of Conditional Sentences may be exhibited as follows: —

PARTICULAR CONDITIONS

A. Simple Conditions (nothing implied as to fulfilment)

1. Present Time

Present Indicative in both clauses: —

sī adest, bene est, *if he is* [now] *here, it is well.*

2. Past Time

Imperfect or Perfect Indicative in both clauses: —

sī aderat, bene erat, *if he was* [then] *here, it was well.*

sī adfuit, bene fuit, *if he has been* [was] *here, it has been* [was] *well.*

B. Future Conditions (as yet unfulfilled)

1. More Vivid

a. Future Indicative in both clauses: —

sī aderit, bene erit, *if he is* (shall be) *here, it will be well.*

b. Future Perfect Indicative in protasis, Future Indicative in apodosis: —

sī adfuerit, bene erit, *if he is* (shall have been) *here, it will* [then] *be well.*

2. Less Vivid

a. Present Subjunctive in both clauses: —

sī adsit, bene sit, *if he should be* (*or* were to be) *here, it would be well.*

b. Perfect Subjunctive in protasis, Present Subjunctive in apodosis: —

sī adfuerit, bene sit, *if he should be* (should have been) *here, it would* [then] *be well.*

C. Conditions Contrary to Fact

1. Present Time

Imperfect Subjunctive in both clauses: —

sī adesset, bene esset, *if he were* [now] *here, it would be well* (but he is NOT here).

2. Past Time

Pluperfect Subjunctive in both clauses: —

sī adfuisset, bene fuisset, *if he had* [then] *been here, it would have been well* (but he was NOT here).

NOTE. — The use of tenses in Protasis is very loose in English. Thus *if he is alive now* is a PRESENT condition, to be expressed in Latin by the Present Indicative; *if he is alive next year* is a FUTURE condition, expressed in Latin by the Future Indicative. Again, *if he were here now* is a PRESENT condition contrary to fact, and would be expressed by the Imperfect Subjunctive; *if he were to see me thus* is a FUTURE condition less vivid, to be expressed by the Present Subjunctive; and so too, *if you advised him, he would attend* may be future less vivid.[1]

D. GENERAL CONDITIONS

General Conditions do not usually differ in form from Particular Conditions (*A*, *B*, and *C*), but are sometimes distinguished in the cases following: —

1. Present General Condition (Indefinite Time)

a. Present Subjunctive second person singular (Indefinite Subject) in protasis, Present Indicative in apodosis: —

sī hōc dīcās, crēditur, *if any one* [ever] *says this, it is* [always] *believed.*

b. Perfect Indicative in protasis, Present Indicative in apodosis:

sī quid dīxit, crēditur, *if he* [ever] *says anything, it is* [always] *believed.*

[1] In most English verbs the Preterite (or Past) Subjunctive is identical in form with the Preterite Indicative. Thus in such a sentence as *if he loved his father, he would not say this*, the verb *loved* is really a Preterite Subjunctive, though this does not appear from the inflection. In the verb *to be*, however, the Subjunctive *were* has been preserved and differs in form from the indicative *was*.

2. **Past General Condition** (Repeated Action in Past Time)

a. Pluperfect Indicative in protasis, Imperfect Indicative in apodosis: —

sī quid dīxerat, crēdēbātur, *if he* [ever] *said anything, it was* [always] *believed.*

b. Imperfect Subjunctive in protasis, Imperfect Indicative in apodosis: —

sī quid dīceret, crēdēbātur, *if he* [ever] *said anything, it was* [always] *believed* (= whatever he said was always believed).[1]

PARTICULAR CONDITIONS

Simple Present and Past Conditions — Nothing Implied

515. In the statement of Present and Past conditions *whose falsity is* NOT *implied*, the Present and Past tenses of the Indicative are used in both Protasis and Apodosis: —

sī tū exercitusque **valētis,** bene **est** (Fam. v. 2), *if you and the army are well, it is well.* [Present Condition.]

haec igitur, sī Rōmae **es**; sīn abes, aut etiam sī **ades,** haec negōtia sīc sē **habent** (Att. v. 18), *this, then, if you are at Rome; but if you are away — or even if you are there — these matters are as follows.* [Present Condition.]

sī Caesarem **probātis,** in mē **offenditis** (B. C. ii. 32. 10), *if you favor Cæsar, you find fault with me.* [Present Condition.]

sī quī māgnīs ingeniīs in eō genere **exstitērunt,** nōn satis Graecōrum glōriae **respondērunt** (Tusc. i. 3), *if any have shown themselves of great genius in that department, they have failed to compete with the glory of the Greeks.* [Past General Condition, not distinguished in form from Particular.]

accēpī Rōmā sine epistulā tuā fasciculum litterārum in quō, sī modo **valuistī** et Rōmae **fuistī,** Philotīmī dūcō esse culpam nōn tuam (Att. v. 17), *I have received from Rome a bundle of letters without any from you, which, provided you have been well and at Rome, I take to be the fault of Philotimus, not yours.* [Mixed: Past condition and Present conclusion.]

quās litterās, sī Rōmae **es, vidēbis** putēsne reddendās (id. v. 18), *as to this letter, if you are at Rome, you will see whether in your opinion it ought to be delivered.* [Mixed: Present and Future.]

sī nēmō **impetrāvit,** adroganter **rogō** (Lig. 30), *if no one has succeeded in obtaining it, my request is presumptuous.* [Past and Present.]

[1] Cf. the Greek forms corresponding to the various types of conditions: —

A. 1. εἰ πράσσει τοῦτο, καλῶς ἔχει.	2. εἰ ἔπρασσε τοῦτο, καλῶς εἶχεν.
B. 1. ἐὰν πράσσῃ τοῦτο, καλῶς ἕξει.	2. εἰ πράσσοι τοῦτο, καλῶς ἂν ἔχοι.
C. 1. εἰ ἔπρασσε τοῦτο, καλῶς ἂν εἶχεν.	2. εἰ ἔπραξε τοῦτο, καλῶς ἂν ἔσχεν.
D. 1. ἐάν τις κλέπτῃ, κολάζεται.	2. εἴ τις κλέπτοι, ἐκολάζετο.

a. In these conditions the apodosis need not always be in the Indicative, but may assume any form, according to the sense: —

sī placet . . . **videāmus** (Cat. M. 15), *if you please, let us see.* [Hortatory Subjunctive, § 439.]

sī nōndum satis cernitis, **recordāminī** (Mil. 61), *if you do not yet see clearly, recollect.* [Imperative.]

sī quid habēs certius, **velim** scīre (Att. iv. 10), *if you have any trustworthy information, I should like to know it.* [Subjunctive of Modesty, § 447. 1.]

NOTE. — Although the *form* of these conditions does not imply anything as to the truth of the supposition, the sense or the context may of course have some such implication: —

nōlīte, sī in nostrō omnium flētū nūllam lacrimam aspexistis Milōnis, hōc minus eī parcere (Mil. 92), *do not, if amid the weeping of us all you have seen no tear* [in the eyes] *of Milo, spare him the less for that.*

petimus ā vōbīs, iūdicēs, sī qua dīvīna in tantīs ingeniīs commendātiō dēbet esse, ut eum in vestram accipiātis fidem (Arch. 31), *we ask you, judges, if there ought to be anything in such genius to recommend it to us as by a recommendation of the gods, that you receive him under your protection.*

In these two passages, the protasis really expresses *cause:* but the cause is put by the speaker in the form of a non-committal condition. His hearers are to draw the inference for themselves. In this way the desired impression is made on their minds more effectively than if an outspoken causal clause had been used.

Future Conditions

516. Future Conditions may be *more vivid* or *less vivid.*

1. In a more vivid future condition the protasis makes a distinct supposition of a future case, the apodosis expressing what *will be* the logical result.

2. In a less vivid future condition, the supposition is less distinct, the apodosis expressing what *would be* the result in the case supposed.

a. In the *more vivid* future condition the Future Indicative is used in both protasis and apodosis: —

sānābimur, sī **volēmus** (Tusc. iii. 13), *we shall be healed if we wish.*

quod sī legere aut audīre **volētis**, . . . **reperiētis** (Cat. M. 20), *if you will* [shall wish to] *read or hear, you will find.*

NOTE. — In English the protasis is usually expressed by the Present Indicative, rarely by the Future with SHALL. Often in Latin the Present Indicative is found in the protasis of a condition of this kind (cf. § 468): —

sī vincimus, omnia nōbīs tūta erunt; sīn metū cesserimus, eadem illa advorsa fīent (Sall. Cat. 58), *if we conquer, all things will be safe for us; but if we yield through fear, those same things will become hostile.*

sī pereō, hominum manibus periisse iuvābit (Aen. iii. 606), *if I perish, it will be pleasant to have perished at the hands of men.*

b. In the *less vivid* future condition the Present Subjunctive is used in both protasis and apodosis: —

> haec sī tēcum patria **loquātur**, nōnne impetrāre **dēbeat** (Cat. i. 19), *if your country should thus speak with you, ought she not to prevail?*
>
> quod sī quis deus mihi **largiātur**, . . . valdē **recūsem** (Cat. M. 83), *but if some god were to grant me this, I should stoutly refuse.*

NOTE. — The Present Subjunctive sometimes stands in protasis with the Future (or the Present) Indicative in apodosis from a change in the point of view: —[1]

> sī dīligenter **attendāmus**, **intellegēmus** (Inv. ii. 44), *if we attend* (should attend) *carefully, we shall understand.*
>
> nisi hōc **dīcat**, "iūre fēcī," nōn **habet** dēfēnsiōnem (id. i. 18), *unless he should say this, "I acted justifiably," he has no defence.*

c. If the conditional act is regarded as *completed* before that of the apodosis begins, the Future Perfect is substituted for the Future Indicative in protasis, and the Perfect Subjunctive for the Present Subjunctive: —

> sīn cum potuerō nōn **vēnerō**, tum erit inimīcus (Att. ix. 2 A. 2), *but if I do not come when I can, he will be unfriendly.*
>
> sī ā corōnā **relictus sim**, nōn queam dīcere (Brut. 192), *if I should be deserted by the circle of listeners, I should not be able to speak.*

NOTE. — The Future Perfect is often used in the apodosis of a future condition: as, — vehementer mihi grātum **fēceris**, sī hunc adulēscentem hūmānitāte tuā comprehenderis (Fam. xiii. 15), *you will do* (will have done) *me a great favor, if you receive this young man with your usual courtesy.*

d. Any form denoting or implying future time may stand in the apodosis of a future condition. So the Imperative, the participles in **-dus** and **-rus**, and verbs of *necessity, possibility,* and the like: —

> alius fīnis **cōnstituendus est**, sī prius quid maximē reprehendere Scīpiō solitus sit dīxerō (Lael. 59), *another limit must be set, if I first state what Scipio was wont most to find fault with.*
>
> sī mē praecēperit fātum, vōs mandāsse **mementō** (Q. C. ix. 6. 26), *if fate cuts me off too soon, do you remember that I ordered this.*
>
> nisi oculīs vīderitis īnsidiās Milōnī ā Clōdiō factās, nec **dēprecātūrī sumus** nec **postulātūrī** (Mil. 6), *unless you see with your own eyes the plots laid against Milo by Clodius, I shall neither beg nor demand,* etc.
>
> nōn **possum** istum accūsāre, sī cupiam (Verr. iv. 87), *I cannot accuse him, if I should* (so) *desire.*

[1] It often depends entirely upon the view of the writer at the moment, and not upon the nature of the condition, whether it shall be stated vividly or not; as in the proverbial "If the sky falls, we shall catch larks" the impossible condition is ironically put in the vivid form, to illustrate the absurdity of some other supposed condition stated by some one else.

e. Rarely the Perfect Indicative is used in apodosis with a Present or even a Future (or Future Perfect) in protasis, to represent the conclusion rhetorically as *already accomplished:* —

sī hōc bene fīxum in animō est, **vīcistis** (Liv. xxi. 44), *if this is well fixed in your minds, you have conquered.* [For *you will have conquered.*]

sī eundem [animum] habueritis, **vīcimus** (id. xxi. 43), *if you shall have kept the same spirit, we have conquered.*

f. A future condition is frequently thrown back into past time, without implying that it is contrary to fact (§ 517). In such cases the Imperfect or Pluperfect Subjunctive may be used: —

nōn poterat, **nisi** dēcertāre **vellet** (B. C. iii. 44), *he was not able, unless he wished to fight.*

tumulus appāruit, . . . sī lūce palam **īrētur** hostis praeventūrus erat (Liv. xxii. 24), *a hill appeared . . . if they should go openly by daylight, the enemy would prevent.* [The first two appear like Indirect Discourse, but are not. An observer describing the situation in the first example as *present* would say **nōn potest nisi velit** (see *d*), and no indirect discourse would be thought of.]

Caesar **sī peteret,** . . . nōn quicquam prōficeret (Hor. S. i. 3. 4), *if even Cæsar were to ask, he would gain nothing.* [Here the construction is not contrary to fact, but is simply **sī petat, nōn prōficiat,** thrown into past time.]

Conditions Contrary to Fact

517. In the statement of a supposition *impliedly false*, the Imperfect and Pluperfect Subjunctive are used in both protasis and apodosis.[1] The Imperfect refers to *present time*, the Pluperfect to *past:* —

sī **vīveret**, verba êius **audīrētis** (Rosc. Com. 42), *if he were living, you would hear his words.* [Present.]

nisi tū **āmīsissēs**, numquam **recēpissem** (Cat. M. 11), *unless you had lost it, I should not have recovered it.* [Past.]

sī meum cōnsilium **valuisset**, tū hodiē **egērēs**, rēs pūblica nōn tot ducēs **āmīsisset** (Phil. ii. 37), *if my judgment had prevailed* [as it did not], *you would this day be a beggar, and the republic would not have lost so many leaders.* [Mixed Present and Past.]

[1] The implication of falsity, in this construction, is not inherent in the subjunctive; but comes from *the transfer of a future condition to past time.* Thus the time for the happening of the condition has, at the moment of writing, already passed; so that, if the condition remains a *condition*, it must be contrary to fact. So past forms of the indicative implying a future frequently take the place of the subjunctive in apodosis in this construction (see *c*, *d*, below, and § 511).

a. In conditions contrary to fact the Imperfect often refers to *past time*, both in protasis and apodosis, especially when a *repeated or continued action* is denoted, or when the condition *if true would still exist:*

sī nihil litterīs **adiuvārentur**, numquam sē ad eārum studium contulissent (Arch. 16), *if they had not been helped at all by literature, they never would have given their attention to the study of it.* [Without the condition, **adiuvābantur.**]

hīc sī mentis **esset** suae, ausus esset ēdūcere exercitum (Pison. 50), *if he were of sane mind, would he have dared to lead out the army?* [Here **esset** denotes a continued state, past as well as present.]

nōn concidissent, nisi illud receptāculum classibus nostrīs **patēret** (Verr. ii. 3), [the power of Carthage] *would not have fallen, unless that station had been* [constantly] *open to our fleets.* [Without the condition, **patēbat.**]

b. In the apodosis of a condition contrary to fact the past tenses of the Indicative may be used to express what was *intended*, or *likely*, or *already begun.* In this use, the Imperfect Indicative corresponds in time to the Imperfect Subjunctive, and the Perfect or Pluperfect Indicative to the Pluperfect Subjunctive: —

sī licitum esset, mātrēs **veniēbant** (Verr. v. 129), *the mothers were coming if it had been allowed.*

in amplexūs fīliae **ruēbat**, nisi līctōrēs obstitissent (Tac. Ann. xvi. 32), *he was about rushing into his daughter's arms, unless the lictors had opposed.*

iam tūta **tenēbam**, nī gēns crūdēlis ferrō invāsisset (Aen. vi. 358), *I was just reaching a place of safety, had not the fierce people attacked me.*

NOTE 1. — Here the apodosis may be regarded as elliptical. Thus, — mātrēs veniēbant (et vēnissent), *the matrons were coming* (and would have kept on) *if*, etc.

NOTE 2. — With **paene** (and sometimes **prope**), *almost*, the Perfect Indicative is used in the apodosis of a past condition contrary to fact: as, — pōns iter **paene** hostibus **dedit**, nī ūnus vir fuisset (Liv. ii. 10), *the bridge had almost given a passage to the foe, if it had not been for one hero.*

c. Verbs and other expressions denoting *necessity*, *propriety*, *possibility*, *duty*, when used in the apodosis of a condition contrary to fact, may be put in the Imperfect or Perfect Indicative.

Such are **oportet, decet, dēbeō, possum, necesse est, opus est**, and the Second Periphrastic Conjugation: —[1]

nōn **potuit** fierī sapiēns, nisi nātus esset (Fin. ii. 103), *he could not have become a sage, if he had not been born.*

sī prīvātus esset hōc tempore, tamen is **erat dēligendus** (Manil. 50), *if he were at this time a private citizen, yet he ought to be appointed.*

[1] Observe that all these expressions contain the idea of futurity (cf. p. 328, footnote). Thus, **decet mē** [**hodiē**] **īre crās**, means *it is proper for me* [to-day] *to go to-morrow;* and, **decēbat mē** [**herī**] **īre hodiē**, *it was proper for me* [yesterday] *to go to-day*, usually with the implication that *I have not gone as I was bound to do.*

quod esse caput **dēbēbat**, sī probārī posset (Fin. iv. 23), *what ought to be the main point, if it could be proved.*

sī ita putāsset, certē **optābilius** Milōnī **fuit** (Mil. 31), *if he had thought so, surely it would have been preferable for Milo.*

NOTE 1.—In Present conditions the Imperfect Subjunctive (**oportēret, possem**, etc.) is the rule, the Indicative being rare; in Past conditions both the Subjunctive (usually Pluperfect) and the Indicative (usually Perfect) are common.

For **pār erat, melius fuit**, and the like, followed by the infinitive, see § 521. N.

NOTE 2.—The indicative construction is carried still further in poetry: as,—sī nōn alium iactāret odōrem, laurus erat (Georg. ii. 133), *it were a laurel, but for giving out a different odor.*

d. The participle in **-ūrus** with **eram** or **fuī** may take the place of an Imperfect or Pluperfect Subjunctive in the apodosis of a condition contrary to fact:—

quid enim **futūrum fuit** [= fuisset], sī . . . (Liv. ii. 1), *what would have happened if*, etc.

relictūrī agrōs erant, nisi ad eōs Metellus litterās mīsisset (Verr. iii. 121), *they would have abandoned their fields, if Metellus had not sent them a letter.*

neque ambigitur quīn . . . id **factūrus fuerit**, sī . . . (Liv. ii. 1), *nor is there any question that he would have done it, if*, etc. [Direct: **fēcisset**.]

adeō parāta sēditiō fuit ut Othōnem **raptūrī fuerint**, nī incerta noctis timuissent (Tac. H. i. 26), *so far advanced was the conspiracy that they would have seized upon Otho, had they not feared the hazards of the night.* [In a main clause: **rapuissent, nī timuissent**.]

e. The Present Subjunctive is sometimes used in poetry in the protasis and apodosis of conditions contrary to fact:—

nī comes **admoneat, inruat** (Aen. vi. 293), *had not his companion warned him, he would have rushed on.* [Cf. tū sī hīc sīs, aliter **sentiās** (Ter. And. 310), *if you were in my place, you would think differently.*]

NOTE 1.—This is probably a remnant of an old construction (see next note).

NOTE 2.—In old Latin the Present Subjunctive (as well as the Imperfect) is used in present conditions contrary to fact and the Imperfect (more rarely the Pluperfect) in past conditions of the same kind. Thus it appears that the Imperfect Subjunctive, like the Imperfect Indicative, once denoted past time, even in conditional sentences. Gradually, however, in conditional sentences, the Present Subjunctive was restricted to the less vivid future and the Imperfect (in the main) to the present contrary to fact, while the Pluperfect was used in past conditions of this nature. The old construction, however, seems to have been retained as an archaism in poetry.

f. In Plautus and Terence **absque mē** (**tē**, etc.) is sometimes used to introduce conditions contrary to fact:—

absque tē **esset**, hodiē nusquam **vīverem** (Pl. Men. 1022), *if it were not for you, I should not be alive to-day.*

absque eō **esset**, rēctē ego mihi **vīdissem** (Ter. Ph. 188), *if it had not been for him, I should have looked out for myself.*

GENERAL CONDITIONS

518. General Conditions (§ 513. 2) have usually the same forms as Particular Conditions. But they are sometimes distinguished in the following cases: —

a. The Subjunctive is often used in the *second person singular*, to denote the act of an indefinite subject (*you* = *any one*). Here the Present Indicative of a *general truth* may stand in the apodosis: —

> vīta hūmāna prope utī ferrum est: sī **exerceās, conteritur**; sī nōn **exerceās**, tamen rōbīgō **interficit** (Cato de M.), *human life is very like iron: if you use it, it wears away; if you don't use it, rust still destroys it.*
>
> virtūtem necessāriō glōria, etiamsī tū id nōn **agās, cōnsequitur** (Tusc. i. 91), *glory necessarily follows virtue, even if that is not one's aim.*
>
> sī prohibita impūne **trānscenderis**, neque metus ultrā neque pudor **est** (Tac. Ann. iii. 54), *if you once overstep the bounds with impunity, there is no fear or shame any more.*

b. In a general condition in present time, the protasis often takes the Perfect Indicative, and the apodosis the Present Indicative. For past time, the Pluperfect is used in the protasis, and the Imperfect in the apodosis: —

> sī quōs aliquā parte membrōrum inūtilīs **nōtāvērunt**, necārī **iubent** (Q. C. ix. 1. 25), *if they* [ever] *mark any infirm in any part of their limbs, they* [always] *order them to be put to death.* [Present.]
>
> sī ā persequendō hostīs dēterrēre **nequīverant**, ab tergō **circumveniēbant** (Iug. 50), *if* [ever] *they were unable to prevent the enemy from pursuing, they* [always] *surrounded them in the rear.* [Past.]

c. In later writers (rarely in Cicero and Cæsar), the Imperfect and Pluperfect Subjunctive are used in protasis, with the Imperfect Indicative in apodosis, to state a *repeated* or *customary* action in past time (*Iterative Subjunctive*): —

> sī quis ā dominō **prehenderētur**, concursū mīlitum **ēripiēbātur** (B. C. iii. 110), *if any* (runaway) *was arrested by his master, he was* (always) *rescued by a mob of soldiers.*
>
> accūsātōrēs, sī facultās **incideret**, poenīs **adficiēbantur** (Tac. Ann. vi. 30), *the accusers, whenever opportunity offered, were visited with punishment.*
>
> sī quis collēgam **appellāsset**, ab eō ita **discēdēbat** ut paenitēret nōn priōris dēcrētō stetisse (Liv. iii. 36. 8), *if any one appealed to a colleague, he* [always] *came off in such case that he repented not having submitted to the decree of the former decemvir.* [Cf. Sōcratēs, quam sē cumque in partem **dedisset**, omnium **fuit** facile prīnceps (De Or. iii. 60), *in whatever direction Socrates turned himself, he was* (always) *easily the foremost* (if in any, etc.).]

Conditional Relative Clauses

519. A clause introduced by a Relative Pronoun or Relative Adverb may express a condition and take any of the constructions of Protasis[1] (§ 514): —

quī enim vitiīs modum **adpōnit**, is partem suscipit vitiōrum (Tusc. iv. 42), *he who* [only] *sets a limit to faults, takes up the side of the faults.* [= **sī quis adpōnit.** Present, nothing implied.]

quī mentīrī **solet**, pēierāre cōnsuēvit (Rosc. Com. 46), *whoever is in the habit of lying, is accustomed to swear falsely.* [= **sī quis solet.** Present, nothing implied.]

quicquid potuit, potuit ipsa per sē (Leg. Agr. i. 20), *whatever power she had, she had by herself.* [= **sī quid potuit.** Past, nothing implied.]

quod **quī faciet**, nōn aegritūdine sōlum vacābit, sed, etc. (Tusc. iv. 38), *and he who does* (shall do) *this, will be free not only*, etc. [= **sī quis faciet.** Future, more vivid.]

quisquis hūc **vēnerit**, vāpulābit (Pl. Am. 309), *whoever comes here shall get a thrashing.* [= **sī quis vēnerit.** Future, more vivid.]

quō volēs, sequar (Clu. 71), *whithersoever you wish* (shall wish), *I will follow.* [= **sī quō volēs.** Future, more vivid.]

philosophia, cui **quī pāreat**, omne tempus aetātis sine molestiā possit dēgere (Cat. M. 2), *philosophy, which if any one should obey, he would be able to spend his whole life without vexation.* [= **sī quis pāreat.** Future, less vivid.]

quaecumque vōs causa hūc **attulisset**, laetārer (De Or. ii. 15), *I should be glad, whatever cause had brought you here* (i.e. if any other, as well as the one which did). [= **sī . . . attulisset.** Contrary to fact.]

The relative in this construction is always indefinite in *meaning*, and very often in *form*.

520. The special constructions of General Conditions are sometimes found in Conditional Relative Clauses: —

1. The Second Person Singular of the Subjunctive in the protasis with the Indicative of a *general truth* in the apodosis (§ 518. *a*): —

bonus tantum modo sēgnior **fit ubi neglegās**, at malus improbior (Iug. 31. 28), *a good man merely becomes less diligent when you don't watch him, but a bad man becomes more shameless.* [Present General Condition.]

2. The Perfect or Pluperfect Indicative in the protasis and the Present or Imperfect Indicative in the apodosis (§ 518. *b*): —

cum hūc **vēnī**, hōc ipsum nihil agere mē **dēlectat** (De Or. ii. 24), *whenever I come here, this very doing nothing delights me* (whenever I have come, etc.). [Present General Condition.]

[1] As in the Greek ὃς ἄν, ὅταν, etc.; and in statutes in English, where the phrases *if any person shall* and *whoever shall* are used indifferently.

cum rosam **vīderat,** tum incipere vēr **arbitrābātur** (Verr. v. 27), *whenever he saw* (had seen) *a rose, then he thought spring was beginning.* [Past General Condition.]

3. In later writers (rarely in Cicero and Cæsar) the Imperfect or Pluperfect Subjunctive in the protasis and the Imperfect Indicative in the apodosis (§ 518. *c*): —

ubi imbēcillitās māteriae postulāre **vidērētur,** pīlae **interpōnuntur** (B. C. ii. 16), *wherever the weakness of the timber seemed to require, piles were put between.* [Past General Condition: **interpōnuntur = interpōnēbantur.**]

quōcumque sē **intulisset,** victōriam sēcum **trahēbat** (Liv. vi. 8), *wherever he advanced, he carried victory with him.* [Past General Condition.]

Condition Disguised

521. In many sentences properly conditional, the Protasis is not expressed by a conditional clause, but is stated in some other form of words or implied in the nature of the thought.

a. The condition may be implied in a Clause, or in a Participle, Noun, Adverb, or some other word or phrase: —

facile mē paterer — illō **ipsō** iūdice **quaerente** — prō Sex. Rōsciō dīcere (Rosc. Am. 85), *I should readily allow myself to speak for Roscius if that very judge were conducting the trial.* [Present contrary to fact: **sī quaereret, paterer.**]

nōn mihi, nisi **admonitō,** vēnisset in mentem (De Or. ii. 180), *it would not have come into my mind unless* [I had been] *reminded.* [Past contrary to fact: **nisi admonitus essem.**]

nūlla alia gēns tantā mōle clādis nōn obruta esset (Liv. xxii. 54), *there is no other people that would not have been crushed by such a weight of disaster.* [Past contrary to fact: **sī alia fuisset.**]

nēmō umquam **sine** māgnā **spē** immortālitātis sē prō patriā offerret ad mortem (Tusc. i. 32), *no one, without great hope of immortality, would ever expose himself to death for his country.* [Present contrary to fact: **nisi māgnam spem habēret.**]

quid hunc paucōrum annōrum **accessiō** iuvāre potuisset (Lael. 11), *what good could the addition of a few years have done him* (if they had been added)? [Past contrary to fact: **sī accessissent.**]

quid igitur mihi ferārum laniātus oberit **nihil sentientī** (Tusc. i. 104), *what harm will the mangling by wild beasts do me if I don't feel anything* (feeling nothing)? [Future more vivid: **sī nihil sentiam.**]

incitāta semel prōclīvī lābuntur sustinērīque nūllō modō possunt (id. iv. 42), *if once given a push, they slide down rapidly and can in no way be checked.* [Present General: **sī incitāta sunt.**]

NOTE.—In several phrases denoting *necessity, propriety*, or the like, the Imperfect, Perfect, or Pluperfect Indicative of esse is used in the apodosis of a condition contrary to fact, the protasis being implied in a subject infinitive (cf. 517. *c*):—

quantō melius fuerat prōmissum nōn esse servātum (Off. iii. 94), *how much better would it have been if the promise had not been kept!* [prōmissum . . . servātum = sī prōmissum nōn esset servātum.]

morī praeclārum fuit (Att. viii. 2. 2), *it would have been honorable to die.*

sed erat aequius Triārium aliquid dē dissēnsiōne nostrā **iūdicāre** (Fin. ii. 119), *but it would be more equitable if Triarius passed judgment on our dispute.* [Triārium iūdicāre = sī Triārius iūdicāret.]

satius fuit āmittere mīlitēs (Inv. ii. 73), *it would have been better to lose the soldiers.* [āmittere = sī āmīsisset.]

b. The condition may be contained in a wish (*Optative Subjunctive*), or expressed as an exhortation or command (*Hortatory Subjunctive* or *Imperative*):—

utinam quidem **fuissem**! molestus nōbīs nōn esset (Fam. xii. 3), *I wish I had been* [chief]: *he would not now be troubling us* (i.e. if I had been). [Optative Subjunctive.]

nātūram **expellās** furcā, tamen ūsque recurret (Hor. Ep. i. 10. 24), *drive out nature with a pitchfork, still she will ever return.* [Hortatory.]

rogēs enim Aristōnem, neget (Fin. iv. 69), *for ask Aristo, he would deny.*

manent ingenia senibus, modo **permaneat** studium et industria (Cat. M. 22), *old men keep their mental powers, only let them keep their zeal and diligence* (§ 528. N.). [Hortatory.]

tolle hanc opīniōnem, lūctum sustuleris (Tusc. i. 30), *remove this notion, and you will have done away with grief.* [Imperative.]

NOTE.—The so-called *Concessive Subjunctive* with ut and nē often has the force of protasis (§ 527. *a.* N.): as,—ut enim ratiōnem Platō nūllam adferret, ipsā auctōritāte mē frangeret (Tusc. i. 49), *even if Plato gave no reasons,* [still] *he would overpower me by his mere authority.*

c. Rarely the condition takes the form of an *independent clause:*

rīdēs: mâiōre cachinnō concutitur (Iuv. iii. 100), *you laugh; he shakes with louder laughter* (= if you laugh, he shakes).

commovē: sentiēs (Tusc. iv. 54), *stir him up,* [and] *you'll find,* etc.

dē paupertāte agitur: multī patientēs pauperēs commemorantur (id. iii. 57), *we speak of poverty; many patient poor are mentioned.*

For Conditional Relative Clauses, see §§ 519, 520.

Condition Omitted

522. The Protasis is often wholly omitted, but may be inferred from the course of the argument:—

poterat Sextilius impūne negāre: quis enim redargueret (Fin. ii. 55), *Sextilius might have denied with impunity; for who would prove him wrong* (if he had denied)?

a. In expressions signifying *necessity, propriety,* and the like, the Indicative may be used in the apodosis of implied conditions, either future or contrary to fact: —

quod contrā **decuit** ab illō meum [corpus cremārī] (Cat. M. 84), *whereas on the other hand mine ought to have been burnt by him.*

nam nōs **decēbat** domum lūgēre ubi esset aliquis in lūcem ēditus (Tusc. i. 115), *for it were fitting for us to mourn the house where a man has been born* (but we do not).

quantō **melius fuerat** (Off. iii. 94), *how much better it would have been.*

illud **erat aptius**, aequum cuique concēdere (Fin. iv. 2), *it would be more fitting to yield each one his rights.*

ipsum enim exspectāre **māgnum fuit** (Phil. ii. 103), *would it have been a great matter to wait for the man himself?*

longum est ea dīcere, sed . . . (Sest. 12), *it would be tedious to tell,* etc. [Future.]

Note 1.—In this construction, the Imperfect Indicative refers to *present time;* the Pluperfect to simple *past* time, like the Perfect. Thus **oportēbat** means *it ought to be* [now], *but is not;* **oportuerat** means *it ought to have been, but was not.*

Note 2.—In many cases it is impossible to say whether a protasis was present to the mind of the speaker or not (see third example above).

Complex Conditions

523. Either the Protasis or the Apodosis may be a complex idea in which the main statement is made with expressed or implied qualifications. In such cases the true logical relation of the parts is sometimes disguised: —

sī quis hōrum dīxisset . . . sī verbum dē rē pūblicā fēcisset . . . multa plūra dīxisse quam dīxisset putārētur (Rosc. Am. 2), *if any of these had spoken, in case he had said a word about politics he would be thought to have said much more than he did say.* [Here the apodosis of **dīxisset** is the whole of the following statement (**sī . . . putārētur**), which is itself conditioned by a protasis of its own: **sī verbum**, etc.].

quod sī in hōc mundō fierī sine deō nōn potest, nē in sphaerā quidem eōsdem mōtūs sine dīvīnō ingeniō potuisset imitārī (Tusc. i. 63), *now if that cannot be done in this universe without divine agency, no more could* [Archimedes] *in his orrery have imitated the same revolutions without divine genius.* [Here **sī potest** (a protasis with nothing implied) has for its apodosis the whole clause which follows, but **potuisset** has a contrary-to-fact protasis of its own implied in **sine . . . ingeniō**.]

peream male sī nōn optimum erat (Hor. S. ii. 1. 6), *confound me* (may I perish wretchedly) *if it would n't be better.* [Here **peream** is apodosis to the rest of the sentence, while the true protasis to **optimum erat**, contrary to fact, is omitted.]

Clauses of Comparison (Conclusion Omitted)

524. Conditional Clauses of Comparison take the Subjunctive, usually in the Present or Perfect unless the sequence of tenses requires the Imperfect or Pluperfect.

Such clauses are introduced by the comparative particles **tamquam, tamquam sī, quasi, ac sī, ut sī, velut sī** (later **velut**), poetic **ceu** (all meaning *as if*), and by **quam sī** (*than if*): —

tamquam clausa **sit** Asia (Fam. xii. 9), *as if Asia were closed.*
tamquam sī claudus **sim** (Pl. Asin. 427), *just as if I were lame.*
ita hōs [honōrēs] petunt, quasi honestē **vīxerint** (Iug. 85), *they seek them* (offices) *just as if they had lived honorably.*
quasi vērō nōn speciē vīsa **iūdicentur** (Acad. ii. 58), *as if forsooth visible things were not judged by their appearance.*
similiter facis ac sī mē **rogēs** (N. D. iii. 8), *you do exactly as if you asked me.*
crūdēlitātem horrērent velut sī cōram **adesset** (B. G. i. 32), *they dreaded his cruelty* (they said), *as if he were present in person.*
hīc ingentem pūgnam cernimus ceu cētera nusquam bella **forent** (Aen. ii. 438), *here we saw a great battle, as if there were no fighting elsewhere.* [But sometimes with the indicative in poetry, as id. v. 88.]
magis ā mē abesse vidēbāre quam sī domī **essēs** (Att. vi. 5), *you seemed to be absent from me more than if you were at home.*

NOTE 1.—These subjunctive clauses are really future conditions with apodosis implied in the particle itself. Thus in **tamquam sī claudus sim** the protasis is introduced by **sī**, and the apodosis implied in **tamquam**.

NOTE 2.—The English idiom would lead us to expect the Imperfect and Pluperfect Subjunctive (contrary to fact) with these particles; but the point of view is different in the two languages. Thus the second example above is translated *just as if I were lame*,—as if it were a present condition contrary to fact; but it really means *just as* [it would be] *if I should* [at some future time] *be lame*, and so is a less vivid future condition requiring the Present Subjunctive. Similarly **quasi honestē vīxerint**, *as if they had lived honorably*, is really *as* [they would do in the future] *if they should have lived honorably* and so requires the Perfect Subjunctive (§ 516. *c*).

a. Even after a primary tense, the Imperfect or Pluperfect Subjunctive (*contrary to fact*) is often used in conditional clauses of comparison: —

aequē ā tē petō ac sī mea negōtia **essent** (Fam. xiii. 43), *I entreat you as much as if it were my own business.*
êius negōtium sīc velim suscipiās ut sī **esset** rēs mea (id. vii. 20. 1), *I would have you undertake his business as though it were my affair.*

NOTE.—The practice differs with the different particles. Thus in Cicero a clause with **tamquam** or **quasi** almost always observes the sequence of tenses, but with **quam sī** the Imperfect or Pluperfect is the rule.

Use of *sī* and its Compounds

525. The uses of some of the more common Conditional Particles may be stated as follows: —

a. **Sī** is used for *affirmative*, **nisi** (**nī**) and **sī nōn** for *negative* conditions.

1. With **nisi** (generally *unless*) the apodosis is stated as *universally* true *except* in the single case supposed, in which case it is (impliedly) *not true*: —

nisi Conōn adest, maereō, *unless Conon is here, I mourn* (i.e. I am always in a state of grief except in the single case of Conon's presence, in which case I am not).

2. With **sī nōn** (*if not*) the apodosis is only stated as true *in the* (negative) *case supposed*, but as to other cases no statement is made: —

sī Conōn **nōn** adest, maereō, *if Conon is not here, I mourn* (i.e. I mourn in the single case of Conon's absence, nothing being said as to other cases in which I may or may not mourn).

Note. — It often makes no difference in which of these forms the condition is stated.

3. Sometimes **nisi sī**, *except if, unless*, occurs: —

nōlī putāre mē ad quemquam longiōrēs epistulās scrībere, **nisi sī** quis ad mē plūra scrīpsit (Fam. xiv. 2), . . . *except in case one writes more to me.*

Note. — **Nī** is an old form surviving in a few conventional phrases and reappearing in poets and later writers.

b. **Nisi vērō** and **nisi forte** regularly introduce an objection or exception *ironically*, and take the Indicative: —

nisi vērō L. Caesar crūdēlior **vīsus est** (Cat. iv. 13), *unless indeed Lucius Cæsar seemed too cruel.*

nisi forte volumus Epicūrēōrum opīniōnem sequī (Fat. 37), *unless, to be sure, we choose to follow the notion of the Epicureans.*

Note. — This is the regular way of introducing a *reductio ad absurdum* in Latin. Nisi alone is sometimes used in this sense: as, — nisi ūnum hōc faciam ut in puteō cēnam coquant (Pl. Aul. 365), *unless I do this one thing,* [make them] *cook dinner in the well.*

c. **Sīve** (**seu**) . . . **sīve** (**seu**), *whether . . . or*, introduce a condition in the form of an *alternative*. They may be used with any form of condition, or with different forms in the two members. Often also they are used without a verb: —

nam illō locō libentissimē soleō ūtī, **sīve** quid mēcum ipse cōgitō, **sīve** quid scrībō aut legō (Legg. ii. 1), *for I enjoy myself most in that place, whether I am thinking by myself, or am either writing or reading.*

Note. — Sīve . . . seu and seu . . . sīve are late or poetic.

d. **Sīn**, *but if*, often introduces a supposition contrary to one that precedes: —

accūsātor illum dēfendet sī poterit; sīn minus poterit, negābit (Inv. ii. 88), *the accuser will defend him if he can; but if he cannot, he will deny.*

e. **Nisi** is often used loosely by the comic poets in the sense of *only* when a negative (usually **nesciō**) is expressed, or easily understood, in the main clause: —

nesciō: **nisi** mē dīxisse nēminī certō sciō (Ter. Ph. 952), *I don't know: only I am sure that I have n't told anybody.*

CONCESSIVE CLAUSES

526. The concessive idea is rather vague and general, and takes a variety of forms, each of which has its distinct history. Sometimes concession is expressed by the Hortatory Subjunctive in a sentence grammatically independent (§ 440), but it is more frequently and more precisely expressed by a dependent clause introduced by a concessive particle. The concessive force lies chiefly in the Conjunctions (which are indefinite or conditional in origin), and is often made clearer by an adversative particle (**tamen, certē**) in the main clause. As the Subjunctive may be used in independent clauses to express a concession, it is also employed in concessive clauses, and somewhat more frequently than the indicative.

527. The Particles of Concession (meaning *although, granting that*) are **quamvīs, ut, licet, etsī, tametsī, etiam sī, quamquam,** and **cum.** Some of these take the Subjunctive, others the Indicative, according to the nature of the clause which each introduces.

a. **Quamvīs** and **ut** take the Subjunctive: —

quamvīs ipsī īnfantēs **sint**, tamen . . . (Or. 76), *however incapable of speaking they themselves may be, yet,* etc.

quamvīs scelerātī illī **fuissent** (De Or. i. 230), *however guilty they might have been.*

quamvīs cōmis in amīcīs tuendīs **fuerit** (Fin. ii. 80), *amiable as he may have been in keeping his friends.*

ut nēminem alium **rogāsset** (Mil. 46), *even if he had asked no other.*

ut enim nōn **efficiās** quod vīs, tamen mors ut malum nōn sit efficiēs (Tusc. i. 16), *for even if you do not accomplish what you wish, still you will prove that death is not an evil.*

ut ratiōnem Platō nūllam **adferret** (id. i. 49), *though Plato adduced no reasons.*

NOTE. — **Quamvīs** means literally *as much as you will.* Thus in the first example above, *let them be as incapable as you will, still,* etc. The subjunctive with **quamvīs** is hortatory, like that with **nē** (§ 440); that with **ut** (**ut nōn**) is of uncertain origin.

b. **Licet**, *although*, takes the Present or Perfect Subjunctive: —

licet omnēs mihi terrōrēs perīculaque **impendeant** (Rosc. Am. 31), *though all terrors and perils should menace me.*

NOTE. — **Licet** is properly a verb in the present tense, meaning *it is granted.* Hence the subjunctive is by the sequence of tenses limited to the Present and Perfect. The concessive clause with **licet** is hortatory in origin, but may be regarded as a substantive clause serving as the subject of the impersonal verb (§ 565. N.[1]).

c. **Etsī, etiam sī, tametsī,** *even if,* take the same constructions as **sī** (see § 514): —

etsī abest mātūritās, tamen nōn est inūtile (Fam. vi. 18. 4), *though ripeness of age is wanting, yet it is not useless,* etc.

etsī numquam dubium **fuit**, tamen perspiciō (id. v. 19), *although it has never been doubtful, yet I perceive,* etc.

etsī statueram (id. v. 5), *though I had determined.*

etsī nihil aliud **abstulissētis**, tamen contentōs vōs esse oportēbat (Sull. 90), *even if you had taken away nothing else, you ought to have been satisfied.*

etiam sī quod scrībās nōn **habēbis**, scrībitō tamen (Fam. xvi. 26), *even if you* [shall] *have nothing to write, still write.*

sed ea **tametsī** vōs parvī **pendēbātis** (Sall. Cat. 52. 9), *but although you regarded those things as of small account.*

NOTE 1. — **Tametsī** with the subjunctive is very rare.

NOTE 2. — A protasis with **sī** often has a concessive force: as, — ego, **sī essent** inimīcitiae mihi cum C. Caesare, tamen hōc tempore reī pūblicae cōnsulere . . . dēbērem (Prov. Cons. 47), *as for me, even if I had private quarrels with Cæsar, it would still be my duty to serve the best interests of the state at this crisis.*

d. **Quamquam,** *although,* introduces an *admitted fact* and takes the Indicative: —

omnibus — **quamquam ruit** ipse suīs clādibus — pestem dēnūntiat (Phil. xiv. 8), *though he is breaking down under his disasters, still he threatens all with destruction.*

NOTE. — **Quamquam** more commonly means *and yet,* introducing a *new proposition* in the indicative: as, — **quamquam** haec quidem iam tolerābilia **vidēbantur**, etsī, etc. (Mil. 76), *and yet these, in truth, seemed now bearable, though,* etc.

e. The poets and later writers frequently use **quamvīs** and **quamquam** like **etsī**, connecting them with the Indicative or the Subjunctive, according to the nature of the condition: —

quamquam movērētur (Liv. xxxvi. 34), *although he was moved.*

Polliō amat nostram, **quamvīs est** rūstica, mūsam (Ecl. iii. 84), *Pollio loves my muse, though she is rustic.*

quamvīs pervēnerās (Liv. ii. 40), *though you had come.*

f. **Ut,** *as,* with the Indicative, may be equivalent to a concession:

vērum **ut** errāre **potuistī**, sīc dēcipī tē nōn potuisse quis nōn videt (Fam. x. 20. 2), *suppose you could have been mistaken, who does not see that you cannot have been deceived in this way?*

For **cum** concessive, see § 549; for **quī** concessive, see § 535. *e.* For concession expressed by the Hortatory Subjunctive (negative **nē**), see § 440.

CLAUSES OF PROVISO

528. **Dum, modo, dummodo,** and **tantum ut,** introducing a Proviso, take the Subjunctive. The negative with these particles is **nē**:

ōderint **dum metuant** (Off. i. 97), *let them hate, if only they fear.*

valētūdō **modo** bona **sit** (Brut. 64), *provided the health be good.*

dummodo inter mē atque tē mūrus **intersit** (Cat. i. 10), *provided only the wall* (of the city) *is between us.*

tantum ut sciant (Att. xvi. 11. 1), *provided only they know.*

modo nē sit ex pecudum genere (Off. i. 105), *provided* [in pleasure] *he be not of the herd of cattle.*

id faciat saepe, **dum nē** lassus **fīat** (Cato R. R. v. 4), *let him do this often, provided he does not get tired.*

dummodo ea (sevēritās) **nē variētur** (Q. Fr. i. 1. 20), *provided only it* (strictness) *be not allowed to swerve.*

tantum nē noceat (Ov. M. ix. 21), *only let it do no harm.*

NOTE.—The Subjunctive with **modo** is hortatory or optative; that with **dum** and **dummodo**, a development from the use of the Subjunctive with **dum** in temporal clauses, § 553 (compare the colloquial *so long as my health is good, I don't care*).

a. The Hortatory Subjunctive without a particle sometimes expresses a proviso:—

sint Maecēnātēs, nōn deerunt Marōnēs (Mart. viii. 56. 5), *so there be Mæcenases, Virgils will not be lacking.*

b. The Subjunctive with **ut** (negative **nē**) is sometimes used to denote a proviso, usually with **ita** in the main clause:—

probāta condiciō est, sed **ita ut** ille praesidia **dēdūceret** (Att. vii. 14. 1), *the terms were approved, but only on condition that he should withdraw the garrisons.*

NOTE.—This is a development of the construction of Characteristic or Result. For a clause of Characteristic expressing Proviso, see § 535. *d.*

CLAUSES OF PURPOSE (FINAL CLAUSES)

529. The Subjunctive in the clause of Purpose is *hortatory* in origin, coming through a kind of indirect discourse construction (for which see § 592). Thus, **mīsit lēgātōs quī dīcerent** means *he sent ambassadors who should say,* i.e. *who were directed to say;* in the direct orders the verb would be **dīcite**, which would become **dīcant** in the Indirect Discourse of narrative (§ 588) or **dīcerent** in the past (cf. hortatory subjunctive in past tenses, § 439. *b*). The Subjunctive with **ut** and **nē** is, in general, similar in origin.

530. A clause expressing *purpose* is called a Final Clause.

531. Final Clauses take the Subjunctive introduced by **ut** (**utī**), negative **nē** (**ut nē**), or by a Relative Pronoun or Adverb:—

1. Pure Clauses of Purpose, with **ut** (**utī**) or **nē** (**ut nē**), express the purpose of the main verb in the form of a modifying clause:—

ab arātrō abdūxērunt Cincinnātum, ut dictātor **esset** (Fin. ii. 12), *they brought Cincinnatus from the plough that he might be dictator.*

ut sint auxiliō suīs, subsistunt (B. C. i. 80), *they halt in order to support* (be an aid to) *their own men.*

nē mīlitēs oppidum **inrumperent**, portās obstruit (id. i. 27), *he barricaded the gates, in order that the soldiers might not break into the town.*

scālās parārī iubet, **nē** quam facultātem **dīmittat** (id. i. 28), *he orders scaling-ladders to be got ready, in order not to let slip any opportunity.*

ut nē sit impūne (Mil. 31), *that it be not with impunity.*

NOTE 1.—Sometimes the conjunction has a correlative (**ideō, idcircō, eō cōnsiliō**, etc.) in the main clause (cf. § 561. *a*):—

lēgum **idcircō** servī sumus, **ut** līberī **sīmus** (Clu 146), *for this reason we are subject to the laws, that we may be free.*

cōpiās trānsdūxit **eō cōnsiliō**, **ut** castellum expūgnāret (cf. B. G. ii. 9), *he led the troops across with this design—to storm the fort.*

NOTE 2.—**Ut nōn** sometimes occurs in clauses of purpose when **nōn** belongs to some particular word: as,—**ut** plūra **nōn** dīcam (Manil. 44), *to avoid unnecessary talk.*

2. Relative Clauses of Purpose are introduced by the relative pronoun **quī** or a relative adverb (**ubi, unde, quō**, etc.). The antecedent is expressed or implied in the main clause:—

mittitur L. Dēcidius Saxa **quī** locī nātūram **perspiciat** (B. C. i. 66), *Lucius Decidius Saxa is sent to examine the ground* (who should examine, etc.).

scrībēbat ōrātiōnēs **quās** aliī **dīcerent** (Brut. 206), *he wrote speeches for other men to deliver.*

eō exstīnctō fore **unde discerem** nēminem (Cat. M. 12), *that when he was dead there would be nobody from whom* (whence) *I could learn.*

huic nē **ubi cōnsisteret** quidem contrā tē locum relīquistī (Quinct. 73), *you have left him no ground even to make a stand against you.*

habēbam **quō cōnfugerem** (Fam. iv. 6. 2), *I had* [a retreat] *whither I might flee.*

NOTE.—In this construction **quī = ut is** (etc.), **ubi = ut ibi**, and so on (§ 537. 2).

a. The ablative **quō** (= **ut eō**) is used as a conjunction in final clauses which contain a *comparative*:—

comprimere eōrum audāciam, **quō facilius** cēterōrum animī **frangerentur** (Fam. xv. 4. 10), *to repress their audacity, that the spirit of the others might be broken more easily* (by which the more easily).

lībertāte ūsus est, **quō impūnius** dicāx **esset** (Quinct. 11), *he took advantage of liberty, that he might bluster with more impunity.*

NOTE.—Occasionally **quō** introduces a final clause that does not contain a comparative: as,—L. Sulla exercitum, **quō** sibi fīdum **faceret**, lūxuriōsē habuerat (Sall. Cat. 11), *Lucius Sulla had treated the army luxuriously, in order to make it devoted to him.*

For **quōminus** (= **ut eō minus**) after verbs of *hindering*, see § 558. *b*.

532. The principal clause, on which a final clause depends, is often to be supplied from the context: —

ac nē longum sit . . . iussimus (Cat. iii. 10), *and, not to be tedious, we ordered*, etc. [Strictly, *in order not to be tedious, I say we ordered.*]

sed ut ad Dionȳsium redeāmus (Tusc. v. 63), *but to return to Dionysius.*

sed ut eōdem revertar, causa haec fuit timōris (Fam. vi. 7. 3), *but, to return to the same point, this was the cause of fear.*

satis incōnsīderātī fuit, nē dīcam audācis (Phil. xiii. 12), *it was the act of one rash enough, not to say daring.*

Note 1. — By a similar ellipsis the Subjunctive is used with **nēdum** (sometimes **nē**), *still less, not to mention that*: —

nēdum salvī esse possīmus (Clu. 95), *much less could we be safe.*

nēdum istī nōn statim conquīsītūrī sint aliquid sceleris et flāgitī (Leg. Agr. ii. 97), *far more will they hunt up at once some sort of crime and scandal.*

nēdum in marī et viā sit facile (Fam. xvi. 8), *still less is it easy at sea and on a journey.*

quippe secundae rēs sapientium animōs fatīgant; **nē** illī corruptīs mōribus victōriae temperārent (Sall. Cat. 11), *for prosperity overmasters the soul even of the wise; much less did they with their corrupt morals put any check on victory.*

Note 2. — With **nēdum** the verb itself is often omitted: as, — aptius hūmānitātī tuae quam tōta Peloponnēsus, **nēdum** Patrae (Fam. vii. 28. 1), *fitter for your refinement than all Peloponnesus, to say nothing of Patræ.*

For Substantive Clauses involving *purpose*, see §§ 563–566.

533. The Purpose of an action is expressed in Latin in various ways; but never (except in idiomatic expressions and rarely in poetry) by the simple Infinitive as in English (§ 460).

The sentence, *they came to seek peace*, may be rendered —

(1) vēnērunt ut pācem peterent. [Final clause with **ut** (§ 531. 1).]
(2) vēnērunt quī pācem peterent. [Final clause with Relative (§ 531. 2).]
(3) [vēnērunt ad petendum pācem.] Not found with transitive verbs (§ 506, N. 2), but cf. **ad pārendum senātuī.** [Gerund with **ad** (§ 506).]
(4) vēnērunt ad petendam pācem. [Gerundive with **ad** (§ 506).]
(5) vēnērunt pācem petendī causā (grātiā). [Gen. of Gerund with **causā** (§ 504. *b*).]
(6) vēnērunt pācis petendae causā (grātiā). [Gen. of Gerundive with **causā** (§ 504. *b*).]
(7) vēnērunt pācem petītūrī. [Future participle (§ 499. 2); in later writers.]
(8) vēnērunt pācem petītum. [Supine in **-um** (§ 509).]

These forms are not used indifferently, but —

a. The usual way of expressing purpose is by **ut** (negative **nē**), unless the purpose is *closely connected with some one word*, in which case a relative is more common: —

lēgātōs ad Dumnorīgem mittunt, ut eō dēprecātōre ā Sēquanīs impetrārent (B. G. i. 9), *they send envoys to Dumnorix, in order through his intercession to obtain* (this favor) *from the Sequani.*

mīlitēs mīsit ut eōs quī fūgerant persequerentur (id. v. 10), *he sent the soldiers to follow up those who had fled.*

Cūriō praemittit equitēs quī prīmum impetum sustineant (B. C. ii. 26), *Curio sends forward cavalry to withstand the first attack.*

b. The Gerund and Gerundive constructions of purpose are usually limited to short expressions, where the literal translation, though not the English idiom, is nevertheless not harsh or strange.

c. The Supine is used to express purpose only with verbs of *motion*, and in a few idiomatic expressions (§ 509).

d. The Future Participle used to express purpose is a late construction of inferior authority (§ 499. 2).

For the poetical Infinitive of Purpose, see § 460. *c.* For the Present Participle in a sense approaching that of purpose, see § 490. 3.

CLAUSES OF CHARACTERISTIC

534. The relative clause of Characteristic with the Subjunctive is a development peculiar to Latin. A relative clause in the Indicative merely states something *as a fact* which is true of the antecedent; a characteristic clause (in the Subjunctive) *defines* the antecedent as a person or thing *of such a character* that the statement made is true of him or it and of all others belonging to the same class. Thus,—nōn potest exercitum is continēre imperātor quī sē ipse nōn continet (indicative) means simply, *that commander who does not* (as a fact) *restrain himself cannot restrain his army;* whereas nōn potest exercitum is continēre imperātor quī sē ipse nōn contineat (subjunctive) would mean, *that commander who is not such a man as to restrain himself*, etc., that is, *who is not characterized by self-restraint.*

This construction has its origin in the *potential* use of the subjunctive (§ 445). Thus, in the example just given, quī sē ipse nōn contineat would mean literally, *who would not restrain himself* (in any supposable case), and this potential idea passes over easily into that of *general quality* or *characteristic.* The characterizing force is most easily felt when the antecedent is indefinite or general. But this usage is extended in Latin to cases which differ but slightly from statements of fact, as in some of the examples below.

The use of the Subjunctive to express Result comes from its use in Clauses of Characteristic. Thus, nōn sum ita hebes ut haec dīcam means literally, *I am not dull in the manner* (degree) *in which I should say this*, hence, *I am not so dull as to say this.* Since, then, the characteristic often appears in the form of a *supposed result*, the construction readily passes over into Pure Result, with no idea of characteristic; as,—tantus in cūriā clāmor factus est ut populus concurreret (Verr. ii. 47), *such an outcry was made in the senate-house that the people hurried together.*

535. A Relative Clause with the Subjunctive is often used to indicate a *characteristic* of the antecedent, especially where the antecedent is otherwise *undefined:*—

neque enim tū is es quī nesciās (Fam. v. 12. 6), *for you are not such a one as not to know.* [Here is is equivalent to *such*, and is defined only by the relative clause that follows.]

multa dīcunt quae vix intellegam (Fin. iv. 2), *they say many things which* (such as) *I hardly understand.*

pācī quae nihil habitūra sit īnsidiārum semper est cōnsulendum (Off. i. 35), *we must always aim at a peace which shall have no plots.*

a. A Relative Clause of Characteristic is used after general expressions of *existence* or *non-existence*, including questions which imply a negative.

So especially with **sunt quī**, *there are* [some] *who;* **quis est quī**, *who is there who?* —

sunt quī discessum animī ā corpore **putent** esse mortem (Tusc. i. 18), *there are some who think that the departure of soul from body constitutes death.*

erant quī cēnsērent (B. C. ii. 30), *there were some who were of the opinion*, etc.

erant quī Helvidium **miserārentur** (Tac. Ann. xvi. 29), *there were some who pitied Helvidius.* [Cf. **est cum** (N. 3, below).]

quis est quī id nōn maximīs **efferat** laudibus (Lael. 24), *who is there that does not extol it with the highest praise?*

nihil videō **quod timeam** (Fam. ix. 16. 3), *I see nothing to fear.*

nihil est **quod** adventum nostrum **extimēscās** (Fam. ix. 26. 4), *there is no reason why you should dread my coming.*

unde agger comportārī **posset** nihil erat reliquum (B. C. ii. 15), *there was nothing left from which an embankment could be got together.*

NOTE 1. — After general negatives like **nēmō est quī**, the Subjunctive is regular; after general affirmatives like **sunt quī**, it is the prevailing construction, but the Indicative sometimes occurs; after **multī** (**nōn nūllī, quīdam**) **sunt quī**, and similar expressions in which the antecedent is partially defined, the choice of mood depends on the shade of meaning which the writer wishes to express: —

sunt bēstiae quaedam in quibus inest aliquid simile virtūtis (Fin. v. 38), *there are certain animals in which there is something like virtue.*

But, — **inventī multī** sunt **quī** vītam prōfundere prō patriā **parātī essent** (Off. i. 84), *many were found of such a character as to be ready to give their lives for their country.*

NOTE 2. — Characteristic clauses with **sunt quī** etc. are sometimes called Relative Clauses with an Indefinite Antecedent, but are to be carefully distinguished from the Indefinite Relative in *protasis* (§ 520).

NOTE 3. — The phrases **est cum, fuit cum**, etc. are used like **est quī, sunt quī**: as, — **ac fuit cum** mihi quoque initium requiēscendī fore iūstum **arbitrārer** (De Or. i. 1), *and there was a time when I thought a beginning of rest would be justifiable on my part.*

b. A Relative Clause of Characteristic may follow **ūnus** and **sōlus**:

nīl admīrārī prope **rēs est ūna sōlaque quae possit** facere et servāre beātum (Hor. Ep. i. 6. 1), *to wonder at nothing is almost the sole and only thing that can make and keep one happy.*

sōlus es cûius in victōriā **ceciderit** nēmō nisi armātus (Deiot. 34), *you are the only man in whose victory no one has fallen unless armed.*

c. A clause of Result or Characteristic with **quam ut, quam quī** (rarely with **quam** alone), may be used after comparatives: —

Canachī sīgna **rigidiōra** sunt **quam ut imitentur** vēritātem (Brut. 70), *the statues of Canachus are too stiff to represent nature* (stiffer than that they should).

māiōrēs arborēs caedēbant **quam quās** ferre mīles **posset** (Liv. xxxiii. 5), *they cut trees too large for a soldier to carry* (larger than what a soldier could carry).

NOTE. — This construction corresponds in sense to the English *too . . . to.*

d. A relative clause of characteristic may express *restriction* or *proviso* (cf. § 528. *b*): —

quod sciam, *so far as I know* (lit. as to what I know).

Catōnis ōrātiōnēs, **quās** quidem **invēnerim** (Brut. 65), *the speeches of Cato, at least such as I have discovered.*

servus est nēmō, **quī** modo tolerābilī condiciōne **sit** servitūtis (Cat. iv. 16), *there is not a slave, at least in any tolerable condition of slavery.*

e. A Relative Clause of Characteristic may express *cause* or *concession*: —

peccāsse mihi videor **quī** ā tē **discesserim** (Fam. xvi. 1), *I seem to myself to have done wrong because I have left you.* [Causal.]

virum simplicem **quī** nōs nihil cēlet (Or. 230), *O guileless man, who hides nothing from us!* [Causal.]

egomet **quī** sērō Graecās litterās **attigissem,** tamen complūrēs Athēnīs diēs sum commorātus (De Or. i. 82), *I myself, though I began Greek literature late, yet,* etc. (lit. [a man] who, etc.). [Concessive.]

NOTE 1. — In this use the relative is equivalent to **cum is** etc. It is often preceded by **ut, utpote,** or **quippe**: —

nec cōnsul, **ut quī** id ipsum **quaesīsset,** moram certāminī fēcit (Liv. xlii. 7), *nor did the consul delay the fight, since he had sought that very thing* (as [being one] who had sought, etc.).

Lūcius, frāter ēius, **utpote quī** peregrē **dēpūgnārit,** familiam dūcit (Phil. v. 30), *Lucius, his brother, leads his household, inasmuch as he is a man who has fought it out abroad.*

convīvia cum patre nōn inībat, **quippe quī** nē in oppidum quidem nisi perrārō **venīret** (Rosc. Am. 52), *he did not go to dinner parties with his father, since he did not even come to town except very rarely.*

NOTE 2. — The Relative of Cause or Concession is merely a variety of the Characteristic construction. The quality expressed by the Subjunctive is connected with the action of the main verb either as *cause on account of which* (SINCE) or as *hindrance in spite of which* (ALTHOUGH).

f. **Dīgnus, indīgnus, aptus, idōneus** take a subjunctive clause with a relative (rarely **ut**). The negative is **nōn**: —

dīgna **in quibus ēlabōrārent** (Tusc. i. 1), (things) *worth spending their toil on* (worthy on which they should, etc.).

dīgna rēs est **ubi** tū nervōs **intendās** tuōs (Ter. Eun. 312), *the affair is worthy of your stretching your sinews* (worthy wherein you should, etc.).

idōneus quī impetret (Manil. 57), *fit to obtain.*
indīgnī ut redimerēmur (Liv. xxii. 59. 17), *unworthy to be ransomed.*

NOTE 1. — This construction is sometimes explained as a relative clause of purpose, but it is more closely related to characteristic.

NOTE 2. — With **dīgnus** etc., the poets often use the Infinitive: —

fōns rīvō **dare** nōmen idōneus (Hor. Ep. i. 16. 12), *a source fit to give a name to a stream.*

aetās mollis et apta **regī** (Ov. A. A. i. 10), *a time of life soft and easy to be guided.*

vīvere dīgnus erās (Ov. M. x. 633), *you were worthy to live.*

CLAUSES OF RESULT (CONSECUTIVE CLAUSES)

536. The Subjunctive in Consecutive Clauses is a development of the use of that mood in Clauses of Characteristic (as explained in § 534).

537. Clauses of Result take the Subjunctive introduced by **ut**, *so that* (negative, **ut nōn**), or by a relative pronoun or relative adverb.

1. Pure Clauses of Result, with **ut** or **ut nōn**, express the result of the main verb in the form of a modifying clause: —

tanta vīs probitātis est **ut** eam in hoste **dīligāmus** (Lael. 29), *so great is the power of goodness that we love it even in an enemy.*

pūgnātur ācriter ad novissimum agmen, adeō **ut** paene terga **convertant** (B. C. i. 80), *there is sharp fighting in the rear, so* (to such a degree) *that they almost take flight.*

multa rūmor adfingēbat, **ut** paene bellum cōnfectum **vidērētur** (id. i. 53), *rumor added many false reports, so that the war seemed almost ended.*

2. Relative Clauses of Result are introduced by the relative pronoun **quī** or a relative adverb (**ubi, unde, quō**, etc.). The antecedent is expressed or implied in the main clause.

The Relative in this construction is equivalent to **ut** with the corresponding demonstrative: — **quī** = **ut is** (etc.), **ubi** = **ut ibi**, and so on:

nam est innocentia affectiō tālis animī **quae noceat** nēminī (Tusc. iii. 16), *for innocence is such a quality of mind as to do harm to no one.*

sunt aliae causae **quae** plānē **efficiant** (Top. 59), *there are other causes such as to bring to pass.*

nūlla est celeritās **quae possit** cum animī celeritāte contendere (Tusc. i. 43), *there is no swiftness which can compare with the swiftness of the mind.*

quis nāvigāvit **quī nōn** sē mortis perīculō **committeret** (Manil. 31), *who went to sea who did not incur the peril of death?*

NOTE 1. — Since the relative clause of Result is a development from the relative clause of Characteristic (§ 534), no sharp line can be drawn between the two constructions. In doubtful cases, it is better to attempt no distinction or to describe the clause as one of Characteristic.

NOTE 2. — Clauses of Result are often introduced by such correlative words as **tam, tālis, tantus, ita, sīc, adeō, ūsque eō**, which belong to the main clause.

a. A Negative Result is introduced by **ut nōn, ut nēmō, quī nōn,** etc., not by **nē**: —

multīs gravibusque volneribus cōnfectus **ut** iam sē sustinēre **nōn posset** (B. G. ii. 25), *used up with many severe wounds so that he could no longer stand.*

tantā vī in Pompêī equitēs impetum fēcērunt **ut** eōrum **nēmō cōnsisteret** (B. C. iii. 93), *they attacked Pompey's cavalry with such vigor that not one of them stood his ground.*

nēmō est tam senex **quī** sē annum **nōn putet** posse vīvere (Cat. M. 24), *nobody is so old as not to think that he can live a year.*

Note. — When the result implies *an effect intended* (not a simple purpose), **ut nē** or **nē** is sometimes used as being less positive than **ut nōn**: — [librum] ita corrigās **nē mihi noceat** (Caecina, Fam. vi. 7. 6), *correct the book so that it may not hurt me.*

b. Frequently a clause of result or characteristic is used in a *restrictive* sense, and so amounts to a Proviso (cf. § 535. *d*): —

hōc ita est ūtile **ut nē** plānē **inlūdāmur** ab accūsātōribus (Rosc. Am. 55), *this is so far useful that we are not utterly mocked by the accusers* (i.e. useful only on this condition, that, etc.).

nihil autem est molestum **quod** nōn **dēsīderēs** (Cat. M. 47), *but nothing is troublesome which* (= provided that) *you do not miss.*

c. The clause of result is sometimes expressed in English by the Infinitive with TO or SO AS TO or an equivalent: —

tam longē aberam ut nōn vidērem, *I was too far away to see* (so far that I did not see; cf. § 535. *c*).

Note. — Result is never expressed by the Infinitive in Latin except by the poets in a few passages (§ 461. *a*).

538. The constructions of Purpose and Result are precisely alike in the *affirmative* (except sometimes in *tense sequence*, § 485. *c*); but, in the *negative*, Purpose takes **nē**, Result **ut nōn** etc.: —

cūstōdītus est **nē** effugeret, *he was guarded in order that he* MIGHT *not escape.*
cūstōdītus est **ut nōn** effugeret, *he was guarded so that he* DID *not escape.*

So in negative Purpose clauses **nē quis, nē quid, nē ūllus, nē quō, nē quandō, nēcubi,** etc. are almost always used; in negative Result clauses, **ut nēmō, ut nihil, ut nūllus,** etc.: —

(1) cernere **nē quis** eōs, **neu quis** contingere posset (Aen. i. 413), *that no one might see them, no one touch them.* [Purpose.]

nē quandō līberīs prōscrīptōrum bona patria reddantur (Rosc. Am. 145), *lest at some time the patrimony of the proscribed should be restored to their children.*

ipse **nē quō** inciderem, revertī Formiās (Att. viii. 3. 7), *that I might not come upon him anywhere, I returned to Formiæ.*

dispositīs explōrātōribus **nēcubi** Rōmānī cōpiās trādūcerent (B. G. vii. 35), *having stationed scouts here and there in order that the Romans might not lead their troops across anywhere.*

(2) multī ita sunt imbēcillī senēs **ut nūllum** officī mūnus exsequī possint (Cat. M. 35), *many old men are so feeble that they cannot perform any duty to society.* [Result.]

quī summum bonum sīc īnstituit **ut nihil** habeat cum virtūte coniūnctum (Off. i. 5), *who has so settled the highest good that it has nothing in common with virtue.*

For clauses of Result or Characteristic with **quīn**, see § 559. For Substantive Clauses of Result, see §§ 567–571.

CAUSAL CLAUSES

539. Causal Clauses take either the Indicative or the Subjunctive, according to their construction; the idea of *cause* being contained, not in the mood itself, but in the form of the argument (by implication), in an antecedent of causal meaning (like **propterea**), or in the connecting particles.

Quod is in origin the relative pronoun (stem **quo-**) used adverbially in the accusative neuter (cf. § 214. *d*) and gradually sinking to the position of a colorless relative conjunction (cf. English *that* and see § 222). Its use as a *causal particle* is an early special development. **Quia** is perhaps an accusative plural neuter of the relative stem **qui-**, and seems to have developed its causal sense more distinctly than **quod**, and at an earlier period. It is used (very rarely) as an interrogative, *why?* (so in classical Latin with **nam** only), and may, like **quandō**, have developed from an interrogative to a relative particle.

Quoniam (for **quom iam**) is also of relative origin (**quom** being a case-form of the pronominal stem **quo-**). It occurs in old Latin in the sense of *when* (cf. **quom, cum**), from which the causal meaning is derived (cf. **cum** causal). The Subjunctive with **quod** and **quia** depends on the principle of Informal Indirect Discourse (§ 592).

Quandō is probably the interrogative **quam** (*how?*) compounded with a form of the pronominal stem **do-** (cf. **dum, dō-nec**). It originally denoted *time* (first interrogatively, then as a relative), and thus came to signify *cause*. Unlike **quod** and **quia**, it is not used to state a reason in informal indirect discourse and therefore is never followed by the Subjunctive.

540. The Causal Particles **quod** and **quia** take the Indicative, when the reason is given on the authority of the *writer* or *speaker;* the Subjunctive, when the reason is given on the authority of *another:*—

1. Indicative:—

cum tibi agam grātiās **quod** mē vīvere **coēgistī** (Att. iii. 3), *when I may thank you that you have forced me to live.*

cūr igitur pācem nōlō? **quia** turpis **est** (Phil. vii. 9), *why then do I not wish for peace? Because it is disgraceful.*

ita fit ut adsint propterea **quod** officium sequuntur, taceant autem **quia** perīculum vītant (Rosc. Am. 1), *so it happens that they attend because they follow duty, but are silent because they seek to avoid danger.*

2. Subjunctive: —

mihi grātulābāre **quod audīssēs** mē meam prīstinam dīgnitātem obtinēre (Fam. iv. 14. 1), *you congratulated me because* [as you said] *you had heard that I had regained my former dignity.*

noctū ambulābat Themistoclēs **quod** somnum capere nōn **posset** (Tusc. iv. 44), *Themistocles used to walk about at night because* [as he said] *he could not sleep.*

mea māter īrāta est **quia** nōn **redierim** (Pl. Cist. 101), *my mother is angry because I did n't return.*

Note 1. — **Quod** introduces either a *fact* or a *statement*, and accordingly takes either the Indicative or the Subjunctive. **Quia** regularly introduces a fact; hence it rarely takes the Subjunctive. **Quoniam**, *inasmuch as, since, when now, now that*, has reference to motives, excuses, justifications, and the like and takes the Indicative.

Note 2. — Under this head what the speaker himself thought under other circumstances may have the Subjunctive (§ 592. 3. n.): as, — ego laeta vīsa sum **quia** soror **vēnisset** (Pl. Mil. 387), *I seemed* (in my dream) *glad because my sister had come.*

So with **quod** even a verb of *saying* may be in the Subjunctive: as, — rediit **quod** sē oblītum nesciō quid dīceret (Off. i. 40), *he returned because he said he had forgotten something.*

Note 3. — **Nōn quod, nōn quia, nōn quō**, introducing a reason *expressly to deny it*, take the Subjunctive; but the Indicative sometimes occurs when the statement is *in itself* true, though not the *true reason*. In the negative, **nōn quīn** (with the Subjunctive) may be used in nearly the same sense as **nōn quod nōn**. After a comparative, **quam quō** or **quam quod** is used: —

pugilēs ingemēscunt, **nōn quod doleant**, sed quia profundendā vōce omne corpus intenditur (Tusc. ii. 56), *boxers groan, not because they are in pain, but because by giving vent to the voice the whole body is put in a state of tension.*

nōn quia rēctior ad Alpīs via **esset**, sed crēdēns (Liv. xxi. 31. 2), *not because the route to the Alps was more direct, but believing*, etc.

nōn quīn parī virtūte et voluntāte aliī **fuerint**, sed tantam causam nōn habuērunt (Phil. vii. 6), *not that there were not others of equal courage and good-will, but they had not so strong a reason.*

haec amōre magis impulsus scrībenda ad tē putāvī, **quam quō** tē **arbitrārer** monitīs et praeceptīs egēre (Fam. x. 3. 4), *this I thought I ought to write to you, rather from the impulse of* (prompted by) *affection than because I thought that you needed advice and suggestion.*

a. **Quoniam** and **quandō**, *since*, introduce a reason given on the authority of the writer or speaker, and take the Indicative: —

locus est ā mē, **quoniam** ita Murēna **voluit**, retrāctandus (Mur. 54), *I must review the point, since Murena has so wished.*

quandō ita **vīs**, dī bene vortant (Pl. Trin. 573), *since you so wish, may the gods bless the undertaking.*

quandō ad māiōra **nātī sumus** (Fin. v. 21), *since we are born for greater things.*

Note. — The Subjunctive with **quoniam** is unclassical. **Quandō**, *since*, in the causal sense, is mostly archaic or late. **Quandō**, *when*, is used as interrogative, relative, and indefinite: as, — **quandō? hodiē**, *when? to-day*; **sī quandō**, *if ever.*

b. Causal clauses introduced by **quod, quia, quoniam,** and **quandō** take the Subjunctive in Indirect Discourse, like any other dependent clause (see § 580).

c. A Relative, when used to express *cause*, regularly takes the Subjunctive (see § 535. *e*).

d. **Cum** causal takes the Subjunctive (see § 549).

For Substantive Clauses with **quod**, see § 572.

TEMPORAL CLAUSES

541. Temporal Clauses are introduced by particles which are almost all of relative origin. They are construed like other relative clauses, except where they have developed into special idiomatic constructions.[1]

For list of Temporal Particles, see p. 138.

Temporal Clauses may be classified as follows: —

I. Conditional Relative Clauses: **ubi, ut, cum, quandō,** in Protasis (§ 542).
II. Clauses with **postquam, ubi,** etc. (Indicative), (§ 543).
III. Clauses with **cum** { 1. **Cum** temporal (§§ 545–548). 2. **Cum** causal or concessive (§ 549).
IV. Clauses with **antequam** and **priusquam** (Indicative or Subjunctive) (§ 551).
V. Clauses with **dum, dōnec,** and **quoad** (Indicative or Subjunctive) (§§ 552–556).

Conditional Relative Clauses

542. The particles **ubi, ut, cum, quandō,** either alone or compounded with **-cumque,** may be used as Indefinite Relatives (in the sense of *whenever*), and have the constructions of Protasis (cf. § 514): —

cum id malum **negās** esse, capior (Tusc. ii. 29), *whenever you* (the individual disputant) *deny it to be an evil, I am misled.* [Present general condition.]

quod profectō **cum** mē nūlla vīs **cōgeret**, facere nōn audērem (Phil. v. 51), *which I would surely not venture to do, as long as no force compelled me.* [Present, contrary to fact: cf. § 517.]

cum videās eōs dolōre nōn frangī, dēbeās exīstimāre, etc. (Tusc. ii. 66), *when you see that those are not broken by pain, you ought to infer,* etc. [Present general condition: cf. § 518. *a.*]

cum rosam **vīderat,** tum incipere vēr arbitrābātur (Verr. v. 27), *whenever he saw a rose he thought spring had begun.* [Past general condition: cf. § 518. *b.*]

id **ubi dīxisset,** hastam in fīnīs eōrum ēmittēbat (Liv. i. 32. 13), *when he had said this, he would cast the spear into their territories.* [Past General Condition, repeated action: see § 518. *c.*]

[1] With all temporal particles the Subjunctive is often found depending on some other principle of construction. (See Intermediate Clauses, § 591.)

Temporal Clauses with *postquam, ubi*, etc.

543. The particles **postquam** (**posteāquam**), **ubi**, **ut** (**ut prīmum**, **ut semel**), **simul atque** (**simul ac**, or **simul** alone), take the Indicative (usually in the *perfect* or the *historical present*): —

mīlitēs **postquam** victōriam **adeptī sunt**, nihil reliquī victīs fēcēre (Sall. Cat. 11), *when the soldiers had won the victory, they left nothing to the vanquished.*

posteāquam forum **attigistī**, nihil fēcistī nisi, etc. (Fam. xv. 16. 3), *since you came to the forum, you have done nothing except*, etc.

ubi omnīs idem sentīre **intellēxit**, posterum diem pūgnae cōnstituit (B. G. iii. 23), *when he understood that all agreed* (thought the same thing), *he appointed the next day for the battle.*

Catilīna, **ubi** eōs convēnisse **videt**, sēcēdit (Sall. Cat. 20), *when Catiline sees that they have come together, he retires.*

Pompêius **ut** equitātum suum pulsum **vīdit**, aciē excessit (B. C. iii. 94), *when Pompey saw his cavalry beaten, he left the field.*

ut·semel ē Pīraeeō ēloquentia **ēvecta est** (Brut. 51), *as soon as eloquence had set sail from the Piræus.*

nostrī **simul** in āridō **cōnstitērunt**, in hostīs impetum fēcērunt (B. G. iv. 26), *our men, as soon as they had taken a position on dry ground, made an attack on the enemy.*

simul atque intrōductus est, rem cōnfēcit (Clu. 40), *as soon as he was brought in, he did the job.*

a. These particles less commonly take the Imperfect or Pluperfect Indicative. The Imperfect denotes a past state of things; the Pluperfect, an action completed in past time: —

postquam strūctī utrimque **stābant**, ducēs in medium prōcēdunt (Liv. i. 23), *when they stood in array on both sides, the generals advance into the midst.*

P. Āfricānus **posteāquam** bis cōnsul et cēnsor **fuerat** (Caecil. 69), *when Africanus had been* (i.e. had the dignity of having been) *twice consul and censor.*

postquam id difficilius vīsum est, neque facultās perficiendī **dabātur**, ad Pompêium trānsiērunt (B. C. iii. 60), *when this seemed too hard, and no means of effecting it were given, they passed over to Pompey.*

post diem quīntum **quam** iterum barbarī male **pūgnāverant** [= victī sunt], lēgātī ā Bocchō veniunt (Iug. 102), *the fifth day after the barbarians were beaten the second time, envoys come from Bocchus.*

haec iuventūtem, **ubi** familiārēs opēs **dēfēcerant**, ad facinora incendēbant (Sall. Cat. 13), *when their inherited resources had given out*, etc.

ubi perīcula virtūte **prōpulerant** (id. 6), *when they had dispelled the dangers by their valor.*

For the use of **ubi**, **ut**, either alone or compounded with **-cumque**, as Indefinite Relatives, see § 542.

Uses of *Cum*

544. The conjunction **cum** (**quom**) is a case-form of the relative pronoun **quī**. It inherits from **quī** its subordinating force, and in general shares its constructions. But it was early specialized to a temporal meaning (cf. **tum**, **dum**), and its range of usage was therefore less wide than that of **quī**; it could not, for example, introduce clauses of purpose or of result.

With the Indicative, besides the simple expression of definite time (corresponding to simple relative clauses with the Indicative), it has a few special uses, — conditional, explicative, **cum** *inversum* — all easily derived from the temporal use.

With the Subjunctive, **cum** had a development parallel to that of the **quī**-clause of Characteristic, — a development not less extensive and equally peculiar to Latin. From *defining* the time the **cum**-clause passed over to the *description* of the time by means of its attendant circumstances of cause or concession (cf. *since, while*).

In particular, **cum** with the Subjunctive was used in narrative (hence the past tenses, Imperfect and Pluperfect) as a descriptive clause of time. As, however, the present participle in Latin is restricted in its use and the perfect active participle is almost wholly lacking, the historical or narrative **cum**-clause came into extensive use to supply the deficiency. In classical writers the narrative **cum**-clause (with the Subjunctive) has pushed back the defining clause (with the Imperfect or Pluperfect Indicative) into comparative infrequency, and is itself freely used where the descriptive or characterizing force is scarcely perceptible (cf. the **quī**-clause of Characteristic, § 534).

Cum Temporal

545. A temporal clause with **cum**, *when*, and some past tense of the Indicative *dates* or *defines the time* at which the action of the main verb occurred: —

eō [lituō] regiōnēs dīrēxit tum **cum** urbem **condidit** (Div. i. 30), *he traced with it the quarters* [of the sky] *at the time he founded the city.*

cum occīditur Sex. Rōscius, ibīdem fuērunt servī (Rosc. Am. 120), *when Roscius was slain, the slaves were on the spot.* [**occīditur** is historical present.]

quem quidem **cum** ex urbe **pellēbam**, hōc prōvidēbam animō (Cat. iii. 16), *when I was trying to force him* (conative imperfect) *from the city, I looked forward to this.*

fulgentīs gladiōs hostium vidēbant Deciī **cum** in aciem eōrum **inruēbant** (Tusc. ii. 59), *the Decii saw the flashing swords of the enemy when they rushed upon their line.*

tum **cum** in Asiā rēs māgnās permultī **āmīserant** (Manil. 19), *at that time, when many had lost great fortunes in Asia.*

Note 1. — This is the regular use with all tenses in early Latin, and at all times with the Perfect and the Historical Present (as with **postquam** etc.). With the Imperfect and Pluperfect the Indicative use is (in classical Latin) much less common than the Subjunctive use defined below (§ 546).

Note 2. — This construction must not be confused with that of **cum**, *whenever*, in General Conditions (§ 542).

a. When the time of the main clause and that of the temporal clause are *absolutely identical*, **cum** takes the Indicative in the same tense as that of the main verb: —

> maximā sum laetitiā adfectus **cum audīvī** cōnsulem tē factum esse (Fam. xv. 7), *I was very much pleased when I heard that you had been elected consul.*

546. A temporal clause with **cum** and the Imperfect or Pluperfect Subjunctive *describes the circumstances* that accompanied or preceded the action of the main verb: —

> **cum essem** ōtiōsus in Tusculānō, accēpī tuās litterās (Fam. ix. 18. 1), *when I was taking my ease in my house at Tusculum, I received your letter.*
>
> **cum** servīlī bellō **premerētur** (Manil. 30), *when she* (Italy) *was under the load of the Servile War.*
>
> **cum** id **nūntiātum esset**, mātūrat (B. G. i. 7), *when this had been reported, he made* (makes) *haste.*
>
> **cum** ad Cybistra quīnque diēs **essem morātus**, rēgem Ariobarzānem īnsidiīs līberāvī (Fam. xv. 4. 6), *after remaining at Cybistra for five days, I freed King Ariobarzanes from plots.*
>
> is **cum** ad mē Lāodicēam **vēnisset** mēcumque ego eum **vellem**, repente percussus est atrōcissimīs litterīs (id. ix. 25. 3), *when he had come to me at Laodicea and I wished him to remain with me, he was suddenly*, etc.

Note 1. — This construction is very common in narrative, and **cum** in this use is often called *narrative* cum.

Note 2. — **Cum** with the Imperfect or Pluperfect Indicative does not (like **cum** with the Imperfect or Pluperfect Subjunctive) *describe the time by its circumstances;* it *defines the time* of the main verb by denoting a coëxistent state of things (Imperfect Indicative) or a result attained when the action of the main verb took place (Pluperfect). Thus the construction is precisely that of **postquam** etc. (§ 543. *a*).

Note 3. — The distinction between the uses defined in §§ 545, 546, may be illustrated by the following examples: (1) *He had a fever when he was in Spain* (Shakspere). Here the *when*-clause *defines the time* when Cæsar had the fever, — namely, in the year of his Spanish campaign (B.C. 49). In Latin we should use **cum** with the Imperfect Indicative. (2) *Columbus discovered America when he was seeking a new route to India;* here the *when*-clause does not define or date the time of the discovery; it merely *describes the circumstances* under which America was discovered, — namely, in the course of a voyage undertaken for another purpose. In Latin we should use the Imperfect Subjunctive.

Note 4. — The distinction explained in Note 3 is unknown to early Latin. In Plautus **quom** always has the Indicative unless the Subjunctive is required for some other reason.

a. When the principal action is expressed in the form of a temporal clause with **cum**, and the definition of the time becomes the main clause, **cum** takes the Indicative.

Here the logical relations of the two clauses are inverted; hence **cum** is in this use called **cum** *inversum:* —

diēs nōndum decem intercesserant, **cum** ille alter fīlius īnfāns **necātur** (Clu. 28), *ten days had not yet passed, when the other infant son was killed.* [Instead of *when ten days had not yet passed*, etc.]

iamque lūx appārēbat **cum prōcēdit** ad mīlitēs (Q. C. vii. 8. 3), *and day was already dawning when he appears before the soldiers.*

hōc facere noctū apparābant, **cum** mātrēs familiae repente in pūblicum **prōcurrērunt** (B. G. vii. 26), *they were preparing to do this by night, when the women suddenly ran out into the streets.*

547. Present time with **cum** temporal is denoted by the Present Indicative; future time, by the Future or Future Perfect Indicative: —

incidunt tempora, **cum** ea, quae maximē videntur dīgna esse iūstō homine, **fīunt** contrāria (Off. i. 31), *times occur when those things which seem especially worthy of the upright man, become the opposite.*

nōn dubitābō dare operam ut tē videam, **cum** id satis commodē facere **poterō** (Fam. xiii. 1), *I shall not hesitate to take pains to see you, when I can do it conveniently.*

longum illud tempus **cum** nōn **erō** (Att. xii. 18), *that long time when I shall be no more.*

cum vēneris, cōgnōscēs (Fam. v. 7. 3), *when you come* (shall have come), *you will find out.*

548. **Cum**, *whenever*, takes the construction of a relative clause in a general condition (see § 542).

For present time, either the Present or the Perfect Indicative is used; for past time, regularly the Pluperfect Indicative.

For **est cum** etc., see § 535. *a.* N.[3].

Cum Causal or Concessive

549. **Cum** *causal* or *concessive* takes the Subjunctive: —

id difficile nōn est, **cum** tantum equitātū **valeāmus** (B. C. iii. 86), *this is not difficult since we are so strong in cavalry.* [Causal.]

cum sōlitūdō īnsidiārum et metūs plēna **sit**, ratiō ipsa monet amīcitiās comparāre (Fin. i. 66), *since solitude is full of treachery and fear, reason itself prompts us to contract friendships.* [Causal.]

cum prīmī ōrdinēs **concidissent**, tamen ācerrimē reliquī resistēbant (B. G. vii. 62), *though the first ranks had fallen, still the others resisted vigorously.* [Concessive.]

brevī spatiō legiōnēs numerō hominum explēverat, **cum** initiō nōn amplius duōbus mīlibus **habuisset** (Sall. Cat. 56), *in a short time he had filled out the legions with their complement of men, though at the start he had not had more than two thousand.* [Concessive.]

Cum causal may usually be translated by *since;* **cum** concessive by *although* or *while;* either, occasionally, by *when.*

NOTE 1.—**Cum** in these uses is often emphasized by **ut, utpote, quippe, praesertim**: as,—nec reprehendō: **quippe cum** ipse istam reprehēnsiōnem nōn fūgerim (Att. x. 3 A), *I find no fault; since I myself did not escape that blame.*

NOTE 2.—These causal and concessive uses of **cum** are of relative origin and are parallel to **quī** causal and concessive (§ 535. *e*). The attendant circumstances are regarded as the *cause* of the action, or as tending to *hinder* it.

NOTE 3.—In early Latin **cum (quom)** causal and concessive usually takes the Indicative: as,—**quom** tua rēs **distrahitur**, utinam videam (Pl. Trin. 617), *since your property is being torn in pieces, O that I may see,* etc.

a. **Cum** with the Indicative frequently introduces an explanatory statement, and is sometimes equivalent to **quod**, *on the ground that:*—

> **cum tacent**, clāmant (Cat. i. 21), *when they are silent, they cry out* (i.e. their silence is an emphatic expression of their sentiments).
>
> grātulor tibi **cum** tantum **valēs** apud Dolābellam (Fam. ix. 14. 3), *I congratulate you that you are so strong with Dolabella.*

NOTE.—This is merely a special use of **cum** temporal expressing coincident time (§ 545. *a*).

b. **Cum . . . tum**, signifying *both . . . and*, usually takes the Indicative; but when **cum** approaches the sense of *while* or *though*, the Subjunctive is used (§ 549):—

> **cum** multa nōn **probō**, **tum** illud in prīmīs (Fin. i. 18), *while there are many things I do not approve, there is this in chief.* [Indicative.]
>
> **cum** difficile **est**, **tum** nē aequum quidem (Lael. 26), *not only is it difficult but even unjust.*
>
> **cum** rēs tōta **ficta sit** puerīliter, **tum** nē efficit quidem quod vult (Fin. i. 19), *while the whole thing is childishly got up, he does not even make his point* (accomplish what he wishes). [Subjunctive; approaching **cum** causal.]

Antequam and *Priusquam*

550. **Antequam** and **priusquam**, *before*, introduce Clauses of Time which resemble those with **cum** temporal in their constructions. **Priusquam** consists of two parts (often written separately and sometimes separated by other words), the comparative adverb **prius**, *sooner* (*before*), which really modifies the main verb, and the relative particle **quam**, *than*, which introduces the subordinate clause. The latter is therefore a relative clause, and takes the Indicative or the Subjunctive (like other relative clauses) according to the sense intended. The Subjunctive with **priusquam** is related to that of purpose (§ 529) and is sometimes called the Anticipatory or Prospective Subjunctive. **Antequam**, like **priusquam**, consists of two words, the first of which is the adverb **ante**, *before*, modifying the main verb. Its constructions are the same as those of **priusquam**, but the latter is commoner in classic prose.

551. **Antequam** and **priusquam** take sometimes the Indicative sometimes the Subjunctive.

a. With **antequam** or **priusquam** the Perfect Indicative *states a fact* in past time:—

antequam tuās **lēgī** litterās, hominem īre cupiēbam (Att. ii. 7. 2), *before I read your letter, I wished the man to go.*

neque **ante** dīmīsit eum **quam** fidem **dedit** adulēscēns (Liv. xxxix. 10), *and she did not let the young man go till he pledged his faith.*

neque **prius** fugere dēstitērunt **quam** ad flūmen **pervēnērunt** (B. G. i. 53), *nor did they stop running until they reached the river.*

NOTE.—The Perfect Indicative in this construction is regular when the main clause is negative and the main verb is in an historical tense. The Imperfect Indicative is rare; the Pluperfect Indicative, very rare. The Perfect Subjunctive is rare and ante-classical, except in Indirect Discourse.

b. With **antequam** or **priusquam** the Imperfect Subjunctive is common when the subordinate verb implies *purpose* or *expectancy* in past time, or when the action that it denotes *did not take place:*—

ante pūgnārī coeptum est **quam** satis **īnstruerētur** aciēs (Liv. xxii. 4. 7), *the fight was begun before the line could be properly formed.*

priusquam tū suum sibi **vénderēs**, ipse possēdit (Phil. ii. 96), *before you could sell him his own property, he took possession of it himself.*

priusquam tēlum abicī **posset** aut nostrī propius **accēderent**, omnis Vārī aciēs terga vertit (B. C. ii. 34), *before a weapon could be thrown or our men approached nearer, the whole line about Varus took flight.*

NOTE 1.—The Pluperfect Subjunctive is rare, except in Indirect Discourse by sequence of tenses for the Future Perfect Indicative (§ 484. *c*): as,—**antequam** hominēs nefāriī dē meō adventū audīre **potuissent**, in Macedoniam perrēxī (Planc. 98), *before those evil men could learn of my coming, I arrived in Macedonia.*

NOTE 2.—After an historical present the Present Subjunctive is used instead of the Imperfect: as,—neque ab eō **prius** Domitiānī mīlitēs discēdunt **quam** in cōnspectum Caesaris **dēdūcātur** (B. C. i. 22), *and the soldiers of Domitius did* (do) *not leave him until he was* (is) *conducted into Cæsar's presence.* So, rarely, the Perfect Subjunctive (as B. G. iii. 18).

c. **Antequam** and **priusquam**, when referring to future time, take the Present or Future Perfect Indicative; rarely the Present Subjunctive:

priusquam dē cēterīs rēbus **respondeō**, dē amīcitiā pauca dīcam (Phil. ii. 3), *before I reply to the rest, I will say a little about friendship.*

nōn dēfatīgābor **antequam** illōrum ancipitēs viās **percēperō** (De Or. iii. 145), *I shall not weary till I have traced out their doubtful ways.*

antequam veniat litterās mittet (Leg. Agr. ii. 53), *before he comes, he will send a letter.*

NOTE 1.—The Future Indicative is very rare.

NOTE 2.—In a few cases the Subjunctive of *present general condition* is found with **antequam** and **priusquam** (cf. § 518. *a*): as,—in omnibus negōtiīs **priusquam aggrediāre**, adhibenda est praeparātiō dīligēns (Off. i. 73), *in all undertakings, before you proceed to action, careful preparation must be used.*

Dum, Dōnec, and *Quoad*

552. As an adverb meaning *for a time, awhile,* **dum** is found in old Latin, chiefly as an enclitic (cf. **vixdum, nōndum**). Its use as a conjunction comes either through correlation (cf. **cum . . . tum, sī . . . sīc**) or through substitution for a conjunction, as in the English *the moment I saw it, I understood.* **Quoad** is a compound of the relative **quō**, *up to which point,* with **ad**. The origin and early history of **dōnec** are unknown.

553. Dum and **quoad**, *until,* take the Present or Imperfect Subjunctive in temporal clauses implying *intention* or *expectancy :* —

exspectās fortasse **dum dīcat** (Tusc. ii. 17), *you are waiting perhaps for him to say* (until he say). [**Dum** is especially common after **exspectō**.]

dum reliquae nāvēs **convenīrent**, ad hōram nōnam exspectāvit (B. G. iv. 23), *he waited till the ninth hour for the rest of the ships to join him.*

comitia dīlāta [sunt] **dum** lēx **ferrētur** (Att. iv. 17. 3), *the election was postponed until a law should be passed.*

an id exspectāmus, **quoad** nē vestīgium quidem Asiae cīvitātum atque urbium **relinquātur** (Phil. xi. 25), *shall we wait for this until not a trace is left of the states and cities of Asia?*

Epamīnōndās exercēbātur plūrimum luctandō ad eum fīnem **quoad** stāns complectī **posset** atque contendere (Nep. Epam. 2), *Epaminondas trained himself in wrestling so far as to be able* (until he should be able) *to grapple standing and fight* (in that way).

Note 1.—**Dōnec** is similarly used in poetry and later Latin: as,—et dūxit longē **dōnec** curvāta **coīrent** inter sē capita (Aen. xi. 860), *and drew it* (the bow) *until the curved tips touched each other.*

Note 2.—**Dum**, *until,* may be used with the Present or Future Perfect Indicative to state a future fact when there is no idea of intention or expectancy; but this construction is rare in classic prose. The Future is also found in early Latin. **Dōnec**, *until,* is similarly used, in poetry and early Latin, with the Present and Future Perfect Indicative, rarely with the Future: —

ego in Arcānō opperior **dum** ista **cōgnōscō** (Att. x. 3), *I am waiting in the villa at Arcæ until I find this out.* [This is really **dum**, *while*.]

mihi ūsque cūrae erit quid agās, **dum** quid ēgeris **scierō** (Fam. xii. 19. 3), *I shall always feel anxious as to what you are doing, until I actually know* (shall have known) *what you have done.*

dēlicta mâiōrum luēs **dōnec** templa **refēceris** (Hor. Od. iii. 6. 1), *you shall suffer for the sins of your ancestors until you rebuild the temples.*

ter centum rēgnābitur annōs, **dōnec** geminam partū **dabit** Īlia prōlem (Aen. i. 272), *sway shall be held for thrice a hundred years, until Ilia shall give birth to twin offspring.*

554. Dōnec and **quoad**, *until,* with the Perfect Indicative denote an *actual fact* in past time: —

dōnec rediit silentium fuit (Liv. xxiii. 31. 9), *there was silence until he returned.*

ūsque eō timuī **dōnec** ad rêiciendōs iūdicēs **vēnimus** (Verr. ii. 1. 17), *I was anxious until the moment when we came to challenge the jurors.*

Rōmae fuērunt **quoad** L. Metellus in prōvinciam **profectus est** (id. ii. 62), *they remained at Rome until Lucius Metellus set out for the province.*

NOTE.—**Dum**, *until*, with the Perfect Indicative is rare: as,—mānsit in condiciōne ūsque ad eum fīnem **dum iūdicēs rêiectī sunt** (Verr. i. 16), *he remained true to the agreement until the jurors were challenged.*

555. Dum, dōnec, and **quoad,** *as long as*, take the Indicative:—

dum anima est, spēs esse dīcitur (Att. ix. 10. 3), *as long as there is life, there is said to be hope.*

dum praesidia ūlla **fuērunt**, in Sullae praesidiīs fuit (Rosc. Am. 126), *so long as there were any garrisons, he was in the garrisons of Sulla.*

dum longius ā mūnītiōne **aberant** Gallī, plūs multitūdine tēlōrum prōficiēbant (B. G. vii. 82), *so long as the Gauls were at a distance from the fortifications, they had the advantage because of their missiles.*

dōnec grātus **eram** tibī, Persārum viguī rēge beātior (Hor. Od. iii. 9. 1), *as long as I enjoyed thy favor, I flourished happier than the king of the Persians.*

quoad potuit fortissimē restitit (B. G. iv. 12), *he resisted bravely as long as he could.*

NOTE 1.—**Dōnec** in this use is confined to poetry and later writers.

NOTE 2.—**Quam diū**, *as long as*, takes the Indicative only: as,—sē oppidō tam diū tenuit **quam diū** in prōvinciā Parthī **fuērunt** (Fam. xii. 19. 2), *he kept himself within the town as long as the Parthians were in the province.*

556. Dum, *while*, regularly takes the Present Indicative to denote continued action in past time.

In translating, the English Imperfect must generally be used:—

dum haec **geruntur**, Caesarī nūntiātum est (B. G. i. 46), *while this was going on, a message was brought to Cæsar.*

haec **dum aguntur**, intereā Cleomenēs iam ad Elōrī lītus pervēnerat (Verr. v. 91), *while this was going on, Cleomenes meanwhile had come down to the coast at Elorum.*

hōc **dum nārrat**, forte audīvī (Ter. Haut. 272), *I happened to hear this while she was telling it.*

NOTE.—This construction is a special use of the Historical Present (§ 469).

a. A past tense with **dum** (usually *so long as*) makes the time emphatic by contrast; but a few irregular cases of **dum** with a past tense occur where no contrast is intended:

nec enim **dum eram** vōbīscum, animum meum vidēbātis (Cat. M. 79), *for while I was with you, you could not see my soul.* [Here the time when he was alive is contrasted with that after his death.]

coörta est pūgna, pār **dum cōnstābant** ōrdinēs (Liv. xxii. 47), *a conflict began, well matched as long as the ranks stood firm.*

But,—**dum** oculōs hostium certāmen āverterat (id. xxxii. 24), *while the struggle kept the eyes of the enemy turned away.*

dum ūnum adscendere gradum **cōnātus est**, vēnit in perīculum (Mur. 55), *while he attempted to climb one step* [in rank] *he fell into danger.*

NOTE. — In later writers, **dum** sometimes takes the Subjunctive when the classical usage would require the Indicative, and **dōnec**, *until*, is freely used in this manner (especially by Tacitus): —

dum ea in Samniō **gererentur**, in Etruriā interim bellum ingēns concītur (Liv. x. 18), *while this was being done in Samnium, meanwhile a great war was stirred up in Etruria.*

illa quidem **dum** tē **fugeret**, hydrum nōn vīdit (Georg. iv. 457), *while she was fleeing from you she did not see the serpent.*

dum per vīcōs **dēportārētur**, condormiēbat (Suet. Aug. 78), *while he was being carried through the streets he used to fall dead asleep.*

Rhēnus servat nōmen et violentiam cursūs (quā Germāniam praevehitur) **dōnec** Ōceanō **misceātur** (Tac. Ann. ii. 6), *the Rhine keeps its name and rapid course (where it borders Germany) until it mingles with the ocean.*

temporibusque Augustī dīcendīs nōn dēfuēre decōra ingenia **dōnec** glīscente adūlātiōne **dēterrērentur** (id. i. 1), *for describing the times of Augustus there was no lack of talent until it was frightened away by the increasing servility of the age.*

For **dum**, *provided that*, see § 528.

CLAUSES WITH *QUĪN* AND *QUŌMINUS*

557. The original meaning of **quīn** is *how not? why not?* (**quī-nē**), and when used with the Indicative or (rarely) with the Subjunctive it regularly implies a general negative. Thus, **quīn ego hōc rogem?** *why should n't I ask this?* implies that there is no reason for not asking. The implied negative was then expressed in a main clause, like **nūlla causa est** or **fierī nōn potest**. Hence come the various dependent constructions introduced by **quīn**.

Quōminus is really a phrase (**quō minus**), and the dependent constructions which it introduces have their origin in the relative clause of purpose with **quō** and a comparative (see § 531. *a*).

558. A subjunctive clause with **quīn** is used after verbs and other expressions of *hindering, resisting, refusing, doubting, delaying*, and the like, when these are *negatived*, either expressly or by implication: —

nōn hūmāna ūlla neque dīvīna obstant **quīn** sociōs amīcōs **trahant exscindant** (Sall. Ep. Mith. 17), *no human or divine laws prevent them from taking captive and exterminating their friendly allies.*

ut nē Suessiōnēs quidem dēterrēre potuerint **quīn** cum **hīs cōnsentīrent** (B. G. ii. 3), *that they were unable to hinder even the Suessiones from making common cause with them.*

nōn posse mīlitēs continērī **quīn** in urbem **inrumperent** (B. C. ii. 12), *that the soldiers could not be restrained from bursting into the city.*

nōn recūsat **quīn iūdicēs** (Deiot. 43), *he does not object to your judging.*

neque recūsāre **quīn** armīs **contendant** (B. G. iv. 7), *and that they did not refuse to fight.*

praeterīre nōn potuī **quīn scrīberem** ad tē (Caesar ap. Cic. Att. ix. 6 A), *I could not neglect to write to you.*

Trēverī tōtīus hiemis nūllum tempus intermīsērunt **quīn** lēgātōs **mitterent** (B. G. v. 55), *the Treveri let no part of the winter pass without sending ambassadors.* [Cf. B. G. v. 53; B. C. i. 78.]

nōn cūnctandum exīstimāvit **quīn** pūgnā **dēcertāret** (B. G. iii. 23), *he thought he ought not to delay risking a decisive battle.*

paulum āfuit **quīn** Vārum **interficeret** (B. C. ii. 35), *he just missed killing Varus* (it lacked little but that he should kill).

neque multum āfuit **quīn** castrīs **expellerentur** (id. ii. 35), *they came near being driven out of the camp.*

facere nōn possum **quīn** cotīdiē ad tē **mittam** (Att. xii. 27. 2), *I cannot help sending to you every day.*

fierī nūllō modō poterat **quīn** Cleomenī **parcerētur** (Verr. v. 104), *it was out of the question that Cleomenes should not be spared.*

ut efficī nōn possit **quīn** eōs **ōderim** (Phil. xi. 36), *so that nothing can prevent my hating them.*

a. **Quīn** is especially common with **nōn dubitō**, *I do not doubt*, **nōn est dubium**, *there is no doubt*, and similar expressions: —

nōn dubitābat **quīn** eī **crēderēmus** (Att. vi. 2. 3), *he did not doubt that we believed him.*

illud cavē dubitēs **quīn** ego omnia **faciam** (Fam. v. 20. 6), *do not doubt that I will do all.*

quis īgnōrat **quīn** tria Graecōrum genera **sint** (Flacc. 64), *who is ignorant that there are three races of Greeks?*

nōn erat dubium **quīn** Helvētiī plūrimum **possent** (cf. B. G. i. 3), *there was no doubt that the Helvetians were most powerful.*

neque Caesarem fefellit **quīn** ab iīs cohortibus initium victōriae **orīrētur** (B. C. iii. 94), *and it did not escape Cæsar's notice that the beginning of the victory came from those cohorts.*

NOTE 1.—**Dubitō** without a negative is regularly followed by an Indirect Question; so sometimes **nōn dubitō** and the like: —

nōn nūllī dubitant **an** per Sardiniam **veniat** (Fam. ix. 7), *some doubt whether he is coming through Sardinia.*

dubitāte, sī potestis, ā **quō sit** Sex. Rōscius **occīsus** (Rosc. Am. 78), *doubt, if you can, by whom Sextus Roscius was murdered.*

dubitābam tū hās ipsās litterās **essēsne** acceptūrus (Att. xv. 9), *I doubt whether you will receive this very letter.* [Epistolary Imperfect (§ 479).]

quālis sit futūrus, nē vōs quidem dubitātis (B. C. ii. 32), *and what it* (the outcome) *will be, you yourselves do not doubt.*

nōn dubitō **quid sentiant** (Fam. xv. 9), *I do not doubt what they think.*

dubium illī nōn erat **quid futūrum esset** (id. viii. 8. 1), *it was not doubtful to him what was going to happen.*

NOTE 2.—**Nōn dubitō** in the sense of *I do not hesitate* commonly takes the Infinitive, but sometimes **quīn** with the Subjunctive: —

nec dubitāre illum **appellāre** sapientem (Lael. 1), *and not to hesitate to call him a sage.*

dubitandum nōn exīstimāvit **quīn proficīscerētur** (B. G. ii. 2), *he did not think he ought to hesitate to set out.*

quid dubitās **ūtī** temporis opportūnitāte (B. C. ii. 34), *why do you hesitate to take advantage of the favorable moment?* [A question implying a negative.]

b. Verbs of *hindering* and *refusing* often take the subjunctive with **nē** or **quōminus** (= **ut eō minus**), especially when the verb is not negatived: —

plūra **nē dīcam** tuae mē lacrimae impediunt (Planc. 104), *your tears prevent me from speaking further.*

nec aetās impedit **quōminus** agrī colendī studia **teneāmus** (Cat. M. 60), *nor does age prevent us from retaining an interest in tilling the soil.*

nihil impedit **quōminus** id facere **possīmus** (Fin. i. 33), *nothing hinders us from being able to do that.*

obstitistī **nē** trānsīre cōpiae **possent** (Verr. v. 5), *you opposed the passage of the troops* (opposed lest the troops should cross).

NOTE. — Some verbs of *hindering* may take the Infinitive: —

nihil obest **dīcere** (Fam. ix. 13. 4), *there is nothing to prevent my saying it.*
prohibet **accēdere** (Caec. 46), *prevents him from approaching.*

559. A clause of Result or Characteristic may be introduced by **quīn** after a general negative, where **quīn** is equivalent to **quī (quae, quod) nōn**: —

1. Clauses of Result: —

nēmō est tam fortis **quīn** [= quī nōn] reī novitāte **perturbētur** (B. G. vi. 39), *no one is so brave as not to be disturbed by the unexpected occurrence.*

nēmō erat adeō tardus **quīn putāret** (B. C. i. 69), *no one was so slothful as not to think*, etc.

quis est tam dēmēns **quīn sentiat** (Balb. 43), *who is so senseless as not to think*, etc.?

nīl tam difficilest **quīn** quaerendō investīgārī **possiet** (Ter. Haut. 675), *nothing's so hard but search will find it out* (Herrick).

2. Clauses of Characteristic: —

nēmō nostrum est **quīn** [= quī nōn] **sciat** (Rosc. Am. 55), *there is no one of us who does not know.*

nēmō fuit mīlitum **quīn vulnerārētur** (B. C. iii. 53), *there was not one of the soldiers who was not wounded.*

ecquis fuit **quīn lacrimāret** (Verr. v. 121), *was there any one who did not shed tears?*

quis est **quīn intellegat** (Fin. v. 64), *who is there who does not understand?*

hōrum nihil est **quīn** [= quod nōn] **intereat** (N. D. iii. 30), *there is none of these* (elements) *which does not perish.*

nihil est illōrum **quīn** [= quod nōn] ego illī **dīxerim** (Pl. Bac. 1012), *there is nothing of this that I have not told him.*

NOTE. — **Quīn** sometimes introduces a pure clause of result with the sense of **ut nōn**: as, — numquam tam male est Siculīs **quīn** aliquid facētē et commodē **dīcant** (Verr. iv. 95), *things are never so bad with the Sicilians but that they have something pleasant or witty to say.*

For **quīn** in independent constructions, see § 449. *b.*

SUBSTANTIVE CLAUSES

560. A clause which is used as a noun may be called a Substantive Clause, as certain relative clauses are sometimes called adjective clauses. But in practice the term is restricted to clauses which represent a nominative or an accusative case, the clauses which stand for an ablative being sometimes called adverbial clauses.

Even with this limitation the term is not quite precise (see p. 367, footnote 1). The fact is rather that the clause and the leading verb are mutually complementary; each reinforces the other. The simplest and probably the earliest form of such sentences is to be found in the paratactic use (see § 268) of two verbs like **volō abeās, dīcāmus cēnseō, adeam optimum est.** From such verbs the usage spread by analogy to other verbs (see lists on pp. 363, 367, footnotes), and the complementary relation of the clause to the verb came to resemble the complementary force of the accusative, especially the accusative of cognate meaning (§ 390).

561. A clause used as a noun is called a Substantive Clause.

a. A Substantive Clause may be used as the Subject or Object of a verb, as an Appositive, or as a Predicate Nominative or Accusative.

NOTE 1.—Many ideas which in English take the form of an abstract noun may be rendered by a substantive clause in Latin. Thus, *he demanded an investigation* may be **postulābat ut quaestiō habērētur.** The common English expression *for* with the infinitive also corresponds to a Latin substantive clause: as,—*it remains for me to speak of the piratic war*, **reliquum est ut dē bellō dīcam pīrāticō.**

NOTE 2.—When a Substantive Clause is used as subject, the verb to which it is subject is called *impersonal*, and the sign of the construction in English is commonly the so-called *expletive* IT.

562. Substantive Clauses are classified as follows:—

1. Subjunctive Clauses (**ut, nē, ut nōn**, etc.).
   - *a.* Of purpose (*command, wish, fear*) (§§ 563, 564).
   - *b.* Of result (*happen, effect*, etc.) (§ 568).
2. Indicative Clauses with **quod**: Fact, Specification, Feeling (§ 572).
3. Indirect Questions: Subjunctive, introduced by an Interrogative Word (§§ 573–576).
4. Infinitive Clauses
   - *a.* With verbs of *ordering, wishing*, etc. (§ 563).
   - *b.* Indirect Discourse (§ 579 ff.).

NOTE.—The Infinitive with Subject Accusative is not strictly a clause, but in Latin it has undergone so extensive a development that it may be so classed. The uses of the Infinitive Clause are of two kinds: (1) in constructions in which it replaces a subjunctive clause with **ut** etc.; (2) in the Indirect Discourse. The first class will be discussed in connection with the appropriate subjunctive constructions (§ 563); for Indirect Discourse, see § 579 ff.

Substantive Clauses of Purpose

563. Substantive Clauses of Purpose with **ut** (negative **nē**) are used as the object of verbs denoting an action *directed toward the future.*

Such are, verbs meaning to *admonish, ask, bargain, command, decree, determine, permit, persuade, resolve, urge,* and *wish:* —[1]

monet **ut** omnēs suspīciōnēs **vītet** (B. G. i. 20), *he warns him to avoid all suspicion.*

hortātur eōs **nē** animō **dēficiant** (B. C. i. 19), *he urges them not to lose heart.*

tē rogō atque ōrō **ut** eum **iuvēs** (Fam. xiii. 66), *I beg and pray you to aid him.*

hīs **utī conquīrerent** imperāvit (B. G. i. 28), *he ordered them to search.*

persuādet Casticō **ut** rēgnum **occupāret** (id. i. 3), *he persuades Casticus to usurp royal power.*

suīs imperāvit **nē** quod omnīnō tēlum **rêicerent** (id. i. 46), *he ordered his men not to throw back any weapon at all.*

NOTE. — With any verb of these classes the poets may use the Infinitive instead of an object clause: —

hortāmur **fārī** (Aen. ii. 74), *we urge* [him] *to speak.*

nē quaere **docērī** (id. vi. 614), *seek not to be told.*

temptat **praevertere** (id. i. 721), *she attempts to turn,* etc.

For the Subjunctive without **ut** with verbs of *commanding,* see § 565. *a.*

a. **Iubeō,** *order,* and **vetō,** *forbid,* take the Infinitive with Subject Accusative: —

Labiēnum iugum montis **ascendere** iubet (B. G. i. 21), *he orders Labienus to ascend the ridge of the hill.*

līberōs ad sē **addūcī** iussit (id. ii. 5), *he ordered the children to be brought to him.*

ab opere **lēgātōs discēdere** vetuerat (id. ii. 20), *he had forbidden the lieutenants to leave the work.*

vetuēre [**bona**] **reddī** (Liv. ii. 5), *they forbade the return of the goods* (that the goods be returned).

NOTE. — Some other verbs of *commanding* etc. occasionally take the Infinitive: —

pontem imperant **fierī** (B. C. i. 61), *they order a bridge to be built.*

rēs monet **cavēre** (Sall. Cat. 52. 3), *the occasion warns us to be on our guard.*

b. Verbs of *wishing* take either the Infinitive or the Subjunctive. With **volō** (**nōlō, mālō**) and **cupiō** the Infinitive is commoner, and the subject of the infinitive is rarely expressed when it would be the same as that of the main verb.

With other verbs of *wishing* the Subjunctive is commoner when the subject changes, the Infinitive when it remains the same.

1. Subject of dependent verb same as that of the verb of *wishing:* —

augur **fierī** voluī (Fam. xv. 4. 13), *I wished to be made augur.*

cupiō vigiliam meam tibi **trādere** (id. xi. 24), *I am eager to hand over my watch to you.*

[1] Such verbs or verbal phrases are id agō, ad id veniō, caveō (nē), cēnseō, cōgō, concēdō, cōnstituō, cūrō, dēcernō, ēdīcō, flāgitō, hortor, imperō, īnstō, mandō, metuō (nē), moneō, negōtium dō, operam dō, ōrō, persuādeō, petō, postulō, praecipiō, precor, prōnūntiō, quaerō, rogō, scīscō, timeō (nē), vereor (nē), videō, volō.

iūdicem **mē** **esse**, nōn doctōrem volō (Or. 117), *I wish to be a judge, not a teacher.*

mē Caesaris mīlitem **dīcī** voluī (B. C. ii. 32. 13), *I wished to be called a soldier of Cæsar.*

cupiō **mē esse** clēmentem (Cat. i. 4), *I desire to be merciful.* [But regularly, cupiō **esse clēmēns** (see § 457).]

omnīs hominēs, quī **sēsē** student **praestāre** cēterīs animālibus (Sall. Cat. 1), *all men who wish to excel other living creatures.*

2. Subject of dependent verb different from that of the verb of *wishing:*

volō **tē scīre** (Fam. ix. 24. 1), *I wish you to know.*

vim volumus **exstinguī** (Sest. 92), *we wish violence to be put down.*

tē tuā **fruī** virtūte cupimus (Brut. 331), *we wish you to reap the fruits of your virtue.*

cupiō **ut impetret** (Pl. Capt. 102), *I wish he may get it.*

numquam optābō **ut audiātis** (Cat. ii. 15), *I will never desire that you shall hear.*

For **volō** and its compounds with the Subjunctive without **ut**, see § 565.

c. Verbs of *permitting* take either the Subjunctive or the Infinitive. **Patior** takes regularly the Infinitive with Subject Accusative; so often **sinō**: —

permīsit **ut faceret** (De Or. ii. 366), *permitted him to make.*

concēdō tibi **ut** ea **praetereās** (Rosc. Am. 54), *I allow you to pass by these matters.*

tabernācula statuī passus nōn est (B. C. i. 81), *he did not allow tents to be pitched.*

vīnum importārī nōn sinunt (B. G. iv. 2), *they do not allow wine to be imported.*

d. Verbs of *determining, decreeing, resolving, bargaining,* take either the Subjunctive or the Infinitive: —

cōnstituerant **ut** L. Bēstia **quererētur** (Sall. Cat. 43), *they had determined that Lucius Bestia should complain.*

proeliō **supersedēre** statuit (B. G. ii. 8), *he determined to refuse battle.*

dē bonīs rēgis **quae reddī** cēnsuerant (Liv. ii. 5), *about the king's goods, which they had decreed should be restored.*

dēcernit **utī** cōnsulēs dīlēctum **habeant** (Sall. Cat. 34), *decrees that the consuls shall hold a levy.*

ēdictō **nē** quis iniussū **pūgnāret** (Liv. v. 19), *having commanded that none should fight without orders.*

Note 1. — Different verbs of these classes with the same meaning vary in their construction (see the Lexicon). For verbs of *bargaining* etc. with the Gerundive, see § 500. 4.

Note 2. — Verbs of *decreeing* and *voting* often take the Infinitive of the Second Periphrastic conjugation: — Rēgulus **captīvōs reddendōs** [**esse**] nōn cēnsuit (Off. i. 39), *Regulus voted that the captives should not be returned.* [He said, in giving his formal opinion: **captīvī nōn reddendī sunt.**]

e. Verbs of *caution* and *effort* take the Subjunctive with **ut.** But **cōnor,** *try,* commonly takes the Complementary Infinitive: —

cūrā **ut** quam prīmum **intellegam** (Fam. xiii. 10. 4), *let me know as soon as possible* (take care that I may understand).

dant operam **ut habeant** (Sall. Cat. 41), *they take pains to have* (give their attention that, etc.).

impellere **utī** Caesar **nōminārētur** (id. 49), *to induce them to name Cæsar* (that Cæsar should be named).

cōnātus est Caesar **reficere** pontīs (B. C. i. 50), *Cæsar tried to rebuild the bridges.*

NOTE 1. — **Cōnor sī** also occurs (as B. G. i. 8); cf. **mīror sī** etc., § 572. *b.* N.

NOTE 2. — **Ut nē** occurs occasionally with verbs of *caution* and *effort* (cf. § 531): — cūrā et prōvidē **ut nēquid eī dēsit** (Att. xi. 3. 3), *take care and see that he lacks nothing.*

For the Subjunctive with **quīn** and **quōminus** with verbs of *hindering* etc., see § 558.

564. Verbs of *fearing* take the Subjunctive, with **nē** affirmative and **nē nōn** or **ut** negative.

In this use **nē** is commonly to be translated by *that,* **ut** and **nē nōn** by *that not:* —

timeō **nē** Verrēs **fēcerit** (Verr. v. 3), *I fear that Verres has done,* etc.

nē animum **offenderet** verēbātur (B. G. i. 19), *he feared that he should hurt the feelings,* etc.

nē exhērēdārētur veritus est (Rosc. Am. 58), *he feared that he should be disinherited.*

ōrātor metuō **nē languēscat** senectūte (Cat. M. 28), *I fear the orator grows feeble from old age.*

vereor **ut** tibi **possim** concēdere (De Or. i. 35), *I fear that I cannot grant you.*

haud sānē perīculum est **nē nōn** mortem optandam **putet** (Tusc. v. 118), *there is no danger that he will not think death desirable.*

NOTE. — The subjunctive in **nē**-clauses after a verb of fearing is optative in origin. To an independent **nē**-sentence, as **nē accidat,** *may it not happen,* a verb may be prefixed (cf. § 560), making a complex sentence. Thus, **vidē nē accidat; ōrō nē accidat; cavet nē accidat;** when the prefixed verb is one of fearing, **timeō nē accidat** becomes *let it not happen, but I fear that it may.* The origin of the **ut**-clause is similar.

565. Volō and its compounds, the impersonals **licet** and **oportet,** and the imperatives **dīc** and **fac** often take the Subjunctive without **ut:** —

volō **amēs** (Att. ii. 10), *I wish you to love.*

quam vellem mē **invītāssēs** (Fam. x. 28. 1), *how I wish you had invited me!*

māllem Cerberum **metuerēs** (Tusc. i. 12), *I had rather you feared Cerberus.*

sint enim oportet (id. i. 12), *for they must exist.*

querāmur licet (Caec. 41), *we are allowed to complain.*

fac **dīligās** (Att. iii. 13. 2), *do love!* [A periphrasis for the imperative **dīlige,** *love* (cf. § 449. *c*).]

dīc **exeat,** *tell him to go out.*

NOTE 1.—In such cases there is no ellipsis of **ut**. The expressions are idiomatic remnants of an older construction in which the subjunctives were *hortatory* or *optative* and thus really independent of the verb of *wishing* etc. In the classical period, however, they were doubtless felt as subordinate. Compare the use of **cavē** and the subjunctive (without **nē**) in Prohibitions (§ 450), which appears to follow the analogy of **fac.**

NOTE 2.—**Licet** may take (1) the Subjunctive, usually without **ut**; (2) the simple Infinitive; (3) the Infinitive with Subject Accusative; (4) the Dative and the Infinitive (see § 455. 1). Thus, *I may go* is **licet eam, licet īre, licet mē īre,** or **licet mihi īre.**

For **licet** in concessive clauses, see § 527. *b*.

NOTE 3.—**Oportet** may take (1) the Subjunctive without **ut**; (2) the simple Infinitive; (3) the Infinitive with Subject Accusative. Thus *I must go* is **oportet eam, oportet īre,** or **oportet mē īre.**

a. Verbs of *commanding* and the like often take the subjunctive without **ut**:—

huic mandat Rēmōs **adeat** (B. G. iii. 11), *he orders him to visit the Remi.*
rogat fīnem **faciat** (id. i. 20), *he asks him to cease.*
Mnēsthea vocat, classem **aptent** sociī (Aen. iv. 289), *he calls Mnestheus* [and orders that] *his comrades shall make ready the fleet.*

NOTE.—The subjunctive in this construction is the hortatory subjunctive used to express a command in Indirect Discourse (§ 588).

Substantive Clauses of Purpose with Passive Verbs

566. A Substantive Clause used as the object of a verb becomes the subject when the verb is put in the passive (*Impersonal Construction*):—

Caesar **ut cōgnōsceret** postulātum est (B. C. i. 87), *Cæsar was requested to make an investigation* (it was requested that Cæsar should make an investigation).
sī erat Hēracliō ab senātū mandātum **ut emeret** (Verr. iii. 88), *if Heraclius had been instructed by the senate to buy.*
sī persuāsum erat Cluviō **ut mentīrētur** (Rosc. Com. 51), *if Cluvius had been persuaded to lie.*
putō concēdī nōbīs oportēre **ut** Graecō verbō **ūtāmur** (Fin. iii. 15), *I think we must be allowed to use a Greek word.*
nē quid eīs **noceātur** ā Caesare cavētur (B. C. i. 86), *Cæsar takes care that no harm shall be done them* (care is taken by Cæsar lest, etc.).

a. With verbs of *admonishing*, the personal object becomes the subject and the object clause is retained:—

admonitī sumus **ut cavērēmus** (Att. viii. 11 D. 3), *we were warned to be careful.*
cum monērētur **ut** cautior **esset** (Div. i. 51), *when he was advised to be more cautious.*
monērī vīsus est **nē** id **faceret** (id. 56), *he seemed to be warned not to do it.*

b. Some verbs that take an infinitive instead of a subjunctive are used impersonally in the passive, and the infinitive becomes the subject of the sentence: —

loquī nōn concēditur (B. G. vi. 20), *it is not allowed to speak.*

c. With **iubeō, vetō,** and **cōgō,** the *subject accusative* of the infinitive becomes the *subject nominative* of the main verb, and the infinitive is retained as complementary (*Personal Construction*): —

adesse iubentur postrīdiē (Verr. ii. 41), *they are ordered to be present on the following day.*

īre in exsilium iussus est (Cat. ii. 12), *he was ordered to go into exile.*

Simōnidēs vetitus est **nāvigāre** (Div. ii. 134), *Simonides was forbidden to sail.*

Mandubiī **exīre** cōguntur (B. G. vii. 78), *the Mandubii are compelled to go out.*

Substantive Clauses of Result (Consecutive Clauses)

567. Clauses of Result may be used substantively, (1) as the object of **faciō** etc. (§ 568); (2) as the subject of these same verbs in the passive, as well as of other verbs and verbal phrases (§ 569); (3) in apposition with another substantive, or as predicate nominative etc. (see §§ 570, 571).[1]

568. Substantive Clauses of Result with **ut** (negative **ut nōn**) are used as the object of verbs denoting the *accomplishment of an effort.*[2]

Such are especially **faciō** and its compounds (**efficiō, cōnficiō,** etc.): —

efficiam **ut intellegātis** (Clu. 7), *I will make you understand* (lit. effect that you, etc.). [So, **faciam ut intellegātis** (id. 9).]

commeātūs **ut** portārī **possent** efficiēbat (B. G. ii. 5), *made it possible that supplies could be brought.*

perfēcī **ut** ē rēgnō ille **discēderet** (Fam. xv. 4. 6), *I brought about his departure from the kingdom.*

quae lībertās **ut** laetior **esset** rēgis superbia fēcerat (Liv. ii. 1), *the arrogance of the king had made this liberty more welcome.*

ēvincunt īnstandō **ut** litterae **darentur** (id. ii. 4), *by insisting they gain their point, — that letters should be sent.* [Here **ēvincunt** = **efficiunt.**]

[1] In all these cases the clause is not strictly subject or object. The main verb originally conveyed a meaning sufficient in itself, and the result clause was merely complementary. This is seen by the frequent use of ita and the like with the main verb (**ita accidit ut,** etc.). In like manner purpose clauses are only apparently subject or object of the verb with which they are connected.

[2] Verbs and phrases taking an ut-clause of result as subject or object are **accēdit, accidit, additur, altera est rēs, committō, cōnsequor, contingit, efficiō, ēvenit, faciō, fit, fierī potest, fore, impetrō, integrum est, mōs est, mūnus est, necesse est, prope est, rēctum est, relinquitur, reliquum est, restat, tantī est, tantum abest,** and a few others.

NOTE 1.—The expressions **facere ut, committere ut**, with the subjunctive, often form a periphrasis for the simple verb: as,—**invītus fēcī ut Flāminium ē senātū ēicerem** (Cat. M. 42), *it was with reluctance that I expelled Flaminius from the senate.*

569. Substantive Clauses of Result are used as the subject of the following:—

1. Of passive verbs denoting the *accomplishment of an effort:*—

impetrātum est **ut** in senātū **recitārentur** (litterae) (B. C. i. 1), *they succeeded in having the letter read in the senate* (it was brought about that, etc.).
ita efficitur **ut** omne corpus mortāle **sit** (N. D. iii. 30), *it therefore is made out that every body is mortal.*

2. Of Impersonals meaning *it happens, it remains, it follows, it is necessary, it is added,* and the like (§ 568, footnote):—

accidit **ut esset** lūna plēna (B. G. iv. 29), *it happened to be full moon* (it happened that it was, etc.). [Here **ut esset** is subject of **accidit.**]
reliquum est **ut** officiīs **certēmus** inter nōs (Fam. vii. 31), *it remains for us to vie with each other in courtesies.*
restat **ut** hōc **dubitēmus** (Rosc. Am. 88), *it is left for us to doubt this.*
sequitur **ut doceam** (N. D. ii. 81), *the next thing is to show* (it follows, etc.).

NOTE 1.—The infinitive sometimes occurs: as,—**nec enim acciderat mihi opus esse** (Fam. vi. 11. 1), *for it had not happened to be necessary to me.*

NOTE 2.—**Necesse est** often takes the subjunctive without **ut**: as,—**concēdās** necesse est (Rosc. Am. 87), *you must grant.*

3. Of **est** in the sense of *it is the fact that,* etc. (mostly poetic):—

est **ut** virō vir lātius **ōrdinet** arbusta (Hor. Od. iii. 1. 9), *it is the fact that one man plants his vineyards in wider rows than another.*

a. **Fore** (or **futūrum esse**) **ut** with a clause of result as subject is often used instead of the Future Infinitive active or passive; so necessarily in verbs which have no supine stem:—

spērō **fore ut contingat** id nōbīs (Tusc. i. 82), *I hope that will be our happy lot.*
cum vidērem **fore ut nōn possem** (Cat. ii. 4), *when I saw that I should not be able.*

570. A substantive clause of result may be in apposition with another substantive (especially a neuter pronoun):—

illud etiam restiterat, **ut** tē in iūs **ēdūcerent** (Quinct. 33), *this too remained—for them to drag you into court.*

571. A substantive clause of result may serve as predicate nominative after **mōs est** and similar expressions:—

est mōs hominum, **ut nōlint** eundem plūribus rēbus excellere (Brut. 84), *it is the way of men to be unwilling for one man to excel in several things.*

a. A result clause, with or without **ut**, frequently follows **quam** after a comparative (but see § 583. *c*): —

Canachī sīgna rigidiōra sunt **quam ut imitentur** vēritātem (Brut. 70), *the statues of Canachus are too stiff to represent nature* (stiffer than that they should).

perpessus est omnia potius **quam indicāret** (Tusc. ii. 52), *he endured all rather than betray*, etc. [Regularly without **ut** except in Livy.]

b. The phrase **tantum abest**, *it is so far* [from being the case], regularly takes two clauses of result with **ut**: one is *substantive*, the subject of **abest**; the other is *adverbial*, correlative with **tantum**: —

tantum abest **ut** nostra **mīrēmur**, **ut** ūsque eō difficilēs ac mōrōsī **sīmus**, **ut** nōbīs nōn **satis faciat** ipse Dēmosthenēs (Or. 104), *so far from admiring my own works, I am difficult and captious to that degree that not Demosthenes himself satisfies me.* [Here the first **ut**-clause is the subject of **abest** (§ 569. 2); the second, a result clause after **tantum** (§ 537); and the third, after **ūsque eō**.]

c. Rarely, a *thought* or an *idea* is considered as a result, and is expressed by the subjunctive with **ut** instead of the accusative and infinitive (§ 580). In this case a demonstrative usually precedes:

praeclārum illud est, **ut** eōs . . . **amēmus** (Tusc. iii. 73), *this is a noble thing, that we should love*, etc.

vērī simile nōn est **ut** ille **antepōneret** (Verr. iv. 11), *it is not likely that he preferred.*

For Relative Clauses with **quīn** after verbs of *hindering* etc., see § 558.

Indicative with *Quod*

572. A peculiar form of Substantive Clause consists of **quod** (in the sense of *that, the fact that*) with the Indicative.

The clause in the Indicative with **quod** is used when the statement is *regarded as a fact:* —

alterum est vitium, **quod** quīdam nimis māgnum studium **cōnferunt** (Off. i. 19), *it is another fault that some bestow too much zeal*, etc. [Here **ut cōnferant** could be used, meaning *that* some *should* bestow; or the accusative and infinitive, meaning *to bestow* (abstractly); **quod** makes it a fact that men *do* bestow, etc.]

inter inanimum et animal hōc maximē interest, **quod** animal **agit** aliquid (Acad. ii. 37), *this is the chief difference between an inanimate object and an animal, that an animal aims at something.*

quod rediit nōbīs mīrābile vidētur (Off. iii. 111), *that he* (Regulus) *returned seems wonderful to us.*

accidit perincommodē **quod** eum nusquam **vīdistī** (Att. i. 17. 2), *it happened very unluckily that you nowhere saw him.*

opportūnissima rēs accidit **quod** Germānī **vēnērunt** (B. G. iv. 13), *a very fortunate thing happened,* (namely) *that the Germans came.*

praetereō **quod** eam sibi domum sēdemque **dēlēgit** (Clu. 188), *I pass over the fact that she chose that house and home for herself.*

mittō **quod possessa** per vim (Flacc. 79), *I disregard the fact that they were seized by violence.*

NOTE.—Like other substantive clauses, the clause with **quod** may be used as subject, as object, as appositive, etc., but it is commonly either the subject or in apposition with the subject.

a. A substantive clause with **quod** sometimes appears as an *accusative of specification,* corresponding to the English *whereas* or *as to the fact that:*—

quod mihi dē nostrō statū **grātulāris**, minimē mīrāmur tē tuīs praeclārīs operibus laetārī (Fam. i. 7. 7), *as to your congratulating me on our condition, we are not at all surprised that you are pleased with your own noble works.*

quod dē domō **scrībis**, ego, etc. (Fam. xiv. 2. 3), *as to what you write of the house, I,* etc.

b. Verbs of *feeling* and the *expression of feeling* take either **quod** (**quia**) or the accusative and infinitive (Indirect Discourse):—

quod scrībis . . . gaudeō (Q. Fr. iii. 1. 9), *I am glad that you write.*

faciō libenter **quod** eam nōn **possum** praeterīre (Legg. i. 63), *I am glad that I cannot pass it by.*

quae perfecta esse vehementer laetor (Rosc. Am. 136), *I greatly rejoice that this is finished.*

quī **quia** nōn **habuit** ā mē turmās equitum fortasse suscēnset (Att. vi. 3. 5), *who perhaps feels angry that he did not receive squadrons of cavalry from me.*

molestē tulī **tē** senātuī grātiās nōn **ēgisse** (Fam. x. 27. 1), *I was displeased that you did not return thanks to the senate.*

NOTE.—**Mīror** and similar expressions are sometimes followed by a clause with **sī**.[1] This is apparently substantive, but really protasis (cf. § 563. *e.* N.[1]). Thus,—mīror sī quemquam amīcum habēre potuit (Lael. 54), *I wonder if he could ever have a friend.* [Originally, *If this is so, I wonder at it.*]

Indirect Questions

573. An Indirect Question is any sentence or clause which is introduced by an interrogative word (pronoun, adverb, etc.), and which is itself the subject or object of a verb, or depends on any expression implying uncertainty or doubt.

In grammatical form, *exclamatory* sentences are not distinguished from *interrogative* (see the third example below).

[1] Cf. the Greek *θαυμάζω εἰ.*

574. An Indirect Question takes its verb in the Subjunctive:

quid ipse **sentiam** expōnam (Div. i. 10), *I will explain what I think.* [Direct: **quid sentiō?**]

id **possetne** fierī cōnsuluit (id. i. 32), *he consulted whether it could be done.* [Direct: **potestne?**]

quam sīs audāx omnēs intellegere potuērunt (Rosc. Am. 87), *all could understand how bold you are.* [Direct: **quam es audāx!**]

doleam necne doleam nihil interest (Tusc. ii. 29), *it is of no account whether I suffer or not.* [Double question.]

quaesīvī ā Catilīnā in conventū apud M. Laecam **fuisset necne** (Cat. ii. 13), *I asked Catiline whether he had been at the meeting at Marcus Lœca's or not.* [Double question.]

rogat mē **quid sentiam**, *he asks me what I think.* [Cf. **rogat mē sententiam**, *he asks me my opinion.*]

hōc dubium est, **uter** nostrum **sit** inverēcundior (Acad. ii. 126), *this is doubtful, which of us two is the less modest.*

incertī quātenus Volerō **exercēret** victōriam (Liv. ii. 55), *uncertain how far Volero would push victory.* [As if **dubitantēs quātenus**, etc.]

Note.—An Indirect Question may be the subject of a verb (as in the fourth example), the direct object (as in the first), the secondary object (as in the sixth), an appositive (as in the seventh).

575. The Sequence of Tenses in Indirect Question is illustrated by the following examples:—

dīcō quid faciam, *I tell you what I am doing.*
dīcō quid factūrus sim, *I tell you what I will (shall) do.*
dīcō quid fēcerim, *I tell you what I did (have done, was doing).*
dīxī quid facerem, *I told you what I was doing.*
dīxī quid fēcissem, *I told you what I had done (had been doing).*
dīxī quid factūrus essem, *I told you what I would (should) do* (was going to do).
dīxī quid factūrus fuissem, *I told you what I would (should) have done.*

a. Indirect Questions referring to *future time* take the subjunctive of the First Periphrastic Conjugation:—

prōspiciō **quī concursūs futūrī sint** (Caecil. 42), *I foresee what throngs there will be.* [Direct: **quī erunt?**]

quid sit futūrum crās, fuge quaerere (Hor. Od. i. 9. 13), *forbear to ask what will be on the morrow.* [Direct: **quid erit** or **futūrum est?**]

posthāc nōn scrībam ad tē **quid factūrus sim**, sed quid fēcerim (Att. x. 18), *hereafter I shall not write to you what I am going to do, but what I have done.* [Direct: **quid faciēs** (or **factūrus eris**)? **quid fēcistī?**]

Note.—This Periphrastic Future avoids the ambiguity which would be caused by using the Present Subjunctive to refer to future time in such clauses.

b. The Deliberative Subjunctive (§ 444) remains unchanged in an Indirect Question, except sometimes in tense:—

quō mē **vertam** nesciō (Clu. 4), *I do not know which way to turn.* [Direct: **quō mē vertam**?]
neque satis cōnstābat **quid agerent** (B. G. iii. 14), *and it was not very clear what they were to do.* [Direct: **quid agāmus**?]
nec quisquam satis certum habet, **quid** aut **spēret** aut **timeat** (Liv. xxii. 7. 10), *nor is any one well assured what he shall hope or fear.* [Here the future participle with **sit** could not be used.]
incertō **quid peterent** aut **vītārent** (id. xxviii. 36. 12), *since it was doubtful* (ablative absolute) *what they should seek or shun.*

c. Indirect Questions often take the Indicative in early Latin and in poetry: —

vīneam **quō** in agrō cōnserī **oportet** sīc observātō (Cato R. R. 6. 4), *in what soil a vineyard should be set you must observe thus.*

d. **Nesciō quis,** when used in an indefinite sense (*somebody or other*), is not followed by the Subjunctive.

So also **nesciō quō** (**unde**, etc.), and the following idiomatic phrases which are practically adverbs: —

mīrum (nīmīrum) quam, *marvellously* (marvellous how).
mīrum quantum, *tremendously* (marvellous how much).
immāne quantum, *monstrously* (monstrous how much).
sānē quam, *immensely.*
valdē quam, *enormously.*

Examples are: —

quī istam **nesciō quam** indolentiam māgnopere laudant (Tusc. iii. 12), *who greatly extol that freedom from pain, whatever it is.*
mīrum quantum prōfuit (Liv. ii. 1), *it helped prodigiously.*
ita fātō **nesciō quō** contigisse arbitror (Fam. xv. 13), *I think it happened so by some fatality or other.*
nam suōs **valdē quam** paucōs habet (id. xi. 13 A. 3), *for he has uncommonly few of his own.*
sānē quam sum gāvīsus (id. xi. 13 A. 4), *I was immensely glad.*
immāne quantum discrepat (Hor. Od. i. 27. 5), *is monstrously at variance.*

576. In colloquial usage and in poetry the subject of an Indirect Question is often attracted into the main clause as object (*Accusative of Anticipation*): —

nōstī **Mārcellum** quam **tardus sit** (Fam. viii. 10. 3), *you know how slow Marcellus is.* [For **nōstī quam tardus sit Mārcellus.** Cf. "I know thee who thou art."]
Cf. potestne igitur **eārum rērum**, quā rē futūrae sint, ūlla esse praesēnsiō (Div. ii. 15), *can there be, then, any foreknowledge as to those things, why they will occur?* [A similar use of the Objective Genitive.]

NOTE.—In some cases the Object of Anticipation becomes the Subject by a change of *voice*, and an apparent mixture of relative and interrogative constructions is the result:—

> **quīdam** saepe in parvā pecūniā perspiciuntur quam sint levēs (Lael. 63), *it is often seen, in a trifling matter of money, how unprincipled some people are* (some people are often seen through, how unprincipled they are).
>
> quem ad modum Pompêium oppūgnārent ā mē indicātī sunt (Leg. Agr. i. 5), *it has been shown by me in what way they attacked Pompey* (they have been shown by me, how they attacked).

a. An indirect question is occasionally introduced by **sī** in the sense of *whether* (like *if* in English, cf. § 572. *b.* N.):—

> circumfunduntur hostēs **sī** quem aditum reperīre **possent** (B. G. vi. 37), *the enemy pour round* [to see] *if they can find entrance.*
>
> vīsam **sī** domī **est** (Ter. Haut. 170), *I will go see if he is at home.*

NOTE.—This is strictly a Protasis, but usually no Apodosis is thought of, and the clause is virtually an Indirect Question.

For the Potential Subjunctive with **forsitan** (originally an Indirect Question), see § 447. *a.*

INDIRECT DISCOURSE

577. The use of the Accusative and Infinitive in Indirect Discourse (*ōrātiō oblīqua*) is a comparatively late form of speech, developed in the Latin and Greek only, and perhaps separately in each of them. It is wholly wanting in Sanskrit, but some forms like it have grown up in English and German.

The essential character of Indirect Discourse is, that the language of some other person than the writer or speaker is compressed into a kind of Substantive Clause, the verb of the main clause becoming Infinitive, while modifying clauses, as well as all hortatory forms of speech, take the Subjunctive. The *person* of the verb necessarily conforms to the new relation of persons.

The construction of Indirect Discourse, however, is not limited to reports of the language of some person other than the speaker; it may be used to express what any one—whether the speaker or some one else—*says, thinks,* or *perceives,* whenever that which is *said, thought,* or *perceived* is capable of being expressed in the form of a complete sentence. For anything that can be *said* etc. can also *be reported* indirectly as well as directly.

The use of the Infinitive in the main clause undoubtedly comes from its use as a *case-form* to complete or modify the action expressed by the verb of *saying* and its object together. This object in time came to be regarded as, and in fact to all intents became, the subject of the infinitive. A transition state is found in Sanskrit, which, though it has no indirect discourse proper, yet allows an indirect predication after verbs of saying and the like by means of a predicative apposition, in such expressions as "The maids told the king [that] his daughter [was] bereft of her senses."

The simple form of indirect statement with the accusative and infinitive was afterwards amplified by introducing dependent or modifying clauses; and in Latin it became a common construction, and could be used to report whole speeches etc., which in other languages would have the direct form. (Compare the style of reporting speeches in English, where only the person and tense are changed.)

The Subjunctive in the subordinate clauses of Indirect Discourse has no significance except to make more distinct the fact that these clauses are subordinate; consequently no direct connection has been traced between them and the uses of the mood in simple sentences. It is probable that the subjunctive in indirect questions (§ 574), in informal indirect discourse (§ 592), and in clauses of the integral part (§ 593) represents the earliest steps of a movement by which the subjunctive became in some degree a mood of subordination.

The Subjunctive standing for hortatory forms of speech in Indirect Discourse is simply the usual hortatory subjunctive, with only a change of person and tense (if necessary), as in the reporter's style.

578. A Direct Quotation gives the exact words of the original speaker or writer (*Ōrātiō Rēcta*).

An Indirect Quotation adapts the words of the speaker or writer to the construction of the sentence in which they are quoted (*Ōrātiō Oblīqua*).

NOTE.—The term Indirect Discourse (*ōrātiō oblīqua*) is used in two senses. In the wider sense it includes all clauses—of whatever kind—which express the words or thought of any person *indirectly*, that is, in a form different from that in which the person said the words or conceived the thought. In the narrower sense the term Indirect Discourse is restricted to those cases in which some *complete proposition* is cited in the form of an Indirect Quotation, which may be extended to a narrative or an address of any length, as in the speeches reported by Cæsar and Livy. In this book the term is used in the restricted sense.

Formal Indirect Discourse

579. Verbs and other expressions of *knowing*, *thinking*, *telling*, and *perceiving*,[1] govern the Indirect Discourse.

NOTE.—**Inquam**, *said I* (etc.) takes the Direct Discourse except in poetry.

Declaratory Sentences in Indirect Discourse

580. In Indirect Discourse the *main clause* of a Declaratory Sentence is put in the Infinitive with Subject Accusative. All *subordinate clauses* take the Subjunctive:—

scīō mē paene incrēdibilem rem pollicērī (B. C. iii. 86), *I know that I am promising an almost incredible thing.* [Direct: polliceor.]

nōn arbitror tē ita sentīre (Fam. x. 26. 2), *I do not suppose that you feel thus.* [Direct: sentīs.]

spērō mē līberātum [esse] dē metū (Tusc. ii. 67), *I trust I have been freed from fear.* [Direct: līberātus sum.]

[1] Such are: (1) *knowing*, sciō, cōgnōscō, compertum habeō, etc.; (2) *thinking*, putō, exīstimō, arbitror, etc.; (3) *telling*, dīcō, nūntiō, referō, polliceor, prōmittō, certiōrem faciō, etc.; (4) *perceiving*, sentiō, comperiō, videō, audiō, etc. So in general any word that denotes thought or mental and visual perception or their expression may govern the Indirect Discourse.

[dīcit] esse nōn **nūllōs** quōrum auctōritās plūrimum **valeat** (B. G. i. 17), *he says there are some, whose influence most prevails.* [Direct: **sunt nōn nūllī . . . valet.**]

nisi iūrāsset, scelus **sē factūrum** [**esse**] arbitrābātur (Verr. ii. 1. 123), *he thought he should incur guilt, unless he should take the oath.* [Direct: **nisi iūrāverō, faciam.**]

a. The verb of *saying* etc. is often not expressed, but implied in some word or in the general drift of the sentence: —

cōnsulis alterīus nōmen invīsum cīvitātī fuit: **nimium Tarquiniōs rēgnō adsuēsse; initium ā Prīscō factum; rēgnāsse** dein **Ser. Tullium,** etc. (Liv. ii. 2), *the name of the other consul was hateful to the state; the Tarquins* (they thought) *had become too much accustomed to royal power,* etc. [Here **invīsum** implies a thought, and this thought is added in the form of Indirect Discourse.]

ōrantēs ut urbibus saltem — iam enim **agrōs dēplōrātōs esse** — opem senātus ferret (id. xli. 6), *praying that the senate would at least bring aid to the cities — for the fields* [they said] *were already given up as lost.*

b. The verb **negō**, *deny*, is commonly used in preference to **dīcō** with a negative: —

[Stōicī] negant **quidquam** [esse] bonum nisi quod honestum **sit** (Fin. ii. 68), *the Stoics assert that nothing is good but what is right.*

c. Verbs of *promising, hoping, expecting, threatening, swearing,* and the like, regularly take the construction of Indirect Discourse, contrary to the English idiom: —

minātur **sēsē abīre** (Pl. Asin. 604), *he threatens to go away.* [Direct: **abeō**, *I am going away.*]

spērant sē maximum frūctum **esse captūrōs** (Lael. 79), *they hope to gain the utmost advantage.* [Direct: **capiēmus.**]

spērat **sē absolūtum īrī** (Sull. 21), *he hopes that he shall be acquitted.* [Direct: **absolvar.**]

quem inimīcissimum **futūrum esse** prōmittō ac spondeō (Mur. 90), *who I promise and warrant will be the bitterest of enemies.* [Direct: **erit.**]

dolor fortitūdinem sē **dēbilitātūrum** minātur (Tusc. v. 76), *pain threatens to wear down fortitude.* [Direct: **dēbilitābō.**]

cōnfīdō **mē** quod velim facile ā tē **impetrātūrum** (Fam. xi. 16. 1), *I trust I shall easily obtain from you what I wish.* [Direct: **quod volō, impetrābō.**]

NOTE. — These verbs, however, often take a simple Complementary Infinitive (§ 456) So regularly in early Latin (except **spērō**): —[1]

pollicentur obsidēs **dare** (B. G. iv. 21), *they promise to give hostages.*

prōmīsī dōlium vīnī **dare** (Pl. Cist. 542), *I promised to give a jar of wine.*

[1] Compare the Greek aorist infinitive after similar verbs.

d. Some verbs and expressions may be used either as verbs of *saying*, or as verbs of *commanding*, *effecting*, and the like. These take as their object either an Infinitive with subject accusative or a Substantive clause of Purpose or Result, according to the sense.

1. Infinitive with Subject Accusative (Indirect Discourse): —

laudem sapientiae statuō **esse** maximam (Fam. v. 13), *I hold that the glory of wisdom is the greatest.* [Indirect Discourse.]

rēs ipsa monēbat **tempus esse** (Att. x. 8. 1), *the thing itself warned that it was time.* [Cf. **monēre ut**, *warn to do something.*]

fac mihi **esse persuāsum** (N. D. i. 75), *suppose that I am persuaded of that.* [Cf. **facere ut**, *bring it about that.*]

hōc volunt persuādēre, **nōn interīre animās** (B. G. vi. 14), *they wish to convince that souls do not perish.*

2. Subjunctive (Substantive Clause of Purpose or Result): —

statuunt **ut** decem mīlia hominum **mittantur** (B. G. vii. 21), *they resolve that 10,000 men shall be sent.* [Purpose clause (cf. § 563).]

huic persuādet **utī** ad hostīs **trānseat** (id. iii. 18), *he persuades him to pass over to the enemy.*

Pompêius suīs praedīxerat **ut** Caesaris impetum **exciperent** (B. C. iii. 92), *Pompey had instructed his men beforehand to await Cæsar's attack.*

dēnūntiāvit **ut essent** animō parātī (id. iii. 86), *he bade them be alert and steadfast* (ready in spirit).

NOTE. — The infinitive with subject accusative in this construction is Indirect Discourse, and is to be distinguished from the simple infinitive sometimes found with these verbs instead of a subjunctive clause (§ 563. *d*).

581. The Subject Accusative of the Infinitive is regularly expressed in Indirect Discourse, even if it is wanting in the direct:

ōrātor sum, *I am an orator;* dīcit **sē** esse ōrātōrem, *he says he is an orator.*

NOTE 1. — But the subject is often omitted if easily understood: —

īgnōscere imprūdentiae dīxit (B. G. iv. 27), *he said he pardoned their rashness.*

eadem ab aliīs quaerit: reperit esse vēra (id. i. 18), *he inquires about these same things from others; he finds that they are true.*

NOTE 2. — After a relative, or **quam** (*than*), if the verb would be the same as that of the main clause, it is usually omitted, and its subject is attracted into the accusative: —

tē suspicor eīsdem rēbus quibus **mē ipsum** commovērī (Cat. M. 1), *I suspect that you are disturbed by the same things as I.*

cōnfīdō tamen haec quoque tibi nōn minus grāta quam **ipsōs librōs** futūra (Plin. Ep. iii. 5. 20), *I trust that these facts too will be no less pleasing to you than the books themselves.*

NOTE 3. — In poetry, by a Greek idiom, a Predicate Noun or Adjective in the indirect discourse sometimes agrees with the subject of the main verb: —

vir bonus et sapiēns ait esse **parātus** (Hor. Ep. i. 7. 22), *a good and wise man says he is prepared*, etc. [In prose: **ait sē esse parātum.**]

sēnsit mediōs **dēlāpsus** in hostīs (Aen. ii. 377), *he found himself fallen among the foe.* [In prose: **sē esse dēlāpsum.**]

582. When the verb of *saying* etc. is *passive*, the construction may be either Personal or Impersonal. But the Personal construction is more common and is regularly used in the tenses of incomplete action: —

beātē vīxisse **videor** (Lael. 15), *I seem to have lived happily.*

Epamīnōndās fidibus praeclārē cecinisse **dīcitur** (Tusc. i. 4), *Epaminondas is said to have played excellently on the lyre.*

multī idem factūrī esse **dīcuntur** (Fam. xvi. 12. 4), *many are said to be about to do the same thing.* [Active: **dīcunt multōs factūrōs (esse).**]

prīmī **trāduntur** arte quādam verba vīnxisse (Or. 40), *they first are related to have joined words with a certain skill.*

Bibulus **audiēbātur** esse in Syriā (Att. v. 18), *it was heard that Bibulus was in Syria* (Bibulus was heard, etc.). [Direct: **Bibulus est.**]

cēterae Illyricī legiōnēs secūtūrae **spērābantur** (Tac. H. ii. 74), *the rest of the legions of Illyricum were expected to follow.*

vidēmur enim quiētūrī fuisse, nisi essēmus lacessītī (De Or. ii. 230), *it seems that we should have kept quiet, if we had not been molested* (we seem, etc.). [Direct: **quiēssēmus . . . nisi essēmus lacessītī.**]

Note. — The poets and later writers extend the personal use of the passive to verbs which are not properly *verba sentiendī* etc.: as, — **colligor dominae placuisse** (Ov. Am. ii. 6. 61), *it is gathered* [from this memorial] *that I pleased my mistress.*

a. In the compound tenses of verbs of *saying* etc., the impersonal construction is more common, and with the gerundive is regular: —

trāditum est etiam Homērum caecum fuisse (Tusc. v. 114), *it is a tradition, too, that Homer was blind.*

ubi tyrannus est, ibi nōn vitiōsam, sed **dīcendum est** plānē nūllam esse rem pūblicam (Rep. iii. 43), *where there is a tyrant, it must be said, not that the commonwealth is evil, but that it does not exist at all.*

Note. — An indirect narrative begun in the personal construction may be continued with the Infinitive and Accusative (as De Or. ii. 299; Liv. v. 41. 9).

Subordinate Clauses in Indirect Discourse

583. A Subordinate Clause *merely explanatory*, or containing statements which are regarded as true independently of the quotation, takes the Indicative: —

quis neget haec omnia **quae vidēmus** deōrum potestāte administrārī (Cat. iii. 21), *who can deny that all these things we see are ruled by the power of the gods?*

cūius ingeniō putābat ea **quae gesserat** posse celebrārī (Arch. 20), *by whose genius he thought that those deeds which he had done could be celebrated.* [Here the fact expressed by **quae gesserat**, though not explanatory, is felt to be true without regard to the quotation: **quae gessisset** would mean, what Marius *claimed* to have done.]

NOTE.—Such a clause in the indicative is not regarded as a part of the Indirect Discourse; but it often depends merely upon the feeling of the writer whether he shall use the Indicative or the Subjunctive (cf. §§ 591–593).

a. A subordinate clause in Indirect Discourse occasionally takes the Indicative when the *fact* is emphasized:—

factum êius hostis perīculum . . . **cum**, Cimbrīs et Teutonīs . . . pulsīs, nōn minōrem laudem exercitus quam ipse imperātor meritus **vidēbātur** (B. G. i. 40), *that a trial of this enemy had been made when, on the defeat of the Cimbri and Teutoni, the army seemed to have deserved no less credit than the commander himself.*

b. Clauses introduced by a relative which is equivalent to a demonstrative with a conjunction are not properly subordinate, and hence take the Accusative and Infinitive in Indirect Discourse (see § 308. *f*):—

Mārcellus requīsīsse dīcitur Archimēdem illum, **quem** cum audīsset interfectum permolestē **tulisse** (Verr. iv. 131), *Marcellus is said to have sought for Archimedes, and when he heard that he was slain, to have been greatly distressed.* [**quem** = **et eum.**]

cēnsent ūnum quemque nostrum mundī esse partem, **ex quō** [= et ex eō] illud nātūrā **cōnsequī** (Fin. iii. 64), *they say that each one of us is a part of the universe, from which this naturally follows.*

NOTE.—Really subordinate clauses occasionally take the accusative and infinitive: as,—**quem ad modum** sī nōn dēdātur obses prō ruptō foedus sē **habitūrum**, sīc dēditam inviolātam ad suōs **remissūrum** (Liv. ii. 13), [he says] *as in case the hostage is not given up he shall consider the treaty as broken, so if given up he will return her unharmed to her friends.*

c. The infinitive construction is regularly continued after a comparative with **quam**:—

addit sē **prius** occīsum īrī ab eō **quam mē violātum īrī** (Att. ii. 20. 2), *he adds that he himself will be killed by him, before I shall be injured.*

nōnne adfīrmāvī quidvīs mē **potius** perpessūrum quam ex Ītaliā **exitūrum** (Fam. ii. 16. 3), *did I not assert that I would endure anything rather than leave Italy?*

NOTE.—The subjunctive with or without ut also occurs with **quam** (see § 535. *c*).

Tenses of the Infinitive in Indirect Discourse

584. The Present, the Perfect, or the Future Infinitive[1] is used in Indirect Discourse, according as the time indicated is *present*, *past*, or *future* with reference to the verb of *saying* etc. by which the Indirect Discourse is introduced:—

[1] For various ways of expressing the Future Infinitive, see § 164. 3. *c*.

cadō, *I am falling.*
dīcit sē cadere, *he says he is falling.*
dīxit sē cadere, *he said he was falling.*

cadēbam, *I was falling;* **cecidī**, *I fell, have fallen;*
cecideram, *I had fallen.*
dīcit sē cecidisse, *he says he was falling, fell, has fallen, had fallen.*
dīxit sē cecidisse, *he said he fell, had fallen.*

cadam, *I shall fall.*
dīcit sē cāsūrum [**esse**], *he says he shall fall.*
dīxit sē cāsūrum [**esse**], *he said he should fall.*

ceciderō, *I shall have fallen.*
dīcit fore ut ceciderit [rare], *he says he shall have fallen.*
dīxit fore ut cecidisset [rare], *he said he should have fallen.*

a. All varieties of past time are usually expressed in Indirect Discourse by the Perfect Infinitive, which may stand for the Imperfect, the Perfect, or the Pluperfect Indicative of the Direct.

Note.—Continued or repeated action in past time is sometimes expressed by the Present Infinitive, which in such cases stands for the Imperfect Indicative of the Direct Discourse and is often called the *Imperfect Infinitive*.

This is the regular construction after **meminī** when referring to a matter of actual experience or observation: as,—**tē meminī haec dīcere**, *I remember your saying this* (that you said this). [Direct: **dīxistī** or **dīcēbās**.]

b. The present infinitive **posse** often has a future sense:—

totīus Galliae sēsē potīrī posse spērant (B. G. i. 3), *they hope that they shall be able to get possession of all Gaul.*

Tenses of the Subjunctive in Indirect Discourse

585. The tenses of the Subjunctive in Indirect Discourse follow the rule for the Sequence of Tenses (§ 482). They depend for their sequence on the verb of *saying* etc. by which the Indirect Discourse is introduced.

Thus in the sentence, **dīxit sē Rōmam itūrum ut cōnsulem vidēret**, *he said he should go to Rome in order that he might see the consul*, **vidēret** follows the sequence of **dīxit** without regard to the Future Infinitive, **itūrum** [**esse**], on which it directly depends.

Note.—This rule applies to the subjunctive in subordinate clauses, to that which stands for the imperative etc. (see examples, § 588), and to that in questions (§ 586).

a. A subjunctive depending on a Perfect Infinitive is often in the Imperfect or Pluperfect, even if the verb of *saying* etc. is in a primary tense (cf. § 485. *j*); so regularly when these tenses would have been used in Direct Discourse:—

Tarquinium **dīxisse ferunt** tum exsulantem sē **intellēxisse** quōs fīdōs amīcōs **habuisset** (Lael. 53), *they tell us that Tarquin said that then in his exile he had found out what faithful friends he had had.* [Here the main verb of saying, **ferunt**, is *primary*, but the time is carried back by **dīxisse** and **intellēxisse**, and the sequence then becomes secondary.]

tantum **prōfēcisse vidēmur** ut ā Graecīs nē verbōrum quidem cōpiā **vincerēmur** (N. D. i. 8), *we seem to have advanced so far that even in abundance of words we* ARE *not surpassed by the Greeks.*

NOTE 1.—The proper sequence may be seen, in each case, by turning the Perfect Infinitive into that tense of the Indicative which it represents. Thus, if it stands for an *imperfect* or an *historical perfect*, the sequence will be secondary; if it stands for a *perfect definite*, the sequence may be either primary or secondary (§ 485. *a*).

NOTE 2.—The so-called imperfect infinitive after **meminī** (§ 584. *a*. N.) takes the secondary sequence: as,—ad mē **adīre** quōsdam **meminī**, quī **dīcerent** (Fam. iii. 10. 6), *I remember that some persons visited me, to tell me*, etc.

b. The Present and Perfect Subjunctive are often used in dependent clauses of the Indirect Discourse even when the verb of *saying* etc. is in a secondary tense:—

dīcēbant . . . totidem Nerviōs (pollicērī) quī longissimē **absint** (B. G. ii. 4), *they said that the Nervii, who live farthest off, promised as many.*

NOTE.—This construction comes from the tendency of language to refer all time in narration to the time of the speaker (*repraesentātiō*). In the course of a long passage in the Indirect Discourse the tenses of the subjunctive often vary, sometimes following the sequence, and sometimes affected by *repraesentātiō*. Examples may be seen in B. G. i. 13, vii. 20, etc.

Certain constructions are never affected by *repraesentātiō*. Such are the Imperfect and Pluperfect Subjunctive with **cum** temporal, **antequam**, and **priusquam**.

Questions in Indirect Discourse

586. A Question in Indirect Discourse may be either in the Subjunctive or in the Infinitive with Subject Accusative.

A *real question*, asking for an answer, is generally put in the Subjunctive; a *rhetorical* question, asked for effect and implying its own answer, is put in the Infinitive:—

quid sibi **vellet**? cūr in suās possessiōnēs **venīret** (B. G. i. 44), *what did he want? why did he come into his territories?* [Real question. Direct: **quid vīs? cūr venīs?**]

num recentium iniūriārum memoriam [sē] dēpōnere **posse** (id. i. 14), *could he lay aside the memory of recent wrongs?* [Rhetorical Question. Direct: **num possum?**]

quem sīgnum **datūrum** fugientibus? **quem ausūrum** Alexandrō succēdere (Q. C. iii. 5. 7), *who will give the signal on the retreat? who will dare succeed Alexander?* [Rhetorical. Direct: **quis dabit . . . audēbit.**]

NOTE 1.—No sharp line can be drawn between the Subjunctive and the Infinitive in questions in the Indirect Discourse. Whether the question is to be regarded as *rhetorical* or *real* often depends merely on the writer's point of view:—

utrum partem rēgnī **petītūrum esse**, an tōtum **ēreptūrum** (Liv. xlv. 19. 15), *will you ask part of the regal power* (he said), *or seize the whole?*

quid tandem praetōrī **faciendum fuisse** (id. xxxi. 48), *what, pray, ought a prætor to have done?*

quid repente **factum** [esse] cūr, etc. (id. xxxiv. 54), *what had suddenly happened, that*, etc.?

NOTE 2.—Questions coming immediately after a verb of *asking* are treated as Indirect Questions and take the Subjunctive (see § 574). This is true even when the verb of asking serves also to introduce a passage in the Indirect Discourse. The question may be either real or rhetorical. See **quaesīvit**, etc. (Liv. xxxvii. 15).

For the use of tenses, see § 585.

587. A Deliberative Subjunctive (§ 444) in the Direct Discourse is always retained in the Indirect:—

cūr aliquōs ex suīs **āmitteret** (B. C. i. 72), *why* (thought he) *should he lose some of his men?* [Direct: **cūr āmittam**?]

Commands in Indirect Discourse

588. All Imperative forms of speech take the Subjunctive in Indirect Discourse:—

reminīscerētur veteris incommodī (B. G. i. 13), *remember* (said he) *the ancient disaster*. [Direct: **reminīscere.**]

fīnem **faciat** (id. i. 20), *let him make an end.* [Direct: **fac.**]

ferrent opem, **adiuvārent** (Liv. ii. 6), *let them bring aid, let them help.*

a. This rule applies not only to the Imperative of the direct discourse, but to the Hortatory and the Optative Subjunctive as well.

NOTE 1.—Though these subjunctives stand for independent clauses of the direct discourse, they follow the rule for the sequence of tenses, being in fact dependent on the verb of *saying* etc. (cf. §§ 483, 585).

NOTE 2.—A Prohibition in the Indirect Discourse is regularly expressed by **nē** with the present or imperfect subjunctive, even when **nōlī** with the infinitive would be used in the Direct: as,—**nē perturbārentur** (B. G. vii. 29), *do not* (he said) *be troubled.* [Direct: **nōlīte perturbārī**. But sometimes **nōllet** is found in Indirect Discourse.]

Conditions in Indirect Discourse

589. Conditional sentences in Indirect Discourse are expressed as follows:—

1. The Protasis, being a *subordinate clause*, is always in the Subjunctive.

2. The Apodosis, if independent and not hortatory or optative, is always in some form of the Infinitive.

a. The Present Subjunctive in the apodosis of *less vivid* future conditions (§ 516. *b*) becomes the Future Infinitive like the Future Indicative in the apodosis of *more vivid* future conditions.

Thus there is no distinction between more and less vivid future conditions in the Indirect Discourse.

Examples of Conditional Sentences in Indirect Discourse are —

1. Simple Present Condition (§ 515): —

(dīxit) sī ipse populō Rōmānō nōn **praescrīberet** quem ad modum suō iūre ūterētur, nōn **oportēre** sēsē ā populō Rōmānō in suō iūre impedīrī (B. G. i. 36), *he said that if he did not dictate to the Roman people how they should use their rights, he ought not to be interfered with by the Roman people in the exercise of his rights.* [Direct: **sī nōn praescrībō . . . nōn oportet.**]

praedicāvit . . . sī pāce ūtī **velint**, inīquum **esse**, etc. (id. i. 44), *he asserted that if they wished to enjoy peace, it was unfair*, etc. [Direct: **sī volunt . . . est.** Present tense kept by *repraesentātiō* (§ 585. *b.* N.).]

2. Simple Past Condition (§ 515): —

nōn dīcam nē illud quidem, sī maximē in culpā **fuerit** Apollōnius, tamen in hominem honestissimae cīvitātis honestissimum tam graviter animadvertī, causā indictā, nōn **oportuisse** (Verr. v. 20), *I will not say this either, that, even if Apollonius was very greatly in fault, still an honorable man from an honorable state ought not to have been punished so severely without having his case heard.* [Direct: **sī fuit . . . nōn oportuit.**]

3. Future Conditions (§ 516): —

(dīxit) quod sī praetereā nēmō **sequātur**, tamen sē cum sōlā decimā legiōne **itūrum** (B. G. i. 40), *but if nobody else should follow, still he would go with the tenth legion alone.* [Direct: **sī sequētur . . . ībō.** Present tense by *repraesentātiō* (§ 585. *b.* N.).]

Haeduīs sē obsidēs redditūrum nōn esse, neque eīs . . . bellum **illātūrum**, sī in eō **manērent**, quod convēnisset, stipendiumque quotannīs **penderent**: sī id nōn **fēcissent**, longē eīs frāternum nōmen populī Rōmānī **āfutūrum** (id. i. 36), *he said that he would not give up the hostages to the Haedui, but would not make war upon them if they observed the agreement which had been made, and paid tribute yearly; but that, if they should not do this, the name of brothers to the Roman people would be far from aiding them.* [Direct: **reddam . . . īnferam . . . sī manēbunt . . . pendent: sī nōn fēcerint . . . aberit.**]

id Datamēs ut audīvit, sēnsit, sī in turbam **exīsset** ab homine tam necessāriō sē relictum, **futūrum** [esse] **ut** cēterī cōnsilium **sequantur** (Nep. Dat. 6), *when Datames heard this, he saw that, if it should get abroad that he had been abandoned by a man so closely connected with him, everybody else would follow his example.* [Direct: **sī exierit . . . sequentur.**]

(putāvērunt) nisi mē cīvitāte **expulissent**, obtinēre sē nōn **posse** licentiam cupiditātum suārum (Att. x. 4), *they thought that unless they drove me out of the state, they could not have free play for their desires.* [Direct: **nisi (Cicerōnem) expulerimus, obtinēre nōn poterimus.**]

b. In changing a Condition *contrary to fact* (§ 517) into the Indirect Discourse, the following points require notice: —

1. The Protasis always remains *unchanged in tense.*
2. The Apodosis, if *active*, takes a peculiar infinitive form, made by combining the Participle in **-ūrus** with **fuisse.**
3. If the verb of the Apodosis is *passive* or has no supine stem, the periphrasis **futūrum fuisse ut** (with the Imperfect Subjunctive) must be used.
4. An Indicative in the Apodosis becomes a Perfect Infinitive.

Examples are: —

nec sē superstitem fīliae **futūrum fuisse**, nisi spem ulcīscendae mortis êius in auxiliō commīlitōnum **habuisset** (Liv. iii. 50. 7), *and that he should not now be a survivor*, etc., *unless he had had hope*, etc. [Direct: **nōn superstes essem, nisi habuissem.**]

illud Asia cōgitet, nūllam ā sē neque bellī externī neque discordiārum domesticārum calamitātem **āfutūram fuisse**, sī hōc imperiō nōn **tenērētur** (Q. Fr. i. 1. 34), *let Asia* (personified) *think of this, that no disaster*, etc., *would not be hers, if she were not held by this government.* [Direct: **abesset, sī nōn tenērer.**]

quid inimīcitiārum crēditis [mē] **exceptūrum fuisse**, sī īnsontīs **lacessīssem** (Q. C. vi. 10. 18), *what enmities do you think I should have incurred, if I had wantonly assailed the innocent?* [**excēpissem . . . sī lacessīssem.**]

invītum sē dīcere, nec **dictūrum fuisse**, nī cāritās reī pūblicae **vinceret** (Liv. ii. 2), *that he spoke unwillingly and should not have spoken, did not love for the state prevail.* [Direct: **nec dīxissem . . . nī vinceret.**]

nisi eō tempore quīdam nūntiī dē Caesaris victōriā . . . **essent allātī**, exīstimābant plērīque **futūrum fuisse utī** [oppidum] **āmitterētur** (B. C. iii. 101), *most people thought that unless at that time reports of Cæsar's victory had been brought, the town would have been lost.* [Direct: **nisi essent allātī . . . āmissum esset.**]

quōrum sī aetās **potuisset** esse longinquior, **futūrum fuisse ut** omnibus perfectīs artibus hominum vīta **ērudīrētur** (Tusc. iii. 69), *if life could have been longer, human existence would have been embellished by every art in its perfection.* [Direct: **sī potuisset . . . ērudīta esset.**]

at plērīque exīstimant, sī ācrius īnsequī **voluisset**, bellum eō diē **potuisse** fīnīre (B. C. iii. 51), *but most people think that, if he had chosen to follow up the pursuit more vigorously, he could have ended the war on that day.* [Direct: **sī voluisset . . . potuit.**]

Caesar respondit . . . sī alicûius iniūriae sibi cōnscius **fuisset**, nōn **fuisse** difficile cavēre (B. G. i. 14), *Cæsar replied that if* [the Roman people] *had been aware of any wrong act, it would not have been hard for them to take precautions.* [Direct: **sī fuisset, nōn difficile fuit** (§ 517. *c*).]

NOTE 1. — In Indirect Discourse Present Conditions contrary to fact are not distinguished in the *apodosis* from Past Conditions contrary to fact, but the *protasis* may keep them distinct.

NOTE 2. — The periphrasis **futūrum fuisse ut** is sometimes used from choice when there is no necessity for resorting to it, but not in Cæsar or Cicero.

NOTE 3. — Very rarely the Future Infinitive is used in the Indirect Discourse to express the Apodosis of a Present Condition contrary to fact. Only four or five examples of this use occur in classic authors: as, — Titurius clāmābat sī Caesar **adesset** neque Carnutēs, etc., neque Eburōnēs tantā cum contemptiōne nostra ad castra **ventūrōs esse** (B. G. v. 29), *Titurius cried out that if Cæsar were present, neither would the Carnutes*, etc., *nor would the Eburones be coming to our camp with such contempt.* [Direct: sī adesset . . . venīrent.]

590. The following example illustrates some of the foregoing principles in a connected address: —

INDIRECT DISCOURSE

Sī pācem populus Rōmānus cum Helvētiīs **faceret**, in eam partem **itūrōs** atque ibi **futūrōs Helvētiōs**, ubi eōs Caesar **cōnstituisset** atque esse **voluisset**: sīn bellō persequī **persevērāret**, **reminīscerētur** et veteris incommodī populī Rōmānī, et prīstinae virtūtis Helvētiōrum. Quod imprōvīsō ūnum pāgum **adortus esset**, cum eī quī flūmen **trānsīssent** suīs auxilium ferre nōn **possent**, nē ob eam rem aut **suae** māgnō opere virtūtī **tribueret**, aut **ipsōs dēspiceret**: **sē** ita ā patribus mâiōribusque **suīs didicisse**, ut magis virtūte quam dolō **contenderent**, aut īnsidiīs **nīterentur**. Quā rē **nē committeret**, ut is locus ubi **cōnstitissent** ex calamitāte populī Rōmānī et interneciōne exercitūs nōmen **caperet**, aut memoriam **prōderet**. — B. G. i. 13.

DIRECT DISCOURSE

Sī pācem populus Rōmānus cum Helvētiīs **faciet**, in eam partem **ībunt** atque ibi **erunt Helvētiī**, ubi eōs tū **cōnstitueris** atque esse **volueris**: sīn bellō persequī **persevērābis**, **reminīscere** [inquit] et veteris incommodī populī Rōmānī, et prīstinae virtūtis Helvētiōrum. Quod imprōvīsō ūnum pāgum **adortus es**, cum eī quī flūmen **trānsierant** suīs auxilium ferre nōn **possent**, nē ob eam rem aut **tuae** māgnō opere virtūtī **tribueris**, aut **nōs dēspexeris**: **nōs** ita ā patribus mâiōribusque **nostrīs didicimus**, ut magis virtūte quam dolō **contendāmus**, aut īnsidiīs **nītāmur**. Quā rē **nōlī committere**, ut **hīc** locus ubi **cōnstitimus** ex calamitāte populī Rōmānī et interneciōne exercitūs nōmen **capiat**, aut memoriam **prōdat**.

INTERMEDIATE CLAUSES

591. A Subordinate clause takes the Subjunctive —

1. When it expresses the thought of some other person than the speaker or writer (*Informal Indirect Discourse*), or

2. When it is an integral part of a Subjunctive clause or equivalent Infinitive (*Attraction*).[1]

[1] See note on Indirect Discourse (§ 577).

Informal Indirect Discourse

592. A Subordinate Clause takes the Subjunctive when it expresses the thought of some other person than the writer or speaker: —

1. When the clause depends upon another containing a *wish*, a *command*, or a *question*, expressed indirectly, though not strictly in the form of Indirect Discourse: —

animal sentit quid sit quod **deceat** (Off. i. 14), *an animal feels what it is that is fit.*

huic imperat quās **possit** adeat cīvitātēs (B. G. iv. 21), *he orders him to visit what states he can.*

hunc sibi ex animō scrūpulum, quī sē diēs noctīsque **stimulat** ac **pungit**, ut ēvellātis postulat (Rosc. Am. 6), *he begs you to pluck from his heart this doubt that goads and stings him day and night.* [Here the relative clause is not a part of the Purpose expressed in **ēvellātis**, but is an assertion made by the subject of **postulat**.]

2. When the main clause of a quotation is merged in the verb of *saying*, or some modifier of it: —

sī quid dē hīs rēbus dīcere **vellet**, fēcī potestātem (Cat. iii. 11), *if he wished to say anything about these matters, I gave him a chance.*

tulit dē caede quae in Appiā viā **facta esset** (Mil. 15), *he passed a law concerning the murder which* (in the language of the bill) *took place in the Appian Way.*

nisi **restituissent** statuās, vehementer minātur (Verr. ii. 162), *he threatens them violently unless they should restore the statues.* [Here the main clause, "that he will inflict punishment," is contained in **minātur**.]

iīs auxilium suum pollicitus sī ab Suēbīs **premerentur** (B. G. iv. 19), *he promised them his aid if they should be molested by the Suevi.* [= **pollicitus sē auxilium lātūrum**, etc.]

prohibitiō tollendī, nisi **pactus esset**, vim adhibēbat pactiōnī (Verr. iii. 37), *the forbidding to take away unless he came to terms gave force to the bargain.*

3. When a *reason* or an *explanatory fact* is introduced by a relative or by **quod** (rarely **quia**) (see § 540): —

Paetus omnīs librōs **quōs** frāter suus **relīquisset** mihi dōnāvit (Att. ii. 1. 12), *Pætus presented to me all the books which* (he said) *his brother had left.*

NOTE. — Under this head even what the speaker himself thought under other circumstances may have the Subjunctive. So also with **quod** even the verb of *saying* may be in the Subjunctive (§ 540. N.[2]). Here belong also **nōn quia, nōn quod**, introducing a reason *expressly to deny it.* (See § 540. N.[3].)

Subjunctive of Integral Part (Attraction)

593. A clause depending upon a Subjunctive clause or an equivalent Infinitive will itself take the Subjunctive if regarded *as an integral part of that clause:* —[1]

imperat, dum rēs **iūdicētur**, hominem adservent: cum iūdicāta **sit**, ad sē ut addūcant (Verr. iii. 55), *he orders them, till the affair should be decided, to keep the man; when it is judged, to bring him to him.*

etenim quis tam dissolūtō animō est, quī haec cum **videat**, tacēre ac neglegere possit (Rosc. Am. 32), *for who is so reckless of spirit that, when he sees these things, he can keep silent and pass them by?*

mōs est Athēnīs laudārī in cōntiōne eōs quī **sint** in proeliīs interfectī (Or. 151), *it is the custom at Athens for those to be publicly eulogized who have been slain in battle.* [Here **laudārī** is equivalent to **ut laudentur.**]

a. But a dependent clause may be closely connected *grammatically* with a Subjunctive or Infinitive clause, and still take the Indicative, if it is not regarded as a necessary *logical* part of that clause: —

quōdam modō postulat ut, quem ad modum **est**, sīc etiam appellētur, tyrannus (Att. x. 4. 2), *in a manner he demands that as he is, so he may be called, a tyrant.*

nātūra fert ut eīs faveāmus quī eadem perīcula quibus nōs **perfūnctī sumus** ingrediuntur (Mur. 4), *nature prompts us to feel friendly towards those who are entering on the same dangers which we have passed through.*

nē hostēs, quod tantum multitūdine **poterant**, suōs circumvenīre possent (B. G. ii. 8), *lest the enemy, because they were so strong in numbers, should be able to surround his men.*

sī mea in tē essent officia sōlum tanta quanta magis ā tē ipsō praedicārī quam ā mē ponderārī **solent**, verēcundius ā tē . . . peterem (Fam. ii. 6), *if my good services to you were only so great as they are wont rather to be called by you than to be estimated by me, I should,* etc.

NOTE 1.—The use of the Indicative in such clauses sometimes serves to emphasize the *fact*, as true independently of the statement contained in the subjunctive or infinitive clause. But in many cases no such distinction is perceptible.

NOTE 2.—It is often difficult to distinguish between Informal Indirect Discourse and the Integral Part. Thus in **imperāvit ut ea fierent quae opus essent, essent** may stand for **sunt**, and then will be Indirect Discourse, being a part of the thought, but not a part of the order; or it may stand for **erunt**, and then will be Integral Part, being a part of the order itself. The difficulty of making the distinction in such cases is evidence of the close relationship between these two constructions.

[1] The subjunctive in this use is of the same nature as the subjunctive in the main clause. A dependent clause in a clause of purpose is really a part of the purpose, as is seen from the use of *should* and other auxiliaries in English. In a result clause this is less clear, but the result construction is a branch of the characteristic (§ 534), to which category the dependent clause in this case evidently belongs when it takes the subjunctive.

594. IMPORTANT RULES OF SYNTAX

1. A noun used to describe another, and denoting the same person or thing, agrees with it in Case (§ 282).

2. Adjectives, Adjective Pronouns, and Participles agree with their nouns in Gender, Number, and Case (§ 286).

3. Superlatives (more rarely Comparatives) denoting order and succession — also **medius**, (**cēterus**), **reliquus** — usually designate not *what object*, but *what part of it*, is meant (§ 293).

4. The Personal Pronouns have two forms for the genitive plural, that in **-um** being used *partitively*, and that in -ī oftenest *objectively* (§ 295. *b*).

5. The Reflexive Pronoun (**sē**), and usually the corresponding possessive (**suus**), are used in the predicate to refer to the subject of the sentence or clause (§ 299).

6. To express Possession and similar ideas the Possessive Pronouns must be used, not the genitive of the personal or reflexive pronouns (§ 302. *a*).

7. A Possessive Pronoun or an Adjective implying possession may take an appositive in the genitive case agreeing in gender, number, and case with an implied noun or pronoun (§ 302. *e*).

8. A Relative Pronoun agrees with its Antecedent in Gender and Number, but its Case depends on its construction in the clause in which it stands (§ 305).

9. A Finite Verb agrees with its Subject in Number and Person (§ 316).

10. Adverbs are used to modify Verbs, Adjectives, and other Adverbs (§ 321).

11. A Question of *simple fact*, requiring the answer *yes* or *no*, is formed by adding the enclitic **-ne** to the emphatic word (§ 332).

12. When the enclitic **-ne** is added to a negative word, — as in **nōnne**, — an *affirmative* answer is expected. The particle **num** suggests a *negative* answer (§ 332. *b*).

13. The Subject of a finite verb is in the Nominative (§ 339).

14. The Vocative is the case of direct address (§ 340).

15. A noun used to limit or define another, and *not* meaning the same person or thing, is put in the Genitive (§ 342).

16. The Possessive Genitive denotes the person or thing to which an object, quality, feeling, or action belongs (§ 343).

17. The genitive may denote the Substance or Material of which a thing consists (§ 344).

18. The genitive is used to denote Quality, but only when the quality is modified by an adjective (§ 345).

19. Words denoting a *part* are followed by the Genitive of the *whole* to which the part belongs (*Partitive Genitive*, § 346).

20. Nouns of *action*, *agency*, and *feeling* govern the Genitive of the object (*Objective Genitive*, § 348).

21. Adjectives denoting *desire*, *knowledge*, *memory*, *fulness*, *power*, *sharing*, *guilt*, and their opposites; participles in **-ns** when used as adjectives; and verbals in **-āx**, govern the Genitive (§ 349. *a*, *b*, *c*).

22. Verbs of *remembering* and *forgetting* take either the Accusative or the Genitive of the object (§ 350).

23. Verbs of *reminding* take with the Accusative of the person a Genitive of the thing (§ 351).

24. Verbs of *accusing*, *condemning*, and *acquitting* take the Genitive of the *charge* or *penalty* (§ 352).

25. The Dative is used of the object *indirectly affected* by an action (*Indirect Object*, § 361).

26. Many verbs signifying to *favor*, *help*, *please*, *trust*, and their contraries; also, to *believe*, *persuade*, *command*, *obey*, *serve*, *resist*, *envy*, *threaten*, *pardon*, and *spare*, take the Dative (§ 367).

27. Many verbs compounded with **ad**, **ante**, **con**, **in**, **inter**, **ob**, **post**, **prae**, **prō**, **sub**, **super**, and some with **circum**, admit the Dative of the indirect object (§ 370).

28. The Dative is used with **esse** and similar words to denote Possession (§ 373).

29. The Dative of the Agent is used with the Gerundive, to denote the person on whom the necessity rests (§ 374).

30. The Dative often depends, not on any *particular word*, but on the *general meaning* of the sentence (*Dative of Reference*, § 376).

31. Many verbs of *taking away* and the like take the Dative (especially of a *person*) instead of the Ablative of Separation (§ 381).

32. The Dative is used to denote the Purpose or End, often with another Dative of the person or thing affected (§ 382).

33. The Dative is used with adjectives (and a few adverbs) of *fitness*, *nearness*, *likeness*, *service*, *inclination*, and their opposites (§ 384).

34. The Direct Object of a transitive verb is put in the Accusative (§ 387).

35. An intransitive verb often takes the Accusative of a noun of kindred meaning, usually modified by an adjective or in some other manner (*Cognate Accusative*, § 390).

36. Verbs of *naming*, *choosing*, *appointing*, *making*, *esteeming*, *showing*, and the like, may take a Predicate Accusative along with the direct object (§ 393).

37. Transitive verbs compounded with prepositions sometimes take (in addition to the direct object) a Secondary Object, originally governed by the preposition (§ 394).

38. Some verbs of *asking* and *teaching* may take two Accusatives, one of the Person, and the other of the Thing (§ 396).

39. The subject of an Infinitive is in the Accusative (§ 397. *e*).

40. Duration of Time and Extent of Space are expressed by the Accusative (§§ 424. *c*, 425).

41. Words signifying *separation* or *privation* are followed by the Ablative (*Ablative of Separation*, § 400).

42. The Ablative, usually with a preposition, is used to denote the *source* from which anything is derived or the *material* of which it consists (§ 403).

43. The Ablative, with or without a preposition, is used to express *cause* (§ 404).

44. The Voluntary Agent after a passive verb is expressed by the Ablative with **ā** or **ab** (§ 405).

45. The Comparative degree is often followed by the Ablative signifying *than* (§ 406).

46. The Comparative may be followed by **quam**, *than*. When **quam** is used, the two things compared are put in the same case (§ 407).

47. The Ablative is used to denote the *means* or *instrument* of an action (§ 409).

48. The deponents, **ūtor**, **fruor**, **fungor**, **potior**, and **vēscor**, with several of their compounds, govern the Ablative (§ 410).

49. **Opus** and **ūsus**, signifying *need*, are followed by the Ablative (§ 411).

50. The *manner* of an action is denoted by the Ablative, usually with **cum** unless a limiting adjective is used with the noun (§ 412).

51. *Accompaniment* is denoted by the Ablative, regularly with **cum** (§ 413).

52. With Comparatives and words implying comparison the Ablative is used to denote the *degree of difference* (§ 414).

53. The *quality* of a thing is denoted by the Ablative with an adjective or genitive Modifier (§ 415).

54. The *price* of a thing is put in the Ablative (§ 416).

55. The Ablative of Specification denotes that *in respect to which* anything *is* or *is done* (§ 418).

56. The adjectives **dīgnus** and **indīgnus** take the Ablative (§ 418. *b*).

57. A noun or pronoun, with a participle in agreement, may be put in the Ablative to define the *time* or *circumstances* of an action (*Ablative Absolute*, § 419).

An adjective, or a second noun, may take the place of the participle in the ablative absolute construction (§ 419. *a*).

58. Time *when*, or *within which*, is denoted by the Ablative; time *how long* by the Accusative (§ 423).

59. Relations of Place are expressed as follows:—

1. The *place from which*, by the Ablative with **ab, dē, ex.**
2. The *place to which* (or *end of motion*), by the Accusative with **ad** or **in.**
3. The *place where*, by the Ablative with **in** (*Locative Ablative*). (§ 426.)

60. With names of *towns* and *small islands*, and with **domus** and **rūs**, the relations of place are expressed as follows:—

1. The *place from which*, by the Ablative without a preposition.
2. The *place to which*, by the Accusative without a preposition.
3. The *place where*, by the Locative. (§ 427.)

61. The Hortatory Subjunctive is used in the present tense to express an *exhortation*, a *command*, or a *concession* (§§ 439, 440).

62. The Optative Subjunctive is used to express a *wish*. The present tense denotes the wish as *possible*, the imperfect as *unaccomplished* in present time, the pluperfect as *unaccomplished* in past time (§ 441).

63. The Subjunctive is used in questions implying (1) *doubt, indignation*, or (2) an *impossibility* of the thing's being done (*Deliberative Subjunctive*, § 444).

64. The Potential Subjunctive is used to suggest an action as *possible* or *conceivable* (§ 446).

65. The Imperative is used in *commands* and *entreaties* (§ 448).

66. Prohibition is regularly expressed in classic prose (1) by **nōlī** with the Infinitive, (2) by **cavē** with the Present Subjunctive, (3) by **nē** with the Perfect Subjunctive (§ 450).

67. The Infinitive, with or without a subject accusative, may be used with **est** and similar verbs (1) as the Subject, (2) in Apposition with the subject, or (3) as a Predicate Nominative (§ 452).

68. Verbs which imply *another action of the same subject* to complete their meaning take the Infinitive without a subject accusative (*Complementary Infinitive*, § 456).

69. The Infinitive, with subject accusative, is used with verbs and other expressions of *knowing, thinking, telling,* and *perceiving* (*Indirect Discourse*, see § 459).

70. The Infinitive is often used for the Imperfect Indicative in narration, and takes a subject in the Nominative (*Historical Infinitive*, § 463).

71. SEQUENCE OF TENSES. In complex sentences, a *primary* tense in the main clause is followed by the Present or Perfect Subjunctive in the dependent clause; a *secondary* tense by the Imperfect or Pluperfect (§ 483).

72. Participles denote time as *present, past,* or *future* with respect to the time of the verb in their clause (§ 489).

73. The Gerund and the Gerundive are used, in the oblique cases, in many of the constructions of nouns (§§ 501–507).

74. The Supine in **-um** is used after verbs of *motion* to express Purpose (§ 509).

75. The Supine in **-ū** is used with a few adjectives and with the nouns **fās, nefās,** and **opus,** to denote Specification (§ 510).

76. **Dum, modo, dummodo,** and **tantum ut,** introducing a Proviso, take the Subjunctive (§ 528).

77. Final clauses take the Subjunctive introduced by **ut (utī)**, negative **nē (ut nē)**, or by a Relative Pronoun or Relative Adverb (§ 531).

78. A Relative Clause with the Subjunctive is often used to indicate a *characteristic* of the antecedent, especially where the antecedent is otherwise *undefined* (§ 535).

79. **Dīgnus, indīgnus, aptus,** and **idōneus,** take a Subjunctive clause with a relative (rarely with **ut**) (§ 535. *f*).

80. Clauses of Result take the Subjunctive introduced by **ut**, *so that* (negative, **ut nōn**), or by a Relative Pronoun or Relative Adverb (§ 537).

81. The Causal Particles **quod, quia**, and **quoniam** take the Indicative when the reason is given on the authority of the *writer* or *speaker;* the Subjunctive when the reason is given on the authority of *another* (§ 540).

82. The particles **postquam (posteāquam), ubi, ut (ut prīmum, ut semel), simul atque (simul ac**, or **simul** alone) take the Indicative (usually in the *perfect* or the *historical present*) (§ 543).

83. A Temporal clause with **cum**, *when*, and some past tense of the Indicative *dates* or *defines the time* at which the action of the main verb occurred (§ 545).

84. A Temporal clause with **cum** and the Imperfect or Pluperfect Subjunctive *describes the circumstances* that accompanied or preceded the action of the main verb (§ 546).

85. **Cum** Causal or Concessive takes the Subjunctive (§ 549).

For other concessive particles, see § 527.

86. In Indirect Discourse the *main clause* of a Declaratory Sentence is put in the Infinitive with Subject Accusative. All *subordinate clauses* take the Subjunctive (§ 580).

87. The Present, the Perfect, or the Future Infinitive is used in Indirect Discourse, according as the time indicated is *present, past,* or *future* with reference to the verb of *saying* etc. by which the Indirect Discourse is introduced (§ 584).

88. In Indirect Discourse a *real question* is generally put in the Subjunctive; a *rhetorical question* in the Infinitive (§ 586).

89. All Imperative forms of speech take the Subjunctive in Indirect Discourse (§ 588).

90. A Subordinate clause takes the Subjunctive when it expresses the thought of some other person than the writer or speaker (*Informal Indirect Discourse*, § 592).

91. A clause depending on a Subjunctive clause or an equivalent Infinitive will itself take the Subjunctive if regarded as an *integral part* of that clause (*Attraction*, § 593).

For Prepositions and their cases, see §§ 220, 221.
For Conditional Sentences, see § 512 ff. (Scheme in § 514.)
For ways of expressing Purpose, see § 533.

ORDER OF WORDS

595. Latin differs from English in having more freedom in the arrangement of words for the purpose of showing the relative importance of the ideas in a sentence.

596. As in other languages, the Subject tends to stand first, the Predicate last. Thus,—

> **Pausāniās** Lacedaemonius māgnus homō sed varius in omnī genere vītae **fuit** (Nep. Paus. 1), *Pausanias the Lacedæmonian was a great man, but inconsistent in the whole course of his life.*

NOTE.—This happens because, from the speaker's ordinary point of view, the subject of his discourse is the most important thing in it, as singled out from all other things to be spoken of.

a. There is in Latin, however, a special tendency to place the verb itself *last of all*, after all its modifiers. But many writers purposely avoid the monotony of this arrangement by putting the verb last but one, followed by some single word of the predicate.

597. In *connected discourse* the word most prominent in the speaker's mind comes first, and so on in order of prominence.

This relative prominence corresponds to that indicated in English by a graduated stress of voice (usually called *emphasis*).

a. The difference in *emphasis* expressed by difference in order of words is illustrated in the following passages:—

> apud Xenophōntem **autem moriēns** Cȳrus māior haec dīcit (Cat. M. 79), IN XENOPHON *too, on his* **death-bed** *Cyrus the elder utters these words.*
>
> Cȳrus quidem haec moriēns; nōs, sī placet, nostra videāmus (id. 82), CYRUS, *to be sure, utters these words on his death-bed; let* US, *if you please, consider our own case.*
>
> Cȳrus quidem apud Xenophōntem eō sermōne, quem moriēns habuit (id. 30), CYRUS, *to be sure, in* **Xenophon**, *in that speech which he uttered on his death-bed.*

NOTE.—This stress or emphasis, however, in English does not necessarily show any violent contrast to the rest of the words in the sentence, but is infinitely varied, constantly increasing and diminishing, and often so subtle as to be unnoticed except in careful study. So, as a general rule, the precedence of words in a Latin sentence is not mechanical, but corresponds to the prominence which a good speaker would mark by skilfully managed stress of voice. A Latin *written* sentence, therefore, has all the clearness and expression which could be given to a *spoken* discourse by the best actor in English. Some exceptions to the rule will be treated later.

The first chapter of Cæsar's Gallic War, if rendered so as to bring out as far as possible the shades of emphasis, would run thus:—

GAUL,[1] *in the widest sense*, is **divided**[2] into three *parts*,[3] which are *inhabited*[4] (as follows): **one**[5] by the Belgians, **another**[6] by the Aquitani, **the third** by a people called in *their own*[7] language Celts, in *ours* Gauls. THESE[8] in their **language**,[9] **institutions**, and **laws are** *all* of them[10] different. The GAULS[11] (proper) are separated[12] from the **Aquitani** by the river *Garonne*, from the **Belgians** by the *Marne and Seine*. Of THESE[13] (TRIBES) the bravest of **all**[14] are the *Belgians*, for the reason that they live **farthest**[15] *away*

Gallia est omnis dīvīsa in partīs trīs, quārum ūnam incolunt Belgae, aliam Aquītānī, tertiam quī ipsōrum linguā Celtae, nostrā Gallī appellantur. Hī omnēs linguā, īnstitūtīs, lēgibus inter sē differunt. Gallōs ab Aquītānīs Garumna flūmen, ā Belgīs Mātrona et Sēquana dīvidit. Hōrum omnium fortissimī sunt Belgae, proptereā quod ā cultū atque hūmānitāte

[1] GAUL: emphatic as the *subject of discourse*, as with a title or the like.

[2] **Divided**: opposed to the false conception (implied in the use of **omnis**) that the country called Gallia by the Romans is one. This appears more clearly from the fact that Cæsar later speaks of the *Gallī* in a narrower sense as distinct from the other two tribes, who with them inhabit *Gallia* in the wider sense.

[3] *Parts*: continuing the emphasis begun in **dīvīsa**. Not *three* parts as opposed to any other number, but into *parts* at all.

[4] *Inhabited*: emphatic as the next subject, "*The inhabitants* of these parts are, etc."

[5] **One**: given more prominence than it otherwise would have on account of its close connection with **quārum**.

[6] **Another**, etc.: opposed to *one*.

[7] *Their own, ours*: strongly opposed to each other.

[8] THESE (tribes): the main subject of discourse again, collecting under one head the names previously mentioned.

[9] **Language**, etc.: these are the most prominent ideas, as giving the striking points which distinguish the tribes. The emphasis becomes natural in English if we say "these have a different *language*, different *institutions*, different *laws*."

[10] *All* of them: the emphasis on *all* marks the distributive character of the adjective, as if it were "*every one* has its own, etc."

[11] GAULS: emphatic as referring to the Gauls proper in distinction from the other tribes.

[12] Separated: though this word contains an indispensable idea in the connection, yet it has a subordinate position. It is not emphatic in Latin, as is seen from the fact that it cannot be made emphatic in English. The sense is: The *Gauls* lie between the *Aquitani* on the one side, and the *Belgians* on the other.

[13] Of THESE: the subject of discourse.

[14] **All**: emphasizing the superlative idea in "bravest"; they, as Gauls, are assumed to be warlike, but the most so of *all* of them are the *Belgians*.

[15] **Farthest** *away*: one might expect **absunt** (are away) to have a more emphatic place, but it is dwarfed in importance by the predominance of the main idea, the *effeminating influences* from which the Belgians are said to be free. It is not that they live *farthest off* that is insisted on, but that the *civilization of the Province* etc., which would *soften* them, comes less in their way. It is to be noticed also that **absunt** has already been anticipated by the construction of **cultū** and still more by **longissimē**, so that when it comes it amounts only to a formal part of the sentence. Thus,— "because the *civilization* etc. of the Province (which would soften them) is *farthest* from them."

from the CIVILIZATION and REFINEMENT of the **Province**, and because **they** are LEAST[1] of all of them subject to the visits of *traders*,[2] and to the (consequent) importation of **such things as**[3] tend to *soften*[4] their warlike spirit; and are also **nearest**[5] to the *Germans*, who live *across the Rhine*,[6] and with whom they are *incessantly*[7] at war. For **the same** reason the HELVETIANS, as well, are superior to all the *other* Gauls in valor, because they are engaged in *almost daily* battles with the Germans, either defending **their own** boundaries from *them*, or **themselves** making war on *those of the Germans.* Of ALL THIS country, **one** part — the one which, **as** has been said, the *Gauls* (proper) occupy — BEGINS at the river Rhone. Its **boundaries** are the *river Garonne*, the *ocean*, and the *confines* of the Belgians. It even REACHES on the side of the *Sequani* and *Helvetians* the river Rhine. Its *general direction* is towards the north. The BELGIANS begin at the **extreme** *limits* of Gaul; they **reach** (on this side) as far as the lower part of the Rhine. They *spread* to the northward and eastward.

prōvinciae longissimē absunt, minimēque ad eōs mercātōrēs saepe commeant atque ea quae ad effēminandōs animōs pertinent important, proximīque sunt Germānīs, quī trāns Rhēnum incolunt, quibuscum continenter bellum gerunt. Quā dē causā Helvētiī quoque reliquōs Gallōs virtūte praecēdunt, quod ferē cotīdiānīs proeliīs cum Germānīs contendunt, cum aut suīs fīnibus eōs prohibent, aut ipsī in eōrum fīnibus bellum gerunt. Eōrum ūna pars, quam Gallōs obtinēre dictum est, initium capit ā flūmine Rhodanō; continētur Garumnā flūmine, Ōceanō, fīnibus Belgārum; attingit etiam ab Sēquanīs et Helvētiīs flūmen Rhēnum; vergit ad septentriōnēs. Belgae ab extrēmīs Galliae fīnibus oriuntur: pertinent ad īnferiōrem partem flūminis Rhēnī; spectant in septentriōnem et orientem sōlem. Aquītānia ā Garumnā flūmine ad Pȳrēnaeōs montīs et eam partem Ōceanī quae est ad Hispāniam pertinet; spectat inter occāsum sōlis et septentriōnēs.

AQUITANIA extends from the **Garonne** to the Pyrenees, and that part of the ocean that lies towards Spain. **It runs off** westward and northward.

b. The more important word is never placed last for emphasis. The apparent cases of this usage (when the emphasis is not misconceived) are cases where a word is added as an afterthought, either real or affected, and so has its position not in the sentence to which it is appended, but, as it were, in a new one.

[1] LEAST: made emphatic here by a common Latin order, the *chiasmus* (§ 598. *f*).

[2] *Traders:* the fourth member of the *chiasmus*, opposed to **cultū** and **hūmānitāte**.

[3] **Such things as**: the importance of the *nature* of the importations overshadows the fact that they are *imported*, which fact is anticipated in *traders*.

[4] *Soften:* cf. what is said in note 15, p. 394. They are *brave* because they have less to *soften* them, their native barbarity being *taken for granted*.

[5] **Nearest**: the same idiomatic prominence as in note 1 above, but varied by a special usage combining *chiasmus* and *anaphora* (§ 598. *f*).

[6] *Across the Rhine:* i.e. and so are perfect savages.

[7] *Incessantly:* the continuance of the warfare becomes the all-important idea, as if it were "and not a day passes in which they are not at war with them."

598. The main rules for the Order of Words are as follows: —

a. In any phrase the determining and most significant word comes first: —

1. Adjective and Noun: —

omnīs hominēs decet, EVERY *man ought* (opposed to some who do not).

Lūcius Catilīna **nōbilī** genere nātus fuit, **māgnā** vī et animī et corporis, sed **ingeniō** malō prāvōque (Sall. Cat. 5), *Lucius Catiline was born of a* NOBLE *family, with* GREAT *force of mind and body, but with a* NATURE *that was evil and depraved.* [Here the adjectives in the first part are the emphatic and important words, no antithesis between the nouns being as yet thought of; but in the second branch the *noun* is meant to be opposed to those before mentioned, and immediately takes the prominent place, as is seen by the natural English emphasis, thus making a *chiasmus.*[1]]

2. Word with modifying case: —

quid magis Epamīnōndam, **Thēbānōrum** imperātōrem, quam **victōriae** Thēbānōrum cōnsulere decuit (Inv. i. 69), *what should Epaminondas, commander of the* THEBANS, *have aimed at more than the* VICTORY *of the Thebans?*

lacrimā nihil citius ārēscit (id. i. 109), *nothing dries quicker than a* TEAR.

nēmō ferē **laudis** cupidus (De Or. i. 14), *hardly any one desirous of* GLORY (cf. Manil. 7, **avidī** laudis, EAGER *for glory*).

b. Numeral adjectives, adjectives of quantity, demonstrative, relative, and interrogative pronouns and adverbs, tend to precede the word or words to which they belong: —

cum **aliquā** perturbātiōne (Off. i. 137), *with* SOME *disturbance.*

hōc ūnō praestāmus (De Or. i. 32), *in* THIS *one thing we excel.*

cēterae ferē artēs, *the* OTHER *arts.*

NOTE. — This happens because such words are usually emphatic; but often the words connected with them are more so, and in such cases the pronouns etc. yield the emphatic place: —

causa aliqua (De Or. i. 250), *some* CASE.

stilus ille tuus (id. i. 257), *that well-known* STYLE *of yours* (in an antithesis; see passage). [Ille is idiomatic in this sense and position.]

Rōmam quae apportāta sunt (Verr. iv. 121), *what were carried to* ROME (in contrast to what remained at Syracuse).

c. When **sum** is used as the Substantive verb (§ 284. *b*), it regularly stands first, or at any rate before its subject: —

est virī māgnī pūnīre sontīs (Off. i. 82), *it is the duty of a great man to punish the guilty.*

[1] So called from the Greek letter X (*chi*), on account of the criss-cross arrangement of the words. Thus, ${}^{a}_{b}\mathrm{X}^{b}_{a}$ (see *f* below).

d. The verb may come first, or have a prominent position, either (1) because the *idea* in it is emphatic; or (2) because the *predication of the whole statement* is emphatic; or (3) the *tense* only may be emphatic: —

(1) **dīcēbat** idem Cotta (Off. ii. 59), *Cotta used to* SAY *the same thing* (opposed to others' *boasting*).

idem **fēcit** adulēscēns M. Antōnius (id. ii. 49), *the same thing was* DONE *by Mark Antony in his youth.* [Opposed to **dīxī** just before.]

facis amīcē (Lael. 9), *you* ACT *kindly.* [Cf. **amīcē** facis, *you are very* KIND (you act KINDLY).]

(2) prōpēnsior benīgnitās esse dēbēbit in calamitōsōs nisi forte **erunt** dīgnī calamitāte (Off. ii. 62), *liberality ought to be readier toward the unfortunate unless perchance they* REALLY DESERVE *their misfortune.*

praesertim cum **scrībat** (Panaetius) (id. iii. 8), *especially when he* DOES SAY (in his books). [Opposed to something omitted by him.]

(3) **fuimus** Trōes, **fuit** Īlium (Aen. ii. 325), *we have* CEASED *to be Trojans, Troy is now no* MORE.

loquor autem dē commūnibus amīcitiīs (Off. iii. 45), *but I am* SPEAKING NOW *of common friendships.*

e. Often the connection of two emphatic phrases is brought about by giving the precedence to the most prominent part of each and leaving the less prominent parts to follow in inconspicuous places: —

plūrēs solent esse causae (Off. i. 28), *there are* USUALLY SEVERAL *reasons.*

quōs āmīsimus cīvīs, eōs Mārtis vīs perculit (Marc. 17), WHAT *fellow-citizens we have* LOST, *have been stricken down by the violence of war.*

maximās tibi omnēs grātiās agimus (id. 33), *we* ALL *render you the* WARMEST *thanks.*

haec rēs ūnīus est propria Caesaris (id. 11), THIS *exploit belongs to Cæsar* ALONE.

obiūrgātiōnēs etiam nōn numquam incidunt necessāriae (Off. i. 136), OCCASIONS FOR REBUKE *also* SOMETIMES *occur which are unavoidable.*

f. Antithesis between two pairs of ideas is indicated by placing the pairs either (1) in the same order (*anaphora*) or (2) in exactly the opposite order (*chiasmus*): —

(1) rērum cōpia verbōrum cōpiam gignit (De Or. iii. 125), ABUNDANCE *of* MATTER *produces* COPIOUSNESS *of* EXPRESSION.

(2) lēgēs suppliciō improbōs afficiunt, dēfendunt ac tuentur bonōs (Legg. ii. 13), *the laws* VISIT PUNISHMENTS *upon the* WICKED, *but the* GOOD *they* DEFEND *and* PROTECT.

NOTE. — Chiasmus is very common in Latin, and often seems in fact the more inartificial construction. In an artless narrative one might hear, "The women were all *drowned*, they *saved* the men."

nōn igitur ūtilitātem amīcitia sed ūtilitās amīcitiam cōnsecūta est (Lael. 51), *it is not then that friendship has followed upon advantage, but advantage upon friendship.* [Here the chiasmus is only grammatical, the ideas being in the parallel order.] (See also p. 395: **longissimē, minimē, proximī.**)

g. A modifier of a phrase or some part of it is often embodied within the phrase (cf. *a*): —

dē commūnī hominum memoriā (Tusc. i. 59), *in regard to the* UNIVERSAL *memory of man.*

h. A favorite order with the poets is the *interlocked*, by which the attribute of one pair comes between the parts of the other (*synchysis*): —

et superiectō pavidae natārunt aequore dammae (Hor. Od. i. 2. 11).

NOTE.—This is often joined with chiasmus: as,—arma nōndum expiātīs ūncta cruōribus (id. ii. 1. 5).

i. Frequently unimportant words follow in the train of more emphatic ones with which they are grammatically connected, and so acquire a prominence out of proportion to their importance: —

dictitābat sē hortulōs aliquōs emere velle (Off. iii. 58), *he gave out that he wanted to buy some gardens.* [Here **aliquōs** is less emphatic than **emere**, but precedes it on account of the emphasis on **hortulōs**.]

j. The copula is generally felt to be of so little importance that it may come in anywhere where it sounds well; but usually under cover of more emphatic words: —

cōnsul ego quaesīvī, cum vōs mihi essētis in cōnsiliō (Rep. iii. 28), *as consul I held an investigation in which you attended me in council.*
falsum est id tōtum (id. ii. 28), *that is all false.*

k. Many expressions have acquired an invariable order: —

rēs pūblica; populus Rōmānus; honōris causā; pāce tantī virī.

NOTE.—These had, no doubt, originally an emphasis which required such an arrangement, but in the course of time have changed their shade of meaning. Thus, **senātus populusque Rōmānus** originally stated with emphasis the official bodies, but became fixed so as to be the only permissible form of expression.

l. The Romans had a fondness for emphasizing *persons*, so that a name or a pronoun often stands in an emphatic place: —

[dīxit] vēnālīs quidem **sē** hortōs nōn habēre (Off. iii. 58), [said] *that he did n't have any gardens for sale, to be sure.*

m. Kindred words often come together (*figūra etymologica*): —

ita sēnsim sine sēnsū aetās senēscit (Cat. M. 38), *thus gradually, without being perceived, man's life grows old.*

Special Rules

599. The following are special rules of arrangement: —

a. The negative precedes the word it especially affects; but if it belongs to no one word in particular, it generally precedes the verb; if it is especially emphatic, it begins the sentence. (See example, 598. *f.* N.)

b. **Itaque** regularly comes first in its sentence or clause; **enim, autem, vērō, quoque,** never first, but usually second, sometimes third if the second word is emphatic; **quidem** never first, but after the emphatic word; **igitur** usually second; **nē . . . quidem** include the emphatic word or words.

c. **Inquam, inquit,** are always used parenthetically, following one or more words. So often **crēdō, opīnor,** and in poetry sometimes **precor.**

d. (1) Prepositions (except **tenus** and **versus**) regularly precede their nouns; (2) but a monosyllabic preposition is often placed between a noun and its adjective or limiting genitive: —

> quem ad modum; quam ob rem; māgnō cum metū; omnibus cum cōpiīs; nūllā in rē (cf. § 598. *i*).

e. In the arrangement of clauses, the Relative clause more often comes first in Latin, and usually contains the antecedent noun: —

> **quōs āmīsimus cīvīs,** eōs Mārtis vīs perculit (Marc. 17), *those citizens whom we have lost*, etc.

f. Personal or demonstrative pronouns tend to stand together in the sentence: —

> cum **vōs mihi** essētis in cōnsiliō (Rep. iii. 28), *when you attended me in counsel.*

Structure of the Period

600. Latin, unlike modern languages, expresses the relation of words to each other by *inflection* rather than by *position*. Hence its structure not only admits of great variety in the arrangement of words, but is especially favorable to that form of sentence which is called a Period. In a period, the sense is expressed by the sentence *as a whole*, and is held in suspense till the delivery of the last word.

An English sentence does not often exhibit this form of structure. It was imitated, sometimes with great skill and beauty, by many of the earlier writers of English prose; but its effect is better seen in poetry, as in the following passage: —

> High on a throne of royal state, which far
> Outshone the wealth of Ormus and of Ind,
> Or where the gorgeous East with richest hand
> Showers on her kings barbaric pearl and gold,
> Satan exalted sat. — *Paradise Lost*, ii. 1–5.

But in argument or narrative, the best English writers more commonly give short clear sentences, each distinct from the rest, and saying one thing by itself. In Latin, on the contrary, the story or argument is viewed as a whole; and the logical relation among all its parts is carefully indicated.

601. In the structure of the Period, the following rules are to be observed: —

a. In general the main subject or object is put in the main clause, not in a subordinate one: —

> Hannibal cum recēnsuisset auxilia Gādēs profectus est (Liv. xxi. 21), *when Hannibal had reviewed the auxiliaries. he set out for Cadiz,*

Volscī exiguam spem in armīs, aliā undique abscissā, cum tentāssent, praeter cētera adversa, locō quoque inīquō ad pūgnam congressī, inīquiōre ad fugam, cum ab omnī parte caederentur, ad precēs ā certāmine versī dēditō imperātōre trāditīsque armīs, sub iugum missī, cum singulīs vestīmentīs, īgnōminiae clādisque plēnī dīmittuntur (Liv. iv. 10). [Here the main fact is *the return of the Volscians*. But the striking circumstances of the surrender etc., which in English would be detailed in a number of brief independent sentences, are put into the several subordinate clauses within the main clause so that the passage gives a complete picture in one sentence.]

b. Clauses are usually arranged in the order of prominence in the mind of the speaker; so, usually, *cause* before *result; purpose, manner*, and the like, before the *act*.

c. In coördinate clauses, the copulative conjunctions are frequently omitted (*asyndeton*). In such cases the connection is made clear by some antithesis indicated by the position of words.

d. A change of subject, when required, is marked by the introduction of a pronoun, if the new subject has already been mentioned. But such change is often purposely avoided by a change in structure, — the less important being merged in the more important by the aid of participles or of subordinate phrases: —

quem ut barbarī incendium effūgisse vīdērunt, tēlīs ēminus missīs interfēcērunt (Nep. Alc. 10), *when the barbarians saw that he had escaped,* THEY *threw darts at* HIM *at long range and killed* HIM.

celeriter cōnfectō negōtiō, in hīberna legiōnēs redūxit (B. G. vi. 3), *the matter was soon finished,* AND *he led the legions*, etc.

e. So the repetition of a noun, or the substitution of a pronoun for it, is avoided unless a different case is required: —

dolōrem sī nōn potuerō frangere occultābō (Phil. xii. 21), *if I cannot conquer the pain, I will hide* IT. [Cf. *if I cannot conquer I will hide the pain.*]

f. The Romans were careful to close a period with an agreeable succession of long and short syllables. Thus, —

quod scīs nihil prōdest, quod nescīs multum obest (Or. 166), *what you know is of no use, what you do not know does great harm.*

NOTE. — In rhetorical writing, particularly in oratory, the Romans, influenced by their study of the Greek orators, gave more attention to this matter than in other forms of composition. Quintilian (ix. 4. 72) lays down the general rule that a clause should not open with the beginning of a verse or close with the end of one.

PROSODY

QUANTITY

602. The poetry of the Indo-European people seems originally to have been somewhat like our own, depending on accent for its metre and disregarding the natural quantity of syllables. The Greeks, however, developed a form of poetry which, like music, pays close attention to the natural quantity of syllables; and the Romans borrowed their metrical forms in classical times from the Greeks. Hence Latin poetry does not depend, like ours, upon accent and rhyme; but is measured, like musical strains, by the length of syllables. Especially does it differ from our verse in not regarding the prose accent of the words, but substituting for that an entirely different system of metrical accent or *ictus* (see § 611. *a*). This depends upon the character of the measure used, falling at regular intervals of time on a long syllable or its equivalent. Each syllable is counted as either long or short in Quantity; and a long syllable is generally reckoned equal in length to two short ones (for exceptions, see § 608. *c–e*).

The quantity of radical (or stem) syllables — as of short **a** in **păter** or of long **a** in **māter** — can be learned only by observation and practice, unless determined by the general rules of quantity. Most of these rules are only arbitrary formulas devised to assist the memory; the syllables being long or short *because the ancients pronounced them so*. The actual practice of the Romans in regard to the quantity of syllables is ascertained chiefly from the usage of the poets; but the ancient grammarians give some assistance, and in some inscriptions long vowels are distinguished in various ways, — by the apex, for instance, or by doubling (§ 10. *e*. N.).

Since Roman poets borrow very largely from the poetry and mythology of the Greeks, numerous Greek words, especially proper names, make an important part of Latin poetry. These words are generally employed in accordance with the Greek, and not the Latin, laws of quantity. Where these laws vary in any important point, the variations will be noticed in the rules below.

GENERAL RULES

603. The following are General Rules of Quantity (cf. §§ 9–11):

Quantity of Vowels

***a*. Vowels.** A vowel before another vowel or **h** is short: as, **vĭa**, **trăhō**.

Exceptions. — 1. In the genitive form **-ius**, **ī** is long: as, **utrīus**, **nūllīus**. It is, however, sometimes short in verse (§ 113. *c*).

2. In the genitive and dative singular of the fifth declension, **e** is long between two vowels: as, **diēī**; otherwise usually short, as in **fidĕī**, **rĕī**, **spĕī**.

NOTE. — It was once long in these also: as, **plēnu**[s] **fidēī** (Ennius, at the end of a hexameter). **A** is also long before **ī** in the old genitive of the first declension: as, **aulāī**.

3. In the conjugation of **fīō**, **i** is long except when followed by **er**. Thus, **fīō**, **fīēbam**, **fīam**, but **fierī**, **fierem**; so also **fit** (§ 606. *a*. 3).

4. In many Greek words the vowel in Latin represents a long vowel or diphthong, and retains its original long quantity: as, **Trōes** (Τρῶες), **Thalīa** (Θαλεῖα), **hērōas** (ἥρωας), **āēr** (ἀήρ).

NOTE.—But many Greek words are more or less Latinized in this respect: as, **Acadēmīa, chorēa, Malĕa, platĕa.**

5. In **dīus**, in **ēheu** usually, and sometimes in **Dīāna** and **ōhe**, the first vowel is long.

***b.* Diphthongs.** A Diphthong is long: as, **foedus, cui,**[1] **aula.**

Exception.—The preposition **prae** in compounds is generally shortened before a vowel: as, **praĕ-ustīs** (Aen. vii. 524), **praĕ-eunte** (id. v. 186).

NOTE.—**U** following **q, s,** or **g,** does not make a diphthong with a following vowel (see § 5. N. 2). For **â-iō, mâ-ior, pê-ior,** etc., see § 11. *d* and N.

***c.* Contraction.** A vowel formed by contraction (*crasis*) is long: as, **nīl,** from **nihil**; **cōgō** for †**co-agō**; **mālō** for **mā-volō.**

NOTE.—Two vowels of different syllables may be run together without full contraction (*synizēsis*, § 642): as, **d͡einde** (for **deinde**), **m͡eōs** (for **meōs**); and often two syllables are united by Synæresis (§ 642) without contraction: as when **părĭĕtĭbŭs** is pronounced *parўĕtĭbus*.

d. A vowel before **ns, nf, gn,** is long: as, **īnstō, īnfāns, sīgnum.**

Quantity of Syllables

e. A syllable is long if it contains a long vowel or a diphthong: as, **cā-rus, ō-men, foe-dus.**

***f.* Position.** A syllable is long by *position* if its vowel, though short, is followed by two consonants or a double consonant: as, **adventus, cortex.**

But if the two consonants are a mute followed by **l** or **r** the syllable may be either long or short (*common*); as, **alacris** or **alăcris**; **patris** or **pătris.**

Vowels should be pronounced long or short in accordance with their natural quantity without regard to the length of the syllable by position.

NOTE 1.—The rules of Position do not, in general, apply to final vowels before a word beginning with two consonants.

NOTE 2.—A syllable is long if its vowel is followed by consonant **i** (except in **bĭiugis, quadrĭiugis**): see § 11. *d*.

NOTE 3.—Compounds of **iaciō**, though written with one **i**, commonly retain the long vowel of the prepositions with which they are compounded, as if before a consonant, and, if the vowel of the preposition is short, the first syllable is long by position on the principle of § 11. *e*.

obicis hostī (at the end of a hexameter, Aen. iv. 549).
inicit et saltū (at the beginning of a hexameter, Aen. ix. 552).
prōice tēla manū (at the beginning of a hexameter, Aen. vi. 836).

Later poets sometimes shorten the preposition in trisyllabic forms, and prepositions ending in a vowel are sometimes contracted as if the verb began with a vowel:

(1) **cūr an|nōs ŏbĭ|cis** (Claud. iv C. H. 264).
(2) **rēīcĕ că|pellās** (Ecl. iii. 96, at end).

NOTE 4.—The **y** or **w** sound resulting from *synæresis* (§ 642) has the effect of a consonant in making position: as, **abietis** (*abyetis*), **fluviōrum** (*fluvyōrum*). Conversely, when the semivowel becomes a vowel, position is lost: as, **sĭlŭae**, for **silvae.**

[1] Rarely dissyllabic **cŭĭ** (as Mart. i. 104. 22).

FINAL SYLLABLES

604. The Quantity of Final Syllables is as follows: —

a. Monosyllables ending in a vowel are long: as, **mē, tū, hī, nē.**

1. The attached particles **-nĕ, -quĕ, -vĕ, -cĕ, -ptĕ,** and **rĕ- (rĕd-)** are short; **sē- (sēd-)** and **dī-** are long. Thus, **sēcēdit, sēditiō, exercitumquĕ rĕdūcit, dīmittō.** But **re-** is often long in **rēligiō (relligiō), rētulī (rettulī), rēpulī (reppulī).**

b. Nouns and adjectives of one syllable are long: as, **sōl, ōs (ōris), bōs, pār, vās (vāsis), vēr, vīs.**

Exceptions. — **cŏr, fĕl, lăc, mĕl, ŏs (ossis), văs (vădis), vĭr, tŏt, quŏt.**

c. Most monosyllabic Particles are short: as, **ăn, ĭn, cĭs, nĕc.** But **crās, cūr, ēn, nōn, quīn, sīn** — with adverbs in **c**: as, **hīc, hūc, sīc** — are long.

d. Final **a** in words declined by cases is short, except in the ablative singular of the first declension; in all other words final **a** is long. Thus, **eă stellă** (nominative), **cum eā stellā** (ablative); **frūstrā, vocā** (imperative), **posteā, trīgintā.**

Exceptions. — **ēiă, ită, quiă, pută** (*suppose*); and, in late use, **trīgintă** etc.

e. Final **e** is short: as in **nūbĕ, dūcitĕ, saepĕ.**

Exceptions. — Final **e** is long — 1. In adverbs formed from adjectives of the first and second declension, with others of like form: as, **altē, longē, miserē, apertē, saepissimē.** So **ferē, fermē.**

But it is short in **benĕ, malĕ; īnfernĕ, supernĕ.**

2. In nouns of the fifth declension: as, **fidē** (also **famē**), **faciē, hodiē, quārē (quā rē).**

3. In Greek neuters plural of the second declension: as, **cētē**; and in some other Greek words: **Phoebē, Circē, Andromachē,** etc.

4. In the imperative singular of the second conjugation: as, **vidē.**

But sometimes **cavĕ, habĕ, tacĕ, valĕ, vidĕ** (cf. § 629. *b.* 1).

f. Final **i** is long: as in **turrī, fīlī, audī.**

Exceptions. — Final **i** is common in **mihi, tibi, sibi, ibi, ubi**; and short in **nisĭ, quasĭ, sīcutĭ, cuĭ** (when making two syllables), and in Greek vocatives: as, **Alexĭ.**

g. Final **o** is common: but long in datives and ablatives; also in nouns of the third declension. It is almost invariably long in verbs before the time of Ovid.

Exceptions. — **citŏ, modŏ (dummodŏ), immŏ, profectŏ, egŏ, duŏ, cedŏ** (the imperative); so sometimes **octŏ, īlicŏ,** etc., particularly in later writers.

h. Final **u** is long. Final **y** is short.

i. Final **as, es, os,** are long; final **is, us, ys,** are short: as, **nefās, rūpēs, servōs** (accusative), **honōs; hostĭs, amīcŭs, Tethÿs.**

Exceptions. — 1. **as** is short in Greek plural accusatives: as, **lampadăs**; and in **anăs**.

2. **es** is short in the nominative of nouns of the third declension (lingual) having a short vowel in the stem[1]: as, **mīlĕs** (-ĭtis), **obsĕs** (-ĭdis), — except **abiēs, ariēs, pariēs, pēs**; in the present of **esse** (**ĕs, adĕs**); in the preposition **penĕs**, and in the plural of Greek nouns: as, **hērōĕs, lampadĕs.**

3. **os** is short in **compŏs, impŏs**; in the Greek nominative ending: as, **barbitŏs**; in the old nominative of the second declension: as, **servŏs** (later **servus**).

4. **is** in plural cases is long: as in **bonīs, nōbīs, vōbīs, omnīs** (accusative plural).

5. **is** is long in the verb forms **fīs, sīs, vīs** (with **quīvīs** etc.), **velīs, mālīs, nōlīs, edīs**; in the second person singular of the present indicative active in the fourth conjugation: as, **audīs**; and sometimes in the forms in **-eris** (future perfect indicative or perfect subjunctive).

6. **us** is long in the genitive singular and nominative, accusative, and vocative plural of the fourth declension; and in nouns of the third declension having **ū** (long) in the stem: as, **virtūs** (-ūtis), **incūs** (-ūdis). But **pecŭs, -ŭdis.**

j. Of other final syllables, those ending in a single consonant are short. Thus, **amăt, amātŭr**; **dōnĕc, făc, procŭl, iubăr.**

Exceptions. — **hīc** (also **hĭc**); **allēc**; the ablatives **illōc**, etc.; certain adverbs in **-c**: as, **illīc, istūc**; **liēn**, and some Greek nouns: as, **āēr, aethēr, crātēr.**

Perfects and Perfect Participles

605. Perfects and Perfect Participles of two syllables have the first syllable long: as, **iūvī, iūtum** (**iŭvō**), **vīdī, vīsum** (**vĭdeō**); **fūgī** (**fŭgiō**); **vēnī** (**vĕniō**).

Exceptions. — **bĭbī, dĕdī, fĭdī, scĭdī, stĕtī, stĭtī, tŭlī**; **cĭtum, dătum, ĭtum, lĭtum, quĭtum, rătum, rŭtum, sătum, sĭtum, stătum.** In some compounds of **stō, stātum** is found (long), as **praestātum.**

a. In reduplicated perfects the vowel of the reduplication is short; the vowel of the following syllable is, also, usually short: as, **cĕcĭdī** (**cădō**), **dĭdĭcī** (**discō**), **pŭpŭgī** (**pungō**), **cŭcŭrrī** (**currō**), **tĕtĕndī** (**tendō**), **mŏmŏrdī** (**mordeō**). But **cĕcīdī** from **caedō**, **pepēdī** from **pēdō.**

Derivatives

606. Rules for the Quantity of Derivatives are: —

a. Forms from the same stem have the same quantity: as, **ămō, ămāvistī**; **gĕnus, gĕneris.**

Exceptions. — 1. **bōs, lār, mās, pār, pēs, sāl,** — also **arbōs,** — have a long vowel in the nominative, though the stem-vowel is short (cf. genitive **bŏvis** etc.).

[1] The quantity of the stem-vowel may be seen in the genitive singular.

2. Nouns in **-or**, genitive **-ōris**, have the vowel shortened before the final **r**: as, **honŏr.** (But this shortening is comparatively late, so that in early Latin these nominatives are often found long.)

3. Verb-forms with vowel originally long regularly shorten it before final **m**, **r**, or **t**: as, **amĕm, amĕr, dīcerĕr, amĕt** (compare **amēmus**), **dīcerĕt, audĭt, fĭt.**

NOTE. — The final syllable in **t** of the perfect was long in old Latin, but is short in the classic period.

4. A few long stem-syllables are shortened: as, **ācer, ăcerbus.** So **dē-iĕrō** and **pē-iĕrō**, weakened from **iūrō.**

b. Forms from the same root often show inherited variations of vowel quantity (see § 17): as, **dīcō** (cf. **maledĭcus**); **dūcō** (**dŭx, dŭcis**); **fīdō** (**perfĭdus**); **vōx, vōcis** (**vŏcō**); **lēx, lēgis** (**lĕgō**).

c. Compounds retain the quantity of the words which compose them: as, **oc-cĭdō** (**cădō**), **oc-cīdō** (**caedō**), **in-īquus** (**aequus**).

NOTE. — Greek words compounded with πρό have **o** short: as, **prŏphēta, prŏlŏgus.** Some Latin compounds of **prō** have **o** short: as, **prŏficīscor, prŏfiteor.** Compounds with **ne** vary: as, **nĕfās, nĕgō, nĕqueō, nēquam.**

RHYTHM

607. The essence of Rhythm in poetry is the regular recurrence of syllables pronounced with more stress than those intervening. To produce this effect in its perfection, precisely equal times should occur between the recurrences of the stress. But, in the application of rhythm to words, the exactness of these intervals is sacrificed somewhat to the necessary length of the words; and, on the other hand, the words are forced somewhat in their pronunciation, to produce more nearly the proper intervals of time. In different languages these adaptations take place in different degrees; one language disregarding more the intervals of time, another the pronunciation of the words.

The Greek language early developed a very strict rhythmical form of poetry, in which the intervals of time were all-important. The earliest Latin, on the other hand, — as in the Saturnian and Fescennine verse, — was not so restricted. But the purely metrical forms were afterwards adopted from the Greek, and supplanted the native forms of verse. Thus the Latin poetry with which we have to do follows for the most part Greek rules, which require the formal division of words (like music) into measures of equal times, technically called Feet. The strict rhythm was doubtless more closely followed in poetry that was *sung* than in that which was *declaimed* or *intoned.* In neither language, however, is the time perfectly preserved, even in single measures; and there are some cases in which the regularity of the time between the ictuses is disturbed.

The Greeks and Romans distinguished syllables of two kinds in regard to the time required for their pronunciation, a *long* syllable having twice the metrical value of a *short* one. But it must not be supposed that all long syllables were of equal length, or even that in a given passage each long had just twice the length of the contiguous shorts. The ratio was only approximate at best, though necessarily more exact in singing than in recitation. Nor are longs and shorts the only forms of syllables that are found. In some cases a long syllable was protracted, so as to have the time of three or even of four shorts, and often one long or two shorts were pronounced in less than their proper time, though they were perhaps distinguishable in time from one short (see § 608. *c*, *d*). Sometimes a syllable naturally short seems to have been slightly prolonged, so as to represent a long, though in most (not all) cases the apparent irregularity can be otherwise explained. In a few cases, also, a pause takes the place of one or more syllables to fill out the required length of the measure. This could, of course, take place only at the end of a word: hence the importance of Cæsura and Diæresis in prosody (§ 611. *b*, *c*).

Measures

608. Rhythm consists of the division of musical sound into equal intervals of time called Measures or Feet.

The most natural division of musical time is into measures consisting of either two or three equal parts. But the ancients also distinguished measures of five equal parts.

NOTE.—The divisions of *musical* time are marked by a stress of voice on one or the other part of the measure. This stress is called the Ictus (*beat*), or metrical accent (see § 611. *a*).

a. The unit of length in Prosody is *one short syllable*. This is called a Mora. It is represented by the sign ⏑, or in musical notation by the eighth note or *quaver* (♪).

b. A long syllable is regularly equal to two moræ, and is represented by the sign —, or by the quarter note or *crotchet* (♩).

c. A long syllable may be *protracted*, so as to occupy the time of three or four moræ. Such a syllable, if equal to three moræ, is represented by the sign ∟ (or dotted quarter ♩.); if equal to four, by ⊔ (or the half note or *minim*, 𝅗𝅥).

d. A long syllable may be *contracted*, so as to take practically the time of a short one. Such a syllable is sometimes represented by the sign >.

e. A short syllable may be contracted so as to occupy less than one mora.

f. A pause sometimes occurs at the end of a verse or a series of verses, to fill up the time. A pause of one mora in a measure is indicated by the sign ∧; one of two moræ by the sign ∧̄.

g. One or more syllables are sometimes placed before the proper beginning of the measure. Such syllables are called an Anacrūsis or *prelude*.[1]

The anacrusis is regularly equal to the unaccented part of the measure.

[1] The same thing occurs in modern poetry, and in modern music any unaccented syllables at the beginning are treated as an anacrusis, i.e. they make an incomplete measure before the first bar. This was not the case in ancient music. The ancients seem to have treated any unaccented syllable at the beginning as belonging to the following accented ones, so as to make with them a foot or measure. Thus it would seem that there was an original form of Indo-European poetry which was iambic in its structure, or which, at least, accented the second syllable rather than the first.

609. The feet most frequently employed in Latin verse, together with their musical notation, are the following: —

a. Triple or Unequal Measures ($\frac{3}{8}$)[1]

1. Trochee (–́ ⏑ =): as, *rēgĭs.*
2. Iambus (⏑ –́ =): as, *dŭcēs.*
3. Tribrach[2] (⏑ ⏑ ⏑ =): as, *hŏmĭnĭs.*

b. Double or Equal Measures ($\frac{2}{4}$)

1. Dactyl (– ⏑ ⏑ =): as, *cōnsŭlĭs.*
2. Anapæst (⏑ ⏑ – =): as, *mŏnĭtōs.*
3. Spondee (– – =): as, *rēgēs.*

c. Six-timed Measures ($\frac{3}{4}$)

1. Ionic *ā mâiōre* (– – ⏑ ⏑ =): as, *cōnfēcĕrăt.*
2. Ionic *ā minōre* (⏑ ⏑ – – =): as, *rĕtŭlissent.*
3. Choriambus (– ⏑ ⏑ – =): as, *contŭlĕrant.*

d. Quinary or Hemiolic[3] Measures ($\frac{5}{8}$)

1. Cretic (– ⏑ – =): as, *cōnsŭlēs.*
2. Pæon *prīmus* (– ⏑ ⏑ ⏑ =): as, *cōnsŭlĭbŭs.*
3. Pæon *quārtus* (⏑ ⏑ ⏑ – =): as, *ĭtĭnĕrī.*
4. Bacchīus (⏑ – – =): as, *ămīcōs.*

[1] Called *diplasic*, the two parts (Thesis and Arsis) being in the ratio of 2 to 1.
[2] Not found as a fundamental foot, but only as the resolution of a Trochee or Iambus.
[3] Called *hemiolic*, the two parts being in the ratio of 1 to $1\frac{1}{2}$, or of 2 to 3.

Note.—Several compound feet are mentioned by the grammarians, viz. *Pyrrhic* (⏑ ⏑); *Amphibrach* (⏑ — ⏑); *Antibacchīus* (— — ⏑); *Proceleusmatic* (⏑ ⏑ ⏑ ⏑); the *Molossus* (— — —); the 2d and 3d *Pæon*, having a long syllable in the 2d or 3d place, with three short ones; 1st, 2d, 3d, and 4th *Epitrĭtus*, having a short syllable in the 1st, 2d, 3d, or 4th place, with three long ones.

Irrational Feet

e. Feet with these apparent quantities do not always occupy equal time, but may be contracted or prolonged to suit the series in which they occur. They are then called *irrational*, because the thesis and arsis do not have their normal ratio.[1] Such are:—

Irrational Spondee:

(in place of a Trochee) –́ >
(in place of an Iambus) > –́
or

Cyclic Dactyl (in place of a Trochee):

–́ ⏑⏑ or –́⏑ ⏑ = or

Cyclic Anapæst (in place of an Iambus):

⏑⏑ –́ or ⏑ ⏑–́ = or

The apparent dactyl > ⏑́ ⏑, as a substitute for an iambus, and the apparent anapæst ⏑́ ⏑ >, as a substitute for a trochee, occur frequently in the dramatic writers.

Note.—Narrative poetry was written for rhythmical recitation, or chant, with instrumental accompaniment; and Lyrical poetry for rhythmical melody, or singing. It must be borne in mind that in ancient music—which in this differs widely from modern—the rhythm of the melody was identical with the rhythm of the text. The lyric poetry was to be sung; the poet was musician and composer, as well as author. To this day a poet is said conventionally to "sing."

Thus a correct understanding of the rhythmical structure of the verse gives us the *time*, though not the *tune*, to which it was actually sung. The exact time, however, as indicated by the succession of long and short syllables, was varied according to certain laws of so-called "Rhythmic," as will be explained below. In reading ancient verse it is necessary to bear in mind not only the variations in the relative length of syllables, but the occasional pause necessary to fill out the measure; and to remember that the rhythmical accent is the only one of importance, though the words should be distinguished carefully, and the sense preserved. Poetry should not be *scanned*, but read metrically.

[1] It seems probable that both thesis and arsis of an irrational foot were affected by the necessity of preserving the rhythmical time of the foot.

Substitution

610. In many cases measures of the same time may be substituted for each other, a long syllable taking the place of two short ones, or two short syllables the place of a long one.

In the former case the measure is said to be *contracted;* in the latter, to be *resolved:* —

a. A Spondee (— —) may take the place of a Dactyl (— ⏑ ⏑) or an Anapæst (⏑ ⏑ —); and a Tribrach (⏑ ⏑ ⏑) may take the place of a Trochee (— ⏑) or an Iambus (⏑ —). The optional substitution of one long syllable for two short ones is represented by the sign ⏕.

b. When a long syllable having the Ictus (§ 611. *a*) is resolved, the ictus properly belongs to both the resulting short syllables; but for convenience the mark of accent is placed on the first: —

núnc ex|pĕ́rĭar | sítn*e* ă|cétō | tĭ́bĭ cŏr | ắcr*e* in | péctŏ|rĕ́. — Pl. Bac. 405.

—́ > | ⏑́ ⏑ > | —́ ⏑ | —́ > | ⏑́ ⏑ ⏑ | —́ > | —́ ⏑ | ⏑́̄ ∧

The Musical Accent

611. That part of the measure which receives the *stress of voice* (the musical accent) is called the Thesis; the unaccented part is called the Arsis.[1]

a. The stress of voice laid upon the Thesis is called the Ictus (*beat*). It is marked thus: —́ ⏑ ⏑.

b. The ending of a word within a measure is called Cæsura. When this coincides with a rhetorical pause, it is called *the* Cæsura of the verse, and is of main importance as affecting the melody or rhythm.

c. The coincidence of the end of a word with that of a measure is called Diæresis.

[1] The Thesis signifies properly the *putting down* (*θέσις*, from *τίθημι, put, place*) of the foot in beating time, in the march or dance ("downward beat"), and the Arsis the *raising* (*ἄρσις*, from *ἀείρω, raise*) of the foot ("upward beat"). By the Latin grammarians these terms were made to mean, respectively, the ending and the beginning of a measure. By a misunderstanding which has prevailed till recently, since the time of Bentley, their true signification has been reversed. They will here be used in accordance with their ancient meaning, as has now become more common. This metrical accent, recurring at regular intervals of time, is what constitutes the essence of the rhythm of poetry as distinguished from prose, and should be constantly kept in mind. The error mentioned arose from applying to trochaic and dactylic verse a definition which was true only of iambic or anapæstic.

VERSIFICATION

THE VERSE

612. A single line of poetry — that is, a series of feet set in a recognized order — is called a Verse.[1]

NOTE. — Most of the common verses originally consisted of two series (*hemistichs*), but the joint between them is often obscured. It is marked in Iambic and Trochaic Tetrameter by the *Diæresis*, in Dactylic Hexameter by the *Cæsura*.

a. A verse lacking a syllable at the end is called Catalectic, that is, having a pause to fill the measure; when the end syllable is not lacking, the verse is called Acatalectic, and has no such pause.

b. A final syllable, regularly short, is sometimes lengthened before a pause:[2] it is then said to be long by *Diastole*: —

nostrōr*um* obrui<u>mur</u>, — oriturque miserrima caedēs. — Aen. ii. 411.

c. The last syllable of any verse may be indifferently long or short (*syllaba anceps*).

Scansion and Elision

d. To divide the verse into its appropriate measures, according to the rules of quantity and versification, is called *scanning* or *scansion* (**scānsiō**, a *climbing* or advance by steps, from **scandō**).

NOTE. — In *reading* verse rhythmically, care should be taken to preserve the measure or time of the syllables, but at the same time not to destroy or confuse the words themselves, as is often done in *scanning*.

e. In scanning, a vowel or diphthong at the end of a word (unless an interjection) is partially suppressed when the next word begins with a vowel or with **h**. This is called Elision (*bruising*).[3]

In reading it is usual entirely to suppress elided syllables. Strictly, however, they should be sounded lightly.

[1] The word Verse (*versus*) signifies *a turning back*, i.e. to begin again in like manner, as opposed to Prose (*prŏrsus* or *prŏversus*), which means *straight ahead*.

[2] This usage is comparatively rare, most cases where it appears to be found being caused by the retention of an originally long quantity.

[3] The practice of Elision is followed in Italian and French poetry, and is sometimes adopted in English, particularly in the older poets: —

T' inveigle and invite th' unwary sense. — *Comus* 538.

In early Latin poetry a final syllable ending in *s* often loses this letter even before a consonant (cf. § 15. 7): —

seniō cōnfectu*s* quiēscit. — Enn. (Cat. M. 14).

NOTE.—Elision is sometimes called by the Greek name Synalœpha (*smearing*). Rarely a syllable is elided at the end of a verse when the next verse begins with a vowel: this is called Synapheia (*binding*).

f. A final **m**, with the preceding vowel, is suppressed in like manner when the next word begins with a vowel or **h**: this is called Ecthlipsis (*squeezing out*):—

> mōnstr^{um} horrend^{um}, īnform^{e}, ingēns, cui lūmen adēmptum.
> —Aen. iii. 658.

NOTE 1.—Final **m** has a feeble nasal sound, so that its partial suppression before the initial vowel of the following word was easy.

NOTE 2.—The monosyllables **dō, dem, spē, spem, sim, stō, stem, quī** (plural), and monosyllabic interjections are never elided; nor is an iambic word elided in dactylic verse. Elision is often evaded by skilful collocation of words.

g. Elision is sometimes omitted when a word ending in a vowel has a special emphasis, or is succeeded by a pause. This omission is called Hiatus (*gaping*).

NOTE.—The final vowel is sometimes shortened in such cases.

FORMS OF VERSE

613. A verse receives its name from its dominant or fundamental foot: as, *Dactylic*, *Iambic*, *Trochaic*, *Anapæstic;* and from the number of measures (single or double) which it contains: as, *Hexameter*, *Tetrameter*, *Trimeter*, *Dimeter*.

NOTE.—Trochaic, Iambic, and Anapæstic verses are measured not by single feet, but by pairs (*dipodia*), so that six Iambi make a *Trimeter*.

614. A Stanza, or Strophe, consists of a definite number of verses ranged in a fixed order.

Many stanzas are named after some eminent poet: as, *Sapphic* (from Sappho), *Alcaic* (from Alcæus), *Archilochian* (from Archilochus), *Horatian* (from Horace), and so on.

DACTYLIC VERSE

Dactylic Hexameter

615. The Dactylic Hexameter, or *Heroic Verse*, consists theoretically of six dactyls. It may be represented thus:—

–́ ⏑ ⏑ | –́ ⏑ ⏑ | –́ || ⏑ ⏑ | –́ ⏑ ⏑ | –́ ⏑ ⏑ | –́ ⏓

NOTE.—The last foot is usually said to be a spondee, but is in reality a trochee standing for a dactyl, since the final syllable is not measured.

a. For any foot, except the fifth, a spondee may be substituted.

b. Rarely a spondee is found in the fifth foot; the verse is then called *spondaic* and usually ends with a word of four syllables.

Thus in Ecl. iv. 49 the verse ends with **incrēmentum.**

c. The hexameter has regularly one *principal cæsura*—sometimes two—almost always accompanied by a pause in the sense.

1. The principal cæsura is usually *after the thesis* (less commonly *in the arsis*) *of the third foot*, dividing the verse into two parts in sense and rhythm. See examples in *d.*

2. It may also be *after the thesis* (less commonly *in the arsis*) *of the fourth foot.* In this case there is often another cæsura in the second foot, so that the verse is divided into three parts:—

> **pártĕ fĕ|rṓx || ār|dḗnsqu^e ŏcŭ|lís || et | síbĭlă | cóllă.**—Aen. v. 277.

NOTE.—Often the only indication of the *principal* among a number of cæsuras is the break in the sense.

A cæsura occurring after the first syllable of a foot is called *masculine.* A cæsura occurring after the second syllable of a foot is called *feminine* (as in the fifth foot of the third and fourth verses in *d*). A cæsura may also be found in any foot of the verse, but a proper *cæsural pause* could hardly occur in the first or sixth.

When the fourth foot ends a word, the break (properly a diæresis) is sometimes improperly called *bucolic cæsura*, from its frequency in pastoral poetry.

d. The first seven verses of the Æneid, divided according to the foregoing rules, will appear as follows. The principal cæsura in each verse is marked by double lines:—

> Armă vĭ|rumquĕ că|nō || Trō|iae quī | prīmŭs ăb | ōrīs
> Ītălĭ|am fā|tō prŏfŭ|gus || Lā|vīnĭăquĕ | vēnĭt
> lītŏră, | mult^um il|l^e et ter|rīs || iac|tātŭs ĕt | altō
> vī sŭpĕ|rum || sae|vae mĕmŏ|rem Iū|nōnĭs ŏb | īrăm;
> multă quŏ|qu^e et bel|lō pas|sus || dum | condĕrĕt | urbĕm,
> īnfer|retquĕ dĕ|ōs Lătĭ|ō, || gĕnŭs | undĕ Lă|tīnum,
> Albā|nīquĕ pă|trēs, || at|qu^e altae | moenĭă | Rōmae.

1. The *feminine cæsura* is seen in the following:—

> Dīs gĕnĭ|tī pŏtŭ|ērĕ: || tĕ|nent mĕdĭ|^a omnĭă| silvae.—Aen. vi. 131.

NOTE.—The Hexameter is thus illustrated in English verse:—

> Over the sea, past Crete, on the Syrian shore to the southward,
> Dwells in the well-tilled lowland a dark-haired Æthiop people,
> Skilful with needle and loom, and the arts of the dyer and carver,
> Skilful, but feeble of heart; for they know not the lords of Olympus,
> Lovers of men; neither broad-browed Zeus, nor Pallas Athené,
> Teacher of wisdom to heroes, bestower of might in the battle;
> Share not the cunning of Hermes, nor list to the songs of Apollo,
> Fearing the stars of the sky, and the roll of the blue salt water.
>
> —Kingsley's *Andromeda.*

Elegiac Stanza

616. The Elegiac Stanza consists of two verses, — a Hexameter followed by a Pentameter.[1]

The Pentameter verse is the same as the Hexameter, except that it omits the last half of the third foot and of the sixth foot: —

´ ◡◡ | ´ ◡◡ | ´ ⩘ || ´ ◡ ◡ | ´ ◡ ◡ | ´ ⩘

a. The Pentameter verse is therefore to be scanned as *two half-verses*, the second of which always consists of two dactyls followed by a single syllable.

b. The Pentameter has no regular Cæsura; but the first half-verse must always end with a word (*diæresis*, § 611. *c*), which is followed by a pause to complete the measure.[2]

c. The following verses will illustrate the forms of the Elegiac Stanza: —

cum sŭbĭt | illī|us || trīs|tissĭmă | noctĭs ĭ|māgō
  quā mĭhĭ | suprē|mum ⩘ || tempŭs ĭn | urbĕ fŭ|ĭt, ⩘
cum rĕpĕ|tō noc|tem || quā | tot mĭhĭ | cāră rĕ|līquī,
  lābĭtŭr | ex ŏcŭ|līs ⩘ || nunc quŏquĕ | guttă mĕ|īs. ⩘
iam prŏpĕ | lūx ădĕ|rat || quā | mē dis|cēdĕrĕ | Caesar
  fīnĭbŭs | extrē|mae ⩘ || iussĕrăt | Ausŏnĭ|ae. ⩘
— Ov. Trist. i. 3.

NOTE. — The Elegiac Stanza differs widely in character from hexameter verse (of which it is a mere modification) by its division into Distichs, each of which must have its own sense complete. It is employed in a great variety of compositions, — epistolary, amatory, and mournful, — and was especially a favorite of the poet Ovid. It has been illustrated in English verse, imitated from the German: —

In the Hex|ameter | rises || the | fountain's | silvery | column;
In the Pen|tameter | aye || falling in | melody | back.

Other Dactylic Verses

617. Other dactylic verses or half-verses are occasionally used by the lyric poets.

[1] Called *pentameter* by the old grammarians, who divided it, formally, into five feet (two dactyls or spondees, a spondee, and two anapæsts), as follows: —

|| — ◡ ◡ | — ◡ ◡ | — || — | ◡ ◡ — | ◡ ◡ — ||

[2] The time of this pause, however, may be filled by the *protraction* of the preceding syllable: —

´ ◡ ◡ | ´ ◡ ◡ | ⊔́ || ´ ◡ ◡ | ´ ◡ ◡ | ´ ⩘

a. The Dactylic Tetrameter alternates with the hexameter, forming the *Alcmanian Strophe*, as follows: —

ō for|tēs pê|iōrăquĕ | passī
mēcum | saepĕ vĭ|rī, || nunc | vīnō | pellĭtĕ | cūrās;
crās in|gēns ĭtĕ|rābĭmŭs | aequŏr.
— Hor. Od. i. 7 (so 28; Ep. 12).

b. The Dactylic Penthemim (five half-feet) consists of half a pentameter verse. It is used in combination with the Hexameter to form the *First Archilochian Strophe*: —

diffū|gērĕ nĭ|vēs, || rĕdĕ|unt iam | grāmĭnă | campīs,
arbŏrĭ|busquĕ cŏ|mae;
mūtat | terră vĭ|cēs || et | dēcrēs|centĭă | rīpās
flūmĭnă | praetĕrĕ|unt. — Hor. Od. iv. 7.

For the Fourth Archilochian Strophe (Archilochian heptameter, alternating with iambic trimeter catalectic), see § 626. 11.

Iambic Verse

Iambic Trimeter

618. The Iambic Trimeter is the ordinary verse of dramatic dialogue. It consists of three measures, each containing a double iambus (*iambic dipody*). The cæsura is usually in the third foot.

≿ –́ ⏑ –́ | ≿ || –́ ⏑ –́ | ≿ –́ ⏑ –́

NOTE. — The sign ≿–́ denotes possible substitution of an irrational spondee (>–́) for an iambus (⏑–́).

a. The Iambic Trimeter is often used in lyric poetry (1) as an independent system, or (2) alternating with the Dimeter to form the *Iambic Strophe*, as follows: —

(1) iam i^am^ éffĭcā́|cī || dṓ mănū́s | scĭéntĭaé
supplḗx ĕt ṓ|rō || rḗgnă pḗr | Prŏsḗrpĭnaé,
pĕr ét Dĭā́|nae || nṓn mŏvḗn|dă nū́mĭnā́,
pĕr átquĕ lī́b|rōs || cármĭnū́m | vălḗntĭū́m
dēfī́xă caé|lō || dḗvŏcā́|rĕ sī́dĕrā́,
Cănī́d*i*ă, pár|cĕ || vṓcĭbū́s | tandḗm săcrī́s,
cĭtū́mquĕ rḗt|rŏ || rḗtrŏ sṓl|vĕ tū́rbĭnḗm. — Hor. Epod. 17.

The last two lines may be thus translated, to show the movement in English: —

Oh! stay, Canidia, stay thy rites of sorcery,
Thy charm unbinding backward let thy swift wheel fly!

(2) bĕā́tŭs ī́l|lĕ || quí prŏcúl | nĕgṓtĭī́s,
ut príscă gḗns | mortā́lĭū́m,
pătérnă rū́|ră || bū́bŭs éx|ercḗt sŭī́s,
sŏlū́tŭs óm|nī fḗnŏrĕ́;
nĕqu^e éxcĭtā́|tur || clā́ssĭcṓ | mīlés trŭcí,
nĕqu^e hórrĕt ī́|rātúm mărĕ́. — Hor. Epod. 2.

b. In the stricter form of Iambic Trimeter an irrational spondee (> ⏑́) or its equivalent (a cyclic anapæst ⏑ ⏑́ or an apparent dactyl > ⏑́ ⏑, § 609. *e*) may be regularly substituted for the first iambus of any dipody. A tribrach (⏑ ⏑́ ⏑) may stand for an iambus anywhere except in the last place. In the comic poets any of these forms or the proceleusmatic (⏑⏑ ⏑́ ⏑) may be substituted in any foot except the last: —[1]

ō lū́cĭs ál|mĕ rḗctŏr || ét | caelí dĕcū́s!
qu^ī altérnă cúr|rū spătĭă || flā́m|mĭfĕr^ō ámbĭḗns,
illū́strĕ laé|tīs || éxsĕrís | terrís căpū́t.
— Sen. Herc. Fur. 592–94.

quid quaérĭs? án|nōs || séxāgín|tā nā́tŭs ḗs.
— Ter. Haut. 62.

hŏmṓ s^um: hūmā́|nī || nī́l ā m^ē ā́lĭ|ēnúm pŭtṓ.
vel mḗ mŏnḗ|r^e hōc || vél percṓn|tārí pŭtā́.
— id. 77, 78.

c. The Choliambic (*lame Iambic*) substitutes a trochee for the last iambus: —

|| ⏒ ⏑́ ⏑ ⏑́ | ⏒ || ⏑́ ⏑ ⏑́ | ⏑ ⏑́ ⏑́ ⏑ ||

aequ^ē ést bĕā́|tŭs || ác pŏḗ|mă cúm scríbĭt:
tam gaúdĕt ín | sē, || támquĕ s^ē íp|sĕ mī́rā́tŭr.
— Catull. xxiii. 15, 16.

NOTE. — The verse may also be regarded as trochaic with anacrusis: as, —

⏒ : ⏑́ ⏑ ⏑́ ⏒ | ⏑́ ⏑ ⏑́ ⏑ | ⏑́ ⏑́ ⏑

d. The Iambic Trimeter Catalectic is represented as follows: —

|| ⏒ ⏑́ ⏑ ⏑́ | ⏒ || ⏑́ ⏑ ⏑́ | ⏒ ⏑́ ⏑́ ||

It is used in combination with other measures (see § 626. 11), and is shown in the following: —

Vulcā́nŭs ā́r|dēns || ū́rĭt óf|fĭcī́nā́s. — Hor. Od. i. 4.

or in English: —

On purple peaks a deeper shade descending. — *Scott.*

[1] The greater freedom of substitution in the comedy is due to the fact that the verse is regarded as made up of separate feet rather than of dipodies.

Other Iambic Measures

619. Other forms of Iambic verse are the following: —

a. The Iambic Tetrameter Catalectic (*Septēnārius*). This consists of seven and a half iambic feet, with diæresis after the fourth and with the same substitutions as in Iambic Trimeter: —

n^{am} idcírc^{ō} arcés|sor, nū́ptĭā́s || quod m$^{\bar{\imath}}$ ádpărā́|rī sḗnsĭt.
quĭbus quĭ́dĕm quam fắcĭ|lĕ pŏ́tŭĕrát || quĭéscī s$^{\bar{\imath}}$ híc | quĭḗssĕt!
—Ter. And. 690, 691.

The metrical scheme of these two verses may be represented as follows: —

|| > –́ > –́ | > –́ ⏑ –́ || > –́ ⏑ –́ | > –́ ⏑ ⊼ ||
|| ⏖ ⏑́ ⏑ > ⏑́ ⏑ | ⏑ ⏑́ ⏑ ⏑ –́ || ⏑ –́ > –́ | ⏑ –́ ⏑ ⊼ ||

Its movement is like the following: —

In góod king Chárles's gólden daýs, when lóyaltý no hárm meant.
— *Vicar of Bray.*

b. The Iambic Tetrameter Acatalectic (*Octōnārius*). This consists of eight full iambic feet with the same substitutions as in Iambic Trimeter. Like the Septenarius it is used in lively dialogue: —

dīcắt ĕam dắrĕ | nōs Phórmĭṓ|nī || nū́ptum nḗ | suscḗnsĕắt;
et mắgĭs ess^{e} íl|l^{um} ĭdṓnĕúm, || qu$^{\bar{\imath}}$ ipsí sit fắmĭ|lĭắrĭṓr.
—Ter. Ph. 720, 721.

The metrical scheme of these two verses may be represented as follows: —

|| > ⏑́ ⏑ > ⏑́ ⏑ | > –́ ⏑ –́ | > || –́ > –́ | > –́ ⏑ ⏑́ ||
|| > ⏑́ ⏑ > –́ | ⏑ –́ ⏑ –́ || > –́ > ⏑́ ⏑ | ⏑ –́ ⏑ ⏑́ ||

c. The Iambic Dimeter. This may be either acatalectic or catalectic.

1. The Iambic Dimeter Acatalectic consists of four iambic feet. It is used in combination with some longer verse (see § 618. *a*).

2. The Iambic Dimeter Catalectic consists of three and a half iambic feet. It is used only in choruses: —

quōnám crŭén|tă Maénās,
praecéps ămṓ|rĕ saévō,
răpĭtúr quŏd ím|pŏténtī
făcĭnús părát | fŭrṓrĕ? — Sen. Med. 850–853.

Note. — Owing to the fact that in modern music each measure begins with a downward beat, some scholars regard all these forms of Iambic verse as Trochaic verse with anacrusis (§ 618. *c.* N.).

Trochaic Verse

620. The most common form of Trochaic verse is the Tetrameter Catalectic (*Septēnārius*), consisting of four dipodies, the last of which lacks a syllable. There is regularly diæresis after the fourth foot: —

|| –́ ⏑ –́ ⏒ | –́ ⏑ –́ ⏒ || –́ ⏑ –́ ⏒ | –́ ⏑ –́ ∧ ||

In musical notation: —

ád t^{ē} advḗnĭō, spém, sălū́tem, || consĭlĭ^{um}, aúxĭlĭ^{um} éxpĕtḗns.
— Ter. And. 319.

In English verse: —

Téll me nót in moúrnful númbers || lífe is bút an émpty dreám.
— *Longfellow.*

a. In the stricter form of the Septenarius substitutions are allowed only in the even feet, but in comedy the tribrach ⏑́ ⏑ ⏑, or an irrational spondee –́ >, cyclic dactyl –́ ⏕, or apparent anapæst ⏑́ ⏑ >, may be substituted for any of the first six feet; a tribrach for the seventh: —

ítĭd^{em} hăbét pĕtă|s^{um} ác vestī́tum: || tám cōnsímĭlist | átqu^{e} ĕgṓ.
sū́ră, pḗs, stă|tū́ră, tṓnsŭs, || ṓcŭlī, nā́sum, | vél lăbrắ,
mā́lae, méntum, | bárbă, cóllus; || tṓtus! quíd ver|bís ŏpúst?
sí tergúm cĭ|cātrīcṓsum, || n*i*híl hōc símĭlist | símĭlĭús.
— Pl. Am. 443–446.

The metrical scheme of these four verses is as follows: —

	⏑́ ⏑ ⏑ –́ ⏕	–́ > –́ >		–́ > ⏑́ ⏑ >	–́ ⏑ –́ ∧	
	–́ ⏑ –́ ⏑	–́ ⏑ –́ ⏑		⏑́ ⏑ > –́ >	–́ ⏑ –́ ∧	
	–́ > –́ >	–́ ⏑ –́ >		–́ > –́ >	–́ ⏑ –́ ∧	
	–́ > –́ ⏑	–́ > –́ >		–́ > ⏑́ ⏑ >	⏑́ ⏑ ⏑ –́ ∧	

b. The Trochaic Tetrameter Acatalectic (*Octōnārius*), consisting of four complete dipodies, occurs in the lyrical parts of comedy.

Substitutions as in the Septenarius are allowed except in the last foot.

c. Some other forms of trochaic verse are found in the lyric poets, in combination with other feet, either as whole lines or parts of lines: —

nṓn ĕbúr nĕ|qu^{e} aúrĕúm. [Dimeter Catalectic.]
mĕá rĕní|dĕt ín dŏmṓ | lăcū́năr. [Iambic Trimeter Catalectic.]
— Hor Od. ii. 18.

Mixed Measures

621. Different measures may be combined in the same verse in two different ways. Either (1) a series of one kind is simply joined to a series of another kind (compare the changes of rhythm not uncommon in modern music); or (2) single feet of other measures are combined with the prevailing measures, in which case these odd feet are adapted by changing their quantity so that they become *irrational* (see § 609. *e*).

When enough measures of one kind occur to form a series, we may suppose a change of rhythm; when they are isolated, we must suppose adaptation. Of the indefinite number of possible combinations but few are found in Latin poetry.

622. The following verses, combining different rhythmical series, are found in Latin lyrical poetry:—

1. Greater Archilochian (Dactylic Tetrameter; Trochaic Tripody):—

|| –́ ⏖ | –́ ⏖ | –́ ⏖ | –́ ⏖ || –́ ⏑ | –́ ⏑ | –́ ⏓ ||

sólvĭtŭr | ā́crĭs hĭ|éms grā|tā́ vĭcĕ || vḗrĭs | ét Fă|vṓnī. — Hor. Od. i. 4.

Note. — It is possible that the dactyls were cyclic; but the change of measure seems more probable.

2. Verse consisting of Dactylic Trimeter catalectic (*Dactylic Penthemim*); Iambic Dimeter:—

|| –́ ⏑ ⏑ | –́ ⏑ ⏑ | –́ || ⏒ –́ ⏑ –́ | ⏒ –́ ⏑ –́ ||

scríbĕrĕ | vérsĭcŭ|lōs || ămṓrĕ pér|culsúm grăví. — Hor. Epod. 11. 2.

Logaœdic Verse

623. Trochaic verses, containing in regular prescribed positions irrational measures or irrational feet (cf. § 609. *e*), are called Logaœdic. The principal logaœdic forms are —

1. Logaœdic Tetrapody (*four feet*): Glyconic.
2. Logaœdic Tripody (*three feet*): Pherecratic (often treated as a syncopated Tetrapody Catalectic).
3. Logaœdic Dipody (*two feet*): this may be regarded as a *short Pherecratic.*

Note. — This mixture of irrational measures gives an effect approaching that of prose: hence the name Logaœdic (λόγος, ἀοιδή). These measures originated in the Greek lyric poetry, and were adopted by the Romans. All the Roman lyric metres not belonging to the regular iambic, trochaic, dactylic, or Ionic systems, were constructed on the basis of the three forms given above: viz., Logaœdic systems consisting respectively of four, three, and two feet. The so-called Logaœdic *Pentapody* consists of five feet. but is to be regarded as composed of two of the others.

624. Each logaœdic form contains a single dactyl,[1] which may be either in the first, second, or third place. The verse may be catalectic or acatalectic: —

	Glyconic	*Pherecratic*
i.	‖ –́⏑ ⏑ | –́ ⏑ | –́ ⏑ | –́ (⏑) ‖	‖ –́⏑ ⏑ | –́ ⏑ | –́ (⏑) ‖
ii.	‖ –́ ⏑ | –́⏑ ⏑ | –́ ⏑ | –́ (⏑) ‖	‖ –́ ⏑ | –́⏑ ⏑ | –́ (⏑) ‖ or ‖ –́ ⏑ | –́⏑ ⏑ | ⌞́ | –́ ∧
iii.	‖ –́ ⏑ | –́ ⏑ | –́⏑ ⏑ | –́ (⏑) ‖	‖ –́⏑ ⏑ | –́ (⏑) ‖

Note. — The shorter Pherecratic (*dipody*) (–́⏑ ⏑ | –́ ⏑), if catalectic, appears to be a simple Choriambus (— ⏑ ⏑ | — ∧); and, in general, the effect of the logaœdic forms is Choriambic. In fact, they were so regarded by the later Greek and Latin metricians, and these metres have obtained the general name of Choriambic. But they are not true choriambic, though they may very likely have been felt to be such by the composer, who imitated the forms without much thought of their origin. They may be read (scanned), therefore, on that principle. But it is better to read them as *logaœdic* measures; and that course is followed here.

625. The verses constructed upon the several Logaœdic forms or models are the following: —

1. Glyconic (*Second Glyconic*, catalectic): —

‖ –́ > | –́⏑ ⏑ | –́ ⏑ | –́ ‖ (or)

Rṓmae | prī́ncĭpĭs | ū́rbĭ|ūm.

In English: —

Fórms more réal than líving mán. — *Shelley*.

Note. — In this and most of the succeeding forms the foot preceding the dactyl is always irrational in Horace, consisting of an irrational spondee (— >).

2. Aristophanic (*First Pherecratic*): —

‖ –́⏑ ⏑ | –́ ⏑ | –́ ⏒ ‖

témpĕrăt |ṓră | frḗnīs. — Hor. Od. i. 8.

Note. — It is very likely that this was made equal in time to the preceding by protracting the last two syllables: —

‖ –́⏑ ⏑ | –́ ⏑ | ⌞́ | –́ ∧ ‖

[1] Different Greek poets adopted fixed types in regard to the place of the dactyls, and so a large number of verses arose, each following a strict law, which were imitated by the Romans as distinct metres.

3. Adonic (*First Pherecratic*, shortened): —

‖ ⏖ ⏑ | ⏗ ⏓ ‖

Térrŭĭt | úrbĕm. — Hor.

Or perhaps: —

‖ ⏖ ⏑ | ⏗ | ⏗ ∧ ‖

4. Pherecratic (*Second Pherecratic*): —

‖ ⏗ ⩾ | ⏖ ⏑ | ⏗ | ⏗ ∧ ‖

crā́s dōnā́bĕrĭs haédṓ. — Hor.

Often scanned as follows: —

⏗ ⩾ | ⏖ ⏑ | ⏗ ⏓

5. Lesser Asclepiadic (*Second Pherecratic* with syncope and *First Pherecratic* catalectic): —

‖ ⏗ > | ⏖ ⏑ | ⏗ ‖ ⏖ ⏑ | ⏗ ⏑ | ⏗ ∧ ‖

Maécēnā́s ătăvī́s édĭtĕ rḗgĭbū́s. — Hor.

6. Greater Asclepiadic (the same as 5, with a syncopated *Logaœdic Dipody* interposed): —

‖ ⏗ > | ⏖ ⏑ | ⏗ ‖ ⏖ ⏑ | ⏗ ‖ ⏖ ⏑ | ⏗ ⏑ | ⏗ ∧ ‖

tū́ nē quaésĭĕrís — scírĕ nĕfā́s — quém mĭhĭ, quém tĭbí. — Hor.

7. Lesser Sapphic (*Logaœdic Pentapody*, with dactyl in the third place): —

‖ ⏗ ⏑ | ⏗ > | ⏗ ‖ ⏕ | ⏗ ⏑ | ⏗ | ⏓ ∧ ‖

íntĕgér vītaé scĕlĕrísquĕ pū́rūs. — Hor.

Or in English: —

Brílliant hópes, all wóven in górgeous tíssùes. — *Longfellow.*

8. Greater Sapphic (*Third Glyconic; First Pherecratic*): —

‖ ⏗ ⏑ | ⏗ > | ⏖ ⏑ | ⏗ ‖ ⏖ ⏑ | ⏗ ⏑ | ⏗ | ⏓ ∧ ‖

tḗ dĕṓs ōrṓ Sўbărín ‖ cū́r prŏpĕrā́s ămándṓ. — Hor.

9. Lesser Alcaic (*Logaœdic Tetrapody*, two irrational dactyls, two trochees): —

‖ ⏖ ⏑ | ⏖ ⏑ | ⏗ ⏑ | ⏗ ⏓ ‖

vírgĭnĭbús pŭĕrísquĕ cántō. — Hor.

10. Greater Alcaic (*Logaœdic Pentapody*, catalectic, with anacrusis, and dactyl in the third place, — compare *Lesser Sapphic*): —

|| ˃ ⁝ ´ ᴗ | ´ > || ´ᴗ ᴗ | ´ ᴗ | ´ᴗ ∧ ||

iūst*um* ét tĕnácem || prṓpŏsĭtí vĭrúm. — Hor.

Note. — Only the above logaœdic forms are employed by Horace.

11. Phalæcean (*Logaœdic Pentapody*, with dactyl in the second place): —

|| ´ᴗ > | ´ᴗ ᴗ | ´ ᴗ | ´ ᴗ | ´ ᴗ ||

quaénam tḗ mălă ménș, mĭsélli Rā́*u*idī,
ā́git praécĭpĭt*em* ín mĕṓs ĭámbōs? — Catull. xl.

In English: —

Górgeous flowerets ín the súnlight shíning. — *Longfellow.*

12. Glyconic Pherecratic (*Second Glyconic* with syncope, and *Second Pherecratic*): —

|| ´ ˃ | ´ᴗ ᴗ | ´ ᴗ | ⌊´ || ´ ˃ | ´ᴗ ᴗ | ⌊´ | ´ ∧ ||

ṓ Cŏlṓnĭă quaé cŭpís || póntĕ lū́dĕrĕ lóngō̆. — Catull. xvii.

METRES OF HORACE

626. The Odes of Horace include nineteen varieties of stanza. These are: —

1. Alcaic, consisting of two Greater Alcaics (10), one Trochaic Dimeter with anacrusis, and one Lesser Alcaic (9)[1]: —

iūst*um* ét tenácem || prṓpositī́ virúm
nōn cívi*um* ā́rdor || prā́va iubéntiúm,
nōn vúltus ínstantís tyránnī
ménte quatít solidā́, nequ*e* Aúster. — Od. iii. 3.

(Found in Od. i. 9, 16, 17, 26, 27, 29, 31, 34, 35, 37; ii. 1, 3, 5, 7, 9, 11, 13, 14, 15, 17, 19, 20; iii. 1, 2, 3, 4, 5, 6, 17, 21, 23, 26, 29; iv. 4, 9, 14, 15.)

Note. — The Alcaic Strophe is named after the Greek poet Alcæus of Lesbos, and was a special favorite with Horace, of whose Odes thirty-seven are in this form. It is sometimes called the *Horatian Stanza.*

2. Sapphic (*minor*), consisting of three Lesser Sapphics (7) and one Adonic (3): —

iám satís terrís || nivis átque dírae
grándinís mīsít || pater ét rubénte
déxterā́ sacrā́s || iaculā́tus ā́rcīs
térruit úrbem. — Od. i. 2.

(Found in Od. i. 2, 10, 12, 20, 22, 25, 30, 32, 38; ii. 2, 4, 6, 8, 10, 16; iii. 8, 11, 14, 18, 20, 22, 27; iv. 2, 6, 11; Carm. Saec.)

[1] The figures refer to the foregoing list (§ 625).

NOTE.—The Sapphic Stanza is named after the poetess Sappho of Lesbos, and was a great favorite with the ancients. It is used by Horace in twenty-five Odes—more frequently than any other except the Alcaic.

3. Sapphic (*major*), consisting of one Aristophanic (2) and one Greater Sapphic (8):—

Lȳ́dia dī́c, per ómnī́s
tḗ deṓs ōrṓ, Sybarī́n || cū́r properā́s amándṓ.—Od. i. 8.

4. Asclepiadean I (*minor*), consisting of Lesser Asclepiadics (5):—

éxēgī́ monumént*um* || aére perénniū́s
rḗgālī́que sitū́ || pȳ́ramid*um* áltiū́s.—Od. iii. 30.

(Found in Od. i. 1; iii. 30; iv. 8.)

5. Asclepiadean II, consisting of one Glyconic (1) and one Lesser Asclepiadic (5):—

nā́vis quaé tibi crḗditū́m
dḗbēs Vérgiliū́m, || fī́nibus Ā́tticī́s
réddās íncolumém, precór,
ét servḗs animaé || dī́midiū́m meaé.—Od. i. 3.

(Found in Od. i. 3, 13, 19, 36; iii. 9, 15, 19, 24, 25, 28; iv. i, 3.)

6. Asclepiadean III, consisting of three Lesser Asclepiadics (5) and one Glyconic (1):—

quī́s dēsī́deriṓ || sī́t pudor aút modū́s
tám cārī́ capitī́s? || praécipe lū́gubrī́s
cántūs, Mélpomenḗ, || cuí liquidám patér
vṓcem cúm citharā́ dedī́t.—Od. i. 24.

(Found in Od. i. 6, 15, 24, 33; ii. 12; iii. 10, 16; iv. 5, 12.)

7. Asclepiadean IV, consisting of two Lesser Asclepiadics (5), one Pherecratic (4), and one Glyconic (1):—

ṓ fōns Bándusiaé || spléndidiór vitrṓ,
dúlcī dígne merṓ, || nṓn sine flṓribū́s,
crā́s dōnā́beris haédṓ
cuí frōns túrgida córnibū́s.—Od. iii. 13.

(Found in Od. i. 5, 14, 21, 23; iii. 7, 13; iv. 13.)

8. Asclepiadean V (*major*), consisting of Greater Asclepiadics (6):—

tū́ nē quaésierī́s, || scī́re nefā́s! || quém mihi, quém tibī́
fī́nem dī́ dederī́nt, || Leúconoḗ, || néc Babylṓniṓs
téntārī́s numerṓs.—Od. i. 11.

(Found in Od. i. 11, 18; iv. 10.)

9. Alcmanian, consisting of Dactylic Hexameter (§ 615) alternating with Tetrameter (§ 617. *a*). (Od. i. 7, 28; Epod. 12.)

10. Archilochian I, consisting of a Dactylic Hexameter alternating with a Dactylic Penthemim (see § 617. *b*). (Od. iv. 7.)

11. Archilochian IV, consisting of a Greater Archilochian (*heptameter*, § 622. 1), followed by Iambic Trimeter Catalectic (§ 618. *d*). The stanza consists of two pairs of verses: —

sólvitur ácris hiéms grātá vice || Vḗris ét Favṓnī,
trahúntque síccās || mā́chinaé carī́nā́s;
ác neque iám stabulī́s gaudét pecus, || aút arā́tor ī́gnī,
nec prā́ta cā́nīs || álbicánt pruī́nī́s. — Od. i. 4.

12. Iambic Trimeter alone (see § 618). (Epod. 17.)

13. Iambic Strophe (see § 618. *a*). (Epod. 1–10.)

14. Dactylic Hexameter alternating with Iambic Dimeter: —

nóx erat, ét caelṓ || fulgḗbat lū́na serḗnō
intér minṓra sī́derá,
cúm tū, mā́gnōrúm || nūmén laesū́ra deṓrum,
in vérba iū́rābā́s meá. — Epod. 15. (So in Epod. 14.)

15. Dactylic Hexameter with Iambic Trimeter (§ 618): —

áltera iám teritúr || bellī́s cīvī́libus aétās,
suī́s et ī́psa Rṓma || vī́ribús ruít. — Epod. 16.

16. Verse of Four Lesser Ionics (§ 609. *c*. 2): —

miserār^{um} est | nequ^{e} amōrī | dare lūdum | neque dulcī
mala vīnō | laver^{e} aut ex|animārī | metuentīs. — Od. iii. 12.

17. Iambic Trimeter (§ 618); Dactylic Penthemim (§ 617. *b*); Iambic Dimeter: —

Pettī́, nihī́l mē || sī́cut ánteā́ iuvát
scrī́bere vérsiculṓs || amṓre pérculsúm graví́. — Epod. 11.

18. Dactylic Hexameter; Iambic Dimeter; Dactylic Penthemim (§ 617. *b*):

hórrida témpestā́s || caelúm contrā́xit, et ī́mbrēs
nivḗsque dédūcúnt Iovém; || núnc mare, núnc silüaé . . .
— Epod. 13.

19. Trochaic Dimeter, Iambic Trimeter, each catalectic (see § 620. *c*).

INDEX TO THE METRES OF HORACE

Lib. I

1. Maecēnās atavīs: 4.
2. Iam satis terrīs: 2.
3. Sīc tē dīva: 5.
4. Solvitur ācris hiems: 11.
5. Quis multā: 7.
6. Scrībēris Variō: 6.
7. Laudābunt aliī: 9.
8. Lȳdia dīc: 3.
9. Vidēs ut altā: 1.
10. Mercurī fācunde nepōs: 2.
11. Tū nē quaesieris: 8.
12. Quem virum: 2.
13. Cum tū Lȳdia: 5.
14. Ō nāvis: 7.

15. Pāstor cum traheret: 6.
16. Ō mātre pulchrā: 1.
17. Vēlōx amoenum: 1.
18. Nūllam Vāre: 8.
19. Māter saeva: 5.
20. Vīle pōtābis: 2.
21. Dīānam tenerae: 7.
22. Integer vītae: 2.
23. Vītās īnuleō: 7.
24. Quis dēsīderiō: 6.
25. Parcius iūnctās: 2.
26. Mūsīs amīcus: 1.
27. Nātīs in ūsum: 1.
28. Tē maris: 9.
29. Iccī beātīs: 1.
30. Ō Venus: 2.
31. Quid dēdicātum: 1.
32. Poscimur: 2.
33. Albī nē doleās: 6.
34. Parcus deōrum: 1.
35. Ō dīva: 1.
36. Et tūre: 5.
37. Nunc est bibendum: 1.
38. Persicōs ōdī: 2.

Lib. II

1. Mōtum ex Metellō: 1.
2. Nūllus argentō: 2.
3. Aequam mementō: 1.
4. Nē sit ancillae: 2.
5. Nōndum subāctā: 1.
6. Septimī Gādēs: 2.
7. Ō saepe mēcum: 1.
8. Ūlla sī iūris: 2.
9. Nōn semper imbrēs: 1.
10. Rēctius vīvēs: 2.
11. Quid bellicōsus: 1.
12. Nōlīs longa: 6.
13. Ille et nefāstō: 1.
14. Ēheu fugācēs: 1.
15. Iam pauca: 1.
16. Ōtium dīvōs: 2.
17. Cūr mē querellīs: 1.
18. Nōn ebur: 19.
19. Bacchum in remōtīs: 1.
20. Nōn ūsitātā: 1.

Lib. III

1. Ōdī profānum: 1.
2. Angustam amīcē: 1.
3. Iūstum et tenācem: 1.
4. Dēscende caelō: 1.
5. Caelō tonantem: 1.
6. Dēlicta māiōrum: 1.
7. Quid flēs: 7.
8. Mārtiīs caelebs: 2.
9. Dōnec grātus: 5.
10. Extrēmum Tanain: 6.
11. Mercurī nam tē: 2.
12. Miserārum est: 16.
13. Ō fōns Bandusiae: 7.
14. Herculis rītū: 2.
15. Uxor pauperis: 5.
16. Inclūsam Danaēn: 6.
17. Aelī vetustō: 1.
18. Faune nymphārum: 2.
19. Quantum dīstet: 5.
20. Nōn vidēs: 2.
21. Ō nāta mēcum: 1.
22. Montium cūstōs: 2.
23. Caelō supīnās: 1.
24. Intāctīs opulentior: 5.
25. Quō mē Bacche: 5.
26. Vīxī puellīs: 1.
27. Impiōs parrae: 2.
28. Fēstō quid: 5.
29. Tyrrhēna rēgum: 1.
30. Exēgī monumentum: 4.

Lib. IV

1. Intermissa Venus: 5.
2. Pindarum quisquis: 2.
3. Quem tū Melpomenē: 5
4. Quālem ministrum: 1.
5. Dīvīs orte bonīs: 6.
6. Dīve quem prōlēs: 2.
7. Diffūgēre nivēs: 10.
8. Dōnārem paterās: 4.
9. Nē forte crēdās: 1.
10. Ō crūdēlis adhūc: 8.
11. Est mihī nōnum: 2.
12. Iam vēris comitēs: 6.
13. Audīvēre Lycē: 7.
14. Quae cūra patrum: 1.
15. Phoebus volentem: 1.

Carmen Saeculāre: 2.

EPODES

1. Ībis Liburnīs: 13.
2. Beātus ille: 13.
3. Parentis ōlim: 13.
4. Lupīs et āgnīs: 13.
5. At ō deōrum: 13.
6. Quid immerentīs: 13.
7. Quō quō scelestī: 13.
8. Rogāre longō: 13.
9. Quandō repostum: 13.
10. Malā solūta: 13.
11. Pettī nihil: 17.
12. Quid tibi vīs: 9.
13. Horrida tempestās: 18.
14. Mollis inertia: 14.
15. Nox erat: 14.
16. Altera iam: 15.
17. Iam iam efficācī: 12.

627. Other lyric poets use other combinations of the above-mentioned verses: —

a. *Glyconics* with one *Pherecratic* (both imperfect): —

Díā|naé sŭmŭs | ín fĭdḗ
pŭ́el|l*ae* ét pŭĕ|r*ī* íntĕgrí:
Díā|nám, pŭĕ|r*ī* íntĕgrí
pŭ́el|laéquĕ că|nā́|mŭ́s. — Catull. xxxiv.

b. *Sapphics*, in a series of single lines, closing with an *Adonic:* —

Án mă|gís dī|rí trĕmŭ|érĕ | Mā́nēs
Hércŭ|l*em*? ét vī|súm cănīs | ínfĕ|rṓrŭm
fŭ́gĭt | ábrup|tī́s trĕpĭ|dús că|tḗnīs?
fállĭ|múr: lae|tḗ vĕnĭt | éccĕ | vúltū,
quém tŭ|lít Poe|ā́s; hŭmĕ|rísquĕ | tḗlă
géstăt | ét nō|tā́s pŏpŭ|lís phă|rétrās
Hércŭlīs | hḗrēs. — Sen. Herc. Oet. 1600-1606.

c. *Sapphics* followed by *Glyconics*, of indefinite number (id. Herc. Fur. 830-874, 875-894).

MISCELLANEOUS

628. Other measures occur in various styles of poetry.

a. Anapæstic (§ 609. *b*. 2) verses of various lengths are found in dramatic poetry. The spondee, dactyl, or proceleusmatic may be substituted for the anapæst: —

hĭc hŏmóst | omnĭ*um* hŏ́mĭ|num praé|cĭpŭ́ŏs
vŏlŭptā́|tĭbŭs gaú|d*i*īsqu*e* án|tĕpŏténs.
ĭtă cóm|mŏdă quaé | cŭpĭ*ō* é|vĕnĭúnt,
quŏd ăgṓ | sŭbĭt, ád|sĕcŭḗ | sĕquĭtŭ́r:
ĭtă gaú|d*i*um súp|pĕdĭtā́t. — Pl. Trin. 1115-1119.

b. Bacchiac (§ 609. *d*. 4) verses (five-timed) occur in the dramatic poets, — very rarely in Terence, more commonly in Plautus, — either in verses of two feet (Dimeter) or of four (Tetrameter). They are treated very freely, as are all measures in early Latin. The long syllables may be resolved, or the *molossus* (three longs) substituted: —

multā́s rēs | sĭmī́t$^{\bar{u}}$ in | mĕó cor|dĕ vórsō,
mult^{um} ín cō|gĭtándō | dŏlṓr^{em} in|dĭpíscŏr.
ĕgŏmét mē | cōg$^{\bar{o}}$ ét mā|cĕr$^{\bar{o}}$ ét dē|fătígō;
măgíster | mĭh^{i} éxer|cĭtṓr ănĭ|mŭs núnc est.
— Pl. Trin. 223–226.

c. Cretic measures (§ 609. *d.* 1) occur in the same manner as the Bacchiac, with the same substitutions. The last foot is usually incomplete: —

ắmŏr ămī|cús mĭhī | nḗ fŭās | úmquăm.
hī́s ĕgō | d$^{\bar{e}}$ ártĭbus | grắtĭam | fắcĭō.
nī́l ĕg^{o} is|tṓs mŏror | faécĕōs | mṓrēs. — id. 267, 293, 297.

d. Saturnian Verse. In early Latin is found a rude form of verse, not borrowed from the Greek like the others, but as to the precise nature of which scholars are not agreed.[1]

1. According to one view the verse is based on quantity, is composed of six feet, and is divided into two parts by a cæsura before the fourth thesis. Each thesis may consist of a long syllable or of two short ones, each arsis of a short syllable, a long syllable, or two short syllables; but the arsis, except at the beginning of the verse and before the cæsura, is often entirely suppressed, though rarely more than once in the same verse: —

dăbúnt mălúm Mĕtéllī || Naévĭṓ pŏḗtae.

2. According to another theory the Saturnian is made up, without regard to quantity, of alternating accented and unaccented syllables; but for any unaccented syllable two may be substituted, and regularly are so substituted in the second foot of the verse: —

dábunt málum Metéllī || Naéviṓ poḗtae.

EARLY PROSODY

629. The prosody of the earlier poets differs in several respects from that of the later.[2]

a. At the end of words s, being only feebly sounded, does not make *position* with a following consonant; it sometimes disappeared altogether. This usage continued in all poets till Cicero's time (§ 15. 7).

[1] The two principal theories only are given. There are numerous variations, particularly of the second theory here stated.

[2] Before the Latin language was used in literature, it had become much changed by the loss of final consonants and the shortening of final syllables under the influence of accent. In many cases this change was still in progress in the time of the early poets. This tendency was arrested by the study of grammar and by literature, but shows itself again in the Romance languages.

b. A long syllable immediately preceded or followed by the ictus may be shortened (*iambic shortening*): —

1. In a word of two syllables of which the first is short (this effect remained in a few words like **pută, cavĕ, valĕ, vidĕ, egŏ, modŏ, duŏ** [1]): —

ắbĭ (Ter. Ph. 59); bŏ́nĭ (id. 516); hŏmŏ suắvis (id. 411).

2. If it is either a monosyllable or the first syllable of a word which is preceded by a short monosyllable: —

sĕ́d hăs tabellās (Pl. Pers. 195); quĭ́d hĭc nunc (id. Epid. 157); pĕr ĭnplŭ́vium (Ter. Ph. 707); ĕg° ŏsténderem (id. 793).

3. When preceded by a short initial syllable in a word of more than three syllables:—

vĕnŭstắtis (Ter. Hec. 848); sĕnĕctū́tem (id. Ph. 434); Sȳrăcū́sās (Pl. Merc. 37); ămĭcĭ́tia (id. Ps. 1263).

c. In a few isolated words position is often disregarded.[2] Such are **ĭlle, ĭmmo, ĭnde, ĭste, ŏmnis, nĕmpe, quĭppe, ŭnde.**

d. The original long quantity of some final syllables is retained.

1. The ending **-or** is retained long in nouns with long stem-vowel (original **r**-stems or original **s**-stems): —

módo quom díct^a in m^ē íngerébās ódium nṓn **uxṓr** erám (Pl. Asin. 927).
íta m^ī in péctor^e átque córde fácit **amṓr** incéndiúm (id. Merc. 500).
átque quántō nóx fuístī **lóngiṓr** hāc próxumắ (id. Am. 548).

2. The termination **-es** (**-ĭtis**) is sometimes retained long, as in **mīlēs, superstēs.**

3. All verb-endings in **-r, -s,** and **-t** may be retained long where the vowel is elsewhere long in inflection: —

régrediṓr audísse mḗ (Pl. Capt. 1023); átqu^e ut quí fuerīs et quí nunc (id. 248); mē nṓminắt haec (id. Epid. iv. 1. 8); faciắt ut sémper (id. Poen. ii. 42); īnfuscābāt, amābō (cretics, id. Cist. i. 21); quī amēt (id. Merc. 1021); ut fī́t in béllō cápitur álter fíliús (id. Capt. 25); tibi sī́t ad mḗ revísắs (id. Truc. ii. 4. 79).

e. *Hiatus* (§ 612. *g*) is allowed somewhat freely, especially at a pause in the sense, or when there is a change of speaker.[3]

[1] Cf. **ambō** (also a dual, p. 59, footnote), in which the ō is retained because of the length of the first syllable.

[2] Scholars are not yet agreed upon the principle or the extent of this irregularity.

[3] The extent of this license is still a question among scholars; but in the present state of texts it must sometimes be allowed.

MISCELLANEOUS

Reckoning of Time

630. The Roman Year was designated, in earlier times, by the names of the Consuls; but was afterwards reckoned from the building of the City (*ab urbe conditā*, *annō urbis conditae*), the date of which was assigned by Varro to a period corresponding with B.C. 753. In order, therefore, to reduce Roman dates to those of the Christian era, *the year of the city is to be subtracted from* 754: e.g. A.U.C. 691 (the year of Cicero's consulship) corresponds to B.C. 63.

Before Cæsar's reform of the Calendar (B.C. 46), the Roman year consisted of 355 days: March, May, Quīntīlis (July), and October having each 31 days, February having 28, and each of the remainder 29. As this calendar year was too short for the solar year, the Romans, in alternate years, at the discretion of the *pontificēs*, inserted a month of varying length (*mēnsis intercalāris*) after February 23, and omitted the rest of February. The "Julian year," by Cæsar's reformed Calendar, had 365 days, divided into months as at present. Every fourth year the 24th of February (VI. Kal. Mārt.) was counted twice, giving 29 days to that month: hence the year was called *bissextīlis*. The month Quīntīlis received the name *Iūlius* (July), in honor of Julius Cæsar; and Sextīlis was called *Augustus* (August), in honor of his successor. The Julian year (see below) remained unchanged till the adoption of the Gregorian Calendar (A.D. 1582), which omits leap-year three times in every four hundred years.

631. Dates, according to the Roman Calendar, are reckoned as follows: —

a. The *first* day of the month was called **Kalendae** (*Calends*).

NOTE. — **Kalendae** is derived from **calāre**, *to call*, — the Calends being the day on which the pontiffs publicly announced the New Moon in the *Comitia Calāta*. This they did, originally, from actual observation.

b. On the *fifteenth* day of March, May, July, and October, but the *thirteenth* of the other months, were the **Īdūs** (*Ides*), the day of Full Moon.

c. On the *seventh* day of March, May, July, and October, but the *fifth* of the other months, were the **Nōnae** (*Nones* or *ninths*).

d. From the three points thus determined, the days of the month were reckoned *backwards* as so many days before the *Nones*, the *Ides*, or the *Calends*. The point of departure was, by Roman custom, counted in the reckoning, the *second* day being *three* days before, etc. This gives the following rule for determining the date: —

If the given date be Calends, add *two* to the number of days in the month preceding, — if Nones or Ides, add *one* to that of the day on which they fall, — and from the number thus ascertained subtract the given date. Thus, —

VIII. Kal. Feb. $(31 + 2 - 8) =$ Jan. 25.
IV. Nōn. Mār. $(7 + 1 - 4) =$ Mar. 4.
IV. Īd. Sept. $(13 + 1 - 4) =$ Sept. 10.

NOTE. — The name of the month appears as an adjective in agreement with **Kalendae, Nōnae, Īdūs.**

For peculiar constructions in dates, see § 424. *g*.

e. The days of the Roman month by the Julian Calendar, as thus ascertained, are given in the following table: —

	January	*February*	*March*	*April*
1.	KAL. IĀN.	KAL. FEB.	KAL. MĀRTIAE	KAL. APRĪLĒS
2.	IV. Nōn. Iān.	IV. Nōn. Feb.	VI. Nōn. Mārt.	IV. Nōn. Apr.
3.	III. " "	III. " "	V. " "	III. " "
4.	prīd." "	prīd." "	IV. " "	prīd." "
5.	NŌN. IĀN.	NŌN. FEB.	III. " "	NŌN. APRĪLĒS
6.	VIII. Īd. Iān.	VIII. Īd. Feb.	prīd." "	VIII. Īd. Apr.
7.	VII. " "	VII. " "	NŌN. MĀRTIAE	VII. " "
8.	VI. " "	VI. " "	VIII. Īd. Mārt.	VI. " "
9.	V. " "	V. " "	VII. " "	V. " "
10.	IV. " "	IV. " "	VI. " "	IV. " "
11.	III. " "	III. " "	V. " "	III. " "
12.	prīd. " "	prīd. " "	IV. " "	prīd. " "
13.	ĪDŪS IĀN.	ĪDŪS FEB.	III. " "	ĪDŪS APRĪLĒS.
14.	XIX. Kal. Feb.	XVI. Kal. Mārtiās	prīd. " "	XVIII. Kal. Māiās.
15.	XVIII. " "	XV. " "	ĪDŪS MĀRTIAE	XVII. " "
16.	XVII. " "	XIV. " "	XVII. Kal. Aprīlīs.	XVI. " "
17.	XVI. " "	XIII. " "	XVI. " "	XV. " "
18.	XV. " "	XII. " "	XV. " "	XIV. " "
19.	XIV. " "	XI. " "	XIV. " "	XIII. " "
20.	XIII. " "	X. " "	XIII. " "	XII. " "
21.	XII. " "	IX. " "	XII. " "	XI. " "
22.	XI. " "	VIII. " "	XI. " "	X. " "
23.	X. " "	VII. " "	X. " "	IX. " "
24.	IX. " "	VI. " "	IX. " "	VIII. " "
25.	VIII. " "	V. " "	VIII. " "	VII. " "
26.	VII. " "	IV. " "	VII. " "	VI. " "
27.	VI. " "	III. " "	VI. " "	V. " "
28.	V. " "	prīd. " "	V. " "	IV. " "
29.	IV. " "	[prīd. Kal. Mārt. in	IV. " "	III. " "
30.	III. " "	leap-year, the VI.	III. " "	prīd. " "
31.	prīd. " "	Kal. (24th) being	prīd. " "	(So June, Sept.,
	(So Aug., Dec.)	counted twice.]	(So May, July, Oct.)	Nov.)

NOTE. — Observe that a date before the Julian Reform (B.C. 46) is to be found not by the above table, but by taking the earlier reckoning of the number of days in the month.

Measures of Value, etc.

632. The money of the Romans was in early times wholly of copper. The unit was the **as**, which was nominally a pound in weight, but actually somewhat less. It was divided into twelve **unciae** (*ounces*).

In the third century B.C. the **as** was gradually reduced to one-half of its original value. In the same century silver coins were introduced, — the **dēnārius** and the **sēstertius**. The denarius = 10 asses; the sestertius = 2½ asses.

633. The Sestertius was probably introduced at a time when the **as** had been so far reduced that the value of the new coin (2½ asses) was equivalent to the original value of the **as**. Hence, the Sestertius (usually abreviated to ~~HS~~ or HS) came to be used as the unit of value, and **nummus**, *coin*, often means simply **sēstertius**. As the reduction of the standard went on, the sestertius became equivalent to 4 asses. Gold was introduced later, the **aureus** being equal to 100 sesterces. The approximate value of these coins is seen in the following table : —

2½	asses = 1 sēstertius or nummus,	value nearly	5 cents	(2½ d.).
10	asses or 4 sēstertiī = 1 dēnārius .	" "	20 "	(10 d.).
1000	sēstertiī = 1 sēstertium . . .	" "	$50.00	(£10).

NOTE. — The word **sēstertius** is a shortened form of **sēmis-tertius**, *the third one, a half*. The abbreviation ~~HS~~ or HS = **duo et sēmis**, *two and a half*.

634. The **sēstertium** (probably originally the genitive plural of **sēstertius** depending on **mīlle**) was a sum of money, not a coin; the word is inflected regularly as a neuter noun: thus, **tria sēstertia** = $150.00.

When **sēstertium** is combined with a numeral adverb, **centēna mīlia**, *hundreds of thousands*, is to be understood: thus **deciēns sēstertium** (**deciēns** HS) = **deciēns centēna mīlia sēstertium** = $50,000. **Sēstertium** in this combination may also be inflected: **deciēns sēstertiī, sēstertiō**, etc.

In the statement of large sums **sēstertium** is often omitted as well as **centēna mīlia**: thus **sexāgiēns** (Rosc. Am. 2) signifies, **sexāgiēns** [**centēna mīlia sēstertium**] = 6,000,000 sesterces = $300,000 (nearly).

635. In the statement of sums of money in Roman numerals, a line above the number indicates thousands; lines above and at the sides also, hundred-thousands. Thus HS DC = 600 **sēstertiī**; HS $\overline{\text{DC}}$ = 600,000 **sēstertiī**, or 600 **sēstertia**; HS $|\overline{\text{DC}}|$ = 60,000,000 **sēstertiī**, or 60,000 **sēstertia**.

636. The Roman Measures of Length are the following: —

12 inches (*unciae*) = 1 Roman Foot (*pēs:* 11.65 English inches).
1½ Feet = 1 Cubit (*cubitum*). — 2½ Feet = 1 Step (*gradus*).
5 Feet = 1 Pace (*passus*). — 1000 Paces (*mīlle passuum*) = 1 Mile.

The Roman mile was equal to 4850 English feet.

The **iūgerum**, or unit of measure of land, was an area of 240 (Roman) feet long and 120 broad; a little less than $\frac{2}{3}$ of an English acre.

637. The Measures of Weight are —

12 unciae (*ounces*) = one pound (*libra*, about $\frac{3}{4}$ lb. avoirdupois).

Fractional parts (weight or coin) are —

$\frac{1}{12}$, *uncia.*	$\frac{5}{12}$, *quīncunx.*	$\frac{3}{4}$, *dōdrāns.*
$\frac{1}{6}$, *sextāns.*	$\frac{1}{2}$, *sēmis.*	$\frac{5}{6}$, *dextāns.*
$\frac{1}{4}$, *quadrāns.*	$\frac{7}{12}$, *septunx.*	$\frac{11}{12}$, *deunx.*
$\frac{1}{3}$, *triēns.*	$\frac{2}{3}$, *bēs* or *bēssis.*	$\frac{12}{12}$, **as.**

The Talent (*talentum*) was a Greek weight (τάλαντον) = 60 *librae.*

638. The Measures of Capacity are —

12 *cyathī* = 1 *sextārius* (nearly a pint).
16 *sextāriī* = 1 *modius* (peck).
6 *sextāriī* = 1 *congius* (3 quarts, liquid measure).
8 *congiī* = 1 *amphora* (6 gallons).

GLOSSARY

OF TERMS USED IN GRAMMAR, RHETORIC, AND PROSODY

639. Many of these terms are pedantic names given by early grammarians to forms of speech used naturally by writers who were not conscious that they were using figures at all — as, indeed, they were not. Thus when one says, "It gave me no little pleasure," he is unconsciously using *litotes;* when he says, "John went up the street, James down," *antithesis;* when he says, "High as the sky," *hyperbole.* Many were given under a mistaken notion of the nature of the usage referred to. Thus **mēd** and **tēd** (§ 143. *a.* N.) were supposed to owe their **d** to *paragoge*, **sūmpsī** its **p** to *epenthesis*. Such a sentence as "See my coat, how well it fits!" was supposed to be an irregularity to be accounted for by *prolepsis*.

Many of these, however, are convenient designations for phenomena which often occur; and most of them have an historic interest, of one kind or another.

640. Grammatical Terms

Anacoluthon: a change of construction in the same sentence, leaving the first part broken or unfinished.

Anastrophe: inversion of the usual order of words.

Apodosis: the conclusion of a conditional sentence (see *Protasis*).

Archaism: an adoption of old or obsolete forms.

Asyndeton: omission of conjunctions (§ 323. *b*).

Barbarism: adoption of foreign or unauthorized forms.

Brachylogy: brevity of expression.

Crasis: contraction of two vowels into one (§ 15. 3).

Ellipsis: omission of a word or words necessary to complete the sense.

Enallage: substitution of one word or form for another.

Epenthesis: insertion of a letter or syllable.

Hellenism: use of Greek forms or constructions.

Hendiadys (ἓν διὰ δυοῖν): the use of two nouns, with a conjunction, instead of a single modified noun.

Hypallage: interchange of constructions.

Hysteron proteron: a reversing of the natural order of ideas.

This term was applied to cases where the natural sequence of events is violated in language because the later event is of more importance than the earlier and so comes first to the mind. This was supposed to be an artificial embellishment in Greek, and so was imitated in Latin. It is still found in artless narrative; cf. "Bred and Born in a Brier Bush" (Uncle Remus).

Metathesis: transposition of letters in a word.

Paragoge: addition of a letter or letters to the end of a word.

Parenthesis: insertion of a phrase interrupting the construction.

Periphrasis: a roundabout way of expression (*circumlocution*).

Pleonasm: the use of needless words.

Polysyndeton: the use of an unnecessary number of copulative conjunctions.

Prolepsis: the use of a word in the clause preceding the one where it would naturally appear (*anticipation*).

Protasis: a clause introduced by a conditional expression (*if, when, whoever*), leading to a conclusion called the *Apodosis* (§ 512).

Syncope: omission of a letter or syllable from the middle of a word.

Synesis (*cōnstrūctiō ad sēnsum*): agreement of words according to the sense, and not the grammatical form (§ 280. *a*).

Tmesis: the separation of the two parts of a compound word by other words (*cutting*).

This term came from the earlier separation of prepositions (originally adverbs) from the verbs with which they were afterwards joined; so in **per ecastor scītus puer**, *a very fine boy, egad!* As this was supposed to be intentional, it was ignorantly imitated in Latin; as in **cere- comminuit -brum** (Ennius).

Zeugma: the use of a verb or an adjective with two different words, to only one of which it strictly applies (*yoking*).

641. Rhetorical Figures

Allegory: a narrative in which abstract ideas figure as circumstances, events, or persons. in order to enforce some moral truth.

Alliteration: the use of several words that begin with the same sound.

Analogy: argument from resemblances.

Anaphora: the repetition of a word at the beginning of successive clauses (§ 598. *f*).

Antithesis: opposition, or contrast of parts (for emphasis: § 598. *f*).

Antonomasia: use of a proper for a common noun, or the reverse: —

sint Maecēnātēs, nōn deerunt, Flacce, Marōnēs, *so there be patrons* (like Mæcenas), *poets* (like Virgil) *will not be lacking, Flaccus* (Mart. viii. 56. 5).

illa furia et pestis, *that fury and plague* (i.e. Clodius); **Homēromastīx,** *scourge of Homer* (i.e. Zoilus).

Aposiopesis: an abrupt pause for rhetorical effect.

Catachresis: a harsh metaphor (*abūsiō*, misuse of words).

Chiasmus: a reversing of the order of words in corresponding pairs of phrases (§ 598. *f*).

Climax: a gradual increase of emphasis, or enlargement of meaning.

Euphemism: the mild expression of a painful or repulsive idea: —

sī quid eī acciderit, *if anything happens to him* (i.e. if he dies).

Euphony: the choice of words for their agreeable sound.

Hyperbaton: violation of the usual order of words.

Hyperbole: exaggeration for rhetorical effect.

Irony: the use of words which naturally convey a sense contrary to what is meant.

Litotes: the affirming of a thing by denying its contrary (§ 326. *c*).

Metaphor: the figurative use of words, indicating an object by some resemblance.

Metonymy: the use of the name of one thing to indicate some kindred thing.

Onomatopœia: a fitting of sound to sense in the use of words.

Oxymoron: the use of contradictory words in the same phrase:—

īnsāniēns sapientia, *foolish wisdom.*

Paronomasia: the use of words of like sound.

Prosopopœia: personification.

Simile: a figurative comparison (usually introduced by *like*, or *as*).

Synchysis: the interlocked order (§ 598. *h*).

Synecdoche: the use of the name of a part for the whole, or the reverse.

642. Terms of Prosody

Acatalectic: complete, as a verse or a series of feet (§ 612. *a*).

Anaclasis: breaking up of rhythm by substituting different measures.

Anacrusis: the unaccented syllable or syllables preceding a verse (§ 608. *g*).

Antistrophe: a series of verses corresponding to one which has gone before (cf. *strophe*).

Arsis: the unaccented part of a foot (§ 611).

Basis: a single foot preceding the regular movement of a verse.

Cæsura: the ending of a word within a metrical foot (§ 611. *b*).

Catalectic: see Catalexis.

Catalexis: loss of a final syllable (or syllables) making the series *catalectic* (incomplete, § 612. *a*).

Contraction: the use of one long syllable for two short (§ 610).

Correption: shortening of a long syllable, for metrical reasons.

Diæresis: the coincidence of the end of a foot with the end of a word within the verse (§ 611. *c*).

Dialysis: the use of **i** (consonant) and **v** as vowels (*silüa* = *silva*, § 603. *f*. N.[4]).

Diastole: the lengthening of a short syllable by emphasis (§ 612. *b*).

Dimeter: consisting of two like measures.

Dipody: consisting of two like feet.

Distich: a system or series of two verses.

Ecthlipsis: the suppression of a final syllable in **-m** before a word beginning with a vowel (§ 612. *f*).

Elision: the cutting off of a final before a following initial vowel (§ 612. *e*).

Heptameter: consisting of seven feet.

Hexameter: consisting of six measures.
Hexapody: consisting of six feet.
Hiatus: the meeting of two vowels without contraction or elision (§ 612. *g*).
Ictus: the metrical accent (§ 611. *a*).
Irrational: not conforming strictly to the unit of time (§ 609. *e*).
Logaœdic: varying in rhythm, making the effect resemble prose (§ 623).
Monometer: consisting of a single measure.
Mora: the unit of time, equal to one short syllable (§ 608. *a*).
Pentameter: consisting of five measures.
Pentapody: consisting of five feet.
Penthemimeris: consisting of five *half-feet.*
Protraction: extension of a syllable beyond its normal length (608. *c*).
Resolution: the use of two short syllables for one long (§ 610).
Strophe: a series of verses making a recognized metrical whole (*stanza*), which may be indefinitely repeated.
Synæresis: **i** (vowel) and **u** becoming consonants before a vowel (§ 603. *c*. N., *f*. N.[4]).
Synalœpha: the same as elision (§ 612. *e*. N.).
Synapheia: elision between two verses (§ 612. *e*. N.).
Syncope: loss of a short vowel.
Synizesis: the running together of two vowels without full contraction (§ 603. *c*. N.).
Systole: shortening of a syllable regularly long.
Tetrameter: consisting of four measures.
Tetrapody: consisting of four feet.
Tetrastich: a system of four verses.
Thesis: the accented part of a foot (§ 611).
Trimeter: consisting of three measures.
Tripody: consisting of three feet.
Tristich: a system of three verses.

INDEX OF VERBS

Regular verbs of the First, Second, and Fourth Conjugations are given only in special cases. Compounds are usually omitted when they are conjugated like the simple verbs. The figures after the verbs indicate the conjugation. References are to sections. For classified lists of important verbs see § 209 (First Conjugation), § 210 (Second Conjugation), § 211 (Third Conjugation), § 212 (Fourth Conjugation), §§ 190, 191 (Deponents), § 192 (Semi-Deponents).

nectō [NEC], 3, nexī (nexuī), nexum.
neglegō, 3, neglēxī, -lēctum, 211. *e*, footnote 2.
neō, 2, nēvī, —.
nequeō, defect., 206. *d*.
nigrēscō, 3, nigruī, —.
ningit, 3, nīnxit (impers.), 208. *a*.
niteō, 2, —, —.
nitēscō, 3, nituī, —.
nītor, -ī, nīsus (nīxus).
-nīveō, 2, -nīvī (-nīxī), —.
nō, 1, nāvī, —, 179. *a*.
noceō, 2, nocuī, —.
nōlō, nōlle, nōluī, —, 199 (nevīs, nevolt, id. N.).
nōscō [GNO], 3, nōvī, nōtum [āg-, cōg-, dī(g)-, īg-nōscō], 205. *b*. N.[2] (nōsse, 181. *a*).
nōtēscō, 3, -uī, —.
nūbō, 3, nūpsī, nūptum.
-nuō, 3, -nuī, — [ab-, ad-nuō].

ob-dō, 3, -didī, -ditum, 209. *a*. N.
ob-līvīscor, -ī, oblītus.
ob-mūtēscō, 3, -mūtuī, —.
ob-sideō, 2, -sēdī, -sessum [sideō].
ob-sīdō, 3, —, —.
ob-sistō, 3, -stitī, -stitum.
ob-solēscō, 3, -ēvī, -ētum.
ob-stō, 1, -stitī, (-stātūrus).
ob-tineō, 2, -uī, -tentum [teneō].
ob-tingit (impers.), 208. *c*.
ob-tundō, 3, -tudī, -tūsum (-tūnsum).
ob-venit (impers.), 208. *c*.
oc-callēscō, 3, -calluī, —.
oc-cidō, 3, -cĭdī, - cāsum [cadō].
oc-cīdō, 3, -cīdī, -cīsum [caedō].
oc-cinō, 3, -cinuī, — [canō].
oc-cipiō, 3, -cēpī, -ceptum.
occulō, 3, occuluī, occultum.
oc-currō, 3, -currī (-cucurrī), -cursum.
ōdī, ōdisse, ōsūrus (perōsus), 205.
of-ferō, -ferre, obtulī, oblātum.
-oleō (*grow*) [see ab-, ad-].
oleō (*smell*), 2, oluī, —.
operiō, 4, operuī, opertum.
oportet, -ēre, -uit (impers.), 208. *c*.
op-pangō, 3, -pēgī, -pāctum [pangō].
opperior, -īrī, oppertus.
op-primō, 3, -pressī, -pressum [premō].
ōrdior, -īrī, ōrsus.
orior (3d), -īrī, ortus (oritūrus) (so comps.), 174, 191.
os-tendō, 3, -tendī, -tentum.
ovāre, ovātus, defect., 206. *f*.

paciscor, -ī, pactus.
paenitet (impers.), -ēre, -uit, 208. *b* (-tūrus, -tendus, id. N.).
palleō, 2, palluī, —.
pallēscō, 3, palluī, —.
pandō, 3, pandī, pānsum (passum) [dis-].
pangō [PAG], 3, pepigī (-pēgī), pāctum [im-pingō; op-pangō].
parcō, 3, pepercī (parsī), (parsūrus).
pāreō, 2, -uī, pāritum (late).
pariō, 3, peperī, partum (paritūrus) [com-, re-periō].
partior, -īrī, -ītus, 190.
parturiō, 4, —, —.
pāscō, 3, pāvī, pāstum.
pateō, 2, patuī, —.
patior, -ī, passus [per-petior].
paveō, 2, pāvī, —.
pavēscō, 3, -pāvī, — [ex-].
pectō, 3, pexī, pexum.
pel-liciō, 3, -lexī, -lectum [-liciō].
pellō, 3, pepulī, pulsum, 176. *d*. N.[2], 178. *b*. N.[4] [ap-pellō, com-pellō, etc.].
pendeō, 2, pependī, -pēnsum.
pendō, 3, pependī, pēnsum.
per-agō, 3, -ēgī, -āctum.
per-cellō, 3, -culī, -culsum.
per-ciō, see ciō; p.p. -cĭtus.
per-currō, 3, -currī (-cucurrī), -cursum.
per-dō, 3, -didī, -ditum, 209. *a*. N.
per-ficiō, 3, -fēcī, -fectum [faciō].
per-fringō, 3, -frēgī, -frāctum [frangō].
pergō, 3, perrēxī, perrēctum.
per-legō, 3, -lēgī, -lēctum [legō].
per-ōsus, see ōdī.
per-petior, -ī, -pessus.
per-quīrō, 3, -quīsīvī, -quīsītum [quaerō].
per-spiciō, 3, -spexī, -spectum.
per-stō, 1, -stitī, —.
per-tineō, 2, -uī, — [teneō].
per-tundō, 3, -tudī, -tūsum.
pessum-dō, like dō, 209. *a*. N., 428. *i*.
petessō (petissō), 3, —, —, 263. 2. *b*.
petō, 3, petīvī (-iī), petītum, 177. *f*.
piget (impers.), -ēre, piguit, 208. *b* (pigitum est, id. N.).
pingō [PIG], 3, pīnxī, pictum.
pīnsō, 3, -sī, pīns- (pīnstum, pīstum).
pīsō, 3, pīsīvī (-iī), pīstum (see pīnsō).
placeō, 2, -uī, -itum (placet, impers., 208. *c*.).
plangō, 3, plānxī, plānctum.
plaudō, 3, plausī, plausum [ex-plōdō, etc.; ap-plaudō].
plectō, 3, plexī, plexum, 174, 176. *b*. 1.
-plector, -ī, -plexus.
-pleō, 2, -plēvī, -plētum (only in comps., as com-pleō).
plicō, 1, -plicuī (-plicāvī), -plicitum (-plicātum).
pluit, 3, pluit (plūvit), 174, 208. *a* (pluunt, id. N.).
polleō, 2, —, —.
polluō, 3, -uī, -ūtum [luō].
pōnō, 3, posuī, positum.
porr-iciō, 3, —, -rectum [iaciō].
por-rigō (porgō), 3, -rēxī, -rēctum.

pōscō, 3, popōscī, — (so comps.).
possideō, 2, -sēdī, -sessum [sedeō].
possīdō, 3, -sēdī, -sessum.
possum, posse, potuī, —, 198. *b* (potis sum, pote sum, possiem, poterint, potisit, potestur, possitur, id., footnote).
potior, -īrī, potītus.
pōtō, 1, -āvī, -ātum (pōtum).
praebeō, 2, -uī, -itum [habeō].
prae-cellō, 3, —, — [-cellō].
prae-cinō, 3, -cinuī, — [canō].
prae-currō, 3, -currī (-cucurrī), -cursum.
prae-fātur, 206. *c*.
prae-legō, 3, -lēgī, -lēctum [legō].
prae-sāgiō, 4, -īvī, —.
prae-sēns, 170. *b* (see sum).
prae-sideō, 2, -sēdī, — [sedeō].
prae-stō, 1, -stitī, -stitum (-stātum) (praestat, impers., 208. *c*).
prae-sum, -esse, -fuī, (-futūrus).
prandeō, 2, prandī, prānsum.
prehendō (prēndō), 3, -dī, prehēnsum (prēnsum).
premō, 3, pressī, pressum [re-primō].
prēndō, see prehendō.
prō-currō, 3, -currī (-cucurrī), -cursum.
prōd-eō, 4, -iī, -itum, 203. *e*.
prōd-igō, 3, -ēgī, -āctum [agō].
prō-dō, 3, -didī, -ditum, 209. *a*. N.
prō-fātus, 206. *c*.
prō-ficiō, 3, -fēcī, -fectum.
pro-ficīscor, -ī, profectus.
prō-fiteor, -ērī, -fessus.
prō-mineō, -ēre, -uī, —.
prōmō, 3, -mpsī, -mptum, 15. 3.
prō-siliō, 3, -uī (-īvī), — [saliō].
prō-sum, prōdesse, prōfuī (-futūrus), 198. *a*.
prō-tendō, 3, -dī, -tentus (-sus).
psallō, 3, -ī, —.
pūbēscō, 3, pūbuī, —.
pudet (impers.), pudēre, puduit or puditum est, 208. *b* (pudendus, id. N.).
puerāscō, 3, —, —.
pungō [PUG], 3, pupugī, pūnctum [com-].
pūtēscō, 3, pūtuī, —.

quaerō, 3, quaesīvī, quaesītum [re-quīrō] (cf. quaesō).
quaesō, 3, defect., 206. *e* (cf. quaerō).
quassō, 1, reg., 263. 2.
quatiō, 3, -cussī, quassum [con-cutiō].
queō, quīre, quīvī, quitus, 206. *d* (quītur, etc., id. N.); cf. nequeō.
queror, -ī, questus.
quiēscō, 3, quiēvī, quiētum.

rabō (rabiō), 3, —, —.
rādō, 3, rāsī, rāsum.
rapiō, 3, rapuī, raptum (ērēpsēmus, 181. *b*. N.[2] [ab-ripiō etc.].
re-cidō, 3, reccīdī, (recāsūrus) [cadō].
re-cīdō, 3, -cīdī, -cīsum [caedō].
re-cipiō, 3, -cēpī, -ceptum [capiō] (recēpsō, 183. 3).
re-clūdō, 3, -sī, -sum.
red-dō, 3, reddidī, redditum, 209. *a*. N.
red-igō, 3, -ēgī, -āctum [agō].
red-imō, 3, -ēmī, -ēmptum.
re-fellō, 3, -fellī, — [fallō].
re-ferciō, 4, -fersī, -fertum [farciō].
re-ferō, -ferre, rettulī, relātum [ferō].
rē-fert, -ferre, -tulit (impers.), 208. *c*.
re-ficiō, 3, -fēcī, -fectum.
regō, 3, rēxī, rēctum [ar-rigō etc.; pergō, surgō].
re-linquō, 3, -līquī, -lictum [linquō].
re-minīscor, -ī, —.
renīdeō, 2, —, —.
reor, rērī, ratus.
re-pellō, 3, reppulī (repulī), repulsum.
reperiō, 4, repperī, repertum.
rēpō, 3, rēpsī, —.
re-primō, 3, -pressī, -pressum [premō].
re-quīrō, 3, -sīvī, -sītum [quaerō].
re-sideō, 2, -sēdī, —.
re-siliō, 4, -uī (-iī), —.
re-sipīscō, 3, -sipīvī, — [sapiō].
re-sistō, 3, -stitī, —.
re-spergō, 3, -sī, -sum [spargō].
re-spondeō, 2, -dī, -spōnsum [spondeō].
re-stat (impers.), 208. *c*.
re-stō, 1, -stitī, —, 209. *a*. N.
re-tendō, 3, -dī, -tum (-sum).
re-tineō, 2, -tinuī, -tentum [teneō].
re-tundō, 3, rettudī, retūnsum (-tūsum).
re-vertor, -ī, reversus, 191 (revertī, -eram, id. N.).
rīdeō, 2, rīsī, -rīsum.
rigeō, 2, riguī, —.
rigēscō, 3, riguī, —.
ringor, 3, rictus.
rōdō, 3, rōsī, rōsum.
rubeō, 2, —, —.
rubēscō, 3, rubuī, —.
rudō, 3, rudīvī, —.
rumpō [RUP], 3, rūpī, ruptum.
ruō, 3, ruī, rutum (ruitūrus), 176. *e* [dī-, cor-].

saepiō, 4, saepsī, saeptum.
sāgiō, 4, see prae-sāgiō.
saliō, 4, saluī (saliī), [saltum] [dē-siliō].
salvē, salvēre, 206. *g*.
sanciō [SAC], 4, sānxī, sānctum, 177. *b*. N.
sānēscō, 3, -sānuī, — [con-].
sapiō, 3, sapiī, —.
sarciō, 4, sarsī, sartum.
satis-dō, -dăre, -dedī, -dătum, 209. *a*. N.
scabō, 3, scābī, —.
scalpō, 3, scalpsī, scalptum.
scandō, 3, -scendī, -scēnsum [a-scendō, etc.].

scateō (scatō), -ēre or -ĕre, —, —.
scatūriō, 4, —, —.
scīn' (=scīsne), 13. N. (see sciō).
scindō [SCID], 3, scidī, scissum, 177. c. N.
sciō, 4, -īvī, scītum (scīn', 13. N.).
scīscō, 3, scīvī, scītum.
scrībō, 3, scrīpsī, scrīptum, 178. b. N.[1].
sculpō, 3, sculpsī, sculptum.
sē-cernō, 3, -crēvī, -crētum.
secō, 1, -uī, sectum (also secātūrus).
sedeō, 2, sēdī, sessum [ad-, pos-sideō, etc.; super-sedeō].
sē-ligō, 3, -lēgī, -lēctum [legō].
senēscō, 3, -senuī, —.
sentiō, 4, sēnsī, sēnsum.
sepeliō, 4, sepelīvī, sepultum.
sequor, -ī, secūtus, 190.
serō (*entwine*), 3, seruī, sertum.
serō (*sow*), 3, sēvī, satum.
serpō, 3, serpsī, —.
sīdō, 3, sīdī (-sēdī), -sessum.
sileō, 2, -uī, —.
singultiō, 4, -īvī, —.
sinō, 3, sīvī, situm (sīris, etc., 181. b. N.[1]).
sistō [STA], 3, stitī, statum.
sitiō, 4, -īvī, —.
sōdēs (=sī audēs), 13. N.
soleō, solēre, solitus, 192.
solvō, 3, solvī, solūtum, 177. e, 261. N.
sonō, 1, -uī, -itum (-ātūrus).
sorbeō, 2, sorbuī (rarely sorpsī), —.
spargō, 3, sparsī, sparsum [ad-spergō].
spernō, 3, sprēvī, sprētum, 177. a. N.
-spiciō, 3, -spexī, -spectum.
splendeō, 2, -uī, —.
spondeō, 2, spopondī, spōnsum [re-].
spuō, 3, -spuī, —.
squāleō, 2, —, —.
statuō, 3, -uī, -ūtum, 176. d [con-stituō].
sternō, 3, strāvī, strātum, 177. a. N.
sternuō, 3, sternuī, —.
stertō, 3, -stertuī, —.
-stinguō, 3, -stīnxī, -stīnctum (in comp., as ex-).
stō, stāre, stetī, -statum (-stit-), 209. a, and N.
strepō, 3, strepuī, —.
strīdeō, 2, strīdī, —.
strīdō, 3, strīdī, —.
stringō, 3, strīnxī, strictum.
struō, 3, strūxī, strūctum.
studeō, 2, -uī, —.
stupeō, 2, stupuī, —.
stupēscō, 3, -stupuī, —.
suādeō, 2, suāsī, suāsum.
sub-dō, 3, -didī, -ditum, 209. a. N.
sub-igō, 3, -ēgī, -āctum [agō].
suc-cidō, 3, -cĭdī, — [cadō].
suc-cīdō, 3, -cīdī, -cīsum [caedō].
suc-currō, 3, -currī, -cursum.
suēscō, 3, suēvī, suētum.
suf-ferō, sufferre, sustulī, sublātum.
suf-ficiō, 3, -fēcī, -fectus [faciō].
suf-fodiō, 3, -fōdī, -fossum.
sug-gerō, 3, -gessī, -gestum.
sūgō, 3, sūxī, sūctum.
sūltis (= sī vultis), 13. N.
sum, esse, fuī, (futūrus), 170; fuī (forem, fore, 170. a; †sōns, -sēns, ēns, id. b; fūvimus, fūvisset, siem, fuam, fuās, escit, escunt, id. b. N.; homōst, etc., 13. N.).
sūmō, 3, sūmpsī, sūmptum, 15. 11.
suō, 3, suī, sūtum.
super-dō, -dăre, -dedī, -dătum, 209. a. N.
super-fit, defect., 204. c.
super-fluō, 3, —, — [fluō].
super-stō, 1, -stetī, —.
super-sum, see sum (superest, impers., 208. c).
surdēscō, 3, surduī, —.
surgō (sur-rigō), 3, surrēxī, surrēctum.
sur-ripiō, 3, -uī (surpuī), -reptum [rapiō].

tābeō, 2, -uī, —.
tābēscō, 3, tābuī, —.
taedet (impers.), -ēre, taeduit, pertaesum est, 208. b.
tangō [TAG], 3, tetigī, tāctum, 176. c. 2 [con-tingō].
tegō, 3, tēxī, tēctum, 186.
temnō, 3, -tempsī, -temptum, 176. b. 1.
tendō [TEN], 3, tetendī, tentum.
teneō, 2, tenuī, -tentum [con-tineō, etc.].
tepēscō, 3, tepuī, —.
tergeō, 2, tersī, tersum.
tergō, 3, tersī, tersum.
terō, 3, trīvī, trītum.
texō, 3, texuī, textum.
timeō, 2, -uī, —.
-timēscō, 3, -timuī, —.
tingō (tinguō), 3, tīnxī, tīnctum, 178. b. N.[2].
tollō, 3, sustulī, sublātum, 211. f. N. [at-tollō].
tondeō, 2, -totondī (-tondī), tōnsum, 177. c.
tonō, 1, -uī, -tonitum (-tonātum).
torpeō, 2, —, —.
torqueō, 2, torsī, tortum.
torreō, 2, torruī, tostum.
trā-dō, 3, -didī, -ditum, 209. a. N.
trahō, 3, trāxī, trāctum (trāxe, 181. b. N.[2]).
trāns-currō, 3, -currī (-cucurrī), -cursum.
tremō, 3, tremuī, —.
tribuō, 3, tribuī, tribūtum.
trūdō, 3, trūsī, trūsum.
tueor, -ērī, tuitus (tūtus, adj.).
tumeō, 2, —, —.
tumēscō, 3, -tumuī, — [in-].
tundō [TUD], 3, tutudī, tūnsum (-tūsum) [ob-tundō].
turgeō, 2, tursī, —.
tussiō, 4, —, —.

ulcīscor, -ī, ultus.
ungō (-uō), 3, ūnxī, ūnctum.
urgeō, 2, ursī, —.
ūrō, 3, ussī, ustum (so comps., cf. also combūrō).
ūtor, -ī, ūsus.

vacat (impers.), 208. *c*.
vādō, 3, -vāsī, -vāsum.
vāgiō, 4, -iī, —.
valeō, 2, -uī, (-itūrus).
valēscō, 3, -uī, —.
vānēscō, 3, -vānuī, — [ē-].
vehō, 3, vēxī, vectum.
vellō (vollō), 3, vellī (-vulsī), vulsum.
vēndō, 3, -didī, -ditum, 428. *i*.
vēneō (*be sold*), 4, -iī, -itum, 428. *i*.
veniō (*come*), 4, vēnī, ventum, 19, 174.
vēnum-dō, -dăre, -dedī, -dătum, 209. *a*. N., 428. *i*.
vereor, -ērī, -itus, 190.
vergō, 3, —, —.
verrō (vorrō), 3, -verrī, versum.
vertō (vortō), 3, vertī, versum, 178. *b*. N.[1] (vertor, mid., 156. *a*. N.).
vescor, -ī, —.
vesperāscit (impers.), 208. *a*, 263. 1.
veterāscō, 3, veterāvī, —.
vetō, 1, -uī, -itum.
videō, 2, vīdī, vīsum.
videor (*seem*), -ērī, vīsus (vidētur, impers., 208. *c*).
vieō, 2, [viēvī], -ētum.
vigeō, 2, -uī, —.
vīn' (= vīsne, see volō).
vinciō, 4, vīnxī, vīnctum.
vincō [VIC], 3, vīcī, victum.
vireō, 2, -uī, —.
vīsō [VID], 3, vīsī, —, 263. 4. N.
vīvīscō, 3, -vīxī, —, [re-].
vīvō, 3, vīxī, vīctum (vīxet, 181. *b*. N.[2]).
volō, velle, voluī, 199 (sūltis, 13. N., 199. N.; vīn', 13. N.).
volvō, 3, volvī, volūtum.
vomō, 3, vomuī, —.
voveō, 2, vōvī, vōtum.

INDEX OF WORDS AND SUBJECTS

NOTE. — The numerical references are to sections, with a few exceptions in which the page (p.) is referred to. The letters and some numerals refer to subsections. The letter N. signifies Note; ftn., footnote. Abl. = ablative; acc. = accusative; adj. = adjective; adv. = adverb or adverbial; apod. = apodosis; app. = appositive or apposition; cf. = compare; comp. = compound or composition; compar. = comparative or comparison; conj. = conjugation or conjunction; constr. = construction; dat. = dative; gen. = genitive; gend. = gender; imv. = imperative; ind. disc. = indirect discourse; loc. = locative; nom. = nominative; prep. = preposition; subj. = subject; subjv. = subjunctive; vb. = verb; w. = with. (Other abbreviations present no difficulty.)

LATIN AUTHORS AND THEIR WORKS CITED IN THIS BOOK

NOTE.—In the citations the names Cæsar, Cicero, Sallust (with *Iugurtha*), and Virgil are not generally given. Thus, "B. G." refers to Cæsar's *Bellum Gallicum*; "Fam." to Cicero's letters *ad Familiares*; "Iug." to Sallust's *Iugurtha*; "Aen." to Virgil's *Æneid*, etc.

Ap., Apuleius (A.D. 125–?):
- Met., *Metamorphoses*.
- ——, B. Afr., *Bellum Africum*.

Cæsar (B.C. 100–44):
- B. C., *Bellum Civile*.
- B. G., *Bellum Gallicum*.

Cato (B.C. 234–149):
- de M., *de Moribus*.
- R. R., *de Re Rustica*.

Catull., Catullus (B.C. 87–54).

Cic., Cicero (B.C. 106–43):
- Acad., *Academica*.
- Ad Her., [*ad Herennium*].
- Arch., *pro Archia*.
- Att., *ad Atticum*.
- Balb., *pro Balbo*.
- Brut., *Brutus de Claris Oratoribus*.
- Caec., *pro Caecina*.
- Caecil., *Divinatio in Caecilium*.
- Cael., *pro M. Caelio*.
- Cat., *in Catilinam*.
- Cat. M., *Cato Maior* (*de Senectute*).
- Clu., *pro Cluentio*.
- Deiot., *pro Deiotaro*.
- De Or., *de Oratore*.
- Div., *de Divinatione*.
- Dom., *pro Domo Sua*.
- Fam., *ad Familiares*.
- Fat., *de Fato*.
- Fin., *de Finibus*.
- Flacc., *pro Flacco*.
- Font., *pro M. Fonteio*.
- Har. Resp., *de Haruspicum Responsis*.
- Inv., *de Inventione Rhetorica*.

Cic. Lael., *Laelius* (*de Amicitia*).
- Leg. Agr., *de Lege Agraria*.
- Legg., *de Legibus*.
- Lig., *pro Ligario*.
- Manil., *pro Lege Manilia*.
- Marc., *pro Marcello*.
- Mil., *pro Milone*.
- Mur., *pro Murena*.
- N. D., *de Natura Deorum*.
- Off., *de Officiis*.
- Or., *Orator*.
- Par., *Paradoxa*.
- Part. Or., *de Partitione Oratoria*.
- Phil., *Philippicae*.
- Planc., *pro Plancio*.
- Pison., *in Pisonem*.
- Prov. Cons., *de Provinciis Consularibus*.
- Q. Fr., *ad Q. Fratrem*.
- Quinct., *pro Quinctio*.
- Rabir., *pro Rabirio*.
- Rab. Post., *pro Rabirio Postumo*.
- Rep., *de Re Publica*.
- Rosc. Am., *pro Roscio Amerino*.
- Rosc. Com., *pro Roscio Comoedo*.
- Scaur., *pro Scauro*.
- Sest., *pro Sestio*.
- Sull., *pro Sulla*.
- Tim., *Timaeus* (*de Universo*).
- Top., *Topica*.
- Tull., *pro Tullio*.
- Tusc., *Tusculanae Disputationes*.
- Vat., *in Vatinium*.

Cic. Verr., *in Verrem*.

Claud., Claudianus (abt. A.D. 400):
- iv C. H., *de Quarto Consulatu Honorii*.

Enn., Ennius (B.C. 239–169).

Gell., A. Gellius (d. A.D. 175).

Hirtius (d. B.C. 43):
- ? B. Al., *Bellum Alexandrinum*.

Hor., Horace (B.C. 65–8):
- A. P., *de Arte Poetica*.
- C. S., *Carmen Saeculare*.
- Ep., *Epistles*.
- Epod. *Epodes*.
- Od. *Odes*.
- S. *Satires*.

Iust., Justinus (abt. A.D. 150).

Iuv., Juvenal (abt. A.D. 60–140).

Liv., Livy (B.C. 59–A.D. 17).

Lucr., Lucretius (B.C. 96–55).

Mart., Martial (A.D. 43–? 104):
- Ep., *Epigrams*.

Nep., Nepos (B.C. 99–24):
- Ages., *Agesilaus*.
- Alc., *Alcibiades*.
- Att., *Atticus*.
- Dat., *Datames*.
- Dion, *Dion*.
- Epam., *Epaminondas*.
- Eum., *Eumenes*.
- Hann., *Hannibal*.
- Milt., *Miltiades*.
- Paus., *Pausanias*.
- Them., *Themistocles*.
- Timoth., *Timotheus*.

Ov., Ovid (B.C. 43–A.D. 17):
A. A., *Ars Amatoria.*
F., *Fasti.*
H., *Heroides.*
M., *Metamorphoses.*
Pont., *Epistulae ex Ponto.*
Trist., *Tristia.*
Pers., Persius (A.D. 34–62):
Sat., *Satires.*
Phaed., Phaedrus (abt. A.D. 40).
Pl., Plautus (B.C. 254–184):
Am., *Amphitruo.*
Asin., *Asinaria.*
Aul., *Aulularia.*
Bac., *Bacchides.*
Capt., *Captivi.*
Cist., *Cistellaria.*
Curc., *Curculio.*
Epid., *Epidicus.*
Men., *Menaechmi.*
Merc., *Mercator.*
Mil., *Miles Gloriosus.*
Most., *Mostellaria.*
Pers., *Persa.*
Poen., *Poenulus.*
Ps., *Pseudolus.*
Rud., *Rudens.*
Stich., *Stichus.*
Trin., *Trinummus.*
Truc., *Truculentus.*

Plin., Pliny, senior (A.D. 23–79):
H. N., *Historia Naturalis.*
Plin., Pliny, junior (A.D. 62–113):
Ep., *Epistles.*
Prop., Propertius (B.C. 49–15).
Pub. Syr., Publilius Syrus (abt. B.C. 44).
Q. C., Q. Curtius (abt. A.D. 50).
Quint., Quintilian (abt. A.D. 35–95).
Sall., Sallust (B.C. 86–34):
Cat., *Catilina.*
Ep. Mith., *Epistula Mithridatis.*
Iug., *Iugurtha.*
——, S. C. de Bac., *Senatus Consultum de Bacchanalibus* (B.C. 186).
Sen., Seneca (B.C. 4–A.D. 65):
Dial., *Dialogues.*
Ep., *Epistles.*
Herc. Fur., *Hercules Furens.*
Herc. Oet., *Hercules Oetaeus.*
Med., *Medea.*

Sen. Q. N., *Quaestiones Naturales.*
Sil., Silius Italicus (abt. A.D. 25–101).
Suet., Suetonius (abt. A.D. 75–160):
Aug., *Augustus.*
Dom., *Domitianus.*
Galb., *Galba.*
Tac., Tacitus (abt. A.D. 55–120):
Agr., *Agricola.*
Ann., *Annales.*
H., *Historiae.*
Ter., Terence (d. B.C. 159):
Ad., *Adelphi.*
And., *Andria.*
Eun., *Eunuchus.*
Haut., *Hautontimorumenos.*
Hec., *Hecyra.*
Ph., *Phormio.*
Val., Valerius Maximus (abt. A.D. 26).
Varr., Varro (B.C. 116–27):
R. R., *de Re Rustica.*
Vell., Velleius Paterculus (abt. B.C. 19–A.D. 31).
Verg., Virgil (B.C. 70–19).
Aen., *Æneid.*
Ecl., *Eclogues.*
Georg., *Georgics.*

A CATALOG OF SELECTED

DOVER BOOKS

IN ALL FIELDS OF INTEREST

A CATALOG OF SELECTED DOVER BOOKS IN ALL FIELDS OF INTEREST

STICKLEY CRAFTSMAN FURNITURE CATALOGS, Gustav Stickley and L. & J. G. Stickley. Beautiful, functional furniture in two authentic catalogs from 1910. 594 illustrations, including 277 photos, show settles, rockers, armchairs, reclining chairs, bookcases, desks, tables. 183pp. 6½ x 9¼. 0-486-23838-5

AMERICAN LOCOMOTIVES IN HISTORIC PHOTOGRAPHS: 1858 to 1949, Ron Ziel (ed.). A rare collection of 126 meticulously detailed official photographs, called "builder portraits," of American locomotives that majestically chronicle the rise of steam locomotive power in America. Introduction. Detailed captions. xi+ 129pp. 9 x 12. 0-486-27393-8

AMERICA'S LIGHTHOUSES: An Illustrated History, Francis Ross Holland, Jr. Delightfully written, profusely illustrated fact-filled survey of over 200 American lighthouses since 1716. History, anecdotes, technological advances, more. 240pp. 8 x 10¾. 0-486-25576-X

TOWARDS A NEW ARCHITECTURE, Le Corbusier. Pioneering manifesto by founder of "International School." Technical and aesthetic theories, views of industry, economics, relation of form to function, "mass-production split" and much more. Profusely illustrated. 320pp. 6⅛ x 9¼. (Available in U.S. only.) 0-486-25023-7

HOW THE OTHER HALF LIVES, Jacob Riis. Famous journalistic record, exposing poverty and degradation of New York slums around 1900, by major social reformer. 100 striking and influential photographs. 233pp. 10 x 7⅞. 0-486-22012-5

FRUIT KEY AND TWIG KEY TO TREES AND SHRUBS, William M. Harlow. One of the handiest and most widely used identification aids. Fruit key covers 120 deciduous and evergreen species; twig key 160 deciduous species. Easily used. Over 300 photographs. 126pp. 5⅜ x 8½. 0-486-20511-8

COMMON BIRD SONGS, Dr. Donald J. Borror. Songs of 60 most common U.S. birds: robins, sparrows, cardinals, bluejays, finches, more–arranged in order of increasing complexity. Up to 9 variations of songs of each species.
Cassette and manual 0-486-99911-4

ORCHIDS AS HOUSE PLANTS, Rebecca Tyson Northen. Grow cattleyas and many other kinds of orchids–in a window, in a case, or under artificial light. 63 illustrations. 148pp. 5⅜ x 8½. 0-486-23261-1

MONSTER MAZES, Dave Phillips. Masterful mazes at four levels of difficulty. Avoid deadly perils and evil creatures to find magical treasures. Solutions for all 32 exciting illustrated puzzles. 48pp. 8¼ x 11. 0-486-26005-4

MOZART'S DON GIOVANNI (DOVER OPERA LIBRETTO SERIES), Wolfgang Amadeus Mozart. Introduced and translated by Ellen H. Bleiler. Standard Italian libretto, with complete English translation. Convenient and thoroughly portable–an ideal companion for reading along with a recording or the performance itself. Introduction. List of characters. Plot summary. 121pp. 5¼ x 8½. 0-486-24944-1

FRANK LLOYD WRIGHT'S DANA HOUSE, Donald Hoffmann. Pictorial essay of residential masterpiece with over 160 interior and exterior photos, plans, elevations, sketches and studies. 128pp. 9¼ x 10¾. 0-486-29120-0

THE CLARINET AND CLARINET PLAYING, David Pino. Lively, comprehensive work features suggestions about technique, musicianship, and musical interpretation, as well as guidelines for teaching, making your own reeds, and preparing for public performance. Includes an intriguing look at clarinet history. "A godsend," *The Clarinet,* Journal of the International Clarinet Society. Appendixes. 7 illus. 320pp. 5⅜ x 8½. 0-486-40270-3

HOLLYWOOD GLAMOR PORTRAITS, John Kobal (ed.). 145 photos from 1926-49. Harlow, Gable, Bogart, Bacall; 94 stars in all. Full background on photographers, technical aspects. 160pp. 8⅜ x 11¼. 0-486-23352-9

THE RAVEN AND OTHER FAVORITE POEMS, Edgar Allan Poe. Over 40 of the author's most memorable poems: "The Bells," "Ulalume," "Israfel," "To Helen," "The Conqueror Worm," "Eldorado," "Annabel Lee," many more. Alphabetic lists of titles and first lines. 64pp. 5$\frac{3}{16}$ x 8¼. 0-486-26685-0

PERSONAL MEMOIRS OF U. S. GRANT, Ulysses Simpson Grant. Intelligent, deeply moving firsthand account of Civil War campaigns, considered by many the finest military memoirs ever written. Includes letters, historic photographs, maps and more. 528pp. 6⅛ x 9¼. 0-486-28587-1

ANCIENT EGYPTIAN MATERIALS AND INDUSTRIES, A. Lucas and J. Harris. Fascinating, comprehensive, thoroughly documented text describes this ancient civilization's vast resources and the processes that incorporated them in daily life, including the use of animal products, building materials, cosmetics, perfumes and incense, fibers, glazed ware, glass and its manufacture, materials used in the mummification process, and much more. 544pp. 6⅛ x 9¼. (Available in U.S. only.) 0-486-40446-3

RUSSIAN STORIES/RUSSKIE RASSKAZY: A Dual-Language Book, edited by Gleb Struve. Twelve tales by such masters as Chekhov, Tolstoy, Dostoevsky, Pushkin, others. Excellent word-for-word English translations on facing pages, plus teaching and study aids, Russian/English vocabulary, biographical/critical introductions, more. 416pp. 5⅜ x 8½. 0-486-26244-8

PHILADELPHIA THEN AND NOW: 60 Sites Photographed in the Past and Present, Kenneth Finkel and Susan Oyama. Rare photographs of City Hall, Logan Square, Independence Hall, Betsy Ross House, other landmarks juxtaposed with contemporary views. Captures changing face of historic city. Introduction. Captions. 128pp. 8¼ x 11. 0-486-25790-8

NORTH AMERICAN INDIAN LIFE: Customs and Traditions of 23 Tribes, Elsie Clews Parsons (ed.). 27 fictionalized essays by noted anthropologists examine religion, customs, government, additional facets of life among the Winnebago, Crow, Zuni, Eskimo, other tribes. 480pp. 6⅛ x 9¼. 0-486-27377-6

TECHNICAL MANUAL AND DICTIONARY OF CLASSICAL BALLET, Gail Grant. Defines, explains, comments on steps, movements, poses and concepts. 15-page pictorial section. Basic book for student, viewer. 127pp. 5⅜ x 8½. 0-486-21843-0

THE MALE AND FEMALE FIGURE IN MOTION: 60 Classic Photographic Sequences, Eadweard Muybridge. 60 true-action photographs of men and women walking, running, climbing, bending, turning, etc., reproduced from rare 19th-century masterpiece. vi + 121pp. 9 x 12. 0-486-24745-7

ANIMALS: 1,419 Copyright-Free Illustrations of Mammals, Birds, Fish, Insects, etc., Jim Harter (ed.). Clear wood engravings present, in extremely lifelike poses, over 1,000 species of animals. One of the most extensive pictorial sourcebooks of its kind. Captions. Index. 284pp. 9 x 12. 0-486-23766-4

1001 QUESTIONS ANSWERED ABOUT THE SEASHORE, N. J. Berrill and Jacquelyn Berrill. Queries answered about dolphins, sea snails, sponges, starfish, fishes, shore birds, many others. Covers appearance, breeding, growth, feeding, much more. 305pp. $5\frac{1}{4}$ x $8\frac{1}{4}$. 0-486-23366-9

ATTRACTING BIRDS TO YOUR YARD, William J. Weber. Easy-to-follow guide offers advice on how to attract the greatest diversity of birds: birdhouses, feeders, water and waterers, much more. 96pp. $5\frac{3}{16}$ x $8\frac{1}{4}$. 0-486-28927-3

MEDICINAL AND OTHER USES OF NORTH AMERICAN PLANTS: A Historical Survey with Special Reference to the Eastern Indian Tribes, Charlotte Erichsen-Brown. Chronological historical citations document 500 years of usage of plants, trees, shrubs native to eastern Canada, northeastern U.S. Also complete identifying information. 343 illustrations. 544pp. $6\frac{1}{2}$ x $9\frac{1}{4}$. 0-486-25951-X

STORYBOOK MAZES, Dave Phillips. 23 stories and mazes on two-page spreads: Wizard of Oz, Treasure Island, Robin Hood, etc. Solutions. 64pp. $8\frac{1}{4}$ x 11. 0-486-23628-5

AMERICAN NEGRO SONGS: 230 Folk Songs and Spirituals, Religious and Secular, John W. Work. This authoritative study traces the African influences of songs sung and played by black Americans at work, in church, and as entertainment. The author discusses the lyric significance of such songs as "Swing Low, Sweet Chariot," "John Henry," and others and offers the words and music for 230 songs. Bibliography. Index of Song Titles. 272pp. $6\frac{1}{2}$ x $9\frac{1}{4}$. 0-486-40271-1

MOVIE-STAR PORTRAITS OF THE FORTIES, John Kobal (ed.). 163 glamor, studio photos of 106 stars of the 1940s: Rita Hayworth, Ava Gardner, Marlon Brando, Clark Gable, many more. 176pp. $8\frac{3}{8}$ x $11\frac{1}{4}$. 0-486-23546-7

YEKL and THE IMPORTED BRIDEGROOM AND OTHER STORIES OF YIDDISH NEW YORK, Abraham Cahan. Film Hester Street based on *Yekl* (1896). Novel, other stories among first about Jewish immigrants on N.Y.'s East Side. 240pp. $5\frac{3}{8}$ x $8\frac{1}{2}$. 0-486-22427-9

SELECTED POEMS, Walt Whitman. Generous sampling from *Leaves of Grass*. Twenty-four poems include "I Hear America Singing," "Song of the Open Road," "I Sing the Body Electric," "When Lilacs Last in the Dooryard Bloom'd," "O Captain! My Captain!"–all reprinted from an authoritative edition. Lists of titles and first lines. 128pp. $5\frac{3}{16}$ x $8\frac{1}{4}$. 0-486-26878-0

SONGS OF EXPERIENCE: Facsimile Reproduction with 26 Plates in Full Color, William Blake. 26 full-color plates from a rare 1826 edition. Includes "The Tyger," "London," "Holy Thursday," and other poems. Printed text of poems. 48pp. $5\frac{1}{4}$ x 7. 0-486-24636-1

THE BEST TALES OF HOFFMANN, E. T. A. Hoffmann. 10 of Hoffmann's most important stories: "Nutcracker and the King of Mice," "The Golden Flowerpot," etc. 458pp. $5\frac{3}{8}$ x $8\frac{1}{2}$. 0-486-21793-0

THE BOOK OF TEA, Kakuzo Okakura. Minor classic of the Orient: entertaining, charming explanation, interpretation of traditional Japanese culture in terms of tea ceremony. 94pp. $5\frac{3}{8}$ x $8\frac{1}{2}$. 0-486-20070-1

FRENCH STORIES/CONTES FRANÇAIS: A Dual-Language Book, Wallace Fowlie. Ten stories by French masters, Voltaire to Camus: "Micromegas" by Voltaire; "The Atheist's Mass" by Balzac; "Minuet" by de Maupassant; "The Guest" by Camus, six more. Excellent English translations on facing pages. Also French-English vocabulary list, exercises, more. 352pp. 5⅜ x 8½. 0-486-26443-2

CHICAGO AT THE TURN OF THE CENTURY IN PHOTOGRAPHS: 122 Historic Views from the Collections of the Chicago Historical Society, Larry A. Viskochil. Rare large-format prints offer detailed views of City Hall, State Street, the Loop, Hull House, Union Station, many other landmarks, circa 1904-1913. Introduction. Captions. Maps. 144pp. 9⅜ x 12¼. 0-486-24656-6

OLD BROOKLYN IN EARLY PHOTOGRAPHS, 1865-1929, William Lee Younger. Luna Park, Gravesend race track, construction of Grand Army Plaza, moving of Hotel Brighton, etc. 157 previously unpublished photographs. 165pp. 8⅞ x 11¾. 0-486-23587-4

THE MYTHS OF THE NORTH AMERICAN INDIANS, Lewis Spence. Rich anthology of the myths and legends of the Algonquins, Iroquois, Pawnees and Sioux, prefaced by an extensive historical and ethnological commentary. 36 illustrations. 480pp. 5⅜ x 8½. 0-486-25967-6

AN ENCYCLOPEDIA OF BATTLES: Accounts of Over 1,560 Battles from 1479 B.C. to the Present, David Eggenberger. Essential details of every major battle in recorded history from the first battle of Megiddo in 1479 B.C. to Grenada in 1984. List of Battle Maps. New Appendix covering the years 1967-1984. Index. 99 illustrations. 544pp. 6½ x 9¼. 0-486-24913-1

SAILING ALONE AROUND THE WORLD, Captain Joshua Slocum. First man to sail around the world, alone, in small boat. One of great feats of seamanship told in delightful manner. 67 illustrations. 294pp. 5⅜ x 8½. 0-486-20326-3

ANARCHISM AND OTHER ESSAYS, Emma Goldman. Powerful, penetrating, prophetic essays on direct action, role of minorities, prison reform, puritan hypocrisy, violence, etc. 271pp. 5⅜ x 8½. 0-486-22484-8

MYTHS OF THE HINDUS AND BUDDHISTS, Ananda K. Coomaraswamy and Sister Nivedita. Great stories of the epics; deeds of Krishna, Shiva, taken from puranas, Vedas, folk tales; etc. 32 illustrations. 400pp. 5⅜ x 8½. 0-486-21759-0

MY BONDAGE AND MY FREEDOM, Frederick Douglass. Born a slave, Douglass became outspoken force in antislavery movement. The best of Douglass' autobiographies. Graphic description of slave life. 464pp. 5⅜ x 8½. 0-486-22457-0

FOLLOWING THE EQUATOR: A Journey Around the World, Mark Twain. Fascinating humorous account of 1897 voyage to Hawaii, Australia, India, New Zealand, etc. Ironic, bemused reports on peoples, customs, climate, flora and fauna, politics, much more. 197 illustrations. 720pp. 5⅜ x 8½. 0-486-26113-1

THE PEOPLE CALLED SHAKERS, Edward D. Andrews. Definitive study of Shakers: origins, beliefs, practices, dances, social organization, furniture and crafts, etc. 33 illustrations. 351pp. 5⅜ x 8½. 0-486-21081-2

THE MYTHS OF GREECE AND ROME, H. A. Guerber. A classic of mythology, generously illustrated, long prized for its simple, graphic, accurate retelling of the principal myths of Greece and Rome, and for its commentary on their origins and significance. With 64 illustrations by Michelangelo, Raphael, Titian, Rubens, Canova, Bernini and others. 480pp. 5⅜ x 8½. 0-486-27584-1

PSYCHOLOGY OF MUSIC, Carl E. Seashore. Classic work discusses music as a medium from psychological viewpoint. Clear treatment of physical acoustics, auditory apparatus, sound perception, development of musical skills, nature of musical feeling, host of other topics. 88 figures. 408pp. 5⅜ x 8½. 0-486-21851-1

LIFE IN ANCIENT EGYPT, Adolf Erman. Fullest, most thorough, detailed older account with much not in more recent books, domestic life, religion, magic, medicine, commerce, much more. Many illustrations reproduce tomb paintings, carvings, hieroglyphs, etc. 597pp. 5⅜ x 8½. 0-486-22632-8

SUNDIALS, Their Theory and Construction, Albert Waugh. Far and away the best, most thorough coverage of ideas, mathematics concerned, types, construction, adjusting anywhere. Simple, nontechnical treatment allows even children to build several of these dials. Over 100 illustrations. 230pp. 5⅜ x 8½. 0-486-22947-5

THEORETICAL HYDRODYNAMICS, L. M. Milne-Thomson. Classic exposition of the mathematical theory of fluid motion, applicable to both hydrodynamics and aerodynamics. Over 600 exercises. 768pp. 6⅛ x 9¼. 0-486-68970-0

OLD-TIME VIGNETTES IN FULL COLOR, Carol Belanger Grafton (ed.). Over 390 charming, often sentimental illustrations, selected from archives of Victorian graphics–pretty women posing, children playing, food, flowers, kittens and puppies, smiling cherubs, birds and butterflies, much more. All copyright-free. 48pp. 9¼ x 12¼. 0-486-27269-9

PERSPECTIVE FOR ARTISTS, Rex Vicat Cole. Depth, perspective of sky and sea, shadows, much more, not usually covered. 391 diagrams, 81 reproductions of drawings and paintings. 279pp. 5⅜ x 8½. 0-486-22487-2

DRAWING THE LIVING FIGURE, Joseph Sheppard. Innovative approach to artistic anatomy focuses on specifics of surface anatomy, rather than muscles and bones. Over 170 drawings of live models in front, back and side views, and in widely varying poses. Accompanying diagrams. 177 illustrations. Introduction. Index. 144pp. 8⅜ x11¼. 0-486-26723-7

GOTHIC AND OLD ENGLISH ALPHABETS: 100 Complete Fonts, Dan X. Solo. Add power, elegance to posters, signs, other graphics with 100 stunning copyright-free alphabets: Blackstone, Dolbey, Germania, 97 more–including many lower-case, numerals, punctuation marks. 104pp. 8⅛ x 11. 0-486-24695-7

THE BOOK OF WOOD CARVING, Charles Marshall Sayers. Finest book for beginners discusses fundamentals and offers 34 designs. "Absolutely first rate . . . well thought out and well executed."–E. J. Tangerman. 118pp. 7¾ x 10⅝. 0-486-23654-4

ILLUSTRATED CATALOG OF CIVIL WAR MILITARY GOODS: Union Army Weapons, Insignia, Uniform Accessories, and Other Equipment, Schuyler, Hartley, and Graham. Rare, profusely illustrated 1846 catalog includes Union Army uniform and dress regulations, arms and ammunition, coats, insignia, flags, swords, rifles, etc. 226 illustrations. 160pp. 9 x 12. 0-486-24939-5

WOMEN'S FASHIONS OF THE EARLY 1900s: An Unabridged Republication of "New York Fashions, 1909," National Cloak & Suit Co. Rare catalog of mail-order fashions documents women's and children's clothing styles shortly after the turn of the century. Captions offer full descriptions, prices. Invaluable resource for fashion, costume historians. Approximately 725 illustrations. 128pp. 8⅜ x 11¼. 0-486-27276-1

HOW TO DO BEADWORK, Mary White. Fundamental book on craft from simple projects to five-bead chains and woven works. 106 illustrations. 142pp. 5⅜ x 8. 0-486-20697-1

THE 1912 AND 1915 GUSTAV STICKLEY FURNITURE CATALOGS, Gustav Stickley. With over 200 detailed illustrations and descriptions, these two catalogs are essential reading and reference materials and identification guides for Stickley furniture. Captions cite materials, dimensions and prices. 112pp. 6½ x 9¼. 0-486-26676-1

EARLY AMERICAN LOCOMOTIVES, John H. White, Jr. Finest locomotive engravings from early 19th century: historical (1804–74), main-line (after 1870), special, foreign, etc. 147 plates. 142pp. 11⅜ x 8¼. 0-486-22772-3

LITTLE BOOK OF EARLY AMERICAN CRAFTS AND TRADES, Peter Stockham (ed.). 1807 children's book explains crafts and trades: baker, hatter, cooper, potter, and many others. 23 copperplate illustrations. 140pp. 4⅝ x 6. 0-486-23336-7

VICTORIAN FASHIONS AND COSTUMES FROM HARPER'S BAZAR, 1867–1898, Stella Blum (ed.). Day costumes, evening wear, sports clothes, shoes, hats, other accessories in over 1,000 detailed engravings. 320pp. 9⅜ x 12¼. 0-486-22990-4

THE LONG ISLAND RAIL ROAD IN EARLY PHOTOGRAPHS, Ron Ziel. Over 220 rare photos, informative text document origin (1844) and development of rail service on Long Island. Vintage views of early trains, locomotives, stations, passengers, crews, much more. Captions. 8⅞ x 11¾. 0-486-26301-0

VOYAGE OF THE LIBERDADE, Joshua Slocum. Great 19th-century mariner's thrilling, first-hand account of the wreck of his ship off South America, the 35-foot boat he built from the wreckage, and its remarkable voyage home. 128pp. 5⅜ x 8½. 0-486-40022-0

TEN BOOKS ON ARCHITECTURE, Vitruvius. The most important book ever written on architecture. Early Roman aesthetics, technology, classical orders, site selection, all other aspects. Morgan translation. 331pp. 5⅜ x 8½. 0-486-20645-9

THE HUMAN FIGURE IN MOTION, Eadweard Muybridge. More than 4,500 stopped-action photos, in action series, showing undraped men, women, children jumping, lying down, throwing, sitting, wrestling, carrying, etc. 390pp. 7⅞ x 10⅝. 0-486-20204-6 Clothbd.

TREES OF THE EASTERN AND CENTRAL UNITED STATES AND CANADA, William M. Harlow. Best one-volume guide to 140 trees. Full descriptions, woodlore, range, etc. Over 600 illustrations. Handy size. 288pp. 4½ x 6⅜. 0-486-20395-6

GROWING AND USING HERBS AND SPICES, Milo Miloradovich. Versatile handbook provides all the information needed for cultivation and use of all the herbs and spices available in North America. 4 illustrations. Index. Glossary. 236pp. 5⅜ x 8½. 0-486-25058-X

BIG BOOK OF MAZES AND LABYRINTHS, Walter Shepherd. 50 mazes and labyrinths in all–classical, solid, ripple, and more–in one great volume. Perfect inexpensive puzzler for clever youngsters. Full solutions. 112pp. 8⅛ x 11. 0-486-22951-3

PIANO TUNING, J. Cree Fischer. Clearest, best book for beginner, amateur. Simple repairs, raising dropped notes, tuning by easy method of flattened fifths. No previous skills needed. 4 illustrations. 201pp. 5⅜ x 8½. 0-486-23267-0

HINTS TO SINGERS, Lillian Nordica. Selecting the right teacher, developing confidence, overcoming stage fright, and many other important skills receive thoughtful discussion in this indispensible guide, written by a world-famous diva of four decades' experience. 96pp. 5⅜ x 8½. 0-486-40094-8

THE COMPLETE NONSENSE OF EDWARD LEAR, Edward Lear. All nonsense limericks, zany alphabets, Owl and Pussycat, songs, nonsense botany, etc., illustrated by Lear. Total of 320pp. 5⅜ x 8½. (Available in U.S. only.) 0-486-20167-8

VICTORIAN PARLOUR POETRY: An Annotated Anthology, Michael R. Turner. 117 gems by Longfellow, Tennyson, Browning, many lesser-known poets. "The Village Blacksmith," "Curfew Must Not Ring Tonight," "Only a Baby Small," dozens more, often difficult to find elsewhere. Index of poets, titles, first lines. xxiii + 325pp. 5⅜ x 8¼. 0-486-27044-0

DUBLINERS, James Joyce. Fifteen stories offer vivid, tightly focused observations of the lives of Dublin's poorer classes. At least one, "The Dead," is considered a masterpiece. Reprinted complete and unabridged from standard edition. 160pp. 5³⁄₁₆ x 8¼. 0-486-26870-5

GREAT WEIRD TALES: 14 Stories by Lovecraft, Blackwood, Machen and Others, S. T. Joshi (ed.). 14 spellbinding tales, including "The Sin Eater," by Fiona McLeod, "The Eye Above the Mantel," by Frank Belknap Long, as well as renowned works by R. H. Barlow, Lord Dunsany, Arthur Machen, W. C. Morrow and eight other masters of the genre. 256pp. 5⅜ x 8½. (Available in U.S. only.) 0-486-40436-6

THE BOOK OF THE SACRED MAGIC OF ABRAMELIN THE MAGE, translated by S. MacGregor Mathers. Medieval manuscript of ceremonial magic. Basic document in Aleister Crowley, Golden Dawn groups. 268pp. 5⅜ x 8½. 0-486-23211-5

THE BATTLES THAT CHANGED HISTORY, Fletcher Pratt. Eminent historian profiles 16 crucial conflicts, ancient to modern, that changed the course of civilization. 352pp. 5⅜ x 8½. 0-486-41129-X

NEW RUSSIAN-ENGLISH AND ENGLISH-RUSSIAN DICTIONARY, M. A. O'Brien. This is a remarkably handy Russian dictionary, containing a surprising amount of information, including over 70,000 entries. 366pp. 4½ x 6⅛. 0-486-20208-9

NEW YORK IN THE FORTIES, Andreas Feininger. 162 brilliant photographs by the well-known photographer, formerly with *Life* magazine. Commuters, shoppers, Times Square at night, much else from city at its peak. Captions by John von Hartz. 181pp. 9¼ x 10¾. 0-486-23585-8

INDIAN SIGN LANGUAGE, William Tomkins. Over 525 signs developed by Sioux and other tribes. Written instructions and diagrams. Also 290 pictographs. 111pp. 6⅛ x 9¼. 0-486-22029-X

ANATOMY: A Complete Guide for Artists, Joseph Sheppard. A master of figure drawing shows artists how to render human anatomy convincingly. Over 460 illustrations. 224pp. 8⅜ x 11¼. 0-486-27279-6

MEDIEVAL CALLIGRAPHY: Its History and Technique, Marc Drogin. Spirited history, comprehensive instruction manual covers 13 styles (ca. 4th century through 15th). Excellent photographs; directions for duplicating medieval techniques with modern tools. 224pp. 8⅜ x 11¼. 0-486-26142-5

DRIED FLOWERS: How to Prepare Them, Sarah Whitlock and Martha Rankin. Complete instructions on how to use silica gel, meal and borax, perlite aggregate, sand and borax, glycerine and water to create attractive permanent flower arrangements. 12 illustrations. 32pp. 5⅜ x 8½. 0-486-21802-3

EASY-TO-MAKE BIRD FEEDERS FOR WOODWORKERS, Scott D. Campbell. Detailed, simple-to-use guide for designing, constructing, caring for and using feeders. Text, illustrations for 12 classic and contemporary designs. 96pp. 5⅜ x 8½. 0-486-25847-5

THE COMPLETE BOOK OF BIRDHOUSE CONSTRUCTION FOR WOODWORKERS, Scott D. Campbell. Detailed instructions, illustrations, tables. Also data on bird habitat and instinct patterns. Bibliography. 3 tables. 63 illustrations in 15 figures. 48pp. 5¼ x 8½. 0-486-24407-5

SCOTTISH WONDER TALES FROM MYTH AND LEGEND, Donald A. Mackenzie. 16 lively tales tell of giants rumbling down mountainsides, of a magic wand that turns stone pillars into warriors, of gods and goddesses, evil hags, powerful forces and more. 240pp. 5⅜ x 8½. 0-486-29677-6

THE HISTORY OF UNDERCLOTHES, C. Willett Cunnington and Phyllis Cunnington. Fascinating, well-documented survey covering six centuries of English undergarments, enhanced with over 100 illustrations: 12th-century laced-up bodice, footed long drawers (1795), 19th-century bustles, 19th-century corsets for men, Victorian "bust improvers," much more. 272pp. 5⅝ x 8¼. 0-486-27124-2

ARTS AND CRAFTS FURNITURE: The Complete Brooks Catalog of 1912, Brooks Manufacturing Co. Photos and detailed descriptions of more than 150 now very collectible furniture designs from the Arts and Crafts movement depict davenports, settees, buffets, desks, tables, chairs, bedsteads, dressers and more, all built of solid, quarter-sawed oak. Invaluable for students and enthusiasts of antiques, Americana and the decorative arts. 80pp. 6½ x 9¼. 0-486-27471-3

WILBUR AND ORVILLE: A Biography of the Wright Brothers, Fred Howard. Definitive, crisply written study tells the full story of the brothers' lives and work. A vividly written biography, unparalleled in scope and color, that also captures the spirit of an extraordinary era. 560pp. 6⅛ x 9¼. 0-486-40297-5

THE ARTS OF THE SAILOR: Knotting, Splicing and Ropework, Hervey Garrett Smith. Indispensable shipboard reference covers tools, basic knots and useful hitches; handsewing and canvas work, more. Over 100 illustrations. Delightful reading for sea lovers. 256pp. 5⅜ x 8½. 0-486-26440-8

FRANK LLOYD WRIGHT'S FALLINGWATER: The House and Its History, Second, Revised Edition, Donald Hoffmann. A total revision–both in text and illustrations–of the standard document on Fallingwater, the boldest, most personal architectural statement of Wright's mature years, updated with valuable new material from the recently opened Frank Lloyd Wright Archives. "Fascinating"–*The New York Times*. 116 illustrations. 128pp. 9¼ x 10¾. 0-486-27430-6

PHOTOGRAPHIC SKETCHBOOK OF THE CIVIL WAR, Alexander Gardner. 100 photos taken on field during the Civil War. Famous shots of Manassas Harper's Ferry, Lincoln, Richmond, slave pens, etc. 244pp. 10⅝ x 8¼. 0-486-22731-6

FIVE ACRES AND INDEPENDENCE, Maurice G. Kains. Great back-to-the-land classic explains basics of self-sufficient farming. The one book to get. 95 illustrations. 397pp. 5⅜ x 8½. 0-486-20974-1

A MODERN HERBAL, Margaret Grieve. Much the fullest, most exact, most useful compilation of herbal material. Gigantic alphabetical encyclopedia, from aconite to zedoary, gives botanical information, medical properties, folklore, economic uses, much else. Indispensable to serious reader. 161 illustrations. 888pp. 6½ x 9¼. 2-vol. set. (Available in U.S. only.) Vol. I: 0-486-22798-7 Vol. II: 0-486-22799-5

HIDDEN TREASURE MAZE BOOK, Dave Phillips. Solve 34 challenging mazes accompanied by heroic tales of adventure. Evil dragons, people-eating plants, bloodthirsty giants, many more dangerous adversaries lurk at every twist and turn. 34 mazes, stories, solutions. 48pp. 8¼ x 11. 0-486-24566-7

LETTERS OF W. A. MOZART, Wolfgang A. Mozart. Remarkable letters show bawdy wit, humor, imagination, musical insights, contemporary musical world; includes some letters from Leopold Mozart. 276pp. 5⅜ x 8½. 0-486-22859-2

BASIC PRINCIPLES OF CLASSICAL BALLET, Agrippina Vaganova. Great Russian theoretician, teacher explains methods for teaching classical ballet. 118 illustrations. 175pp. 5⅜ x 8½. 0-486-22036-2

THE JUMPING FROG, Mark Twain. Revenge edition. The original story of The Celebrated Jumping Frog of Calaveras County, a hapless French translation, and Twain's hilarious "retranslation" from the French. 12 illustrations. 66pp. 5⅜ x 8½. 0-486-22686-7

BEST REMEMBERED POEMS, Martin Gardner (ed.). The 126 poems in this superb collection of 19th- and 20th-century British and American verse range from Shelley's "To a Skylark" to the impassioned "Renascence" of Edna St. Vincent Millay and to Edward Lear's whimsical "The Owl and the Pussycat." 224pp. 5⅜ x 8½. 0-486-27165-X

COMPLETE SONNETS, William Shakespeare. Over 150 exquisite poems deal with love, friendship, the tyranny of time, beauty's evanescence, death and other themes in language of remarkable power, precision and beauty. Glossary of archaic terms. 80pp. 5³⁄₁₆ x 8¼. 0-486-26686-9

HISTORIC HOMES OF THE AMERICAN PRESIDENTS, Second, Revised Edition, Irvin Haas. A traveler's guide to American Presidential homes, most open to the public, depicting and describing homes occupied by every American President from George Washington to George Bush. With visiting hours, admission charges, travel routes. 175 photographs. Index. 160pp. 8¼ x 11. 0-486-26751-2

THE WIT AND HUMOR OF OSCAR WILDE, Alvin Redman (ed.). More than 1,000 ripostes, paradoxes, wisecracks: Work is the curse of the drinking classes; I can resist everything except temptation; etc. 258pp. 5⅜ x 8½. 0-486-20602-5

SHAKESPEARE LEXICON AND QUOTATION DICTIONARY, Alexander Schmidt. Full definitions, locations, shades of meaning in every word in plays and poems. More than 50,000 exact quotations. 1,485pp. 6½ x 9¼. 2-vol. set. Vol. 1: 0-486-22726-X Vol. 2: 0-486-22727-8

SELECTED POEMS, Emily Dickinson. Over 100 best-known, best-loved poems by one of America's foremost poets, reprinted from authoritative early editions. No comparable edition at this price. Index of first lines. 64pp. 5³⁄₁₆ x 8¼. 0-486-26466-1

THE INSIDIOUS DR. FU-MANCHU, Sax Rohmer. The first of the popular mystery series introduces a pair of English detectives to their archnemesis, the diabolical Dr. Fu-Manchu. Flavorful atmosphere, fast-paced action, and colorful characters enliven this classic of the genre. 208pp. 5³⁄₁₆ x 8¼. 0-486-29898-1

THE MALLEUS MALEFICARUM OF KRAMER AND SPRENGER, translated by Montague Summers. Full text of most important witchhunter's "bible," used by both Catholics and Protestants. 278pp. 6⅝ x 10. 0-486-22802-9

SPANISH STORIES/CUENTOS ESPAÑOLES: A Dual-Language Book, Angel Flores (ed.). Unique format offers 13 great stories in Spanish by Cervantes, Borges, others. Faithful English translations on facing pages. 352pp. 5⅜ x 8½. 0-486-25399-6

GARDEN CITY, LONG ISLAND, IN EARLY PHOTOGRAPHS, 1869–1919, Mildred H. Smith. Handsome treasury of 118 vintage pictures, accompanied by carefully researched captions, document the Garden City Hotel fire (1899), the Vanderbilt Cup Race (1908), the first airmail flight departing from the Nassau Boulevard Aerodrome (1911), and much more. 96pp. 8⅞ x 11¾. 0-486-40669-5

OLD QUEENS, N.Y., IN EARLY PHOTOGRAPHS, Vincent F. Seyfried and William Asadorian. Over 160 rare photographs of Maspeth, Jamaica, Jackson Heights, and other areas. Vintage views of DeWitt Clinton mansion, 1939 World's Fair and more. Captions. 192pp. 8⅞ x 11. 0-486-26358-4

CAPTURED BY THE INDIANS: 15 Firsthand Accounts, 1750-1870, Frederick Drimmer. Astounding true historical accounts of grisly torture, bloody conflicts, relentless pursuits, miraculous escapes and more, by people who lived to tell the tale. 384pp. 5⅜ x 8½. 0-486-24901-8

THE WORLD'S GREAT SPEECHES (Fourth Enlarged Edition), Lewis Copeland, Lawrence W. Lamm, and Stephen J. McKenna. Nearly 300 speeches provide public speakers with a wealth of updated quotes and inspiration–from Pericles' funeral oration and William Jennings Bryan's "Cross of Gold Speech" to Malcolm X's powerful words on the Black Revolution and Earl of Spenser's tribute to his sister, Diana, Princess of Wales. 944pp. 5⅜ x 8⅜. 0-486-40903-1

THE BOOK OF THE SWORD, Sir Richard F. Burton. Great Victorian scholar/adventurer's eloquent, erudite history of the "queen of weapons"–from prehistory to early Roman Empire. Evolution and development of early swords, variations (sabre, broadsword, cutlass, scimitar, etc.), much more. 336pp. 6⅛ x 9¼. 0-486-25434-8

AUTOBIOGRAPHY: The Story of My Experiments with Truth, Mohandas K. Gandhi. Boyhood, legal studies, purification, the growth of the Satyagraha (nonviolent protest) movement. Critical, inspiring work of the man responsible for the freedom of India. 480pp. 5⅜ x 8½. (Available in U.S. only.) 0-486-24593-4

CELTIC MYTHS AND LEGENDS, T. W. Rolleston. Masterful retelling of Irish and Welsh stories and tales. Cuchulain, King Arthur, Deirdre, the Grail, many more. First paperback edition. 58 full-page illustrations. 512pp. 5⅜ x 8½. 0-486-26507-2

THE PRINCIPLES OF PSYCHOLOGY, William James. Famous long course complete, unabridged. Stream of thought, time perception, memory, experimental methods; great work decades ahead of its time. 94 figures. 1,391pp. 5⅜ x 8½. 2-vol. set. Vol. I: 0-486-20381-6 Vol. II: 0-486-20382-4

THE WORLD AS WILL AND REPRESENTATION, Arthur Schopenhauer. Definitive English translation of Schopenhauer's life work, correcting more than 1,000 errors, omissions in earlier translations. Translated by E. F. J. Payne. Total of 1,269pp. 5⅜ x 8½. 2-vol. set. Vol. 1: 0-486-21761-2 Vol. 2: 0-486-21762-0

MAGIC AND MYSTERY IN TIBET, Madame Alexandra David-Neel. Experiences among lamas, magicians, sages, sorcerers, Bonpa wizards. A true psychic discovery. 32 illustrations. 321pp. 5⅜ x 8½. (Available in U.S. only.) 0-486-22682-4

THE EGYPTIAN BOOK OF THE DEAD, E. A. Wallis Budge. Complete reproduction of Ani's papyrus, finest ever found. Full hieroglyphic text, interlinear transliteration, word-for-word translation, smooth translation. 533pp. 6½ x 9¼. 0-486-21866-X

HISTORIC COSTUME IN PICTURES, Braun & Schneider. Over 1,450 costumed figures in clearly detailed engravings–from dawn of civilization to end of 19th century. Captions. Many folk costumes. 256pp. 8⅜ x 11¾. 0-486-23150-X

MATHEMATICS FOR THE NONMATHEMATICIAN, Morris Kline. Detailed, college-level treatment of mathematics in cultural and historical context, with numerous exercises. Recommended Reading Lists. Tables. Numerous figures. 641pp. 5⅜ x 8½. 0-486-24823-2

PROBABILISTIC METHODS IN THE THEORY OF STRUCTURES, Isaac Elishakoff. Well-written introduction covers the elements of the theory of probability from two or more random variables, the reliability of such multivariable structures, the theory of random function, Monte Carlo methods of treating problems incapable of exact solution, and more. Examples. 502pp. 5⅜ x 8½. 0-486-40691-1

THE RIME OF THE ANCIENT MARINER, Gustave Doré, S. T. Coleridge. Doré's finest work; 34 plates capture moods, subtleties of poem. Flawless full-size reproductions printed on facing pages with authoritative text of poem. "Beautiful. Simply beautiful."–*Publisher's Weekly.* 77pp. 9¼ x 12. 0-486-22305-1

SCULPTURE: Principles and Practice, Louis Slobodkin. Step-by-step approach to clay, plaster, metals, stone; classical and modern. 253 drawings, photos. 255pp. 8⅛ x 11. 0-486-22960-2

THE INFLUENCE OF SEA POWER UPON HISTORY, 1660–1783, A. T. Mahan. Influential classic of naval history and tactics still used as text in war colleges. First paperback edition. 4 maps. 24 battle plans. 640pp. 5⅜ x 8½. 0-486-25509-3

THE STORY OF THE TITANIC AS TOLD BY ITS SURVIVORS, Jack Winocour (ed.). What it was really like. Panic, despair, shocking inefficiency, and a little heroism. More thrilling than any fictional account. 26 illustrations. 320pp. 5⅜ x 8½. 0-486-20610-6

ONE TWO THREE . . . INFINITY: Facts and Speculations of Science, George Gamow. Great physicist's fascinating, readable overview of contemporary science: number theory, relativity, fourth dimension, entropy, genes, atomic structure, much more. 128 illustrations. Index. 352pp. 5⅜ x 8½. 0-486-25664-2

DALÍ ON MODERN ART: The Cuckolds of Antiquated Modern Art, Salvador Dalí. Influential painter skewers modern art and its practitioners. Outrageous evaluations of Picasso, Cézanne, Turner, more. 15 renderings of paintings discussed. 44 calligraphic decorations by Dalí. 96pp. 5⅜ x 8½. (Available in U.S. only.) 0-486-29220-7

ANTIQUE PLAYING CARDS: A Pictorial History, Henry René D'Allemagne. Over 900 elaborate, decorative images from rare playing cards (14th–20th centuries): Bacchus, death, dancing dogs, hunting scenes, royal coats of arms, players cheating, much more. 96pp. 9¼ x 12¼. 0-486-29265-7

MAKING FURNITURE MASTERPIECES: 30 Projects with Measured Drawings, Franklin H. Gottshall. Step-by-step instructions, illustrations for constructing handsome, useful pieces, among them a Sheraton desk, Chippendale chair, Spanish desk, Queen Anne table and a William and Mary dressing mirror. 224pp. 8⅛ x 11¼. 0-486-29338-6

NORTH AMERICAN INDIAN DESIGNS FOR ARTISTS AND CRAFTSPEOPLE, Eva Wilson. Over 360 authentic copyright-free designs adapted from Navajo blankets, Hopi pottery, Sioux buffalo hides, more. Geometrics, symbolic figures, plant and animal motifs, etc. 128pp. 8⅜ x 11. (Not for sale in the United Kingdom.) 0-486-25341-4

THE FOSSIL BOOK: A Record of Prehistoric Life, Patricia V. Rich et al. Profusely illustrated definitive guide covers everything from single-celled organisms and dinosaurs to birds and mammals and the interplay between climate and man. Over 1,500 illustrations. 760pp. 7½ x 10⅛. 0-486-29371-8

VICTORIAN ARCHITECTURAL DETAILS: Designs for Over 700 Stairs, Mantels, Doors, Windows, Cornices, Porches, and Other Decorative Elements, A. J. Bicknell & Company. Everything from dormer windows and piazzas to balconies and gable ornaments. Also includes elevations and floor plans for handsome, private residences and commercial structures. 80pp. 9⅜ x 12¼. 0-486-44015-X

WESTERN ISLAMIC ARCHITECTURE: A Concise Introduction, John D. Hoag. Profusely illustrated critical appraisal compares and contrasts Islamic mosques and palaces–from Spain and Egypt to other areas in the Middle East. 139 illustrations. 128pp. 6 x 9. 0-486-43760-4

CHINESE ARCHITECTURE: A Pictorial History, Liang Ssu-ch'eng. More than 240 rare photographs and drawings depict temples, pagodas, tombs, bridges, and imperial palaces comprising much of China's architectural heritage. 152 halftones, 94 diagrams. 232pp. 10¾ x 9⅞. 0-486-43999-2

THE RENAISSANCE: Studies in Art and Poetry, Walter Pater. One of the most talked-about books of the 19th century, *The Renaissance* combines scholarship and philosophy in an innovative work of cultural criticism that examines the achievements of Botticelli, Leonardo, Michelangelo, and other artists. "The holy writ of beauty."–Oscar Wilde. 160pp. 5⅜ x 8½. 0-486-44025-7

A TREATISE ON PAINTING, Leonardo da Vinci. The great Renaissance artist's practical advice on drawing and painting techniques covers anatomy, perspective, composition, light and shadow, and color. A classic of art instruction, it features 48 drawings by Nicholas Poussin and Leon Battista Alberti. 192pp. 5⅜ x 8½. 0-486-44155-5

THE MIND OF LEONARDO DA VINCI, Edward McCurdy. More than just a biography, this classic study by a distinguished historian draws upon Leonardo's extensive writings to offer numerous demonstrations of the Renaissance master's achievements, not only in sculpture and painting, but also in music, engineering, and even experimental aviation. 384pp. 5⅜ x 8½. 0-486-44142-3

WASHINGTON IRVING'S RIP VAN WINKLE, Illustrated by Arthur Rackham. Lovely prints that established artist as a leading illustrator of the time and forever etched into the popular imagination a classic of Catskill lore. 51 full-color plates. 80pp. 8⅜ x 11. 0-486-44242-X

HENSCHE ON PAINTING, John W. Robichaux. Basic painting philosophy and methodology of a great teacher, as expounded in his famous classes and workshops on Cape Cod. 7 illustrations in color on covers. 80pp. 5⅜ x 8½. 0-486-43728-0

LIGHT AND SHADE: A Classic Approach to Three-Dimensional Drawing, Mrs. Mary P. Merrifield. Handy reference clearly demonstrates principles of light and shade by revealing effects of common daylight, sunshine, and candle or artificial light on geometrical solids. 13 plates. 64pp. 5⅜ x 8½. 0-486-44143-1

ASTROLOGY AND ASTRONOMY: A Pictorial Archive of Signs and Symbols, Ernst and Johanna Lehner. Treasure trove of stories, lore, and myth, accompanied by more than 300 rare illustrations of planets, the Milky Way, signs of the zodiac, comets, meteors, and other astronomical phenomena. 192pp. 8⅜ x 11. 0-486-43981-X

JEWELRY MAKING: Techniques for Metal, Tim McCreight. Easy-to-follow instructions and carefully executed illustrations describe tools and techniques, use of gems and enamels, wire inlay, casting, and other topics. 72 line illustrations and diagrams. 176pp. 8¼ x 10⅞. 0-486-44043-5

MAKING BIRDHOUSES: Easy and Advanced Projects, Gladstone Califf. Easy-to-follow instructions include diagrams for everything from a one-room house for bluebirds to a forty-two-room structure for purple martins. 56 plates; 4 figures. 80pp. 8¾ x 6⅜. 0-486-44183-0

LITTLE BOOK OF LOG CABINS: How to Build and Furnish Them, William S. Wicks. Handy how-to manual, with instructions and illustrations for building cabins in the Adirondack style, fireplaces, stairways, furniture, beamed ceilings, and more. 102 line drawings. 96pp. 8¾ x 6⅜. 0-486-44259-4

THE SEASONS OF AMERICA PAST, Eric Sloane. From "sugaring time" and strawberry picking to Indian summer and fall harvest, a whole year's activities described in charming prose and enhanced with 79 of the author's own illustrations. 160pp. 8¼ x 11. 0-486-44220-9

THE METROPOLIS OF TOMORROW, Hugh Ferriss. Generous, prophetic vision of the metropolis of the future, as perceived in 1929. Powerful illustrations of towering structures, wide avenues, and rooftop parks–all features in many of today's modern cities. 59 illustrations. 144pp. 8¼ x 11. 0-486-43727-2

THE PATH TO ROME, Hilaire Belloc. This 1902 memoir abounds in lively vignettes from a vanished time, recounting a pilgrimage on foot across the Alps and Apennines in order to "see all Europe which the Christian Faith has saved." 77 of the author's original line drawings complement his sparkling prose. 272pp. 5⅜ x 8½. 0-486-44001-X

THE HISTORY OF RASSELAS: Prince of Abissinia, Samuel Johnson. Distinguished English writer attacks eighteenth-century optimism and man's unrealistic estimates of what life has to offer. 112pp. 5⅜ x 8½. 0-486-44094-X

A VOYAGE TO ARCTURUS, David Lindsay. A brilliant flight of pure fancy, where wild creatures crowd the fantastic landscape and demented torturers dominate victims with their bizarre mental powers. 272pp. 5⅜ x 8½. 0-486-44198-9

Paperbound unless otherwise indicated. Available at your book dealer, online at **www.doverpublications.com**, or by writing to Dept. GI, Dover Publications, Inc., 31 East 2nd Street, Mineola, NY 11501. For current price information or for free catalogs (please indicate field of interest), write to Dover Publications or log on to **www.doverpublications.com** and see every Dover book in print. Dover publishes more than 500 books each year on science, elementary and advanced mathematics, biology, music, art, literary history, social sciences, and other areas.